JOURNALISM
RESEARCH AND
INVESTIGATION IN
A DIGITAL WORLD

JOURNALISM RESEARCH AND INVESTIGATION IN A DIGITAL WORLD

EDITED BY
STEPHEN TANNER
AND NICK RICHARDSON

OXFORD
UNIVERSITY PRESS
AUSTRALIA & NEW ZEALAND

OXFORD
UNIVERSITY PRESS

Oxford University Press is a department of the University of Oxford.

It furthers the University's objective of excellence in research, scholarship, and education by publishing worldwide. Oxford is a registered trademark of Oxford University Press in the UK and in certain other countries.

Published in Australia by
Oxford University Press
253 Normanby Road, South Melbourne, Victoria 3205, Australia

© Stephen Tanner and Nick Richardson 2013

The moral rights of the authors have been asserted.

First published 2013

National Library of Australia Cataloguing-in-Publication entry

Author: Tanner, Stephen J. (Stephen John)
Title: Journalism research and investigation in a digital world / Stephen Tanner, Nick Richardson.
ISBN: 9780195518337 (pbk.)
Notes: Includes index.
Subjects: Journalism—Research.
          Digital media.
          Online journalism.
Other Authors/Contributors: Richardson, Nick.

Dewey Number: 070.43

Edited by Natasha Broadstock
Typeset by diacriTech, Chennai, India
Proofread by Valina Rainer
Indexed by Jeanne Rudd
Printed in Singapore by Markono Media Pte Ltd

CONTENTS

ABOUT THE AUTHORS   viii

ACKNOWLEDGMENTS   xiv

PART 1: CONTEXT

INTRODUCTION   3
Stephen Tanner and Nick Richardson

CHAPTER 1: THE HISTORY OF INVESTIGATIVE JOURNALISM IN AUSTRALIA   10
Andrea Carson

Case Study: The Making of an Investigative Journalist   25
Richard Baker

CHAPTER 2: LESSONS FROM ABROAD: PARTNERSHIPS   28
Bill Birnbauer

CHAPTER 3: *WIKILEAKS* AND TWO NEW MODELS FOR INVESTIGATIVE JOURNALISM   39
Suelette Dreyfus and Kristinn Hrafnsson

CHAPTER 4: HUMAN SOURCES: THE JOURNALIST AND THE WHISTLE-BLOWER IN THE DIGITAL ERA   48
Suelette Dreyfus, Reeva Lederman, A.J. Brown, Simon Milton, Marcia P. Miceli, Rachelle Bosua, Andrew Clausen and Jessie Schanzle

PART 2: APPROACHES AND TOOLS

CHAPTER 5: THE RESEARCH PROCESS   65
Wendy Bacon

CHAPTER 6: RESEARCH STRATEGIES   77
Rod Kirkpatrick

CHAPTER 7: THE 'TWITTERISATION' OF INVESTIGATIVE JOURNALISM   88
Julie Posetti

Case Study: Investigative Social Journalism and the Arab Spring   101
Jess Hill

CHAPTER 8: MATHS AND STATS FOR JOURNALISTS   103
Stephen Tanner

CHAPTER 9: DATA JOURNALISM (1)   116
Stephen K. Doig

CHAPTER 10: DATA JOURNALISM (2)   123
Kerry Green

Case Study: The Sin Index   137
Fiona Hudson

CHAPTER 11: INTERPRETING FINANCIAL DOCUMENTS   139
Stephen Tanner and Nick Richardson

Case Study: The Numbers Never Lie   149
John Beveridge

CHAPTER 12: WORKING WITH THE PR INDUSTRY   151
Jane Johnston

Case Study: Strategic Communications   163
Nino Tesorierio

CHAPTER 13: LEGAL ISSUES   166
Mark Pearson

Case Study: Intellectually Disabled People Fight for Equal Access to Justice   178
Nance Haxton

CHAPTER 14: DIRTY HANDS AND INVESTIGATIVE JOURNALISM   181
Ian Richards

Case Study: The Day I Went Silent   188
Sharon Mascall-Dare

PART 3: APPLIED INVESTIGATIONS

CHAPTER 15: POLITICS   193
Nick Richardson

Case Study: In Search of a Truth Serum   204
Hedley Thomas

CHAPTER 16: CRIME WRITING   208
Andrew Rule and Nick Richardson

Case Study: Intelligence-led Reporting   217
Mark Solomons

CHAPTER 17: ON FLAK, BALANCE AND ACTIVISM: THE UPS AND
DOWNS OF ENVIRONMENTAL JOURNALISM   221

Libby Lester

CHAPTER 18: HEALTH REPORTING: OPPORTUNITIES AND CHALLENGES?   232

Trevor Cullen

Case Study: Harnessing the Digital Era for Health Investigations 243

Melissa Sweet

CHAPTER 19: SCIENCE JOURNALISM   246

Karina Kelly

CHAPTER 20: REPORTING INDIGENOUS AFFAIRS   254

Michael Meadows

Case Study: Taking Journalists on the Journey   267

Heather Stewart

CHAPTER 21: INVESTIGATIVE ESSENTIALS FOR JOURNALISTS
IN MULTICULTURAL AND DIVERSE COMMUNITIES   269

Angela Romano

CHAPTER 22: NOT JUST ABOUT THE MONEY   282

Nigel McCarthy

Case Study: BHP and Ok Tedi   291

Mary Kaidonis

CHAPTER 23: INDUSTRIAL RELATIONS   297

Kayt Davies

Case Study: IR Reporting   305

Mark Skulley

CHAPTER 24: INVESTIGATIVE JOURNALISM AND SPORTS REPORTING   308

Roger Patching

Case Study: Harness Racing Exposé   318

Caro Meldrum-Hanna

CHAPTER 25: PUBLISHING YOUR WORK   320

Lawrie Zion

Case Study: Tipping Point   330

Ruth Fogarty

INDEX   333

ABOUT THE AUTHORS

WENDY BACON is a Professor with the Australian Centre for Independent Journalism at the University of Technology Sydney, where she previously headed the journalism program. She is an award-winning investigative journalist and is currently a contributing editor with the daily online magazine *New Matilda*. She blogs at http://wendybacon.com.

RICHARD BAKER joined *The Age's* investigative unit in 2005 after four years covering Victorian politics and, before that, rural affairs. He soon broke major stories, including exposing BHP Billiton's link to the AWB Iraqi kickbacks scandal and China's secret bid to buy uranium mines in Australia. He has a strong interest in foreign affairs, business, law enforcement and defence. His work with colleague Nick McKenzie has won several Melbourne Press Club and Walkley awards.

JOHN BEVERIDGE writes a daily business column for the *Herald Sun* in Melbourne. He has been writing business for many years after a long career with News Ltd as an overseas correspondent, based in Los Angeles, and as a senior feature writer for the *Herald Sun*.

BILL BIRNBAUER is a Senior Lecturer in Journalism at Monash University, Melbourne, where he teaches investigative reporting and feature writing. Before moving to academia in 2008, he was a senior journalist at *The Age* and *The Sunday Age*. He is a member of the International Consortium of Investigative Journalists.

DR RACHELLE BOSUA is a Lecturer in the Department of Computing and Information Systems, at The University of Melbourne. She holds graduate qualifications in three IT disciplines: Computer Science, Software Engineering and Information Systems. She teaches web development, business process modelling and design and knowledge management at both undergraduate and graduate level.

A.J. BROWN is John F. Kearney Professor of Public Law at Griffith University. Born and raised in Canberra, and educated at the University of New South Wales in Sydney, he has worked as a senior investigator for the Commonwealth Ombudsman, as associate to Justice G.E. 'Tony' Fitzgerald AC, President of the Queensland Court of Appeal, and as a ministerial policy advisor in the Queensland Government. He is the foundation lead researcher of the Australian Research Council-funded Australian Constitutional Values Survey, and has been project leader of the world's largest empirical research project into public interest whistleblowing, *Whistling While They Work* (2005–09). He also wrote the biography of former High Court judge Michael Kirby.

ANDREA CARSON is a journalist, author, lecturer and PhD candidate at The University of Melbourne. She is researching the watchdog role of newspapers in the internet age. Andrea started her journalism career at the *Colac Herald* before commencing a cadetship at *The Age*. She has worked as a reporter, producer and broadcaster in radio (ABC, 3RRR), television (*The 7.30 Report*) and online.

DR ANDREW CLAUSEN is an Economics Lecturer at the University of Edinburgh. His research involves designing incentives for institutions that are prone to fraud, corruption and scandal. He also develops mathematical tools to simplify economic theory research. He recently completed his PhD at the University of Pennsylvania. He has a background in mathematics and computer science, and has developed free software that is widely used in the GNU/Linux community.

TREVOR CULLEN is Associate Professor and Program Director for Communications and Head of Journalism at Edith Cowan University in Perth, Western Australia. His degrees are from Louvain University in Belgium, City University in London and Queensland University in Australia, and he has won both university and national tertiary teaching and research awards. Trevor is the author of more than 25 peer-reviewed articles, book chapters and conference papers on reporting HIV, and he has led UN, AusAid, CPU, SPC and PIAF-sponsored workshops in Asia and the Pacific region for editors and journalists on reporting health and HIV.

DR KAYT DAVIES is a Senior Lecturer in Journalism at Edith Cowan University in Perth, Western Australia. She has worked as a business journalist and magazine editor, and her professional interests include the development of journalism as an academic research methodology, Indigenous issues and global journalism ethics.

STEPHEN K. DOIG teaches at the Cronkite School of Journalism at Arizona State University (ASU). Before joining ASU in 1996, he spent 19 years as a *Miami Herald* investigative reporter. His data analysis work has won the Pulitzer Prize, the IRE Award, the Goldsmith Prize, the George Polk Award and other recognition.

DR SUELETTE DREYFUS is a Research Fellow at The University of Melbourne's Department of Computing and Information Systems. She worked as reporter on the staff of the *Herald Sun* in Melbourne and was previously a member of the *WikiLeaks* Advisory Board. She wrote *Underground*, the 1997 cult-classic book about computer hacking, with Julian Assange. It has been translated into seven languages.

RUTH FOGARTY is a website producer with ABC Television in Sydney. Much of Ruth's work has appeared on *Four Corners*, where she and a team—made up of Ruth, reporter Marian Wilkinson, cameraman Neale Maude, researcher Kate Wild—compiled the 'Tipping Point' program that won a Walkley Award in 2008 and also a Eureka Science prize.

KERRY GREEN is Professor of Communication in the School of Communication, International Studies and Languages at the University of South Australia. He is a former newspaper editor who teaches print journalism and conducts research into traumatising reporting practices. He is a past president of the Journalism Education Association of Australia.

NANCE HAXTON is an award-winning ABC radio journalist. Based in South Australia, she reports to flagship programs *AM*, *PM* and *The World Today*. Nance has a Master of Journalism. She won the 2001 Radio Walkley for her coverage of the Woomera Detention Centre, received a Walkley commendation in 2000 and was a finalist in 2001 and 2007. Other prizes include the 2003 United Nationa Media Peace Prize, the 2004 South Australian Media Award and the 2011 Yooralla Media Award for Excellence at the National Disability Awards for the story she talks about in her case study.

JESS HILL was the Middle East correspondent for *The Global Mail*, based in Cairo. In 2011, before moving to Egypt, she was a producer/reporter at ABC Radio Current Affairs, and spearheaded the network's new approach to conflict reporting, using social media to help investigate and report hundreds of original stories about the Arab uprisings, from across the region. In 2008, Jess drove across the USA covering the presidential election for the website *New Matilda*. She returned to the USA in 2011 as a visiting scholar at the Edward R. Murrow program for journalists. You can follow Jess on Twitter @jessradio.

KRISTINN HRAFNSSON is an Icelandic investigative journalist and the public spokesman for the *WikiLeaks* organisation. He has worked in various media jobs, including at the Icelandic National Broadcasting Service and in newspapers. He also hosted the television program *Kompás*, where he and his team exposed criminal activity and corruption in high places. Kristinn has been awarded the Icelandic Journalism awards three times in 2004, 2007 and 2010 (Journalist of the Year).

FIONA HUDSON is a senior journalist with the *Herald Sun*. She has become expert at data journalism and has compiled a number of feature packages for the paper and its website after crunching data from diverse sources. She has been a chief of staff, News Ltd European correspondent, feature writer and run the iPad app for the paper before her current role. She has also won several Melbourne Press Club awards for her reporting.

JANE JOHNSTON is Associate Professor of Journalism and PR at Bond University. She is the author of *Media Relations: Issues and Strategies* (Allen & Unwin, 2007, 2013) and co-editor of *Public Relations: Theory and Practice* (fourth edition currently under way). She is a keen researcher into the connections between journalism and PR and has worked in both industries.

MARY KAIDONIS is Associate Professor in the School of Accounting and Finance at the University of Wollongong. She has over 20 years' experience as an academic and in public practice (taxation) and industry. Her research is informed by interdisciplinary perspectives, with an emphasis in the critique of accounting in its environmental, organisational, political and social contexts.

KARINA KELLY worked in television news for SBS and the Seven Network before moving to the ABC's *Quantum* for 11 years and *Catalyst* for four. She has been awarded the Michael Daly award for science journalism, a World Gold Medal at the New York Film and Television Festivals, and holds an Honorary Doctorate of Letters from the University of Wollongong for contributions to journalism and science in Australia.

DR ROD KIRKPATRICK, an independent scholar, is a semi-retired journalism lecturer and a former New South Wales regional daily newspaper editor. He has written published histories of the Queensland, New South Wales and Victorian provincial press and a biography of a Queensland newspaper editor. He gained a PhD in history from the University of Queensland in 1995, with a thesis charting the end of six Queensland provincial newspaper dynasties, 1930–89. He lectured in journalism at the three different universities—based in Toowoomba, Bathurst and Brisbane—over a total of 25 years.

DR REEVA LEDERMAN is a faculty member in the Department of Computing and Information Systems (IS) at The University of Melbourne. Her research interests involve the theoretical foundations of IS, and she is the winner of the 2012 Stafford Beer Medal for IS research. She is currently involved in projects that examine reluctant users of IS, ranging from whistle-blowers to organisational managers, doctors and patients. Recent problems examined include the use of hospital risk reporting software and modes of health data presentation. She has been published in prestigious IS journals such as the *European Journal of Information Systems*.

LIBBY LESTER is Professor of Journalism, Media and Communications at the University of Tasmania. Recent books include *Media and Environment: Conflict, Politics and the News* and *Transnational Protests and the Media*, co-edited with Simon Cottle.

DR NIGEL MCCARTHY is a journalist, documentary film producer and director, consultant and educator with extensive international experience. He has reported business, economics and politics and held executive roles in public and commercial television. Nigel has a BA, MLit (Economic History) and a PhD. He has taught at several Australian universities and presents seminars for journalists.

SHARON MASCALL-DARE produces radio documentaries for the BBC World Service and teaches journalism at the University of South Australia. An award-winning journalist, she has been named Best Radio Broadcaster three times at the South Australian Media Awards. Her radio documentary *The Big House* won 'Best Radio Current Affairs' and 'Best Radio Broadcaster' at the 2012 South Australian Media Awards. The documentary was also highly commended by the 2011 Walkley Awards' judging panel.

MICHAEL MEADOWS worked as a print and broadcast journalist for 10 years before moving into Journalism education in the late 1980s. His research interests include media representation of minorities, community media audiences, policy and practice. He is Professor of Journalism in the School of Humanities at Griffith University's Nathan Campus in Brisbane.

CARO MELDRUM-HANNA joined the ABC in 2006, starting as a radio presenter before branching into television as the only video journalist for the Sydney newsroom. She became a researcher, working on documentaries including *Jihad Sheilas* and *The Howard Years* before joining *Four Corners* as a researcher in 2009. She was nominated for a Walkley Award in 2009 and 2010 for two of her *Four Corners* stories. She joined *7.30 NSW* as a reporter and won a Walkley Award for her harness racing story.

MARCIA P. MICELI is Professor of Management at the McDonough School of Business, Georgetown University, Washington DC, USA. Her research concerns whistle-blowing and employee voice in organisations. She also studies compensation systems. Together with Janet Near and Terry Dworkin, she has published two books on whistle-blowing. Her earlier articles have appeared in a range of journals, including *Academy of Management Journal, Academy of Management Review, Administrative Science Quarterly* and *Business Ethics Quarterly.*

DR SIMON MILTON received his PhD from the University of Tasmania's Department of Information Systems. His dissertation reported the first comprehensive analysis of data modelling languages using a commonsense realistic ontology. Simon continues his interests in the ontological foundations of data modelling languages and the implications of top-level ontological commitments in information systems modelling. His interests have recently extended to the value and use of ontologies to business and biomedicine, and to the use of anonymising technology in transparency. He holds a senior lectureship in the Department of Computing and Information Systems at The University of Melbourne.

ROGER PATCHING is an adjunct Associate Professor of Journalism at Bond University on Queensland's Gold Coast. He spent 18 years in mainstream print and broadcast media, before entering tertiary education in 1979. He has taught broadcast journalism, ethics and sports reporting at three Australian universities. He is the co-author of seven journalism texts and is a life member of the Journalism Education Association of Australia.

MARK PEARSON is Professor of Journalism at Bond University on Queensland's Gold Coast. He is a prolific researcher who has published widely on a range of topics, including, most recently,

The Journalist's Guide to Media Law (with Mark Polden, Allen & Unwin, 2011), and *Blogging and Tweeting Without Getting Sued* (Allen & Unwin, 2012). He is Australian correspondent for *Reporters Sans Frontières*, tweets from @journlaw and blogs from journlaw.com/. He is also a widely respected consultant and media trainer.

JULIE POSETTI lectures in broadcast journalism at the University of Canberra, Australia. A former senior journalist with the ABC, she has been a Walkley Awards finalist in the Investigative Journalism category and she won the 1993 Tim Mugridge Award for Investigative Journalism, along with the title Journalist of the Year, for her radio coverage of allegations of waterfront corruption. Julie's academic research centres on journalism and social media, talk radio, public broadcasting, political reporting and broadcast coverage of Muslims post-9/11. She is currently writing her PhD dissertation on 'The Twitterisation of Journalism'. She is also the Australian correspondent for *PBS MediaShift* and a regular commentator on journalism and social media. You can follow her on Twitter: @julieposetti.

IAN RICHARDS is Professor of Journalism at the University of South Australia, Adelaide. His research interests include journalism and communication ethics and his publications include *Quagmires and Quandaries: Exploring Journalism Ethics* (2005). Ian is also editor of *Australian Journalism Review*, Australia's leading refereed journal in the academic field of journalism. A former newspaper journalist, he has worked and studied in Australia and the UK.

DR NICK RICHARDSON has been a journalist for 30 years. He has worked on newspapers and magazines in the UK and Australia, including *The (Melbourne) Herald*, *The Australian* and *The Bulletin*. He was an Associate Editor of the *Herald Sun* and a weekly columnist. He also taught journalism at RMIT University in Melbourne, where he ran the postgraduate program. He has a PhD in history from The University of Melbourne and is the author or editor of five books. He is adjunct Professor of Journalism at La Trobe University in Melbourne and national editorial training manager for News Ltd.

DR ANGELA ROMANO teaches journalism at the Queensland University of Technology. She conducts research on a wide range of issues, including ethnic and cultural diversity, refugees and asylum seekers, democracy and politics, gender, and media education. Her major publications include *Politics and the Press in Indonesia*, *Journalism and Democracy in Asia* (co-edited with Michael Bromley) and *International Journalism and Democracy*. She is the winner of the 2005 Media Peace Award, organised by the UN Association of Australia.

ANDREW RULE has written, edited and published more than 30 true crime books—including the best-selling *Underbelly* series, with John 'Sly of the Underworld' Silvester. Their work inspired the hit *Underbelly* television drama on Melbourne's gangland war. After starting in country newspapers, he wrote variously for *The Age*, *The Herald*, *The Sun*, and *The Sunday Age* and *Good Weekend* magazine before becoming deputy editor of *The Sunday Age* in 2007. He joined *The Herald Sun* as writer at large in early 2011. He has won many national journalism awards … and claims to be the only Australian Journalist of the Year to have ridden a winner as an amateur jockey.

JESSIE SCHANZLE holds a Bachelor of Arts from the University of Toronto in Cinema Studies and Anthropology, and a Master of Communication (Journalism) from RMIT University.

MARK SKULLEY has been a journalist for 16 years with *The Australian Financial Review*, where he writes about national IR—unions and workplace issues across most industries. He also covers the Australian car industry and has a strong interest in thoroughbred horse racing; he has covered 12 Melbourne Cups for the paper. He is a former *AFR* Melbourne bureau chief and previously worked for *The Sydney Morning Herald* as a finance reporter and feature writer based in Melbourne. He is originally from Perth, where he worked for *The West Australian* newspaper, the now-defunct *Western Mail*, mining publications and country newspapers.

MARK SOLOMONS is a British journalist based in Australia. He has been Investigations Editor of *The Courier Mail* in Brisbane since October 2010, following a stint as Chief of Staff. He previously spent 10 years at the *Financial Times* in London, where he was Assistant News Editor. He occasionally lectures at the University of Queensland.

HEATHER STEWART is a freelance journalist based in Queensland, a Visiting Fellow at Queensland University of Technology, leading the First Nations' Voices For the Future AIATSIS Grant Project. She is a co-founder of the University of Queensland's Indigenous Voice Project 2009–11 and winner of the 2010 UQ Equity Award.

MELISSA SWEET is an independent journalist, media columnist, author, blogger and enthusiastic tweeter who specialises in covering public health matters. She has been writing about health and medical issues since the late 1980s, working for *The Sydney Morning Herald* and Australian Associated Press. She coordinates *Crikey*'s health blog, Croakey, and is involved in various research and teaching activities. She is Adjunct Senior Lecturer in the Sydney School of Public Health at the University of Sydney.

STEPHEN TANNER is Professor of Journalism at the University of Wollongong. He has previously worked as a journalist and government media adviser. Stephen is an active researcher, having published widely on a range of topics, including media ethics, politics and teaching practice. He is the author or editor of a number of texts, including *Feature Writing: Telling the Story* (with Nick Richardson and Molly Blair, OUP, 2009 and 2012); *Journalism Ethics at Work* (with Gail Phillips, Chris Smyth and Suellen Tapsall, Pearson, 2005) and *Journalism Investigation and Research* (Longman, 2002). He is currently lead researcher on an OLT grant looking at employer attitudes towards the qualifications of journalism graduates.

NINO TESORIERO is a public affairs and communications specialist with nearly 20 years' experience in Australia and the UK. He has worked as Press Secretary to Prime Minister Julia Gillard, as a communications advisor to a former New South Wales Deputy Premier, and as an advisor to a Director-General of the Department of Education. Nino was a journalist with the ABC, covering industrial relations, and was then a television reporter and senior political correspondent in Sydney.

HEDLEY THOMAS is a Queensland-based senior journalist for *The Australian* newspaper. He began his career at *The Gold Coast Bulletin*, followed by lengthy periods at *The Courier Mail* in Brisbane and *The South China Morning Post* in Hong Kong. He has been a London-based foreign correspondent for News Ltd and is one of Australia's best-known investigative journalists. He has won five Walkley awards, including a Gold Walkley, the Sir Keith Murdoch Award and others, including a Queensland Premier's Literary Award.

LAWRIE ZION is Associate Professor of Journalism at LaTrobe University. He has extensive experience in a range of media, including as a broadcaster on triple j, and as a journalist for *The Age* and *The Australian*. In 2007 he wrote the award-winning documentary *The Sounds of Aus*. He appears regularly on ABC radio and ABC *News Breakfast*.

ACKNOWLEDGMENTS

This is the third major book project we've worked on together—all under the auspices of Oxford University Press. In the first two we were co-authors, along with Molly Kasinger, in the feature writing text *Feature Writing: Telling the Story*. The first edition of *Feature Writing* appeared in 2009, and the second in 2012.

This project, however, is in some respects far more ambitious. We wanted to produce a book that drew on the vast knowledge and expertise that exists in Australia, both journalistic and academic. We wanted to produce a book that was pitched at both journalism students and practising journalists who were dedicated to higher forms of journalism, to seeking out and finding answers to the more complex questions that are often ignored or overlooked in the daily grind of 24/7 journalism. We also wanted to produce a book that reinforced the value and relevance of a journalist's curiosity, passion and determination to make a difference. At a time when journalism feels so precarious, it is important to underline the important contribution it makes to our public debate and to emphasise ways that journalistic activity can be maintained.

We believe this book achieves our goals—and it does so because of the willingness of the following journalists and academics who so willingly agreed to participate when approached. Our thanks—and a sincere debt of gratitude—go to: Richard Baker, Wendy Bacon, John Beveridge, William Birnbauer, Rachelle Bosua, A.J. Brown, Andrea Carson, Andrew Clausen, Trevor Cullen, Kayt Davies, Stephen K. Doig, Suelette Dreyfus, Kerry Green, Nance Haxton, Jess Hill, Kristinn Hrafnsson, Fiona Hudson, Jane Johnston, Mary Kaidonis, Karina Kelly, Rod Kirkpatrick, Reeva Lederman, Libby Lester, Sharon Mascall-Dare, Nigel McCarthy, Michael Meadows, Caro Meldrum-Hanna, Marcia P. Miceli, Simon Milton, Roger Patching, Mark Pearson, Julie Posetti, Ian Richards, Angela Romano, Andrew Rule, Jessie Schanzle, Mark Skulley, Mark Solomons, Heather Stewart, Melissa Sweet, Nino Tesorierio, Hedley Thomas and Lawrie Zion, for their outstanding contributions. We believe that the list of contributions provides a solid mix of journalistic and academic talent, brought together by a love for, and commitment to, journalism and journalism education.

On a personal level, Nick would also like to thank Sue and Patrick, who farewell him every night as he takes the short journey to the bungalow where some of the thinking and writing in this book germinated. It is often difficult for non-journalists to understand what it is about journalism that works like some exotic (or sinister) bug on otherwise rational people, but thankfully my family do understand it. And they have, as a consequence, been inoculated against it. Yet there is still something deeply satisfying about journalism. And to all those journos I've worked with and met over the years, thanks for the wonderful stories, the fun and the perspective you've given me. One of those journos was Stephen Tanner, whom it has been one of my great life pleasures to spend time with, reflecting on what it was then—and what it is now—that makes journalism so frustrating and so compelling.

As always, Stephen is indebted to Kath, Emilija, Hamish and Lucy for their love and forbearance. Not only have they had to endure Kath's life-threatening accident and my wishes to build a new family home, but they've also had to put up with multiple books and other academic projects over the past two years. Sometimes I wish I could say no, but I know I never will, certainly when it comes to projects such as this.

Stephen would also like to pay special tribute to Nick. We've come a long way since we started our journalism together at the Launceston *Examiner* in the early 1980s, and while our careers may have taken different twists and turns, we've continued to maintain a shared passion for the good things in life, namely journalism, journalism education and, as we age, increasingly better quality red wine.

Finally, to the wonderful staff at OUP. To Karen Hildebrandt, the Senior Publisher and Development Manager of OUP's Higher Education Division, thank you for believing in this project and running with it on our behalf. We've enjoyed working with you on this project, as we did the feature writing book, and we trust that it meets your exacting standards. To Estelle Tang for managing the project, and to Natasha Broadstock for editing the manuscript: thank you both. Natasha, we're delighted—for the sake of the contributors—that you couldn't find too many words to cut.

The author and the publisher wish to thank the following copyright holders for reproduction of their material.

ABC AM, 'Government will continue negotiations to pass MRRT: Wong' and the text from Black Saturday 'About Black Saturday, the website' reproduced by permission of the Australian Broadcasting Corporation and ABC Online. © 2011 ABC. All rights reserved;

Creative Tropical City: Mapping Darwin's creative industries. Sydney: CAMRA (2009). reproduced with permission of Lea, T., Luckman, S., Gibson, C., Fitzpatrick, D., Brennan-Horley, C., Willoughby-Smith, J., and Hughes, K.

Every effort has been made to trace the original source of copyright material contained in this book. The publisher will be pleased to hear from copyright holders to rectify any errors or omissions.

PART 1

CONTEXT

Introduction   3

Chapter 1: The History of Investigative Journalism in Australia   10
Case Study: The Making of an Investigative Journalist   25

Chapter 2: Lessons from Abroad: Partnerships   28

Chapter 3: *WikiLeaks* and Two New Models for Investigative Journalism   39

Chapter 4: Human Sources: The Journalist and the
        Whistle-blower in the Digital Era   48

Introduction

STEPHEN TANNER AND NICK RICHARDSON

Much has been written in recent years about the death of journalism, particularly in its longer investigative form. Various reasons have been posited for this, including the impact of technology, changing media consumption habits, and a decline in the profitability of traditional media platforms. In fact, this last-mentioned commercial perspective has driven some extraordinary pronouncements about the link between falling profits and significant journalism. Consider this: in September 2012 Simon Marais, who runs the funds management group that was the second-largest shareholder in Fairfax Media, told one of Australia's most respected journalists, Gideon Haigh, that what Haigh stood for actually didn't matter any more. 'If you don't make money you're gone. Not only must you make money you must also maximise your profits. That's what you're there for. You're not there to provide great-quality journalism' (Haigh 2012).

Working journalists everywhere should be appalled by a statement that tells them their job is actually not about 'great-quality journalism'. It is professionally, morally and ethically offensive to suggest that most of those who labour in the industry don't care about doing their best-possible work. Or indeed that there is no value attached to doing your job well. But here's the rub—the industry is so economically vulnerable that it has become financially linked to some people who don't appear to care about journalism. And if they don't care, what hope do the news consumers have? Well, we believe they should have every hope. Why? Because great-quality journalism will always have a market.

Certainly, traditional journalism has been going through a rough period, with media outlets closing or amalgamating, and journalists losing their jobs. But we believe that talk about its death is misguided. In fact we believe that journalism has a great future: that the elements that have contributed to the ructions of recent times may well provide the foundations for its survival. And that we need to avoid confusion about the future of journalism and the future of newspapers or any other content platform. It is a sombre fact that opportunities for full-time journalism careers as they were 15 or even 10 years ago have considerably lessened, but this does not mean there are fewer opportunities to actually create significant and quality journalism. In reality, the opposite is true. Newspapers are indeed undergoing enormous challenges that may prove terminal. But good journalism, as we know, can exist outside the legacy (or traditional) content models. We know that already.

Technology is the key to the future of journalism, just as it always has been. From its earliest days journalism has embraced technology. Looking back, it is easy to identify the technological milestones that have helped journalism grow. These include, but are not limited to: Gutenberg's invention of movable type, the typewriter, photography, the electric telegraph, the telephone, the facsimile machine, colour printing, radio, television, videography, the personal computer and the internet.

History has shown that those organisations and individuals that embrace new technology will survive. Those that are intimidated by it, or are dismissive of its potential, however, have often struggled. Recent history in particular has highlighted the extent to which those companies that fail to adapt to the new technology will struggle, while the early adapters will often flourish. Added to this is the fact that current technological developments—particularly those associated with computers, software, smartphones, tablets and internet-based communication, including social media—have opened up great possibilities for newcomers.

Recent technological advances—including more powerful yet smaller personal computers, greater storage capacity, better software, wireless technology, and faster internet speeds—have created tremendous opportunities for media organisations. And that's why we are excited about the future. While technology may be responsible for changes in the way we receive our news, or even the way journalists approach their information-gathering and story-telling, the fact is, it can't be blamed for the death of journalism as we know it. Journalism has always been adaptable, and the current environment highlights that.

One particularly exciting area that has responded to the challenges posed by technology is investigative journalism. For a number of years now, journalists have bemoaned the fact that media organisations have been slashing their investigative budgets, requiring their staff writers to push their investigative interests to the side while they meet the daily challenges of what one of our contributors calls 'churnalism'; that is, meeting the demands of the daily news cycle. This has led to a reduction in in-depth research and reporting, and an increasing reliance on information produced and packaged for immediate consumption by PR advisers employed by larger companies and interest groups, or in-house media people working for these groups and governments. Today, a significant percentage of material appearing in newspapers or on radio and television news bulletins is generated by PR people. A 2010 study by the University of Technology Sydney's Australian Centre for Independent Journalism suggests this may be as high as 55 per cent across major newspapers (McNamara 2012, p. 38).

PR people—and the organisations they work for—not only recognise the importance of traditional (or legacy) media, they also realise that to get their message out, they need to tap into the so-called social media. If you look at the websites of our politicians, major companies and special interest groups, you'll see that they all have Twitter, YouTube and Facebook links. They know that this is the only way to reach younger people.

While some long-established Australian media organisations are only now recognising the audience reach of social media, others have been long-time adopters, with considerable success from a circulation or ratings perspective. Journalists too have recognised the key role that social media can play in helping them to research stories.

And the benefits of tapping into such technology are numerous. First, the technology is both cheap to access and easy to use. Any device that can access the internet—smartphones, tablets, laptops and other hand-held devices—are social-media-ready, thus people can access Twitter, Facebook or YouTube while on the move or at their desk. This has proved a boon to journalists who are able to use social media to float ideas, seek information, or even enlist people to help them on their projects. As such, the introduction of social media has proved a great time-saver to journalists—both generalist, round-specific and investigative.

Second, with advances in computer hardware have come innovations in software that have changed not only the way we access media content, but also (from a journalistic perspective) the way in which stories are researched, and data is interpreted. This means that potentially the quality of journalism will improve. In fact, we're seeing that already. Journalists are now able to harness the power of computers and software applications to undertake investigations that a few years ago would have been beyond their capacity—they would have needed the support of a computer specialist, a forensic accountant, or even a private investigator to track down and interpret material. Today, such investigations are within the capacity of competent generalist and specialist journalists, as some of the case studies featured in this book reveal.

There is, however, one important caveat: technology is a wonderful tool, but it does not—and never will—replace the need for cultivating contacts and sources, and the journalist's determination and desire to talk to people. Technology brings information to your lap, or your desk, but it doesn't help you develop a relationship based on trust with a contact who can help reveal the path to the right document or data chain. Wearing out shoe leather still matters. And you will see this in the book's contributions from working journalists.

WHAT IS THE BOOK ABOUT?

As the title suggests, this book has been designed to help journalism students and journalists who are only just embarking on their career learn how to conduct complex investigations. In so doing, we are drawing on a strong history of journalism that can be traced back hundreds of years. The first known dissertation on the hows and whys of journalism was produced by Tobias Peucer in 1690 (Lloyd 2002). Peucer's thesis, *De relationibus novellis*, provides the fundamentals of news gathering that has evolved into what we see today (Lloyd 2002), both in its generalist and specialist forms. As Lloyd points out, Peucer did not embrace the notion of the media as the Fourth Estate, or watchdog; the foundations of such an idea more likely having their genesis in the writings of John Milton, whose 1644 pamphlet *Aeropagitica*, was a call for press freedom (Lloyd 2002, p. 3). Milton was writing in the mid-seventeenth century—when the idea of a free press was anathema to those in positions of power. It nonetheless appeared at a time when newspaper proprietors were beginning to lobby for greater freedoms, including the right to report on and criticise government. While a number were censored and jailed for their actions, the battles they fought paved the way for the emergence of modern journalism and the notion of journalism as the Fourth Estate.

By the early nineteenth century the fight for press freedom was being fought on a number of fronts. One of the intellectual leaders was the British philosopher John Stuart Mill, whose 1825 treatise *Liberty of the Press* highlighted the need for change:

> Mill was no great admirer of the press of his time, describing its potential offences as co-equal with the whole field of delinquency. He did acknowledge that in achieving fundamental change the press was the principal instrument. By investigation and disclosure, government would be forced to bring about reform in its own self interest. In effect, journalists acted as agitators, enforcing social reform (Lloyd 2002, p. 5).

The arguments of Milton, Mill and other intellectuals found great favour among the editors of the day. In the UK and the USA, the eighteenth and nineteenth centuries saw a maturing of journalism—both in style and output. In Australia, the early to mid-nineteenth century saw a number of battles fought between newspaper editors and their colonial governors. While the journalism of this era could hardly be described as investigative, some did begin to embrace Mill's social agitation role and the battles that were fought in the name of press freedom certainly laid some of the groundwork for the later emergence of investigative journalism, both here and abroad. In this could be seen the fundamentals of watchdog journalism, although without our modern attachment to notions of balance and fairness.

If we want to find the origins of modern investigative journalism, we need to look forward to the late nineteenth and early twentieth centuries. Having won their battles over the right to report on government without fear or favour, the liberal democratic press began to change the way in which it reported news events. Major developments came with the emergence of the 'yellow press' in the late nineteenth century, and the muckraking journalism in the early twentieth century. The latter, while generally considered a US phenomenon, also found favour in a range of Australian newspapers (Lloyd 2002).

While these movements informed the development of the modern investigative tradition, the real impetus can be traced to the so-called New Journalism of the 1960s and 70s. This form of journalism marked a noticeable change in the way journalists approached their tasks. Rather than simply reporting on events, journalists began to immerse themselves in their stories to investigate social and political wrongs. The results were significant and gave journalism not only greater credibility, but also encouragement. Journalists—and the organisations for which they worked—began to feel that they could play an important role in exposing high-level corruption, much as their muckraking forebears had done at the turn of the century, but with impunity. This was highlighted by a number of landmark cases in the 1970s, including the so-called Watergate affair in the USA, which led to the resignation of President Richard Nixon, and the thalidomide scandal in the UK. These stories kick-started the modern investigative tradition in newsrooms around the world, including Australia.

DEFINING INVESTIGATIVE JOURNALISM

This leads to the question: what is investigative journalism and how does it differ from daily journalism? Investigative journalism is often defined in ways that set it apart from daily journalism. Definitions of daily journalism, for example, tend to contain references to providing 'history's first draft', or of telling people about themselves and the communities in which they live, including those who rule them. Investigative journalism, on the other hand, is often defined as journalism in a super-added form. Take Williams' definition, for example:

> [Investigative journalism is] an intellectual process. It is a business of gathering and sorting ideas and facts, building patterns, analyzing options and making decisions based on logic rather than emotion—including the decision to say no at any of several stages (cited in Protess et al. 1991, p. 4).

However, the reality is that all journalism is—or should be—an intellectual process. While much of what journalists do tends to take a templated form, all journalism involves 'gathering and sorting ideas and facts, building patterns, analyzing options and making decisions based on logic rather than emotion'.

To gain a better insight into what investigative journalism entails, it is important to turn first to an organisation such as the American-based Investigative Reporters and Editors (IRE) for a traditional view. According to IRE, investigative journalism is:

> the reporting, through one's own work product and initiative, matters of importance which some persons or organisations wish to keep secret. The three basic elements are that the investigation be the work of the reporter, not the report of an investigation made by someone else: that the subject of the story involves something of reasonable importance to the reader or viewer: and that others are attempting to hide these matters from the public (Investigative Reporters and Editors 1983, pp. vii–viii).

However, while this definition may have been applicable in the 1960s and 70s when the Watergate and thalidomide stories were broken by journalists, or even in the 1980s and 90s, the reality is that technological advances mean that journalists cannot—and should not—expect to work in isolation. While technology is clearly the journalist's friend, enabling them to do so much more than they would previously have attempted, the reality is that investigations are no longer conducted by a journalist working alone, or in a team with a small number of colleagues from the one organisation. Today, we're finding that many of the tips that lead to journalistic exposés are provided by non-journalists—often whistle-blowers, or people who have been defrauded or jilted by the individual or organisation that becomes the subject of the journalistic inquiry. Journalists who wish to conduct investigations should not be put off by the fact that much of the initial work is undertaken by others, who then pass it on to the journalist for completion, or corroboration, and then for publication or broadcast. In fact, the truth is that the Watergate story would probably never have occurred if it had not been for the guiding hand of the then deputy director of the CIA, W. Mark Felt, who provided journalists with the initial tip-off and kept them heading down the right path throughout, particularly when they began to lose the information trail.

Felt's involvement did not amount to a formal report as such, but the reality is that reports prepared by others can certainly provide the basis of other investigations, be they a single sentence in a company's annual report, a line item in a budget, or a comment in the dissenting report of a parliamentary committee. Viewed with the right eyes, such documents—while prepared by others—can lead to major exposés by journalists.

The second and third elements identified by IRE do, however, retain their currency. Investigative journalism deals in matters of public importance, not trivialities. In that sense it can, sadly, be differentiated from a great deal of daily journalism. The reality is that much daily journalism is the product of the 24-hour news cycle. A lot of it has a limited life, and the amount of time taken to produce it is similarly short. This means that the daily product tends not to have the same energies devoted to it as its investigative sibling. While the goals of all journalism are to inform, educate and entertain, the routine of daily journalism tends to emphasise the latter, rather than the first two. Investigative reporting, on the other hand, focuses on the first two legs of the journalistic mantra—to inform and educate.

Investigative journalism focuses on the critical issues: those that have the capacity to change our world in a positive or negative way, rather than simply providing us with short-term entertainment.

Add to that the third element identified by IRE—secrecy—and the story can take on a new layer of significance. Traditionally, investigative journalism has tackled the tough stories: the politicians with their snouts in the trough, the businesses that are ripping customers off, the doctors who are mistreating patients, the medical companies that are releasing drugs onto the market prematurely, the industries that are recklessly polluting the environment. These are the big stories: the ones that have the capacity to change the world around us.

However, these stories have traditionally taken a great deal of time to pull together. They have required a considerable commitment—of time and energy by the journalist concerned, as well as a willingness on the part of their employer to give them the time and the financial resources to undertake such stories. Today, there are few media organisations with the capacity—or willingness—to devote such resources to investigations that may or may not produce a story of political, economic or moral wrongdoing.

But the good news is that by changing the way they tackle investigative stories, media outlets will continue to play an important watchdog role, without too much risk to their profitability. The answer— as this book will explain—lies in technology and teamwork. By adopting the new technology and being prepared to share the workload and the ultimate plaudits, media organisations will continue to hold governments and business to account, thereby fulfilling a role that has been nearly 400 years in the making; one that can date back at least to Tobias Peucer's thesis of 1690.

There will be echoes throughout this book of the legendary investigative journalism that made the reputation of two *Washington Post* reporters, Bob Woodward and Carl Bernstein. Almost four decades after the Watergate story triggered a presidential resignation, this example still has much to tell us about journalism in the age of digital technology. In early 2012, Woodward asked a class of journalism students at the prestigious Ivy League university, Yale, how the story would unfold in the digital age. The results shocked him to his professional bootlaces (Crovitz 2012). 'I came as close as I ever have to having an aneurysm,' he explained, 'because the students wrote that, "Oh, you would just use the Internet."' Supposedly, the details of the break-in at the Watergate building and President Richard Nixon's involvement would be contained somewhere in cyberspace. Woodward described the students' thinking as: 'somehow the Internet was a magic lantern that lit up all events'. One student wrote: 'Solid evidence proving their [the burglars'] guilt would have spread everywhere on the Internet. As a result, the Nixon Administration would have almost immediately confessed the truth of the scandal.'

Woodward's horror at this view may sound old-fashioned, but nonetheless it is vital in the current environment to remember that 'the truth resides with people', as Woodward puts it. In other words: the truth is found in human sources, not the internet (Crovitz 2012). So when you are reading this book, please remember that information and data usually needs to be tested and checked—for meaning, context and accuracy. And humans provide that testing, not the internet.

It is important to offer one final word before outlining the structure of this book. While investigative reporting is often considered a super-added form of journalism—one that is the domain of the best and brightest (Tanner 2002)—recent technological changes mean that need not be the case. There is no reason why the skills normally associated with investigative journalism should not inform, and add to, the armoury of the generalist reporter or round's specialist. Journalists should not be afraid to utilise the technology that is available both to research their stories and then present the finished product.

STRUCTURE OF THE BOOK

This book is divided into three parts. The first we've headed 'Context', because it contains a number of chapters and case studies that provide a historical background to the emergence of investigative reporting in Australia, as well as discussions about more recent trends, including collaboration between not-for-profit organisations and media companies. This section finishes with detailed discussions on *Wikileaks* and whistle-blowing.

The second part is headed 'Approaches and tools'. It contains 10 chapters and six case studies. These cover a range of topics, including research methods and approaches. Individual chapters and case studies provide tips on data analysis, including an introduction to maths and stats, and strategies for interpreting financial documents. There are also chapters on law and ethics.

The third section is headed 'Applied investigations'. This heading can apply equally to much of the material in Part 2, although we have sought to differentiate between the two by devoting the third section to round-specific approaches. In this section our contributors—via their chapters and case studies—provide strategies on how to tackle stories across a range of areas, including politics, crime, the environment, health, science, Indigenous affairs, multiculturalism, business, industrial relations and sport. The final chapter and case study provide a guide to writing up and presenting your story in an online environment.

This book has been designed to allow readers to pick and choose the chapters and case studies to suit their immediate needs. The various contributions can be read in isolation, or they can be coupled with other chapters and case studies to provide readers with the skills they require to tackle similar tasks themselves.

Whichever approach you adopt, we hope that the book both stimulates and informs. If it achieves one—or both—of these goals, then it has been successful.

Good luck with your journalism.

REFERENCES

Australian Centre for Independent Journalism. 2010. 'Over Half Your News is Spin', *Crikey*, 15 March: www.crikey.com.au (log-in required) (accessed 24 September 2012).

Crovitz. L.G. 2012. 'Before Watergate could be Googled', 17 April, *The Wall Street Journal*: http://online.wsj.com/article/SB1000142405270230 435660457734188324409625.6.html (accessed 30 September 2012).

Haigh, G. 2012. 'Brave New World', *Crikey*, 24 September: www.crikey.com.au (log-in required) (accessed 24 September 2012).

Investigative Reporters and Editors (IRE) Inc. 1983. *The Reporter's Handbook: An Investigator's Guide to Documents and Techniques*, J. Ullmann & S. Honey eds, New York: St Martin's Press.

Lloyd, C. 2002. 'The Historical Roots', in S.J. Tanner, ed., *Journalism: Investigation and Research*, Frenchs Forest, NSW: Longman.

McNamara, J. 2012. 'Journalism and Public Relations: Unpacking Myths and Stereotypes', *Australian Journalism Review*, 34(1), pp. 33–50.

Protess, D., Cook, F.L., Doppelt, J.C., Ettema, J.S., Gordon, M.T., Leff, D.R. & Miller, P. 1991. *The Journalism of Outrage: Investigative Reporting and Agenda Building in America*, New York: The Guildford Press.

Tanner, S.J. 2002. 'Introduction,' in S.J. Tanner, ed., *Journalism: Investigation and Research*, Frenchs Forest, NSW: Longman.

1

The History of Investigative Journalism in Australia

ANDREA CARSON

INTRODUCTION

The tradition of Australian investigative journalism began with newspapers. It was a slow start. The first newspapers were printed in colonial times under government control. As restrictive controls were lifted, more mastheads appeared, freer to report the news of the day. But editors for the most part remained deferential to the authorities during the nation's early years. Journalism evolved as Australians became more literate and the number of readers grew.

Developments in the UK and the USA influenced Australian reporting too. This was evident leading up to the twentieth century with the rise of muckraking tabloids, and again in the 1960s with the establishment of specialist investigative teams following successes in the UK with similar units. During the 1970s, the high-profile Watergate investigation, which ended Richard Nixon's US presidency, glamorised investigative journalism, bringing it to vogue in Australian newsrooms. But such high-impact investigative stories are rare.

This chapter is divided into three broad sections. The first details the origins of Australian investigative reporting; the second examines the growth of Australia's press and the rise of investigative journalism in all media; and the third focuses on the evolving digital media landscape and its impact on investigative journalism in the twenty-first century. Case studies illustrate particular characteristics of investigative journalism and showcase the media organisations that did it best.

THE ORIGINS OF AUSTRALIAN INVESTIGATIVE REPORTING

Australia's first newspaper—*The Sydney Gazette and New South Wales Advertiser*—was first published on 5 March 1803. It was a weekly paper with the specific purpose of delivering information from the UK to the colonies and was under government control. By 1824 government censorship had lifted, and independent newspapers emerged (Mayer 1964). Among the earliest were the broadsheets—*The Sydney Morning Herald* (*SMH*) (1831)[1] in New South Wales and *The Age* (1854) in Victoria. The noisy political debates and emerging social issues of the day began to play out in the free press.

There were some early, but rare, examples of reporting that held those with power to account. Hobart's *Colonial Times* editor Henry Melville spent time in prison for challenging the harsh treatment of prisoners in the 1830s, and exposing widespread bribery in the public houses of Hobart (Gapps 2010, p. 93). An earlier example in Sydney was the Sudd/Thompson case of 1826.

Sudd/Thompson case

William Charles Wentworth and Dr Robert Wardell (owners of *The Australian*—unrelated to the modern-day *Australian*), along with Edward Smith Hall (editor of *The Monitor*), publicly chastised New South Wales Governor Ralph Darling for the excessive punishment of Sudds and Thompson, two soldiers caught stealing calico. Sudds died within five days of being cast in iron rings, while Thompson spent a year in jail before his sentence was ruled illegal. Wentworth interviewed Thompson before accusing Darling of cruelty and torture. In response, the colony's papers were threatened with punitive licensing arrangements, while Wardell was accused of seditious libel. Darling was eventually recalled to London, and the press rejoiced (State Library of New South Wales (undated)).

REPORTING IN THE TWENTIETH CENTURY

In the late nineteenth century, British and US newspapers embraced the rise of 'yellow journalism' and the penny press—its key ingredients: sensationalist writing and scandalous content. These papers were so dubbed because they initially either featured the iconic yellow comic character 'the yellow kid', or cost a penny a paper. Tabloid in format, they attracted a mass readership (Lloyd 2002, p. 10). By the early twentieth century, these US papers had been labelled 'muckrakers' by then US President Theodore Roosevelt, who decried the behaviour of journalists he considered had crossed the line in their efforts to expose deviance in government and beyond (Mitford 1979, p. 4). By the 1950s and 60s, however, the term had gained respectability (Mitford 1979).

At the turn of the century, the Australian weekly press revelled in muckraking, using the advantage of a weekly deadline to break exclusives about shysters and charlatans, with its left-leaning journalism usually defending the common man (Lloyd 2002, p. 12). Another term for this was 'nosey journalism' (Carroll 2012). 'Nosey journalists are likely to upset long-established non-inquisitive relationships between the media and officialdom,' said Vic Carroll (2012). 'Crimes and accidents which police and politicians might find embarrassing were early rewarding targets for such nosey journalism.' Examples could be found in *The Bulletin*, John Norton's *Truth* and, a little later, *Smith's Weekly* (1919–50).

McKnight (1999, p. 156) identifies two peaks of Australian investigative journalism in the twentieth century: the first in the immediate postwar period 'when the hopes of a post war "new order" were high'; the second responding to the 'cultural and political' revolution of the 1960s, leading to an upsurge in the 1970s and early 80s. The first was usually directed at single targets, such as an unscrupulous doctor. The second involved more systemic reporting with wider targets, such as corruption within a state health department.

REPORTING AND THE COLD WAR

The transition from single-issue muckraking to systemic investigative reporting was interrupted by another period of complacency, much like the early reporting in colonial newspapers, although this time not officially under government control. By the mid-twentieth century, the mass media in Australia, as in Europe and the USA, had become largely complicit with anti-communism as the organising principle of a broader cultural Cold War (McKnight 2008). Exceptions included labour movement publications such as *The Worker* (Suich 2012). The collaborating relationship between the press and the establishment only started to pull apart as social and political movements such as feminism and Vietnam War protests gained strength. Evan Whitton (2012), a multi-award-winning investigative journalist, believed that 'the media did not tell the customer what was really going on until relatively recently'.

According to Whitton, investigative journalism did not really appear until the late 1950s (Whitton 2012). By 1956 the Walkley Awards for journalism excellence had begun. Among the few award winners (there were only five categories; today there are 34), the Melbourne *Herald* provided investigative journalism with a human interest focus.

INVESTIGATIVE JOURNALISM IN THE 1950S

In early 1957 the *Herald's* police reporter Lionel Hogg did what Victoria police were unable to do and tracked down a missing Ukrainian stewardess who deserted her ship while it was docked in Melbourne for the 1956 Olympic Games. Hogg used his extensive contacts to find the stewardess, Nina Paranyuk, who moved between three safe houses across Melbourne during her two months on the run. In Hogg's four-part series, Paranyuk told how tough life was in the Baltic states during the Cold War. The series began with Paranyuk telling Hogg:

> Ever since Stalin ordered the demolition of our tiny stone Church, I have prayed for somebody or something to take me away from the USSR. That was 24 years ago. I was only 10. I had to wait a long time before my prayers were answered (Hogg 1957).

Following the series, Paranyuk was granted asylum in Australia.

Douglas Lockwood was another early investigative journalist working for the *Herald*. Lockwood tracked down a 15-year-old Indigenous girl, Ruth Daylight. Months earlier, Daylight had trekked from her remote Halls Creek community in Western Australia to visit the Queen Mother in Canberra. Lockwood contrasted the Queen Mother's regal Canberra accommodation with the 'filthy hovel, only 3 ft high, where Ruth lives with her mother and four other Daylight children' (Lockwood 1958). The story examined the poor living conditions of Aboriginal Australians.

In 1958, the *SMH* finance editor, Tom Fitzgerald, began a small-circulation journal, *Nation*, as an outlet for explainer or investigative journalism. Whitton (2012) recalled that in 1961, Max Newton began a similar type of financial journalism at the *Australian Financial Review*, while the ABC launched its dedicated television investigative program 'Four Corners'. 'They started to query the Establishment,' said Whitton. By 1965, the editor-in-chief of Brisbane's *Courier Mail*, Sir Theodore Bray, signalled a revival of the press as the Fourth Estate in Australia:

> I would maintain that to be the Fourth Estate is still one of the main functions of the press … It has also to be a watchdog of civil liberties and a protector against the petty tyranny of bureaucrats and all those clothed with or assuming authority against the common man … Newspapers clearly have a function beyond mere reporting and recording—a function of probing behind the straight news, of interpreting and explaining and sometimes of exposing (Schultz 1998, p. 43).

INVESTIGATIVE JOURNALISM IN THE 1960S

During the Cold War, journalism was used as the cover for spies on both sides of the American–Russian divide. A famous example was that of British civil servant Kim Philby. Philby, an undercover MI6 agent, used his journalism posting in the Middle East not only to report back to the UK, but also to act as a double agent, giving secrets to Moscow. In 1963, an Australian journalist, Phillip Knightley, was part of the London *Sunday Times* investigative team 'Insight' that exposed Philby's treachery (Evans 2010).

Knightley and the 'Insight' team significantly influenced Australian investigative reporting. The editor of *The Age*, Graham Perkin, was so impressed with the work of the *Sunday Times* and its editor, Harold Evans, that he bought the rights to republish its stories in Australia, including the Philby spy ring story (Hills 2010, p. 294). Perkin then created *The Age's* own specialist investigative unit in 1967, borrowing the *Sunday Times'* investigative title 'Insight' (Hills 2010, pp. 293–4). Under Perkin's reign, *The Age* was listed as one of the world's 10 best newspapers.

Perkin also published Knightley's iconic stories about lapses in the testing of the drug thalidomide, which was sold around the world to treat morning sickness, but which instead caused thousands of birth defects. The London 'Insight' team later wrote a book appropriately titled *Suffer the Children* ('Insight' team 1979) based on their early investigations, but they did not break the story as such.[2] That was the role of Australian obstetrician William McBride, who first identified the link between birth defects and the drug, and German paediatrician Widukind Lenz, who proved the link in 1961. The drug was subsequently removed from the market. In 2012, half a century later, thalidomide victims finally received an apology from the drug's German inventors (*The Telegraph* 2012).

Despite Perkin's newly established investigative unit, it was the tabloids and their muckraking that dominated investigative reporting in the 1960s (Carson 2012). Weekend and weekly tabloids, with their longer deadlines, led the way. Sydney's *Sunday Telegraph* was the most successful, at least in terms of its number of award-winning investigative stories. Its reporter Wallace J. Crouch won the 1963 Best Feature Walkley Award for an investigation questioning widespread kangaroo culling in New South Wales. Denis O'Brien won the same award in 1966 for investigating the damaging effects of alcohol on Indigenous communities.

The tabloid *Truth*—its circulation exceeding 400 000—was also winning awards for its investigative journalism with 'big target' stories that marked the second wave of investigative journalism. Under the editorship of Sol Chandler (1965–67), Evan Whitton started experimenting with New Journalism, inspired by US writers such as Tom Wolfe. Whitton combined Chandler's demand for insignificant details and applied Wolfe's notion of using literary techniques to write vivid non-fiction news. One of Whitton's investigations from this time blew the whistle on police corruption.

Abortion and police corruption (1969)

In the late 1960s Dr Bertram Wainer was making allegations of a police protection racket involving Victorian abortionists. For a fee, police would not pursue doctors and backyard abortionists who performed illegal abortions. Whitton seized on these allegations, publishing details of six sworn affidavits alleging police extortion. The *Truth's* revelations led to a government board of inquiry chaired by Melbourne silk Bill Kaye. Three homicide detectives were jailed. The stories and Wainer's dedicated campaign led to law reform. Whitton earned his second Walkley. He said:

> The task was made easier by the failure of other organs of the media to turn up during Dr Wainer's campaign to show that bad laws made bad cops. Police roundsmen tend to be prisoners of the source. I suspect editors made the error of believing them when they said Dr Wainer was mad and bad and there was nothing in the police corruption story' (Whitton 2012).

THE GROWTH OF AUSTRALIA'S PRESS AND THE RISE OF INVESTIGATIVE JOURNALISM

In the 1960s and early 70s—a time of great political and social change—two national newspapers appeared: *The Australian* and *The National Times*. *The Australian*, established by Rupert Murdoch in 1964, did what no other paper was doing at the time: it combined the latest overseas design with clever, innovative journalism (Hills 2010, p. 227).

Seven years later, in 1971, Fairfax started its national weekly broadsheet, *The National Times*. Founded by Vic Carroll (then the *Australian Financial Review* managing editor), its mission was to analyse and uncover news behind the news (Fairfax Media 2011). Over 16 years, it broke many national stories through investigative journalism. Under the editorships of Max Suich and Whitton, its circulation exceeded 100 000. Subsequent editors David Marr, Brian Toohey and Jefferson Penberthy shifted its focus from social issues to investigating corruption and networks of influence (Schultz 1998, p. 200). But the financial woes of proprietor Warwick Fairfax Jr saw it sink.

INVESTIGATIVE JOURNALISM IN THE 1970S

By the 1970s investigative journalism was in fashion for several reasons, including the glamorisation of Bob Woodward and Carl Bernstein's Watergate investigation for the *Washington Post* (Henningham, 1990). And no discussion of Australian investigative journalists would be complete without John Pilger, the controversial, Australian documentary maker who started his career in print with Sydney's *Sunday Sun* before eventually moving to London. Walkley-winning investigative journalist Paul Robinson recalls: 'his 1970 documentary about dissension in the ranks during the Vietnam War was profound and timely, as were his documentaries about the atrocities of the Pol Pot regime in Cambodia' (2012).

Former tabloid and broadsheet editor Bruce Guthrie (2010) said the maverick editorship of *The Age's* Perkin (1966–75) also contributed to the rise of investigative journalism in local newsrooms. In addition, this period heralded the start of university graduates choosing journalism as a career, as opposed to it being seen as a craft. Robinson, who was one of the first university graduates entering journalism, explains:

> I was part of a changing world that rebelled against the Vietnam War, was suspicious of authority and contemptuous of the strict morality of past generations. Journalism was the job of a lifetime. It presented the opportunity to challenge authority, to be close to the decision-making process and a chance to play a critical part in political life (Robinson 2012).

Perkin's *Age* investigative unit, initially made up of reporter John Tidey and writer John Larkin, took time to develop. By November 1973, it was a 'dedicated investigative outfit with a full-time staff of three', headed by Ben Hills (Robinson 2012). Early successes included Hills' and Philip Chubb's revelations about Victoria's corrupt housing commission land deals (1974), which contributed to the Hamer/Thompson Government's downfall (Robinson 2012).

The author's own research shows investigative journalism in the 1970s had a broad social reform agenda, with the majority of stories targeting corporate or government power. *The National Times* and *The West Australian* produced the most Walkley-winning investigative journalism in the 1970s (Carson 2012).

The National Times won four consecutive Walkley Awards for best newspaper feature in 1975, 1976, 1977 and 1978. It was unusual compared to other newspapers of the era, in that it regularly engaged in commentary and feature writing. Its investigative stories would sometimes run beyond 10 000 words. Other papers tended to report news 'straight'.

The National Times' award-winning investigative stories included: a three-part series about Vietnam (Whitton 1974); the collapse of Australian commodities trading company the Gollin group (Gottliebsen 1978) and an inside account of when prison guards attacked inmates at Sydney's Long Bay jail (Summers 1976). The paper had several pioneering female Australian investigative journalists, including Marian Wilkinson, Anne Summers, Wendy Bacon, Deborah Snow and Adele Horin.

The West Australian published some quality investigations and won a number of Walkleys in the 1970s due to the work of Catherine Martin. Her investigation into the use of the now disreputable Tronado microwave machine then used to treat cancer (Martin 1975, p. 1) won the 1975 Walkley for Best Piece of Reporting. Two years earlier she had won a Best Feature Walkley for her two-week expedition reporting on the health conditions of Indigenous Australians and how bush nurses coped with treating diseases and malnourishment (Hurst 1988, p. 135). Martin's celebrated investigative series in 1978 exposed the deadly effects of blue asbestos on mining workers' health. Her final story in this series led to CSR, the owner of Western Australia's blue asbestos mine, establishing the Wittenoom Trust. The trust provided $2 million to affected former employees over 10 years, but CSR did not acknowledge legal liability at the time (Hurst 1988, p. 57). For this, Martin won not only the Best Piece of Reporting award, but also the inaugural Gold Walkley.

In terms of examining government power, the standout example during the 1970s came from Melbourne broadsheet *The Herald*, which ultimately contributed to the end of the Whitlam Government.

The loans affair: 'Khemlani tells' (1975)

The Whitlam Government sought to borrow about $4 billion from oil-rich Arab nations to fund large-scale natural resource and energy projects. The Federal Minister for Minerals and Energy, Rex Connor, was accused of bypassing the Treasury-approved model for raising funds by using an intermediary to tap into monies from the Middle East. By mid-1975, the controversy over the attempt to secure the funds saw Connor's authority to raise the money revoked.

Herald journalist Peter Game (1975) located and interviewed the London-based commodity trader and intermediary, Tirath Khemlani. Connor denied Khmelani's version of events. Khemlani, a meticulous record keeper, flew to Australia and provided Game with telexes between himself and Connor contradicting the minister's denials. *The Herald* published the evidence on 8 October 1975. A week later, after receiving a copy of the telexes and a statutory declaration from Khemlani, Prime Minister Gough Whitlam dismissed Connor as minister for misleading Parliament. Opposition Leader Malcolm Fraser used the 'extraordinary and reprehensible' example as one reason for using his numbers in the Senate to block supply. This led to the Australian constitutional crisis that saw Whitlam dismissed from office by the Governor-General, Sir John Kerr.

INVESTIGATIVE JOURNALISM IN THE 1980S

At its best, investigative journalism provides transparency and accountability of public figures and institutions. It shines a light where cover-ups and corruption prosper. Crime reporter David Richards achieved this when he investigated corruption within the Federated Ships, Painters and Dockers' Union.

Union murders and mayhem (1980)

Richards' 1980 four-part series in Australia's oldest news magazine, *The Bulletin* (1880–2008), was the ammunition the Fraser Government needed to launch the Costigan Royal Commission.

Richards' research involved funeral parlour stake-outs, secret interviews at Pentridge with criminal Billy 'The Texan' Longley, and working closely with police. He uncovered murders, thefts, and a 'ghosting' scheme where waterside workers collected pay packets for hours not worked. The subsequent Royal Commission unearthed much more.

The Costigan Royal Commission (1980–84) found evidence of 36 murders and attempted murders of union associates. It also discovered wrongdoing beyond union ranks. It used advanced computer programming to expose white collar crime and tax evasion, including the infamous 'bottom of the harbour' schemes. This caused the Fraser Government embarrassment because it had failed to outlaw them. The final report, filling 20 volumes, led to the reversal of High Court tax decisions, and the establishment of the National Crime Authority. At one point, the reputation of media magnate Kerry Packer—ironically *The Bulletin's* owner—was called into question by the *National Times*. No charges were brought against Packer, who strenuously denied any wrongdoing, but he was branded with the everlasting moniker, 'the Goanna'.

'The Age tapes' (1983–84)

Australia's major media organisations often argue that self-regulation is an important element of a free press, and that the media are best able to judge what is in the public interest. But this is not always a simple judgment. Sometimes the end is thought to justify the means. Take, for example, the investigative story known as '*The Age* tapes' (1984).

The Age faced a dilemma: to publish the transcripts of illegal Australian Federal Police recordings, or to refrain because of their dubious acquisition and legal status. *The Age* chose to publish (interestingly, the *SMH* chose not to) (Schultz 1998, p. 215).

The controversial series of reports documented links between organised crime in New South Wales, police and government, resulting in corruption allegations against former Attorney-General and High Court justice Lionel Murphy. The transcripts of police telephone intercepts were of calls between Murphy and New South Wales solicitor Morgan Ryan who was facing criminal charges at the time. Ryan had high-profile 'underworld' clients and the transcripts allegedly showed that he sought information from Murphy about whether certain police were corruptible (Wilson 1986, p. 1). Murphy was charged with attempting to pervert the course of justice and was tried twice; he was found guilty on the first hearing, but not guilty on the second. Ryan had been convicted in 1983 of conspiring to help 22 Koreans enter Australia illegally, but the conviction was quashed on appeal, and the retrial was later dropped (Robinson 1987, p. 1).

The Age tapes led to seven separate inquiries and the Stewart Royal Commission. The New South Wales Government responded to the series by passing the *Listening Devices Act 1984*, to tighten the law (Schultz 1998, p. 215).

Fairfax produced the most investigative journalism in the 1980s (Carson 2012). It was a prolific freelancer in Western Australia, Jan Mayman, who collected the 1984 Gold Walkley for *The Age*. Her stories about police brutality within a West Australian Indigenous community exposed the death of 16-year-old John Pat, who died in police custody at Roebourne.

The 1980s was also a golden era for television investigative reporting. Chris Masters' report for *Four Corners* about police corruption in Queensland, 'The Moonlight State', proved that Sir Larry Lamb, the former editor of *The Australian*, was wrong when in 1982 he told *The Bulletin* that, 'Television is no good at all at the big investigative type of story' (Schultz 1998, p. 61). 'The Moonlight State' confirmed that the media had become 'equal contenders' in the existing power dynamic, and not, as previously thought, 'cooperating servants' to authoritative figures (Schultz 1998, p. 224).

'The Moonlight State' (1987)

Queensland's Fitzgerald Inquiry was sparked days after 'The Moonlight State' aired. This enormously important story, which was separately investigated by *The Courier Mail's* Phil Dickie, documented the role played by Queensland's senior police and government officials in illegal drug, gambling and prostitution rackets. It resulted in the imprisonment of Police Commissioner Sir Terence Lewis and several government ministers, and the later resignation of the Premier, Sir Joh Bjelke-Petersen.

Allegations of corruption and unethical practices against the National Party Government were not new. Quentin Dempster's earlier ABC documentary, *The Sunshine System*, showed how Queensland had not worked properly for 70 years. However, what Dickie and Masters did was to firmly establish a pattern, and provide an historical context for how the corruption had been able to develop and flourish. Masters (2011) explains:

> It wasn't just the revelation of a set of facts that indicated that police and government had a corrupt relationship with criminal entities, etc; there was a three-dimensional story there about institutional corruption and the exploitation of public innocence. There was a history story there as well as a news story.

FROM PRINT TO BROADCAST AND BEYOND

The ABC hired its first radio journalist in 1934. It was not until 1967, however, that it began its half-hour morning current affairs program, *AM*, which had occasional investigative stories, as did niche programs such as *The Health Report*, hosted by Dr Norman Swan. Swan won the 1988 Gold Walkley for exposing the fraudulent medical research of Dr William McBride (unrelated to McBride's famous work linking thalidomide to birth deformities). Yet radio's only dedicated investigative program is Radio National's *Background Briefing*, which has consistently won Walkley Awards for its investigations, including Mark Aaron's series in the 1980s on Australia's policy of accepting ex-Nazis as refugees.

The ABC also pioneered television investigative journalism, broadcasting *Four Corners* (from 1961), then *This Day Tonight* (1967–79). Graeme Turner (2005) wrote that 1967 was about the time that hard-hitting investigative reports replaced *This Day Tonight's* polite interviews. Hosted by Bill Peach, the program produced a generation of Australian journalists, among them: Gerald Stone, Richard Carleton, Caroline Jones, Mike Willesee, Mike Carlton, Allan Hogan, George Negus, Peter Luck,

Andrew Olle, Clive Hale, Manning and Stuart Littlemore. In 1973, Mike Carlton, Littlemore and Peach's report into illegal gambling in New South Wales highlighted the program's financial and editorial commitment to investigative reporting.

Investigative television programs at Channel Nine have included *Sunday* (1981–2008) and long-time stalwart *60 minutes* (from 1979). Even in its last days, *Sunday* was winning awards, including three Walkleys for Ross Coulthart and Nick Farrow's 'Butcher of Bega' story. They found victims to tell the story of Dr Graeme Stephen Reeves, who deliberately mutilated and sexually abused up to 500 female patients while working as a gynaecologist and obstetrician at various hospitals across Sydney and the New South Wales hamlet of Bega. Reeves was deregistered and jailed.

Channel Seven's past investigative program contributions have included *Witness* (1996–98), hosted by investigative journalist Paul Barry, and *Real Life* (1992), which enticed Gerald Stone to come back to Australia from the USA. Seven currently produces *Sunday Night*, with Coulthart on staff.

Many award-winning investigative television programs were unable to hold audiences and were replaced with populist, tabloid formats offering consumer and celebrity stories. This was the case for Ten's *Page One* (1988–89) and its successor *Public Eye* (1989). Despite luring journalists such as Kerry O'Brien, Chris Masters and Maxine McKew, they were unable to attract large audiences (Turner 2005, p. 41). Current programs that do some investigative reporting include SBS's *Dateline* and the ABC's *Foreign Correspondent*, *7.30* and *Lateline*.

INVESTIGATIVE JOURNALISM IN THE 1990S

Following the Australian stock market crash in 1987, and some high-profile business collapses such as Victoria's Pyramid Building Society, the 1990s was the start of an upswing in investigative business reporting, which peaked in the 2000s (Carson 2012). This was particularly evident at the *Australian Financial Review*, with many examples including Pamela Williams' Gold Walkley-winning series about the political manoeuvrings behind the 1998 Waterfront dispute. Jonathan Holmes (2011) observes that in the 1990s investigative reporters followed up the collapse of the stock market, but they were slow to expose wrongdoers as the drama was unfolding. 'The big bank collapses that happened in Victoria and South Australia went largely unnoticed and were not exposed by anyone's journalism as they should have been,' he said. According to Holmes, it was not investigative journalism's best decade, although there were some exceptions, such as Paul Barry's exposé of the dodgy dealings of billionaire Alan Bond.

The standout award-winning papers in this decade were *The Courier Mail* and the weekly *Sunday Age* (Carson 2012). In 1993 the *Sunday Age*'s Paul Robinson undertook a three-month investigation into Australians involved in sex tourism in Thailand and the Philippines. The exposé led to the enactment of new laws making it an offence to commit sexual offences against children while travelling abroad.

The Courier Mail's most notable investigations included David Bentley's 1995 Gold Walkley for exposing author Helen Darville as a literary hoax. Darville wrote the award-winning novel *The Hand that Signed the Paper*, claiming to be Helen Demindenko, an author with Ukrainian heritage writing from family experience about the Holocaust. *The Courier Mail*'s Paul Whittaker also won two Walkleys for exposing government corruption. The first was for the 'Net Bet affair' in 1999, with Hedley Thomas. This investigation linked the company that won Queensland's first internet gaming licence to three Labor Party figures who were likely to financially benefit from the deal. Two ministers were forced to stand down as a result. The other was 'Operation Wallah', which revealed a secret investigation where the Criminal Justice Commission and the Australian Federal Police were at odds about pursuing prostitution and gambling rackets in Queensland, raising the question of political intervention. The Criminal Justice Commission probe uncovered possible breaches of US and Australian laws relating to a multimillion-dollar fraud involving government defence contracts, the bribery of company officials and the illicit trade of huge quantities of computer semi-conductors (Whittaker 1995).

The Courier Mail produced many investigative stories in the 1980s and 90s, but when it became a tabloid in 2006, like its sister paper the *Adelaide Advertiser* (which converted from broadsheet to compact in 1997), their Walkley Award-winning investigative journalism all but ended.

THE EVOLVING DIGITAL MEDIA LANDSCAPE AND INVESTIGATIVE JOURNALISM IN THE TWENTY-FIRST CENTURY

The changing economic and technological landscape of the news media has led some critics to argue that Australian news media no longer fulfils its Fourth Estate function. Among them is former Federal Minister Lindsay Tanner, who criticises shallow, sensationalist reporting, particularly of political personalities at the expense of policy coverage (2011).

Criticism of the news media is also expressed more broadly through increased public cynicism. Regular polling shows that the media lacks public trust and that journalists are poorly regarded compared to other professionals (Essential Research 2008). British academic Bob Franklin (2008, p. 3) said a widespread downmarket approach to news is a direct threat to investigative journalism. Franklin (2008, p. 15) used the term 'newszak' to describe a raft of changes to the style and content of newspapers, including, 'a retreat from investigative journalism and hard news to the preferred territory of "softer" or "lighter" stories'. This trend is also sometimes referred to as 'dumbing down' and the 'tabloidisation' of news (Schudson 2003, p. 93).

Another threat to investigative journalism is the time, commitment and cost required to authenticate or discard a story. In the digital age, the media cycle is fast and focused on breaking news, and—increasingly—opinion and commentary. Investigative journalism needs employers who are committed to producing it. 'It can get very expensive,' said multi-award-winning investigative television reporter Ross Coulthart (2011), who also said he feels lucky to still have the support of his commercial network, which recently allowed him to travel to four countries while pursuing one investigative story.

Investigative journalism yields a greater chance for lengthy litigation against the journalist, the publisher or both. And there is also the emotional cost. Masters (2011) said that even when you want to say goodbye to stories, you can't because sometimes you spend years defending them in court. 'It is easy to get really angry with how lonely you feel, when you are in a big fight that goes on forever, and it seems that so often you have to wear most of it on your own,' he said.

INVESTIGATIVE JOURNALISM 2000–20

Despite this, investigative journalism hit a second peak in the early 2000s, even higher than that of the 1970s (Carson 2012). Against the predictions of many, and noting that *The National Times* ceased publication in 1987, the volume of investigative stories increased. The most popular story topics were crime and corporate corruption. While Australian masthead circulations fell, the amount of investigative reporting did not —at least not at the end of the first decade of the 2000s.

In the early 2000s, Fairfax continued the trend of the previous two decades and produced more investigative journalism than any other print organisation. In this decade, the financial tabloid, the *Australian Financial Review*, produced more investigative stories than previously. Its topics were evenly divided between individual and corporate corruption. It included a profile on high-flying stockbroker Rene Rivkin and his undisclosed Swiss bank accounts (Chenoweth et al. 2003, p. 1). This team effort won both the 2004 Gold Walkley and the Business Journalism Award. The following year, the late Morgan Mellish wrote a 3500-word profile on Liberal Party donor and multimillionaire businessman Robert Gerard, who was being investigated by the Australian Tax Office for allegedly avoiding tax using an elaborate and fraudulent offshore insurance scheme. Gerard had been awarded a medal of the Order of Australia by Prime Minister John Howard and appointed to the board of the Reserve Bank for five years (Mellish 2005, p. 58). Corporate stories focused on shareholders who lost millions following the collapses of financial companies, including Opes Prime and Storm (Chenoweth et al. 2008, p. 1; Hughes 2009, p. 1).

Two other trends became apparent in that decade. The first was the increase in syndicating stories across mastheads within the same group. Fairfax began this in the late 1980s and by 2010 the practice had grown exponentially. The other was print media's collaboration with outside media organisations; for example, the use of *WikiLeaks* material as a starting point for investigative stories in Fairfax mastheads.

The Age and the ABC have also teamed up to gain greater audience share, most notably on the 'Money Makers'. Mark Baker (2012) explains the decision to share resources with the ABC:

> I saw it as a good opportunity to raise the profile of the story because we had been plugging away at it for over a year or so, at that stage, and we had had significant impact: the police investigation was under way and all the rest of it. But the story was hard to get traction outside of Victoria. After 'Four Corners' the story got a new lease of life and got a better national profile and we were then able to drive it to new heights, and then of course we saw charges being laid and the story continues to evolve, so it was a good deal.

The 'Money Makers' (2009)

Journalists Richard Baker and Nick McKenzie uncovered Australia's biggest bribery scandal involving the Reserve Bank of Australia's subsidiary currency firms, Note Printing Australia and Securency. Australia's foreign bribery laws were enacted for the first time, charging the firms and local and international senior managers with corruption offences. *The Age* stories claimed bribes were paid to secure bank-note-making contracts overseas, including in Vietnam, Malaysia, Indonesia and Nepal. Three years after the story broke, Reserve Bank Governor Glenn Stevens told a 2012 federal parliamentary committee that his deputy was warned in writing of corruption inside the bank's operations in 2007 (McKenzie & Baker 2012, p. 2).

Despite the official ABC collaboration, there was remarkably little acknowledgment or follow-up from other media about this international corruption story, particularly from print. Several journalists have privately attributed this to the toxic competition between Fairfax Media and News Limited. Masters (2011) said the media's failure to follow up a good story is a grave disservice to the public. 'One of the reasons that these stories aren't going further, is because sometimes the competition is so poisonous that a story won't have carriage because competitors refuse to acknowledge that it existed,' he said.

INVESTIGATIVE JOURNALISM TODAY

The future of investigative journalism in the 2010s is unclear. Up until 2010, the *SMH* and *The Age* had produced more investigative journalism than any other masthead in the past seven decades. In June 2012, however, Australian newspapers suffered a crushing blow. Both News Limited and Fairfax announced major changes to the operations of their newspapers. Fairfax would close its Sydney and Melbourne printing presses, and the *SMH* and *The Age* would become tabloid in 2013. Fairfax announced paywalls for its online content from 2013 and the loss of 1900 jobs, with a quarter of these coming from the editorial floor. Similarly, News Limited announced editorial job losses, the number undisclosed, and greater sharing of its content and resources across its mastheads (Norrie 2012).

The then Managing Editor at Fairfax Media, Mark Baker, acknowledges that legal costs, salaries to retain experienced journalists, and travel and time expenses make investigative journalism a multimillion dollar enterprise (2012). However, Baker also said that the digital media landscape provides new opportunities for investigative journalism. In an environment where news is ubiquitous and free, investigative journalism offers readers unique information for which they might be prepared to pay. 'We need to do more of it, not less … where we want to make money is on the strength and credibility of our investigative journalism,' he said prior to Fairfax's restructure. Similarly, in 2010, *The Australian* emphasised investigative journalism in its national mantle, launching a dedicated unit led by Hedley Thomas (Mitchell 2011).

Even after the announcement of cutbacks, newspapers are still the largest employers of journalists in Australia. Few Australian stand-alone websites have the resources to perform ongoing investigative journalism. The online sphere only began receiving Walkley Awards for its investigative journalism in the early 2000s. Those winners were almost entirely made up of the traditional print media producing online stories, with the exception of the ABC, which won a Walkley for its online coverage in 2002 with 'The Timber Mafia'.

As Birnbauer discusses in Chapter 2, media websites have collaborated with traditional media internationally with great success. For example, *The New York Times* partnered with online newsroom *ProPublica* to win the 2010 US Pulitzer Prize for investigative journalism. *ProPublica* is a not-for-profit organisation that secures philanthropic funds to produce investigative journalism in the public interest. Its philanthropic model offers a future for investigative journalism, and has been replicated elsewhere, including Australia.

Another online model that might provide a future for investigative journalism is *WikiLeaks*, which is discussed in detail by Hrafnsson and Dreyfus in Chapter 3. Like *ProPublica*, *WikiLeaks* has collaborated with traditional media to extend its audience reach. Whitton (2012) said that by definition *WikiLeaks* is investigative reporting because 'it exposes wrongdoing'. In 2011, the Walkley Board awarded *WikiLeaks* the prize for most outstanding contribution to Australian journalism for delivering an 'avalanche of inconvenient truths'.

The honour divided industry opinion. Some viewed the web-based organisation as akin to a warehouse for information, which is then retailed by others. Nonetheless, *WikiLeaks'* recognition did underscore a successful partnership with traditional media to expose wrongdoing and hidden truths.

CONCLUSION

This chapter has outlined the origins of the Australian investigative journalism tradition, evolving from the deferential media of the colonial era, to the muckraking stories of the late nineteenth century, with its antecedents belonging to both the UK and USA. Australian watchdog reporting has experienced peaks and troughs in newsrooms, with a notable lull during the Cold War years when the fear of communism was high. With some exceptions, this period engendered a largely unquestioning relationship between the press and the establishment. The social and political upheaval of the late 1960s, the US Watergate scandal in the 1970s, university education, and the standout *Age* editorship of Graham Perkin inspired a second wave of watchdog-style reporting in Australian newsrooms, resulting in historic outcomes in the public interest.

Each decade in recent times has offered a different contribution to investigative journalism. The evening papers had early success in the 1950s, followed by the weekly tabloids in the 1960s. Broadcast investigative journalism evolved throughout the 1960s and 70s and experienced great success thereafter. But to date, it has been Australia's broadsheet newspapers that have done more investigative reporting than any other media. In the digital era, *WikiLeaks* and other story collaborations between various media organisations seem to be heralding a new approach to investigative reporting. While the print business model supporting investigative journalism has changed—making its future less certain—the need for public scrutiny and accountability of those with power remains as necessary as ever.

QUESTIONS TO CONSIDER

1   To what extent have 'yellow journalism' and muckraking journalism influenced the development of modern investigative journalism?

2   In what ways have the types of stories undertaken by investigative journalists changed over time?

3   Of the journalists and editors mentioned in this chapter, who do you consider has had the strongest influence and why?

TASK

1   Access two of the stories discussed in this chapter (one from an early era (pre-1970s), and the other from a later era (1990s and beyond)). See if you can identify how the stories were researched. List the sources and documents mentioned, any strategies the journalist may have used, and any difficulties they may have encountered in pulling this story together.

What does the story say about the difficulties confronting investigative journalists? Have the approaches changed over time?

REFERENCES

Baker, M. 2012. Interview with the author, 11 January.

Carroll, V.J. 2012. Interview with Evan Whitton for the author, 8 February.

Carson, A. 2012. 'Investigative Journalism, the Public Sphere and Australian Democracy: The Watchdog Role of Newspapers in the Digital Age', unpublished PhD thesis, University of Melbourne.

Chenoweth, N., Drummond, M., Nicholas, K. & A. White. 2008. 'Inside Job: Who Killed Opes Prime?', *Australian Financial Review*, 12 June.

Chenoweth N., Elam. S., Ryan. C. 2003. 'Rivkin's Swiss Bank Scandal', *Australian Financial Review*, 30 October.

Coulthard, R. 2011. Interview with the author, 28 December.

Essential Research. 2008. *MEAA—Research on the Future of Journalism*, Sydney: Essential Research.

Evans, H. 2010. *My Paper Chase: True Stories of Vanished Times*, London: Abacus.

Fairfax Media. 'History of the National Times'. Sydney: Fairfax Media: www.nationaltimes.com.au/aboutnationaltimes (accessed 25 February 2011).

Franklin, B. (ed.). 2008. *Pulling Newspapers Apart: Analysing Print Journalism*, Abingdon: Routledge.

Game, P. 1975. 'Khemlani Tells', *Herald*, 8 November.

Gapps, S. 2010. *Front Pages that Shaped Australia*, Millers Point: Murdoch Books Australia.

Gottliebsen, R. 1978. '"Gollin" the $120 million crash', *National Times*, 3 October.

Guthrie, B. 2010. Interview with the author, 11 February.

Henningham, J. 1990. *Issues in Australian Journalism*, Melbourne: Longman Cheshire Pty Limited.

Hills, B. 2010. *Breaking News: The Golden Age of Graham Perkin*, Melbourne: Scribe.

Hogg, L. 1957. 'Nina Tells: Why I Fled', *Herald*, 9 February.

Holmes, J. 2011. Interview with the author, 19 December.

Hughes, D. 2009. 'ASIC knew about Storm for Months', *Australian Financial Review*, 2 April.

Hurst, J. 1988. *The Walkley Awards: Australia's Best Journalists in Action*, Melbourne: John Kerr Pty Ltd.

'Insight' team. 1979. 'Suffer the Children', London: *Sunday Times*.

Lloyd, C. 2002. 'The Historical Roots', in S.J. Tanner, ed., *Journalism: Investigation and Research*, Frenchs Forest, NSW: Longman.

Lockwood, D. 1958. 'Now Ruth is Back in Native Hovel', *Herald*.

Martin, C. 1975. 'Tronado Cancer Device Blasted', *West Australian*, 16 April.

Masters, C. 2011. Interview with the author, 15 February.

Mayer, H. 1964. *The Press in Australia*, Melbourne: Lansdowne Press.

Mayman, J. 1983. 'A Town with Two Names and Two Laws', *The Age*, 14 October.

McKenzie, N. & Baker, R. 2012. 'Reserve Chief Admits Bank Knew of Corruption', *The Age*, 25 February.

McKnight, D. 1999. 'The Investigative Tradition in Australian Journalism 1945–1965', in A. Curthoys & J. Schultz, eds, *Journalism: Print, Politics and Popular Culture*, St Lucia: University of Queensland Press, pp. 155–67.

McKnight, D. 2008. '"Not Attributable to Official Sources": Counter-Propaganda and the Mass Media', *Media International Australia, Incorporating Culture & Policy*, 128 (Aug), pp. 5–17.

Mellish, M. 2005. 'The Rise and Fall of a Liberal Bankroller', *Australian Financial Review*, 29 November.

Mitchell, C. 'Award-Winning Journalists to Undertake Special Investigations', *The Australian*: www.theaustralian.com.au/national-affairs/award-winning-journalists-to-undertake-special-investigations/story-fn59niix-1225942450312 (accessed 3 March 2011).

Mitford, J. 1979. *The Making of a Muckraker*, London: Michael Joseph.

Norrie, J. 'Fairfax to Cut 1900 Jobs, Shut Printers in Huge Downsize', Melbourne: The Conversation: www.theconversation.edu.au (accessed 18 June 2012).

Robinson, P. 1987. 'Morgan Ryan Faces False Evidence Count', *The Age*, 27 February.

Robinson, P. 2012. Interview with the author, 20 January.

Schudson, M. 2003. *The Sociology of News*, San Diego: W.W. Norton & Company.

Schultz, J. 1998. *Reviving the Fourth Estate: Democracy, Accountability and the Media*, Melbourne: Cambridge University Press.

State Library of New South Wales. Undated. *The Sudds and Thompson Case*, Discover Collections, Sydney: State Library of New South Wales: www.sl.nsw.gov.au/discover_collections/history_nation/justice/sudds/index.html (accessed 4 February 2012).

Suich, M. 2012. Interview with Evan Whitton for the author, 8 February.

Summers, A. 1976. 'The Day the Screws were Turned Loose', *National Times*, 19 April.

Tanner, L. 2011. *Sideshow: Dumbing Down Democracy*, Melbourne: Scribe Publications.

The Telegraph. 2012. 'Thalidomide: Timeline of a Scandal', 1 September: www.telegraph.co.uk/health/healthnews/9513903/Thalidomide-timeline-of-a-scandal.html (accessed 1 September 2012).

Turner, G. 2005. *Ending the Affair: The Decline of Television Current Affairs in Australia,* Sydney: University of New South Wales Press.

Whittaker, P. 1995. 'FBI Probes Richo Mate', *Courier Mail*, 13 March.

Whitton, E. 1974. 'The Truth about Vietnam', *National Times*, 28 April.

Whitton, E. 2012. Interview with the author, 8 February.

Wilson, D. 1986. 'Issues the Murphy Judges will Examine', *The Age*, 15 May.

WEBSITE REFERENCES

ProPublica: About Us: www.propublica.org/about/.

FURTHER READING

de Burgh, H. 2000. *Investigative Journalism*, London: Routledge.

McNair, B. 2007. *An Introduction to Political Communication*, J. Curran, ed., 4th edn, Abingdon: Routledge.

O'Donnell, P. 2009. 'That's Gold! Thinking About Excellence in Australian Journalism', *Australian Journalism Review*, 31(2), pp. 47–60.

O'Donnell, P. & McKnight, D. 2010. 'The Future of Quality Journalism', in *Life in the Clickstream 2: The Future of Journalism*, Sydney: Media Arts and Entertainment Alliance.

Ricketson, M. 1999. 'Newspaper Feature Writing in Australia 1956–1996', in A. Curthoys & J. Schultz, eds, *Journalism: Print, Politics and Popular Culture*, St Lucia: University of Queensland Press.

Schudson, M. 2008. *Why Democracies Need an Unlovable Press*, Cambridge: Polity Press.

Simons, M. 2007. *The Content Makers: Understanding the Media in Australia*, Melbourne: Penguin.

Tiffen, R. 2010. 'The Press', in S. Cunningham & G. Turner, eds, *The Media and Communications in Australia*, Sydney: Allen and Unwin, pp. 81–96.

Tiffen, R. 1999. *Scandals, Media, Politics & Corruption in Contemporary Australia*, Sydney: University of News South Wales Press.

Tiffen, R. & Gittins, R. 2009. *How Australia Compares*, 2nd edn, Melbourne: Cambridge University Press.

Wilkinson, M. 2012. Interview with the author, 30 January.

NOTES

1   *The Sydney Morning Herald* was first called *The Sydney Herald*, and it is the oldest continuously published newspaper in Australia. It become a daily in 1840 and changed its name to *The Sydney Morning Herald* in 1842.

2   However, it was not until Knightley and the investigative team's long-running newspaper campaign in the 1970s that £28 million compensation was paid out to UK victims, a substantial increase on the earlier 1968 settlement, by the UK manufacturers Diageo.

THE MAKING OF AN INVESTIGATIVE JOURNALIST

Richard Baker

I knew I wanted to be a journalist when I turned 16.

My family had moved to London for a few months and I spent weekends ploughing through editions of newspapers such as *The Guardian*, *The Times, The Sunday Times* and *The Observer*.

I found I was getting to the end of stories about people or subjects I knew nothing about—and not just stories from the sports pages (I was and remain a sports nut).

Perhaps it was because winter was looming, the days short and dark, and I had little else to do.

But I prefer to think that it was the great writing, the immense variety of topics and the sating of my natural curiosity that inspired me to pursue a career in journalism.

Of all the stories I read, the ones that had me most hooked were those that took me somewhere new and gave an insight into a world that had, hitherto, been secret.

These were the stories the rich and powerful wanted kept from the public. Although it has become a cliché, it remains a pithy and accurate description of investigative journalism.

When I arrived back in Australia and returned to my high school, I was set on becoming a journalist: the journalist who got the story behind the story.

After completing an arts degree majoring in journalism, I was fortunate enough to begin a cadetship at *The Age* in 1999. But I would have gone to the smallest country paper to get a start.

From there I had stints as the rural reporter and covering Victorian politics. Both were good training grounds for an aspiring investigative reporter.

Rural reporting for a city paper forced you to think outside the square just to get a run and taught you the importance of making the effort to meet people face to face. I found country people had far more time for a reporter from a big city paper if you actually travelled to see them rather than just talked over the phone.

Politics was a place to build a network of contacts across political parties, the public service, police and lobbying types. It was also a competitive environment that kept you sharp.

And so in 2005, I joined *The Age*'s investigative team under the editorship of the mercurial Andrew Jaspan. The senior man in the team was Gary Hughes, a multiple Walkley-Award-winning journalist.

What struck me about Hughes was the meticulous nature of his research. When he got his teeth into an issue, he made sure he had a mouthful of flesh before he published.

Though the membership of the investigative team has undergone several changes, I have remained and continue to enjoy my work there.

My definition of investigative journalism has sharpened over the years. In essence, I believe all journalism should have an investigative edge. After all, there is no point giving the public what it already knows. Good journalism should be motivated by the desire for truth.

But in today's ever-shrinking, budget-conscious newsrooms, the rounds reporters are so stretched to file across the day for print, online, iPad and smartphones that they do not always have the opportunity to probe as deep as they would like.

That privilege and responsibility rests with the few in the investigative team who are given time and resources to peel back the layers of a story.

I believe classic hard-core investigative journalism can be boiled down to two elements.

First, as I mentioned before, it is giving the public information that they should know but would not if it were not for good journalism.

Second, the real power of investigative journalism is unearthing something that is of benefit to society.

This can range from exposing corruption at the highest levels of government to giving a voice to those without one in order to right a wrong.

A recent example of this at *The Age* was when my colleague Nick McKenzie and I uncovered 36 unexpected, unnatural or violent deaths of patients in Victoria's public mental health system.

We spent months with the families of three of the victims and told the story of their frustration because health authorities had, to varying degrees, covered up rather than explain what happened.

In the wake of the September 2011 series, Premier Ted Baillieu announced a review of the 36 deaths. Six months later, his government declared a series of reforms about the way deaths in the mental health system are responded to by health services, with an emphasis on respect for the grieving families.

It is an example of investigative journalism in the public interest leading to change for the better.

So what is a typical day like for me at *The Age's* investigative team? Apart from beginning with a strong coffee, a common feature is a conversation with McKenzie.

Over the past few years, we've worked successfully on several big stories as a team. It works because we have compatible personalities and work ethics.

We share tips, contacts and pool our knowledge. It means we can cover more bases faster and have more stories bubbling away.

We collaborate and, at times, argue over the strength of our information and quality of our writing. This process has proven to be a vital element in ensuring one reporter does not become captive to a source or too bent on a particular theory.

While it might not be for everyone, we have found working as a team to be an invaluable asset.

Perhaps our most successful joint effort is our three-year (and ongoing) project to unearth bribery and corruption across Asia and Africa by the Reserve Bank of Australia's currency-printing subsidiaries, Securency and Note Printing Australia.

There is no way we could have uncovered the network of agents and tax havens through which federal police allege bribes were paid to government officials in Malaysia, Indonesia, Vietnam and Nepal if we did not pool contacts and share the fruits of our labours.

This is an example of a story that can only be done by a dedicated, well-funded investigative team. There is no way a reporter answering daily to the whims of the news desk could have got a tenth of the story.

The Reserve Bank of Australia scandal is a perfect example of the difference that investigative journalism can make. It has led to Australia's first prosecutions for foreign bribery and to proposed legislative change to beef up anti-corruption laws.

One of the most important facets of investigative reporting is getting out and talking to people. Not many good stories come from sitting in the office and staring at the screen. It was something I learned doing the rural round.

Human conversation in this day is more important than ever for several reasons. First, contacts or sources feel more comfortable spending time face to face. It's about establishing a relationship and trust.

Each week I make an effort to get out and see various people from all walks of life. I may have no pressing reason to have a coffee with a particular person, but I know they value you making the time just to have a chat about what is going on without feeling they are being pressed for information.

I find that these conversations might not immediately lead to a story. But they may plant the germ of an idea in your head that you build upon months later.

Face-to-face contact is also important for source protection. With more government agencies and private corporations taking an aggressive attitude to leaks of information—even those clearly in the public interest—one way to protect a source is to minimise all electronic contact.

It is routine for call-charge records to be checked to trace phone calls and triangulate on a source. Email leaves a trail.

So, despite the advances in modern technology, it is increasingly preferable to go back to methods of communication from another age.

These can be using snail mail to a PO box. Or an agreed meeting point away from CCTV for a face-to-face chat.

For all an investigative journalist's skill and determination, the biggest key to successful reporting is the whistle-blower.

They are the people on the inside who have the conscience to expose corruption and wrongdoing, often at considerable personal and professional risk.

They are the sparks that lead to the best and most important stories. Investigative journalists, no matter how skilled, cannot possibly know what is going on inside the crooked mining company that is dumping toxic waste or in the police squad that is leaking information to bikie gangs.

The only people who do are the whistle-blowers.

It is the responsibility of investigative journalists and those who publish or broadcast their work to do all they can to protect and look after those who come to them seeking to expose wrongdoing.

It is a delicate and often complicated balancing act, for the journalist also has a duty to report in the public interest.

The biggest danger to investigative journalism is the willingness of governments, police and security agencies, private corporations and wealthy individuals to go after the source of the story.

This is evidenced by leak investigations in the public sector, phone-bugging operations by police and anti-corruption bodies, and legal action by corporations and individuals.

Such situations are immensely stressful for both the journalist and source. In addition, they are a further financial drain on the media companies that fund investigative journalism—an already expensive way of gathering news.

But protection of whistle-blowers is fundamental for any media outlet or individual journalist that takes public interest reporting seriously.

Investigative reporters also need a thick skin. You have to expect some blowback when so much of your work threatens, rightly or wrongly, the reputations, careers and finances of many powerful entities or people.

But for all the threat of legal action, government investigations and hostile critics, the job is addictive.

Nothing has ever compared to the thrill of going home the night before publishing a big, important story, knowing that all hell will break loose in the morning.

2

Lessons from Abroad: Partnerships

BILL BIRNBAUER

INTRODUCTION

Today, the odds are stacked against investigative journalism as traditional media models collapse and newspapers cut staff and other resources to safeguard their short-term profitability. Lengthy, resource-hungry investigations are easy targets for media managers looking to cut costs.

In the USA, the internet has shattered newspaper revenues and circulations resulting in some 13 400 fewer newspaper jobs in 2010 than four years earlier, a drop of more than 25 per cent (Edmonds et al. 2011). Surprisingly, the reaction to this crisis by philanthropic foundations, wealthy individuals and journalists provides potential pathways and unexpected hope for the future of quality journalism in Australia.

Recognising that traditional outlets were struggling to provide the accountability and scrutiny vital for a healthy democracy, US philanthropic foundations pumped tens of millions of dollars into non-profit investigative reporting centres. In 2011, there were at least 75 non-profit news centres in the USA compared to a handful five years earlier.

The impact of the bigger centres on traditional reporting has been significant—serious media such as *The Washington Post*, *The New York Times* and public broadcasters routinely publish or collaborate with non-profit centres on investigative projects, and their work appears daily in media across the USA. Innovative new models have been created for investigative reporting, including university-based centres where journalism students work under supervision on complex stories.

Australian investigative journalism remains robust and supported by employers such as Fairfax, News Limited and the ABC. But Australia has few media proprietors and the question must be asked whether the current outlets will be pursuing watchdog journalism in five, 10 or 15 years' time. The US experience contains valuable lessons—but only if we embrace them.

THE US EXPERIENCE

In late August 2005, Hurricane Katrina scrambled New Orleans, Louisiana, destroying much of the city and its low-lying surrounding suburbs. The storm and subsequent flooding, due mainly to collapsed levee banks, killed more than 700 people in New Orleans and for weeks crippled everyday necessities such as electricity, water, hospital and transport services, and law enforcement. Chaos ensued, with widespread reports of looting, sexual assaults, murders and carjackings—concern enough for thousands of National Guard and federal troops to be called in with cocked M16s.

Almost two years after the devastating hurricane, investigative reporter A.C. Thompson received a disturbing tip-off that would absorb him professionally and emotionally for years to come. A friend who was researching a book on disasters had heard that following the hurricane, residents in a predominantly White New Orleans neighbourhood had shot at, and possibly killed, a number of unarmed African American men.

Thompson was a staff investigative journalist at the Center for Investigative Reporting, not far from San Francisco in Berkeley, California. The Center, founded in 1977, is the oldest non-profit investigative reporting centre in the USA and Thompson had joined it after spending a decade working for alternative news magazines in the San Francisco area.

He started investigating the rumours in 2007. They led him to quite unexpected discoveries that delivered shocking truths and a degree of justice to poor and largely powerless Black families. His findings shook the heart of policing and justice in the USA. Thompson's journey is of interest because of what it says about the model of non-profit investigative reporting, the state of the mainstream media in the USA and the contrast with what might have occurred in Australia.

Hundreds of US reporters, victims of cutbacks and buyouts, joined or created non-profit news centres after 2006 when economic forces, industry shifts and technologies devastated the US press. The growth and impact of non-profit investigative news outlets appear to have reinvigorated and energised investigative reporting in the USA, though it remains, as always, a sideshow to most journalism.

Bigger centres such as ProPublica, The Center for Public Integrity (CIP) and the Center for Investigative Reporting (CIR) have multimillion-dollar budgets and employ dozens of reporters in what amount to specialised 'factories' that churn out investigative projects. They have been recognised in many of journalism's top awards including the Pulitzer Prize.

US non-profit investigative reporting centres employ professional reporters, editors, digital producers, data analysts and others to conduct complex, long-term investigations that are carried on their own websites, but attract far bigger audiences in traditional media which routinely publish and broadcast their projects.

The centres often spend months collaborating on projects with old media such as *The New York Times, The Washington Post*, PBS's *Frontline* and National Public Radio stations. Collaborations that previously would have been unthinkable now abound. California Watch, an initiative of the CIR, has collaborative syndication relationships with dozens of media organisations. Associated Press announced in 2009 that it would distribute stories produced by the CIP, the Investigative Reporting Workshop, the CIR and ProPublica to its 1500 newspaper members. Thomson Reuters in May 2011 announced it would offer its subscribers investigative stories produced by the 60 investigative centres that belong to the Investigative News Network, and *The Huffington Post* runs all stories produced by the CPI.

Charles Lewis is the founding executive editor of the CPI and more recently the Investigative Reporting Workshop, a university-based reporting centre in Washington DC. He says established media knock on his door constantly looking for quality content:

> we have to tell them to go away … we have more than we can deal with. It's slightly amusing on one level and slightly depressing on another. They are desperately seeking content because they have eviscerated their newsrooms (Birnbauer 2011).

Unlike the aggressive 'scoop' culture that pervades Australian media, one impact of the US phenomenon has been a greater willingness by non-profit and for-profit media to collaborate in researching and distributing stories, rather than competing for the same story. When he was editor of the *Philadelphia Inquirer* between 1998 and 2002, Robert Rosenthal and his colleagues opposed collaborating with other news groups. As executive director of the CIR, which has partnerships with 25 major media groups and hundreds of smaller outlets, he says: 'now we're collaboration whores' (Francisco et al. 2011). 'The need for exclusivity, once so sacrosanct throughout print as well as broadcast fell by the wayside' (Rosenthal 2011).

In 2011, the 75 US non-profit reporting centres had annual funding of $US135 million and employed 1300 full-time staff (Lewis et al. 2011). Seventeen centres were based at, or linked to, a university journalism school. Most of the funding for these centres was provided by philanthropic foundations and wealthy individuals (Lewis et al. 2011). The Knight Foundation has estimated that only 10 per cent of journalism outlets that receive philanthropic support would survive if the grants were to disappear (Waldman 2011a).

US charitable foundations play a far bigger role in education, science, arts, health, the environment and civil society than they do in Australia. Philanthropy is integral to US culture: there are about 50 000 private, corporate, community and operating foundations with combined assets of about $US425 billion (Dowie 2001). The biggest US foundations were founded in the late nineteenth and early twentieth centuries by immensely wealthy industrialists such as John D. Rockefeller, Andrew Carnegie and Henry and Edsel Ford.

A.C. Thompson was fortunate to be working at a time when several large foundations were so concerned at the demise of mainstream media that they decided to support non-profit news centres. He secured funding from the Investigative Fund at The Nation Institute, which continued its support when he left the CIR and later quit New America Media to join ProPublica. Thompson was among the first group of reporters hired by ProPublica, which had attracted 850 job applications before its launch in 2008. By then, he had been working on the story for more than a year and ProPublica's editors were keen for him to continue. For the next six months he was in the unusual situation of reporting to editors at both *The Nation* and ProPublica.

When his first stories were published at the end of 2008 and early 2009 on both ProPublica's website and in *The Nation* magazine, they were accompanied by credits to Thompson whose reporting was 'directed and underwritten by the Investigative Fund at The Nation Institute. ProPublica provided additional support, as did the Centre for Investigative Reporting and New America Media'.

GLOVER, ALGIERS POINT AND DANZIGER BRIDGE

Thompson's story 'Body of Evidence' (2008a) told of the discovery by police of human ash and bone fragments in a burned-out car on the banks of the Mississippi River: the remains of African American father of four Henry Glover. Thompson had located eye witnesses who helped him reconstruct the last hours of Glover's life. Glover had been shot in the chest by an unknown gunman (subsequent investigations uncovered that it was a policeman) while walking with his brother and a friend along a shopping strip in the Algiers district of New Orleans, days after the hurricane.

In a desperate fight to save Glover's life, his brother had flagged down passing motorist William Tanner and they sped to a nearby school used by police as a temporary base. Rather than treating the badly injured Glover, Thompson reported, the police had ignored him and assaulted Tanner, Glover's brother and another man, suspecting them of looting. Eventually the men were freed, except for Glover. Police confiscated Tanner's car and drove away with Glover bleeding to death in the back seat. 'If the NOPD [New Orleans Police Department] ever bothers to learn who set fire to Glover, the department's first step should be questioning its own personnel: a trail of clues leads right back to the police force', Thompson wrote (2008a).

Thompson's next story, 'Katrina's Hidden Race War' (Thompson 2008b), described how a White enclave called Algiers Point had withstood the flooding Mississippi River to become a refuge for those seeking shelter. But local White residents were less than welcoming: they formed an armed version of Neighbourhood Watch, setting up barricades and looking out for Black intruders. African American Donnell Herrington was walking in the area when a shotgun blast blew a hole in his neck. Another hit his back and peppered his two friends. No one was charged over the shooting. Thompson wrote:

> Over the course of an eighteen-month investigation, I tracked down figures on all sides of the gunfire, speaking with the shooters of Algiers Point, gunshot survivors and those who witnessed the bloodshed. I interviewed police officers, forensic pathologists, firefighters, historians, medical doctors and private

citizens, and studied more than 800 autopsies and piles of state death records. What emerged was a disturbing picture of New Orleans in the days after the storm, when the city fractured along racial fault lines as its government collapsed (Thompson 2008b).

The FBI began probing the Glover death and the other shootings Thompson had uncovered. The investigative reporter kept digging.

At the end of 2009, two reporters from *The Times Picayune*, a New Orleans-based daily newspaper, and a producer from PBS's *Frontline* joined Thompson's investigation, which by then had expanded to police shootings of 11 people, at least four of whom had died.

Once again, rather than competing for stories, ProPublica's editors figured that collaboration with *The Times Picayune* and *Frontline* would boost reporting resources, take advantage of local knowledge and better inform locals of what was happening in their neighbourhoods. Interestingly, the media partnerships did not involve a formal contractual arrangement. 'It was kind of just like people were chipping in money because they wanted this story to happen' (Thompson 2010).

Throughout 2009 and 2010, the FBI broadened its inquiries into the Glover death, the shootings at Algiers Point, a police shooting at Danziger Bridge in which two people were killed and four others were wounded, and other shooting incidents. The US Justice Department launched an inquiry into the conduct of the New Orleans Police Department. Thompson and the other reporters continued jointly publishing damning evidence about the lack of a proper police inquiry into the shootings. In August 2010, *Frontline* broadcast an hour-long documentary seen by about one million people.

By the end of 2010—almost six years after the hurricane—a federal jury had convicted three serving or former New Orleans police officers over the death of Henry Glover and another federal jury had convicted five police officers over the Danziger Bridge shootings. A total of 16 current or former New Orleans police officers were convicted of crimes, with one conviction later being set aside. The former policeman who shot Glover was jailed for 25 years; the former officer who incinerated his car received more than 17 years jail.

The US Department of Justice released a report on the New Orleans Police Department that identified systemic failings, and a separate investigation by Louisiana State Police concluded that the department's former assistant superintendent had shown 'a lack of both good judgment and maturity' in his handling of the Glover case, noting that either [he] has 'an incredibly poor memory or he has been deceptive' (McCarthy 2011).

Thompson's investigations over three years took him around the country from Dallas and Houston in Texas, Norwich in Connecticut, Richmond Virginia, Washington DC, rural Georgia, and New Orleans.

ProPublica allowed him to work exclusively on the story with no pressure to publish regularly, unlike his colleagues at *The Times Picayune*. He believes he would not have been able to devote as much time to the story had he been employed by a mainstream newspaper. The pressure he faced was different: 'There is not pressure to crank out lots of stories. There is pressure to crank out very, very good stories' (Thompson 2010).

THE NON-PROFIT MODEL

Most non-profits are supported by a number of donors—the CPI, for example, has more than 40 funders. New York-based ProPublica was established by the billionaire former banker Herbert Sandler and his wife Marion who committed to giving it $US10 million a year for three years from 2008 and are believed to have continued their support. By 2011, however, more than half of ProPublica's $10 million budget came from donors other than the Sandlers (ProPublica 2011). Its top editors include former senior newspaper executives: editor-in-chief, president and chief executive is Paul Steiger, a former managing editor of *The Wall Street Journal* and a trustee of the John S. and James L. Knight Foundation; managing editor is Stephen Engelberg, a former managing editor of *The Oregonian* in Portland, Oregon, and a former investigative editor of *The New York Times*.

Sandler is chairman of ProPublica's board. A key donor to Democrat-related causes, he sold his bank to a bigger one, pocketing $US2.4 billion (Nocera 2008). He told *The New York Times* that outrage motivated him to create ProPublica: 'You go a little crazy when power takes advantage of those without power' (Nocera 2008). Several conservative commentators have linked Sandler's political leanings to ProPublica's reporting, attacking its 'left-wing hit pieces' (Chumley 2009).

Former newspaper investigative reporter Brant Houston was executive director of the investigative resource centre, Investigative Reporters and Editors (IRE), for more than a decade and is the John S. and James L. Knight chair in investigative and enterprise reporting at the University of Illinois at Urbana-Champaign. He is critical of the idea of investigative centres having a key single donor or source of revenue. 'The idea of the philanthropist who doles out a few million dollars who hopes for the best and walks away doesn't occur that often' (Birnbauer 2011). Charles Lewis describes the Sandlers' donations to the Democrat Party as 'an unsavoury appearance if you're trying to be non-partisan and have some detachment in your reporting' (Lewis 2010). Thompson, however, insists that a 'bright line' separates the newsroom from its funders:

> We don't tell them about stories that we're working on and we don't tell them what we are doing and we don't ask them for input … they don't influence anything on the newsgathering side, they just have no role in that at all, which is pretty remarkable (2010).

The motives of foundations and wealthy donors are less obvious than those of advertisers, raising questions about their influence and agendas. Writing in a special edition of the *Poynter Report*, Edmonds likened foundations to emperors and archbishops who commissioned concertos. 'Mozart did the composing but his benefactors could stipulate the size and shape of the thing' (Edmonds 2001). 'Some of them would actually think, "we're going to give you this money and we're going to get this result", said Noyes (2010).

Just how sustainable the foundation-funded, non-profit model of investigative journalism will prove is unclear. Foundation support is notoriously fickle, according to Lewis (2010) and several US foundations spoken to by the author agree that relying on philanthropy is not a long-term business model. The Knight Foundation's John Bracken said:

> Building your fiscal model on the vagaries of foundations is precarious at best. Foundations have new interests, they move on … it's not a long-term sustainable thing to expect the MacArthur Foundation to write you a cheque every year for perpetuity (2012).

Thompson (2010) also worries about the sustainability of the foundation model: 'Foundation funders don't necessarily fund one thing year after year, they want to change their areas of emphasis; they want to do this, this year and something different next year … I also realise that history is littered with the carcasses of non-profit enterprises that have gone belly-up and have collapsed.'

Lewis notes (Lewis et al. 2011) that Capitol News Connection—a congressional watchdog that at its peak was heard by 3.1 million people on 211 public radio stations—was forced to close in 2011 due to the loss of funding. Further, at least 10 of the 75 non-profit centres he identified had budgets of less than $US100 000, meaning the staff worked for no or very little pay, 'operating substantially on sweat equity, heart and hope' (Lewis et al. 2011). Lewis found that the operating budgets of at least 10 centres had decreased in 2011.

Steve Waldman and the Working Group on the Information Needs of Communities notes in a Federal Communications Commission report that foundations have focused on seed funding, but non-profits needed to develop ongoing sources of revenue to survive (Waldman 2011a). Funabiki and Yoshihara (2011) surveyed 32 journalism start-ups in 2011 to assess the challenges they faced in becoming sustainable and found that as centres evolved beyond being journalism experiments, donors became less interested in funding them.

One of the reasons non-profit journalism has grown rapidly in the USA is that donors have been able to claim tax deductions for contributions under the Internal Revenue Code. However this relies on the Internal Revenue Service approving individual applications, because news reporting is not one of the 'exempt purposes' listed under the code. Non-profits have been able to claim charitable status by stating they advanced 'educational purposes' (Waldman 2011a).

Some experts fear this route may limit the ability of new entities to thrive as non-profits (Waldman 2011a). Questions persist about how much advertising non-profit centres can accept without risking their tax-deductible status. This concern has been exacerbated by long delays—up to two years in one case—in processing deductibility for news start-ups (Waldman 2011b).

It must be remembered that while the foundation millions are generous they do not come close to replacing the cutbacks in mainstream journalism, estimated to be worth $US1.6 billion (Edmonds 2009). However, without philanthropists and foundations, 'the practice of investigative reporting might not be long for this world' (Westphal 2009).

LESSONS FOR AUSTRALIA

Journalism in Australia has not been as adversely impacted as in the USA. The ABC, Fairfax and News Limited continue to produce investigations that result in public outrage and force government and its agencies to act or respond.

Josephi (2011) notes that the watchdog function is considered to be a central role by Australian journalists and media. She concludes that Australian journalists are fulfilling this role. However, investigative reporting in Australia, other than by public broadcasters, is predominantly done by publishers that are cutting staff and editorial budgets and, in the case of Fairfax, outsourcing key editorial roles such as sub-editing. Some commentators have expressed concern about the impact of such cuts on investigative and quality journalism: 'Though the Australian experience lags behind that of the United States in time, it is no less severe' (Attard 2011).

It is reasonable to conclude that had Thompson lived in Australia, he would not have been able to dedicate three years of full-time investigation to a similar story. In the author's experience, investigative units generally spend several months on projects, although reporters such as *The Age's* Nick McKenzie and Richard Baker pursued the payment of bribes to overseas middlemen by companies owned by the Reserve Bank of Australia for years while working on other projects. However, it is unimaginable that any Australian media company would grant a reporter the right to dedicate years of full-time research to any story. Media managers with an eye on the bottom line increasingly see investigative reports as 'vainglorious indulgences: high risk, high maintenance, high priced impracticalities' (Lewis 2006). What, then, are the alternatives to and the lessons to be gained from the US experience?

For historic, political and cultural reasons, Australian philanthropic foundations and wealthy individuals generally do not regard investigative journalism in the same way as some of their US counterparts, nor are Australian foundations as wealthy as those in the USA. Nevertheless there are non-profit journalism stirrings in Australia, with millionaire wotif.com founder Graeme Wood reportedly pledging between $15 million and $20 million to an online news, features and analysis site, *The Global Mail* (Manning 2011). The project has 13 staff including five overseas correspondents and an investigative reporter who will be assisted by an intern. Its founders believe there is a 'crisis for the maintenance of serious, independent and thoughtful journalism' in Australia due to the disintegration of the traditional business model (Manning 2011).

The Global Mail, several academics (Bacon 2010; Birnbauer 2010; Simons 2010) and The Greens have separately called on the Federal Government to follow US practice and allow donations to non-profit reporting centres to be tax deductible in the belief that this could increase the diversity of outlets undertaking quality journalism.

Another emerging source of public interest journalism is the hundreds of journalism students enrolled in university courses. Lewis, Butts and Musselwhite (2011) found that the number of university-based or linked centres in the USA had increased from 14 to 17 in 2011—a trend that US academics (Downie & Schudson 2009) believe will continue.

Usually supported by philanthropic foundations, such US centres use students as researcher/writers and endeavour to cover issues missed or under-reported by mainstream media. Many employ professional journalists to lead projects. Each summer, students from 12 journalism schools cooperate to produce investigative reports under the News21 program supported by the Carnegie Corporation and the John S. and James L. Knight Foundation.

The deans of 13 US journalism schools in 2010 wrote to the Federal Communications Commission noting that some schools were 'like the communications equivalent of university teaching hospitals, by partnering with local news outlets to undertake journalistic work that also emphasises pedagogical and professional best practices' (Waldman 2011a). This is what the Knight Foundation's Eric Newton has called teaching journalism with the 'live ammunition that results in real journalism that has real use for their communities' (Downie & Schudson 2009). This, in turn, has created 'new hybrid entities ... such as cluster relationships between university-based centres and major commercial news' (Lewis 2008).

US academics (Francisco et al. 2011) note that three factors are behind the growth of university-based journalism. Experienced reporters laid off by their employers are available to manage university programs; the internet has made publication cheap and convenient; and journalism schools are 'trying hard to keep up-to-date to justify their own existence when young people are able to become "journalists" just by putting up a website or starting to blog'.

Several Australian journalism schools have been active in pursuing and publishing investigative reports. The Australian Centre for Independent Journalism at the University of Technology, Sydney, uses students and experienced staff such as veteran reporters Wendy Bacon and Tom Morton to produce investigative articles, and Swinburne University in Melbourne teamed with the *Crikey* news website to comb over tabled state parliamentary reports, most of which were ignored by mainstream journalists. Monash University's investigative journalism students each year update the *Dangerous Ground* website that scrutinises environmental regulation in Victoria. Reports by these student journalists have been published in mainstream newspapers and elsewhere.

Student-led journalism will succeed if academic supervisors are skilled journalistic practitioners themselves. Anecdotally it seems that an increasing number of former senior Australian journalists have moved into academia in the past few years. However, the university system does not reward academics who devote additional time and skills to fact checking and editing student work outside of routine assignments. Projects have generally been funded by the schools themselves or by short courses such as those on feature writing and video journalism.

In 2011, the author advocated that Australian and New Zealand journalism schools might collaborate under the 'UniMuckraker' banner to produce projects on issues of common public concern to each locale:

> Under the proposed model, students studying investigative reporting or in-depth reporting at the participating universities in Australia, New Zealand and the Pacific would undertake assignments on the same issue or theme. After normal assessments have been completed, selected assignments would be improved or enhanced by editing, videos and graphics either in collaboration with a manager/producer or by lecturers and students (Birnbauer 2011).

While enthusiastically received by academics, funding the administrative and editing tasks involved proved problematic without government or philanthropic support. Perhaps UniMuckraker was ahead of its time. Perhaps.

There is little doubt that the next few years will be years of transition as the models and revenue streams that have sustained quality journalism for decades disintegrate and are replaced by ... what? A.C. Thompson, who won the I.F. Stone Medal for Journalistic Independence for his reporting on the Katrina shootings in 2011, is pessimistic about the future of mainstream investigative media: 'It may be that serious reporting is no longer done by for-profit enterprises ... it's entirely possible that you will see the near complete extinction of reporting done by for-profit businesses' (Thompson 2010).

Kevin Davis, who heads the Investigative News Network, an umbrella organisation for US non-profit centres, warns that a big consolidation in the number of non-profit centres will occur unless the Internal Revenue Service approves tax deductibility more readily (Davis 2012). Concern about the sustainability of foundation funding and the lack of commercially based revenue has led to a growing belief that the National Public Radio (and affiliate stations') model of funding from individuals, fees, corporate sponsorship, government, universities and grants may be the answer. It remains to be seen if this would be acceptable in the USA where any government involvement often is equated to intervention and is bound to be attacked by conservative voices.

CONCLUSION

The media's transition to an online environment has trashed the business model that has sustained investigative and other reporting, but has also created unprecedented opportunities for journalists to present the most complex of issues in a more accessible and useful way. It is an extraordinarily exciting and energising time to be an investigative journalist. Highly motivated entrepreneurial journalists are moving away from the teat of 'Big Media' to create their own online platforms; new technologies are being used to present data in a cost-effective way; and universities are increasingly producing quality journalistic output. New and recent players such as *Crikey, New Matilda, Inside Story, The Global Mail, The Conversation* and others are producing quality news and analysis, and groups such as OurSay and GetUp, in their own way, are exploring and drawing attention to social issues.

Australia has neither the foundations nor the degree of understanding of US philanthropists that journalism is instrumental to a vibrant democracy. They should heed the words of the US Federal Communications Commission, which concluded that 'without strong reporting, the issues that philanthropists care about—whether health, environment, children, fiscal responsibility—are all shortchanged' (Waldman 2011a).

The early stirrings mentioned above are likely to gather momentum as more and more people realise that newspapers that once were the bastions of accountability journalism can no longer do it on their own.

Disconcertingly, many Australians seem more able to name the characters of a popular sitcom than the levels of government or ministers responsible for key portfolios. The question remains: do Australian citizens and philanthropists care enough about the quality of information they receive, or that someone is independently scrutinising governments and politicians for waste and political chicanery or exposing corruption and systemic failures, to reach into their pockets and support investigative journalism, as their US counterparts have?

Ultimately, do they want a robust democracy?

QUESTIONS TO CONSIDER

1   What lessons can Australian media organisations gain from the US experience with investigative journalism?

2   What are the benefits associated with collaborations between not-for-profit organisations such as ProPublica and mainstream news organisations working together on investigations?

3   What are the risks?

TASK

1   Log on to the ProPublica website:. Pick one of the investigations its journalists have undertaken and try to prepare a summary that helps explain the processes they went through in pulling the story together.

REFERENCES

Attard, M. 2011. 'Submission by The Global Mail to the Independent Inquiry into Media and Media Regulation': www.dbcde.gov.au/__data/assets/pdf_file/0008/143639/The_Global_Mail.pdf/.

Bacon, W. 2010. 'Submission by Wendy Bacon to the Independent Inquiry into Media and Media Regulation': www.dbcde.gov.au/__data/assets/pdf_file/0015/143421/Professor_Wendy_Bacon-Part_1.pdf/.

Birnbauer, B. 2010. 'Submission by Bill Birnbauer to the Independent Inquiry into Media and Media Regulation': www.dbcde.gov.au/__data/assets/pdf_file/0020/142931/Bill_Birnbauer.pdf/.

Birnbauer, B. 2011. 'Student Muckrakers: Applying Lessons from Non-profit Investigative Reporting in the US', *Pacific Journalism Review*, 17(1), pp. 26–44.

Bracken, J. 2012. Personal interview with the author, 17 February.

Chumley, C.K. 2009. 'ProPublica: Investigative Journalism or Liberal Spin?', *Foundation Watch*: www.phoenix.edu/about_us/media-center/fact-checker/ProPublica-Investigative-Journalism-or-Liberal-Spin.html/.

Davis, K. 2012. Personal interview with the author, 31 January.

Dowie, M. 2001. *American Foundations: An Investigative History*, Cambridge, Massachusetts; London, England: The MIT Press.

Downie, L. & Schudson, M. 2009. 'The Reconstruction of American Journalism', *Columbia Journalism Review*: www.scribd.com/doc/21268382/Reconstruction-of-Journalism/.

Edmonds, R. 2001. 'Behind the Scenes: How Foundations have Quietly Seized a Role in Journalism, Commissioning Content', *Poynter Report*, Poynter Institute.

Edmonds, R. 2009. 'Shrinking Newspapers Have Created $1.6 Billion News Deficit', *Poynter.org*: www.poynter.org/latest-news/business-news/the-biz-blog/98784/shrinking-newspapers-have-created-1-6-billion-news-deficit/.

Edmonds, R., Guskin, E. & Rosenstiel, T. 2011. 'Newspapers: By the Numbers', *The State of the News Media 2011*: http://stateofthemedia.org/2011/newspapers-essay/data-page-6/.

Francisco, T., Lenhoff, A. & Schudson, M. 2011. 'The Classroom as Newsroom: Leveraging University Resources for Public Affairs Reporting', unpublished.

Funabiki, J. & Yoshihara, N. 2011. 'Online Journalism Enterprises: From Startup to Sustainability', *Renaissance Journalism Centre, San Francisco State University*: www.ncg.org/s_ncg/bin.asp?CID=18909&DID=51626&DOC=FILE.PDF/.

Josephi, B. 2011. 'Supporting Democracy: How Well do the Australian Media Perform?', *Australian Journalism Monographs*, 13.

Lewis, C. 2006. 'The Growing Importance of Nonprofit Journalism', *Working Paper for the Joan Shorenstein Centre on the Press, Politics and Public Policy*: www.hks.harvard.edu/presspol/publications/papers/working_papers/2007_03_lewis.pdf/.

Lewis, C. 2008. 'Seeking New Ways to Nurture the Capacity to Report', *Nieman Reports*, Spring 2008: www.nieman.harvard.edu/reportsitem.aspx?id=100060/.

Lewis, C. 2010. Personal interview with the author, 8 November.

Lewis, C., Butts, B. & Musselwhite, K. 2011. 'A Second Look: The New Journalism Ecosystem', *Investigative Reporting Workshop*: http://investigativereportingworkshop.org/ilab/story/second-look/.

Manning, P. 2011. 'What if Public-interest Journalism had a White Knight: A Media Start-up is Born, Packed with Pedigree', *The Age*: www.theage.com.au/national/what-if-publicinterest-journalism-had-a-white-knight-a-media-startup-is-born-packed-with-pedigree-20111230-1pffl.html/.

McCarthy, B. 2011. 'Marlon Defillo's handling of Henry Glover Case Slammed in Louisiana State Police Report', *The Times-Picayune*: www.nola.com/crime/index.ssf/2011/08/marlon_defillos_handling_of_he.html/.

Nocera, J. 2008. 'Self-Made Philanthropists', *The New York Times*: www.nytimes.com/2008/03/09/magazine/09Sandlers-t.html?pagewanted=all/.

Noyes, D. 2010. Personal interview with the author, 4 November.

ProPublica. 2011. 'Making a Difference—With Our Work, In Our Field', *Annual Report, 2011*:

http://propublica.s3.amazonaws.com/assets/about/2011%20Annual%20Report_final.pdf/.

Rosenthal, R. 2011. 'Reinventing Journalism: An Unexpected Personal Journey from Journalist to Publisher', *California Watch*: http://californiawatch.org/project/reinventing-journalism/.

Simons, M. 2010. 'Submission by Margaret Simons to the Independent Inquiry into Media and Media Regulation': www.dbcde.gov.au/_data/assets/pdf_file/0003/143418/Dr_Margaret_Simons.pdf/.

Thompson, A.C. 2008a. 'Body of Evidence', *The Nation*: www.thenation.com/article/body-evidence/.

Thompson, A.C. 2008b. 'Katrina's Hidden Race War', *The Nation*: www.thenation.com/article/katrinas-hidden-race-war/.

Thompson, A.C. 2010. Personal interview with the author, 15 November.

Waldman, S. 2011a. 'The Information Needs of Communities: The Changing Media Landscape in a Broadband Age', *Federal Communications Commission, United States*: www.fcc.gov/info-needs-communities/.

Waldman, S. 2011b. 'Will the IRS Derail Nonprofit Journalism?', *Columbia Journalism Review*: www.cjr.org/the_news_frontier/will_the_irs_derail_nonprofit_journalism.php/.

Westphal, D. 2009. 'Philanthropic Foundations: Growing Funders of News', *Centre on Communication Leadership & Policy*, Research Series July, 2009: http://communicationleadership.usc.edu/pubs/PhilanthropicFoundations.pdf/.

WEBSITE REFERENCES

Dangerous Ground: http://artsonline.monash.edu.au/dangerousground/.

ProPublica: www.propublica.org/.

The case study for Chapter 2, 'Hack the Turkmenet! The Journalistic Challenge in Central Asia', is available online at http://oup.com.au/tanner.

3

WikiLeaks and Two New Models for Investigative Journalism

SUELETTE DREYFUS AND KRISTINN HRAFNSSON

INTRODUCTION

Journalists are taught from their earliest assignments to be highly competitive. Get out there, get the story—and get it exclusively. The idea that two competing media organisations would work together, sharing information and expertise, to achieve a joint publishing outcome flies in the face of that training. Yet in 2010–11 online publisher *WikiLeaks* did just that by bringing together 89 media organisations in a world-first joint publishing exercise for the release of leaked US State Department diplomatic cables.

Although many in the old world of traditional media sniffed their noses at the brash new publisher, there can be little doubt that *WikiLeaks* is a watershed in recent journalism history. During 2010, 2011 and 2012, the online journalism site released large tranches of leaked material to the public for free by publishing it online. It generated analysis and reporting based on the leaked material, but also provided the original data *en masse* so that readers could verify the accuracy of what they were reading by accessing the original documents.

The content of these publications has been covered elsewhere. The purpose of this chapter is to explore the innovative models of journalistic publishing turning large collections of secret documents into front-page news stories day after day.

Although *WikiLeaks* had been publishing online since 2006, it was not until April 2010 that it gained widespread public attention with the release of the 'Collateral Murder' video featuring some of the most confronting footage from any modern war (*WikiLeaks* 2012a). It revealed US soldiers in Baghdad indiscriminately firing on civilians, including two children and Reuters news staff. The US soldiers killed Reuters photographer Namir Noor-Eldeen, 22, and assistant Saeed Chmagh, 40. Then they slayed a Good Samaritan, father of four Saleh Matasher Tomal, who had stopped to help the dying Reuters men. The US soldiers shot and seriously wounded Saleh's two children. Other innocent civilians were also seriously injured in the unprovoked attack. The video footage, viewed through the gunsight of an Apache helicopter, included audio of the soldiers joking about their civilian victims. The Pentagon covered up the events. It fobbed off requests from Reuters for information about the attack—until *WikiLeaks* revealed the truth.

In July 2010, *WikiLeaks* released the 'Afghan War Diary' from a collection of more than 76 000 previously unreleased documents written by coalition soldiers about the war. It painted a bleak picture of life on the ground for the soldiers. *The Guardian* described it as 'a devastating portrait of the failing war in Afghanistan' (AP/*Huffington Post* 2010).

Then in October 2010, *WikiLeaks* began publishing the 'Iraq War Logs', from a compilation of almost 400 000 unreleased documents about the Iraq War. With this publication for the first time it was possible to do a proper accounting of related deaths in Iraq (Rogers 2010). The logs revealed 15 000 previously unknown civilian deaths (Iraq Body Count 2010). It was more evidence of another war that was going very badly.

The following month, *WikiLeaks* began publishing more than 250 000 leaked US embassy cables in a redacted form. To do this, it partnered with media organisations in different countries. It is this model that we explore in this chapter.

BACKGROUND

As a not-for-profit online media publisher, *WikiLeaks* had received from sources more than 250 000 US Department of State diplomatic cables, written from US embassies around the world to US government departments in Washington DC and other US embassies. The cables contained descriptions of local people and events in the country where they were written, as told through the frequently insightful eyes of the US diplomatic corps.

For a journalist, these documents were pure gold. They revealed what US ambassadors really thought (and knew) about leaders in different countries. There was much in the cables about each country that would be in the public interest to report. Yet, as a small online publisher, *WikiLeaks* faced a number of hurdles in deciding how to handle the material. First, it did not have the resources to hand-sift through such a large amount of data, despite the importance of the material. Second, because the material covered events in dozens of different countries, *WikiLeaks* did not have the local expertise in each country to provide context to the hundreds of journalism stories contained in the data. There was a third issue as well: the data could contain information that any responsible journalist would remove or redact; for example, information that could cause a human rights worker to be put in harm's way in repressive regimes. Identifying such potentially dangerous information in the more than 250 000 cables would be exceptionally difficult for one publisher to do on its own—a proverbial hunt for the needle in a haystack.

Redaction is a tricky issue. Earlier in 2010, before the release of any 'Cablegate' material, *WikiLeaks* had received some criticism regarding how much information had been included in the Iraq and Afghan 'War Logs' publications. The criticism of the 'Afghan War Logs' release, made two months earlier, was that too much potentially sensitive information had been left in the public release. *WikiLeaks* stated publicly that it had pulled approximately 15 000 of the more than 91 000 reports to undergo what it described as a 'further harm minimisation review'. Ironically, a converse criticism of the 'Iraq War Logs', released later, was that *too* much information had been redacted and, while names and sensitive sources had been removed, it was not as publicly usable as it could have been. Balancing responsible redaction with the public interest of publishing information proved to be a challenging task.

For the release of the 'Afghan War Diary' and the 'Iraq War Logs', *WikiLeaks* had partnered with other media organisations. *The New York Times*, the London-based *Guardian* newspaper and the German weekly *Der Spiegel* were partners for the Afghan material. For the 'Iraq War Logs', *WikiLeaks* expanded the media partnership. In the initial breaking story, *WikiLeaks* included *Al Jazeera* (Doha), *Le Monde* (Paris), SVT (the Swedish Public Broadcaster), Channel 4's 'Dispatches' and the Bureau of Investigative Journalism in London. It added in non-government organisation Iraq Body Count (Heald 2010) and also the human rights firm Public Interest Lawyers.

For the release of the diplomatic cables that followed these earlier releases, *WikiLeaks* took a much more expansive approach when it came to the number of media outlets. The principle behind the larger scale partnership arrangement was that many dozens of media organisations would pool their significant professional expertise and workforce with *WikiLeaks* to publish as much material as possible after screening it for harm minimisation. *WikiLeaks* would work with these media partners to analyse the cables and explain their relevance to the local people in the locations where the stories were published. The traditional media partners, such as newspapers, would be able to give local context to the material and would write and publish the contextualised news stories. They would also sift the material for information that might cause harm, and redact that material before passing it back to *WikiLeaks* in a 'cleaned' state. *WikiLeaks* would then run another review process of the edited material to determine if the level of redaction was appropriate. This would provide two sets of 'eyeball checks' on the published material. After that, *WikiLeaks* would publish the original documents, now redacted for harm minimisation, in an online searchable format. The local partners would publish stories, but *WikiLeaks* would also publish its own news articles highlighting what was important and newsworthy about the original cables from a particular country, either individually or in aggregate. These news pieces might cover similar ground to a particular media partner's reporting for a specific country, or might show *WikiLeaks*' own differing analysis of the newsworthy elements.

In this way, the media partners and *WikiLeaks* were able to calibrate their news analysis with each other on key stories from the large quantity of data, but each also had the freedom to publish different news stories if they had different views about the same raw data. Thus the partnership model was resilient, providing mutual support without being prescriptive. This calibration may also have proved important to interpreting the large data.

WikiLeaks chose media partners to join its publishing cluster based on a range of criteria, including how 'they are funded, their political line and how independent they are, and that they are responsible' (*WikiLeaks* 2012b). *WikiLeaks* screened the media partners to ensure that they didn't give the selection of cables provided to any third parties, and that they did a 'fair' journalistic job on the material, 'not skewed one way or another' (WikiLeaks 2012b).

The pool of people who worked on turning the raw material that was at the heart of 'Cablegate' into news stories for the global audience is difficult to estimate. It could easily be in the vicinity of 800–1000 people around the world (*WikiLeaks* 2012b). This approximation is based on a conservative estimate of about 10 people per media outlet *on average* working on the material obtained from *WikiLeaks*. *WikiLeaks* estimated that the larger media partners might have had up to 20 staff working on the material. This includes all media production people, such as graphic designers, because their role in conveying a story can be as important as that of traditional journalists. Smaller media partners might only have had three to five staff working on the material. Some countries, such as the Scandinavian nations, might only have had 600–800 cables directly related to them, and thus smaller analysis teams, while others such as Japan had about 10 times that number, with an estimated 6000 cables.

The model provides an interesting merging of two things. The first is data journalism: the sophisticated analysis of large-scale data sets to reveal public interest stories. The second is sunshine journalism: where the original documents on which a story is based are provided in full (usually online) so that a reader can see the unvarnished evidence behind the article or report.

The *WikiLeaks* publishing site contain some meta analysis of the pool of cables. For example, of all the cables some 15 652 are marked 'secret', 101 748 are 'confidential' and 133 887 'unclassified' (*WikiLeaks* 2012c). It is interesting to note that the most frequently discussed subjects, according to the US Department of State labelling system, are 'external political relations' (145 451) and 'internal government affairs' (122 896) (*WikiLeaks* 2012c). By comparison, 'human rights' cables total only 55 211. Even more interesting, cables labelled 'terrorists and terrorism' amount to about 28 801—about only half the human rights cables (*WikiLeaks* 2012c).

At the time of writing, *WikiLeaks*' 'connective publishing' model included 89 media organisations, with many different media owners, across 50 countries (*WikiLeaks* 2012b) in a cooperative partnership that could only have been imagined just a few years ago.

CONNECTIVE PUBLISHING

We have called *WikiLeaks'* new model for collaborative publishing between media outlets 'connective publishing'. This is because so many different media organisations were connected by the large-scale publishing effort that would otherwise be unlikely to publish in partnership, either due to geographic barriers or because they were in competition with each other. This term is also apt because it suggests the individual publishers in each country were connected with a larger whole, in this case *WikiLeaks* and the other partners via the entire archive of US diplomatic cables. It also implies conduits, with information flowing *both* ways (between *WikiLeaks* and the traditional publisher, such as a newspaper). This model was a world-first and provided valuable lessons to the media, the citizenry and government. Its success also has implications for whistle-blowers seeking to right wrongs on a global scale through sweeping data releases.

Comparisons can be drawn between *WikiLeaks'* role and that of an old-fashioned wire service, where many newspapers take the same story from one service. However, in the classic wire service model, information is only flowing in one direction—from the news agency as a supplier of news to the newspaper, radio or television program. For example, the newspaper does not send information back for the wire service to publish on the wires. The connective publishing model is far more collaborative. In this model, the media partners not only transfer raw material for the story back to *WikiLeaks* for publication, there is also two-way communication surrounding analysis of the material.

Two of the greatest barriers to good data journalism in many media organisations are a lack of skills to conduct the analysis (often technology-based skills) and a lack of resources with special expertise to interpret the analysis. This is particularly true in a world where traditional media organisations such as newspapers are being asked to report more with fewer staff, and with less-experienced junior reporters who command cheaper salaries. The cooperative media model rolled out by *WikiLeaks* appears to have gone some of the way to addressing these chronic problems. In practice, the model brought together the technical expertise inside *WikiLeaks* with the seasoned reporting staff of established media partners such as *The Hindu Times* in India and *Asahi Shimbun* in Japan. The pooling of journalism staff from both *WikiLeaks* and the mainstream media outlets also presumably led to better news analysis, with more hands on deck to do the detailed work of good journalism.

The model included media partners from all types of media, including online publishing, television, radio, daily newspapers and weeklies. In some cases, such as Finland and the Netherlands, the partnerships were with state television or radio. In others, such as Haiti, the partners were media organisations publishing purely online. It is estimated, however, that at least 70–80 per cent of the media partners came from the print media category, with the vast majority being daily newspapers (*WikiLeaks* 2012b). The financial implications for daily print publishing is interesting, with sales anecdotally reported to have risen by 20 per cent among some media partners when the Cablegate stories ran. Sales improved even more dramatically for weekly publications, with increases of up to 40 per cent reported to *WikiLeaks* by some media partners in this category (*WikiLeaks* 2012b). These increases in sale figures may hint at a way forward for an industry—the print media—that is struggling financially. If one assumes that the cables represent unspun reality about news that matters (as opposed to reality TV), then it seems the truth sells well.

Interestingly, the model also included partnering media outlets that compete in the same country or city-based market, either directly or indirectly. With Cablegate, for example, *WikiLeaks* brought both *L'Expresso*, an Italian weekly, and *La Repubblica*, Italy's second-largest daily paper, into its media circle. This required the Italian publications to coordinate how to publish news stories around the Italian cables in a way that worked for both outlets. While both are owned by the same publisher, they are independent and rarely cooperate. In another example, *WikiLeaks* partnered for the Brazilian cables release with two different media partners and with the independent, not-for-profit journalism centre Apublica. *Wikileaks* brought *The Telegraph* in the UK into the publishing coterie to examine the British cables. *The Guardian*, another daily British daily, already had a copy of the cables, having been one of *WikiLeaks* earliest partners. The two papers could not be more opposed in their political outlooks, with the former being right-leaning and the latter firmly in the left camp. According to *WikiLeaks*, *The Telegraph* was able to find new angles to stories in the cables (*WikiLeaks* 2012b): 'The different way they treated the [same] material pertaining to Labour or the Conservative government was quite interesting.' It seems unlikely this particular three-way media partnership was as amicable as others given the well-documented falling-out between *WikiLeaks* and *The Guardian*. Nonetheless the public benefited from more media analysing the material through different lenses.

The cooperative aspect to the model has had its share of road bumps, with significant tensions between *WikiLeaks* and some of its media partners, and also between those media partners. However, despite these issues, the proof of the model and the significance of the contributions ultimately made by *all* the media players who participated can be judged by the outcomes of important information made available to the public. The model's success at pushing out information into the public arena, across numerous languages and geographies on such a large scale is surprising, given that this was a world-first attempt. *WikiLeaks* and the other media simply made their best efforts, plunged in and discovered that it worked.

It is interesting to note that this model appears to have entered a new stage of advancement. A different online publisher, the Associated Whistle-blowing Press (AWP) (based in Reykjavik, Iceland), constructed a special online technology in late 2012 to broaden the crowdsourcing of news stories from the Cablegate files (AWP 2012). The core goal of this technology is to enable better crowdsourcing of stories. The AWP wanted to 'create a database of cables filtered manually for their content, produce summaries and notes collaboratively, map their relationships visually using their own references network (REFTEL) in order to [motivate] … collaboration to investigate and write news' (AWP 2012). The AWP also developed a wiki to cross-analyse the many releases made by other publishers from the connective publishing event, in order to produce the AWP's own 'hard news' (AWP 2012). The tool—which allows the harvesting of new stories from both the raw data *and* the output of connective publishing—points to a maturing of the model.

Through this joint effort, the media lifted the veil on the world of those who still believe government information should only go out to the public on a need-to-know basis.

CROWDSOURCED DECLASSIFICATION OF DOCUMENTS

Governments, the citizenry and secrecy make for an uncomfortable triumvirate at times. One reason for this is that governments have traditionally had a monopoly on state secrets and on the processes for releasing them. The tendency of governments has been to hoard information, particularly information that is in the public interest (or that the public has paid for by taxes) but which might be considered embarrassing. Governments have a conflict of interest in the current method of declassifying information and making it public. They cannot fairly be both the keeper of the secrets and also a truly independent judge of whether the public release of those secrets would be in the best interest of the citizens.

What if that decision-making power was passed from the government to someone else? If that happened, who would be able to do it in a truly independent, arms-length manner?

The model used to release the redacted US cables provides an interesting real-world answer. We call it 'crowdsourced declassification'. 'Crowdsourcing' was originally used to describe business behaviour:

> Simply defined, crowdsourcing represents the act of a company or institution taking a function once performed by employees and outsourcing it to an undefined (and generally large) network of people in the form of an open call. This can take the form of peer-production (when the job is performed collaboratively), but is also often undertaken by sole individuals. The crucial prerequisite is the use of the open call format and the large network of potential laborers … crowdsourcing …[is] taking place any time a company makes a choice to employ the crowd to perform labor that could alternatively be performed by an assigned group of employees or contractors (Howe 2006).

However the term 'crowdsourcing' has taken on an even broader meaning outside the business realm in more recent years, particularly in new media forums such as Twitter (Gao et al. 2011; Starbird 2011; Zook et al. 2010). The large-scale redaction process spearheaded by *WikiLeaks* is a function that had previously only been conducted by governments, or possibly private defence contractors working as agents of government. Redaction is what makes the 'declassification' and publication of sensitive leaked material possible. In this new model the 'cleaning and declassifying' of secret and confidential documents was done by a crowd of journalists from many organisations. While the concept probably left some government intelligence analysts stunned, the model has merits. It marks a profound shift in the democratisation of state information.

The release of the redacted cables is almost certainly the first time in history that this core function has been 'outsourced' to a civilian community without security clearance on such a large scale. The closest similar event may be *The Guardian* newspaper's 2009 release of 170 000 documents about MPs' expenses (Andersen 2009). An estimated 20 000 members of the general public analysed the documents, and the crowdsourcing project was considered a success. However, the crowd was only analysing the documents, not classifying them. Analysis is different from redaction. Further, the subject matter was primarily of interest to only one country, and thus did not build the same international partnerships.

The *WikiLeaks'* crowdsourcing for redaction and reporting was based on a crowd that was not truly public (that is, not the general population). Rather, it was a crowd of professionals (primarily journalists). However, the journalists could be considered to be a close approximation of a public crowd, both in content and flavour, with an overlay of professional experience. Their profession brought them into daily proximity to the public and to current issues, which gave them an excellent understanding of public sentiment. Like most citizens, they did not have security clearances. They volunteered into the process, as crowdsourcing participants do. This *WikiLeaks* 'first' provides a real-world example of a 'how-to' model for crowdsourcing the declassification of documents. Like true crowdsourcers, the professional journalists were independent of the entity that owned the information (government)—and had an interest in keeping the information secret. They were also independent of *Wikileaks*.

However, rather than being neutral, they were public advocates. As journalists, they sought to make as much information public as possible, unlike government. In this way they played a sort of 'devil's advocate' role when assessing whether to redact material. Presumably this was tempered by their professional experience and training, which teaches journalists to be true to their professional duty to report responsibly and not endanger innocent people's lives. Often journalists' unions have codes of conduct or ethical standards, just like other professional bodies (Media Entertainment and Arts Alliance (MEAA) 2001). With a few high-visibility exceptions, most media outlets expect journalists to adhere to these codes. The crowdsourcing of the declassification process created a different form of check and balance on the release of the information than is normally the case.

Traditionally this work has been done in government by the secret keepers—often current or semi-retired intelligence officers or foreign affairs officers. While professional standards provided protections in the crowdsourced declassification process, the onus had fundamentally shifted from one of 'only release information if we have to' to one of 'only hold information back if we have to'. The premise was, in essence, that nothing should be kept secret unless there was a real reason for doing so. While some governments have claimed to follow this policy, it would be rare to find one that actually does so universally.

While there are a few earlier examples of the media 'declassifying' (redacting and then releasing) large quantities of leaked classified material—notably the Pentagon Papers reported on by *The New York Times* in 1971—these primarily worked on the basis of one media outlet analysing the secret material from a source, rather than a partnership of many publishers bringing different knowledge. The earlier redaction examples lacked key elements of 'crowdsourcing', either of publication or of redaction. In the past, this also meant that a lone newspaper might run a series of stories with a few quoted extracts, but the vast majority of the secret material would not necessarily be made public in a timely fashion. At best, a book might eventually be published with some or all of the secret material. However, the book would not be free, unlike *WikiLeaks'* publishing site. The technologies used in the 2011 crowdsourcing declassification meant that much more material could be made public, and quickly. Importantly, the information would be put in searchable formats, such as in a redacted database that could be queried. This empowered others—from the public 'crowd', no less—to search the database for other, deeper stories. In this sense the entire structure also effectively contributed to crowdsourced data journalism.

This world-first combined model is important for three reasons. First the model's successful implementation illustrates that governments' claim that certain information must be kept under lock and key for national security reasons is overstated. The cry of 'national security' that attended the first release of the chilling video, then the redacted war logs and cables in no way matched the known outcomes. The redacted cables were not so much a national security issue as an issue of embarrassment to the relevant governments. In some cases that embarrassment was caused by unethical or bad behaviour, either by US or foreign government officials. Embarrassment is not a good reason to keep government information secret. Indeed, it is a very good reason to make it public. In a Supreme Court decision, Justice Black ruled in the Pentagon Papers that 'only a free and unrestrained press can effectively expose deception in government' (*New York Times Co. v United States 1971*). The unethical behaviour that was exposed showed that there was a positive argument for releasing the information, above and beyond the basic foundation premise that governments should not keep information secret unless there is a good reason to do so.

The second reason the crowdsourced declassification model is important is because it may show the way forward for small online media organisations handling big data stories in future. It is a model that can be replicated relatively easily and cheaply, while providing enormous public interest. This is particularly so now it has been done at least once in practice.

Third, the model reveals for the first time an alternative way for government information to be released in the public interest, using an arm's-length method that employs non-government citizens to screen the data for anything that might be dangerous to innocent people before it is released. Without doubt, it is confronting to some, particularly those who believe the people—that is, the general population of voters—cannot handle the truth. However, new approaches are often confronting; this is not a reason to discount them.

This crowdsourced declassification may have interesting implications for whistle-blowers in the digital age. It has shown that the world's media are able to redact very large quantities of sensitive material themselves, without the hand of government in the redacting process. One of the key motivations of whistle-blowers is the desire to right a wrong (see the following chapter). They tend to not want to destroy the organisations of which they are part. Usually they simply want a change from unethical behaviour. The success of this model may hearten whistle-blowers considering releasing large-scale evidence of wrongdoing, as they see that change can happen through the pressure of public opinion without destroying their 'home' organisations.

CONCLUSION

WikiLeaks has introduced two provocative new models to news publishing. 'Connective publishing' and 'crowdsourced declassification' are both counter-intuitive ideas. They involve working in partnership with potential competitors and devolving power from the state to the media.

No doubt the crowdsourced declassification model jolts diplomatic and intelligence officers. It removes a significant amount of power from their traditional roles and devolves it to less-closed sections of society. Such change may seem threatening and disturbing. In many ways it echoes the outsourcing changes a number of traditional industries have undergone in the past two decades. However, in this case the 'outsourcing' is not motivated by saving money or improving production-line efficiency. It is motivated by transparency and democratic accountability. One of the core benefits of crowdsourced declassification is that it removes the conflict inside government between the obligation to make as much information available to the public as possible, and the desire to cover up things that are embarrassing or that reveal serious wrongdoing.

These two models illustrate how it is possible to release and publish large volumes of secret documents in the public interest across dozens of media organisations. *WikiLeaks* provided a real-life experiment with these models. Savvy publishers of the future may adapt these models and use them in new and interesting ways.

QUESTIONS TO CONSIDER

1   What are the benefits of connective publishing and crowdsourcing declassification, as defined by *WikiLeaks*?

2   What are the potential risks or downsides of these two approaches to investigative journalism?

3   To what extent do you consider that redaction should be undertaken by journalists and media organisations when dealing with confidential documents?

4   To what extent do you consider that *WikiLeaks* is justified in publishing documents that may have been given to it in breach of a country's secrecy laws?

5   Are media organisations justified in publishing these documents? What tests should be applied in making these decisions?

TASK

1   Log on to the *WikiLeaks* site and identify a story that was co-published by an Australian media organisation. Go onto the Australian media organisation's site and locate the stories relating to the *WikiLeaks* documents. To what extent were the documents redacted for the purposes of publication? Do you see any ethical issues with this process?

Acknowledgments

This work draws on research from The Australian Research Council Project DP1095696: *Blowing Boldly: The Changing Roles, Avenues and Impacts of Public Interest Whistleblowing in the Era of Secure Online Technologies*.

REFERENCES

Andersen, M. 2009. 'Four Crowdsourcing Lessons from *The Guardian's* (Spectacular) Expenses-scandal Experiment', Nieman Journalism Lab, Nieman Foundation, Harvard University, 23 June: www.niemanlab.org/2009/06/four-crowdsourcing-lessons-from-the-guardians-spectacular-expenses-scandal-experiment (accessed 25 May 2012).

AP/*Huffington Post*. 2010. '*WikiLeaks* "Afghan War Diary" Provides Ground-level Account of Afghanistan War', 25 May: www.huffingtonpost.com/2010/07/25/wikileaks-afghan-war-diary_n_658743.html (accessed 25 May 2012).

AWP. 2012. 'AWP Presents New Tools for Collaborative Investigation', Associated Whistle-Blowing Press, Reykjavik, Press Release No. 3: http://whistle.is/?p=728 (accessed 29 November 2012).

Gao, H., Wang, X., Barbier, G. & Liu, H. 2011. 'Promoting Coordination for Disaster Relief—From Crowdsourcing to Coordination', *Lecture Notes in Computer Science*, Berlin/Heidelberg, Vol. 6589, pp. 197–204.

Heald, E. 2010. '*Wikileaks*' Iraq War Logs: A Week On', 29 October: www.editorsweblog.org/2010/10/29/wikileaks-iraq-war-logs-a-week-on (accessed 25 May 2012).

Howe, J. 2006. 'Crowdsourcing: A Definition', Crowdsourcing.com, 2 June: http://crowdsourcing.typepad.com/cs/2006/06/crowdsourcing_a.html (accessed 20 November 2012).

Iraq Body Count 2010. 'Iraq War Logs: What the Numbers Reveal', 23 October: www.iraqbodycount.org/analysis/numbers/warlogs (accessed 25 May 2012).

Media Entertainment and Arts Alliance (MEAA). 2001. *Australian Journalists' Association Code of Ethics*: www.alliance.org.au/code-of-ethics.html (accessed 21 November 2012).

New York Times Co. v United States 1971, 403 U.S. pp. 714–20.

Rogers, S. 2010. '*WikiLeaks* Iraq War Logs: Every Death Mapped', *The Guardian*, Datablog, 23 October: www.guardian.co.uk/world/datablog/interactive/2010/oct/23/wikileaks-iraq-deaths-map (accessed 25 May 2012).

Starbird, K. 2011. 'Digital Volunteerism During Disaster: Crowdsourcing Information Processing', *CHI 2011 Workshop on Crowsourcing and Human Computation: Systems, Studies and Platforms*, 8 May: http://crowdresearch.org/chi2011-workshop/papers/starbird.pdf (accessed 25 May 2012).

WikiLeaks. 2012a. 'Collateral Murder': www.collateralmurder.com (accessed 21 November 2012).

WikiLeaks. 2012b. On-the-record conversation with a *WikiLeaks* representative conducted for this piece, July 2011. ('The specific date is not provided for privacy reasons.)

WikiLeaks. 2012c. 'Secret US Embassy Cables': http://wikileaks.org/cablegate.html (accessed 21 May 2012).

Zook, M., Graham M., Shelton, T & Gorman, S. 2010. 'Volunteered Geographic Information and Crowdsourcing Disaster Relief: A Case Study of the Haitian Earthquake', *World Medical & Health Policy*, 2(2), pp. 7–33.

FURTHER READING

Howe, J. 2006. 'The Rise of Crowdsourcing', *Wired Magazine*, June: www.wired.com/wired/archive/14.06/crowds_pr.html (accessed 20 November 2011).

Rich, R. 2012. 'Kiss This War Goodbye', in E. Star, ed., *Open Secrets*: WikiLeaks, *War and American Diplomacy*: http://books.google.com.au/books?id=6VVHgoCt9KQC&pg=PT239&lpg=PT239&dq=wikileaks+changed+the+course+of+war+in+afghanistan&source=bl&ots=GUs1WxUbvl&sig=lHfHwSMNqhVc_1CQh98yjHfevxs&hl=en&sa=X&ei=7lW4T5HvJei1iQfO85HWCA&ved=0CGAQ6AEwCA#v=onepage&q=wikileaks%20changed%20the%20course%20of%20war%20in%20afghanistan&f=false (accessed 20 May 2012).

4

Human Sources: The Journalist and the Whistle-blower in the Digital Era

SUELETTE DREYFUS, REEVA LEDERMAN, A.J. BROWN, SIMON MILTON, MARCIA P. MICELI, RACHELLE BOSUA, ANDREW CLAUSEN AND JESSIE SCHANZLE

INTRODUCTION

Imagine you're sitting in an empty bar and you strike up a conversation with another customer. He's clearly very unhappy. You tell him you're a journalist. Pretty soon he begins unloading to you about the unethical things happening at his work. The next thing you know he's handing you a USB stick with 251 000 US State Department cables on it.

Of course that's not how it *really* happens. In real life, random barflies rarely provide closely guarded government secrets to strangers. Most reporters don't *really* go creeping around darkened car parks waiting for Deep Throat to show up, as in *All the President's Men*. As one national security reporter[1] suggests: 'It happens in Hollywood a lot more than in real life frankly.'

Yet, there is no underestimating the value of human sources. HUMINT ('human intelligence') has long been recognised as one of the core roles of an effective spy organisation. The information-gathering role of an investigative journalist is similar. Most investigative journalists depend on human sources: for leads, to verify a story, or both. These sources may be anonymous, confidential, or their identities may be publicly identified. In recent years, technology-led web publishers, such as *WikiLeaks*, have pioneered new ways to protect anonymity and confidentiality, although technology can also make it easier to link journalists and their sources.

This chapter provides an in-depth look into one of the reporter's most important human sources— the whistle-blower. 'Whistle-blowing' occurs when a member of an organisation discloses 'illegal, immoral or illegitimate practices (including omissions) under the control of their employers, to persons or organisations who may be able to effect action' (Near & Miceli 1985). The authors suggest expanding this definition further: whistle-blowing is the act of revealing inside information about serious wrongdoing to people or authorities who may be able to take action about that wrongdoing. Wrongdoing is when a person or organisation does things that are unlawful, unjust, dangerous or dishonest.

Public interest whistle-blowing is conventionally understood to identify wrongdoing that affects more than the private or personal interests of the whistle-blower (Brown et al. 2008, p. 8). It also *commonly* requires an element of seriousness—sufficient to cause actual harm to the interests of individuals, the organisation or wider society—rather than just 'technical' breaches of rules or procedures.[2] These definitions are important, for they dovetail with the public interest element of journalism in bringing to light important information that exposes wrongdoing.

This chapter addresses three questions:

1   What motivates whistle-blowers to come to the media?

2   What do these sources want when choosing a journalist they can blow the whistle to? and

3   How can journalists help protect whistle-blowers and other human sources?

The chapter highlights high-profile news stories in which whistle-blowers played a key role and suggests some key elements common to many whistle-blowers. It also includes analysis of an international qualitative research study conducted from 2010 to 2012 by the authors of this chapter.

TYPES OF HUMAN SOURCES

Leaks are the journalist's lifeblood. According to Flynn and others, leakers 'disclose unauthorised information to the press that has not been processed by official channels' (Flynn 2006; Bok 1982; Ericson et al. 1989; Sigal 1973; Thompson 1995; Tiffen 1989). Increasingly, whistle-blowers are working through 'citizen journalists'—online bloggers, Twitter and Facebook—users and others who write (sometimes quite expertly) on a topic, but who may not be employed for money by a media organisation.

There are different types of leakers with varying motivations, including the whistle-blower (who intends that the wrongdoing be stopped). Other leakers may have unrelated intentions—such as tactical political gain, or embarrassment. According to veteran Australian political journalist Laurie Oakes, 'leakers, whatever their motivation, serve the public interest' simply because of their importance to free journalism: 'being first with important news is, in essence, what being a reporter is all about' (2010, p. 296). However, whistle-blowers are both particularly valuable in identifying newsworthy issues, and less likely than other more 'tactical' leakers to protect themselves against retaliation or other consequences of their actions.

Only a limited proportion of whistle-blowing involves the media. Workplace fraud, for example, is generally reported through internal channels or to a manager. There is also a range of external channels, including the police or an anti-corruption agency. If a potential whistle-blower thinks these institutions are part of the fraud, however, they may well turn to an MP or to an NGO such as a help group. Whistle-blowers frequently only turn to the media as a last resort, if they feel there is nowhere else to go; or because they have suffered reprisals, and have nothing left to lose (Callahan & Dworkin 1994; Donkin et al. 2008; Smith & Brown 2008). As one of the whistle-blowers interviewed for this study described it: 'What the whistle-blower has been forced into … with the media is looking for a way to short-circuit those entrenched power systems … and achieve what are publicly acceptable legal or moral outcomes.' In such circumstances, the whistle-blower turns to the journalist.

Some of the biggest news stories come from whistle-blowers. These stories often serve the public interest by revealing safety failures or wrongdoing in a way that protects society. An example of this is the 'Dr Death' case from Queensland. In 2005, intensive care nurse unit manager Toni Hoffman revealed wrongdoing by surgeon Jayant M. Patel in a scandal that rocked the Queensland Government, led to a major commission of inquiry, and made international news (ABC 2005; AAP 2005; Davies 2005; CNN 2010). Dubbed 'Dr Death' by the media, Patel was eventually linked to 80 deaths at Bundaberg Base Hospital (Mancuso 2005). It was only when Hoffman's concerns became public that a full picture emerged (Thomas 2007). In 2010, the Queensland Supreme Court sentenced Patel to seven years prison in one of the longest running Supreme Court criminal trials in the state (ABC/AAP 2010), although the High Court in August 2012 ordered a retrial that was still to be heard at the time this book was published.

At times, whistle-blowers reveal their own wrongdoing as well as that of their peers or superiors. One of the most famous examples of this is the 'My Lai Massacre' story from the Vietnam War era. In 1969, at the height of the Vietnam War, investigative journalist Seymour Hersch sat in an Indiana farmhouse listening to young US soldier Paul Meadlo (Hersch 1977). Meadlo was revealing wrongdoing—by himself, his superior and fellow soldiers—in circumstances so awful that they would eventually contribute to the end of the Vietnam War. The news story became known as the 'My Lai Massacre', after the name of the village where US soldiers went on a killing spree, murdering more than 100 women, children and old men in cold blood. Meadlo's mother told Hersch: 'I gave them a good boy, and they made him a murderer' (Hersch 1977, p. 296).

Meadlo told Hersch how the soldiers had 'choppered in … expecting it to be hot; filled with the enemy. Nobody was there'. Army Second Lieutenant William Calley ordered Meadlo to begin shooting villagers. At first Meadlo refused, but after Calley began shooting, Meadlo joined in. 'Meadlo told Hersch, "Calley told me to push them in a ditch, and he named two or three other guys, and then we just shot them in the ditch"' (Hersch 1977, p. 296). Eventually Calley was convicted of war crimes for his role (*Los Angeles Times* 2009).

Meadlo was whistle-blowing. Hersch wrote: 'Meadlo wanted to do it … In his case, expiation was very important' (Hersch 1977, p. 296). This case highlights the complex motivations that bring whistle-blowers to talk to journalists, even when it may not be in their own best interest to do so.

PORTRAIT OF A WHISTLE-BLOWER

Who are whistle-blowers? What motivates them to talk to journalists? What do they want from the journalist? The authors sought answers to these questions by studying whistle-blowers and the investigative journalists who work with them.

Using whistle-blower motivation as an initial unit of analysis, the authors first conducted five pre-interviews with investigative journalists and whistle-blowers. The authors used the data from these and from an extensive literature search to draw up more structured questions for Phase 2 of the data gathering. This involved 24 in-depth interviews with five 'high-impact' whistle-blowers and 19 journalists from news organisations covering 11 countries (Australia, the UK, Iceland, Russia, Germany, Bulgaria, Kyrgyzstan, Kazakhstan, Uzbekistan, Tajikistan and Turkmenistan).

The whistle-blowers' stories were labelled 'high impact' if they had been covered by one or more major media outlets, including metropolitan daily newspapers or national broadcasters. In some cases the whistle-blowers were anonymous in those stories; in others their identities were known. Most of the reporters interviewed had an investigative journalism background. All forms of media were represented, including newspapers, television, radio and online media. Note that all participants in this study have been anonymised, and are referred to as 'he' regardless of their gender.

The rationale behind supplementing the whistle-blowers' stories with those of investigative reporters was because it was not possible to find and gain access to large numbers of high-impact whistle-blowers. The reporters had worked on long-term investigative stories, or had made extensive use of sources or leaks in high-risk or high-impact situations. To ensure the data we collected was valid, the authors tested the journalists' interview data against the data from the interviews with the whistle-blowers themselves for consistency. The authors also wanted to include a wide age range of journalists in order to capture data on the impact of digital technologies. All the interviews were transcribed and then coded using Atlas.ti, a qualitative data analysis software program. The next section describes aspects that motivate whistle-blowers to go to the media.

WHISTLE-BLOWER MOTIVATIONS IN GOING TO THE MEDIA

Whistle-blowers may all be revealing inside information about wrongdoing to the media in the hopes of having that wrongdoing stopped, but their motivations are sometimes quite complex, and frequently there is more than one motivation at work. As part of the data gathering, the authors asked each subject what motivated whistle-blowers. The authors built and expanded the list as the interviews progressed and tested the validity of the motivations in subsequent interviews. The authors also asked subjects to rank the list of motivations from most frequent to least frequent.

Participant A (a journalist) identified three key categories of whistle-blower which were reinforced by subsequent interviewees:

1   seeking justice

2   seeking some form of personal gain

3   were angry or wanted retribution or revenge.

They might all be revealing inside information about wrongdoing to the media in the hopes of having that wrongdoing stopped, but their motivations are quite different. These broad categories were confirmed by other study participants, such as Participant B, an award-winning journalist with more than 20 years' experience:

> You've got the ones that simply are driven by ideals, values and conscience. And there's nothing in it for them but heartache. Then you'll get another subset where they are doing the right thing in highlighting what is going on … but they will get some kind of benefit. Not saying that's a bad thing. And then there is a third sort of subset: they're pissed off and they're going to get back. There's a bit of revenge …
>
> It doesn't mean you don't do the story. You get every side of it. But the ones I like dealing with are the first [category].

There were additional motivations identified by participants, but these were effectively subsets of the earlier categories (see Table 4.1).

TABLE 4.1: THE PALETTE OF WHISTLE-BLOWER MOTIVATIONS

	MOTIVATION	HOW COMMON?
1	Justice seekers/altruism/moral outrage—the genuine desire to correct or stop something that is wrong or unjust, regardless of whether this benefits or costs them personally	The most common motivation identified, with almost all listing it
2	Retribution—getting back at a person or organisation perceived to have injured the whistle-blower or friends/allies	The second most common motivation listed
3	Patriotism	Less common
5	Fame or acknowledgment	Less common
6	Power/manoeuvring within an organisation/politics/leverage	Less common
7	Information trading	Less common
8	Stirrers/people who want to 'stir things up'	Less common
9	Personal or financial gain	Less common

Often the motivations would blend or merge together. This is why we refer to them as a 'palette'. However, two stood out: justice seekers/altruism/moral outrage and retribution.

By the former, the authors mean the genuine desire to correct or stop something that is unjust or wrong, regardless of whether this personally benefited the whistle-blower. Participants also sometimes called it 'public spirit'. Almost all study participants listed this, and many listed it as the most frequent motivation. Participant C (a journalist) described it as follows:

> It is altruistic. It's also sort of reforming in their minds. It's doing it for a reason, which they believe will change something … a foreign intervention or a change in policy by somebody or it will create something. It's not just for the sake of the information getting out there. They want to effect a change.

Some participants (all of whom were journalists) doubted that this motivation occurred as frequently as the public believed, and a few doubted that it existed on its own. They viewed it as always being combined with other motives.

Retribution was also commonly listed by the investigative journalists in the study, but not by the whistle-blowers. Some journalists did not believe this was a motivation by 'true whistle-blowers', but rather by some other sort of leaker. In most cases where retribution was listed as a major motivation, the journalists making the observation had spent much of their careers focusing on major crime, particularly organised crime.

Among the whistle-blowers, retribution did not loom large, except possibly after they tried to blow the whistle and were badly treated. This was the case with Participant D, whose whistle-blowing involved the revelation of activities that led to the deaths of children. As a result of the mistreatment he received after blowing the whistle on the activity, he was now motivated by retribution: 'I don't want revenge from the original thing,' he said. 'I want revenge from the reprisal.'

Other, less frequent motivations included patriotism, fame-seeking, power and information trading (described by one journalist as 'horse trading'). This cluster of motivations was much less frequent, with 'horse trading' tending to be most prevalent around political reporting. Note that the desire for power in exchange for whistle-blowing information is not always selfish in the sense of empire building. In corrupt or violent societies, it is sometimes simply self-preservation as a direct result of the first whistle-blowing act. This was described by Participant E (a journalist):

> [The whistle-blower] was reliably informed that they [the people he blew the whistle on] were going to try and assassinate him … He suddenly really, really wanted to talk to us personally, right, because what he was doing was trying to gain leverage. [Something] like 'look, if I die in a car 'accident' or something, the world is going to know who did this' kind of thing. So that is kind of horse trading in a sense.

The 'fame' motivation is also sometimes used by whistle-blowers to protect themselves. However, participants more often confirmed the fame motivation as an after-benefit rather than a primary motivation. Where it was identified as a motivation, the 'fame' tended to be more of an acknowledgment of the whistle-blower's existence than the desire to see their name in lights. Participant F (a journalist) described an example of this:

> I had one just recently where a person sent in some anonymous information that turned out to be absolutely fantastic. It was typed up and it had 'If you want more of this information please put a smiley face on the front page.'
>
> Well, we didn't. Then the person contacted us after a couple of weeks … then rang—that's when I managed to weasel [it] out of them.

Understanding a whistle-blower's motivations is important for any investigative journalist in determining how much to trust the source, and ultimately the information. Whistle-blowers sometimes say that all they have is their integrity. Similarly, all journalists have is their credibility. Destroying credibility can remove pesky investigative journalists who reveal unpleasant truths. False human intelligence provides an excellent way to do that. The stereotype of the greying journalist full of bitter cynicism has some basis in fact, in part because most working journalists have faced the problem of being duped by false information. Participant G (a journalist) noted:

> People always present as having some noble motive that they wish to improve the system. And I don't normally take them at their word. I think quite carefully about what their other motives might be—underlying motives might be—because I need to know. The first thing I need to know about a source is what their motive is so I can evaluate the veracity of what is going on.

Participant H (a journalist), who worked in a non-Western country, was concerned at having misinformation deliberately 'planted' on him as a way of discrediting him. This concern was repeated by other journalist-participants, particularly those who worked in countries where the rule of law had failed or who had broken particularly high-profile stories of wrongdoing by powerful individuals.

A COMPLEX RELATIONSHIP

The relationship between the journalist and the whistle-blower is complex. While journalists may have to protect themselves against the whistle-blower providing inaccurate information, they may also end up having to defend the whistle-blower.

All the whistle-blower participants and some of the journalists observed that the first thing an organisation does when the news story breaks is attempt to discredit the whistle-blower. Participant K (a whistle-blower who now supports other whistle-blowers in public service roles) described this as a 'textbook' approach: 'It's always very quick, the retaliation, when anyone speaks up ... the attack on the person occurs to put the focus on that person and take away from what the whistle-blower is actually speaking about.'

In attacking the whistle-blower, however, the organisation may also turn against the journalist, with their reputation also becoming a casualty. Many journalist participants discussing this sub-topic were adamant about the need for documentary evidence—not just for secondary confirmation of a story, but also as a possible defence against this problem in high-impact whistle-blower story transactions. For Participant G (a journalist), providing documents is the definition of a 'valuable whistle-blower'.

While it is possible for documents to be faked, participants generally agreed that documents lend a degree of legitimacy to whistle-blowers' statements that is much harder to undermine. It's interesting to note that whistle-blower participants say they always suggest getting documents as proof of the wrongdoing before taking the big step of going to the media.

The journalist's request for documentary evidence is important for another reason: the whistle-blower is in most cases completely unprepared for the maelstrom on the horizon and may not even have thought about it. Participant K (a whistle-blower) observed:

> There's a bit of autism in a lot of whistle-blowers I've noticed. People that are on the autism spectrum don't have the social cues. They don't care about what other people think and they have a very strong sense of right and wrong—very black and white. So when they see corruption they go: 'Hey, the rule is: report corruption ... This is wrong. I'm going to report corruption.'
>
> There's no benefit. It's actually a detriment. Whistle-blowers ... get crushed. Their careers are ruined; they end up in dead corridors. They actually lose more—not just their family and friends—their work colleagues, their jobs ... The organisation doesn't want you and it's only a matter of time before the work environment is unsafe; you're not wanted ... your mental health deteriorates. It's like throwing yourself on the sword; it's not a positive, good thing. A person that had high social skills ... they're not going to do it. The cost is too high.
>
> A lot of whistle-blowers don't even realise they're blowing the whistle ... They're going: 'Hey, I just wanted to point out that something's wrong over here.'

Participant K has special knowledge of autism spectrum disorders, as well as providing support over years to people considering blowing the whistle. Thus the observations made in this area take on a special significance.

Participants of both types repeatedly stated that whistle-blowing to the media was not in the whistle-blower's best interest. Participant G (a journalist) said:

> I would mostly advise whistle-blowers not to do it if I was considering their interests rather than mine, because I would say mostly the whistle-blowers I come across … the consequences for them are not great.
> I don't say I exploit … but I do use what these people have to say as much as I can in order to make things public that I would like to make public.

On this topic, the journalists and whistle-blowers were in strong agreement.

WHAT IS IMPORTANT TO THE WHISTLE-BLOWER IN DEALING WITH A JOURNALIST

The whistle-blowers and journalists had a very similar list of what was commonly important to the whistle-blower who came to the media (as distinct from the things that motivated the whistle-blower to speak up in the first place):

TABLE 4.2: CHARACTERISTICS OF THE MEDIA OUTLET VALUED BY WHISTLE-BLOWERS

MEDIA CHARACTERISTIC	DESCRIPTION
Change agent	Media exposure through given outlet likely to cause change and fix the injustice
Anonymity	Outlet able to keep the whistle-blower's identity secret from all except possibly the journalist (although sometimes even from the journalist too)
Story treatment	How the journalist would treat the story (sympathetically, with a fair eye, etc.)
Reputation	Reputation of the journalist and the publication
Previous related stories	Whether the journalist or outlet had run related stories before
Media outlet's audience	The reach and make-up of the media outlet's audience (big, small but influential, international or not)
Treatment after the story runs	How the journalist treats the whistle-blower after the story runs

The first two items—change agent and anonymity—were the most important on the list for both journalists and whistle-blowers. Surprisingly, a number of whistle-blowers put change before anonymity, despite the risks to themselves. As one observed, many whistle-blowers are taking big risks talking to a journalist in order to win change. So they would not sacrifice that primary desire even at the cost of their identities being exposed. This preference provides evidence for the altruistic motivation identified earlier.

Sometimes the whistle-blower wants to hide their identity from the reporter as well as the rest of the world. This is true anonymity. Confidentiality is when the identity of the source is kept secret from all but a few, such as the journalist and their editor. The desire for full anonymity drew a mixed response from study participants. Some journalists wouldn't accept it, such as Participant G, who often covers crime cases: 'they love sending you anonymous emails. You see that all the time, sometimes done with a Hotmail address … under a fake name. So I'm not going to deal with you on this basis … I have to know who you are.'

Other participants, however, were willing to build a long-term relationship of trust with a person they could not identify. Participant F, a multi-award-winning seasoned journalist, said:

> I've been having a dialogue for years with someone called AlphaBear.[3] I don't know who AlphaBear is, but AlphaBear is very connected to the mafia and gives me terrific information.
>
> Look, once you establish the veracity of some of the information, I don't care if they don't want to reveal who they are … As long as you can establish what they're telling you is accurate, they want to be anonymous, that is fine.

While anonymity can protect whistle-blowers, the reverse can also be true. Some deliberately make themselves very public for protection, believing it is more difficult for tough-minded organisations or individuals to use dirty tricks on someone who is very much in the public eye. Participant K (a whistle-blower) in a Western country said:

> I was offered to go into a [safe] house. There'd been about nine people that died in these [safe] houses … I could run and change my name, but I couldn't hide. These guys were going to kill me.
>
> [So I] hit the media… And I made it very clear out there that I had documents put with different people, and if I died, they were coming out. I had dirt on everyone. And I think everyone was going, 'Oh, shit, what has he got?' That's the only thing that kept me alive.

This approach seems to apply less to things such as losing a job or reputation, and more in cases where personal safety is at risk.

The reputation of the journalist's publication repeatedly appeared in the interview transcripts as a key 'buying criteria' for whistle-blowers. Participant F (a journalist) said: 'having the weight of a major media organisation behind you really impacts on the whistle-blowers'.

Perhaps even more importantly, the whistle-blowers were strategic about the journalist they targeted, in some cases testing journalists by feeding them a titbit of information and seeing how they handled it. This test was mentioned in two contexts: trust about keeping something secret when asked to, and trust that the journalist could make good stories out of it.

For some whistle-blowers, also important was the ability of the journalist to see beyond the story being spun by the powerful in society—often called 'the narrative'—and to present an alternative. In *Political Fictions*, author and journalist Joan Didion defines 'the narrative' as being 'made up of tacit agreements, small and large, to overlook the observable in the interests of obtaining a dramatic story line' (Didion 2001, p. 37). This definition could be expanded to include obtaining an illegal, immoral or illegitimate outcome, as described by Participant J (a journalist):

> It's an ability to see through the narrative … The narrative is … 'We're good, they're terrorists' … That's their narrative and they're sticking to it.
>
> 'If you tell a lie, tell a big one and keep telling it'—that's what they do. And the media has no endurance beyond the seven-day media cycle, *if* they last seven days. Mostly its just 24 hours. So the government just has to stick to the narrative and keep telling the lies. [Sometimes] you get a long narrative, like the one with the Vietnam War or the one we see now with the war in Afghanistan. You've got this … phoney war on terror which has impinged on civil liberties …

This same view about the false story, the made-up tidy tale, was repeated in different words over and over again by whistle-blowers.

Not all whistle-blowers carefully target a particular journalist, however, with the study identifying at least two distinct groups. One group turns to the media after trying all other avenues, and they are often already public or semi-public. A second group appears to turn to the media either first or very early on, usually because they have realised that the wrongdoing comes from the very highest levels of their organisation, and therefore reporting via accepted channels is hopeless. This second group appears highly deliberate in identifying the journalist they approach.

The data suggests that some whistle-blowers have a high degree of sophistication and are subtler than simply choosing a 'warm' journalist. They want a journalist who is able to completely disassemble all that is assumed about a reality before reconstructing it from scratch.

Whistle-blowers also consider whether the journalist (or media outlet) has run stories related to their topic. For example, in the pre-interviews, the authors interviewed a journalist who staffed a submission box. When the journalist's media outlet put out a call for information on a particular topic, people would submit material. However, running a story on the topic would frequently generate a large stream of related information through the submission box, some of it anonymously and some with contact details attached. Interestingly, the journalist noticed that the closer someone seemed to be to the key players in a story topic, the less likely they were to provide original documents.

Whistle-blowers care about the media outlet's audience. Is it an influential audience, such as politicians and policy makers, that might succeed in effecting change? Or is it far-reaching, such as the nightly news audience, that might protect them?

Similarly, while not a core criterion, whistle-blowers care about how the journalist treats them after the story has run its course. This appeared in the interviews numerous times as something that journalists need to be sensitive to when they move on to the next story.

HOW JOURNALISTS CAN HELP TO PROTECT THEIR SOURCES

The primary protection traditionally offered to whistle-blowers is 'an undertaking by the journalist that the identity of the source will not be revealed' (Flynn 2006, p. 258). This is almost always in the journalist's own interest, because it reserves the source as their exclusive asset. It is also typically presumed to be the best protection a whistle-blower can have. However, the reality of whistle-blower protection is not so simple.

One of the investigative journalists interviewed for this study described how a whistle-blower had gone to great effort to hide his identity when telephoning, including using a voice synthesizer. Unfortunately he called from a phone that revealed its number. It was recognised by her caller ID phone. He was surprised when she asked: 'So, can I get back to you on this number?' *WikiLeaks'* creation of an anonymous online dropbox provided some protection for whistle-blowers from such tracking (Dreyfus et al. 2011). However, despite this improvement, tracking communications in the digital world is generally very easy. A senior investigative journalist observed that he found it much harder to get leaks of any sort these days (whistle-blowing or otherwise). He believed the ease of tracing communications along with the severe penalties for leaking are to blame.

For these reasons, media organisations have been strong supporters of legal protection for whistle-blowers. Legal protection can take many forms, from criminalisation of reprisals, to compensation rights, to freedom from prosecution or civil action for having breached confidences or official secrets. In Australia, the effectiveness of whistle-blower protection has been patchy at best (Brown et al. 2008), while internationally the situation is also highly variable (Calland & Dehn 2004; Lewis 2010). Only relatively recently has legislative protection extended explicitly to whistle-blowers who go public, as opposed to those who use official channels; with the UK and, most recently, Queensland's *Public Interest Disclosure Act 2010* providing special leadership in this respect (Brown 2011).

Journalism 'shield laws' are also important. These provide a special legal privilege to confidential communications between journalists and their sources, In Australia, the federal *Evidence Act* was amended to that effect in 2011, although in the USA such reform has foundered over a long period (Brown 2011). However, shield laws function primarily to protect journalists—saving them from jail or fines for contempt of court—and only secondarily to protect whistle-blowers, who may still be prosecuted.

Journalists therefore have a responsibility to give whistle-blowers good advice about how best to protect themselves. They have a responsibility to adopt practical strategies for minimising the chances that their communications with whistle-blowers can be traced or identified. They also need to consider whether they might be compelled to name a source in court.

For extremely risky stories, such as those involving national security or law enforcement, it is best to avoid electronic communications with the whistle-blower entirely. Electronic communications are the most effective (and cheapest) way to link a whistle-blower and a journalist. A trusted go-between, snail mail and agreed drop locations are preferable.

If electronic communication is necessary, however, both the journalist and the whistle-blower should armour themselves properly. The most comprehensive guide for doing this is on the *Surveillance Self-Defense* website by the not-for-profit (and independent) Electronic Frontier Foundation in the USA (see the Website References at the end of this chapter). Beyond this, there are other issues that good journalists should consider regarding how best to manage and protect their sources. Like law enforcement agencies that make good use of whistle-blowers, journalists' sense of responsibility should not always end with the story. News organisations cannot compensate whistle-blowers for *all* the stresses and difficulties that may befall them as a result of providing public interest information to the media— but good journalists and editors are clearly aware that they do owe at least a moral duty of care towards these most valuable of sources. How best to identify and fulfil this duty is likely to be an increasing topic of debate among journalists, publishers, media regulators and the wider public.

CONCLUSION

HUMINT remains an essential source for investigative journalists. People who leak information provide much of this, and whistle-blowers are one of the most important sub-categories of HUMINT sources. Whistle-blowers who choose to go outside their organisations to the media in order to blow the whistle may have a palette of motivations. The desire to reveal wrongdoing in order to seek justice is one of the most common. The desire for retribution or revenge also appears as a motivation in some cases, such as in organised crime stories.

Understanding motivation is important in order to determine how much to trust the source, the accuracy of the leaked information, and the degree of risk that surrounds the source—both the risk of them sharing the information with others, and the risks of retaliation to which they are likely to be exposed if, or when, they are identified. Obtaining documents is often important to verify the whistle-blower's account and to protect the journalist from organisations that try to discredit both the whistle-blower and the journalist's story.

Technology has made it more difficult to hide communication links between journalists and their human sources. This puts whistle-blowers at greater risk. The further exploration of technology's impact on whistle-blowing to the media is a worthwhile area of study that may help to protect the free flow information from what is an important journalistic source of information.

QUESTIONS TO CONSIDER

1   Define the term 'whistle-blower'.

2   Why do whistle-blowers tend to release evidence of wrongdoing to the media rather than keeping it to themselves or advising a senior person within the organisation?

3   What risks do whistle-blowers face in publicly releasing previously confidential information?

4   How can journalists help protect whistle-blowers?

5   What are the ethical questions journalists should consider when considering:

   a   if and how to protect whistle-blowers

   b   whether to publish or broadcast the information that comes into their possession via a whistle-blower?

TASK

1   Go online and find out what legal protections exist for whistle-blowers in Australia and elsewhere. What legislation might they breach when leaking information? Write a 500-word summary of the issues you uncover.

Acknowledgments

This work draws on research from The Australian Research Council Project DP1095696: *Blowing Boldly: The Changing Roles, Avenues and Impacts of Public Interest Whistleblowing in the Era of Secure Online Technologies.*

REFERENCES

AAP. 2005. 'Qld Health Minister Nuttall Resigns', *Sydney Morning Herald*: www.smh.com.au/news/National/Qld-health-minister-Nuttall-quits/2005/07/22/1121539132175.html (accessed 15 April 2012).

ABC. 2005. 'At Death's Door', *Australian Story*, 27 June: www.abc.net.au/austory/content/2005/s1400735.htm (accessed 10 April 2012).

ABC/AAP. 2010. 'Patel Guilty on All Charges', *ABC News*, 30 June: www.abc.net.au/news/2010-06-29/patel-guilty-on-all-charges/886392 (accessed on 16 March 2012).

Bok, S. 1982. *Secrets: On the Ethics of Concealment and Revelation*, London: Oxford University Press.

Brown, A.J. 2011. 'Weeding Out WikiLeaks (And Why It Won't Work): Legislative Recognition of Public Whistleblowing in Australia', *Global Media Journal (Australian Edition)*, Vol. 5, No. 1: www.commarts.uws.edu.au/gmjau/2011_5_1_toc.html (accessed 30 April 2012).

Brown, A.J., Latimer P., McMillan J. & Wheeler, C. 2008. 'Towards Best Practice Whistleblowing Legislation for the Public Sector: The Key Principles', in A.J. Brown, ed., *Whistleblowing in the Australian Public Sector: Enhancing the Theory and Practice of Internal Witness Management in Public Sector Organisations*, Canberra: ANU E-Press.

Callahan, E. & Dworkin, T. 1994. 'Who Blows the Whistle to the Media, and Why: Organizational Characteristics of Media Whistleblowers', *American Business Law Journal*, 32(2), pp. 151–84.

Calland, R. & Dehn, G., eds. 2004. *Whistleblowing Around the World: Law, Culture & Practice*, London: Public Concern At Work.

CNN. 2010. *The Making of a Bad Surgeon*, 2 November: http://edition.cnn.com/video/#/video/international/2010/11/02/wus.dr.death.bk.b.cnn (accessed 25 March 2012).

Davies, G. (Commissioner). 2005. *Queensland Public Hospitals Commission of Inquiry Report*, Brisbane: Queensland Health: www.qphci.qld.gov.au/final_report/Final_Report.pdf (accessed 2 May 2012).

Didion, J. 2001. *Political Fictions*, New York: Vintage Books.

Donkin M., Smith, R. & Brown, A.J. 2008. 'How Do Officials Report? Internal and External Whistleblowing', in A.J. Brown, ed., *Whistleblowing in the Australian Public Sector: Enhancing the Theory and Practice of Internal Witness Management in Public Sector Organisations*, Canberra: Australia & New Zealand School of Government/ANU E-Press.

Dreyfus, S., Lederman, R., Bosua, R. & Milton, S. 2011. 'Can We Handle the Truth? Whistleblowing to the Media in the Digital Era', *Global Media Journal (Australian Edition)*, Vol. 5, No. 1: www.commarts.uws.edu.au/gmjau/v5_2011_1/dreyfus_truth_Essay.html (accessed 2 May 2012).

Ericson, R., Barank, P. & Chan, J. 1989. *Negotiating Control: A Study of News Sources*, Toronto: University of Toronto Press.

Flynn, K. 2006. 'Covert Disclosures: Unauthorized Leaking, Public Officials and the Public Sphere', *Journalism Studies*, 7(2), pp. 256–73.

Hersch, S.M. 1977. 'The My Lai Massacre Uncovered', in L.R. Obst, ed., *The Sixties*, New York: Random House/Rolling Stone Press, pp. 294–8.

Lewis, D., ed. 2010. *A Global Approach to Public Interest Disclosure*, Cheltenham, UK: Edward Elgar.

Los Angeles Times. 2009. 'Calley Expresses Remorse for Role in My Lai Massacre in Vietnam', 22 August.

Manusco, R. 2005. 'Queensland's "Dr Death" Linked to 80 Deaths', *The Age*, 25 May: www.theage.com.au/news/National/Queenslands-Dr-Death-linked-to-80-deaths/2005/05/24/1116700709781.html (accessed 2 March 2012).

Near, J.P. & Miceli, M.P. 1985. 'Organizational Dissidence: The Case of Whistle-blowing', *Journal of Business Ethics*, 1(4), pp. 1–16.

Oakes, L. 2010. *On the Record: Politics, Politicians and Power*, Sydney: Hachette Australia.

Sigal, L. 1973. *Reporters and Officials: The Organization and Politics of Newsmaking*, Lexington, MA: D.C. Heath and Company.

Smith, R. & Brown, A.J. 2008. 'The Good, The Bad and The Ugly: Whistleblowing Outcomes', in A.J. Brown, ed., *Whistleblowing in the Australian Public Sector: Enhancing the Theory and Practice of Internal Witness Management in Public Sector Organisations*, Canberra: Australia & New Zealand School of Government/ANU E-Press, Canberra.

Thomas, H. 2007. *Sick to Death*, Crow's Nest, Sydney: Allen & Unwin.

Thompson, J. 1995. *The Media and Modernity: A Social Theory of the Media*, Stanford, CA: Stanford University Press.

Tiffen, R. 1989. *News and Power*, Sydney: Allen & Unwin.

WEBSITE REFERENCES

Electronic Frontier Foundation: *Surveillance Self-Defense*: https://ssd.eff.org/.

World Online Whistleblowing Survey: https://whistleblowingsurvey.org/.

FURTHER READING

Neuman, W.L. 1997. *Social Research Methods—Qualitative and Quantitative Approaches*, Massachusetts: Allyn and Bacon.

NOTES

1   Participant I in the study described later in this chapter.

2   This is adapted from the World Online Whistleblowing Survey, the first multilanguage online survey (and open to everyone) about whistle-blowing ever to be fielded in so many languages (see the Website References at the end of this chapter). The survey was designed, built and run by a research team composed of the authors.

3   Note the real pseudonym of the whistle-blower has been changed because it was also an email address.

PART 2

APPROACHES AND TOOLS

Chapter 5: The Research Process 65

Chapter 6: Research Strategies 77

Chapter 7: The 'Twitterisation' of Investigative Journalism 88
Case Study: Investigative Social Journalism and the Arab Spring 101

Chapter 8: Maths and Stats for Journalists 103

Chapter 9: Data Journalism (1) 116

Chapter 10: Data Journalism (2) 123
Case Study: The Sin Index 137

Chapter 11: Interpreting Financial Documents 139
Case Study: The Numbers Never Lie 149

Chapter 12: Working with the PR Industry 151
Case Study: Strategic Communications 163

Chapter 13: Legal Issues 166
Case Study: Intellectually Disabled People Fight for Equal Access to Justice 178

Chapter 14: Dirty Hands and Investigative Journalism 181
Case Study: The Day I Went Silent 188

5

The Research Process

WENDY BACON

INTRODUCTION

Research is an essential part of all journalism. Although it is particularly important for in-depth journalism—including investigations, features, profiles and documentaries—even short stories require fact checking and basic background research.

Learning to be an effective researcher is an ongoing practice that is never complete. New stories and questions will arise that throw up new research challenges. Content changes and needs to be updated, and the forms in which information is provided are constantly changing. This chapter provides some ideas about research that I have developed over decades of practice as a journalist, educator and legal researcher. Many of these points may seem simple to readers, but I have always found it useful to revisit basic principles in journalism.

DEVELOPING A STORY RESEARCH STRATEGY

There are two broad types of story idea. The first is when you have a tip-off or some definite information, which, if substantiated, will provide evidence for a story or part thereof. The other is when you select or are given a more general theme—for example, homelessness in your home town—and you need to find if there is a story you can publish, or establish angles that will require more in-depth research. Occasionally you may need to interview some sources immediately, in case they become unavailable, but usually the first step is to develop a solid research plan.

Evidence or empirical material is crucial for all stories. Other elements, including analysis of information, narrative technique and story-telling ability, are also important; but if you do not have a sound basis for making your 'truth' claims, your journalism will be weak. So once you have clarified your starting idea, ask yourself: In order to develop my idea into a strong story, what evidence do I need? Where and how can I find that evidence?

Every researcher has to develop their own style, but one way or another your plan will consist of a list of tasks. Group your tasks under different headings. For example, everything about housing statistics would go in one section, but may come from different sources. Grouping sub-topics and sources of information will save time. You don't want to be revisiting sources of information unnecessarily, so getting a broad overview of what needs to be done will help save time.

Sometimes, you may not know whether information exists publicly, so part of the research process is to establish what information is available and what will require interviews with sources (both on and off the record), direct observation and access to private information.

Establish an order of priority for your research. Some tasks will take longer than others, and some may need to be done in order for you to work out what to do next. As new angles emerge, your research strategy can be reviewed and new tasks added, and perhaps some removed.

Regularly review your plan. If the tasks become overwhelming or impractical in the time available, then prioritise. If this occurs, the key question will be: What information is essential for me to support a strong story? What information or angles are desirable because they will add depth and compelling detail?

Think about the best order in which to do tasks. Where there is time, you should research in advance of interviews. While you may not necessarily initially reveal it, it is good to be sufficiently on top of your information to know whether an interviewee is being honest so you can probe any false or self-serving statements. If you already know information will only be available through a Freedom of Information (FOI) request, you will need a minimum of five weeks, so you need to plan early for this.

MANAGING YOUR INFORMATION

It goes without saying that all research must be accurate. This means you need to have a way of recording and managing your research, making sure that errors do not creep in as you transfer information from one file to another. Very early on in my career as an investigative journalist, I wrote a story about a business liquidation involving fraud. I had original dockets which proved my main points and the article as a whole was sound. On reading it after publication, however, I realised I had got the first name of a leading auditor wrong. While there were no serious repercussions, I immediately realised how stupid this careless error was as it detracted from my credibility with all those readers who were familiar with the auditor's name. From then on, I made a practice of checking and rechecking all names, places and spelling at the end of the process. These days, most files are digital so you can avoid errors by cutting and pasting information from your research files into a draft story file or script as you go. When you revisit the draft later in the story process, you will have the correct names, dates and places already in place and can concentrate on creating a strong narrative.

A single investigative story or in-depth feature can generate literally hundreds of files across a range of media. Managing your information is a core issue. Clear labelling of files, whether hard copy or digital; breaking information up into minor topics or angles that relate to the story; retrieving or highlighting the most relevant information you need from larger files as you go; all help you to get the most from the information you collect and be able to quickly recheck information during the process and in your final fact checking.

RESEARCHING IN A GROUP

By researching in a group you will be able to tackle research tasks on a scale not otherwise possible. Because labour resources are scarce, partnerships with universities provide opportunities for the media to conduct such projects.

If you are working in a group, you may want to work on a collaborative online platform. There are many options, but I find sharing a Google Doc works well. This has the advantage of more than one person being able to enter information from different locations. As group members read new information, they can add ideas for story angles and further research as comments. For investigative classes, we have also used basic educational course software such as Moodle or Blackboard to gather group information together.

It is important when working in a group to establish a strong culture of accuracy and of fact checking before final publication.

If you feel you have lost control of your information, it may pay to take the time to review all the work so far, reassess the angles for your story and ascertain what information you actually need to prove or illustrate each key point.

BE COMPREHENSIVE

After accuracy, the next most important principle is to be comprehensive and up to date, even when a task becomes tedious. If you are not comprehensive, you may miss a crucial detail. But even more importantly, you will not be able to state your conclusions with any certainty, or you may make inaccurate statements. Imagine for example you are producing a piece about BHP Billiton's operations outside Australia and you want to be able to provide an accurate summary of their operations. The latest annual report may give you an excellent and accurate summary of operations at that time, but some projects might have been cancelled or announced during the year. A search of their company announcements, a news archive search, search of the company website or a call to the company will bring you up to date (you will find more on corporate research later in this chapter).

ASSESSING CREDIBILITY AND PROVIDING SOURCES

As you research, critically assess the credibility of your information sources. Some information sources are more likely to be reliable than others. Keep track of where each bit of information comes from so you can provide your audience with your sources for all information other than what is established fact. For example, the year on which a person was elected to Parliament is an established fact and can be very easily verified. The donations that person received during their election campaign is not established fact and may be found on a government electoral funding register in the returns supplied by the politician and/or donor. The source of the information needs to be accurately recorded, both for your editorial supervisors and your audience.

These days, journalists use links to connect audiences with sources. It will save time if you do these as you go along, or manage them in a list, if you are planning online resources to go with a broadcast.

THINK LATERALLY

It is important to hunt down your story. Sometimes this may mean focusing on a single particular piece of information, but at other times you have to move laterally. For example, in 1999, while researching a story about women in prison for the *Sun Herald* in Sydney, I met Roseanne Catt who had been in prison for eight years for crimes she insisted she did not commit. Fellow reporter Tracy Pillemer and I decided to investigate her case. We began by carefully reading hundreds of pages of her committal and trial transcripts. The case seemed weak and there were many conflicts in the evidence, but the material was not strong enough to support a story about a case for which all avenues of appeal had been exhausted. We identified former New South Wales detective Peter Thomas as a key actor in the prosecution case. Thomas had resigned from the police force after the Catt case and become a private inquiry agent. So we stepped sideways and started looking for cases in which Thomas had been involved since the Catt case. This involved legal and news database searches (which are discussed later in this chapter), and calls to people who had been charged by Thomas. We were able to identify several cases, but found little information was available on the internet. At one point, we travelled from Sydney to Brisbane to read a transcript from a Queensland court registry that was not online.

Through this process, we established that in several prosecutions based on Thomas' activities as a private inquiry agent, a judge commented on the flimsy evidence provided by him to support charges. We also conducted company searches to establish where he had worked and, through these, eventually tracked down others who had worked with him, one of whom had talked to him about the Catt prosecution. This person told us off the record that Thomas had told him he had planted a gun on Catt. If proved, this amounted to fresh evidence in the case.

Finally, we had two narratives. The first, 'Fire Trail', told the story of Thomas and his victims. This provided strong evidence to support the second story about the flaws in the Catt case. At about the same time, ABC's *Four Corners* broadcast 'Burned', a program about Thomas which featured a short segment on the Catt case. Interestingly, the ABC had begun by researching Thomas' career and, through that process, found their way to Catt. Although we started with different leads and came at the research process from different directions, we ended up with very similar information.

The ex-colleague of Thomas later came forward to give evidence about the conversation in a New South Wales inquiry, and after that, Catt was released from prison (Bacon & Pillemer 2000a; 2000b).

FOLLOW-UP RESEARCH

As suggested earlier, there will be evidence that you must establish before you have a story, but there will also be additional matters that you may need to research which add to the strength and narrative quality of the story. I always recommend visiting a destination if possible. For example, in 2009, the Australian Centre for Independent Journalism (ACIJ) was researching a story for the *Crikey* website about an aid contractor called GRM International, which had received hundreds of aid contracts from AusAID, Australia's international aid agency. GRM was in the same group as Queensland-based meat company Austrex, and both were owned by companies controlled by James Packer. I knew both companies operated from the same high-rise building, but it was only when I visited the address that I learned they operated out of the same small office. This fact, although not essential, added impact to the story by demonstrating the close connections between the aid and meat export companies (Bacon & Duxfield 2010a).

If new actors emerge in the story, you need to do basic searches on their background and current interests. Have a set of procedures that you follow, including advanced web searches (for example, Google), databases (including news databases such as Factiva or Newsbank) and social media. Media searches are also very important as you may pick up important old information that is not on the internet. Make sure you check media publications that are not on news databases. In Australia this includes commercial television current affairs programs such as '60 Minutes'. I have found LinkedIn useful when gathering background on individuals, although you must remember that this information may not be accurate or comprehensive, as it is the individual's own version of their background and connections.

As new individuals emerge, check their previous connections with other actors in your story by repeating searches.

TIMELINES AND DIAGRAMS

A journalist's ability to read large amounts of material and provide readable and concise summaries is one worth developing. If you are researching a story or topic that stretches over a period of time, creation of your own timelines and diagrams can be helpful in establishing connections between events and individuals and for developing a narrative. You may use these just for story development and research analysis purposes, or they may become a way of making a complex story more accessible for your audience. They can also be useful for recapping or reminding your audience of key points if your story develops after initial publications.

When connections between people and organisations become relevant but difficult to explain in words, draw a sketch or diagram. Even if you do not publish the diagram, it may help you grasp the networks or work out the most important links. It also helps you see how different sets of information can be linked. For example, a casino company may be owned by a public company, and, in backgrounding the public company directors, you find that one is also on the board of a public authority that can ease the way for casino developments. While they may not be on the actual casino company board, the link is still important.

Timelines can be useful when covering a story about political or social policy in relation to which audiences of different ages or from different places have different knowledge or memories of previous events. Recently, when the Gillard Government announced that it would be reopening detention facilities for asylum seekers on Nauru and Manus Island, I realised that many younger Australians had still been in school when the Pacific Solution was introduced in 2001. To prepare the timeline, I began by researching all news coverage through the Factiva news database and the Google News archive search engine, transferring key events and dates to my story file. I followed up court cases, non-government organisation reports, parliamentary records and other media to retrieve the most salient details, including powerful quotations (Bacon 2012a; 2012b).

Links to original material, photos, videos and sound files can also be embedded in story files to enrich the timeline and assist the audience to go as deep as they want. A comment button can allow members of the audience to suggest new entries.

SOURCES OF INFORMATION

Journalism has a lot to do with the day-to-day exercise of power and control over, and access to, resources of all kinds. For example, there is conflict over a proposed development. Resident groups object to the scale and environmental impacts of the development, while the company that owns the land says it will go broke if it does not get a certain height approved. As a journalist wanting to deliver a fair and accurate report on the situation, you need the answers to a range of questions. For example: Who exactly are the developers? Is there anything of interest in their business history? What, if any, are their connections to the government and political decision makers? Who is involved in the resident action groups? How representative are they of the community affected? Are their claims of over-development justified? According to what terms? What is the company's actual financial status? Are its claims justified? What is the company's communications' strategy and tactics? What is the nature of the government consultation process? Is the development approval a foregone conclusion or still open to change? Is a fix in? Or are the possibilities limited by the planning regulations themselves? Has anyone who is voting got a pecuniary or financial interest or received a benefit of any kind? What experts are involved? Who selects them? How independent are they? And what are their ongoing economic interests? Are they connected to any of the other interest groups?

Seen from an organisational point of view, you can divide information sources into several categories.

- company and business records
- property records
- government and parliamentary information (local, state and federal), including information held on elected representatives
- legal information
- other organisations and individuals including academics, other experts, non-government organisations and think-tanks.

COMPANIES AND BUSINESS RECORDS

All companies and business or trading names in Australia must be registered with the Australian Securities & Investment Commission (ASIC). This means that if you have what you think is a company name and you can't find it, you know that you either have the name wrong or the company is not listed in Australia. Once a company is registered, it will continue to exist until it is deregistered. All companies are allocated a nine-digit number. This is called its Australian Company Number (ACN). In fact, it is possible for a company to only have a number and not a name. The names of deregistered companies remain on ASIC records and it is possible to find information about these.

Unless you intend to become a specialist business or finance journalist, or you have studied business, you will only need to develop a fairly basic knowledge of companies to be able to do some useful research. This guide is only intended to provide a starting point. As always, if you do not understand something or need more information, find a source (human or documentary) that can help you.

It is important to understand from the outset that there are two categories of companies—private or proprietary companies, and public companies.

Proprietary companies have two words after their name: 'Pty Limited' or 'Pty Ltd'. These are by far the most common companies in Australia. Public companies have only 'Ltd' after their name.

All companies must have at least one shareholder (owner) and director (responsible for management of the company).

Three differences between public and private companies are:

- proprietary companies must have at least one shareholder but no more than 50 non-employee shareholders

- proprietary companies must have at least one director who must ordinarily be resident in Australia (public companies must have at least three directors), aged over 18 and not bankrupt.

- proprietary companies cannot sell shares to the investing public.

Companies may operate in many countries but they need to be registered separately to operate in each one.

An Australian company comes into legal existence when it is registered with ASIC. Once a company is registered, it can enter into contracts, own property and be sued. This is important from the point of view of even basic journalistic research because if, for example, you are searching electoral donations (see below) you will need to search both company and individual names. Similarly, if you want to establish the property interests of a person, you will need to know both their own name and the names of companies in which they have an interest.

Every private company must supply ASIC with the names of its directors and shareholders at the time of registration and keep ASIC informed about any changes. Do not assume, however, that records are up to date, as many companies are late with returns. The company must have a registered office, which does not have to be the place where it conducts business.

ASIC has a number of searchable registers. These are easily found on the front page of ASIC's website: www.asic.gov.au/asic/asic.nsf/. The key one for basic research is the 'organisational and business names register' which contains all the publicly available information on all companies and business names. To start with, you need a name or number. If you have not used this register before, do an exercise in which you enter any basic name. If you put in 'Apple', for example, you will get a list of all companies which include the word 'Apple', including deregistered or removed companies. You can then click on each one to find out some very basic information, including the suburb, but not address, in which it is (or was) registered and when the company was established. Assuming you started with a real company, you should by now have identified the company of interest to you. Just occasionally, you will not be sure and may have to do further (paid) searches (see below).

Companies have to file documents giving ASIC notice of changes in office holders, registered office, charges over the company and so on. Up until the 1980s, they also had to file accounts, but now nearly all private companies are required to provide no financial information (although there are some large and foreign-owned company exceptions). If you scroll to the bottom of the screen, you will find the last three documents filed. You can also get a list of all documents ever filed by the company. This information can prove useful in establishing when major changes occurred in the company's history and what other searches might be useful.

Unfortunately for researchers, ASIC provides no other information about private companies. To find out the directors and shareholders of companies, you need to pay either ASIC or an information broker. If you do have to pay, it is worthwhile researching comparative prices. When I last checked in September 2012, ASIC was the cheapest.

By paying for a search, you can find out the current directors and shareholders in a company (a current extract) or perhaps even more usefully, all directors and shareholders since the company was formed (a historical extract). Shareholders are important because as the owners, they are the beneficiaries of the company.

You will often find that one major company has many subsidiaries. Once you know the 'ultimate holding company', you should be careful not to do any unnecessary searches on the subsidiaries.

The names of directors will also help sort out connections between companies and people. As date of birth is usually provided, you often get a sense of age and family connections as well. The names and addresses of past directors and shareholders may lead to useful interviews or give you an understanding of major changes in the history of the company.

You can also do a search to find out all the companies in which a person is a director. This is more expensive but can be important if you are doing a profile, or the person is an important subject in your story.

All the documents that are listed under a company have an individual number and can be searched. For example, when researching the aid contractor GRM International in 2010, the ACIJ noticed in a list of documents one that referred to the government-owned Export and Finance Corporation providing finance to GRM at the time GRM was sold by James Packer. This information had not been publicly released. By searching this document, we were able to find more information, although much remained confidential. (Bacon & Duxfield 2010b). This provided an important fresh angle for our investigation.

Not all businesses are companies. Many find it simpler and cheaper to register a trading name with the relevant state department. But even business names have to be registered with ASIC, so it is still possible to find the identity of the person who has registered the name. If you find a trading name is not registered but you know a business is operating, this may lead to further questions or angles for your story.

Public companies

Public companies that require capital are listed on the Australian Securities Exchange (ASX) for the purpose of making shares available for trading. In order to provide a reliable and fair marketplace, the ASX has an important compliance role in setting minimum standards for disclosure. The end result is much higher levels of accountability and transparency than you will find for proprietary companies. You can easily establish if a company is listed on the stock exchange in Australia by visiting the ASX or the company's own website.

Each public company has a code which you can identify by entering the beginning letters in the company name on the ASX companies page (www.asx.com.au/professionals/companies.htm/). Once you have the code, you can use this to find a summary of the company's activities, the address of its registered office, its phone numbers, a description of the company's 'principal activities' and the current share price. There is also a list of the current company directors.

If a company is listed on the ASX, it is required to ensure the market is kept informed of any matters that could affect its share price by filing 'announcements', which are archived. Major documents such as annual reports are in this archive as well, although these may also be found on the company's website. By searching announcements from earlier years, you can get an overview of past takeovers, court cases and media releases. Companies also do presentations that provide concise descriptions of their activities. Provided you understand that there is a promotional aspect to the material, it is a convenient way to get an overall grasp of the company's activities.

Mining companies with exploration licences have to report their results to the ASX. In 2010, the ACIJ's Reportage/Enviro site (www.reportage-enviro.com) published two features on a pollution incident at Lake Kutubu in PNG. By researching the oil company's earlier announcements, reporter Calliste Weitenberg was able to document the precise date on which a well had been closed down because it was unstable, adding strength to her story (Weitenberg 2010).

For more on the ASX, see Chapter 11.

PROPERTY RECORDS

There are many reasons why you might want to know the identity of a landowner or what property an individual or company owns. For example, you might be investigating a conflict over development, an allegation of bribery or improper influence, patterns of land occupation, or you may simply want to gain an overall picture of the wealth of an individual.

Land and property are registered with a plan number and controlled through state and territory registers. Before records were computerised, if you wanted to research ownership of property you needed to visit your state registry, where for a few dollars you could retrieve an actual title that showed all the previous owners of a particular lot of land on a single document. Today, property information can be quickly obtained online, but it is more expensive. Cost varies between jurisdictions. In New South Wales, for example, in 2012 you could obtain a title and most recent transfer document for approximately $24. The Australian Government Land Titles Search page (http://australia.gov.au/services/service-task/search/land-titles-search/) provides links to relevant state departments managing land.

If you start with an address, you can find the plan number, and if you have the plan number, you can find and search the title. The first schedule on the title will tell you the owner. The second schedule will tell you about dealings such as mortgages and easements, and will also provide a transfer number for the last sale. The transfer document, which needs to be searched separately (more costs), will give you name of the previous owner and purchaser and how much was paid for the property.

The New South Wales Government Spatial Information Exchange provides useful samples that will help explain what you are looking for and the different processes. Go to https://shop.lands.nsw.gov.au and select 'Title search & records'. If you know where a property is but have neither its address nor plan number, you should be able to use Google maps to identify the address.

Mining leases are granted and registered with state and territory government departments. Environmental Impact Statements for lease applications may be available as well, although they need to be critically assessed as they are often conducted by consultants of the applicant's choice.

Significant land and property development applications are also often dealt with by government departments, although most are covered by local councils. The quality and accessibility of this information will vary enormously.

GOVERNMENT AND PARLIAMENTARY INFORMATION

Government information

A comprehensive list of Australian government departments and agencies can be found here: http://australia.gov.au/directories/. This page also provides access points to all state and territory departments and to local government as well.

Other importance government sources for journalists include:

- tenders databases: which document government contracts (www.tenders.gov.au)
- lobbyist registers: which record lobbyists and their owners and clients (http://lobbyists.pmc.gov.au)
- electoral donations databases: which record returns from donors and political organisations recording political donations (http://periodicdisclosures.aec.gov.au)
- the Australian Bureau of Statistics: which has a huge range of freely available statistical information on its 'Statistics' page (www.abs.gov.au)
- the National Pollutant Inventory: which provides emission estimates for 93 toxic substances and the source and location of these emissions: (www.npi.gov.au).

The links provided are federal ones. Many similar databases exist at state and territory levels.

Government databases provide specific pieces of information, but should also be more systematically accessed by journalists. Investigative journalist and Monash University academic Bill Birnbauer and his students developed 'Dangerous Ground', an ongoing text and video project that systematically investigates the management of toxic waste by the Victorian Environmental Agency. This project has already broken stories in mainstream media, but perhaps more importantly provides a continuing public record that 'scrutinises and makes accountable a key government body'.

For more information on advanced searching of government and business sources, including 'grey' literature that can not easily be searched, Maureen Henninger's *Hidden Web* (2008) is a useful source.

Parliamentary information

The news we receive about Parliament barely touches the surface of possible stories. The Parliament of Australia website (www.aph.gov.au) is the source of a huge amount of useful information, not just on political matters but many other topics as well. There are equivalent state and territory parliamentary websites. A good starting point with any of these is to give yourself a tour of the website.

A full record of parliamentary proceedings can be found in *Hansard*, which can be searched online (www.aph.gov.au/Parliamentary_Business/Hansard). Parliamentary committees also publish their proceedings, submissions and reports.

When reading a report, do not make the mistake of only reading the executive summary. While this may capture key issues, it does not necessarily contain the best examples or the strongest material. In 2010, Swinburne University students and the *Crikey* website team trawled through 200 reports that had been tabled in the Victorian Parliament on one day and produced 12 stories that had been missed by the mainstream media (*Crikey* 2010).

Committee submissions will also provide ideas for sources, contact details, background research, allegations of wrongdoing, and the perspectives of different interest groups.

Remember: provided you publish a fair and accurate report on parliamentary proceedings, you have a defence against any claim of defamation (Pearson 2010). This means that people sometimes speak and write more openly in parliamentary proceedings.

Parliamentary Library

The Parliamentary Library (www.aph.gov.au/library) provides a high-quality research service to parliamentarians, much of which is made publicly available. Providing you note the purpose and scope of publications, the library's background briefings and reports will provide you with a strong overview of an issue.

There are other useful ways of accessing parliamentary information. Most parliamentarians now have their own websites where they publish speeches made outside Parliament, media releases and so on. You need to remember, however, that this is information and versions of policy and events that they want you to know.

While the Parliament site provides a massive amount of information, if you are tracking a particular politician or debate, you will find the *OpenAustralia* website useful (www.openaustralia.org). This is a non-profit organisation which seeks to 'help keep people informed about what their representatives are up to'. It can be used for tracking a comprehensive range of parliamentary proceedings and particular politicians and issues.

Pecuniary interests

Pecuniary interest registers are a way of encouraging the integrity of elected representatives and some appointed officials. Such individuals have to regularly lodge forms that contain information about what they owe and own, gifts received and membership of organisations. Registers exist at federal, state and local level, although the requirements differ and you need to research these before using the relevant disclosure forms for investigation.

Many Australian government organisations at all levels of government have been reluctant to make the information easily available online to the public in a searchable form. University of Technology, Sydney (UTS) students working on a local government information project in 2010 found that some New South Wales local councils would not even allow them to take photocopies of the pecuniary interest register, which meant they had to take handwritten notes. There are likely, however, to be improvements in this area as more agitation for the 'public right to know' is successful.

OpenAustralia had the first crack at making the declarations of federal parliamentarians available, but abandoned this in 2010. In 2012, *The Sydney Morning Herald* and journalism students from the University of Technology, Sydney, trawled through the handwritten declarations of interests of federal parliamentarians to create a searchable database of the interests of parliamentarians and their spouses. By sorting and analysing the declarations, they were able to produce a set of stories to highlight the significance of the material (*Sydney Morning Herald* 2012).

LEGAL INFORMATION

The best Australian source of legal information is the Australian Legal Information Institute, or AustLII (www.austlii.edu.au). It provides access to all Australian federal and state laws, as well as links to the laws of some other countries. If someone mentions a section of an act to you, and you have made yourself familiar with the AustLII database, you can read it for yourself in just a few seconds.

AustLII also contains a huge database of case law that includes all key court judgments and an increasing number of judgments from tribunals, including specialist ones. You can search everything by topic or keyword, or read through decisions by year. In addition, there are specialist libraries, for example on aviation law.

Summaries of facts at the head of judgments provide a helpful synopsis, but as with reports of all kinds, you may find stronger material from a journalistic point of view by reading the whole document.

High Court transcripts are available through AustLII, but the vast majority of court transcripts are not. These are usually obtainable on request, but will be expensive. You can, however, often access them through a registry or transcript office. New South Wales provides its guidelines here: www.lawlink.nsw. gov.au/Lawlink/Corporate/ll_corporate.nsf/pages/attorney_generals_department_court_recording/.

The parties to a case can obtain transcripts and this is often the best way for a journalist to gain access.

PUTTING IT ALL TOGETHER

This overview of sources of information is only intended to give you a taste of what is available. You will constantly be looking for and stumbling across new and useful sources. Generally, the development of the internet and 'public right to know' campaigns have provided an impetus towards more government information being available. In 2010, the Australian Parliament amended FOI laws to include a strong presumption in favour of providing information (see www.oaic.gov.au/foi-portal/about_foi.html#what_changed_foi). Similar steps have been taken in some states. As this book goes to press, there is however a review of these new FOI laws under way, which some fear will lead to additional costs for those seeking information. At the same time, the citizens' transparency initiative *OpenAustralia* is educating the public by making FOI applications and government responses accessible: www.openaustraliafoundation.org. au/2012/11/28/you-have-the-right-to-know/.

When you cannot find information, make inquiries about whether it is available or not. Consult someone who knows the field well. Once you have established that you have a right to access the information, make sure you have documentation of that right and insist on access.

Once you have the information, read it carefully—and sometimes read it again, because when you have a stronger understanding of your subject, you may pick up further points. Look for gaps and silences. General and bureaucratic language can often be used to say very little. At this point, you will consider how to get the important extra material you need through interviews, formal questions and more specific requests.

You may need to consider specific FOI requests for documents that are not publicly available. FOI has been used to produce many strong stories, but a detailed explanation is not within the scope of this chapter. However, note that the minimum time for a successful request is 30 days and that costs can be prohibitive, so you should check whether you are eligible for any waiver of charges.

If information of public importance remains secret despite your best efforts, consider making a point of that in your report. This will enhance public interest in openness.

Developing strong research skills needs to be a lifelong process. As you follow investigations by experienced journalists, track their resource sources. I have deliberately emphasised examples involving journalism students in this chapter to suggest that if independent, alternative and younger journalists develop a strong and inquiring approach to journalism, they can play an important role in producing journalism in the public service.

TIPS

1   Make a research plan. If the project is a long one, review and revise the plan if it proves too cumbersome for your timeframe.
2   Make sure you have a process for managing your information. Label all files clearly.
3   Work out the best order in which to do tasks in order to avoid wasting time.
4   Some sources of information will be required often. Bookmark these for speedy use.
5   Develop strong searching techniques, including Boolean searching. This will enable you to target your searches. Advanced searches are also useful.
6   With key documents, read and reread. You may pick up more points as your knowledge of your subject grows.
7   Evaluate the credibility and motivation of your information sources, whether they are documentary or human. Read critically.
8   There will always be new sources of information and research techniques, so never stop developing your knowledge. Take time to revisit sources so you don't lose familiarity with them.
9   Journalism may deal with the past, but its relevance must be contemporary. Make sure you are up to date with developments and with what has already been published.
10 Set up processes to ensure accuracy. Fact-check information, including names and dates, before publication.
11 Don't do unnecessary work. For example, don't wait for court authorities to give you documents if you can obtain a full file from one of the parties in a court case.
12 If your process has been a long one, always check that your information is current before publishing.
13 The internet allows journalists to be more transparent. So long as you are not breaching any confidentiality, share your research sources with your audience.

QUESTIONS TO CONSIDER

1   What is the importance of grouping information?
2   Why should you constantly review your research plan?
3   Why is it important to assess the credibility of sources?
4   What is the key lesson to be learned from the Roseanne Catt story?
5   What are the key differences between public companies and private companies?

TASK

1   Identify a company listed on the ASX. Go online and put together a profile of the company, including its ABN, ASX code, list of directors and the name of the CEO. Also list its market capitalisation. Go onto the ASIC site and see if it had previously traded under a different name.

REFERENCES

Bacon, W. 2012a. 'Our Nauru Amnesia', *New Matilda*, 24 July: http://newmatilda.com/2012/12/06/my-family-calling-justice (accessed 30 November 2012).

Bacon, W. 2012b. 'Three Waves of Anguish', *New Matilda*, 25 July: http://newmatilda.com/2012/07/25/three-waves-nauru-anguish (accessed 30 November 2012).

Bacon, W. & Duxfield, F. 2010a. 'Who Profits from our Foreign Aid—From Cattle Company to Global Aid', *Crikey*, 13 July: www.crikey.com.au/2010/07/13/who-profits-from-our-foreign-aid-from-cattle-company-to-global-aid (accessed 20 September 2012).

Bacon, W. & Duxfield, F. 2010b. 'Who Profits from our Foreign Aid—The Export and Finance Corporation Steps Up', *Crikey*, 14 July: www.crikey.com.au/2010/07/14/who-profits-from-our-foreign-aid-export-finance-and-investment-corporation-steps-up (accessed 20 September 2012).

Bacon, W. & Pillemer, T. 2000a. 'Fire Trail', *Sydney Morning Herald*, 21 October.

Bacon, W. & Pillemer, T. 2000b. 'Should This Woman be in Jail', *Sydney Morning Herald*, 24 October, p. 13.

Crikey. 2010. 'The Brumby Dump': www.crikey.com.au/the-brumby-dump/.

Four Corners. 2000. 'Burned', ABC, 23 October.

Henninger, M. 2008. *The Hidden Web*, Sydney: University of New South Wales Press.

Monash University. 2011. 'Dangerous Ground—The EPA's Toxic Legacy': http://epadangerousground.com (accessed 20 September 2012).

Pearson. 2010.

Sydney Morning Herald. 2012. 'Making Sense of the Perks': www.smh.com.au/opinion/political-news/making-sense-of-the-perks-20120829-2513y.html/.

Weitenberg, C.2010. 'WWF Buries Wetlands Pollution Report', *Reportage-Enviro*: www.reportage-enviro.com/2009/12/wwf-buries-wetlands-pollution-report (accessed 20 September 2012).

WEBSITE REFERENCES

ABS: www.abs.gov.au/.

Australian Centre for Independent Journalism: Reportage/Enviro: www.reportage-enviro.com

Australian Electoral Commission: Annual Returns Locator Service: http://periodicdisclosures.aec.gov.au/.

Australian Government: AusTender: www.tenders.gov.au/.

Australian Government: Directories: http://australia.gov.au/directories/.

Australian Government: Land Titles Search: http://australia.gov.au/services/service-task/search/land-titles-search/.

Australian Government: Register of Lobbyists: http://lobbyists.pmc.gov.au/.

Australian Legal Information Institute (AustLII): www.austlii.edu.au/.

Australian Securities & Investments Commission (ASIC): www.asic.gov.au/asic/asic.nsf/.

Australian Securities Exchange (ASX): www.asx.com.au/.

Australian Securities Exchange (ASX): Companies: www.asx.com.au/professionals/companies.htm/.

Hansard: www.aph.gov.au/Parliamentary_Business/Hansard/.

Monash University: Dangerous Ground: http://artsonline.monash.edu.au/dangerousground/.

National Pollutant Inventory: www.npi.gov.au/.

New South Wales Government: Spatial Information Exchange: https://shop.lands.nsw.gov.au/.

OpenAustralia: www.openaustralia.org/.

OpenAustralia: You Have the Right to Know: www.openaustraliafoundation.org.au/2012/11/28/you-have-the-right-to-know/.

Parliament of Australia: www.aph.gov.au/.

Parliamentary Library: www.aph.gov.au/library/.

6

Research Strategies

ROD KIRKPATRICK

INTRODUCTION

Documents that provide insights into significant events in a nation's past are not all available when a journalist is writing the so-called 'first draft of history'. They don't conveniently fall into the journalist's hands contemporaneously with the first reportage or, sometimes, even within 10, 20 or 30 years of the significant events. Documents—letters, diaries, manuscripts, business records and photographs—are sometimes locked away for a lifetime, either because people have not wanted them to be made public, or because they have been mislaid, forgotten or regarded as insignificant. Government archives have strict rules about when particular documents can be released; access may be denied for 30 years or more.

Why should journalists living in a digital world take the trouble to know how to locate historical resources? Documents—and library and archival resources, including oral history—can provide the bridge from the superficial and the speculative to something much deeper and much closer to 'truth'. Good research makes a story come to life. Librarians and archivists can help you find sources you may not have even dreamed existed, and they can save you a lot of time. Reporters seeking to explain things and embrace ideas must strive to go beyond libraries of newspaper clippings—or their internet equivalent—for background. The whole idea of research is to provide stories that are 'less derivative, less second-hand and superficial' (Murray & White 1985, p. 11–12). This chapter sets out to provide guidelines for locating historical resources in a digital age.

PROVIDING CONTEXT

> If you don't know history, then you don't know anything. You are a leaf that doesn't know it is part of a tree.
>
> Michael Crichton

Until about the 1970s, mythology held that journalists went out and discovered things—the story, the facts, the truth. That belief changed when various US social scientists conducted studies which found that many of the decisions professional journalists made could be explained by the demands of the production routine around which the entire newsroom was built. The studies found that journalists 'manufactured' or 'made' news. They had to feed this news into an assembly line that operated throughout the day. This meant that the latest news had the least chance of being included because there were fewer placement options as the final deadline neared. Ultimately, the content of the newspaper was determined by the production schedule which demanded delivery in time for people to be able to read their newspaper at breakfast or to buy a copy to read on the way to work. The production schedule was god. It could not wait for the journalist to make an extra telephone call to obtain context that would have helped explain the Page 3 'main'. Yet the lack of context might reduce the Page 3 main to 'meaningless noise' (Rosen 2010).

In many instances, journalists who lack a sense of the events of the day as being part of an historical cavalcade will find it difficult to provide suitable context. Such journalists tend not to think automatically about the need to let the readers see the event as part of a bigger picture. Alan Ramsey, when he wrote columns on politics for *The Sydney Morning Herald* between 1987 and 2008, was renowned for providing context. Through the use of information on the record—whether in *Hansard*, the transcript of court records or of press conferences, or other documentary means—Ramsey backgrounded issues that were topical, throwing new light on them by giving them historical context. He raised issues that other political writers had ignored. He was remote from the day-to-day 'hysteria' of newsgathering and sought threads of meaning which could be woven into stories that informed the electorate in ways desired in a democracy. By placing quotes in context, he often revealed the shallowness of the reports presented by other political journalists.[1]

Ramsey was an exception. Many journalists skimp on context, sometimes because they are young and know little about Australian society before 1980 or because they lack an understanding of what sort of resources are held by government and private archives. Sometimes important or intriguing documents survive in private collections, or haphazardly, over the years. For example, a cache of letters found in a recycling depot in Brisbane provided poignant insights into the final months of a sailor who died when HMAS *Sydney* was sunk by the Germans off Western Australia in November 1941 in Australia's worst naval disaster (Kieza 2011). Fresh insights into one of Australia's great poets, Henry Lawson, were obtained through three letters that he wrote in 1914 and 1921 during his drunken and deteriorating years. The letters were written to a friend, Simon Hickey, a Labor MP, when Lawson was lobbying the New South Wales Parliament for a pension. In 1998, the letters were lodged with the Stockman's Hall of Fame, Longreach, by Sir Justin Hickey, Lawson's godson (Wiseman 1998). Ned Kelly's 'Jerilderie Letter', which was concealed until its chance discovery in 1930, is another example of how some important historical records are preserved only by sheer luck. The 8300-word 'rebel manifesto'—considered to be the only document resembling an autobiography of Australia's most infamous murderer—has been lodged with the archives of the State Library of Victoria (Strahan 2000) and can be read online through the Library's website.

Journalists are accustomed to interviewing people in the news and trying to 'get inside their minds', especially when writing profiles. In the same way, journalists keen to make good use of historical resources should try to 'get inside the mind' of the historian. By doing so, journalists will begin to think like historians and come to know what resources may be available and where to go to find them.

In this digital age, many historical resources are available online. A good starting point is Trove, available through the website of the National Library of Australia: www.nla.gov.au/. Through this powerful search engine, you can access more than six million digitised Australian newspaper pages for the period 1803–1954. Also included are pages from the *Australian Women's Weekly* to 1982. In addition, Trove (http://trove.nla.gov.au) allows you to browse other 'zones' of information such as journals, articles and data sets; books; pictures, photos and objects; music, sound and video; maps; diaries, letters and archives; archived websites (1996–now); people and organisations; and lists. In February 2012, Trove provided access to more than 256 million items.

The Trove search engine is managed by the National Library and most of the information comes from reliable sources such as libraries, museums, art galleries, repositories and archives. New contributor data is being added all the time (*Australian Newspaper History Group Newsletter* 2010, Item 59.4.3).

Trove also provides links to archival websites where government records (including births, deaths and marriages) are held.

PRIMARY AND SECONDARY SOURCES

Historians work by building up evidence from primary sources. A primary source, basically, is eyewitness testimony, a contemporaneous document, first-hand testimony or direct evidence. There is no substitute for the painstaking culling of such sources. The essential requirement for the historian is that the evidence should come substantially from primary sources. The historian should analyse such evidence for its authenticity and credibility, and study it in the context of the period in which it was produced. The primary source producing the best evidence from the historian's point of view is the eyewitness with expertise in an area, but one who lacks bias and motives of self-interest.

Startt and Sloan (1989, p. 114) say that primary sources are the 'raw materials of history'. They are contemporaneous records, or records in close proximity to some past occurrence. Or they might be original documents. Secondary sources, on the other hand, rest on primary sources (or they should), and they are not contemporaneous with the subject under study. For example, if you quote details said to have come from a primary source but you have obtained those details from a book or journal article, then you are citing a secondary source. You have not been to the primary source yourself to make sure that what you are citing is correct. Some glaring errors in Australian newspaper history have been made by authors relying on secondary sources which have also relied on secondary sources. No one has located and studied the primary source.

Military historian Barbara Tuchman wrote that she used material *from primary sources only*. Her feeling about secondary sources was that they were helpful but 'pernicious'. She used them as guides at the start of a project to find out the general scheme of what had happened, but she did not take notes from them because she did not want to end up simply rewriting someone else's book. This was Tuchman's approach:

> I plunge as soon as I can into primary sources: the memoirs and the letters, the generals' own accounts of their campaigns, however tendentious, not to say mendacious, they may be. Even an untrustworthy source is valuable for what it reveals about the personality of the author, especially if he is an actor in the events. Bias in a primary source is to be expected. One allows for it and corrects it by reading another version. I try always to read two or more for every episode. Even if an event is not controversial, it will have been seen and remembered from different angles of view by different observers. If the event is in dispute, one has extra obligation to examine both sides (Tuchman 1983, p. 19).

Documentary evidence will often provide, half a century or more later, significant or even startling slants on events of national importance or interest—events that may or may not have been publicised at the time. For example, the Australian Government's program to bring German scientists into the country immediately after the Second World War was kept secret. More than 50 years later, after studying about 10 000 documents, Gerard Ryle and Gary Hughes (1999) reported in the Melbourne *Age* and the *Sydney Morning Herald* that former members of the Nazi Party, the SS and Hitler's stormtroopers were among the scientists brought to Australia. The reporters said it was unclear how much of the truth members of the Chifley Government and, after 1949, of the Menzies Government, knew. As this example demonstrates, a good journalist should develop sound historical research methods for at least two important reasons:

1   History throws new light on significant events in our recent past—sometimes during the lifetime of many who experienced those events.
2   History puts events into context, helping to explain them and interpret them more fully.

Journalists write mainly about people who are or have been in the public eye. It follows that when journalists engage in historical research it is often to obtain biographical information. If the person they are researching is dead, it is worth checking whether the *Australian Dictionary of Biography* (available online) carries an entry on that person. If the person was a parliamentarian, substantial biographical information should be readily available. In addition, the manuscript section of the National Library of Australia holds the papers of many dead Australians of national interest and some living ones. Among the dead are historian Manning Clark (his papers occupy 196 boxes), Indigenous land-rights fighter Eddie Mabo (Powell 2001), and journalists Chester Wilmot and Kenneth Slessor. Among the living are Ian Temby, QC, former head of the Independent Commission Against Corruption, New South Wales; historian Geoffrey Blainey; and Lindy Chamberlain, who spent three years in a Darwin jail after being convicted in 1982 of having murdered her nine-week-old daughter, Azaria, at Ayers Rock in August 1980. The Northern Territory Court of Appeal unanimously quashed her conviction in September 1988. In May 1992 she and her former husband, Michael, received $1.3 million compensation. Lindy's papers are held in 177 boxes, but they are partly closed.[2] In fact, access to the papers of living Australians held at the National Library is generally closed or restricted, as it is for the papers of such organisations as Greenpeace Australia and the Australian Conservation Foundation, Canberra Office.

Journalists can obtain useful and generally reliable details of people from their 'interface'—or connection—with government, business and other organisations, and courts. Many of these sources are available through the various state archives, state libraries, and the National Archives and National Library. Such interfaces include:

1   With government:
  - births, deaths and marriages
  - immigration records
  - registration of companies or being struck from the register of companies
  - election to Parliament (parliamentary directories, *Hansard* for what the person has said in Parliament, and biographical registers of the various Parliaments)
  - employment as a teacher or some other type of public servant
  - letters to local government bodies.

2   With organisations:
  - minutes books
  - wages registers
  - the current executives and board members
  - annual reports (for example from the Australian Securities and Investment Commission).

3   With courts:
  - legal proceedings (for example defamation suits)
  - probate on wills, etc.

CABINET MINUTES

At the government-operated national and state archives offices, journalists are unusual faces among the patient note takers studying volumes of correspondence or other records. Many of the faces belong to family or local historians. One of the reasons why journalists do visit the archives is to obtain access to records of Cabinet meetings and related matters. The repositories for federal and state records vary, just as the quality itself varies, in the degree of detail and reliability. At a federal level, until 1925 there was no regular procedure for recording the decisions of Cabinet. The system has varied over the years, but a significant change came in March 1968 when a separate Department of the Cabinet Office was created. This was placed under the wing of the new Department of the Prime Minister and Cabinet in March 1971. The main Cabinet records are the submissions (agenda) and decisions (minutes).

The records are usually grouped under separate series and registers for each ministry (for example, the Gorton Ministry). The main series of Cabinet Office files—giving background information to Cabinet decisions—covers 1958–67. Cabinet records less than 30 years old are not accessible (Department of the Prime Minister and Cabinet 1984).

In Queensland, you can obtain access to the Queensland Cabinet minutes at the State Archives, from the first Cabinet meeting of the Nicklin Government on 21 October 1957 until Cabinet meetings held up to about 30 years ago. The records for 1859–1957 are haphazard. Decisions were noted on the relevant departmental files by the ministers concerned.

In Victoria, most Cabinet records are in the custody of the Public Record Office Victoria and are closed to the public until January 2026. Before the 1980s there was apparently little formal keeping of Cabinet records, so what is held for the preceding periods is described as 'those records known to be extant'. Two boxes hold all the records dated 1921–69. Also accessible is a Register of Cabinet Decisions, 1983–92, which was required to be created under the *Freedom of Information Act 1982* (Cth). There is also an Index to the Registers of Cabinet Decisions, 1983–88 (McKinnon 2001).

In New South Wales, Cabinet records are generally available at the State Records Authority after 30 years, although they can be withheld for longer (Hunter 2001).

In Tasmania, the *Archives Act 1983* denies access to Cabinet records and formal records of the Executive Council until 25 years after their creation, unless this restriction is specifically removed by the transferring agency—the Department of Premier and Cabinet.

In South Australia, Cabinet records are held by the Department of Premier and Cabinet; but the correspondence series that State Records of South Australia holds for the Department and its predecessor, the Chief Secretary's Office, sometimes contains documents that were produced in Cabinet meetings. A 50-year rule applies (Jeffery 2001).

In Western Australia, several series of Cabinet records have been transferred to the State Records Office from the Department of Premier and Cabinet. Few of these records pre-date 1950. Access to all Cabinet records is restricted for 30 years. These records include: schedules of matters considered for Cabinet's consideration 1903–14; files of Cabinet minutes and decisions 1948–93; and Cabinet indices and agenda 1965–93 (Reynolds 2001).

In the Australian Capital Territory, which achieved self-government in 1989, ArchivesACT makes Cabinet documents that are at least 10 years old are made available from Canberra Day (12 March) each year. Detailed background papers and earlier drafts of the Cabinet papers can be found on the files of the agency that sponsored each submission. These papers reveal the detailed deliberations of the public service on the topic and often include the opinions and guidance of the responsible minister. They are available to the public from Canberra Day after 20 years have passed.

Journalists should note that parliamentarians, party officials and parliamentary staff often leave memoirs, generally unpublished. These are generally to be found in the hands of the family, but may have been lodged with a state library or the National Library. Families may be cautious about showing the memoirs to researchers, but a tactful, responsible and persistent approach may win their confidence and eventually access to the manuscript. State secretaries of the relevant party can often provide names and addresses of relatives holding such memoirs (Murray & White 1985, p. 115).

ARCHIVES JARGON

At an archival office, you do not search for material according to author or subject, but according to what is called 'provenance'. This basically means the creator of the document or the receiver of it (for example, if your great-grandfather wrote to the New South Wales Colonial Secretary in 1869, his letter may well still form part of that department's archival records; so the provenance is the Colonial Secretary's Department). In general, the provenance is the government department or agency that has sent a letter, received a letter, recorded the details of an issue, presented a submission, or drawn up maps for a project. The closest analogy that 'provenance' has in the library system is author, but it is only vaguely similar.

It is better to think of 'creator' or 'initiator' (and sometimes 'receiver') than author. Provenance can also indicate the hands through which the document has passed. The dictionary says of provenance: 'The place of origin, derivation, or earliest known history, especially of a work of art, manuscript, etc. A record of the ultimate derivation and passage of an item through its various owners.'

ARCHIVES: NATIONAL AND STATE

Throughout Australia, federal, state and territory parliaments preserve government records through legislation requiring the establishment of archives. Each of the archives has established preservation policies, but the extent of the records that each archive is now required to make available to the public depends on the seriousness with which the various government departments and authorities have approached preservation over the past century or more. You can find out much about these archives through visiting one of their websites and linking up with the others through it (or through visiting them individually).

You should visit the appropriate website or telephone the particular archive before attempting a visit. Generally a 'reader's ticket' is required when you visit and you will need to allow some time to obtain it. Also, you will need to find out the opening hours and conditions of use of the records (for example, you can write only in pencil or type on a laptop computer in the manuscript room at the National Library of Australia).

Snapshots of some of the federal archives follow.[3]

NATIONAL ARCHIVES OF AUSTRALIA (NAA)

Based in Canberra, with offices in each state capital and Darwin, the NAA holds records that trace the events and decisions that shaped the nation, including: the papers of governors-general, prime ministers and ministers; Cabinet documents; Royal Commission files; and departmental records on defence, immigration, security and intelligence, naturalisation and many other issues involving the Federal Government. The main focus is records created since the formation of the Commonwealth of Australia in 1901.[4] It also holds some nineteenth-century records relating to functions that were transferred by the colonies to the Commonwealth, including shipping and postal services. Cabinet records must be 30 years old and Cabinet notebooks 50 years old before access is permitted.

Generally, records relating to Commonwealth Government functions in a particular state are found in the NAA office of the state's capital. However, all items are on a common catalogue.

SPECIAL COLLECTIONS

Many archives were established to preserve particular collections of records. Among them are the Australian Science Archives Project, the John Curtin Prime Ministerial Library, the Bob Hawke Prime Ministerial Library, ScreenSound Australia (the national film and sound archive), the University of New South Wales Archives, the Monash University Records and Archives Service, the University of Melbourne Archives, the University of Tasmania Archives, the Australian War Memorial, and the Noel Butlin Archives Centre (housed at the Australian National University: a large collection of documents from many Australian business and labour organisations, such as the Australian Journalists' Association).

The National Library, five of the six state libraries and the two territory libraries are all major archival repositories (Powell 2001).

ORAL HISTORY

Oral history allows investigative journalists to obtain qualitative insights into and information on people and events of national significance. Those interviewed in the oral history program conducted by the National Library of Australia are invited to speak frankly and candidly, on the understanding that they can restrict access to their interviews for long periods. This protective framework is designed to encourage a high degree of honesty and truthfulness.

Oral historians regard the personal speaking voice as a rich and unique form of documentation—a primary source of information and understanding, enabling the researcher to experience events, issues and so on, 'from the inside out'. The routine argument in favour of oral history is that it enables gaps in formal records to be filled, especially by providing deep background on the hidden or undisclosed dynamics behind so much that happens. It helps a journalist or historian to detect the underlying layers of the real story. Oral history also provides detail, a sense of 'being there' that is not usually included in the formal records, reports and other documents (Cranfield 2001).

AUSTRALIAN CEMETERIES INDEX

The Australian Cemeteries Index provides a searchable database for all cemetery inscriptions that have been recorded by its authors and contributors over several years. Intended mainly as a useful tool for those researching their family history, the index contains details of headstones from a number of cemeteries in Australia. It initially concentrated on cemeteries in regional New South Wales but is now expanding Australia-wide. Remember that this index is not a record of burials, but a record of inscriptions.

CONCLUSION

Journalists who want to bring a topic to life should remember their ABC: Archives Bring Context. In other words, journalists should seriously consider what records may be held about the person or issue that they are exploring. Documents and oral history can provide clues to understanding actions and decisions that otherwise seem baffling. They can be great aids to discovery. They can lead journalists to pose questions that they may not otherwise have considered. Journalists should be encouraged, in appropriate articles, to take an historical perspective, to place things in context. Events such as the deposing of a prime minister, an economic crisis, or the government's response to a national disaster can be better explained to the general public if historical context is provided.

1   When you plan a feature, remember that context will help you bring an issue or a person to life.

2   Much context can be obtained online, and much can be obtained only in documentary form.

3   Think like an historian: seek out primary sources whenever you can, but test them for authenticity and credibility.

4   Trove, the National Library of Australia's search engine, is a digital goldmine. Note, in particular, that it provides digital access to a growing number of Australian newspapers up to 1954.

5   The best primary source is the eyewitness with expertise in an area, but lacking bias and motives of self-interest.

6   Documentary evidence unearthed many years after a newsworthy event can provide significant new slants on it.

7   You can obtain useful and generally reliable information on people from their connection with government, private organisations and the courts.

8   Cabinet records are generally not available from federal or state archives for 30 years.

9   Archives function differently from libraries and have a different jargon that you need to know.

10 Don't forget oral history: check what is available through the National Library of Australia's oral history program.

QUESTIONS TO CONSIDER

1   What is the difference between primary and secondary materials?

2   What timelines tend to be placed on the release of Cabinet documents in Australia?

3   What is the difference between 'provenance' and 'author' in archival language?

4   What does the Jerilderie Letter reveal about the benefit of online searching to journalists?

TASK

1   Go online to the archives of the state in which your family originates (or that of another person whose history you are interested in). Using the archive tools, see what information you can find about your/their early ancestors, including relationships, births, deaths and marriages, wills, convict history and military records. Using Trove, see if you can find any newspaper articles to support your primary research. Finally, use the Australian Cemeteries Index to see if you can locate any headstones.

REFERENCES

Australian Newspaper History Group Newsletter, 2010, 59.4.3 (October), p. 17.

Cranfield, M. (Curator of Oral History, National Library of Australia). 2001. Email message to the author, 26 July; interview with the author, Canberra, 16 August.

Department of the Prime Minister and Cabinet. 1984. 'The Development of Cabinet Procedures in Australia', *Department of the Prime Minister and Cabinet Annual Report 1983–84*, Australian Government Publishing Service.

Haigh, G. 1993. 'Lindy's Letters Pass into National History', *Weekend Australian*, 2–3 October.

Hunter, W. (Policy Officer, Access and Information, State Records Authority of New South Wales). 2001. Email message to the author, 6 July.

Jeffery, J. (State Records of South Australia). 2001. Typescript and email messages to the author, 12 July.

Kieza, G. 2011. 'Lloyd's Legacy', *Qweekend* (*Courier-Mail* magazine), 19–20 November, pp.18–24.

McKinnon, J. (Manager, Reference Services, Public Records Office Victoria). 2001. Email messages to the author, 26 June and 17 July.

Murray, R. & White, K. 1985. *Research for Writers*, Geelong, Victoria: Deakin University Press.

Powell, G. (Manuscript Librarian, National Library of Australia). 2001. Email messages to the author, 4 and 10 July.

Reynolds, T. (State Records Office of Western Australia). 2001. Email message to the author, 18 July.

Rosen, J. 2010. 'Make the Public King Again', *Walkley Magazine*, Issue 63, October/November, pp. 22–3.

Ryle, G. & Hughes, G. 1999. 'Rocket Science', *Sydney Morning Herald*, 21 August, p. 40.

Startt, J.D. & Sloan, W.D. 1989. *Historical Methods in Mass Communication*, New Jersey: Lawrence Erlbaum Associates.

Strahan, N. 2000. 'Rebel Heart of Ned Kelly Caught on Paper', *The Australian*, 24 November, p. 3.

Tuchman, B. 1983. *Practising History*, London: Papermac.

Wiseman, N. 1998. 'Godson's Gift Captures Lawson to the Letter', *Courier-Mail*, 26 February, p. 5.

WEBSITE REFERENCES

ArchivesACT: www.archives.act.gov.au/.

Australian Cemeteries Index: http://austcemindex.com/.

Australian Dictionary of Biography: http://adb.anu.edu.au/.

Australian Society of Archivists: www.archivenet.gov.au/.

National Archives of Australia: www.naa.gov.au/.

National Archives of Australia: Records of Australia's Security, Intelligence and Law Enforcement: www.naa.gov.au/collection/explore/security/index.aspx/.

National Library of Australia: www.nla.gov.au/.

State Library of Victoria: www.slv.vic.gov.au/.

Trove: http://trove.nla.gov.au/.

FURTHER READING

The Australian Magazine. 2001. 'The Lindy Papers', 2–3 June.

Australian Newspaper History Group Newsletter, 2000, 8.2 (August), p. 1.

Coulthard, R. 2001. *Sunday*, Channel 9, 17 June.

Queensland State Archives. 2003. 'Brief Guide 23: Cabinet Minutes': www.archives.qld.gov.au/ Researchers/CollectionsDownloads/Documents/ BG23Cabinet.pdf/.

Ramsey, A. 1995. 'The Botany Affair in Retrospect', *Sydney Morning Herald*, 29 July, p. 35.

Ramsey, A. 1997. 'The Anatomy of a Cover-up', *Sydney Morning Herald*, 19 April, p. 39.

Ramsey, A. 1999. 'Your Humble Servant, Sir', *Sydney Morning Herald*, 2 October, p. 47.

Ramsey, A. 2000. 'What price leadership?', *Sydney Morning Herald*, 19 February, p. 49.

Ramsey, A. 2009. *A Matter of Opinion*, Sydney: Allen & Unwin.

NOTES

1   See, for example, Ramsey's classic *Sydney Morning Herald* columns on Laurie Brereton ('The Botany Affair in Retrospect', 1995), how Senator Mal Colston had problems with his expenses account over many years ('The Anatomy of a Cover-up', 1997), how nobody told Prime Minister Menzies of the *Voyager* disaster in 1964 ('Your Humble Servant, Sir', 1999), and how Parliament has become just another television studio backdrop ('What price leadership?', 2000). A selection of Ramsey's 2273 *Sydney Morning Herald* columns appears in his book, *A Matter of Opinion* (2009).

2   Temby at MS 9105; Blainey at MS 9225; Chamberlain at MS 9180. See also *The Australian Magazine* 2001, pp. 30–3; Haigh 1993, p. 1.

3   For each of the archives, the main reference for this material has been its website. In several instances, email responses to the author's inquiries have helped embellish the online information.

4   Sometimes, records that should be kept do not make it to the NAA. For example, Ross Coulthard, an investigative reporter for Channel 9, found that the electoral rolls for 1987 were held by no state library in Australia, nor the National Library nor the NAA (2001).

7

The 'Twitterisation' of Investigative Journalism

JULIE POSETTI

Social media platforms such as Twitter and Facebook, the 'social tools' most widely used by journalists in their work, are transforming professional norms and values. The ways journalists engage with these platforms are: challenging notions of objectivity through the convergence of personal and professional lives; propelling the mainstreaming of 'open journalism' models, which promote collaborative research and reportage; and even upending established verification processes. So, what are the implications for investigative journalism? What are the potential benefits of 'social journalism' for research, investigation and verification? How can journalists and news publishers most effectively deploy social media platforms in pursuit of investigative stories? And what are the pitfalls of this brave new world?

This chapter will seek to answer these questions and work towards developing a best-practice approach to social journalism principles in the context of investigative reporting, with an emphasis on the role and impact of Twitter as the tool of choice for most journalists. The data for this chapter is drawn from: online interviews with 25 tweeting journalists conducted in 2009 (Posetti 2009a; 2009b; 2009c); a case study of Twitter and political reporting, based on the 2009 Australian Liberal leadership coup which became known by its hashtag #Spill,[1] featuring interviews with eight Canberra Press Gallery journalists (Posetti 2010b); the record of journalist working group contributions from the 2011 BBC Social Media Summit (Posetti 2011b), at which the author acted as a facilitator and rapporteur; and a 2012 qualitative survey of 10 social media-active Australian journalists engaged in investigative reporting. The data has been analysed[2] with the objective of identifying the risks, pitfalls, strengths, benefits and impacts of social journalism specific to research, source identification, investigation and verification—the hallmarks of traditional investigative journalism practice.

THE 'TWITTERISATION' OF JOURNALISM

> Twitter provides journalists with more potential sources than just about any other platform in history (Posetti 2012).[3]

Twitter, a micro-blogging platform launched in 2006, encourages users to post 140-character-limited messages to 'followers' (that is, those who subscribe to another's tweets). It functions as a 'real-time' (that is, live) interactive, global conversation portal. It could be described as public text messaging on steroids, a collaborative newswire service, or an instantaneous global 'water cooler' zone.

The platform allows users to interact with one another via openly published tweets directed at specific users, who are identified by 'handles' (for example, @julieposetti) or by participating in 'hashtagged' conversations (for example, #Journalism), which aggregate all tweets that include a common hashtag at a single URL. Additionally, tweeters can converse privately via direct message (DM), a function restricted to those following each other.

By late 2011, Twitter was estimated to have 100 million active users globally (Mangalinden 2011). The speed of uptake and its popularity as a site for public communication involving policy makers, news breakers, journalists and other citizens are what make it such a significant platform—despite being dwarfed by Facebook's estimated 850 million users worldwide (Savitz 2012). In Australia, professional journalists have occupied the Twittersphere en masse, using the platform as a diving board into the real-time web and a new model for interactive journalism.

I have adopted the term 'Twitterisation' to describe the transformative impacts of audience engagement and emerging reporting practices facilitated via many journalists' participation in the Twittersphere. These impacts include identifiable shifts in professional journalistic practices, norms and identities that are challenging core elements of traditional journalistic ethics and professionalism in the process (Posetti 2010a; Sheffer & Shulz 2010; Lasorsa et al. 2011).

The three main effects of 'Twitterisation' can be described as:

1   the embedding of real-time audience engagement in the journalistic process

2   the challenges wrought via the convergence/clash of personal/private and professional/public lives

3   new models of verification that challenge traditional professional standards (for example, open verification).

Through these processes, journalists are being re-cast as individual reporter-brands, with a focus on follower engagement, collaborative investigation and the 'crowdsourcing' (see below) of research, verification and story dissemination (Posetti 2009a; 2009b; 2009c).

This shift in journalists' professional identities and practice is playing out against a backdrop of rapid technological change and failing commercial models, along with demands for interaction with journalists and participation in the news production and distribution process by 'the people formerly known as the audience' (Rosen 2006a) leading to the collapsing of boundaries between journalists and media consumers (Posetti 2009d; 2010a). That is, journalists active on social media platforms are also audience members—consumers of citizen-generated journalism, observation and commentary.

Twitter is the logical platform to springboard this transformation (a future foreshadowed by Gillmor (2004) and envisioned by Rosen (2006b): it is both 'cool' in the pop-culture sense of the word, making it the beneficiary of novelty news value which has made it a 'hot' story; and cool in the McLuhan (2001) sense of being a highly interactive medium. This transformation builds on the tradition of participatory media, with its foundations in talkback radio in Australia (compare Phillips 2007; Lee 2007; Griffin-Foley 2004) that the author has identified as the original, albeit mediated, form of social media (ABC Radio National 2008).

Twitter's speed imperative (reflective of the instantaneous nature of the medium), in combination with its role as an incubator for collaborative journalism, is altering processes of verification and reframing the key journalistic value of accuracy. A shift by some practitioners towards what has become known as 'open verification'—a contentious process involving the publication of unconfirmed information together with an invitation to the journalist's followers to collaborate on the verification process—is of particular relevance to investigative journalism.

The transformative impact of Twitter is highlighted by *The Global Mail's* Middle East Correspondent, Jess Hill, an Australian leader in this field:

[Social media] has fundamentally changed the level of access I have to people all over the world … Twitter actually makes me work harder as a journalist, but that's as it should be. It makes me work harder to get to the bottom of stories, rather than just accepting the official line. It makes me work harder to uncover contacts that we previously never had access to. The more I use it, the better it gets, because the profile I'm earning on [Twitter] makes it easier for me to win people's trust [see Hill's accompanying case study at the end of this chapter] (Posetti 2012).

HOW ARE JOURNALISTS USING SOCIAL MEDIA TO RESEARCH, INVESTIGATE AND REPORT?

The main functions of Twitter journalism are:

1   breaking and disseminating news in real time (including live-tweeting)
2   newsgathering: crowdsourcing news monitoring, fact checking, and locating case studies and contacts
3   engaging the audience /building community around content
4   sharing information and discussing journalistic processes/practices/ethics (public reflective practice)
5   making content out of the processes of journalism (for example, tweeting about doing journalism)
6   subverting spin (that is, the coordinated position of official sources)
7   marketing journalists as journalist-brands
8   publicly engaging with one another—working collaboratively across competitive boundaries.

'Often the key to good investigative journalism is finding the right people and Twitter and Facebook make this easier,' one journalist surveyed in 2012 commented (Posetti 2012). For Hill, Twitter is where all investigations begin:

First, I'm looking for information: I'll search to see if anybody's posted links related to the story, or tweeted something that might be a good clue. If I find a clue that looks like it's worth following up, I ask for the tweeter's email address so I can find out more about it. That person may lead me to a source, or just provide a link in the chain (Posetti 2012).

Hill says her next move is to 'crowdsource' sources (see the discussion of crowdsourcing below and in Chapter 3):

That doesn't mean I'm looking to speak to people who are actually on Twitter, but rather to enlist tweeters' help to find the most relevant people to speak to. It's like a fixer relationship—you find somebody who looks knowledgeable in the field you're reporting on, let them know what you're looking for and ask if they're prepared to help (Posetti 2012)

A political journalist who specialises in economics described how he used Twitter to nail a story about Federal Opposition costings:

The people who do the election costings for political parties are secretive. How to get in touch with one and find out what really goes on? Using Twitter, writing about Shadow Treasurer Joe Hockey's claim that a Perth accountant had 'audited' his costings, a commentator tweeted in such a way as to make me suspect he had been on the inside. I messaged him, asking him to follow me so I could DM him. In my DM I asked for his phone number … He used to do the costings for the Coalition at Access Economics and told me lots, so long as I didn't use his name. The background was very valuable (Posetti 2012).

Hill also described her Twitter network as a kind of journalists' travel service:

As a foreign correspondent, Twitter is invaluable. Before I travel to a new city, I can make contact with key people there—journalists, activists, intellectuals, even politicians—ask for advice and contacts, and sometimes arrange to meet them once I get there (Posetti 2012).

Twitter was also an invaluable resource for investigations undertaken to support ABC Radio Current Affairs' remote coverage of the Arab Spring in 2011, according to Hill, who was then on staff as a reporter/producer with the flagship programs *AM*, *The World Today* and *PM*. 'Sometimes we'd find an eye witness on Twitter, tweeting from an event as it happened.' One such case involved Mohammed, a photographer from Bahrain. Hill said:

> Just before *PM* was about to go to air one evening, I was monitoring tweets coming out of Bahrain. We knew that Saudi forces had entered the country and were on their way to confront protesters in the capital—we just didn't know exactly when it would happen. Suddenly, a tweeter, who said he was on the highway leading into the capital, started posting photos of soldiers approaching the main square, then that those soldiers were shooting at civilians. I asked him to follow me so I could DM him, and then got his phone number. *PM's* presenter Mark Colvin recorded an interview with him five minutes later (Posetti 2012).

Another useful function of Twitter for investigative journalism is its ability to act as a platform of record, or content aggregator, for material that may be excluded from mainstream publications due to space limitations or editorial priorities. As Annabel Crabb (then with *The Sydney Morning Herald*) observed when reflecting on the value of Twitter as a reporting tool during the #Spill, Twitter can accommodate the back-story via 'mini-serial narratives' (Clark 2011):

> A story filed for a newspaper at the end of the day would ... be obliged to edit out some of the stranger twists and turns that occurred during the day; the deals that fell over, the partnerships that formed and disintegrated all within the space of an orthodox news cycle (Posetti 2010b).

Similarly, through its role as a platform for audience engagement and reflective practice by journalists, Twitter also has the capacity to increase journalistic transparency (Weinberger 2009), something linked to audience trust in the journalist and their content. Practically, this transparency could be achieved by making content out of process. This could involve journalists describing research, investigation, ethical dilemmas and reporting processes (where appropriate) during or after publication (depending upon the nature of the story and issues of exclusivity) via social media, and facilitating conversations with other users about these issues.

CROWDSOURCING

A portmanteau of 'crowd' and 'outsourcing', 'crowdsourcing' is a term first coined by Jeff Howe (2006). Howe initially observed the rise of online collaborations between producers and users in business settings, and the term has since been co-opted to apply to the collaborative production of journalism.

So, how does crowdsourcing apply to journalism research and investigation? A useful example is the method of research I employed in my 2009 work on Twitter journalism. When I began this research, my first move was to tweet a request for journalists on the platform to respond to questions about why and how they used Twitter, receiving responses including the following:

> **Harleyd** @julie_posetti i'd have responded earlier about how i use twitter as a journo, but i was too busy live tweeting an inquiry on my beat :-) (Dennet 2009).

I received useful feedback and uncovered a number of new contacts via this method, before conducting more extensive online interviews with 25 of the respondents.

Wolf Cocklin, then of ABC Innovation, described the value of Twitter in crowdsourcing elements of the coverage of a large-scale blackout in Sydney in mid-2009. 'I was able to crowdsource the size and approximate location of the affected area in five minutes, faster than calling 100 people to ask them if their power was out' (Posetti 2009a).

In 2012, Jess Hill demonstrated just how far crowdsourcing has come in Australian journalism:

> I ask people on Twitter to help with spot translations. I once crowdsourced three separate Arabic translators to translate a video of the Saudi activist, Manal al-Sharif, breaking the ban on women driving in Saudi Arabia. I had each translator check the last translator's work, until we were satisfied the video had been

translated accurately. When we posted it on YouTube (and promoted it on Twitter), the video received over 80 000 hits (Posetti 2012).

VERIFICATION

The perceived problems associated with social media verification continue to dominate debates about social journalism. This fixation became apparent during #BBCSMS, the BBC Social Media Summit, held in London in May 2011. 'The biggest issue with social media is verification,' one journalist said (Posetti 2011b). That statement was met with vigorous nods of agreement—from newspaper reporters and online editors to radio producers.

But how do you define verification? Can it evolve in the manner of a radio news story, filling in blanks over time, with details unfolding hour by hour? Can it be crowdsourced, with media consumers acting as widely distributed fact checkers with collective expertise? And what standards of verification and accuracy do audiences expect of professional journalists in the social media sphere?

Twitter's role in the aftermath of the 2009 Iranian election highlighted some of the key issues with research and verification being faced by professional journalists in the Twittersphere. Questions like: Does re-tweeting ('RTing')—republishing someone else's tweet—equate to your giving their tweets your imprimatur? If you are passing on information to your followers, do you have an obligation to first establish its authenticity or acknowledge it as 'unconfirmed'—something many journalists would assume if they were doing the same for a newspaper or broadcaster. And what should you do if you inadvertently report an inaccuracy? In the example in Figure 7.1, London's *The Guardian* quickly tweeted an apology for misinforming followers after another tweeter corrected the record.

This approach to social media correction is now quite well entrenched. Asked in 2012 how they would respond upon discovering that information they had redistributed via Twitter was false, one journalist said: 'If I RT something later shown to be wrong, for example Phillip Coorey's initial tweet [McGregor 2012] on the ballot numbers for the Gillard/Rudd leadership spill, I RT subsequent corrections' (Posetti 2012).

Twitter's potential to send errors 'viral' was highlighted by several journalists responding to my 2012 survey. 'The rush to report breaking stories like celebrity deaths, the recent leadership ballot, mean

FIGURE 7.1: *THE GUARDIAN'S* APOLOGETIC TWEET

Twitter mistakes are amplified before they can be properly checked,' one observed. Another journalist cogently summarised these risks: 'as a story is breaking, there is lots of incorrect and exaggerated information. Sometimes people claim to be "there" when they're not, others have a political slant or opinion that can affect the way they Tweet.' The same journalist said crowdsourced content needs particularly careful vetting and matching with traditional research methods: 'I still tend to gravitate towards other reputable journalists for information if I am not on the spot ... I try to build an accurate picture using that information combined with other sources—such as direct checking and wires' (Posetti 2012).

Signifying a radical shift in verification practice, one #BBCSMS participant reported in 2011: 'Our default is to publish unchecked information with a disclaimer that it's unverified' (Posetti 2011a). Such an approach has become relatively standard for some of the world's big news brands on breaking news stories, but many journalists remain concerned about the implications of this shift for professional practice and traditional ethics.

During #BBCSMS, there was debate about the emerging verification method, 'open verification'; that is, the publication of stages of verification, including the crowdsourcing of verification (such as publishing a rumour on Twitter and seeking followers' assistance to verify or debunk it) often attributed to US National Public Radio's Andy Carvin (@acarvin). One of the respondents to my 2012 survey explained the process of Twitter-based 'open verification' as follows: 'You can RT with a question posed. This opens debate and the truth can be found ... or at least be attempted.'

Asked whether they would ever publish material sourced from social media before independently verifying it, the 2012 survey respondents reinforced the shifting standards of verification. Two answered 'Certainly' and eight responded 'Yes, but with some hesitation', while none chose the options 'Only in exceptional circumstances', or 'Never'.

One journalist indicated that their qualifier for redistributing unchecked Twitter-sourced information was the perceived trustworthiness of the tweeter: 'If Mark Colvin [respected presenter of ABC Radio's *PM* and exemplary journalistic tweeter] were to tweet that the Prime Minister had been shot, I would probably RT it. Some random follower? Probably not' (Posetti 2012).

However, another journalist indicated that the number of times an unverified fact had been re-posted by others would influence their decision to RT:

> For example, I was working the day Whitney Houston died and RTd an unknown and unverified source before it broke via AP, because it had been RTd by someone I trusted and was also an unsubstantiated fact that was getting widely trafficked (Posetti 2012).

Another commented that they would never knowingly redistribute inaccurate information: 'I don't publish or RT material I know to be wrong or misguided—at least not without some commentary to this effect' (Posetti 2012). The addition of explanatory information or a question to an RT containing potentially inaccurate content is a useful method for tweeting journalists.

A point raised by other respondents is relevant here: most journalists now view RTs as they would quotes; they do not necessarily endorse the content, they are just redistributing it, believing it may be of interest to their followers. As one commented:

> I RT a large volume of information. I can't possibly verify every article that I RT. I RT what I think might be interesting, useful, relevant or just entertaining ... my disclaimer is that I don't necessarily agree with everything that I RT or publish (Posetti 2012).

Jess Hill's social journalism verification methodology enables better exposure of spin:

> After verifying information about events occurring in real time on the ground, and then hearing/viewing contradictory 'official statements' on traditional media, I have come to question the latter's willingness to broadcast such statements from official sources, especially after such sources have been proven to make false statements (Posetti 2012).

Hill places 'official sources' on par with reliable social media reporters:

> I now pit these versions of the truth against each other: if the [social media] info contradicts the traditional media sources, I confront the source with it; but more critically, I can challenge sources making their trad media statements with the eye-witness accounts from the scenes they're speaking about (Posetti 2012).

This is a significant benefit of social media verification—the capacity to upturn attempts at traditional message control and call out falsehoods with evidence acquired in real time. 'The shift is essentially one engendered by the different speeds of social media and traditional media,' Hill said, and continued:

> Many sources are used to making statements that take time to verify, and do so knowing that any gaps in their stories will not be news by the time they're revealed. With [social media], these statements are made to answer to the voices on the ground (Posetti 2012).

On the flipside is the phenomenon of 'astroturfing'—organised social media campaigns designed to mimic organic public reaction. It can be difficult to determine what is authentic in public outcries on social media, sometimes described as 'Twitstorms'. Online journalism pioneer Paul Bradshaw has observed that the journalist's task of verification in such cases is especially difficult when content is post-moderated. 'Although there's a skill to be built in knowing when to respond and when to ignore bait, it's not so clear how to manage disinformation,' he said (Bradshaw 2011).

This was a concern also raised by respondents to my 2012 survey. One said:

> I have seen well-intentioned journalists attacked for asking basic questions. This can be because there is a crowd of bored people out there, but it also ties into the widespread astroturfing efforts going to misinform, befuddle and endanger journalists. I have seen journalists sucked into false breaking news and others sucked into the ease of Twitter. This may lead to them ending the chase of an investigative story as it is too hard (Posetti 2012).

Hill detailed a forensic approach to verification:

> Clues are everywhere on Twitter, if you have the patience to comb through [them]. For example, I'm about to go to the Turkish-Syrian border to report. Colonel Riad al-Asaad, the leader of the Free Syrian Army, is based in a town close to there. When I decided to try and contact him, I knew I'd have to find someone who'd either met with him recently, or was closely connected to him. But how to find someone like that? On a whim, I thought I'd see if Twitter could turn up any clues. So I searched his name, and found this tweet from @lauandomar: 'My Dad just back from Antakya, meeting Riad Al-Asaad/FreeSyrianArmy, difficult times, no support from Syrian National Council @miafarrow' (Posetti 2012).

The tweeter, @lauandomar, had attempted to draw the attention of high-profile tweeter Mia Farrow (who regularly commentates on human rights and politics) to his tweet by including her Twitter handle. Hill said her first reaction was curiosity, laced heavily with skepticism:

> Lauand was trying to bring a celebrity's attention to this tweet. Why? Is he an activist? I checked his feed, and couldn't see any examples of intentional misinformation. In fact, there was very little about Syria in his feed at all—he's a young film director, originally from Northern Iraq. With that checked, I thought there was a chance this tweet could be genuine (Posetti 2012).

Hill's next move was to ask Lauand to follow her on Twitter so they could send DMs to one another:

> I then inquired a bit more about his Dad, and told him that I was looking to meet with Colonel Asaad, if it was possible. He emailed me with a detailed précis of who his Dad was (a Kurdish-Syrian community leader), what he was doing with Asaad (talking about how to protect Kurdish soldiers defecting from Syria), and how I could get in touch with him (a phone number for someone who works closely with Colonel Asaad in Antakya) (Posetti 2012).

Hill said Lauand's DMs were rich in detail, enabling her to Google his father and confirm his identity:

> I also researched Lauand, and found details about a movie he'd recently filmed on Northern Iraq. So now I'm content that Lauand is almost certainly telling the truth, the next step is to enlist a fixer, someone who can speak Syrian Arabic, to call this contact, use their own gut to confirm finally that it is legitimate, and if so, arrange a meeting (Posetti 2012).

Other journalists spoke of simply transposing traditional processes of verification onto the Twitterverse; for example, by following up public tweets with DMs, phone calls and face-to-face meetings where appropriate. 'I use Twitter to find people and contact them. I ask potential contacts to follow me and we DM. I've been independently contacted by people on Twitter about stories. Most of the traffic is via DM and usually moves later to email,' one said. Another commented: 'I also DM people I am trying to get in touch with. It can be more effective than a phone call, as it was today!' (Posetti 2012).

The prevalence of anonymity and pseudonymity on social media sites also makes verification more complex, according to one journalist:

> The ability for the source to be anonymous or to choose a different identity can influence how the information's received by the journalist, credibility tests become more difficult, therefore old methods are needed anyway—to confirm and verify information (Posetti 2012).

However, another journalist pointed to the potential advantages for investigative journalists:

> [anonymous] people are more prepared to share information than they may have been otherwise. Also, on platforms like Twitter and Facebook, people develop a relationship with the journalist they would not have had otherwise, therefore a trust develops which facilitates sharing of information (Posetti 2012).

The concept of various platforms being imbued with different standards of verification and audience expectations emerged from #BBCSMS. For example, one participant spoke of the lower threshold for publication of unverified information on Facebook: 'We might put it out there unverified on our Facebook page, but we wouldn't print it until we'd verified it.' And another print journalist shared a similar approach: 'Our journalists use social media to correct over time, in between print runs' (Posetti 2011a).

These comments reflect a view among journalists that audiences have lower expectations of accuracy and verification from journalists' and media outlets' social media accounts than they do of 'appointment TV' or the printed page, for example. This was a perspective echoed by one of my 2012 survey respondents: 'I think the rules for Twitter are different … it is so much faster than the (mainstream) media at breaking news, there's an inherent understanding that it's a bit fast and loose and not always … right.'

Indeed, since 2009 there has been a slew of headline-grabbing inaccuracies sourced to tweets, from false reports of the recall of the iPhone 4 based on a tweet by a Steve Jobs faker (Axom 2010), to the fabrication of Nelson Mandela's death (Haggarty 2011). The 'Gay Girl in Damascus' story (BBC News Middle East 2011) is another example. The character at the centre of the story was purportedly a 'lesbian Syrian blogger' who was reportedly arrested, but turned out to be a middle-aged US man in Scotland. Jess Hill described *PM's* treatment of the story:

> We didn't report her arrest, for one simple reason—we couldn't find anyone who'd actually met her in person. No relatives, no personal friends. We spent two days looking for people, asking our Syrian contacts to refer us to people who may have had contact with her, but each lead became a dead end. The fact we couldn't find anyone who had actually met her set off major alarm bells, so we didn't report it (Posetti 2012).

A few days later, the true identity of the blogger was discovered by several people who spent days investigating it. 'News agencies who rushed to report that story didn't do the basic job of going back to the source. They reported news based on one blog entry—an unbelievably irresponsible approach,' Hill said.

However, there is a traditional familiarity to these risks, as one journalist observed:

these are the same pitfalls faced by any journalist using unfamiliar sources, and [they] simply require the same amount of care. That means 'triangulating' all information you receive—either via other contacts in the field (checking to see what they know about the source, or the information the source is giving you—this is especially pertinent if the source is pseudonymous) or through background searches to confirm identity, which can often be done simply by Googling (Posetti 2012).

While 'open verification' is likely to find growing acceptance within professional journalism, the flood of information, disseminated at unrelenting speed on Twitter, means that careful research and investigation by journalists is more important than ever. In the meantime, smart media organisations will invest in the development of better systems of social media verification—from human expertise to analytical tools designed to sift, assess and synthesise social data.

Best-practice social journalism at the organisational level requires adequate, targeted resourcing. At the BBC, a critical role is played by a group of journalists attached to the User-Generated Content Hub—a desk located in the physical centre of the London newsroom that seeks to verify social content. And many of the major media outlets present at #BBCSMS said their organisations employed social media editors with a specific editorial brief to oversee social journalism production. In terms of specific investigative units within media organisations, such a resource could be very valuable for aggregating internal interdisciplinary skills and intelligence to develop best-practice methods, in the interests of enhancing social journalism research and verification techniques.

TIPS

The following tips are curated from a survey of investigative journalists (Posetti 2012):

1   Always verify information elsewhere
2   Make sure you know an account is a 'real' person before quoting.
3   Cultivate a varied Twitter feed.
4   Upskill: 'Social media is such a rapidly evolving field, it is very difficult for individuals to stay abreast.'
5   Engage: 'I'm surprised how many journalists are not using social media to help their work and to engage with their audiences. In many quarters, there is a rather patronising, sniffy attitude about blogs, Twitter etc.'
6   Watch and learn from others around the world. It is a time for innovation and experimentation.
7   Make friends with IT-savvy, data-loving types. 'Journalists need to get better at collaborating with other skill sets.'
8   If you are part of the conversation and community in a particular news round, you will get early warning of a hot issue and you will be the go-to reporter for whistle-blowers. 'This means being active in the community when you don't want anything, not just busting in when you do want something.'
9   Be incredibly careful about the line between your professional and private life and opinions. 'The crossover can be potentially career-ending, and social media tends to blur the boundary significantly.'
10   Politely promote your work.
11   Set up an engaging account that is not just about work, but is as professional as work. Be a real person out there and people/contacts will want to engage with you.
12   Reply to those good enough to respond to you—develop personal relationships
13   Don't get dragged into silly, partisan, back-and-forth brawls.
14   Never say anything on Twitter that you wouldn't be prepared to say in front of a television camera.
15   Share and engage with a wide range of stories and views as well as your own, and remember that social media is a two-way street/conversation, not an information dump.

16 Use lists on both Twitter and Facebook—you can keep lots of projects on the boil at once with the click of a button!

17 Social media doesn't replace traditional methods—it's an additional tool. Use it to broaden your contact base and your outlook: 'Not everyone thinks the same as you!'

18 Check and recheck: 'Rigour is even more important when sources are anonymous and therefore less accountable.'

19 Regard Twitter as a water cooler. Use it to pick up the vibe rather than treating it all as gospel.

20 Deploy deeper search functions and third-party applications to augment manual social journalism research, for example Advanced Twittersearch, Facebakers, Topsy, Reverse Google Image Search, Trendsmap and Twtpoll among others.

QUESTIONS TO CONSIDER

1 Which social media platforms do you currently use? How do you use these networks journalistically?

2 What are the potential benefits of using social media to collaborate with audiences on investigative journalism projects?

3 What are the implications of a journalist tweeting unverified information that turns out to be incorrect?

4 How should journalists respond to criticism levelled against them about their work by other social media participants?

5 How can you apply the examples of 'social journalism' discussed in this chapter to a story you're current working on?

TASK

1 Write five x 500-word blog posts that consider academic and journalistic thought on the issues raised in the above questions, while critically reflecting on your own practice and that of professional journalists you follow on Twitter. Include a bibliography at the end of your posts with Harvard-style academic referencing, adding hyperlinks where available.

REFERENCES

ABC Radio National. 2008. *The Audience Talks Back*, The Media Report: www.abc.net.au/rn/mediareport/stories/2008/2410940.htm/.

Axom, S. 2010. *There's No iPhone 4 Recall, No Matter What Twitter Says*, Mashable: http://mashable.com/2010/06/27/iphone-4-recall/.

BBC News Middle East. 2011. *Syria Gay Girl in Damascus Blog a Hoax by US Man*: www.bbc.co.uk/news/world-middle-east-13744980/.

Bradshaw, P. 2011. *Editorial Issues*, BBC College of Journalism: www.bbc.co.uk/journalism/blog/2011/05/editorial-issues.shtml/.

Clark, R.P. 2011. *How Journalists are Using Facebook, Twitter to Write Mini Serial Narratives*, Poynter: www.poynter.org/how-tos/newsgathering-storytelling/writing-tools/115607/how-journalists-are-using-facebook-twitter-to-write-mini-serial-narratives/.

Dennet, H. 2009. (@harleyd on Twitter): www.twitter.com/harleyd (accessed April 2009).

Gillmor, D. 2004. *We the Media: Grassroots Journalism By the People For the People*, Sebastapol: O'Reilly Media.

Glaser, B. & Strauss, A. 1968. *The Discovery of Grounded Theory: Strategies for Qualitative Research*, London: Weidenfeld and Nicolson.

Griffen-Foley, B. 2004. 'From Tit-Bits to Big Brother: A Century of Audience Participation in the Media', in *Media, Culture & Society*, vol. 26, iss. 4, p. 533.

Haggarty, E. 2011. 'Nelson Mandela The Victim of Latest Twitter Death Hoax', *Toronto Star*: www.thestar.com/news/world/article/923174--nelson-mandela-the-victim-of-latest-twitter-death-hoax/.

Howe, J. 2006. 'The Rise of Crowdsourcing', *Wired Magazine*: www.wired.com/wired/archive/14.06/crowds.html/.

Lasorsa, D.L, Lewis, S.C. & Holton, A.E. 2011. 'Normalizing Twitter: Journalism Practice in an Emerging Communication Space', *Journalism Studies*, 13(1), pp. 19–36.

Lee, C. 2007. 'Mornings with Radio 774: Can John Howard's Medium of Choice Enhance Public Sphere Activity?', *Media International Australia incorporating Culture and Policy*, 122, February, pp. 122–31.

Mangalinden, J.P. 2011. 'Dick Costolo: Twitter Has 100 Million Active Users', *CNN Money*: http://tech.fortune.cnn.com/2011/09/08/twitter-has-100-million-users/.

McGregor, K. 2012. 'Twitter Makes Spill a 24/7 Affair', *Adelaide Advertiser*: www.adelaidenow.com.au/twitter-makes-spill-a-247-affair/story-e6frea8c-1226283329346/.

McLuhan, M. 2001. *Understanding Media* (first published 1964), London: Routledge.

Phillips, G. 2007. 'The Interactive Audience: A Radio Experiment in Community-building', *Media International Australia incorporating Culture and Policy*, 122, February, pp. 174–85.

Posetti, J. 2009a. *How Journalists are Using Twitter in Australia*, Mediashift PBS.

Posetti, J. 2009b. *How Journalists Balance Work, Personal Lives on Twitter*, Mediashift PBS.

Posetti, J. 2009c. *Rules of Engagement for Journalists on Twitter*, Mediashift PBS.

Posetti, J. 2009d. *Media140 Brings Old and New Media Together with Explosive Results*, Mediashift PBS: www.pbs.org/mediashift/2009/11/media140-brings-old-and-new-media-together-with-explosive-results317.html/.

Posetti, J. 2010a. *Twitterising Journalism and J-Ed: An Australian Political Journalism Case Study*, Rhodes University, South Africa. Paper published in online proceedings of the 2nd World Journalism Education Congress: http://wjec.ru.ac.za/index.php?option=com_rubberdoc&view=category&id=15%3Anew-media&Itemid=45/.

Posetti, J. 2010b. *The Spill Effect: Twitter Upends Australian Political Journalism*, Mediashift PBS: www.pbs.org/mediashift/2010/03/the-spill-effect-twitter-hashtag-upends-australian-political-journalism061.html/.

Posetti, J. 2011a. *#bbcsms: Session Report—Editorial Issues: Verification, Referral, Privacy*, London: BBC College of Journalism.

Posetti, J. 2011b. *BBC Social Media Summit Fixates on Creating Open Media*, Mediashift PBS: www.pbs.org/mediashift/2011/06/bbc-social-media-summit-fixates-on-creating-open-media158.html/.

Posetti, J. 2012. Unpublished online surveys conducted with 10 Australian journalists who identified as using social media for investigative journalism.

Rosen, J. 2006a. *The People Formerly Known as the Audience*, Press Think: http://archive.pressthink. org/2006/06/27/ppl_frmr.html/.

Rosen, J. 2006b. *Citizen Journalism Expert Jay Rosen Answers Your Questions Slashdot*: http://interviews. slashdot.org/article.pl?sid=06/10/03/1427254 (accessed 24 May 2010).

Savitz, E. 2012. *The Future of Facebook. What's After the Social Graph?* Forbes: www.forbes.com/sites/ ciocentral/2012/03/19/the-future-of-facebook-whats-after-the-social-graph/.

Seidel, J.V. 1998. *Qualitative Data Analysis* (originally published as 'Qualitative Data Analysis', in *The Ethnograph*, Vol. 5.0, Colorado Springs: Qualis Research): www.qualisresearch.com/qda_ paper.htm/.

Sheffer, M.L. & Shulz, B. 2010. 'Paradigm Shift or Passing Fad?' *International Journal of Sport Communication*, 3, pp. 472–84.

Strauss, A. 1987. *Qualitative Analysis for Social Scientists*, Cambridge: Cambridge University Press.

Strauss, A. & Corbin, J. 1990. *Basics of Qualitative Research: Grounded Theory Procedures and Techniques*, London: Sage Publications.

Weinberger, D. 2009 *Truth and Transparency*, Presentation to Personal Democracy Forum, New York, 29 June: www.youtube.com/watch?v=o3qSD LF6lU4&feature=player_embedded (accessed 29 November 2009.

NOTES

1   The '#Spill' hashtag aggregated all tweets referencing the leadership spill that saw the demise of Malcolm Turnbull in November/December 2009. (In Australia, a leadership 'spill' refers to a process in which the leader's chair is vacated and the leadership is thereby thrown open to a party vote.)

2   The author has adapted and combined principles of grounded theory (GT) (Glaser & Strauss 1968) and qualitative data analysis (QDA) (c.f. Seidel 1998) to reflect the research methods of investigative journalism that involve a GT-style 'bottom-up' approach to generating categories/themes/codes and an analytical approach to data familiar to QDA researchers. This methodological approach most closely resembles that of Strauss and Corbin (Strauss 1987; Strauss & Corbin 1990)

3   Note: the only journalist participating in the 2012 surveys of Australian journalists using social media for investigative reporting, referenced here, who elected to be identified for publication purposes, was Jess Hill.

INVESTIGATIVE SOCIAL JOURNALISM AND THE ARAB SPRING

Jess Hill

When protests broke out in Libya in February 2011, there were no foreign journalists there to report it. I was a producer for ABC Radio Current Affairs and realised that the only way to report this was to contact people on the ground.

Gaddafi had cut off the internet, so Libyans were dependent on phones to raise the alarm. Members of the Libyan diaspora were taking that information, translating it into English, and posting it segment by segment on Twitter.

On the first day of the uprising, I spent hours going through Libyan Twitter feeds, ruling out anyone exhibiting signs of hysteria or ideology—clear, balanced information was crucial. I made a shortlist of people calmly tweeting detailed information, and triangulated that information with at least three other sources. Once that checked out, I made contact with individuals, and developed a source relationship, working with them to contact eye witnesses. By the time foreign journalists arrived in Benghazi a few days later, we'd spoken to people across Libya—all facilitated by Twitter.

For me, Twitter has become more vital as an investigative tool than Google. It's like having instant access to a massive room of 'fixers'. Activists, eye witnesses, academics and fellow journalists have all helped connect me to sources outside the Twitter bubble, and assisted with verifying information.

The Libyan uprising was well suited to this type of social media reporting. This was due to a unique combination of social, cultural and political factors. Libya has a small population—just 6.4 million people. It is divided along tribal lines—a surname can be enough to ascertain where somebody is from. This makes Libya a relatively simple society to navigate, and specific people easy to find. Major areas, such as Benghazi, Misrata and the Western Mountains, also had their own military brigade, and most of them had a dedicated media centre, so information was streamlined. For most of the conflict, fighting was contained close to Libya's densely populated coastline, meaning keeping track of the opposition's progress was relatively easy. Most importantly, however, the opposition was united, and represented by one body: the Transitional National Council, based in the freezone of Benghazi.

On Twitter, representatives from the Libyan diaspora (@ShababLibya, @EnoughGaddafi, @ChangeinLibya) gathered information from inside Libya, verified it, and posted it in English. Others on Twitter, like @acarvin, also worked on verification, and there was a strong culture of outing people who were spreading disinformation. I monitored Twitter most hours of the day and night over six months and, over time, developed a very strong network of contacts.

I collaborated with these sources every day. When new sources sent me leads, these trusted contacts helped me verify them. When a Libyan expat from England said he could put me in touch with a rebel fighter in Tripoli, for instance, I first asked several of my contacts what they knew about him. Nobody raised a red flag, but I was still unsure whether the fighter he was connecting me with was legitimate. Even if he was, how could I be sure he would provide accurate information? I interviewed the fighter, listening out for hysteria, propaganda or misinformation. He *sounded* credible, so I emailed the interview to a close contact of mine with family in Tripoli. He confirmed that the information echoed what he was hearing from his family in the capital. After choosing the grabs to broadcast, I cross-checked that information with two more contacts, and triangulated it with recent news reports out of Tripoli. Only then did we put it to air on ABC Radio.

The Syrian uprising

Cultural, political and social dynamics rendered Libya compatible with social media reporting. The Syrian uprising, however, is a different story.

In many ways, the Syrian conflict is antithetical to the Libyan conflict. Syria's population is four times the size of Libya's and is divided along sectarian lines, which means inter-country connections are nowhere near as strong. Unlike the Libyan conflict, which was contained to a slim wedge of the country, the Syrian conflict is being fought over vast terrain, making it harder to keep track of each flashpoint. Even the sheer volume of videos coming out of Syria makes it much harder to contextualise and verify video evidence.

Perhaps most crucially, however, where the Libyan opposition was united, the Syrian opposition is fractured, and preoccupied by in-fighting, which makes it a lot more difficult to know who to trust. This in part reflects Syrian society—the country's secret police apparatus is said to employ up to one in seven Syrian citizens as informants.

At the time of writing, more than a year into the uprising, social media is increasingly being used as a tool for propaganda, by both sides. The information war between opposition activists and regime supporters is making it virtually impossible to separate factual testimonies and videos from fiction. Groups like the 'Syrian Electronic Army' are working to undermine eye-witness accounts circulating on the internet and the media, and the opposition itself is becoming more wise to the power of propaganda, increasingly showing the media only what it wants them to see. Given how dangerous it is for journalists to cover conflict areas in Syria, it's become incredibly difficult to report reliably on Syria at all.

In reporting the Syrian conflict, journalists can still use social media to crowdsource—especially specific, verified contacts—and to compare information with other journalists and experts in the field. But it's becoming much harder to verify what we're seeing and hearing from opposition activists inside Syria—and the quality of reporting is suffering as a result.

8

Maths and Stats for Journalists

STEPHEN TANNER

Let's face it, journalists tend to disavow any love of mathematics. Their stock-in-trade—so they claim—is words, not statistics. Yet the reality is that journalists deal with data on a daily basis. It is integral to almost all journalistic tasks we tackle, from examining match reports on sporting contests, or increases in interest rates, housing prices or the consumer price index; to analysing opinion polls about the popularity of our politicians, budget accounts or share price movements. Despite the common refrain of journalists—'I hated maths when I was at school'—we constantly seem to look for ways to incorporate statistics into our stories. We do so because they seem to provide our stories with an extra level of gravitas and meaning, despite the warning inherent in the old adage: 'lies, damned lies and statistics'.

In this chapter we return to some of the fundamentals everyone learned at school and talk about how they can be incorporated into our writing. In doing so, we also consider some of the traps that can undermine our writing if we are not careful.

SOME DEFINITIONS

THE MEAN

Journalists like to talk in terms of averages, particularly when they are using data sets, for example: the average house price in a suburb or state; the average salary earned by the chief executives of Australia's top 200 companies; the average cost of living across the different states; the average winning margin in a sporting competition; or even the average score among the winning teams. Really what they're talking about is what mathematicians and statisticians call 'the mean'. How is the mean calculated? By adding the total of all figures in the data set and dividing them by the number of values that make up the data set (see Table 8.1).

Let's look at some examples:

TABLE 8.1: BASE SALARIES OF AUSTRALIAN MPS COMPARED

JURISDICTION	BASE REMUNERATION AT 1 JULY 2011 ($)
Commonwealth	140 910
Western Australia	134 526
New South Wales	140 410
Queensland	140 410
South Australia	138 910
Victoria	135 177
Northern Territory	137 910
Australian Capital Territory	121 023
Tasmania	113 866

Source: Western Australia 2011

In the example in Table 8.1, we want to know the mean base salary of Australia's politicians. This is a two-step process:

1   We add together all the figures in Column 2. This provides us with a total of $1 203 142.

2   The second step provides us with the mean. We simply divide the total ($1 203 142) by the number of contributions we have in the data set (in this case nine, being the Commonwealth plus each of the states and territories). This provides us with a mean (or average) base salary of $133 682.44.

Now many people will say there is nothing mean about a salary of this magnitude. In fact they will probably complain that it is very generous—an argument we're not going to buy into for the purpose of this chapter. We're only interested in the comparisons, more so than the justifications. But the question immediately arises, how useful is this data, except in a superficial sense? It shows us that there is $27 000 difference in base pay between the highest-paid MPs (Commonwealth) and the lowest-paid (Tasmania). Does this mean that Tasmania's state-based MPs do less work than their colleagues in other states and territories, or those working in the federal sphere? Or does it mean that over the years Tasmanian MPs have been less effective in negotiating for wage parity with their counterparts elsewhere? The answers to these questions are no.

The differences are influenced by a range of factors journalists need to be aware of before they make superficial comparisons that may influence the views of readers or listeners. To draw meaningful comparisons we really need to add in a range of other data, including the populations of the various states and territories, and how many politicians there are representing them. We also need to consider how the salaries are calculated. Some are pegged against the salary of Commonwealth MPs, while others are calculated by state-based Salaries and Allowances Tribunals (SATs). These tribunals take into account a range of factors, including the 'work value' of MPs, salary levels in the broader community and economic conditions generally. Poor economic conditions in the past have seen some state and federal parliaments defer wage increases for MPs until economic conditions improve.

For example, among the documents the West Australian Tribunal provided in its 2010 report (Western Australia 2011) was a table comparing increases in the base salary of MPs with rises in the Consumer Price Index (CPI) and Wage Price Index (WPI). This is detailed in Table 8.2.

TABLE 8.2: CHANGES IN BASE REMUNERATION OF WEST AUSTRALIAN MPS, COMPARED WITH KEY ECONOMIC INDICATORS

	CPI		WPI		CHANGE IN WEST AUSTRALIAN MPS' BASE SALARY
	NATIONAL	WA	National	WA	
2006	3.3%	4.4%	4.0%	4.6%	4.1%
2007	3.0%	3.0%	4.2%	5.9%	4.5%
2008	3.7%	3.7%	4.3%	5.7%	4.2%
2009	2.5%	2.2%	4.1%	5.4%	0.0%
2010	3.1%	3.5%	3.1%	3.0%	4.3%
2011	3.6%	3.0%	3.9%	4.1%	

Source: CPI: ABS Cat 6401.0; WPI: ABS Cat 6345.0; both cited in Western Australia 2011, p. 6

Many young journalists would probably avoid this part of the report, deterred by the terms 'CPI' and 'WPI'. However, these are critical terms in finance reporting and help to give the SAT determination context. The terms are easily defined. The CPI, for example, is defined as:

> a current social and economic indicator that is constructed to measure changes over time in the general level of prices of consumer goods and services that households acquire, use or pay for consumption. The index aims to measure the change in consumer prices over time. This may be done by measuring the cost of purchasing a fixed basket of consumer goods and services of constant quality and similar characteristics, with the products in the basket being selected to be representative of households' expenditure during a year or other specified period (International Labour Organization 2003; cited in ABS Cat 6461.0 2005).

The Australian Bureau of Statistics (ABS) provides four separate WPIs:

1 ordinary time hourly rates of pay excluding bonuses

2 ordinary time rates of pay including bonuses

3 total hourly rates of pay excluding bonuses index

4 total hourly rates of pay including bonuses.

Of these, it is the first that is used as the 'headline measure', meaning the one that appears in media reports (ABS Cat 6351.0.55.001 2004).

A journalist who is not intimidated by the sea of figures in Table 8.2 can write an incisive story about the increase being justified. This argument is supported, in part, by the fact that there was no increase in MPs' salaries in 2009 (see Column 6). While it would be inappropriate to base the story on the data contained in these tables alone, delving further into the report (Western Australia 2011) provides an even stronger argument in support of the salary increase, despite the fact that MPs are widely considered to be overpaid relative to the average Australian.

However, a journalist who is looking to write a fair story that compares the salaries of MPs across the various jurisdictions will need to dig deeper than this report, helpful though it is. A more useful comparison involves an analysis of the total remuneration paid to MPs. This includes loadings for members who hold additional offices (for example, the Prime Minister, Premiers, Ministers, Speakers and Opposition Leaders). These loadings are calculated as a percentage of the members' base wage and are intended to reflect the additional workload and responsibility involved (for example, the Prime Minister and the Premiers receive a higher loading than do Ministers, who in turn receive more than Parliamentary Secretaries and Chairs of Committee). MPs can also receive an electorate allowance (calculated by taking into account the geographic size of the electorate, as well as the population) and other allowances for travel, accommodation, etc.; however the number of allowances and the dollar amounts vary considerably between jurisdictions.

It is only when all of these elements are taken into account that a fairer picture emerges, and journalists have to be aware of this when writing stories about the latest increase in MPs' salaries and allowances. Equally, this information helps in providing context, particularly when the inevitable comparisons are made between MPs' salaries and those of private sector employees.

Remember, to do this story justice, it is important to draw comparisons over time. Look at how both base salaries and allowances are calculated over a period. If a large increase is proposed—compared with recent increases in, say, public sector wages or lower-level private sector wages—ask why. Is it because MPs endured a wage freeze? Why was the wage freeze imposed? Are they only now playing catch-up? Remember, raw data does not tell us the complete story. Often we have to look behind the data to understand the real story.

THE MEDIAN

Given the complexities involved in trying to explain the differences in salary levels paid to MPs representing the various jurisdictions, it might be more useful to apply another test—'the median'. The median is the mid-point between the highest figure (the salary paid to Commonwealth MPs) and the lowest (that paid to Tasmanian MPs). As Table 8.3 shows, in our data set the median is $137 910 (the salary paid to MPs from the Northern Territory).

TABLE 8.3: THE SALARIES OF AUSTRALIAN MPS COMPARED

	JURISDICTION	BASE REMUNERATION AT 1 JULY 2011 ($)
1	Commonwealth	140 910
2	New South Wales	140 410
3	Queensland	140 410
4	South Australia	138 910
5	Northern Territory	137 910
6	Victoria	135 177
7	Western Australia	134 526
8	Australian Capital Territory	121 023
9	Tasmania	113 866

Source: Western Australia 2011

This produces an interesting result and one that is worth writing about, given that Northern Territory MPs are paid more than their counterparts in two of the more populous states: Western Australia and Victoria. It also shows that MPs from South Australia—one of the smaller states by population—are the fourth highest paid (and third highest among state MPs). Dig deeper and there is more to extract from the use of the median test.

Use of the median test is far more meaningful in this context than it would be in comparing player statistics on a match-by-match basis. Nor is it particularly useful in drawing comparisons in a data set where there are great disparities between the two extremes, for example the salaries paid to the CEO of a company on the one hand and an apprentice working on the factory floor on the other, as the following example shows.

Company XYZ Ltd employs 15 people. Their salaries are set out in Table 8.4.

TABLE 8.4: SALARIES IN XYZ LTD COMPARED

	ROLE	SALARY ($)
1	CEO	586 000
2	Company secretary	221 000
3	Foreman	71 500
4	Leading hand	65 000
5	Boilermaker welder	65 000
6	Boilermaker welder	65 000
7	Electrician	64 000
8	Boilermaker welder	58 000
9	Boilermaker welder	56 000
10	Electrician	56 000
11	Office assistant	49 600
12	Apprentice	34 000
13	Apprentice	34 000
14	Apprentice	27 000
15	Apprentice	19 000
	Total salaries	***1 471 100***
	Mean (average) salary	**98 073**

However you look at it, this table can produce distorting results. The mean (average) salary is $98 073, and yet only two employees earn above or even close to this amount. Thirteen of the 15 employees actually earn considerably less; the mean figure is inflated by the salaries paid to the CEO and the company secretary. While the median ($58 000) provides a more realistic figure, the fact is that only three of the seven employees who earn the median salary or less are close to this figure, with four earning $34 000 or less.

The lesson to come from this is that we need to be careful about jumping to conclusions when dealing with data sets. We also need to consider the spread of values in the data set (the difference between the largest and the smallest). Statisticians provide for this with what they call the 'standard deviation' or σ. This is a measure of the spread of numbers in the data set. It is calculated by working out the square root of the variance (see the MathsIsFun website). First, you need to calculate the mean of your data set. Let's use a different example, based on hypothetical average weekly rents in Australian capital cities: see Table 8.5.

TABLE 8.5: AVERAGE WEEKLY RENTS IN AUSTRALIAN CAPITAL CITIES

	AVERAGE WEEKLY RENT ($)	VARIATION FROM MEAN
SYDNEY	840	125
Melbourne	783	38
Brisbane	620	85
Perth	811	96
Adelaide	640	75
Hobart	532	183
Canberra	761	48
Darwin	733	18
Total rents	**5720**	
Mean (average) rent	**715**	

The variance is calculated as follows (the variation from mean of all numbers in the data set squared):

$$\sigma^2 = 125^2 + 38^2 + -85^2 + 96^2 + -75^2 + -183^2 + 48^2 + 18^2$$

These totals are then added together and divided by the number of entries in the dataset:

$$= \frac{15\,625 + 1444 + 7225 + 9216 + 5625 + 33\,489 + 2304 + 324}{8}$$

$$= \frac{75\,252}{8} = 9406.5$$

Thus the variance = 9406.5.

The standard deviation is the square root of the variance and is calculated as:

$$\sigma = \sqrt{9406.5}$$

$$= 96.987 \text{ (rounded up to 97).}$$

The standard deviation is widely used in a range of disciplines, including scientific research and share market movements (both of the indices and individual stocks). It provides us with a ready way of measuring and monitoring movements from a set point. For more on this, there are a number of websites that provide good explanations of how the standard deviation works and can be applied across a range of disciplines (see, for example, the resources at the end of this chapter).

MODE

'The mode' is the figure that appears the most frequently in a data set. It tends to be used less frequently than the mean or median, but can be useful in looking at sporting statistics or even share market data.

For example, share market investors often track the movement in a company's share price. This may be over the course of an hour, a day, week, month or year. While they are interested in other data as well—including the total number of share transactions during the course of a day, or the total value of share transactions—they may want to know at what price point the greatest number of shares traded hands, or the closing price of a share over a 10-day period. The mode (in this case, the most frequently appearing closing price for Pluto Resources Ltd) is highlighted in the Table 8.6.

TABLE 8.6: PLUTO RESOURCES LTD CLOSING PRICES

DAY	1	2	3	4	5	6	7	8	9	10
Closing price (cents)	0.03	0.02	0.04	0.03	0.03	0.05	0.03	0.02	0.04	0.02

Table 8.6 shows that the mode is 0.03 cents, as this was the closing price for Pluto Resources shares on four out of 10 days. This was followed by 0.02 cents (three days), 0.04 cents (two days) and 0.05 cents (one day). However, presented as a table, this data can appear relatively meaningless, especially if the closing prices for a range of stocks were added to the table. In this case it may be more appropriate to present the data via a simple chart, for example a column or line chart.

PERCENTAGE POINTS AND BASIS POINTS

When dealing with data sets, it is a good idea to break the figures down into something people can understand. Often the conversation focuses on percentages—usually percentage change or difference. A percentage is usually expressed as a portion or fraction of 100. Interest rates, for example, are calculated as a percentage. Increases or decreases in the CPI are expressed as percentages. So too are the results of public opinion polls.

On the first Tuesday of each month, the Reserve Bank of Australia releases its latest interest rates. When journalists report on the Reserve Bank's decision, they refer to increases and falls in terms of percentage points. Some will also refer to these in terms of 'basis points'. There are 100 basis points to each percentage point. Therefore 1 basis point equals 0.01 percentage points. A fall in interest rates from 5.65 to 5.45 per cent represents a cut of 20 basis points. An increase from 5.65 to 6.65 per cent equals an increase of one percentage point (or 100 basis points).

Journalists are very careful when reporting on such rises, because they do not want to generate fear or angst among mortgage holders. For example, say the standard variable interest rate on mortgages was 10 per cent. The Reserve Bank decides to lift official interest rates to 11 per cent. Technically, this represents an increase of 10 per cent, but journalists prefer to talk in terms of basis points or percentage points, as these do not have the same emotive element as a percentage increase.

When writing about percentages, we need to be able to distinguish between percentage difference and percentage change.

Percentage difference

Percentage difference is the difference between two values divided by the average of those values. For example, say you are an avid cricket follower and want to compare the batting performance of two batsmen—Shivnarine Chanderpaul (West Indies) and Michael Clarke (Australia)—during the 2012 Test series in the West Indies. Chanderpaul scored 346 runs and Clarke 188. The difference between their total scores is 158. The average is the mid-point between the two totals (346 + 188 ÷ 2 = 267). To calculate the difference as a percentage of the average, you should use the following formula: (158 ÷ 267) x 100% = 59.17%, where 158 equals the difference between Chanderpaul and Clarke's performance on tour, and 267 is the average number of runs per batsman.

This is a useful comparison, as it gives us a greater insight into the differences in performance between the two players, at the time ranked number one and seven respectively in the International Cricket Council test batting rankings.

This comparison can also be used when comparing team performances, for example the total West Indies batting, bowling or catching performance compared with that of the Australian team, or of the Australian netball team's performance onshore compared with offshore.

Percentage change

Sometimes, however, we want to compare a batsman's performance on his last tour of a particular country. This is useful when trying to predict how that player will perform on a forthcoming tour, or when trying to explain why they performed better or worse in a recently completed tour than they had previously. In such instances, it is worth putting their statistics under the microscope and looking for the percentage change. This is a simple calculation that involves subtracting the old value from the new value, and then dividing the total by the old value.

This measure is also useful when comparing increases or decreases in the price of a basket of food, salaries or even house prices, as the following example reveals.

Max and Betty purchased a house in Sydney in 2001 for $695 000. They sold the property in 2012 for $989 000, an increase of $294 000, or a 42.3 per cent increase over time. To calculate the percentage increase, use the following formula: 989 000 – 695 000 = 294 000. Then divide 294 000 by 695 000 = 0.423. Convert to a percentage by multiplying 0.423 by 100 = 42.3%.

However, what happens if Max and Betty purchased the house for $989 000 in 2001 and were only able to get $695 000 for it in 2012? Does this mean they have made a 42 per cent loss on their investment? No, it doesn't: 695 000 – 989 000 = –294 000; –294 000 ÷ 989 000 = –0.297; –0.297 x 100 = –29.7. Thus they have made a loss of nearly 30 per cent on their investment (see the MathsIsFun website).

Journalists often try to catch out politicians during election campaigns by asking them how much a litre of milk costs, or a loaf of bread. This is a mean question, given that there is no fixed price for either commodity. The cost of milk varies considerably, depending on whether it is purchased from a supermarket chain that is engaged in a price war with its rival, or from a corner store that has higher overheads and lower purchasing power. The price is also influenced by a range of other factors, including whether it is full-cream milk, low-fat milk, high in calcium or soy, etc. The same applies with bread. Prices vary according to where it is purchased and what type of bread it is—ranging from plain white to exotic artisan products.

Despite this, journalists will often chart the increases in the price of such staples over time, linking the increases or decreases to CPI or even cost-of-living salary increases. As the increases in these products tend to be relatively small, journalists often use the term 'percentage change' to track an individual product over time. This is highlighted in Table 8.7.

TABLE 8.7: PERCENTAGE CHANGE IN PRICE OF STAPLES

	2011	2012	PERCENTAGE CHANGE
BREAD (plain white)	$2.11	$2.35	11.37
Milk (full cream)	$2.19	$2.07	–5.48
Unleaded fuel	$1.48	$1.57	6.08

Percentile

It is human nature that we will often seek to compare our performance against that of our peers, for example in examination results. While such results are often expressed in percentage terms, increasingly the conversation will use the term 'percentile' to describe individual performances. For example, a student whose score is equal to or greater than 80 per cent of those attained by others sitting the examination is said to sit in the 80th percentile. Equally, someone who had an outstanding exam, and finished equal to or better than 98 per cent of candidates, is said to sit in the 98th percentile.

OPINION POLLS

Journalists love opinion polls, particularly those that compare the relative performances or prospects of our politicians or the political parties they represent. Early polls involved a head count (Gawiser & Witt 1994, p. 15) and were intended to find out where people lived, or what population growth and declines had occurred (Economou & Tanner 2008, p. 190). Today such polls, known as censuses, have become far more complex, and seek to find out a range of data—including who lives where, how old they are, where they have come from, their gender, how much they earn, how they are employed, and their religion (see Census 2011). These provide a veritable feast for journalists as they give an important insight into the changing demographics of the population. In Australia a census is conducted every five years—the last being in August 2011, the next in 2016. The data is compiled and analysed by the ABS and released in a piecemeal fashion over time. At the time of writing, the first results of the 2011 census were still to be released. When they are, you can be guaranteed that media organisations will be seeking to report on them.

The census is the largest poll conducted in Australia because it seeks to contact every resident; opinion polls, however, only seek to contact a sample. Sometimes these will be representative of the broader population or a subset thereof; frequently they will not. In the latter case, it is not unusual for media organisations to conduct 'straw polls' or 'vox pops'. These generally involve journalists being sent out onto the street to ask people their views on an issue. Increasingly, the journalists don't even leave their desks; they simply invite people to give their views via online polls. Sometimes the issue may be contentious; on other occasions mundane. But one of the weaknesses with such polls is that they try to express issues in black-and-white terms (yes/no, agree/disagree) when there are often considerable shades of grey in between the two options respondents are generally presented with. Another weakness with these polls—particularly the online or ring-in polls—is that they are self-selecting; that is, they are not representative of the wider population and generally only involve people who are passionate about an issue, when it is the views of other people that may be more representative of the majority.

While journalists play this game, they tend to place greater weight on the scientifically valid polls conducted by experienced pollsters. There are a number of different forms of poll that are recognised as being scientifically valid, including those that produce both qualitative and quantitative data. The different types suit different purposes and tend to produce different outcomes, as Moon points out:

> While the basis of quantitative work is the size and representativeness of the sample, which allows a survey sample to speak for the entire population, the basis of qualitative research is far smaller numbers, not seeking to be representative of the whole population, but whose opinions are sought in much more depth. The aim of the quantitative research is to show how many people in the country hold certain types of opinion. The aim of qualitative research is to establish what sorts of opinions are held within the population and, more importantly, the reasons why those opinions might be held. Thus quantitative research is very good at answering the question 'what?' while qualitative research is very good at answering the question 'why?' (Moon 1999, pp. 177–8).

Qualitative data is usually produced by focus groups or via semi-structured questions; whereas quantitative data is the outcome of telephone or face-to-face interviews in which respondents are asked to choose from a range of predetermined responses. With focus groups and semi-structured questions, the interviewee is given scope to explain the reasoning behind their responses. They are also given the capacity to feed off the response of the interviewer or other members of the focus group.

There is less coverage in the media of qualitative polls than quantitative data. There are a number of reasons for this. While qualitative polls can provide great direct quotes for the journalist to insert in their story, the responses rarely fit the journalistic demand for data that can be quantified. With the majority of (quantitative) polls conducted for media consumption, all respondents are asked the same question and provided with the same list of response options (Economou & Tanner 2008, p. 194). The results are then tabulated according to the responses and broken down into percentages which are easy for the journalist to distil and extrapolate. Finally, quantitative polls are much easier to conduct, with the results fed into computers and quickly analysed before they are distributed to the media or other clients.

Journalists using opinion poll data must ask a number of questions before blithely reporting the findings. The first question is: 'How many people were interviewed?' The second question is: 'How representative of the target population is the sample?' Pollsters can use relatively small samples to accurately predict community sentiment. For example, the political polls that appear in *The Australian* newspaper usually involve approximately 2000 people. By carefully ensuring that the sample represents the wider population (in terms of age, occupation, gender, race, religion, education, political preference and geographical distribution), these results can be extrapolated to predict how the broader Australian population of 20-plus million people would have voted if an election had been held on that night.

One of the keys to success is understanding 'sampling error tolerance'. Pollsters tend to use two measures—called 'confidence levels'—when standing by their results. These are 95 and 99 per cent (depending on the extent of the need for accuracy). By confidence levels, pollsters mean the likelihood that the results will reflect the views or opinions of the broader population.

As Table 8.8 reveals, the degree of confidence is also linked to the sample size. There are significantly higher margins of error in smaller samples than there are in larger samples. While the margin of error drops quickly as the size of samples increases (see the changes between sample sizes of 10 and 100 people), there is a point where the increase in certainty is not justified by the costs associated with increasing the size of the poll (see, for example, the difference between 2000, 2500 and 3000 people). Professional pollsters are satisfied that they can confidently predict the outcomes of polls with sampling tolerance levels of 2.2 per cent (2000 people at 95 per cent).

TABLE 8.8: SAMPLE SIZE AND THE DEGREE OF TOLERANCE

SAMPLE SIZE	TOLERANCE AT 95%: LEVEL OF CONFIDENCE	TOLERANCE AT 99%: LEVEL OF CONFIDENCE
10	30.1	40.1
100	9.8	12.9
400	4.9	6.5
600	4.0	5.3
800	3.5	4.6
1000	3.1	4.1
2000	2.2	2.9
2500	2.0	2.6
3000	1.8	2.4
5000	1.4	1.8

Adapted from Wilhoit & Weaver 1980, p. 28

Thus, it is clear that small samples are less reliable than larger samples. Let's look at two examples:

Example 1:
You have been asked to run a poll that predicts the relative performances of two candidates in a local council election. You design a simple questionnaire based on a familiar question: 'will you vote for either Candidate A or Candidate B in the council election?' You decide that because of the need to produce and analyse the results in time for publication in tomorrow's newspaper, you will limit your sample to 100 people. You conduct the poll by telephone, and come up with the following results:

Candidate A: 53 votes (53 per cent)

Candidate B: 47 votes (47 per cent).

According to Table 8.8, it will be difficult to extrapolate this result to the broader population with any degree of confidence, using either the 95 per cent or 99 per cent tests. On the raw data, you could assume that Candidate A would win in a close tussle, but if the sampling tolerance level of 9.8 per cent at the 95 per cent level of confidence is applied, then Candidate's A's vote could be as high as 62.8 per cent (53 + 9.8 = 62.8) or as low as 43.2 per cent (53 – 9.8 = 43.2). Equally, Candidate B's vote could be as high as 56.8 per cent or as low as 37.2 per cent. Using the 98 per cent measure, the variations could potentially be even greater. The result is that with such a small sample you could not confidently predict the outcome of the election.

Example 2:

You want to know who people think will make the better Prime Minister—the incumbent (Julia Gillard), or the Opposition Leader (Tony Abbott). This time, the poll is conducted nationally, with 2000 voters surveyed. On the raw data, you have the following results:

Gillard: 1017 votes (50.85 per cent)

Abbott: 983 votes (49.15 per cent).

According to Table 8.8, with a sample of 2000 voters, at a 95 per cent confidence level the risk of sampling error reduces to 2.2 per cent. Using the same formula, 50.85 +/– 2.2%, you can see that support for Gillard can potentially range between 53.05 per cent and 48.65 per cent, whereas support for Abbott could be as high as 51.35 per cent or as low as 46.95 per cent. While it is tempting to say that Gillard is the more popular choice as Prime Minister, the reality is that they are potentially at level pegging. However, if Gillard's percentage support was at 53 per cent and Abbott's at 47 per cent, you could more confidently proclaim her as the more popular Prime Minister, given that even with the margin of error, the lowest her vote could slip to would be 50.8 per cent (53 – 2.2 = 50.8), while Abbott's could only move up to 49.2 per cent, less than the required 50 per cent.

CONCLUSION

This chapter has attempted to show that journalists need not be afraid of using mathematics or statistics to value-add to their stories. Statistics are a staple of political, financial and sports journalism, as the examples used reveal. Journalists prepared to interrogate statistics or tables of data will be rewarded, even if their purpose is simply to draw comparisons over time, or between different groups. The old adage 'lies, damned lies and statistics' need not be a disincentive to journalists who feel comfortable dealing with terms such mean, median, mode, percentage difference and percentage change. Armed with a knowledge of these terms, journalists can being to interrogate raw data and produce more interesting and revealing stories.

1   Don't be afraid of statistics: they are your friend.
2   Make sure that when you're using statistics to develop a story, you use the most appropriate measure (mean, median or mode) and that you don't misrepresent the situation by using the wrong one.
3   Consider how the statistics can be used to develop the story. Are they the focus or a supplementary element?
4   Don't overwhelm your readers, viewers or listeners with figures.
5   Present the data in a way that is meaningful, for example as a chart rather than as a table swimming with numbers.
6   Make sure that the changes or differences you are using the figures to highlight are clearly noticeable and not explainable by, for example, a margin of error, in the case of opinion poll data.
7   Make sure you understand the meaning of basis points, and the difference between percentage, percentage change, percentage difference and percentile.
8   When conducting or using opinion poll data, make sure that you understand the strengths and weaknesses of qualitative and quantitative polls.
9   Ensure that your sample is representative; that is, that it reflects the demographics of the group you are referring to (in terms of age, gender, ethnic or religious background, employment status, etc.).

QUESTIONS TO CONSIDER

1   What is the difference between mean, median and mode? Give examples of how you would use each of these in writing a news story.
2   What do statisticians mean when they use the term 'percentage difference'?
3   Provide some examples of how the phrase 'lies, damn lies and statistics' can have validity.
4   Give a list of potential sports stories in which statistics can provide context to the story.
5   What are the relative strengths and weaknesses of qualitative and quantitative polls? Give examples.

TASK

1   Go to the ABS website and locate a data set that you can turn into a feature article (it can be on any topic—trawl through the site until you find something you're interested in). Using the tools explained in this chapter, turn the material you uncover into a feature article.

REFERENCES

ABS Cat 6461.0. 2005. *Australian Consumer Price Index: Concepts, Sources and Methods*: www.abs.gov.au/ausstats/abs@.nsf/2f762f95845417aeca25706c00834efa/bb53f0a5b1d2cee4ca25705f001eca60!OpenDocument/.

ABS Cat 6351.0.55.001. 2004. *Labour Price Index: Concepts, Sources and Methods*: www.abs.gov.au/ausstats/abs@.nsf/2f762f95845417aeca25706c00834efa/b0a92aa3cda312a1ca256f4e00799d66!OpenDocument/.

Census. 2011: www.abs.gov.au/websitedbs/d3310114.nsf/home/2011+census/.

Economou, N. & Tanner, S. 2008. *Media Power and Politics in Australia*, Frenchs Forest: Pearson Education Australia.

Gawiser, S. & Witt, G. 1994. *A Journalist's Guide to Public Opinion Polls*, Westport, CT: Praeger.

Moon, N. 1999. *Opinion Polls: History, Theory and Practice*, Manchester: Manchester University Press.

Western Australia. 2011. *Salaries and Allowances Act 1975: Determination of the Salaries and Allowances Tribunal on Remuneration of Members of Parliament Pursuant to Sections 6(1) (a), (ab), (b) and 6AA*, August: www.sat.wa.gov.au/MembersOfParliament/Documents/Determination%20on%20Remuneration%20of%20MPs%20Final%20Version%204.pdf/.

Wilhoit, G. & Weaver, D. 1980. *Newsroom Guide to Polls and Surveys*, Washington, DC: American Newspaper Publishers' Association.

WEBSITE REFERENCES

ABS: *www.abs.gov.au/*.

MathsIsFun: www.mathsisfun.com/.

MathsIsFun: Percentage Change: www.mathsisfun.com/numbers/percentage-change.html/.

MathsIsFun: Standard Deviation and Variance: www.mathsisfun.com/data/standard-deviation.html/.

RobertNiles.com: www.robertniles.com/.

RobertNiles.com: Standard Deviation: www.robertniles.com/stats/stdev.shtml/.

9

Data Journalism (1)

STEPHEN K. DOIG

Every journalist worth a byline knows how to find sources, ask questions, check answers against other sources, read documents, and then tell the story that emerges. Increasingly, though, a special breed of reporter has learned to use computers and simple software to analyse government data to reveal patterns that tell stories which otherwise would be difficult or impossible to find. Such reporters are known as database (or data) journalists, and are doing what is called computer-assisted reporting (CAR).

These days, database journalists are routinely using computer tools to examine crime patterns, political campaign financing, election irregularities, cheating on school test scores, changes in community demographics, government inefficiency, political corruption, environmental dangers, ambulance and fire response times, racial bias in criminal sentencing, and dozens of other important topics. Thanks to the power and speed of modern computers and software, reporters can examine thousands—even millions—of records in a way that just couldn't be done by hand.

THE HISTORY OF CAR

A scattering of reporters in the USA began doing early data journalism projects in the 1960s, gathering court records on paper and painstakingly entering the information onto mainframe key punch cards to look at problems such as racial differences in bail or sentencing for crimes. However, doing this kind of work was very labour intensive back in the days before such information was routinely stored on computers.

Data journalism began to catch more attention with the publication of *Precision Journalism* in 1973. The book was written by *Miami Herald* reporter Philip Meyer, who had learned how to conduct scientifically valid random-sample public opinion polls. He had used those techniques to do groundbreaking surveys of participants in race riots in Miami and Detroit during the conflicts of the civil rights era of the late 1960s. After learning more about social science tools such as statistical analysis during a fellowship at Harvard, Meyer wrote *Precision Journalism* as a call for other reporters to begin applying such methods to reporting problems.

But despite considerable interest in this book, the difficulty of getting access to mainframe computers kept Meyer's ideas from spreading until the first desktop microcomputers began to appear in the early 1980s. A handful of reporters around the USA, many of whom had bought themselves an Apple II or first-generation IBM PC or Atari 800 as a hobby to play with at home, began to discover that the machines could be used to do their jobs better. For instance, another *Miami Herald* reporter covering state government taught himself the computer language BASIC and wrote a program that would analyse the patterns of legislative roll-call votes. This allowed him, even on deadline, to go beyond simple party differences to see if other patterns—such as urban versus rural legislators, or leadership versus rank-and-file, or contributions from interest groups—explained the vote pattern.

In the mid-1980s, a reporter named Elliot Jaspin used a microcomputer and a simple database program to match up a list of all the school bus drivers in his state with a list of all the people who had been arrested for drunk driving, thereby getting a list of school bus drivers with drinking problems. That story caught the attention of other investigative reporters, and Jaspin went to the University of Missouri to start a training program that today is known as the National Institute for Computer-Assisted Reporting (NICAR). Dozens of reporters have begun learning data analysis techniques there.

Around the same time, a young reporter named Bill Dedman did a CAR study of home mortgage lending in the Atlanta area. His work showed that Atlanta banks were deliberately refusing to give loans to most Black residents of the city, even when their incomes and requested loan amounts were comparable to those of White home buyers who were being given mortgage loans. Dedman's powerful project, called *The Color of Money*, forced the banks to widen their lending and earned a Pulitzer Prize in 1989, causing even more interest in database stories from investigative reporters.

The project that really made CAR a must-have skill at a large number of newspapers came in 1992, when Hurricane Andrew damaged or destroyed more than 80 000 homes in South Florida. In the aftermath of the storm, *Miami Herald* reporters used computer analysis of house-by-house damage reports, property tax records, building inspection reports and political campaign finance data to show that the disaster was magnified by building codes that had been weakened drastically in the years since the last big hurricane had hit the region. The *Herald* won the Pulitzer Prize for Public Service for its reporting, and CAR became a skill in demand at papers and a growing number of television stations across the country.

Today, 20 years later, there are thousands of reporters who have at least basic data analysis skills, using tools like the spreadsheet Microsoft Excel. CAR skills also have spread to reporters around the world. Newsrooms from *The Guardian* in London to the Australian Broadcasting Corporation, and organisations such as the European Journalism Center and ABRAJI, the investigative reporting centre in Brazil, are using CAR and teaching it to others. NICAR, now an offshoot of the US-based Investigative Reporters and Editors (IRE) organisation, remains a leader in spreading the CAR gospel, training hundreds of reporters each year at intensive boot camps and workshops around the USA and in other countries.

WHAT IS 'DATA'?

Data is information that is stored in table form, as an organised collection of rows and columns of information. For example, consider a table of crime reports. The columns would be the variables, such as date, time, location, type of crime, number of victims, name of the lead investigator, number of suspects arrested, charges filed, and more. Each row (called a 'record') would contain the information for the above variables about a particular crime report. Another name for such a table would be 'database'.

In the decades before the computer revolution hit newsrooms, reporters who wanted to do a story about some societal problem would find a few instances of that problem—some particularly lurid crimes, a couple of toxic waste dumps, a few instances where a politician voted in favour of something a campaign donor wanted—and then use those few anecdotes to suggest they were the tip of a much larger mess.

But the analysis of government databases allows reporters to go beyond anecdote to add actual evidence to their stories. For instance, given the crime table mentioned above, a database journalist could put details in the story about what kinds of crimes are most common, which parts of town are most afflicted with crime, patterns of criminal activity such as the time or day of the week when most occurred, the names of repeat offenders, the percentage of crimes that result in arrests, and much more. Instead of just suggesting that crime is a problem, the database journalist can give precise measures of it.

HOW DO REPORTERS GET DATA TO ANALYSE?

The same public records laws that allow journalists to get copies of individual government documents and reports also make possible requests for copies of entire government databases. Public records laws vary widely from country to country, and even vary among different jurisdictions within a country. The USA, for instance, has relatively strong public records laws, but news organisations must still sometimes go to court to fight federal or local government officials who try to deny access to database records.

Some other countries have seemingly good laws calling for open records, but those laws aren't much help if journalists just back down when faced with resistance from officials. An aggressive press corps that doesn't simply take 'no' for an answer is necessary to educate public officials that open records, including database records, are important to the watchdog role of journalism.

When requesting a copy of a government database, journalists should know in advance what it contains. Typically, they first request a copy of what is called the 'file layout' or 'data dictionary', which will list the variables in the database and explain any codes that might be used for 'categorical variables', meaning variables that can take on one of a limited number of possibilities, such as gender or race. Having the file layout not only helps reporters draft a well-specified public records request, but also tells them what kinds of questions can—and can't—be answered by the data. For instance, if there is no variable for race in a database of crime victims, the reporter won't be able to see if some racial groups are more likely to be victimised than others.

Database reporters should be prepared for the possibility that obtaining the data they request may cost money, but generally there should be no great charge for getting a copy of a database. Even one with millions of records usually can be copied quickly and painlessly onto a CD-ROM or made available to be downloaded over the internet.

Occasionally, a request for a partial database that contains only specified variables and records might require government computer technicians to write a program to extract the selected data; in that case, a greater charge is likely. However, some officials will quote an outrageously large sum in the thousands of dollars, in the hope that the reporter will just go away. Faced with that, the reporter should insist on a detailed written estimate of why the charge should be so high, and then be ready to fight over it. It is often cheaper to request the entire database than just a part of it; the database journalist can use their own computer to select the records they wants.

Finally, reporters also need to know what format to ask for. Some agencies will try to insist on exporting their database into the so-called Portable Document Format (PDF). Resist this because PDF files can be difficult to import into a spreadsheet or other data analysis program. But other formats such as a 'comma-separated values' text file or the native format for a spreadsheet like Microsoft Excel will work fine.

WHAT TOOLS ARE USED FOR CAR?

The workhorse of CAR is the spreadsheet Microsoft Excel. A spreadsheet—named after the lightly ruled transaction ledgers used by accountants in the days when records were entered by hand—can be thought of as 'smart paper'. The data is lined up in columns and rows like it would on paper, but a spreadsheet allows so much more to be done than would be possible with just paper.

One of the most useful tools of an Excel spreadsheet is the ability to sort the data. Paper tables often are in alphabetical order, which is only good for looking up a particular record. Journalists are interested in other questions—what is the most or the least, the best or the worst—that can't readily be pulled out of stacks of paper. But a spreadsheet can almost instantly change the order of even tens of thousands of records with a click of the mouse. For example, imagine an Excel spreadsheet containing the standardised test scores of every primary and high school in a region. In seconds, the order could be changed to rank the schools in descending order of scores, putting the best at the top and the worst at the bottom. Excel can also do multi-level sorts, such as sorting the schools first by level of school and then within each level by scores in descending order.

Another useful tool is called filtering. The Excel filter allows a reporter to see only the records that meet whatever conditions are set. Assuming the school scores table has a variable for the level of the schools, the filter could be set to show only the primary schools, or only the schools that have scores in a certain range.

Excel also has dozens of mathematical, text, date and logical functions that enable reporters to create new variables or other information. For example, imagine a database showing the number of violent crimes, the number of property crimes, the number of auto thefts and the population of each city in a region. Excel functions can be used to calculate the total number of each kind of crime across the region. In addition, another function could be copied into new columns labelled 'violent crime rate', 'property crime rate' and 'auto theft rate', calculating the rates based on the population of each city and thus allowing direct comparison of crime problems among cities of different sizes.

One of the most powerful tools of Excel is called a 'pivot table'. This tool is typically used to summarise categorical variables. Consider a database of political campaign contributions that shows for each contributor the name of the candidate getting the money, the city and the postal code of each contributor, and the occupation of each contributor (campaign finance laws in the USA require such information be gathered and made public before elections). Using pivot tables, a reporter can in seconds find out the total money collected by each campaign, how much money has come from each city or postal code, and which occupations are most supportive of which candidates.

Excel will handle almost all the data collections a database journalist is likely to encounter. The latest version of Excel will hold just over a million rows of data, and more than 16 000 variables. Excel also can import data from a variety of text and other database formats. In sum, a reporter who gets comfortable with Excel will have the tools to work on most database problems.

OTHER TOOLS

Sometimes, however, there are data stories that require other tools. One example would be really large data sets, such as the multi-year database of more than 50 million hospital admission records that was used by investigative reporters in California in 2011 to search for evidence of fraud in billing the government for the treatment of elderly patients.

Another situation would be when the story requires merging together two or more tables based on some variable they have in common. An example would be that mentioned above: of taking a table of people arrested for dangerous driving and matching it against a table of school bus drivers using driver's licence numbers, thus producing a list of bus drivers who probably shouldn't be transporting children. For these situations, a program such as Microsoft Access is necessary. Access will handle millions of records, and can readily match separate tables based on common variables. There are more powerful database managers like SAS or MySQL that will do the same thing if a program is written, but Access is widely used and relatively easy to understand.

After database journalists master Excel and Access, many go on to learn more specialised tools. One of those is 'computerised mapping'—so-called geographic information systems software. With an expensive commercial program such as ESRI's ArcMap, or the mapping functions built into the free Google Fusion Tables, reporters can quickly see the geographic patterns in data that has location variables—latitudes and longitudes, street addresses, cities, postal codes, etc. And some of these programs will even answer geographic questions such as how many drug arrests in a city have been made within a specified distance from schools.

Other tools include heavy-duty text editors that let database journalists open large text files to see if some odd formatting is causing problems. Reporters are learning to write simple programs in languages such as Python or Perl to handle problems like breaking full names into first, middle and last names. Cutting-edge journalists who may have taken computer-science courses are creating sophisticated interactive graphics and database look-up tables for their newsroom's website. Others are using specialised statistical analysis software to apply techniques such as linear regression to study, for instance, the relationship between poverty and school test scores, or to spot outliers that may signal fraud in an election.

CONCLUSION

The key requirement for a database journalist is to be comfortable with maths (see Chapter 8). This scares many reporters, who are famously maths-phobic. But most of it is very basic maths—addition, subtraction, multiplication and division. The most complicated kinds of problems you are likely to do regularly might involve percentage change, the calculation of crime rates, or correcting for inflation using a consumer price index. It's essential, though, that these be done correctly—a simple maths error in an otherwise strong story will completely destroy its credibility, at least among readers who can do the maths themselves.

The best skill for a database journalist, though, is the ability to see the possibility of a story in the patterns in the data being analysed. Reporters who develop that 'database state of mind' as they learn to use tools such as Excel will be in demand in their newsrooms and will regularly know the thrill of finding stories that others have missed.

QUESTIONS TO CONSIDER

1   What is Philip Meyer's contribution to the development of CAR?

2   What use is a 'data dictionary' to journalists doing CAR?

3   What are the principal tools used by journalists practising CAR?

4   What is the fundamental difference between Excel and Access? Give examples of how each could be used in researching a story.

5   What is the benefit of mapping software such as ArcMap or Google Fusion Tables?

TASK

1   Go to the NICAR website: www.ire.org/nicar/. Have a look at some of the stories researched by NICAR staff. Which of the tools identified in this chapter are utilised for these reports?

REFERENCES

Dedman, B. 1989. 'The Color of Money', *The Atlanta Journal/The Atlanta Constitution*: http://powerreporting.com/color/.

Meyer, P. 1973. *Precision Journalism*: www.unc.edu/~pmeyer/book/.

Miami Herald. 1992. 'What Went Wrong: The Pulitzer Prize-Winning Special Section of the *Miami Herald*, December 20, 1992' (re Hurricane Andrew): www.flickr.com/photos/juggernautco/sets/72157607210036175/detail/.

WEBSITE REFERENCES

The Guardian: DataBlog: www.guardian.co.uk/news/datablog/.

NICAR: www.ire.org/nicar/.

FURTHER READING

ABC News: Coal Seam Gas by the Numbers: www.abc.net.au/news/specials/coal-seam-gas-by-the-numbers/.

Doig, S.K. 2011. 'Precision Journalism Reveals Patterns in Government Data' (re Hospital billing in California): http://californiawatch.org/dailyreport/precision-journalism-reveals-patterns-government-data-14117/.

10

Data Journalism (2)

KERRY GREEN

INTRODUCTION

Journalists are wordsmiths, producing thousands of words daily as they craft reports carefully designed to attract audience members, entertain and inform them, and maybe even educate them. But that facility with words often doesn't translate to a similar facility with numbers, and many journalists feel apprehensive when faced with the need to support their words with figures.

That's a shame, because the wired world is a treasure trove of data, providing information that journalists just 30 years ago could only dream of. And, given the growth of computer programs that are increasingly intuitive to use, this data is not difficult to inspect, analyse and publish. While spreadsheets and relational databases continue to be invaluable repositories of data, now programs specifically designed to inspect text, pictures, audio and video augment journalists' own strengths in these areas. Add to these geographic information systems (GIS) and it's obvious that journalists today are empowered like never before to carry out their various roles in society—but especially to carry out the Fourth Estate function and investigative journalism.

Journalists shouldn't be afraid of figures—the calculations they have to deal with are, for the most part, simple and easily learned (as discussed in the Chapter 8). For everything else there are computers. Journalists should remember, too, that they use databases daily. Using the newsroom's online archive of its own stories is not so very different from using a spreadsheet or a relational database. In the past, journalists have been reduced to doing word or phrase searches in text databases, but the emergence of much more powerful ways of searching has elevated such archives to a higher level of importance for journalists, revealing relationships, trends or anomalies where they weren't obvious from a surface reading—in much the same way as, say, Microsoft's Excel spreadsheet or Access relational database software do with numbers (and text).

Using the power of databases and computers enhances journalists' capacity to identify news—it gives them powerful ways of identifying social, economic and political trends that could have significant impacts on the lives of their audiences. *The Guardian* newspaper in the UK provided one of the best examples of database journalism combined with crowdsourcing. *The Guardian* took a database containing details of expense claims by British MPs and dumped the details into a database of its own. Readers were invited to participate in the time-consuming and onerous job of identifying those expenses that warranted closer inspection, while at the same time revealing trends and anomalies in the claims. The *Guardian* told its readers:

> Now that 500 000 pages of MPs' receipts and claim forms have been uploaded onto our servers, we can finally get some real numbers out of the MP expenses crisis.
>
> For instance, because we've had to convert each receipt and form into an image, we now know exactly how many there are for each MP, by their party. Some MPs filed nearly 2000 pieces of paper over four years, others less than 40.
>
> We're also doing a running total of spending by different categories (i.e., kitchens, soft furnishings, mortgages, etc.).(*Guardian* 2009).

While many of the claims were for reasonably small amounts, in the hundreds rather than thousands of pounds, at least one item for £3817.38, by then Prime Minister Gordon Brown, raised the ire of *The Guardian's* readers because all the information on the claim form had been blacked out. At one stage *The Guardian* noted: 'We have 458 832 pages of documents. 33 041 of you have reviewed 225 922 of them. Only 232 910 to go ... (*Guardian* 2009).

Clearly, when the power of computerised databases is allied with crowdsourcing, the power of journalism to fulfil its Fourth Estate function is significantly enhanced.

You don't have to be a maths whizz to make good use of databases—a good sense of what is newsworthy is the basic requirement. Story ideas are everywhere and can be found in the most mundane places. The following story idea, for example, comes from a cursory browse of the New South Wales Government website. At the most basic level, it is possible to use the website's own search engine to search for 'statistics'. This is a crude search, but it identifies many potentially interesting sites. Figures for crime, health, education, transport, law and many other elements of New South Wales society are provided (other states have similar sites). Included in the various links is one for the State Library (see the Website References at the end of this chapter). The link (to the library's 2010–11 statistics report) provides a number of broad measures of library use and funding, with figures provided in table and chart formats. It also provides detailed membership, use and funding figures for libraries by local authorities—information an enterprising journalist can use as the basis for a number of stories on state and local government spending. Sites such as this provide journalists with data—and hence stories—that would have been impossible to produce only a few years ago.

How, then, should journalists use computer database reporting to improve their reporting skills?

First, the term 'database journalism' presupposes that you know what a database is. For journalism purposes, an electronic database has been defined as a computer program that permits users to store large amounts of information in such a way that individual bits of information can be quickly and easily retrieved. Tom Koch defines a database as 'A single collection of articles or citations stored by one company which may or may not be the vendor' (1991, p. 241).

The definition of database journalism has undergone a seismic shift in recent years. According to one definition, it is journalism that provides data for databases, primarily the raw material for stories—information in the form of text, photos, audio or video. In this case, database journalism refers to journalists producing content *for* databases, for future publication (Holovaty 2006). This chapter, however, employs different definitions that assume a slightly different situation—in which journalists take data *from* databases to facilitate publication.

Database journalism has grown enormously in recent years. In the USA, where its techniques are practised in newsrooms around the country, observers have noted its growth since the mid-1980s. Organisations such as Investigative Reporters and Editors (IRE) number their members in the thousands and have strong links with the National Institute for Computer-Assisted Reporting (NICAR). In Europe, database journalism is a phenomenon of the mid-1990s. In Australia, it remains in its infancy.

Database journalism would seem to be one of four things:

1   searching publicly available or commercially sold online databases and various kinds of electronic bulletin boards to obtain background information on a person, topic or issue

2   the analysis of the electronic records, for the purposes of news media oversight and disclosure, of the activities of organisations such as government and neo-government agencies and business entities

3   the development of a specialised database by a news organisation itself for reporting on some specific type of story

4   providing raw material for reuse via databases. As noted above, this chapter will not address this form.

Journalists have been making good use of databases for the first purpose listed for some time and have become very adept. The second use—the analysis of electronic records—tends to occur in countries where governments have a commitment to providing access to information held on behalf of citizens. Scandinavian countries and the USA have taken this responsibility seriously. Other nations—North Korea being the most obvious example—provide little or no information to the news media. It is self-evident that access to information held on behalf of citizens is vital if the news media are to fulfil their Fourth Estate function. While most governments prefer to 'manage' the dissemination of information, the growth of the internet and the digital world has meant governments are finding it more and more difficult to manage the global explosion of information, so the second use of databases by journalists has flourished.

The third use—newspapers creating their own databases—has been limited by journalists' timidity in the use of databases and the cost of setting up and maintaining them. Certainly many newspapers have in-house databases which contain treasure troves of information, but by and large they are not easily accessible by journalists and are used mostly by advertising and marketing staff.

SOCIAL MEDIA AND DISCUSSION LISTS

As far as the first kind of use is concerned—using public or commercial online databases and bulletin boards—journalists sometimes forget that blogs, forums, chat sites, tweets and email lists contain their own databases. Most archive postings and some present them in a digest form, both of which can be searched. How useful are such sites for journalists? In the author's own experience, they can be very useful—journalists monitor forums, blogs, Twitter feeds and discussion lists for story ideas and to stay ahead of developing stories or issues (see Chapter 7). In a 2011 study, Brunswick Research found that nine out of 10 business journalists claim to have investigated an issue further as a result of information sourced from social media, and two-thirds claim to have written a story that originated via social media, giving rise to up to one in seven of all published stories. The study also found that Twitter provides the most valuable sources of information, but blogs are the most likely to be the foundation of a published article. Blogs, Twitter and 'message boards' rated highest, with 43 per cent of business journalists saying that sources in these sites had contributed to published reports; social networking sites were a distant second at 32 per cent.

Snooping around in the database archives of such sites obviously pays off for journalists.

OTHER TEXT DATABASES

While blogs, Twitter and discussion lists are quite useful for reporters, they do not provide the power of text databases. The text retrieval systems journalists use, such as news libraries or search engines, provide background information or make relationships between issues more apparent. Text databases such as these are invaluable, because they mean a journalist can be fully briefed on a subject; that a shady or unwilling source will be unable to pull the wool over their eyes; and that information that might otherwise have remained buried becomes obvious. The danger is that all databases contain some incorrect or inaccurate information. Sometimes corrections are appended to the mistakes, but at other times there are no corrections. And even when a correction is appended, it is not always obvious. As a result, journalists can be guilty of perpetuating mistakes by republishing them from database information. Additionally, studies have shown that young naïve journalists can republish the work of other people without proper acknowledgment of the original author.

Text retrieval databases are useful to journalists, particularly when they analyse them using statistical analysis techniques. Let's use the statistics report found on the State Library of New South Wales website, introduced earlier (and listed in the Website References at the end of this chapter), to illustrate how journalists can mine databases for story ideas. For example, a list of summary statistics, starting on p. xxiii, shows that for a 16-year period up to 2010–11, the proportion of the New South Wales population using the libraries fell slightly from 49 to 46 per cent. This might prompt a journalist to ask if libraries—and books—are surviving the online onslaught. The figures also show a significant drop (from 37 million to 35.8 million) in library visits in the final two years of the period. This might also prompt a journalist to ask whether the online onslaught has begun to bite (or to probe for some other cause).

But before we get to work on a specific exercise with the data, it's important to know what we are looking at. Scrolling through the site, you see some very broad measures of library use (for example: borrowers as a percentage of population, expenditure on public library services, local government expenditure per capita) until we reach, on p. xxiii, the more detailed figures.

On the following pages of the report, Table 1 (pp. 1–4) provides details of expenditure and subsidies for individual councils, which allows reporters to compare per capita spending on libraries by the various councils listed. The table also provides, in the far right column, the amount of subsidy each council received for its libraries. Because the table also provides the population figures for each of the councils, it is possible to compare the amount of subsidy per head of population by dividing the subsidy by the number of residents. An astute reporter might also want to identify the political party affiliation of the various regions to see if one party is favoured over another with subsidy funding.

Table 1a (pp. 6–9) provides data about 'voted expenditure' for the current year; that is, the amount of expenditure budgeted to be spent. This allows reporters to check the voted expenditure figure for any council in Table 1a against the actual total expenditure for the previous year in Table 1. Such a comparison provides a rough guide to actual and planned spending that should prompt reporters to ask the appropriate questions of council staff.

Table 1b (p. 9) provides a funding comparison for metropolitan, outer urban and rural regions, and Table 1c (pp. 10–11) presents the data by library service (although there is essentially little difference from the data presented in the earlier tables).

Table 1d (pp. 12–13) shows that spending on books is still by far the major element of library resource spending. It would be worthwhile here to check the percentage of overall spending on licensed access to electronic resources. Some councils (Fairfield and Pittwater, for example) seem to have made a greater commitment to electronic resources than others.

The second series of tables provides interesting data, too. Table 2 (p. 15), which simply provides raw circulation figures, is not of itself particularly illuminating. But Table 2a (pp. 16–17) shows circulation by format (books, non-books, etc.); Table 2b (pp. 18–19) shows the circulation of books by category (adult non-fiction, adult fiction, 'young adult non-fiction', etc.); Table 2c (pp. 20–3) shows the circulation of non-book materials (computer games, toys, e-books, etc.); Table 2d (pp. 24–5) shows how collections (family histories, community languages, etc.) have circulated, and so on through the various series of tables. The Table 3 series (pp. 28–42) provides data on stock holdings, and Tables 4 and 4a (pp. 43–6) provide information about registered users of libraries. Other tables provide information about the number of service points available to residents, the opening hours of individual libraries, and the number of full-time and part-time staff. The Table 16 series (pp. 73–6) provide data on circulation per capita and circulation per staff member, while Table 17a (p. 78) provides data on population per staff member.

Clearly the entire data set provides a goldmine of information that could keep an enterprising journalist busy for a long time writing a series of articles on public library use and funding in New South Wales.

The website presents the data in PDF format; we need to change that so we can work with it and the best way to do this is to save the PDF file and use software such as Acrobat Pro V.10 to convert it to (say) Excel format. You may have to convert to Word first, then to Excel.

Table 10.1 of this book reproduces the first few lines of Table 1 of the report, with the addition of identifying the columns by letters. Let's proceed on the basis that this table has been converted into Excel.

A journalist might well want to know which councils receive the most or least funds in subsidies or grants (the figure in Column J). An easy way to see the relative values would be to re-order this column from highest to lowest. To do this, highlight the data set, starting from the term 'URM' in Column A and ending with the last figure in Column J. Then open the Data Menu by clicking on the word 'Data' at the top of the page. Among the options, you'll see a 'Sort A–Z, Z–A' entry. Click on this and, in the dialog box that opens, click on 'Sort By' and choose Column I. Then click on 'Order' and choose 'Largest to Smallest'. Click 'OK'. The order of entries has now changed: Table 10.2.

We can now see that Blacktown has by far the biggest subsidy ($739 319), substantially larger than the second-placed council, Fairfield (with $479 998). In this case, a glance down the 'Population' column (D) and the 'Subsidy' column (J) shows that the funding is generally in line with the size of the population served: Fairfield, which has a population 63 per cent the size of Blacktown's, received a subsidy 65 per cent of Blacktown's.

However, a quick check of the full data set (not reproduced here) reveals there are some anomalies. Clarence Valley, for example, has a population just 17 per cent the size of Blacktown's, but receives a subsidy 27 per cent the size of Blacktown's. Other council areas have similar anomalies, all of which may well be explained by some special circumstances, but the data itself provides sufficient reason for a reporter to seek explanations. You could create a new Column K to do these calculations using Excel formulas. For example, in cell K4, type '=d12/d6*100' to get the percentage figure for Clarence Valley/Blacktown; and in a new Column L type '=j12/j6*100' to get the subsidy percentage. In this case, however, it would be simpler to use a calculator.

Using a similar process with the other tables, it is possible to discover which categories of books are most popular (Table 2b); the areas where computer games are more/less popular than traditional games (Table 2c); and which councils have the highest/lowest rates of circulation per capita (Table 2e). Where per capita figures would be useful but are not supplied—as for example in Tables 4 and 4a—it is possible to copy and paste the 'Population' column from Column D of Table 1 and then to calculate the per capita figure using a formula similar to those above.

The growth and spread of digital technology means that in developed countries, information and raw data are much more accessible than they were a mere decade ago—and the accessibility improves year by year because governments, even if they would prefer not to release potentially embarrassing information, are unable to quarantine it effectively. In many countries, for example, election results are accessible on the internet, so it is possible for journalists to compare detailed electorate-by-electorate results with census data, in order to link voting patterns and geographic location with age, income, religion, race, and education levels.

Reporters who want to play with more sophisticated tools could, for example, import the Excel spreadsheets used above into a relational database such as Access. Relational databases allow users to use data from separate worksheets, provided each worksheet has at least one common field (column). For example, in the library exercise above, Access would enable a reporter to use the 'Population' figures from Table 1 with almost any of the other tables because they all contain the council names—a common field. Access allows users to import data from Excel; but a word of warning—where the data has originally been converted from PDF format, considerable care should be taken in the cleaning process (that is, ensuring data is presented in appropriate format and units; deleting confusing blank columns; and merging or unmerging cells where necessary).

TABLE 10.1: SECTION OF TABLE 1 OF THE DATA SET

TABLE 1—EXPENDITURE AND SUBSIDY

Councils are grouped into categories according to the Australian Classification of Local Government

[COLUMN A] ACLG ABREV.	[COLUMN B]	[COLUMN C] LIBRARY SERVICE BEGAN	[COLUMN D] POPULATION 2010	[COLUMN E] OPERATING EXPENDITURE $	[COLUMN F] PER CAPITA $	[COLUMN G] CAPITAL EXPENDITURE $	[COLUMN H] TOTAL EXPENDITURE JUL 10 – JUN 11 $	[COLUMN I] PER CAPITA $	[COLUMN J] SUBSIDY AND LOCAL PRIORITY GRANT 2010/2011 $
URM	Albury	1945	51 112	2 724 281.00	53.30	181 557.00	2 905 838.00	56.85	133 162
URS	Armidale Dumaresq	1949	25 855	1 017 050.09	39.34	212 664.34	1 229 714.43	47.56	85 353
UDM	Ashfield	1964	42 787	1 901 138.00	44.43	376 488.00	2 277 626.00	53.23	111 660
UDL	Auburn	1961	78 597	3 153 918.00	40.13	255 841.00	3 409 759.00	43.38	198 706

TABLE 10.2: DATA SORTED BY THE FINAL COLUMN ('SUBSIDY AND LOCAL PRIORITY GRANT 2010/2011')

TABLE 1—EXPENDITURE AND SUBSIDY

Councils are grouped into categories according to the Australian Classification of Local Government

ACLG ABREV.		LIBRARY SERVICE BEGAN	POPULATION 2010	OPERATING EXPENDITURE $	PER CAPITA $	CAPITAL EXPENDITURE $	TOTAL EXPENDITURE JUL 10 – JUN 11 $	PER CAPITA $	SUBSIDY AND LOCAL PRIORITY GRANT 2010/2011 $
UDV	Blacktown	1967	307 816	8 659 615.00	28.13	988 866.00	9 648 481.00	31.34	739 319
UDV	Fairfield	1950	196 567	6 638 368.65	33.77	589 202.10	7 227 570.75	36.77	479 998
UDV	Bankstown	1946	188 814	7 425 016.00	39.32	540 536.00	7 965 552.00	42.19	453 926
UFV	Campbelltown	1965	153 222	5 318 039.06	34.71	469 735.77	5 787 774.83	37.77	371 473

TEXT ANALYSIS TOOLS

Spreadsheets and relational databases provide ways of representing relationships via numbers, but there are alternative approaches. Software packages such as Nvivo and Leximancer let us look at relationships contained in words, pictures and sounds, for example. Both are especially useful when journalists want to examine large tracts of, say, text to reveal relationships or to highlight concepts. Academics use both packages largely for content analysis (see the example below on vulnerability), but they are equally useful for journalists who want to examine (for example) large tracts of text in government documents.

Nvivo requires you to makes some decisions about the kind of information you are looking for and to create categories ('nodes') within which Nvivo will contain that information. Leximancer, on the other hand, inspects the text you are examining and produces categories itself. Which has the greater utility? It really depends on the kind of work you want to do and how much you know about the data before you start. The value of Nvivo is that it makes you think carefully about how to categorise data and therefore how you describe it in your reporting. The value of Leximancer is that you don't have to know beforehand how you want to categorise your data—Leximancer will suggest ways of doing it. Both approaches have their strengths and weaknesses, depending on your purpose. In the example below, both are used to provide a more complete overview of the issue being researched.

EXAMPLE: VULNERABILITY

In the following example, Nvivo is used to examine what members of focus groups say about newspaper depictions of people who are deemed 'vulnerable' because of a perceived inability to influence how the news media deal with them. The example is taken from an Australian Research Council-funded project, 'Vulnerability and the News Media', undertaken by a team from five universities (Pearson et al. 2011).

Focus group members were drawn from organisations representing people with physical and/ or mental disabilities, the physical and mentally traumatised, and ethnic and Indigenous minorities. Content analysis of major Australian newspapers had shown that such issues had in general been dealt with fairly and ethically; the focus group responses were designed to reveal whether the perceptions of group members supported that finding.

The researchers created nine categories or 'parent nodes' to describe the kinds of comments about the media that emanated from the focus groups. One of those nodes was 'vulnerability', and within it researchers discerned 11 other 'child nodes' or sub-categories. Nvivo put such references together and provided the following information for the vulnerability node:

1   Vulnerability All Nodes (11 child nodes; 66 references; 6 sources)

　　A sense of powerlessness (21 references; 5 sources)

　　Consent (6 references; 4 sources)

　　Cool and not cool (1 reference; 1 source)

　　Experience helps (4 references; 1 source)

　　Feeling distressed (15 references; 3 sources)

　　Getting information (1 reference; 1 source)

　　Identification (5 references; 3 sources)

　　Lack of trust (3 references; 2 sources)

　　Lucky (1 reference; 1 source)

　　Privacy (4 references; 2 sources)

　　Using humour (5 references; 2 sources)

Nvivo inspected all nine parent nodes and found 66 references to vulnerability, which it categorised into 11 child nodes. Of the 66 references, almost a third (21) related to a 'sense of powerlessness', allied to a quarter (15 references) of respondents' 'feelings of distress'. (The 'powerlessness' related to respondents' inability to influence the way they were portrayed in the news media.)

In the 'sense of powerlessness' child node, Nvivo recorded focus group comments such as the following, to illustrate the issues the child node dealt with:

<Internals\\VRG_Mental_Illness_Focus_Group>—§ 12 references coded [6.33% Coverage]

Reference 1—0.19% Coverage

Person 14 = And it's the most vulnerable that get attacked, when you can't speak up for yourself, that's when you'll find that you're prey to print media.

Reference 2—0.09% Coverage

Person 4 = Not everybody has that power, or that influence you know.

The information above shows that 12 of the 21 references to 'powerlessness' came from the Mental Illness Focus Group, and that those 12 references represented 6.33 per cent of all references recorded in the study overall. The first two of those 12 references are reproduced here to give some idea of the kind of information that is available to anyone who wants to investigate these issues; their percentage figures merely indicate how much of the overall body of references they represent and shouldn't be used to gauge how important the reference itself is—that is a judgment call by the investigator. Clearly, though, investigators will want to probe more deeply into issues of powerlessness and feelings of distress, and ask how these are related to content analyses that seem to show published articles are balanced and fair. Such disparity focuses attention on journalists' interactions with sources—their professional practices—as much as on what is published, and allows investigators to see new directions of discovery.

This investigation also involved the use of Leximancer to cross-reference researchers' perceptions of the important issues with a view less subject to the vagaries of human perception. Leximancer identified the main themes by data mining the text and producing from the transcript of the Mental Illness Focus Group a concept map that shows major relationships.

The main topic of discussion for this focus group was 'people'. This was strongly related to newspapers, with the relationship shown through the colours of the circles (not shown here) and their proximity. Other important themes involved the 'media' and its level of research into mental illness (and hence perceptions of journalists' level of understanding) and references to 'schizophrenia'. Interestingly, issues involving references to 'craziness' and the use of photos were more peripheral, which might well support the content analyses showing newspaper reportage of these issues to be reasonable.

Additionally, Leximancer can display the information in terms of how strongly the themes are connected to the interests of the Mental Illness Focus Group: see Table 10.3.

TABLE 10.3: MENTAL ILLNESS FOCUS GROUP THEMES

THEME	CONNECTIVITY
People	100%
Media	93%
Story	59%

THEME	CONNECTIVITY
Paper	56%
Time	44%
Different	39%
Community	39%
Talking	37%
Name	15%
Article	12%
Disability	9%

This example has been taken from an academic study of the news media, but the process could just as easily have been used by journalists who want to dig deeper into, say, government documents, and who want to better understand the issues those documents address to reveal any relationships they might contain.

GIS SOFTWARE

Journalists also should consider the use of GIS software. As mentioned earlier, GIS stands for geographic information systems. It covers a wide range of applications, but in most cases it involves the combination of maps and data. Data that is specific to a particular geographic area can be represented on a map to identify 'hotspots' of activity or information or, conversely, areas where no activity is occurring or has ceased (see the case study at the end of this chapter).

The following example comes from a research project designed to reveal the impact and potential for economic growth the creative industries have on the Australian city of Darwin, but it could just as easily be used to reveal news agenda issues in any community. The researchers, in this instance, said:

> In our Creative Tropical City project, we mapped these networks according to responses by creative workers about their activities. We recorded the places where inputs, materials and support services were sourced, as well as specific details about where, beyond Darwin, people had clients, sold their works, travelled to network with similar people, or held social relationships with people within their industry. These results indicate how well-networked Darwin is internally, and further afield. Results show that Darwin's creative industries are strongly embedded in the city economy. Sixty-eight percent of all supplier relationships for creative workers occurred within the Darwin metropolitan area. Indeed, creative industries are probably more embedded—and thus create even stronger local multipliers—in Darwin than the same industries in other cities (Lea et al. 2009, p. 24).

Among other things, the researchers combined Australian Bureau of Statistics (ABS) data, data provided by industry partners and 98 one-on-one interviews, including a visual mapping exercise, with those who work in creative industries. The researchers, who used ArcGIS software, were especially interested in defining where creative industries activity occurred in the city. They said:

> Recognising the importance of space to creativity, this project undertook a mapping exercise in order to understand the internal dynamics of creativity within Darwin's urban and suburban matrix. Our results show patterns of employment, 'hidden' creativity and iconic 'hubs' of creativity which planning ought to recognise and be sympathetic towards (Lea et al. 2009, p. 24).

Figure 10.1 is just one of the many maps produced showing where creative industries activity occurs in the city. This information is then combined with further data to show how much the city's creative industries rely on each other, on outside suppliers and influences, and how much they contribute to the city's economy and wellbeing.

FIGURE 10.1: CREATIVE INDUSTRIES MAP

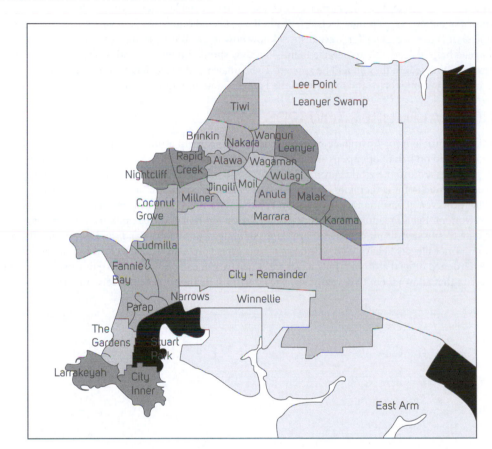

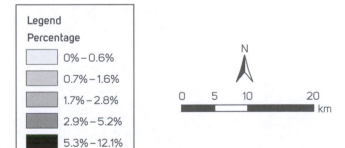

Source: Lea et al. 2009, p. 24

The ArcGIS software used in this instance is an expensive tool, but a number of similar tools based on open-source software are available free or cheaply.

OTHER SOFTWARE AIDS

A number of other, sophisticated software packages exist that are widely used by academics, but hardly, if ever, by journalists—but they should be! Programs such as SPSS and SAS are designed to look at relationships between and among numerical data, and are invaluable when trying to determine how one course of action (say, a policy decision) might have affected outcomes for a variety of citizen groups (variables). It is not necessary for journalists to know how to use these programs themselves—they can always get a helpful academic to operate them—but they should know how and where such programs can be useful and where they should be applied. To be unaware of these details is to miss out on potentially important stories and to perform the Fourth Estate function poorly.

OFFICIAL ATTITUDES TOWARDS DATA

A continuing problem for Australian journalists lies in government attitudes towards the ownership of data collected on behalf of citizens and held in government databases. As mentioned earlier, in many countries around the world, governments recognise they hold data on behalf of their citizens, and access to much of it is therefore available to reporters for publication on behalf of citizens. In Australia, however, governments take the approach that data collected by the government belongs to the government. Even Freedom of Information legislation has failed to free up journalistic access to public data to any significant degree. Commissions of inquiry in Australia and the UK into unethical (and sometimes illegal) behaviour by the news media, especially with regard to invasion of privacy, tend to have hardened official attitudes. Journalists must behave ethically if they are to enjoy useful access to official data that allows them to develop fully the Fourth Estate function of the news media.

CONCLUSION

1   Australian governments—federal, state and local—are not committed to providing data sets for journalistic inspection. By their reluctance to release information, they reveal that they are philosophically disposed to believe the information belongs to governments and not to citizens— and certainly not to the mass media claiming to represent freedom of information on behalf of citizens. Journalists, however, can work towards a change of attitude by demonstrating good database techniques that identify and clarify issues for audiences and hence contribute to the public good.

QUESTIONS TO CONSIDER

1   What lessons are to be learned from *The Guardian's* crowdsourcing experiment discussed above? How do these lessons relate to those discussed in Chapter 3?

2   To what extent has the development of social media sites and other tools changed the way journalists obtain data?

3   What is the link between data retrieval (identified in this chapter) and statistical analysis (discussed in Chapter 8)?

4   To what extent do you believe programs such as Leximancer and Nvivo have the capacity to change the way journalists undertake large-scale research projects?

5   In what ways do Australian governments limit the capacity of journalists to access large data sets that might be turned into stories?

TASK

1   Write a story (500–1000 words) based on your interpretation of the State Library of New South Wales material provided in this chapter. Can you reach other conclusions the author of this chapter has not identified?

REFERENCES

Brunswick Research. 2011. *Use of Social Media among Business Journalists*: www.brunswickgroup.com/Libraries/Reports/Social_Media_-_among_busmedia_web_version_zls_3.sflb.ashx (accessed 25 May 2012).

The Guardian. 2009. 'MPs' Expenses: What You've Told Us. So Far': www.guardian.co.uk/news/datablog/2009/sep/18/mps-expenses-westminster-data-house-of-commons (accessed 23 May 2012).

Holovaty, A. 2006. *A Fundamental Way Newspaper Sites Need to Change*: www.holovaty.com/writing/fundamental-change (accessed 1 June 2012).

Koch, T. 1991. *Journalism in the 21st Century: Online Information, Electronic Databases and the News*, London: Adamantine Press.

Lea, T., Luckman, S., Gibson, C., Fitzpatrick, D., Brennan-Horley, C., Willoughby-Smith, J., & Hughes, K. 2009. *Creative Tropical City: Mapping Darwin's Creative Industries*, Sydney: CAMRA: http://camra.culturemap.org.au/sites/all/files/CreativeTropicalCityreport.pdf (accessed 1 June 2012).

WEBSITE REFERENCES

State Library of New South Wales: Public Library Services: www.sl.nsw.gov.au/services/public_libraries/statistics/docs/2010_11statistics.pdf/.

FURTHER READING

DeFleur, M.H. 1997. *Computer-Assisted Investigative Reporting: Development and Methodology*, Mahwah, New Jersey: Lawrence Erlbaum Associates.

Garrison, B. 1995. *Computer-Assisted Reporting*, Hillsdale: Lawrence Erlbaum Associates.

Houston, B. 1999. *Computer-Assisted Reporting: A Practical Guide*, 2nd edn, Boston: Bedford/St Martin's.

Loosen, W. 2002. 'The Second-Level Digital Divide of the Web, and Its Impact on Journalism', *First Monday*, vol. 7, no. 8, 5 August: http://firstmonday.org/htbin/cgiwrap/bin/ojs/index.php/fm/article/view/977/898 (accessed 24 May 2012).

Miller, T. 1988. 'The Data-base Revolution', *Columbia Journalism Review*, 27(3), pp. 35–8.

Pearson, M., Green, K., Tanner, S., Meadows, M., Romano, A., Skehan, J. & McMahon, C. 2011. 'Vulnerability and the News Media: Investigating Print Media Coverage of Groups Deemed to be Vulnerable in Australian Society and the Media's Understanding of Their Status': www.dbcde.gov.au/__data/assets/pdf_file/0005/142934/ARC_Linkage_Grant_LP0989758_Vulnerability_and_the_News_Media_Research_Project.pdf/.

CASE STUDY

THE SIN INDEX

Fiona Hudson, *Herald Sun*

Glancing at the spreadsheet, you'd hardly guess a dynamic tale of lust, envy, wrath and greed was set to spring from the thousands of cells. It took a couple of weeks to collect and wrangle the data into the tidy rows and columns that would ultimately form the Melbourne Sin Index.

The concept was simple: to capture a snapshot of vice and virtue across Victoria in a fun, interactive way. The index would rank suburbs based on the seven sins and their opposing virtues: pride and humility; greed and charity; envy and kindness; wrath and patience; lust and chastity; gluttony and temperance; and sloth and diligence. The idea was sparked by a similar 'vice maps' developed in the United States, which usually rely on a single measure for each sin, such as violent crime rates for wrath, or chlamydia infections for lust.

We wanted to use three measures per vice, to more accurately rank our wicked ways. That meant sourcing 21 separate data sets, including luxury car ownership, house prices, murders, teen sex rates, love of shopping, use of credit, takeaway consumption, church attendance, volunteerism, and support for charities.

For each sin we sourced a 'serious' measure, a 'fun' measure and an indicator of the opposing virtue. To rank gluttony, for example, we collected figures on:

1   The percentage of people considered overweight or obese in the state government's most recent Victorian Population Health Survey;
2   The percentage of adults who said they like alcoholic drinks 'strong' in a special Roy Morgan survey;
3   The percentage of parents who said they give their children 'as few sweets as possible', also Roy Morgan data.

Most of the figures we used were easily available from public websites such as the ABS, the Victorian health and transport departments, and Victoria Police. It is astonishing how much you can find online if you dig a little. Advanced Google search options make it easy to hunt down data in Excel files or other easy-to-use formats. You can also use one of the many online tutorials to learn basic web 'scraping' skills so you can turn unstructured data into useable formats.

But what if you can't find what you're after? Some of the 'sins' data, such as the brothel-licensing statistics and the Roy Morgan surveys, was prepared especially for the *Herald Sun*. Many agencies are willing to provide unique spreadsheets of information for journalists if asked. As a last resort, we sometimes even use Freedom of Information laws to extract the data sets. For example, a few years back I asked the city council for a database of every ticket issued in a given year so we could map when and where people are most often booked in the CBD. The main downside is the FOI process can take months, so try to negotiate with the agency first.

Because we sourced the 'sins' data from so many different places, it was all in different formats. Some information was collated by postcode, some by local government area, some by police statistical area, and other sets by special geographical zones. Some were raw figures, others were percentages, and one set was an index. Usually I'm a big fan of DIY data projects. I've found in most cases you can either figure things out yourself, or perhaps call on some help from the accounts or IT department to get by. But the complexities of the Sin Index meant self-taught statistics and Excel skills weren't going to be enough, so we partnered with RMIT University. Statisticians Anthony Bedford and Adrian Schembri did the bulk of the data wrangling, transforming all the raw data sets into a statistically valid index that ranked each local government area on each of the 21 individual measures, by each of the seven sins, and overall. Of course, with so many different sets of numbers from so many different sources, there was always a chance of an error creeping in. We triple-checked everything, and at the last minute discovered a glitch which, undiscovered, would have thrown the whole index out of whack. It was a strong reminder of the need for absolute caution and accuracy, especially if you're merging data sets.

Ultimately, we arrived at a spreadsheet showing the final 'sin rankings'. It was still just a mass of numbers though. We needed to sift through, find the best angles, and tell the story in an engaging and compelling way in print and online. We briefly considered using free public tools such as Tableau Public or Google maps, which are quite easy to learn if you take the time to watch the online tutorials. We've used them extensively. Major projects have included a 'Dodgy Dining' map depicting the location of restaurants and cafes convicted of food hygiene breaches, and a 'How Safe Are Our Skies?' interactive showing every reported air safety incident over Victoria. (It's worth noting these simple tools are also useful in the early stages of journalistic research, to help you visualise data and identify trends or outliers that warrant further investigation.) The sheer volume of data underpinning the Sin Index—31 local government areas and 21 measures for each—was a tough ask to display cleanly using open-source tools. No matter how we tinkered, the information was overwhelming.

That's where data visualisation specialists Flink Labs came in. Founder Ben Hosken brainstormed various ways we could present our findings. Despite the rigour we applied to sourcing and analysing the numbers, the Sin Index was very much intended as a fun, 'talk-about' piece to get people thinking about our community. We wanted to find a way readers could explore and interact with the data, and at the same time be entertained and amused. Flink Labs delivered several concept sketches, each a slightly different take on how users might digest the data. Ultimately we decided on an interactive map with bubbles that distorted and moved to show the spread of sin. We also ran accompanying tables online which broke down every measure in some detail. The provision of these extra tables was vital as it allowed readers to drill down and find the information most relevant to them. The first question most people who look at the interactive usually ask is 'where's my suburb?' Everyone wants to know how their area performed, and how it compares to those around them. In the print version of the Sin Index, we had room only to run the 'top five' and 'bottom five' areas for each sin, and an overall saints and sinners table. Online, though, the picture was far more complete. Users were able to see the dynamics of sin shifting between suburbs, and to view the underlying data and rankings for each of the 21 measures.

All of our hi-tech efforts were polished off with some good old-fashioned foot-slogging to flesh out the package. We hit the streets to quiz Greater Dandenong residents on why they 'dress to impress', to ask Stonnington folk about their obsession with luxury cars, and to probe Brimbank dwellers on their low levels of physical activity. Because no matter how you crunch the numbers—or how well you display them—people, not spreadsheets, are the real storytellers.

11

Interpreting Financial Documents

STEPHEN TANNER AND NICK RICHARDSON

INTRODUCTION

While some people may prefer to ignore what governments and business do, the reality—as reflected in the amount of media coverage they receive—is that decisions made in parliamentary chambers and corporate boardrooms within Australia and around the world impact on us. Governments make decisions to expend money on infrastructure projects of varying scales—from re-equipping our armed forces to improve our defence capabilities; to ensuring that health and education standards are maintained, that road and rail networks are sufficient to move people around the country, and that older Australians have sufficient money in their superannuation funds to live on when they retire. To fund these projects—and everything else associated with running the complex structures that make up governments—they are required to raise money. This they do via taxes and charges. Some of these are directed at companies, while others are levied against individuals. We'll look at how governments raise and justify their income and expenditure in the second half of this chapter.

THE BUSINESS SECTOR

Before we do, however, it is important to look at the 'engine room' of the Australian economy: the corporate (private) sector. More people are employed in the private sector than in the government sector. According to the Australian Bureau of Statistics (ABS), there were 1.896 million people employed by government—federal, state and local—across Australia in June 2011, and 11.5 million across all sectors (government and private) in September 2012. Assuming there have been no major increases or decreases in the former, this suggests that the private sector employs approximately 9.6 million Australians (84 per cent).

When we talk about the corporate sector, we are referring to two different categories of business— public and private. The public companies are listed on the Australian Stock Exchange (ASX), while the private companies are unlisted; that is, they are privately controlled (by individuals, families, or partnerships). It is difficult for journalists to investigate private companies because the information about them is tightly controlled and they are not subject to the reporting requirements that apply to listed companies. It is the latter group of entities that we're interested in for the purposes of this chapter, primarily because anyone can invest in them (and many Australians do, either actively as share traders and investors, or passively through their superannuation schemes).

THE AUSTRALIAN SHARE MARKET

In September 2012, there were 2192 companies listed on the ASX, with a combined capitalisation (monetary value) of $1.2 trillion. This figure increases and decreases on a daily basis depending on share price movements. At the time of writing it had fallen significantly from previous highs because of uncertainty over the strength of the European and US economies. This uncertainty was reflected in the fall in the share price of both individual companies, and various industry sectors and indices (a discussion we return to later in this chapter).

There are a number of reasons why companies list on the stock market, rather than remain in private hands. These include: the ability to access additional sources of funding to help expand their operations; increasing their profile; improved valuations; providing a secondary market for shares in the company; allowing early investors—often those who established the company—an exit strategy, or the capacity to reduce their exposure to the company; and aligning employee–management interests through the issuing of readily tradable shares (see the ASX website). Listings occur through what is called an Initial Public Offering (IPO). Sometimes investors will initially flood into a company, as was the case with Google and, more recently, Facebook, when they listed on the US share market. But not all IPOs can produce a bonanza for investors, as the Facebook listing showed. Its share price fell quickly after it was revealed that the company's financial forecasts weren't as strong as promised in the IPO documents.

The number of IPOs (and their success) tends to be linked to market sentiment. When the market is buoyant, the number of IPOs increases, as investors are more willing to risk their money on speculative ventures. However, when the market is in the doldrums, as it was for much of 2011 and 2012, the number of IPOs decreases.

Companies that list on the share market are given a three-letter code that may or may not reflect the name of the company. Rio Tinto's code, for example, is 'RIO', whereas Tatts Group bears the code 'TTS'. Listed companies are also categorised under the Global Industry Classification Standard (GICS). Devised by the rating agency Standard and Poors and by Morgan Stanley Capital International, the sectors are: Australian Real Estate Investment Trusts (A-REIT), Consumer Discretionary, Consumer Staples, Energy, Financials, Financials Excluding A-REITS, Gold Sub-Industry, Health Care, Industrials, Information Technology, Materials, Metals and Mining, Telecommunication Services and Utilities (for definitions of these sectors, see the ASX website).

The sectors also form a number of indices, which are based on various factors including capitalisation and GICS classification. Most people are familiar with the Standard & Poor's (S&P) ASX 200 and S&P ASX 300 indices. Likewise, they would be familiar with the All Ordinaries Index (All Ords), which is made up of the 500 largest companies on the share market; but there are also others, including the S&P ASX 20 and the S&P ASX 50. These are made up of the top 20 and top 50 companies by market capitalisation. Other indices include the S&P ASX Small Ordinaries Index, and the S&P ASX All Australian 50 and All Australian 200 indices. There is even an Emerging Companies Index. Membership of these indices is reassessed regularly, with companies entering and departing according to changes in their fortunes as measured by market capitalisation, liquidity and investability.

Companies listed on the stock market are subject to a number of reporting requirements. There are accounting guidelines which they have to adhere to under legislation, as well as corporate obligations, including the requirement that they submit company reports on both an interim and annual basis. As Kaidonis discusses in her case study at the end of Chapter 22, the information companies provide in these reports can often provide journalists with interesting stories.

In Australia, companies are regulated by a number of bodies, including:

Australian Securities and Investments Commission (ASIC)

Australian Competition and Consumer Commission (ACCC)

Australian Prudential Regulation Authority (APRA)

Australian Taxation Office (ATO).

Companies' decisions are also influenced by the decisions of government and semi-government bodies, including the Reserve Bank of Australia (RBA) which is tasked with setting monetary policy, for example the setting of official interest rates which impacts on the cost of doing business.

Each of the bodies identified above have websites which can provide journalists with great sources of information, particularly ASIC and the ACCC. For example, ASIC has databases that enable journalists to access information about company directors, banned financial and investment advisers, and even companies that that have been required to commit to an enforceable undertaking (see also Chapter 5). The ACCC website has information about consumer scams, consumer rights and other material that helps journalists track the behaviour of errant companies.

TRACKING THE BEHAVIOUR OF COMPANIES

Historically, it was difficult for journalists to track the behaviour of companies. They would have to rely on a paper trail (see Chapter 6 for traditional research strategies), which was often limited to annual reports, media reports, or correspondence between aggrieved parties. Today, however, it is easy for journalists to find information about individual companies via the internet. For example, the majority of companies have their own websites, which provide a great deal of information about the company (both promotional and financial).

For example, the website of Australia's largest company, BHP Billiton, is given at the end of this chapter. The homepage contains a number of links that take the reader to a range of information, including company history, investor updates and sections on BHP's global operations and sustainability. The investor and media section also contains copies of the annual and interim reports, plus exploration, development and production reports, as well as other presentations that provide journalists, analysts and investors with information that helps explain the company's performance and even its future potential.

Obviously the usefulness of this material will depend on the type of story you are researching. If you are writing a story about changes in a company's share price relative to its peers over a 10-year period, then the information will be relatively easy to unearth. While it might not be available on individual company websites, it will certainly be available via one of the online share trading providers (for example Commsec and ETrade) or via the ASX site. However, if you are looking for changes in a company's environmental policies over time, then you will need to comb through a series of annual reports, media releases, media briefings and even media stories dating back some years. This material is more likely to be accessible via the company's website than it will be from the trading platforms, which tend to provide documents over a shorter timeframe.

Sometimes the answers you are seeking are not written down in a publicly accessible form. If that is the case, you can always contact the company's media spokesperson, or if that produces a blank, arrange to have the question (or series of questions) asked from the floor at the AGM. If you are a shareholder, you can attend the AGM and ask questions; if you're not, you could always ask a shareholder to do so on your behalf.

Some of this is not particularly useful, although if you know where to look, or what questions to ask of whom, you might come up with an interesting story.

However, this is not the only source of information about BHP—or other companies for that matter. Journalists looking to research a particular company should go beyond the company's website to look at other sources of information. This can include websites such as the ASX, or one of the online share trading providers. It is also worth investigating the Australian Shareholders Association website, or join one of the many web-based investor forums, where information is freely traded. You may also seek to build a relationship with some of the analysts who cover particular companies or GICS sectors.

Finally, if you have your suspicions about a company, don't forget to return to the ASIC and ACCC sites; or if you are investigating a company that has been delisted (meaning it has been removed from the share market), have a look at the Delisted Australia website. This provides an excellent repository of information about companies that have been suspended, placed in administration, receivership or liquidation, delisted or deregistered, including media releases and copies of letters from administrators, liquidators, etc.

Commsec, ETrade and the ASX provide a wealth of information, including copies of company reports, media releases, and 'please explain' letters from the ASX to the company when share prices shift unexpectedly up or down by more than a reasonable amount. They also provide a snapshot of the company's financial health, share price movements (both historical and immediate, although ASX data is delayed by 20 minutes), earnings and dividends.

While few journalists have accounting, economics or finance backgrounds, it is nonetheless useful to have some insight into how financial statements are structured.

All annual reports (whether for a company, sporting club or community group) are required to contain the following information: a report from the chairman/president; a report from the directors/committee; a declaration by the directors/committee; a report by the independent auditor; a statement of financial performance (also known as the profit and loss statement); a statement summarising the company/organisation's financial position (also known as the balance sheet); a statement of cash flows; notes to and forming part of the financial report; and supplementary information (Hoiberg 2002).

Journalists researching financial stories should understand a range of terms that will appear in an annual or interim report. These include EBITDA (earnings before interest, tax, depreciation and amortisation), EBIT (earnings before interest and tax), ROA (return on assets), ROE (return on equity), debt to equity ratio, gearing, shareholders' equity, and cash flow. To understand these terms, you also need to be familiar with a host of others. For example, what is the difference between assets and liabilities? What is the difference between current and non-current assets and liabilities, or tangible and intangible assets and liabilities? What are depreciation and amortisation? What are operating profits and losses? What are abnormal and extraordinary items? What are dividends and retained earnings? For the sake of space, we're not going to define these terms, preferring to direct you to one of a multitude of websites that provide excellent definitions of these and a whole host of other terms you may come across when writing stories that involve an analysis of a company's financial affairs (see, for example, the glossary of terms provided on the ASX website).

When considering a company report, it is important to look for warning signs that suggest the company or organisation is struggling, or is trying to cover something up. For example, when looking at the statement of financial performance (profit and loss statement), you should look at a number of key features, including:

Sales revenue: Is it up or down compared with the corresponding period? How does it compare historically (say, over five or 10 years)?

Operating profit: This is a key indicator of a company's health and should increase year on year as sales grow or efficiencies of scale are achieved. Is it up or down? Are there unusual circumstances that may have impacted on the company's operating profit, for example, the impact of increased online sales by e-businesses on traditional bricks-and-mortar companies (such as Harvey Norman, JB HiFi and Myer); increased costs associated with the launch of new products; improvements achieved through economies of scale associated with head office cuts; or investments in new equipment?

Abnormal items: These can include costs associated with a rationalisation or restructuring; for example, retrenchments.

Extraordinary items: These include large non-recurring items from transactions that are not part of the company's normal activities, or events outside of its control, such as a loss suffered when a storm damages a factory, causing a slow down in production.

STATEMENT OF FINANCIAL POSITION (BALANCE SHEET)

The statement of financial position lists the company's assets and liabilities at a given date. As such, it is nothing more than a snapshot of a company's financial position, and if any significant change occurs between reporting periods, then the company must advise the market. In Australia, balance sheets are generally prepared as at 30 June (the end of the financial year), although if the entity is a subsidiary of a US company, the reporting date can be 31 December.

As its name suggests, the balance sheet must balance; that is, the total assets (what the entity owns) minus its total liabilities (what it owes) must always equal the shareholders' equity (also known as net assets). This is often expressed as a formula: total assets – total liabilities = net assets.

If a company is vulnerable, this will generally be evident in its liabilities. Current liabilities include debts and other obligations that the company expects to settle inside 12 months, for example accounts payable (money owed to other suppliers for goods and services received), borrowings (short-term loans and overdrafts), and provisions (employee entitlements, taxation and dividend payments). Companies will also make provision in current liabilities for a decrease in an asset's value (for example, in 2012 Fairfax depreciated the value of its mastheads), and provide an estimate of doubtful debts. In the lead-up to the Global Financial Crisis (GFC) a number of companies struck trouble when they arranged short-term loans to purchase long-term assets, such as new companies or factories. When the market crashed, the value of these assets declined, and the companies involved could not meet their obligations to the financiers, causing them to default on the loans.

As journalists, it is important to understand the purpose of a company's borrowings. How much money has the company borrowed? What was the purpose of the loan? What are the terms of the loan (the life of the loan in years and the interest rate at which the money was borrowed)? What is the likelihood of the company being able to renegotiate the loan if the economy contracts? Does the company have the asset backing, credit rating and cash flow to convince the lenders that it can service the loan in the event of a downturn? (In the event of a downturn, banks will look far more favourably on long-term commitments than short-term borrowings if they believe a company is strong enough to service its loans without causing too much stress to its day-to-day operations.)

In considering the health of a company, analysts will look at its gearing levels and debt-to-equity ratio. Gearing is the level of debt a company carries relative to its equity. The debt is normally expressed as a percentage of the equity. While there is no magic figure that analysts rely on (gearing levels vary according to the sector the company is operating in), a gearing level of 30 per cent is considered modest, while anything approximating 75 per cent is viewed as problematic, and levels in excess of 100 per cent are dangerous. The debt-to-equity ratio measures the relationship between net external borrowings incurring interest and funds provided by shareholders. The Australian Shareholders Association considers a ratio of 0.5:1 as conservative, while a ratio of 1:1 is viewed as high.

One of the key measures analysts rely on when assessing the health of a company is the level of shareholders' equity. This figure is achieved by deducting total liabilities from total assets. This is not the same as a company's 'going-concern value', which is the amount likely to be received if a company is sold. The going-concern value will be influenced by a range of factors including the profitability of the company, its debt levels, the market sector within which it is operating, forecasts about its future earnings, the state of the domestic and international economy, and whether it is a forced sale or not. A good indicator of the going-concern value of a company is obtained by multiplying the prevailing price of a single share in the company by the number of shares on issue. If the share price of a company is spiralling downwards, this suggests that investors are wary about its prospects. However, if the economy is strong and/or the company is operating in a sector with strong potential, then prospective purchasers may be prepared to pay a premium to buy in (this was the case during the first years of the twenty-first century, when investors wanted to buy into Australia's iron ore story, or in the early 1990s when they bought the IT story—before that particular bubble burst, leaving many investors with shares that were worthless). Shareholders' equity is reflected various ways on the balance sheet—as share capital, reserves and retained earnings, or accumulated profits or losses (for more on these terms, see the glossary on the ASX website).

CASH FLOW STATEMENT

Journalists looking for an insight into the health of a company or entity (such as a not-for-profit organisation or sporting club) should look beyond the balance sheet to the cash flow statement. This is important because it provides an important comparison of in-goings and out-goings (money in versus money out).

Cash flow statements normally provide data under three headings: operating, investing and financing.

Under the 'operating' heading you will find cash received and paid out by the company. Cash received includes payments from customers; while cash out includes payments to employees, suppliers and others. This heading can also include dividends received, interest received and tax paid.

The 'investing heading' will include details of payments made and received for property, plant and equipment, new businesses, and other investments.

'Financing' will include details of borrowings, loans that have been repaid, proceedings of any new share issue (that is, money received from the release of additional shares in the company), and dividends paid to shareholders. Journalists should question where the money for dividends is coming from. Are the dividends being financed through cash flow, retained earnings, or borrowings? What is the dividend-payout ratio? Has the company increased, decreased or suspended its dividend payments?

SURVIVAL

To survive, a company has to generate a positive cash flow. While established companies can rely on reserves to survive short-term downturns, highly geared or recently established companies may be more vulnerable to changes in economic fortunes. If a company is selling assets (such as subsidiaries or manufacturing plants), journalists should ask why. Is it to cover shortfalls in cash flow or longer term structural problems? It is important to have a look at how much cash the company has at the end of the financial year (calculated by adding the net increase or decrease in cash held for the year to the cash it held at the beginning of the financial year). Has it increased or decreased? An operating cash deficit may be an early warning sign of problems.

OTHER POINTERS

While the financial data may tell the story of a company or organisation in trouble, equally it may not. Reporting requirements, while designed to provide financial transparency, may not tell the real picture if the company's accountants are creative. If you are concerned, have a look at the auditor's report. All financial reports are audited, and while auditors can't look at every transaction, they are expected to provide an overview of the company's financial health. If they are concerned about the state of a company's books, auditors will say so.

Often the most valuable information is hidden in the supporting documentation (the notes that help to explain the financial statements). These can provide interesting information about related party transactions (contracts between the company in question and other companies controlled by the directors, or in which the directors have financial interests), and whether directors have bought or sold shares in the company (directors who do not have an interest in a company, or who don't add to their shareholding following dividend payments can say a great deal about their faith in the future of the company).

At the end of the day, this is a highly specialised area, and journalists who are investigating the financial affairs of a company would be well advised to seek the advice of a forensic accountant who is trained to unpick the complexities of corporate fraud. Companies and individuals intent on defrauding investors or governments will establish complex structures, often involving offshore companies to hide funds from investors and regulatory authorities. If you have an inkling of corporate fraud, it may be prudent to either enlist an accountant to advise you, or talk to the appropriate regulator and try to do a deal with them that gives you first rights to the story, if broken.

BUDGETS: FEDERAL, STATE AND LOCAL

Annual challenges for reporters include budgets—from local council and state government budgets to the Federal Budget. Budgets are vital because they contain so much information that is built around an understanding of mathematics and economics. In addition to financial information—revenue, taxes and expenditure—budgets also contain forecasts and analysis that, with the appropriate expertise to provide a level of understanding, can provide important information about the health of the economy. Sadly, there are some seasoned observers, such as economist Judith Sloan who think the whole thing is a cynical exercise. 'These days, budgets are really a combination of marketing exercises and a snow job' (Sloan 2012, p. 20).

The reality is slightly more subtle. There is often little time given to mining the data in budgets. The problem is twofold. First, many reporters working across local government in particular lack familiarity with budgetary data or indeed the expertise to correctly interpret it. Second, the state and Federal Government controls the flow of budget information, either through selected leaking before the budget is formally released or by putting time constraints around opportunities to digest and report the budget nuts and bolts on the day. Or as media identity Harold Mitchell noted: 'the government organizes the [Budget] leaking through a media-metered irrigation system' (Mitchell 2012, p. 6). Let's take a more considered look at this situation.

State and federal budgets are media events in their own right. Journalists are herded into a secure 'lock-up' for several hours before the formal release of the budget. This mobile phone- and internet-free area, usually strictly monitored by public servants, is to ostensibly give reporters time to delve in to the budget's contents and either write or prepare their stories before they are 'released'. Budgetary information can have stock market implications, so the idea is that security is important to ensure no data, including budgetary forecasts, appears ahead of schedule. However, this premise has been steadily overturned in recent years by the steady drip of budget announcements before the relevant treasurer formally delivers the budget to Parliament. This reached its most comical outcome in the immediate aftermath of the 2012 Federal Budget when the national wire service, Australian Associated Press (AAP), complained to the Treasury about the release of budget details to several media outlets during the lock-up:

> AAP believes the government leaked significant parts of the budget papers to the major television networks and ABC radio in the morning under a 5pm embargo in an attempt to ensure favourable coverage in the nightly television bulletins, one report noted (Christensen 2012, p. 7).

Regardless of the truth of this allegation, the broader issue is that by leaking such details, the capacity for the journalist to actually understand the depth and context of the particular funding initiative is compromised. Every journalist is happy to receive a leak. However, only the most diligent—and only those with the most time—will have the luxury of trying to work out exactly what the numbers in the leak mean.

A companion method to the leaking of budget information is actually limiting the time for understanding what are often complex documents. Budget papers run to several densely typed volumes. Unless you know your way around such documents, or know exactly what you are looking for, it can take ages to identify what some revenue and expenditure measure may mean. The Victorian Budget lock-up is nominally set aside for two-and-a-half hours. In that time, reporters will have to work their way through four volumes of papers, listen to the Treasurer do a presentation on the state's finances, attend the Treasurer's press conference, write a story for online, and then, once they are back in the office, seek reaction for the next day's paper. In practical terms, the reporters in the lock-up will actually have only about 90 minutes to digest the full impact of the Budget.

Media organisations get around this by sending specialists—otherwise known as rounds reporters—into the lock-up so that they can report on their portfolio areas of expertise. These reporters—working on transport, health, justice and economics, for example—have a level of understanding that helps them navigate the data more quickly. But they are still likely to struggle to get the total picture in such a short time.

One of the more reporter-friendly innovations is the Municipal Association of Victoria's (MAV) finance workshop for local or community journalists. The premise of these information sessions is to help local reporters overcome their lack of expertise with budgets but also, as an important consequence, increase the accuracy of reporting local government finances. The reality is that local government budgets are often difficult because local reporters lack the economic or financial expertise—there are rarely financial rounds in suburban publications. It is also true that while local government finances, especially rates, are very important to local readers, they are often the least understood part of council budgets.

The MAV's three-hour workshop covers council budgets in great depth, but for our purposes we can concentrate on several elements that are foundations for understanding budgets across all levels of government.

For example:

Revenue, or the sources of money—what your council or government earns:

Victorian local government (across 72 local councils) recurrent revenue in 2009–10 was $6.4 billion:

- 56.3% or $3.45 billion in rates (at the extremes 25% and 70%)
- 17.1% or $1.05 billion in fees, fines and charges
- 9.2% or $560 million in specific purpose revenue grants
- 7.4% or $450 million in general purpose revenue payments
- 10.0% or $610 million from other (Eg interest, asset sales)

Local government collects 3.5 cents of every $1 raised in Australian taxes. The Commonwealth collects 80.2% (including GST 14%) and the States 16.4% of total taxation revenue.

The importance of these figures is that they explain where the money comes from, and while these sources become more diverse and more lucrative as you escalate the levels of government, the revenue principles remain the same. (It also pays to remember that councils impose rates, while state and federal government have a range of taxes they impose for revenue purposes.)

Once you know where the money comes from, you can start to look at how that money is used and you can start to ask these key financial questions:

1 Is there an operating surplus? (critical for long-term survival)

2 Is working capital positive? (current assets less current liabilities = working capital)

3 Is there adequate cash available? (critical to short-term survival) At the end of each financial year there must be at least enough cash to cover the Provision for [staff] Long Service Leave

4 Is debt being used for appropriate purposes (such as to create value, rather than to fund operating costs)

5 Is depreciation increasing due to the lack of maintenance? (leads to long term problems)

6 Are capital works completed on time and on budget? (if not, why not?)

7 What are the contingent liabilities if any? And what do they mean?

Source: Based on Municipal Association of Victoria 2012

Now, some of these questions are sophisticated and demand a certain level of knowledge. However, they are not insurmountable and they are the questions that financial controllers, auditors and accountants ask of every budget, whether it is a council document or from a small business. The importance of a surplus was the underlying political battle of the 2012 Federal Budget because a surplus represents a pointer to the future health of the organisation, council or government.

Understanding government budgets can be difficult, but knowing the basic building blocks of every budget is the first step to demystifying the data.

One other point is worth making: despite governments' best attempts to avoid or deter journalists from detailed analysis of the extensive budget documents, there are often many stories hidden away in the data that are easy to tease out when you have the time. Deadline-driven budget coverage might well give the impression of a breathless—even cursory—reading of the bottom line, but a more considered approached in the days after a budget can reveal some nuggets of gold. It is important to persevere because budgets are actually current for a year, and sometimes funding initiatives will last longer than that. So in one way, budget stories have a long shelf life. It is worth remembering that when you are released from the lock-up, wondering if you have actually missed something in the four volumes of paper tucked under your arm.

1   Familiarise yourself with the names, acronyms and roles of the various regulators and bodies associated with the finance industry and share market (for example, ASIC, ACCC, APRA, ATO and ASX)

2   Understand how to track information about individual companies, both in hard copy and online. Remember, there are a number of sites that monitor companies and share market activity—such as the Australian Shareholders Association (ASA) site—which can provide invaluable information.

3   Online share-trading platforms (for example Commsec and ETrade) and monitors (such as ASX) provide excellent information on individual companies, as well as on industry sectors.

4   Make sure you are familiar with the key elements of an annual report and the regulatory requirements that exist to manage the behaviour of companies and office holders.

5   When analysing annual reports and government budgets, remember that those involved are trying to present the organisation in the best possible light. You cannot simply rely on the glossy brochures provided; you need to look within, and to question statements or budget items that do not ring true.

6   If you do not feel capable of analysing the financial data yourself, seek advice from a forensic accountant, or someone who has considerable experience in the preparation and interpretation of similar documents.

QUESTIONS TO CONSIDER

1   What are the primary reasons for companies listing on the stock market?

2   What is the Global Industry Classification Standard?

3   Name some of the websites you could use to find out about individual Australian companies.

4   What information are annual reports required by legislation to provide?

5   How do government budgets differ from corporate budgets?

6   What should journalists look for when interpreting government budget documents?

TASK

1   Locate either an annual report produced by an Australian listed company, or the budget documents provided by an Australian government (federal, state or local). Have a look at the supporting documentation and see if you can identify a story from the material. Provide a story plan of the material located and show how you would develop the story.

REFERENCES

ABS Cat 6248.0.55.002. 2011. *Employment and Earnings, Public Sector, Australia, 2010–11*: www.abs.gov.au/ausstats/abs@.nsf/mf/ 6248.0.55.002 (accessed 20 November 2012).

ABS Cat 6202.0. 2012. *Labour Force, Australia, October 2012*: www.abs.gov.au/ausstats/abs@.nsf/mf/6202.0 (accessed 20 November 2012).

Christensen. N. 2012. 'AAP to Complain to Treasury', *The Australian*, 10 May, p. 7.

Hoiberg, P. 2002. 'Understanding Financial Statements', in S.J. Tanner, ed., *Journalism: Investigation and Research*, Frenchs Forest: Pearson.

Mitchell, H. 2012. 'Gushing Leaks Plugged to Digital Drips', *The Age*, 'Business', 11 May, p. 6.

Municipal Association of Victoria. 2012. Local Government Budget Information Pack, Melbourne.

Sloan, J. 2012. 'Doing Time in the Lockup', *The Australian*, 12 May, p. 20.

WEBSITE REFERENCES

Australian Shareholders Association: http:// australianshareholders.com.au/asa_site/.

Australian Stock Exchange: Benefits of Listing: www. asx.com.au/professionals/benefits-of-listing.htm/.

Australian Stock Exchange: Global Industry Classification Standard: www.asx.com.au/products/ gics.htm/.

Australian Stock Exchange: Glossary: www.asx.com. au/glossary/index.htm/.

BHP Billiton: www.bhpbilliton.com/home/Pages/ default.aspx/.

Delisted Australia: www.delisted.com.au/.

FURTHER READING

Kemp, M. 2012. 'Understanding Earnings Reports': www.asx.com.au/resources/investor-update-newsletter/201208-understanding-earnings-reports.htm/.

CASE STUDY

THE NUMBERS NEVER LIE

John Beveridge

Do you want to be the sort of journalist who drives a company into a $60 billion bankruptcy and topples one of the world's largest accounting partnerships at the same time?

That is exactly what happened when *Fortune* journalist Bethany McLean started asking a few very simple questions about Enron's debt levels, erratic cash flow and strange transactions. For her trouble she endured a torrent of abuse and derision from a company that was then a market darling and accusations that she simply didn't understand the complex numbers. In the end her questions about where Enron's money was coming from and how Arthur Andersen behaved as auditor started a process that brought the company down in what was then the biggest bankruptcy in the USA.

Her actions bring into focus two of the great truisms of journalism: (1) that there is no such thing as a stupid question; and (2) that if you know how to analyse them, the numbers never lie.

While Enron might be an extreme example, every day business journalists ask questions and analyse numbers that often lead to lasting changes in the way companies are run or are perceived by investors. There are several much smaller scale Australian versions of Enron, companies that no longer exist because journalists were persistent and courageous enough to keep asking questions in the face of trenchant denials and bluster from chief executives.

The reason these companies and individuals were exposed is that all companies must lodge a significant amount of financial detail with the Australian Securities and Investments Commission (ASIC) and the Australian Securities Exchange (ASX), which runs the stock exchange.

Even when a company such as Enron is involved in significant accounting fraud, those lodged documents still contain enough details to reveal the confusion underlying the company's profits. In Australia, the documents that are most often examined by business journalists are the half-year and full-year profits, which are freely available on the ASX website.

Companies that are not listed on the ASX must still register their results with ASIC, so they too are available for journalists and financial analysts to peruse. Companies are just like people—they want to put the best possible spin on everything they do, including their financial performance, and this is the case with the release of the company accounts or profit and loss accounts.

Often these accounts will include a glossy presentation outlining the achievements of the company in the period under question. These are always worth reading, but the real story is told in the actual accounts, which are usually referred to as 'Appendix 4D'. While the company presentation might be full of artificially derived numbers, such as 'underlying profit' or 'normalised earnings', the actual numbers in all of their grim detail are in the accounts.

While there may be a very good reason for the company to strip out certain figures to get to an 'underlying' number, this can also be a layer of spin and artifice that is hiding the real story.

The prime numbers journalists and investors are interested in are revenue, dividend, net profit after tax (NPAT), EBIT (earnings before interest and tax) and EBITDA (earnings before interest, tax, depreciation and amortisation).

While these terms might seem confusing, they are the basic building blocks of any company's performance. Revenue is simply the total amount of money that came in the company's doors from sales; the dividend is the amount of money the company is paying to its shareholders; NPAT is the profit left when all other payments have been made; and EBIT and EBITDA are different measures of the operating profit and operating cash flow of the company. A company that is struggling will normally show a fall in NPAT and often (but not always) revenue; a company that is booming will see all of these measures rise; while a mixed result will see some up and others down.

These numbers also reveal what is going on inside a company—for example, a business that has recently made a very large acquisition might see its EBIT and EBITDA rising much more strongly than its NPAT.

In the vast majority of cases you are not going to discover an Enron when going through these numbers, but you might well find something that other journalists have not. Some examples might include an auditor's warning that the company may not be a going concern, significant payments to related companies or individuals, or revelations that a business that was bought previously is significantly underperforming. You may also discover that the company is very well run, even if its business is struggling or it may be on the long slide to oblivion.

Thankfully, Enron-style accounting frauds and collapses are reasonably rare but the enduring lesson they leave with all journalists is to always be vigilant in reading the numbers, persistent in pushing for answers, and determined to get to the truth no matter what it takes.

12

Working with the PR Industry

JANE JOHNSTON

INTRODUCTION

For decades, media and communication scholars have been researching and investigating the relationship between journalism and PR. It has been described as a strategic ritual (Tuchman 1972), a dance (Gans 1979), a tug of war (Gans 1979), a parent–child relationship (Tiffen 1989), a shared snake-pit (Hoggart, in Franklin 2003), and a poacher and gamekeeper (Johnston 2013).

These analogies and metaphors provide a range of ways to visualise, imagine and understand a relationship that varies enormously. Indeed, this exchange relationship is both hugely variable and sometimes extremely complex. Fundamentally though, it is a relationship between individuals and, while it is useful to generalise and draw word pictures, a more productive starting point is to consider it as a human exchange rather than a more abstract or generalised one. Rod Tiffen suggests that negative images of PR as 'black magic' and 'propaganda' detract from the reality of the 'flesh and blood' activities that are at the core of the PR–journalist relationship (1989, p. 74). This individual focus is based on the need to develop trust between the individuals. As Shin points out, although journalists might think PR practitioners *in general* lack ethics, they nevertheless believe the practitioners with whom they have contact are significantly more ethical (2006). And Franklin suggests that 'everyday relationships' (2003, p. 46) are less confrontational than idealist notions might suggest. Collectively then, this wisdom suggests the best way to view PR is based on relationships—knowing the professionals with whom you will be working, while at the same time understanding that the journalist and the PR practitioner have different jobs to do.

This chapter will focus on some fundamental and central aspects of this interchange, providing a context and framework for examining it, while also looking at some of the key tactics and techniques used by PR professionals in working with the media. It will also raise some questions and suggest some instances where the investigative reporter's radar should be most attuned within this aspect of their daily work.

THE MEDIA–PR NEXUS

PR is a growth industry found in the corporate, government/political, and not-for-profit or 'third' sector. Just about every industry and sector—from mining to retail, federal politics to tourism, fashion to police—uses professional communicators to tell their story. Part of their communication management lies in working with the media—the role of media relations. While the terms 'public relations' and 'media relations' are often used interchangeably, it is important to understand that some positions will be highly media-focused while others will be far broader in scope. Stockwell explains how it works in politics:

> Modern governments seek to strategically manage their interactions with the mass media in order to build a consensus of support for the government's policies that will ensure its re-election. The PR professionals engaged in this day-to-day management are called 'media minders' (2009, p. 418).

Of course such media management is carried out in conjunction with other communication tactics such as social media and television advertising. Notably, in government PR, practitioners or information officers work with a range of 'publics' (not just media) on, among other things, information and persuasive campaigns, ranging from road safety to anti-smoking; from AIDS to bullying in schools (Stockwell 2009). While these campaigns involve media relations, they also include a range of other tactics, such as paid advertising on bus shelters and cinemas, liaison with professional bodies such as the Australian Medical Association (AMA) and the National Union of Teachers (NUT), and social media tactics that link with targeted demographic and psychographic groups.

Research from around the world has found that media relations material—such as media releases, press conferences, corporate and political documents and tip-offs—has become a fundamental part of the development of news. In Australia, studies by journalism and PR scholars and professionals have come to the same conclusion: that journalism relies heavily on media relations-generated material. A study by the Australian Centre for Independent Journalism (CIJ) and the independent news organisation Crikey.com found nearly 55 per cent of stories were 'driven by some form of public relations—media release, public relations professional or some form of promotion' (*Crikey* 2010). PR consultancy Brumfield Bird and Sandford's (BBS) media survey confirmed that 55 per cent of journalists use media releases to create news (Edwards & Newbery 2007, p. 3). Their 2011 media study found that bloggers' use of PR-generated material was also consistently high, at 42 per cent (Edwards & Newbery 2011, p. 17).

In the UK, similar figures support this widespread use of PR materials. Journalism researchers Lewis, Williams and Franklin (2008) studied 2207 newspaper stories from five newspapers and found that 54 per cent of the stories had some evidence of PR-sourced material. What sectors did this PR material come from? By far the majority of PR-generated stories came from corporate sources (38 per cent); public bodies such as the police, national health and the courts were responsible for 23 per cent; government and politics accounted for 21 per cent; the non-government/not-for-profit sector generated 11 per cent; professional associations accounted for 5 per cent and individuals, 2 per cent. Another study found that, overall, 'items free of PR input are an exceptionally rare phenomenon' (Reich 2010, p. 810).

This trend of PR-generated news has emerged out of what has been described by Gandy as 'information subsidies', which 'reduce the cost of gathering and processing information' (1982, p. 31). Gandy's idea of the information subsidy has gained a great deal of traction since it was first suggested 30 years ago. In their major study of UK news, Lewis et al. suggest that 'news gathering and news reporting is increasingly "outsourced" to public relations professionals' (2008, p. 29). This outsourcing takes the form of media releases, video news releases, media conferences, lobbying, meetings, tip-offs and publications. Given this pervasive influence within the news agenda, it is more important than ever for journalists to know about the way media relations practitioners work, to understand their motivations and tactics and, where possible, establish positive working relationships with individuals. While there will always be times of tension between the two industries, there are aspects of the relationship, such as scoops and tip-offs, that will come the way of trusted journalists.

SOURCE THEORY ON A CONTINUUM

So how does this relationship between journalist and PR practitioner work? Broadly speaking, the journalist–PR relationship is an exchange relationship based on mutual needs and cooperation, but it also includes fundamental conflicts due to differing motivations and objectives. In effect, each profession has its own set of norms and conventions, *plus* there is a set of shared or 'agreed' rules.

The individual norms and conventions are based on internal cultural understandings of what the job is all about. For journalists, this includes using balance, the public's right to know, and the concept of the Fourth Estate. For PR practitioners, it includes using strategic communication to deliver a point of view and linking an organisation to important stakeholders. Shared or 'agreed' rules and conventions include understanding about embargoed stories, concepts such as going 'off the record', the need for access to sources such as politicians and CEOs, and the delivery of quotes and comment. As Franklin points out, if either party 'breaks' one of these rules or conventions, it can trigger confrontation; '[b]ut it is in the interests of both parties to negotiate and repair any breaches to re-establish a viable way of working together' (2003, p. 47). While Franklin's description is about the political–news interchange, the same applies for other sectors that engage with the media in information exchanges. This he calls a process of 'strategic complementarity of interests'—politicians need the media to position themselves and gauge public opinion, and the media need information from politicians to cover political news (2003, p. 47).

Shin talks of a continuum in this relationship from 'pure advocacy to pure accommodation' (2006, p. 7). This is useful because it suggests that relationships between journalists and PR practitioners are not all the same and will vary significantly. As advocates, PR practitioners must consider their organisational needs. As information providers, they must accommodate the needs of the media. Different situations will call for all sorts of information exchanges along this continuum and, at times, it is likely the PR practitioner and the journalist will have different expectations about where on the spectrum their interaction is, or should be, taking place.

In such exchanges they may engage in an understanding of 'collective advocacy'; that is, an agreed view that both parties disagree on certain issues but agree to work together (Spicer, in Shin 2006, p. 29). This is also a useful way of viewing the relationship. It moves away from an adversarial role in which the two are pitted against each other to a role of respecting the differences each other brings to the exchange.

The relationship is represented in Figure 12.1, which combines these various approaches and positions them against the underpinning elements of journalism and PR culture and norms. In the

FIGURE 12.1: THE RELATIONSHIP BETWEEN JOURNALISM AND PR

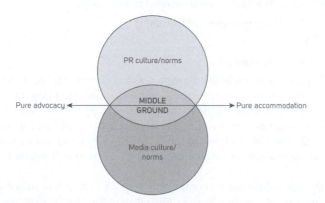

The relationship between journalism and PR incorporates a range of possibilities along a continuum from pure accommodation to pure advocacy, and incorporates PR- and journalism-specific norms, as well as shared and negotiated spaces.

model, the 'middle ground' is made up of the collective advocacy, the strategic complementarity of interests and the shared rules—all of which suggest a degree of negotiation.

MEDIA TRAINING AND INTERVIEW TECHNIQUES

Like journalists, PR practitioners are in the information business. And knowing how to conduct an interview is as important for a PR adviser as it is for a journalist. It stands to reason, then, that these advisers are in the business of training their clients in the art of media interviews. While we expect politicians, government officials and corporate executives will be media trained, this is also becoming standard practice across all professions: athletes, musicians, actors, writers, lawyers—basically any profession that may come into contact with the media. Workshops in this field are easy to find, for example one international opera organisation offers to 'help you raise and maintain your profile throughout your career by working on PR basics, how to work with the press, unlocking your web presence potential, interview techniques and all the media tools necessary for the 21st century singer' (CoOperaco 2012).

We all know that media interviews can vary enormously: from a brief on-camera 'stand-up' or short phone interview, to lengthy formal or informal conversations. For this reason, there are no absolutes about how to best conduct all interviews. However, media training by PR professionals will generally include a few basic rules. These include:

- know your subject
- know the key message you want to get across
- anticipate questions.

International PR company Fleishman-Hillard suggests that interviews can be summed up as: A=Q+1. By this, they are recommending answering the question *plus* adding one key message (Fleishman-Hillard (undated)). While aiming to achieve this, interviewees will also be looking to deflect negative questions.

Two techniques used to manage 'unwelcome' media questions are known as 'bridging' and 'blocking'. 'Blocking means deftly avoiding an unwelcome or unproductive question', while 'bridging means taking the discussion from unfriendly to friendly territory by making a smooth transition from an undesirable question' (Fleishman-Hillard (undated)).

Some blocking and bridging examples include:

- 'You're right, it is serious because ...'
- 'I'm not sure if that's really the issue ... what we need to focus on is ...'
- 'Yes, that's correct ... but it's more important to address ...'
- 'The real issue here is ...'
- 'That's an important point because ...'

Think about the last interview you heard during a political or corporate controversy, or better yet, listen to radio or television news tonight and identify some blocking and bridging in practice. Politicians are generally masters of this and while it is up to the journalist to ensure their questions are answered, this can be difficult as messages become increasingly rehearsed, controlled and scripted. Indeed, it is commonly said these days that politics *is* too scripted, which is why programs such as the ABC's *Q&A*, which takes unplanned questions from a studio audience, has been so well received by the television-viewing public.

As noted earlier though, politicians are not the only ones who know how to bridge in an interview. Following the announcement of Geoffrey Rush as Australian of the Year in 2012, the actor was interviewed on the *Today* show (Channel Nine 2012). In an interview with journalist Lisa Miller, Rush was asked to respond to negative chatter that the award should have gone to someone who worked 'behind the scenes' rather than a multi-award-winning famous actor. In his response Rush deftly bridged to a commentary about the amazing people who had been nominated, how he had spent time with them in the previous few days, named some and then responded that there would always be different opinions about awards, adding that he was used to this from within the movie industry. At no time did he get defensive, remaining gracious throughout the interview. While he answered the question, he also made his own point, turning a potentially negative question into a compliment to the other nominees: A=Q+1.

EXAMPLE

A good way to determine how you might work through practice interviews is to look at real-life examples. In the following interview, the Federal Finance Minister Penny Wong spoke to ABC journalist Sabra Lane on the ABC radio current affairs program *AM* about how the government planned to get the proposed mining tax through Parliament when it needed the support of independent MP Tony Windsor. After reading through the abridged interview, answer the following questions:

1 Did Wong stay on message?

2 What was her key message?

3 Did the media get a response that would satisfy them?

> SABRA LANE: You need the support of four out of six of the crossbenchers in the Lower House to support the minerals resources rent tax through Parliament. Tony Windsor says he won't support it until the issues around coal seam gas are resolved, and he wants a moratorium on further exploration until the results of independent research are in. Will the government agree?
>
> PENNY WONG: Look, we will keep talking to Mr Windsor and the other crossbenchers to obtain the passage of this bill because it's very important legislation. This is about securing the benefits of the boom for all Australians.
>
> We are in the middle of a boom. We are seeing a lot of resources being exported. But we know one thing about this—you can only dig them up once. And it's very important that we spread the benefits of the boom and that's what the Government's package does.
>
> SABRA LANE: Well, what about his concerns that he's linking this to coal seam gas and he wants a moratorium on further exploration? Will the government entertain that?
>
> PENNY WONG: These are discussions which are ongoing. The Prime Minister's made clear that obviously generally these things are dealt with by state governments. But we are very clear that this is important legislation for the nation.
>
> It's important for the future of the nation. So that we secure the benefits of the boom, spread the benefits of the boom for all Australians (ABC 2011).

PR TOOLS

Some of the means by which PR practitioners pass on information to the news media have already been mentioned in this chapter. Set out below is an extensive range of tactics and techniques used in working with the media:

- media releases
- press kits
- media conferences
- media alerts
- one-on-one interviews
- development as a specialist source
- creation of celebrity spokespeople
- speeches
- attendance at public meetings
- events
- sponsorships
- stunts
- freebies/trials
- talkback radio responses

- letters to the editor
- phone calls
- video news releases (VNRs)
- photography
- audio postings/releases (ANRs)
- leaks—managed and unmanaged

- off-the-record conversations/tip-offs
- emails
- Twitter
- Facebook
- YouTube videos
- blogs.

The most common and probably the best-known tactic is the media release (also known as a news or press release). For the media relations practitioner, this is a staple method of sending information out—via email, posted online, linked to Twitter or distributed via a range of other methods such AAP's Medianet or a social media distribution service. Media releases must work at two levels: they must get a key message out for the client organisation, plus they should provide information that is newsworthy to the media. Often, the latter takes second place to the former, resulting in promotional hype with little news value. Seasoned journalists have all seen their share of bad media releases which are poorly written, include puffery and hyperbole, are pitched to the wrong journalist (or are pitched to every journalist), or are not written in the style of the publication or media outlet. In contrast, there are good releases—and these are highly useful. A well-crafted release will be valuable to the journalist because it will provide facts, quotes and background data, contact details and photo opportunities which can be followed up.

In her study of failed and successful media releases used in Melbourne newspapers, Truin noted various accommodation levels in PR practitioner behaviour. Some worked within deadlines, while others ignored them; some localised stories as needed by local papers, others did not; some researched specific requirements about the news organisation's needs and style, others did not, and so on (2007, p. 175). Not surprisingly, Truin found that journalists would block emails from practitioners if they had previously made a nuisance of themselves by pestering them about story uptake. Conversely, where PR practitioners worked to journalists' needs, their releases were more likely to be used.

The other three best-known and most-used tools are press kits, media conferences and media alerts. In general, press kits include a mix of any of the following items: media releases, fact sheets, backgrounders, feature articles, biographies or profiles, newsletters, brochures, maps, a calendar of events, a list of key personnel, an annual report, Q&As, key newspaper clippings, business cards/contacts, and a media pass/application. These are often distributed to the media at media conferences, but they can also work as a stand-alone information source or may be made available under 'Media' or 'News' centres on organisational websites. If logically ordered and clearly written these can, like the media release, provide important shortcuts for journalists who want background information, quotes, contact or personnel details, organisational facts and so on.

Media conferences provide organisations with an opportunity to announce important information to all media at the same time, especially during a time of rumour, controversy or speculation. It is usually the job of the PR practitioner to call these conferences and manage questions. During a 'hot' issue such as a leadership challenge, or in the lead-up to a rumoured announcement, media conferences will be called to gain as much leverage as possible in the news cycle. Sometimes this will be at the end of the day—in order to deal collectively with media questions that have arisen throughout the day—just prior to the evening news. This enables control of the message going out and limited follow-up time in which to gain alternative points of view. So, while media conferences have a sense of fairness about them because of the simultaneous announcement of news, they can also squeeze out individual journalists' needs and homogenise the news.

A media alert is a simple one-pager which is used to make an announcement or invite the media to attend a conference or event. It usually provides details of 'who, what, where and when' to give journalists brief details about an upcoming event or announcement.

SCOOPS

While the media conference provides much the same news to all media, the scoop is a one-off, provided to just one journalist. Media relations practitioners will offer scoops for a variety of reasons:

- if the journalist goes to them with an idea
- if they trust a journalist to break a story in the fairest way
- if it is a story that will suit a particular media style
- if they know the story will gain the most prominence (that is, front page) because only one media outlet has it.

Media selection is therefore clearly a strategic move and it is unlikely that a PR practitioner will offer scoops to journalists they don't trust. Rather, they will seek out journalists who are seen as either 'on-side' or as media agenda setters, depending on their needs. In Australia, such media agenda setters have been identified as AAP, some newspapers (notably broadsheets) and public radio stations ABC and SBS (Pearson & Brand 2001, p. 8).

A variation on the scoop concept is described by Davis (1999) as the 'predicate story', which is intended to set the wider news agenda. This is about 'the selective placement of certain stories and hot documents with a particular news organization':

> The predicate story ideally must be comprehensive and contain all the facts, good and bad. As such, it will become the foundation block for all other reporters and for all future reporting ... By its very nature, a predicate story takes time to investigate and time to write, and thus does not lend itself to the competitive pressures and imminent deadlines that are inevitable when there is a general release to all news organizations. That is why it is necessary to select a single reporter or news organization to help generate such a story (Davis 1999).

Such a story can work for both parties; however, as the following discussion suggests, journalists should remain wary of sources' motivations in releasing stories through them.

TIMING

If news is important enough, it will be the news lead for the day or the hour, no matter what. But in a competitive news environment, some bad news can be buried by other bad news. Likewise, some softer stories will gain prominence on a quiet news day. It is only logical then that media relations practitioners will seek to maximise or minimise the impact of their story—depending on what it is—through its release at the best possible time.

There have been times when this approach has been adopted in the most cynical of ways, most famously by British government adviser Jo Moore, who sent a memo to the government press office within minutes of the attack on the World Trade Center in 2001, suggesting: 'it's now a very good day to get out anything we want to bury' (Sparrow 2001). Among those who condemned Moore's approach was a British clergyman who told the BBC: 'This is basically burying bad news of a fairly insignificant kind under the bodies of 6500 people. That is very, very bad for our nation' (Sparrow 2001). One newspaper columnist said the tactic was part of a system that 'stinks ... it is as old as politicians in a jam. Proclaim bright triumphs from the rooftops and slip the garbage via the back door ... it's what these advisers are there for' (Preston 2001).

Other commentators have gone further in their analysis, suggesting systemic problems in source–media relations. Long-term journalism researcher Bob Franklin explained:

> the significant revelation in this story was not the moral misjudgment and culpability of an individual government spin doctor, but the extent to which politicians' determination to set the news agenda and to use media to inform, shape and manage public discourse about policy and politics, has become a crucial component in a modern statecraft which emphasises what I have described elsewhere as the 'packaging of politics' (2003, p. 45).

Franklin sees this 'packaging of politics' as based on the collaborative nature of the relationship between journalists and sources. This idea places the focus not just on the PR practitioner's placement or timing of news, but on the journalist's critical evaluation of information when it comes their way.

OVERT AND COVERT TACTICS

Information can come from PR practitioners in myriad ways. Tiffen (1989) broadly places these into two categories: overt manoeuvres—those undertaken openly by PR practitioners and covert manoeuvres—leaks and briefings by a range of more nebulous 'sources'. Overt manoeuvres are the public, traceable tactics that we have been discussing so far. Covert manoeuvres are those done in secret, sometimes unofficially or without trace, and may include unethical practices. In truth, both can and do come from PR practitioners, and both are legitimate when undertaken ethically. It would be fair to say that investigative journalism relies on both categories.

LEAKS AND TIP-OFFS

The best known of the covert methods is the leak or tip-off. The fact that PR practitioners provide leaks and tip-offs to the news media is well known and this can be beneficial to both parties. Unfortunately for some though, there are times when this tactic can backfire. At both federal and state levels, political advisers have been caught up in controversies that began with an unofficial tip-off. The now-famous Australia Day protests at Parliament House in 2012, which saw Prime Minister Julia Gillard hurried to her car by security guards, resulted in a prime ministerial press secretary's resignation. The reason? A tip-off to 'an individual' about the whereabouts of Opposition Leader Tony Abbott, who had previously made comments about the Aboriginal Tent Embassy, resulting in the internationally broadcast scuffle that ensued. The Prime Minister's office provided a statement shortly after the event which said: 'A member of the Prime Minister's media unit did call another individual yesterday and disclosed the presence of the Opposition Leader … this action was an error of judgment' (Kenny 2012). Within weeks of the Parliament House incident, a West Australian media adviser also resigned after what was deemed to be inappropriate action. 'His apparent crime was to email a publicly available image of an MP's beachside home to journalists' (Colvin, in ABC 2012). The ABC reported that the West Australian Premier said the emailing of the photo had crossed the line from public to private, describing the incident as 'careless, foolish and silly' (ABC 2012). West Australian Premier Colin Barnett told the ABC:

> Today there is a culture throughout the community, but particularly in media, of people … communicating to each other through texts and emails and twittering all day, every day, 24 hours a day almost and I think that makes people perhaps too familiar and that can lead to carelessness (ABC 2012).

Such familiarity is not unusual. And while leaks can have negative ramifications, as these two did, they can also result in access to valuable information for the investigative journalist. The trick for the journalist in following up any leak or tip-off is to make sure it represents a legitimate story and is not simply being used as a 'kite-flying' exercise; that is, to see if an idea 'flies' in order to gain public support. In any case, in these days of instant, widespread and (largely) irretrievable messaging and publishing, caution should be adopted at all levels. Once the genie is out of the bottle—from either the source or the journalist—it is near impossible to put it back in.

ASTROTURFING AND GREENWASHING

At the darkest end of the covert spectrum are two tactics that are widely considered to be unethical: 'astroturfing' and 'greenwashing'. Astroturfing refers to the development of fake public support at the grassroots level, hence the fake-grass name. As Burton puts it, astroturfing is 'designed to put a community face on a corporate message' (2007, p. 29); but it can also refer to political manipulation.

Astroturfing became well known in the 1990s when environmental researcher and advocate Sharon Bedder exposed the widespread manufacturing of grassroots support. 'The use of such "front groups" enables corporations to take part in public debates and government hearings behind a cover of community concern,' she argued (1998, p. 21). Among others, Bedder identified global PR companies such as Burson-Marsteller, which created the 'National Smokers Alliance' on behalf of Phillip Morris tobacco, and Hydro Quebec's 'Coalition for Clean and Renewable Energy'. As the Public Relations Institute of Australia (PRIA) points out, astroturfing 'is cute terminology for a serious issue that has been around for decades' (PRIA 2006). Early astroturfing techniques included faking talkback radio responses and support, writing letters to the editor under fake names, and fake telemarketing and direct mail. More recently, the internet and social media have enabled the widespread use of astroturfing because websites, blogs and micro-blogging can be so easily established with no authenticity checking.

Astroturfing is repudiated by professional PR associations such as PRIA and the Chartered Institute of Public Relations (CIPR) as unethical and unacceptable practice, however there are nevertheless accounts of its massive growth in the current media-rich environment. A Sydney-based advertising strategist explained how it has fed into contemporary social and political issues:

> Public debate in Australia has been shaped in a profound way by astroturfing. If you look at the debate around the carbon tax, the debate around [the] mining super tax, and the public debate around asylum seekers, the public debates in these major areas of policy are being shaped in meaningful ways by astroturfing (Prasad, in Cohen 2011).

But since few people openly advocate it as a legitimate tactic, there remain many questions around who is involved and the scale of campaigns (Cohen 2011). For the journalist, the message is clear: information, especially on the internet and in social media, should not be taken at face value. There is no substitute for checking the authenticity of sources.

Greenwashing refers to the use of PR techniques to manipulate public perceptions that corporations are acting in environmentally responsible ways when they are not (Demetrious 2009). Greenpeace explains that the name was first coined around 1990, 'when some of America's worst polluters (including DuPont, Chevron, Bechtel, the American Nuclear Society, and the Society of Plastics Industry) tried to pass themselves off as eco-friendly at a trade fair taking place in Washington, DC' (Greenpeace 2001b). As the public and the media's environmental awareness has grown, so too has the sophistication of corporate PR strategies to promote organisations as environmentally friendly (Greenpeace 2001b). Greenpeace identifies cases in which organisations or industries have promoted themselves as green while working against true acceptance of the cause. For example, at the same time as the American Airlines in-flight magazine was running an 'Eco-Skies' environmental campaign, the company was also attempting to block a new law to hold airlines accountable in the European Court of Justice for their global warming pollution. Greenpeace calls this a 'Classic Greenwash' (2001a).

An important point to note here: PR techniques are employed by third-sector groups such as Greenpeace in much the same way as they are by corporations and governments. Therefore, PR can be, and often is, pitted against PR. For the investigative journalist, this means potentially having to deal with practitioners from various sectors, promoting various angles, to uncover and research stories.

CONCLUSION

Sometimes popular culture provides illustrations that help us better understand relationships of all types—including the PR–journalism exchange. In the 2011 film *The Ides of March* we see the crossed purposes of journalism and PR in action. Media minder Stephen Myers, described as 'the best media mind in the country', has a chummy working relationship with *New York Times* investigative reporter Ida Horowicz. They share drinks at the pub, and exchange advice and information; he is her political source and they have what we might call 'an exchange relationship' where each benefits from the other. However, the gloves come off when Horowicz threatens to expose Myers' clandestine meeting with the political opposition, driving home the reality that Horowicz (the journalist) has a job to do and so too has Myers (the media minder)—and separate imperatives drive these two agendas. This is the reality of the journalist–source relationship. Franklin sums it up: 'the relationship between journalists and … sources is essentially symbiotic and consensual although, within this overall framework of collaboration, the prospect for conflict is not merely possible but routine' (2003, p. 60).

As the chapter has described, and Figure 12.1 shows, there can be many variations to the journalist–PR practitioner relationship. With this in mind, some basic ground rules can assist in making this the most productive it can be and getting the most out of the necessary ongoing exchanges that will occur.

TIPS

1   Work with sources rather than against them.
2   Judge individual behaviour rather than generalised patterns.
3   Develop relationships with PR practitioners whom you trust.
4   Understand the implications of overt and covert tactics.
5   Where possible, validate information with independent sources.

QUESTIONS TO CONSIDER

1   What do you understand the term 'information subsidies' to mean?
2   To what extent do you believe Australian media organisations are dependent on PR practitioners?
3   Explain Shin's model of the relationship between PR practitioners and the media.
4   What is the difference between overt and covert strategies? Do you think one is more dangerous than the other from a media perspective?
5   What does Fleishman-Hillard mean by the equation $A=Q+1$?
6   What are the ethical arguments against 'astroturfing' and 'greenwashing'? Do you agree or disagree with the use of these practices?

TASK

1   Go online and identify cases of astroturfing and greenwashing. Explain why you believe these tactics can or cannot be justified in these cases.

REFERENCES

ABC. 2011. 'Government will Continue Negotiations to Pass MRRT: Wong', *AM with Tony Eastley*, 2 November: www.abc.net.au/am/content/2011/s3353745.htm (accessed 2 November 2011).

ABC. 2012. 'WA Labor Calls for Inquiry into Government Media Advisers', *PM with Mark Colvin*, 31 January: www.abc.net.au/pm/content/2012/s3419887.htm (accessed 5 February 2012).

Bedder, S. 1998' 'Public Relations' Role in Manufacturing Artificial Grass Roots Coalitions', *Public Relations Quarterly*, 43(2), pp. 21–3: www.uow.edu.au/~sharonb/PR.html/.

Burton, B. 2007. *Inside Spin: The Dark Underbelly of the PR Industry*, Crows Nest: Allen & Unwin.

Channel Nine. 2012. 'Interview with Geoffrey Rush', *Today*, 27 January.

Cohen, H. 2011. 'Don't Trust the Web', *Radio National: Background Briefing*, 18 September: www.abc.net.au/radionational/programs/backgroundbriefing/dont-trust-the-web/3582912 (accessed 25 December 2011).

CoOperaco. 2012. *Media Training*: www.co-opera-co.org/online/Workshops.html/.

Crikey. 2010 'The Spin Cycle: How your Newspaper Fared', 15 March: www.crikey.com.au/2010/03/15/the-spin-cycle-how-your-newspaper-fared (accessed 1 December 2012).

Davis, L. 1999. 'Scandal Management 101: How to Get the Bad News Out Quickly—And Quietly', *Washington Monthly*: www.washingtonmonthly.com/features/1999/9905.davis.scandal.html (accessed 1 December 2011).

Demetrious, K. 2009. 'Public Relations in the Third Sector', in J. Johnston & C. Zawawi, eds, *Public Relations: Theory and Practice*, 3rd edn, Crows Nest: Allen & Unwin.

Edwards, J. & Newbery, A. 2011. *BBS 2011 Media Survey*, Brisbane: Brumfield, Bird & Sandford Communications, Public Relations and Business Advisors.

Fleishman-Hillard. Undated. *Fleishman-Hillard Media Training Manual*: www.appa-net.org/eweb/Resources/National_Branding/AFORCE_MediaTrainingManual.pdf (accessed 2 November 2011).

Franklin, B. 2003. 'A Good Day to Bury Bad News? Journalists, Sources and the Packaging of Politics', in S. Cottle, ed., *News, Public Relations and Power*, Thousand Oaks: Sage.

Gandy, O.H. 1982. *Beyond Agenda Setting: Information Subsidies and Public Policy*, Norwood, NJ: Ablex Publishing.

Gans, H. 1979. *Deciding What's News: A Study of CBS Evening News, NBC Nightly News, Newsweek and Time*, London: Pantheon Press.

Greenpeace. 2001a. 'Environmental Groups Highlight "Greenwashing" by American, United, Continental Airlines', *Greenwashing*: http://members.greenpeace.org/blog/greenwashing/2011/05/24/environmental-groups-highlight-greenwash (accessed 15 February 2012).

Greenpeace. 2001b. 'Introduction to StopGreenwash.org', *Greenwashing*: http://stopgreenwash.org/introduction (accessed 15 February 2012).

Johnston, J. 2013. *Media Relations: Issues and Strategies*, 2nd edn, Crows Nest: Allen & Unwin.

Kenny, M. 2012. 'Gillard Staffer Sacked over Tip to Tent Embassy Protesters', *Adelaide Now*, 27 January: www.adelaidenow.com.au/gillard-and-abbott-run-protest-gauntlet/story-e6frea6u-1226254435221 (accessed 5 February 2012).

Lewis, J., Williams, A. & Franklin, B. 2008. 'Four Rumours and an Explanation: A Political Economic Account of Journalists' Changing Newsgathering and Reporting Practices', *Journalism Practice*, 2(1), pp. 27–45.

Pearson, M. & Brand, J. 2001. *Sources of News and Current Affairs*, epublications@Bond, Bond University: http://epublications.bond.edu.au/hss_pubs/96 (accessed 1 February 2009).

Preston, P. 2001. 'What That Email Said', *The Guardian*, 15 October: www.guardian.co.uk/politics/2001/oct/15/politicalcolumnists.comment (accessed 15 February 2012).

Public Relations Institute of Australia (PRIA). 2006. *Where the Grass is Not Greener: Astro-turfing is Not an Import Australia Wants to Grow*, 20 July, Appendix C: 'Lobbying in New South Wales: A Submission to the

Independent Commission Against Corruption NSW, 30 June 2010': www.pria.com.au/newsadvocacy/position-statements (accessed 13 February 2012).

Reich, Z. 2010. 'Measuring the Impact of PR on Published News in Increasingly Fragmented News Environments', *Journalism Studies*, 11(6), pp. 799–816.

Shin, J-H. 2006. 'Conflict, Contingency and Continuum: A Conceptual Model of the Source–Reporter Relationship between Public Relations Professionals and Journalists', conference paper, International Communication Association.

Sparrow, A. 2001. 'September 11: A Good Day to Bury Bad News', *The Telegraph*, 10 October: www.telegraph.co.uk/news/uknews/1358985/Sept-11-a-good-day-to-bury-bad-news.html (accessed 15 February 2012).

Stockwell, S. 2009. 'Public Relations and Government', in J. Johnston & C, Zawawi, eds, *Public Relations: Theory and Techniques*, Crows Nest: Allen & Unwin.

Tiffen, R. 1989. *News and Power*, Crows Nest: Allen & Unwin.

Truin, D. 2007. '*Failures and Successes of Media Releases Sent to Suburban Melbourne Press*', *Asia Pacific Public Relations Journal*, Vol. 8, pp. 163–77.

Tuchman, G. 1972. 'Objectivity as Strategic Ritual: An Examination of Newsmen's Notions of Objectivity', *American Journal of Sociology*, 77(4), pp. 660–79.

FURTHER READING

Deitz, M. 2010. *Watch This Space: The Future of Australian Journalism*, Melbourne: Cambridge University Press.

Edwards, J. & Newbery, A. 2007. *BBS 207 Media Survey*, Brisbane: Brumfield, Bird & Sandford Communications, Public Relations and Business Advisors.

Turner, G. Bonner, F. & Marshall, D. 2000. *Fame Games: The Production of Celebrity in Australia*, Melbourne: Cambridge University Press.

CASE STUDY

STRATEGIC COMMUNICATIONS

Nino Tesoriero

There's been a growing chorus of complaint in recent times about the quality of policy development, debate and delivery in Australia.

People have become increasingly frustrated as important policy discussions are often side-tracked by partisan politics or other trivial events.

Governments are accused of developing policy on the run, without proper stakeholder engagement, or simply in response to media pressure.

And there are concerns expressed that public policy is increasingly under threat from the influence of powerful vested interests.

People expect more out of policy, but they have become increasingly disillusioned when those expectations are not met.

Despite all the criticism, governments do actually set out to create good policies. They have a genuine intention to improve our society and environment. That's what they are meant to do.

But without effective strategic communications to support them, good policies often face the real risk of being delayed, derailed or even abandoned if there is poor public engagement and buy-in.

Strategic communications should be an integral part of the policy process from start to end, because the way a government communicates is just as important as what it communicates.

Policy and strategic communications can have the greatest impact when citizens or 'customers' of government are put at the heart of the whole process, from policy development and engagement to implementation and service delivery.

A customer-centric approach builds trust and understanding. It focuses on results for people. It makes policy more flexible and thereby relevant, and it underpins the values of democratic participation.

This approach is widely understood and valued in modern government. But you don't have to look back far to find examples where this relationship has not been strong—where communications was regarded as a service called on at the end of policy design simply to get the message out.

Before the growth of social media, communication was a lot more one-way, where people received information though newspapers and advertising, for example, but had few channels to effectively engage and provide feedback on policy.

Today, with the explosion of digital communication platforms, governments can no longer afford to send out information through traditional media alone.

They need to engage in a two-way conversation with people on policy using the preferred channels and personal networks that audiences trust.

People are also a lot more empowered on where they source their external information and how they would like to receive it—through more personalised services, for example.

This is the challenge for strategic communications: to find these new trusted platforms and re-engage government in conversations where they are currently taking place.

The main aim of strategic communications is to inform, educate and support the implementation of policy from a people-centric approach, so that audiences understand how policy impacts upon them and the wider society.

People rarely separate policy, communications and service delivery in their minds, and neither should governments. That's why an integrated, people-centric approach is so important.

Strategic communications support many disciplines and processes to achieve this, including insight development, behavioural change, public engagement, internal and external messaging, digital communications, events, media and stakeholder management, and marketing.

These approaches and tactics are best described through communications strategies that provide guidance, and outline objectives, audiences and media channels for delivery.

A useful start for the development of a communications strategy involves a scoping exercise to ensure communications are fully integrated with policy and delivery.

A strategy should clearly outline the context in which the policy is being made, namely what the business case and vision is; what the policy objectives are; who are the target audiences; what we already know about them; and what information they have already received.

The next stage is to clearly define the vision, opportunities and communication objectives—which are distinct from business objectives—to show what success looks like and how communications will help to achieve those goals.

Communication objectives are essential to explain what the strategy is trying to achieve, such as changing behaviours, attitudes or awareness. They also provide a mechanism for measurement and evaluation.

The next consideration in a communications strategy is the need to develop an in-depth and customer-focused understanding of the target audiences affected by the policy.

The development of insight—a deep truth on what motivates and drives people based on their experiences, emotions or attitudes—is one of the most important components that drives effective strategic communications and policy delivery.

It also gives communicators a clearer idea on a particular audience's existing relationship with government and their current communication preferences.

Insight helps to explain behaviour and attitudes, and how people will deal with change when new policies are announced and eventually implemented.

With insight, policy and communication teams can determine what behavioural change techniques may be needed to deliver policy effectively.

Policies usually require people to change behaviour through a variety of ways to bring about a desired outcome.

People take time to change, especially when they have entrenched views and beliefs. Effective communications helps to set up the behaviour change environment—to either remove barriers to increase positive actions and behaviour, or increase them to curb certain activity.

The communications task should be to find out what people currently do and why. This informs targeted messaging to take people through the journey of change, starting with initial awareness, inspiring change, helping people make the decision to change, showing them how to change, and then, when change occurs, helping them to lock in the process.

This is the customer or citizen journey—an essential communications tool to highlight the various points at which people's behaviour is likely to be affected and shaped by the chapters in policy design and delivery.

A customer journey also helps to keep the policy and communication plans flexible and responsive to modifications or improvements along the way.

Policies clearly affect multiple groups in society, which is why a communications strategy should segment audiences according to what people do, who they are, and how they think and feel.

Segmentation allows communications to be tailored and targeted to specific groups, rather than speaking to people *en masse*, which can diminish engagement and buy-in.

The identification, relationship and engagement with stakeholders other than key audiences are also critically important for the successful delivery of policy, strongly supported by strategic communications.

Stakeholders can, and usually do, include professional associations, unions, pressure groups, the media, charities and internal audiences, including staff, delivery partners and other departments.

Strategic communications have a key role in mapping stakeholders that are likely to sway or support policy outcomes and then devising engagement strategies to manage their impact and influence.

The way stakeholder relationships are managed—by opening up constructive dialogue where their ideas are listened to—can have significant positive benefits by building trust and understanding around policy.

On the other hand, communication and policy objectives can easily be undermined when stakeholders are not proactively managed and are instead simply informed about policy towards the end of its development.

With all of these strategic communications areas addressed, it will become easier to develop meaningful propositions and key messages for these audiences and stakeholders.

Propositions are the clearest expressions of policy that should be created for each key audience and stakeholder group. They should be able to motivate people to change, even if these people don't benefit directly from a policy objective. Key messages need to support and relate each other. They need to be concise and meaningful.

The next stage in a strategy involves identifying the most appropriate media and communication channels to use, and when to convey the propositions and key messages.

Audience insight and research work will provide a good indication of the most effective channels to use or avoid, and what the role of each channel is in reaching objectives and potential behavioural change.

Clearly, media is an important focus for any government communication. But from a strategic perspective, effective communications planning should go much further, taking a neutral approach when deciding on the myriad of channels to choose from.

All channels—from events and direct marketing to digital media and sponsorships—should be considered in an integrated way, in order to touch the right audiences and help achieve the aims and objectives of the strategy and policy.

Finally, a communications strategy should test whether it does what it is meant to do. A strategy should have evaluation mechanisms built in to test results against its original goals and objectives.

An evaluation of communications should review the real impact of the strategy, focusing on true behavioural outcomes rather than outputs such as the number of web hits or articles published, for example.

The big challenge and opportunity ahead for all governments is to better utilise digital communications as a way to improve engagement.

The power of digital goes beyond just being a great channel in itself—it is an enabler and a pivotal medium that embraces and links all the other key channels in which government communicates.

The digital space can be used a lot more to link up communication strategies across departments that are focused more on audiences than specific policies.

Social media strategies and techniques such as crowdsourcing could also be used by governments as effective ways get to the heart of the big conversations and stimulate new ideas.

If this is done with genuine intentions to listen and engage, it will no doubt help to improve confidence in the design, communication and delivery of good policy.

13

Legal Issues

MARK PEARSON

INTRODUCTION

Ask an investigative journalist the greatest frustration they encounter in their work and many will answer: 'lawyers'. This is because most would have been able to expose so much more if their legal advisers had not insisted they needed more evidence to support an allegation, or cut material they deemed indefensible. Former ABC *Four Corners* reporter and Walkley Award-winning investigative journalist Chris Masters regretted spending so much of his two decades with the program in court rooms and lawyers' offices defending legal actions instead of chasing stories, interviewing sources or sifting through clandestine documents. He wrote: 'The arithmetic of defamation suggested that if you took three months to do a worthwhile story, it would take three full years of work over a 12-year period to defend it' (Masters 2001, p. 22).

Knowledge is power, and reporters can minimise these frustrations if they learn more about the laws related to their investigations. Some become so familiar with media laws that they are able to convince their legal advisers that they do, in fact, have all bases covered in a complex exposé.

This chapter covers some of the main hurdles investigative journalists face in the digital era. It assumes you already have a basic media law understanding from your work or studies. If not, you might read it in tandem with the author's *Blogging and Tweeting Without Getting Sued* (Pearson 2012) and *The Journalist's Guide to Media Law* (Pearson & Polden 2011), which cover the basic laws of publication for the lay blogger and journalist.

THE LEGAL CONTEXT OF JOURNALISM INVESTIGATION

In some ways, the legal difficulties faced by investigative reporters stem from the fact that they are operating in a free, democratic society where journalists are not licensed and, particularly in an era of blogging and 'citizen journalism', anyone can go about the task of reporting corruption or other wrongdoing and publish their findings. Journalists are called upon to defend the investigative role of the media when it is being viewed by its critics as 'just another business'. Courts are all about social mores and attitudes, and if the community perception is that media organisations are more concerned with the bottom line than the public interest, this will lead to a reluctance on the part of legislators and judges to extend any special consideration to investigative journalists.

Unlike in the USA, where the First Amendment to the Constitution enshrines the freedom of the press, in Australia journalists are treated like any other citizen and have no special rights. Australia has no bill of rights and free expression is not mentioned in our Constitution, although the High Court has read into it a freedom to communicate on political matters.

The chapter picks up on the main issues confronting the investigative reporter trying to research and publish Fourth Estate journalism in the digital era. It is divided according to your activities as a journalist—where you go (privacy and trespass); what you access (freedom of information, confidential material and surveillance); who you talk to (source confidentiality); and what you publish (contempt and defamation). Along the way, we consider some of the special legal challenges posed by the internet and social media.

WHERE YOU GO

PRIVACY

Some laws control journalists' access to places—both real and virtual—that other citizens might consider private. The legal right to privacy is enshrined in the Universal Declaration of Human Rights (Article 12), the International Covenant on Civil and Political Rights (Article 17) and many similar documents in other continents and in national constitutions. The International Covenant on Civil and Political Rights states at Article 17:

1 No-one shall be subjected to arbitrary and unlawful interference with his privacy, family, home or correspondence, nor to unlawful attacks on his honour and reputation.

2 Everyone has the right to protection of the law against such interference or attacks.

Despite this, there is still no common law right to privacy in the form of a tort in Australia, although several laws have gone some way towards protecting the privacy of citizens, and the *News of the World* scandal in the UK sparked calls for a statutory right of action against privacy invasion. This was recommended by the Australian Law Reform Commission in 2008 (ALRC 2008). Lower court judges in Queensland and Victoria had ruled against privacy breaches, but superior courts had not followed their lead. The High Court left open the possibility of a privacy tort in the *Lenah Game Meats* case in 2001, after animal liberation protesters trespassed into a Tasmanian abattoir to record on video cameras the slaughter of possums.

Although invasion of privacy may not have all the elements required for a legal breach, investigative reporters still need to be aware that it is a breach of ethics and can be pursued as such under the various industry codes of practice. Only a compelling public interest related to someone's public performance might be considered an overriding factor in a defence.

TRESPASS

Investigative reporters will find it necessary to venture onto property when gathering information for their stories. Sometimes they might be tempted to go beyond a sign reading 'Trespassers will be prosecuted', or perhaps to walk into a business premises, with tape running, filming the activities going on inside and attempting to interview the proprietors.

Trespassers can indeed be prosecuted, but the courts will certainly look at whether their behaviour was reasonable in the circumstances. Some great works of journalism have resulted from trespass. For example, SBS television's Alan Sunderland and Michael O'Brien won the Walkley Award in 1992 for Best Coverage of a Current Story for their work in accompanying and filming a violent raid by protesters upon the Iranian Embassy in Canberra.

Trespass can be both a crime and a civil action. An example of its wording in state-based legislation can be found at s 14B of the *Tasmanian Police Offences Act 1935*, which states:

(1) A person, without reasonable or lawful excuse (proof of which lies on the person), must not enter into, or remain on, any land, building, structure, premises, aircraft, vehicle or vessel without the consent of the owner, occupier or person in charge of the land, building, structure, premises, aircraft, vehicle or vessel.

Similar laws can be found in all Australian jurisdictions. These mirror the law surrounding the civil action for trespass, but make its breach an offence punishable with a fine. If you were sued for trespass in a civil action, the remedies available might be an award of damages against you or the issue of a court order preventing publication.

Briefly, a journalist can be liable for the tort of trespass by:

- entering a property without the occupier's consent
- remaining there after permission to be there has been withdrawn
- placing a listening or surveillance device on someone's property without their permission.

Some courts have also found against media organisations that have entered a property for a purpose other than that for which permission has been granted. For example, a jewellery store opens its doors to the public to enter with the express purpose of purchasing jewellery. This has been interpreted narrowly in some cases to exclude permission for the media to attend with the purpose of conducting an interview.

The courts have been especially sceptical of so-called 'ambush interviews' by sensational television current affairs programs. For example, staff from the Nine Network's *A Current Affair* posed as a husband and wife interested in buying a home in a surprise interview with the owner of a building company after complaints from customers. The New South Wales Court of Appeal held they had breached the misleading and deceptive conduct provisions of the then *Trade Practices Act 1974* (Cth) (now the *Competition and Consumer Act 2010* (Cth)). They failed to win the usual media exemption from that law because their deception was deemed to be part of the building company's business activities and not essential to their media employer's business function. Both the company and journalist Ben Fordham incurred damages awards of $120 000 for the trespass and $20 000 for the misleading and deceptive conduct (the *Craftsman Homes* case, 2008).

WHAT YOU ACCESS

Investigative journalists can find themselves at either end of the legal restrictions on accessing materials. They often wish to get possession of government documents, access other kinds of data and undertake surveillance of the subjects of their stories, either in person or digitally. They sometimes get possession of confidential documents and information. The flipside of this is that journalists are also protective of their own research trail for a host of reasons, with the most important being the confidentiality of their sources and the exclusivity of their story.

FREEDOM OF INFORMATION (FOI)

FOI legislation can add enormous value to investigative journalism. Reforms at a federal level and in some states in recent years have somewhat helped the journalism research enterprise by reducing the time and expense of applications and limiting the avenues by which governments can stymie FOI requests. The targeted use of FOI applications can be a useful device for avoiding many of the legal pitfalls mentioned in this chapter. For example, the formal issue of a government document in response to an FOI application can help a journalist avoid having to reveal a confidential source in court, bypass the need to defend a breach of confidence action, and become a crucial item of evidence in defending a defamation suit. If journalists have the time and resources available to invest in FOI applications, they should take whatever advantage they can gain from them.

CONFIDENTIAL MATERIAL

Investigative journalists are sometimes dependent upon information given to them in confidence, either in the form of verbal information given in an off-the-record context by a confidential source, or documentary information which comes into their possession in a clandestine fashion. Journalists can leave themselves vulnerable to legal dangers in this situation. Of course, the public interest might demand that you go ahead and take these risks, but it is better that you do so on an informed basis, knowing the potential consequences and, if possible, avoiding the traps by establishing defences or minimising your exposure.

One possible consequence of such secret transactions is that you might face an action for breach of confidence, for example when trying to expose information that another individual or company wants kept secret.

To establish an action for breach of confidence, the courts have applied a three-point test, first articulated in the English Court of Appeal in *Saltman Engineering Co Ltd v Campbell Engineering Co Ltd* (1948). This test was summarised by Megarry J in *Coco v A.N. Clark (Engineers) Ltd* as follows:

> First, the information itself … must 'have the necessary quality of confidence about it'. Secondly, that information must have been imparted in circumstances importing an obligation of confidence. Thirdly, there must be an unauthorised use of that information to the detriment of the party communicating it (1969, p. 47).

There is a range of material that could be classified as confidential information, including documents and verbal secrets. The real test is whether the journalist received it in circumstances suggesting it breached an obligation of confidence.

One positive for journalists is that secret information relating to the government or its operations will only qualify for a breach of confidence action if its disclosure would be contrary to the public interest. This gives governments an extra hurdle when launching such an action against the media.

Apart from this public interest provision, however, there is not much solace for journalists in the available defences to a breach of confidence action. The single defence which is sometimes of value is the defence of 'just cause' or 'excuse'. This will not protect journalists in their revelation of trivial secrets, but if they have breached confidence in the interests of some greater cause, such as community health or safety, they may succeed with this defence.

People whose confidences have been broken by the media most commonly seek damages, or an injunction to prevent publication. The most famous Australian breach of confidence case was *Westpac v John Fairfax* (1991). There, *The Sydney Morning Herald* and *The Age* newspapers obtained copies of secret letters written by Westpac's solicitors—Allen, Allen and Hemsley—advising the bank on the dubious foreign exchange dealings of its merchant banking subsidiary, Partnership Pacific Limited. Even though the letters had been widely circulated, even read out in other parliaments, the court upheld an injunction preventing their further publication because they still had a 'quality of confidence' about them. This was despite the public interest in the community, including the bank's customers, learning of the dubious money market dealings of a prominent corporate entity.

Another danger facing journalists dealing with confidential information is that the documents or data that come into their possession might well be stolen. This leaves the journalist open to the criminal charge of receiving stolen goods, or even theft if the journalist was the one who stole the information. The *Crimes Acts* in all jurisdictions feature provisions detailing the penalties for these offences. There are even special provisions relating to the theft of government documents. Investigative journalists would be well advised to look to other methods of obtaining such information, such as FOI laws.

SURVEILLANCE

State and federal laws also affect the use of surveillance and listening devices, and journalists are likely to be breaking state laws if they have not told an interviewee they are being recorded. As noted in *The Journalist's Guide to Media Law* (Pearson & Polden 2011), federal and state laws place a range of restrictions on the publication of reports gained by the use of such devices.

Each of the states and territories has legislation prohibiting the recording of a private conversation, without the consent of all parties to the conversation, by someone who is not a party to the conversation. Victorian, Queensland and Northern Territory laws seem to allow such a recording by a party to a conversation. Reporters would be wise to look closely at their own jurisdiction's law and consult a lawyer on their practices under it.

The New South Wales *Surveillance Devices Act* was updated in 2007 to reflect modern surveillance devices. It states at s 11:

> A person must not publish, or communicate to any person, a private conversation or a record of the carrying on of an activity, or a report of a private conversation or carrying on of an activity, that has come to the person's knowledge as a direct or indirect result of the use of a listening device, an optical surveillance device or a tracking device in contravention of a provision of this Part.

It is a defence to publish with the express or implied permission from all parties to the conversation; if there is an imminent threat of serious violence, property damage or a serious narcotics offence; or if it was recorded by someone else.

The general prohibition on listening devices applies to hidden tape recorders and cameras, as well as emergency services radio scanners and illegal private-eye-type bugging devices; it applies to any equipment used to record or listen to a private conversation.

In June 2007, Channel Seven Perth was prevented from broadcasting a private conversation between an employer and employee, which it had obtained using a hidden camera (the *Seven News* case). The Court of Appeal held that even though the hidden camera recording confirmed that the employee had been terminated after informing a manager that she was pregnant, which the court found was a matter of proper and legitimate public interest, the issue could have been covered adequately without the broadcast of the secret recording.

Karl Quinn (2011) pointed to other examples of Australian media use of private eyes and surveillance techniques, including:

> *The Sydney Morning Herald* used a private eye in 2006 to help find alleged murderer Gordon Wood.

> *A Current Affair* reporter Ben Fordham and producer Andrew Byrne were charged in 2009 over the secret filming of a man as he ordered a $12 000 contract killing. They were found guilty in July 2010 of breaching the New South Wales *Listening Devices Act 1984*, but the charge was later dismissed.

> Private investigators hired by *A Current Affair's* rival tabloid television program *Today Tonight* posed as potential buyers of a helicopter owned by Larry Pickering, former cartoonist for *The Australian*. They secretly filmed and recorded Pickering piloting the helicopter.

> Investigative journalist Paul Barry used a hidden camera when interviewing serial killer Charles Sobhraj in an Indian prison.

Reporters whose poor shorthand skills motivate them to record their telephone interviews would be wise to seek the permission of their sources before doing so and to repeat that request after the recording starts, so they have the permission on record.

WHO YOU TALK TO

SOURCE CONFIDENTIALITY

While breach of confidence involves the unnecessary revelation of secrets, the flipside of the confidentiality issue is the refusal to reveal confidences when ordered to do so by a court. The refusal to answer a question in court is classified as disobedience contempt, because it is one of several types of behaviour deemed to 'interfere with the administration of justice'. Three Australian journalists—Tony Barrass of the Perth *Sunday Times*, Joe Budd of Brisbane's *Courier-Mail* and television freelancer Chris Nicholls from Adelaide—have been jailed for such refusal since 1989, while others have been placed on community service orders or fined.

Each of those jailed found himself in a situation where a court insisted he reveal the identity of a confidential source. This put them in a quandary—their professional code of ethics required that they respect all confidences they had entered into, while the justice system required that they reveal those confidential sources in the interests of justice. Each reporter was conducting an investigative report at the time of his jailing. So too was *The Sydney Morning Herald's* Deborah Cornwall, who was sentenced to a community service order for her refusal to name a source before the New South Wales Independent Commission Against Corruption.

Although reforms at federal level and in some states allow judges to give some consideration to the journalist's obligation to a confidential source in their decision making, a judge is obliged to force the question (and the penalty) if, on balance, the answer is relevant and necessary in the interests of justice.

The only strategy available to journalists is to heed the advice of Clause 3 of the Media, Entertainment and Arts Alliance's Australian Journalists' Association Code of Ethics:

> Aim to attribute information to its source. Where a source seeks anonymity, do not agree without first considering the source's motives and any alternative attributable source. Where confidences are accepted, respect them in all circumstances (MEAA 2001).

In other words, investigative journalists should aim to exhaust all possible avenues for getting information without entering into confidential agreements. Even when it is necessary to take off-the-record information, journalists should negotiate carefully the terms of such arrangements with their source so they both understand the conditions under which the information has been exchanged.

Investigative journalists should also consider the dangers facing their sources, who are often whistle-blowers within government or corporations, facing dismissal or criminal charges if their identities are discovered. Confidential sources face lengthy jail terms in most countries if they reveal state secrets, because officials might not agree there was an ethical or public interest in the material being revealed.

One of the most famous whistle-blowers of the modern era was military analyst Daniel Ellsberg, who leaked the sensitive 'Pentagon Papers' about the true story of the US involvement in Vietnam to the press in 1971. Despite government efforts to stop the publication of the material, the Supreme Court allowed *The New York Times* and *The Washington Post* to go ahead with its release (the *Pentagon Papers* case, 1971). Ellsberg and a co-accused later faced charges of conspiracy, theft of government property and espionage that were dismissed amid allegations of FBI wire-tapping.

In the twenty-first century it is even harder to protect your communications with whistle-blowers against detection by the authorities, so you need to take extraordinary steps if you hope to keep your sources truly confidential. Geolocation technologies, phone records and security cameras are just some of the mechanisms agencies can use to determine who has been talking to the investigative journalist or blogger.

The international whistle-blowing organisation *WikiLeaks* became famous for revealing the twenty-first-century equivalent of the Pentagon Papers when it released thousands of secret US Government files on the Middle East conflicts and broader diplomatic relations throughout 2010 and 2011 (for more on this, see Chapter 3; see also Pearson 2012). *WikiLeaks* reassured sources that its high-security-encrypted submission system, using an electronic drop box, protected their identity; but US soldier Bradley Manning was arrested in 2010 and held in solitary confinement pending trial over the release of the classified material. CNN interviewed several experts about the plethora of similar sites to *WikiLeaks*, who warned whistle-blowers to examine their protocols very carefully if they wanted their identities to remain secret after the authorities discovered the leaks. Some sites reserved the right to disclose leakers' identities if subpoenaed to do so.

Even experienced investigative journalists and organisations specifically set up for handling leaks can find the area a minefield, so you should consider carefully the fact that your colleagues have served jail time throughout the world for either leaking secrets or refusing to name their off-the-record sources in court.

WHAT YOU PUBLISH

CONTEMPT

While some journalists might face disobedience contempt charges for refusing to disclose a source or hand over their documents in court, the other major area of contempt faced by investigative journalists is *sub judice* contempt. This involves publications that tend to prejudice a fair trial. For example, Melbourne radio journalist Derryn Hinch was jailed for 28 days and fined $10 000 for this kind of contempt in 1987, reported in *Hinch v Attorney-General [Victoria]* (1987). (He was also sentenced to home detention in 2011 for breaching suppression orders.)

The media need to be particularly careful with their coverage of a story if an upcoming trial is pending. In criminal cases, this period starts from the instant an accused person is arrested. When juries are involved, the courts are very concerned to protect them from anything that might affect their deliberations, and also to protect witnesses from media coverage that might sway their testimony or tarnish their identification of an accused. With this in mind, journalists need to work within key time zones in the reporting of events that might be the subject of a trial.

If the proceedings are not yet pending, whether criminal or civil, investigative reporters are free to publish a broad range of material without fear of prosecution for *sub judice* contempt. They should be wary of other legal pitfalls in this period, however, such as defamation, discussed below. From the moment a trial is pending, through to the conclusion of the trial, they are restricted to varying degrees in their publishing.

The most restricted period is the time before the trial has started, because reports need to be restricted to the 'bare facts' of the case. This is usually simply a statement of the charges or the cause of action, and a brief account of the basic allegations involved with a minimum of identification for fear of defamation action. Once the court case starts, journalists can write a 'fair and accurate' report on the proceedings. During the *sub judice* period the courts are particularly sensitive to anything that implies the guilt or innocence of an accused; photo identification of an accused where identification might be at issue in the trial; and any mention of an accused person's previous criminal record.

There is, however, a public interest defence available to journalists reporting upon an important public issue. In a 1999 case involving *The Sydney Morning Herald*, the New South Wales Supreme Court went so far as to allow the newspaper to publish the name of an underworld drug syndicate chief and details of previous charges against him in the context of a major exposé on the powerbrokers in Sydney's heroin trade—all while the trial against the individual was pending. This was a major victory for investigative journalism's right to pursue an important matter of public interest despite the fact that a criminal trial was under way (see *Attorney-General for the State of New South Wales v John Fairfax Publications Pty Limited*).

There are also many other restrictions on what may be reported about the criminal justice system covering a gamut of offences and situations, including juveniles, victims of sexual crimes, mental health tribunals, Family Court matters, interviewing prisoners and national security crimes.

Sexual crimes are a special hazard. South Australian and Queensland laws keep the accused's identity secret until later in the criminal process. In South Australia, the identity restriction extends to a ban on any coverage of the preliminary proceedings of a major sexual offence until the accused person has been committed for trial or sentence (*Evidence Act 1929*, s 71A). In Queensland, the preliminary proceedings can be reported, but the identity of the accused must remain secret until after they have been committed for trial (*Criminal Law (Sexual Offences) Act 1978*, s 7). These laws differ from those in other Australian states and territories where the identity of the victim alone is suppressed. There, the accused in a sexual crime can be identified after they have appeared in court unless their identity might lead to the identification of the victim or unless a judge or magistrate decides to suppress the identity on other public interest grounds. Today's communications defy state borders and the postings of bloggers and social media users make a mockery of state-based laws to the disadvantage of traditional media.

DEFAMATION

By far the biggest area of media law of concern to investigative journalists is defamation, the tort of publishing imputations that lower someone's reputation in the eyes of other citizens. Investigative journalists could be said to be in the 'defamation business'. It is their job to erode reputations by setting the record straight on the activities of corrupt and exploitative individuals and businesses. The trick is to be able to defame people within the sanctuary of the available defences.

Near-uniform legislation introduced throughout Australia at the end of 2005 put an end to many of the ridiculous differences in defamation law between states and territories and limited the award of general damages to what stands today at about $300 000 (indexed annually).

Defamation is a technical and complex area of the law for a host of reasons. It is usually a civil action and rarely a criminal charge. Plaintiffs are usually rich and powerful individuals, or those who have the backing of an organisation willing to fund their suits. The reality is that our media products are full of defamatory material; important news often lowers the reputations of people and corporations. However, most of these instances of defamation never make it to court because several defences are available to the media organisation that published or broadcast it or posted it online.

This chapter does not offer the opportunity to go into detail into each of the defamation defences, but investigative reporters should be familiar with them so that they know when to seek expert legal advice on a story. The main defences available to journalists are truth; honest opinion (or fair comment); protected report (of important documents and privileged occasions such as court, parliament and commissions of inquiry, tribunal hearings, council meetings and even public meetings); and qualified privilege (a limited public interest defence).

Truth is not as easy a defence to establish as one might think. You might be called upon to prove the truth of the meaning ('imputation') coming from your story—not just the individual facts themselves. The honest opinion defence is useful for defending commentary pieces about major investigations, and also sometimes for defending the opinions of sources you are quoting within the larger stories, but it has a list of requirements you need to follow. The protected report or 'fair report' defence covers you for fair and accurate reportage privileged occasions including, but again the protection is conditional.

The 2005 reforms to the qualified privilege defence require journalists to show they have been 'reasonable' in their reportage before they can argue the public interest outweighs their inability to prove the truth of their allegations. The court might assess the level of genuine public interest in the defamatory claims; whether they relate to the public role of the plaintiff; their seriousness; your distinction between proven facts and suspicions and allegations; whether you rushed to publish; your sources (sounding alarm bells for confidential sources); whether you gave the other side of the story and the steps you took to obtain it; and what else you have done to verify the information (see for example the *Defamation Act 2005* (NSW), s 30(3)).

The likelihood of defending a defamation action successfully will be enhanced if investigative reporters adopt a professional and systematic approach to their work and maintain a regular communication channel with the media outlet's lawyers. Notebooks should feature a logical system of note-taking, so that when tendered as evidence in court they are viewed credibly. If you are using audio, video or computer-based recordings of interviews, you need a meticulous system of backing up, storing and filing these files. (Of course, investigative reporters also need a system of recording confidential information so they do not breach confidences if their files are subpoenaed.) Lawyers should be consulted on the evidentiary suitability of copied documents, and protocols for obtaining legal documents such as statutory declarations. Journalists should keep a diary of their investigations, particularly their attempts to contact individuals to offer them a right of reply.

One of the key principles of the rules of evidence is that any evidence adduced must be capable of being tested in court, to enable the court to ascribe weight to evidence and determine witness credibility (Pearson & Griffiths 2011).

The court or tribunal process can be a professional minefield for journalists called into the witness box. Their practices and credibility become subject to scrutiny, as BBC journalists Susan Watts, Andrew

Gilligan and Gavin Hewitt discovered when they were called upon to give evidence at the UK's Hutton Inquiry in 2003 into the suicide death of British defence expert Dr David Kelly after he was exposed for leaking intelligence information. During the hearing, the journalists were questioned and at times publicly criticised for their working practices. The inquiry also highlighted the importance of taking and keeping good notes; the journalists' shorthand, longhand and hybrid notes still sit at the inquiry's website (Hutton Inquiry 2004).

Judge-issued injunctions are a particular danger for reporters. Such writs are sometimes known as 'stop', 'slap', 'gag' or 'frightening' writs. Injunctions can be ordered for a range of reasons, such as concern for the safety of an informant or to prevent information being published that might jeopardise another trial. Traditionally, the courts have been reluctant to issue stop writs in defamation actions and have tended to apply a principle known as the 'newspaper rule' which, in the interests of free speech, allows publication to go ahead unless the defence has no chance of success. However, this is discretionary and its application has varied across cases.

CONCLUSION

These are just some of the myriad legal issues facing investigative journalists as they go about their work. Others are not even classed as 'media law'. They include assault, contract law, corporations law and intellectual property. Some investigative journalists are former lawyers or have earned qualifications in this area because they understand the crucial relationship between their work and the law. For the rest of us, while we can learn about media law we are first and foremost reporters. Some legal knowledge can strengthen our journalism, but its main function is to sound the alarm bells to remind us to seek professional legal advice when we really need it.

TIPS

1   Do all the basics properly: take notes accurately, verify facts with independent sources and avoid ambiguities.

2   Work with editors, news directors, producers and lawyers to build protective devices into investigative projects.

3   Carefully negotiate terms such as 'confidentiality' with sources before entering into agreements to accept 'off-the-record' information.

4   Explore alternatives to confidentiality agreements by using devices such as FOI applications.

5   Be aware of the consequences of journalistic actions and weigh them up against the public interest through careful consultation with editors.

6   Don't rush to publish. Accept that time-consuming research deserves equally time-consuming verification and review.

7   Go to great lengths to get all sides of the story and record precisely the steps taken to contact the subjects of allegations.

8   Assume that legal action will follow publication and gather all evidence on the advice of lawyers as you go, rather than having to chase the proof after publication.

9   Maintain an efficient and accessible filing system so that materials and computer files are always on hand to underpin a defence.

10 Build into your filing system a mechanism for protecting the confidentiality of sources.

11 Be aware of the laws of journalism, and the arguments for freedom of the press and the public's right to information.

QUESTIONS TO CONSIDER

1   What are the issues surrounding privacy and trespass for Australian journalists?

2   What legal benefits can be associated with submitting an FOI claim?

3   List the three legs of the breach of confidence test.

4   To what extent should journalists be aware of the provisions of the *Crimes Act* and the various *Surveillance Devices Acts*?

5   Go back over the key areas of the law covered in this chapter and suggest how social media might affect their application. Find and discuss a social media case involving defamation, privacy, surveillance, confidentiality or contempt.

6   How does the qualified privilege defence work?

TASK

1   Locate one of the cases discussed in this chapter. Summarise the facts of the case and the lessons to be learned for investigative journalists.

REFERENCES

Australian Law Reform Commission (ALRC). 2008. *For Your Information: Australian Privacy Law and Practice*, Report 108, Canberra: ALRC: www.alrc.gov.au/publications/report-108/.

Hutton Inquiry. 2004. *Investigation into the Circumstances surrounding the Death of Dr David Kelly*, 'Evidence': www.the-hutton-inquiry.org.uk/content/evidence.htm/.

Masters, C. 2001.'Feisty at Forty', *Weekend Australian Magazine*, 18–19 August, pp. 21–5.

Media Entertainment and Arts Alliance (MEAA). 2001. *Australian Journalists' Association Code of Ethics*: www.alliance.org.au/code-of-ethics.html (accessed 23 November 2001).

Pearson, M. 2012. *Blogging and Tweeting Without Getting Sued: A Global Guide to the Law for Anyone Writing Online*, Sydney: Allen & Unwin.

Pearson, M. & Griffiths, J. 2011. 'From Shorthand to Cyberspace: Journalists' Interview Records as Evidence, *Media & Arts Law Review*, July, 16(2), pp. 144–60.

Pearson, M. & Polden, M. 2011. *The Journalist's Guide to Media Law*, Sydney: Allen & Unwin.

Quinn, K. 2011. 'Private Eyes and Media Lies, *The Age*, 23 July: www.theage.com.au/national/private-eyes-and-media-lies-20110722-1hsvb.html#ixzz1T4Tg57oy/.

CASES CITED

Attorney-General for the State of New South Wales v John Fairfax Publications Pty Limited [1999] NSWSC 318 (9 April 1999).

Australian Broadcasting Corporation v Lenah Game Meats Pty Ltd [2001] HCA 63 (15 November 2001): www.austlii.edu.au (accessed 15 December 2001).

Coco v A.N. Clark (Engineers) Ltd [1969] RPC 41.

Craftsman Homes case: *TCN Channel Nine Pty Ltd v Ilvariy Pty Ltd* [2008] NSWCA 9: www.austlii.edu.au/cgi-bin/sinodisp/au/cases/nsw/NSWCA/2008/9.html/.

Hinch v. Attorney-General [Victoria] (1987) 164 CLR 15.

Pentagon Papers case: *New York Times Co v United States*, 403 U.S. 713 (1971).

Saltman Engineering Co Ltd v Campbell Engineering Co Ltd (1948) 65 RPC 203.

Seven News case: *Channel Seven Perth Pty Ltd v 'S' (a company)* [2007] WASCA 122: www.austlii.edu.au/cgi-bin/sinodisp/au/cases/wa/WASCA/2007/122.html/.

Westpac Banking Corporation v John Fairfax Group Pty Ltd (1991) 19 IPR 513.

INTELLECTUALLY DISABLED PEOPLE FIGHT FOR EQUAL ACCESS TO JUSTICE

Nance Haxton

In South Australia many cases of alleged sexual assault against people with an intellectual disability are dropped before going to trial because the victim has difficulty communicating what happened to them. They are not seen as reliable witnesses in court proceedings due to their disability—because they can't speak well verbally.

The case that prompted my investigation involved a bus driver in Adelaide who allegedly sexually assaulted seven intellectually disabled children on his bus round, some as young as five. But after six months of court proceedings, all charges were dropped because the children cannot speak, even though they can communicate in other ways such as sign language or through a board. The mothers of the children feel they have been abandoned by the justice system.

This story, 'Mothers Speak Out To Prevent Abuse of Disabled Children', should probably be considered as the 'primary' story in my series (ABC 2011a). Two other stories that I highlight in this series are 'Urgent Reform Needed for Disabled to Give Evidence in Court' (ABC 2011b) and 'Chief Justice says Translators in Court for Disabled Victims is Problematic' (ABC 2011c). All the stories were broadcast nationally on ABC Radio Current Affairs, on *AM*, *PM* or *The World Today* over six months in 2011–12. My series culminated in a 20-minute radio documentary which wrapped together the stories of many of the people I had interviewed, and the protests and court hearings I had attended over that time (ABC 2012). I would urge you if possible to read all the transcripts of the reports in my series. If you have the time, listen to the links and download the MP3s. You will then hear the increasing calls from a variety of organisations forcefully arguing for legal reform in South Australia so that the intellectually disabled are not denied access to justice.

Hopefully this series helps prove that radio is still a powerful medium—and is certainly more than 'poor man's TV'. Radio news and radio current affairs is not the consolation prize you get if you aren't pretty enough to be a newsreader or if television was too competitive to get into. It's a challenging and evolving medium that I think will be around for many years to come, despite the increasingly competitive challenges of around-the-clock television and online coverage. I have a great executive producer who told me when I first started in this job how wonderful radio is because it can be subversive. He said that while you have to fight to get people's attention in other mediums—newspapers, television, internet, etc.—often in radio you have a captive audience in the car or in the kitchen. So if you craft a beautiful radio story, even if your listener has no interest in the topic to begin with, you can pull people in. You can have people listen to an issue that they never would have sought out otherwise—which is a wonderful opportunity. It's an aspect of radio current affairs that still excites me to this day. I think it's what inspired me in this series of stories, because while most people did not know about this initially, I don't know anyone who wasn't outraged when they heard about the situation. Most media only covered the initial court story when the charges looked likely to be dropped, but I kept at it and found new angles to keep the story going.

The voice is truly the window to the soul; hearing another person's take on a situation—without the distraction of pictures or reading it on a computer screen—is incredibly powerful and inspires me to keep on working in this medium and keep learning and improving. As I often say, radio is 'theatre of the mind'. Done well, it takes listeners on a journey, like a great book, the story becomes alive in their head in an incredibly personal way. The intimacy of actually hearing people's voices—particularly the mothers I interviewed who are so clearly distressed by the court's treatment of their children—makes these stories more powerful than if I had simply written about the situation. And when you only have the women's voices, you really listen to the story and examine the issue a lot more, and aren't as distracted by other elements such as great visuals or what they look like.

I was the first person to cover this issue on a national level, with follow-up stories appearing in *The Advertiser* and other local media after my first stories appeared. I think this shows the strength of the radio medium to not only break new ground on a story, but also to invite people to examine issues in more detail—something that is often forgotten in people's focus on print and television formats.

I gathered all the interviews myself, and produced and mixed each radio package on my own. I followed this issue through and came up with new angles myself, from interviewing the mothers of some of the victims to interviewing South Australia's Attorney-General and Chief Justice, with the latter admitting that this problem makes intellectually disabled people more vulnerable to abuse. I am proud that a longer, 10-minute version of my interview with Chief Justice John Doyle was added as a special link to the *PM* website for people to listen to his determination on the issue in its full complexity (ABC 2011d).

These stories were broadcast under considerable pressures. One of the difficulties in reporting this complex issue was not being able to go into the details of the cases involved in the early broadcasts because of *sub judice*. Time pressures were also an issue on the days I broadcast the court stories, as I had to travel an hour to the courthouse, do the interviews outside court, and then travel an hour back to the ABC studios and write and put together my package for *PM* by 4.30pm EST. But far more onerous were the legal pressures of having each story checked before going to air by the ABC's legal department. I had to battle with our lawyers to air the interview with the mothers, as the lawyers advised that what they said was potentially *sub judice*. They wanted to pull the story completely 10 minutes before it went to air on *PM*. I had to completely re-edit the package and beg my executive producer to keep a space for the story in the air queue while the legal department debated what could be left in and out. I am extremely pleased that they eventually allowed at least some of the interview to air, so that the mothers could give their important perspective on this issue. So often the parents are not heard in stories such as this because of legal constraints, and yet it is their anguish that drives change and reform in the wider community.

My series was recognised in November 2011 when I received the Yooralla Media Award for Excellence at the National Disability Awards. The judges cited my work as an important contribution to the advancement of disability rights, and as 'one of the best investigative stories of the year in any medium'.

I am passionate about the continuing need for investigative journalism in today's media landscape. Ten years ago I did my Masters thesis on The Death of Investigative Journalism. Thankfully one of my interviewees for that project—respected investigative journalist Chris Masters—inspired me. He said that while investigative journalism was not dead, it was certainly dying. However, he also told me that all journalists should be doing investigative journalism —not just those lucky enough to be assigned to investigative units. There is a responsibility from the organisations we work for to provide the resources required, including the most valuable gift you can ever give a journalist: time. Time to research, time to pursue, and time to put the big picture all together.

My investigative series on disability justice evolved out of nowhere in some ways. I look back now and realise how perhaps we can overplay investigative journalism as if it is some sort of dark art. Basically this series came from me noticing how upset the court reporter was when she came back from the first court appearance. This got me wondering what could upset a seasoned court reporter who has seen a lot of injustice. When I realised the broader scope of what this case involved, I was outraged. And from there I just dug around for new angles to see if this issue was widely known or recognised. Of course it wasn't. Now there is a parliamentary inquiry set up to further investigate the issue. I think one of the best skills we as journalists can nurture is our instinct and gut feeling. We need to trust ourselves when something strikes us as being out of line and pursue that further.

Ultimately all the charges in this case were dropped because of the children's communication difficulties. This is despite the fact that the children can communicate in other ways, but their cases were not deemed able to go to court because they cannot 'talk'. This, however, does not seem to be an impediment for deaf people, who can of course come to court, give evidence and be cross-examined with an interpreter.

When I realised this was likely to happen early on in this series of stories I was disgusted, and wanted to discover why, and how this legal loophole could be addressed. To me if you cannot get a court case up where seven very vulnerable children were all allegedly abused by the same man, then there is little hope of any cases of alleged sexual abuse of intellectually disabled people reaching court.

I intend to follow up this issue, highlighting the injustice that disabled victims of sexual assault face in our justice system. I'm particularly passionate about giving people a voice who are not given access to the media, as I find they often have the best stories to tell and they haven't been heard before. It also gets you out of the press release circus that drives so much news now, and out reporting real issues.

If this serious gap in the law that these stories identified is not remedied, then people with an intellectual disability will become even more of a target of sexual predators, who know how unlikely it is that they will ever be brought to justice. If that isn't enough to inspire you to keep at a series of stories, then to me you're in the wrong game.

FURTHER READING

ABC. 2011a. 'Mothers Speak Out To Prevent Abuse of Disabled Children', *PM*, 12 July: http://www.abc .net.au/pm/content/2011/s3267894.htm/.

ABC. 2011b. 'Urgent Reform Needed for Disabled to Give Evidence in Court', *PM*, 26 July: http://www .abc.net.au/pm/content/2011/s3278580.htm/.

ABC. 2011c. 'Chief Justice says Translators in Court for Disabled Victims is Problematic', *PM*, 10 August: www.abc.net.au/pm/content/2011/s3290440.htm/.

ABC. 2011d. 'Chief Justice says Translators in Court for Disabled Victims is Problematic' (extended version), *PM*, 10 August: http://mpegmedia.abc .net.au/news/audio/pm/201108/20110810pmextra-cheif-justice.mp3/.

ABC. 2012. 'The Full Story: Radio Current Affairs Documentary: Disabilities', *PM*, 11 January: www .abc.net.au/pm/content/2012/s3405854.htm/.

14

Dirty Hands and Investigative Journalism

IAN RICHARDS

INTRODUCTION

One of the ironies of investigative journalism is that some of its best-known practitioners deny its very existence. Thus John Pilger has argued that the term should be 'rejected as a tautology since all journalists should be investigative' (quoted in de Burgh 2000, p. 13), and the late Paul Foot went so far as to describe investigative journalism as a pretentious phrase without genuine meaning 'often used by jumped-up by-lined journalists who want to distinguish themselves from the common ruck' (Foot 1999, p. 80). Despite this, there is plenty of evidence in Western liberal democracies that investigative journalism exists and, indeed, can actually have a major impact—as demonstrated by journalists' investigations of everything from British arms dealing with Iraq and French involvement in the bombing of the Greenpeace ship *Rainbow Warrior*, to the wrongful imprisonment of individuals such as John Button and Roseanne Catt in Australia, and police corruption in Queensland.

While admittedly somewhat blurred at the boundaries, at its core investigative journalism refers to a type of journalism that is more analytical than most other forms and that 'seeks to take the data available and reconfigure it, helping us to ask questions about the situation or statement or see it in a different way' (de Burgh 2000, p. 14). Although much journalism is primarily descriptive, investigative journalism 'at its furthest extent … questions the basis of orthodoxy, challenging the account of reality that the powers that be wish us to accept' (de Burgh 2000, p. 14). As such, it is widely considered to embody journalism's commitment to finding the truth and to working in the public interest (Tapsall & Phillips, 2002, p. 299). As the form of journalism that most closely performs journalism's traditional watchdog role and the one most able to demonstrate journalism's ability 'to act as a check on the state' (Curran 2005, p. 122), investigative journalism is regarded by many as 'the bone structure without which the journalistic body collapses' (Guillermoprieto 2012).

Yet, as Mark Deuze has argued:

> any definition of journalism as a profession working truthfully, operating as a watchdog for the good of society as a whole and enabling citizens to be self-governing is not only naïve, but also one-dimensional and sometimes nostalgic for perhaps the wrong reasons (2005, p. 458).

Historically, the news media have displayed contradictory tendencies of altruism and self-interest, and investigative journalists have been buffeted by the same inconsistent and constantly changing demands and expectations that have affected other journalists. More recently, intense forces ranging from globalisation and multiculturalism to technological change and economic crisis appear to be altering the very nature of journalism. While for centuries the news media were the primary source of information about what was happening for the overwhelming majority of the population, the 'ability to know about the world today extends to aspects of digital connectivity, with the Internet and Twitter becoming important tools in providing a forum for public discussion and participation in the media' (Josephi 2011, p. 8). Indeed, the rise of social media has been so dramatic and its effects so wide-ranging that, among other things, it seems clear that 'a substantial slab of the future of journalism will lie outside today's dominant media companies' (Simons 2012). In recent times, journalism's position has also been undermined by arrogant and unedifying behaviour on the part of some practitioners—epitomised by the revelations associated with the Leveson Inquiry into media ethics in the UK—raising concerns that the term 'investigative journalism' has been used as an umbrella phrase to conceal a range of unethical practices.

Despite these corrosive forces, journalism continues to be the main source of information for major sections of the population. However, it seems clear that, rather than playing one role, journalism today plays a range of roles. Christians and colleagues (2009) describe these roles as follows: the monitorial role (gathering and publishing information of interest to audiences); the facilitative role (supporting and strengthening civil society); the radical role (publication of views that challenge the established order); and the collaborative role (the relationship between the media and sources of political and economic power). Investigative journalism can play a central part in the first three of these roles. Christians and colleagues also argue that the main tasks of journalism in a democracy are observing and informing; participating in public life as an independent actor; and providing a forum or platform for extra-media sources. Further, they argue, under these conditions the occupational tasks of journalists involve four basic activities—discovery, collection and selection of information; processing into publishable accounts; providing background and commentary; and publication. These tasks can be translated into a set of terms that seem to explain what journalism is for, including surveillance of the environment; forming opinion; helping to set the agenda for public discussion; acting as a watchdog on political or economic power; acting as a messenger and public informant; and actively participating in social life. This exposition applies particularly well to investigative journalism, which performs each of these functions to varying degrees.

ETHICS AND INVESTIGATIVE JOURNALISM

Any section of society that has the power to influence public opinion, help set the agenda for public discussion, act as messenger and watchdog and so on, has an ethical obligation to exercise this power in ways that are responsible and in the public interest. This obligation is especially important in the case of investigative journalism, because to undertake this form of journalism is to acknowledge that something in society is wrong and needs righting. While a range of factors influences the decision as to what and when to investigate, all investigative journalists are required to make an initial moral judgment about the gravity of potential topics for investigation and the potential implications for those involved, as well as those likely to be affected by the outcome. This helps explain why investigative journalism tends to focus on such serious social issues as police corruption, criminal activity, political chicanery, miscarriages of justice and cover-ups of various kinds. As with other forms of journalism, an ethical element is present throughout any exercise in investigative journalism, 'from initial decisions regarding what to report, through decisions about the gathering and processing of whatever information is acquired, to decisions about how the information will be presented, and to whom' (Richards 2005, p. x). The last is especially significant because investigative reports are invariably presented in the context of a strong moral judgment—sometimes implicit, sometimes explicit—about the behaviour of the parties involved.

Indeed, through such judgments, investigative journalists not only 'locate, select, interpret, and apply standards for assessing the performance of officials and institutions' (Ettema & Glasser 1998, p. 3), but also contribute to 'the crafting of the moral order' (Ettema & Glasser 1998, p. 185).

Given the ethical basis that infuses and contextualises their role, it might seem that investigative journalists should rigorously apply the ethical requirements of their professional codes at all times. However, for a number of reasons this is not necessarily the case. The central message given to practitioners from these codes is to seek at all times to minimise harm. But while this is excellent advice in general, it raises some questions for investigative journalists.

One of the difficulties is that 'the concept of harm has multiple dimensions and multiple possible meanings' (Pleasance 2009, p. 108). For investigative journalists, this is compounded by the fact that the very nature of their work involves doing harm to someone, as most investigations conclude by pointing the finger at one or more of the parties who were the focus of the investigation. However, it is important to understand that this does not automatically pose an ethical dilemma because, if the party being accused has clearly been engaged in wrongdoing, then in an ethical sense that is really all there is to it; there is no grey area for debate or discussion. As Pleasance says: 'If we're serious about our obligations as moral beings, we don't usually argue whether it's ever okay to defraud or maliciously deceive others' (2009, p. 22). The difficulties arise when the issues are complicated, the conclusions are not necessarily clear cut, and some parties involved in an investigation are more culpable than others.

ON BEING FAIR AND HONEST

A common provision of journalists' ethics codes is a requirement to identify oneself as a journalist prior to acquiring information that may later be published. For example, clause 8 of Australia's Media Entertainment and Arts Alliance (MEAA) code advises journalists to 'Identify yourself and your employer before obtaining any interview for publication or broadcast' (MEAA 2001). Indeed, the clause goes further as it also advises journalists to 'Use fair, responsible and honest means to obtain material'. The underlying message is clear—journalists should not use deception to acquire information.

There are good reasons for the inclusion of such stipulations. Not only are citizens going about their daily business entitled to know the genuine identity of anyone requesting information from them, but they are also entitled not to be snooped upon or lied to by individuals seeking information from or about them. This is especially the case when this information is personal or confidential, and when it could ultimately be published for all the world to see. Such considerations are not only important at the level of the individual practitioner, but also at the wider level of journalism in general. For if journalists are prepared to acquire information by methods that are neither trustworthy nor honest, the wider public can be excused for concluding that journalists in general are not trustworthy and journalism in general is not to be trusted. As the MEAA has argued: 'the audience for a piece of journalism obtained with deception might well ask "If you were willing to deceive them, how do I know you are not deceiving me?"' (MEAA 1997, p. 34).

But despite the strong case that can be made against the use of deception to obtain information, many investigative journalists employ techniques such as hidden cameras and false identities. In most cases, the main reason for this is that such methods are extremely useful and effective tools in the pursuit of evidence of wrongdoing, abuse or fraud—in other words, they work. Given that individuals who are the target of investigative journalism frequently have something to hide, to reveal one's identity at the time of initial contact would succeed merely in alerting them to the fact that they are under investigation. As a result, they could be expected to take active steps to cover their tracks by, for example, destroying or hiding relevant documents or physically removing themselves from the scene, thus potentially undermining or negating the entire investigation. Hidden cameras have been a particular source of controversy. On one hand, they are considered to be an excellent way of finding out what 'really' goes on behind the scenes in the situation under investigation, and have the added advantage that the footage can be published later in order to substantiate the claims being made. On the other hand, hidden cameras also represent a serious form of invasion of privacy and—if used without sufficient justification—provide the wider public with clear evidence that journalists are devious and not to be trusted.

An example of a situation in which the use of hidden cameras was justified is provided by the 2010 Pakistani cricket scandal exposé in the UK. This involved a reporter from the now defunct *News of the World* who posed as an Indian match-fixer and paid £150 000 to sports agent Mazhar Majeed. Pakistani cricketers Salman Butt, Mohammad Amir and Mohammad Asif were subsequently sent to prison after being found guilty of match-fixing (Hughes 2011). As Roy Greenslade has argued, the newspaper appeared to have had prima facie evidence of wrongdoing, and there was a genuine public interest in exposing sporting corruption (Greenslade 2010).

PAYING FOR INFORMATION

Payment for interviews and information is another contentious ethical issue raised by investigative journalism. For while some investigative journalists refuse to pay for information under any circumstances, others are prepared to negotiate the payment of money to informants in certain situations. Although this aspect of what is popularly known as chequebook journalism is commonly defended by journalists—who employ it on the basis that there was no other way of obtaining the necessary information, or that it was an integral part of a 'sting'—there has been an extended debate as to whether such payments are justified.

To summarise, the main arguments against chequebook journalism are that buying someone's information is, in effect, a restriction on press freedom (and hence the people's right to know) because the purchaser retains exclusive rights to the information and keeps it from other media; that paying for stories encourages individuals to exaggerate or distort the information in order to enable them to extract the highest price for it; and that there is a risk that such payments could interfere with or distort the legal process if someone who provides information later appears in court. Against this, it is argued, individuals who have access to the sort of information that would interest an investigative journalist are often whistle-blowers who are placing themselves in peril and some financial return is, in effect, a form of compensation for their troubles. Besides, it is also argued, in contemporary capitalist societies such as Australia, the USA and the UK, it would be unreasonable and unrealistic to expect citizens not to seek to make money by selling to the highest bidder. And if journalists sometimes consider it necessary to fulfil this desire, then so be it.

PROBLEMS OF PRACTICE

Ethical dilemmas can also arise for investigative journalists in relation to standard journalistic practice. Some idea of why can be gained from the experience of US investigative journalist Kristen Lombardi when she was working to expose a clergy sexual-abuse scandal in Boston, Massachusetts. The investigation was complicated because many of those involved had suffered trauma and, as Lombardi has stated publicly, standard journalistic approaches to interviews don't work with trauma victims (Lombardi 2010). Her starting point was to accept that, if the investigation was to get anywhere, she needed to do what few of her professional colleagues would ever willingly agree to—allow her interviewees to control her interviews. In Lombardi's words, 'You must allow interviewees to set the terms—they can lay down the conditions for the interview, and you have to accept them—so they have control' (Lombardi 2010).

Similarly, while dogged persistence of potential sources is an admired quality in many areas of journalism, Lombardi found during her investigations that such approaches would 'only scare them off'. At the same time, other potential sources saw journalists as authority figures to be avoided and still others '[didn't] want to open up a Pandora's box on their emotions' (Lombardi 2010). In order to avoid re-traumatising those involved, Lombardi needed to devote far more time—'many hours'—to her interviews than would be considered acceptable in daily journalism, and also felt obliged to agree not to reveal the identities of most of her interviewees. She also needed to develop long-term relationships with each of her interviewees. Unlike most forms of journalism, where a few minutes of conversation is generally regarded as sufficient to acquire necessary information, she needed to develop a long-term relationship to allow trust to develop. In the process, she became emotionally involved with the lives of her interviewees, thereby also contravening such traditional journalistic notions as professional objectivity.

Taken together, the above examples illustrate the ethical difficulties posed for investigative journalists by some of the ethical principles of their professional work and some of the conventions of the daily practice of journalism. From these (and other examples), it seems clear that investigative journalists would be unsuccessful if they always adhered strictly to the widely accepted ethical principles that underlie their professional role. At first glance, this might seem rather odd, given that—as explained earlier—investigative journalism is widely considered to be the form of journalism which comes closest to journalism's traditional watchdog role. At second glance, however, it is not quite so surprising.

'DIRTY HANDS'

The reality is that investigative journalists are frequently required to deal with individuals who are involved in some form of wrongdoing and those who occupy the seamier side of life. And in order to deal with such individuals, it is sometimes necessary to adopt a different approach. Similar realities in other areas of life have been described as the problem of 'dirty hands'—and, as Matthew Kieran has pointed out, getting one's hands dirty is something that comes with the territory of investigative journalism (2000, p. 158). This is because, in a world that is less than ideal, 'we are often required to sacrifice moral ideals in order to uphold that which is right—and this is itself a moral obligation' (Kieran 2000, p. 159). In other words, not adhering to the provisions of journalists' codes of ethics is sometimes justified because this is the only way to assert right over wrong. And, in practice, many codes of ethics tacitly acknowledge this reality. Thus the MEAA Code, for example, concludes with a guidance clause that states: 'Only substantial advancement of the public interest or risk of substantial harm to people allows any standard to be overridden' (MEAA 1999). In this way, the code acknowledges that its provisions and the principles that underlie them may, on occasion, be justifiably overridden, and, indeed, that to do so is not always unethical.

In such situations, the central dilemma then becomes determining the point at which it is acceptable to override a standard, and knowing how to proceed from that point. The answer to this is, really, that there is no straightforward answer, and that responses will vary case by case. As Werhane has argued, ethical decision making requires moral imagination and the ability to see things from different points of view (cited in Provis 2005. p. 293). Such imagination allows those involved 'to go beyond any one set of mental models or scripts, to a critical awareness of other models and scripts that might properly be applied to the situation that confronts us' (Provis 2005, p. 293). Investigative journalists, then, should be able to come up with an ethically acceptable solution regardless of what their professional codes say, because 'there does not seem to be any ground to believe that the evidence available to us either in theoretical or in practical reasoning is only ever compatible with one reasonable conclusion' (Provis 2005, p. 296). Provis is quick to add that this does not mean that all conclusions are equally reasonable, rather that 'Evidence and reasoning can weigh against some factors and in favour of others' (Provis 2005, p. 296).

CONCLUSION

In any assessment of journalism today, it is important to appreciate that investigative journalism as practised in Western liberal democracies is not an innate component of those societies. Despite the many positive outcomes they have produced in many countries, investigative journalists face many obstacles: within journalism from a lack of resources and declining support from media managements struggling against declining circulations and ratings; and externally, from powerful sections of society that are sometimes prepared to use any means available—legal and illegal, ethical and unethical—to prevent an investigation of their affairs. It is also important to remember that investigative journalism is only one of the forms of journalism alive in the world today. There are many other journalisms, and not all have the legitimacy of investigative journalism. One need only think of the pallid journalism of countries that have dictatorships, or where government control reduces journalists to virtual mouthpieces for the official line.

In summary, the key ethical values of investigative journalism derive from the central role that this form of journalism continues to play in Western liberal democracies and, following on from this, the part such journalism plays in crafting the moral order of those democracies. As such, investigative journalists have a clear ethical duty to exercise their power in ways that are responsible and in the public interest. Paradoxically, at a practical level this does not mean they need to apply the provisions of their professional codes at all times, as overriding these codes is justified when this is the only way to assert right over wrong.

From an ethical perspective, then, one of the most difficult aspects of investigative journalism is determining the point at which it is acceptable to override provisions of ethics codes, and how to proceed from that point. Given that there is seldom, if ever, only one ethical way to respond to an ethical dilemma, what is required is careful and informed exercising of the moral imagination to come up with a solution. As Pleasance has pointed out, media professionals need to develop and cultivate the 'ability to build compelling, rational arguments when their decisions are likely to cause harm' (2009, p. 131). Nowhere in journalism is this more important than with investigative journalists, who need to be constantly alert to the integrity of their decisions, the ethical implications of what they are doing, the ethical options available to them, and the potential harm their decisions could pose. Given the importance of what they do, it is a challenge in which they must succeed.

QUESTIONS TO CONSIDER

1   To what extent is it fair to argue as De Burgh has done that investigative journalism: 'at its furthest extent … questions the basis of orthodoxy, challenging the account of reality that the powers that be wish us to accept' (2000, p. 14). How does your argument sit with those of Pilger and Foot—that the very existence of investigative journalism as a form of its own is questionable?

2   To what extent is there a moral dimension to investigative journalism? How does this moral dimension differ from that applicable to other forms of journalism?

3   What is the problem of 'dirty hands'?

4   Under what circumstances, if any, are investigative journalists permitted to act outside the provisions of their code of conduct or ethics?

5   To what extent, if any, are investigative journalists permitted to pay for information?

TASK

1   To what extent is there a moral dimension to investigative journalism and how does this differ from other forms of journalism? Use examples to justify your answer.

REFERENCES

Christians, C., Glasser, T., McQuail, D., Nordenstreng, K. & White, R. 2009. *Normative Theories of the Media: Journalism in Democratic Societies*, Urbana: University of Illinois Press.

Curran, J. 2005. 'Mediations of Democracy', in J. Curran & M. Gurevitch, eds, *Mass Media and Society*, London: Arnold, pp.122–49.

De Burgh, H., ed. 2000. *Investigative Journalism: Context and Practice*, London: Routledge.

Deuze, M. 2005. 'What is Journalism? Professional Identity and Ideology of Journalists Reconsidered', *Journalism*, 6(4), pp. 442–64.

Ettema, J. & Glasser T. 1998. *Custodians of Conscience: Investigative Journalism and Public Virtue*, New York: Columbia University Press.

Foot, P. 1999. 'The Slow Death of Investigative Journalism', in S. Glover, ed., *Penguin Book of Journalism*, London: Penguin, pp. 79–89.

Greenslade, R. 2010. 'Why the *News of the World's* Pakistan Story was Justified', *The Guardian*, 6 September: www.guardian.co.uk/media/greenslade/2010/sep/06/newsoftheworld-pakistan-cricket-betting-scandal (accessed 29 February 2012).

Guillermoprieto, A. 2012. 'What Others Say about the Center for Public Integrity', The Center for Public Integrity: www.publicintegrity.org/about/our-work/quotes-testimonials (accessed 1 March 2012).

Hughes, S. 2011. 'Pakistan Cricket Stars Face Jail over Match Fix Scandal', *The Sun Online*, 2 November: www.thesun.co.uk/sol/homepage/news/3909236/Pakistan-cricket-stars-facebr-jail-over-match-fix-scandal.html (accessed 24 February 2012).

Josephi, B. 2011. 'Supporting Democracy: How Well do the Australian Media Perform?' *Australian Journalism Monographs*, vol. 13, Griffith Centre for Cultural Research Brisbane, Griffith University.

Kieran, M. 2000. 'The Regulatory and Ethical Framework for Investigative Journalism', in H. de Burgh, ed., *Investigative Journalism: Context and Practice*, London: Routledge.

Lombardi, K. 2010. 'Dart Foundation Address', 19 June, New York: Columbia University.

Media Entertainment and Arts Alliance (MEAA). 1997. *Ethics in Journalism: Report of the Ethics Review Committee*, Melbourne: Melbourne University Press.

Media Entertainment and Arts Alliance (MEAA). 1999. *Australian Journalists' Association Code of Ethics*: www.alliance.org.au/code-of-ethics.html (accessed 23 November 2001).

Pleasance, P. 2009. *Media Ethics: Key Principles for Responsible Practice*, Thousand Oaks: Sage.

Provis, C. 2005. 'Dirty Hands and Loyalty in Organisational Politics', *Business Ethics Quarterly*, 15(2), pp. 283–98.

Richards, I. 2005. *Quagmires and Quandaries: Exploring Journalism Ethics*, Sydney: University of New South Wales Press.

Simons, M. 2012. 'The Bottom Line says a Leaner Fairfax', *Crikey*, 24 February: http://media.crikey.com.au/dm/newsletter/dailymail_5325f386305be3db66c960b3204b126f.html/.

Tapsall, S. & Phillips, G. 2002. 'Investigative Journalism and Ethics—A Slippery Slide Rule', in S. Tanner, ed., *Journalism Investigation and Research*, Sydney: Longman, pp. 298–311.

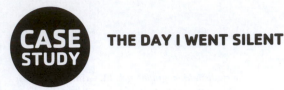

THE DAY I WENT SILENT

Sharon Mascall–Dare

In Australia, we have the term 'silent number'. Strangely, given the investigative work that I have chosen to pursue over the last 20 years or so, I have never 'gone silent'. In the UK, where I began my career with the BBC, the equivalent term is 'ex-directory' and I had never felt the need to withhold my telephone number there, either. In 2011, I was to learn the repercussions of that decision.

It was June and the first instalment of *The Big House* was about to go to air on the BBC World Service. In two parts, *The Big House* told the story of 18 young men as they experienced the hardships of rehabilitation at Port Augusta prison, in South Australia. Many of the men were from Indigenous backgrounds; almost all of them came from broken families, where they had grown up surrounded by domestic violence, substance abuse and crime. My intention was to challenge listeners' assumptions in a radio documentary format: Do 'criminals' think they are 'criminal'? What do we mean by 'prison' and 'rehabilitation'? How can we stop prison's revolving door and break the cycle of crime, punishment and more crime?

From the outset, I used a technique that is well known to documentary makers, particularly in the USA. 'Ethnographic journalism' requires a journalist to immerse him or herself in the environment or culture under study: it can be well suited to investigative assignments. I discovered the theoretical and historical basis of ethnographic journalism only recently even though I, along with many of my colleagues in Australia and the UK, have been using the technique for many years. At the BBC, for example, it shares similarities with a style of documentary commonly known as 'fly on the wall' or 'undercover reporting'. The devil, however, lies in the proverbial detail: ethnographic journalism can raise ethical dilemmas, particularly in an investigative context. As an 'investigator' inside the prison, I found myself questioning interviewees and my methodology.

First, there was the issue of access. Over a three-month period, I spent around 100 hours inside the jail with unfettered access to prisoners and staff. Securing such access required frank discussions with the general manager of the prison, a former military man with a keen interest in anthropology. There was a risk that he would attach conditions to my access; I knew he might use access as a bargaining tool, seeking to influence my interviews or script. To his credit, he did neither. He expressed an interest in ethnography and understood my methodology. The result was a level of trust that I have rarely experienced: I cannot say the same of the South Australian State Government. While the prison trusted my editorial judgment, the minister's office did not, asking me to cut the words 'rack 'em and stack 'em' from one officer's quote. Supported by the BBC's editorial policy and my own commitment to accuracy, I refused to cut those words from the documentary.

Next came the interviews with prisoners. Given the lack of trust that most inmates had for the media and for me, as a 'Pommy woman from the BBC', I asked the men to set the terms, asking them how their stories should be told. At first, it was hard: I spent many hours listening to stories of violence and self-justification: 'I *had* to do the robberies to get money for my girlfriend ...', or 'I had no money, so what was I supposed to do?' Some men said nothing at all; others ignored me. Within a few hours, however, most wanted to talk.

I heard stories of hunting giant lizards in the Simpson Desert, punctuated by rows between an alcoholic father and a violent mother. I heard how one boy (from the age of 10) had learned to run so fast, he had found a way to outrun the cops when caught stealing at the shops. I heard about foster homes and girlfriends, gangs and armed robberies. At times, I had to remind myself that I was there to listen and record, but also to question. I navigated between different roles: I was listener, insider, interrogator and mediator. Above all, I was a mere broadcaster of what the men had to say.

At times, I heard too much. On one occasion, a prison officer told me—off microphone—about a case of child abuse that had recently come to court. The details were harrowing; the story was haunting. I made a decision: I hooked up with the Dart Center for Journalism and Trauma based at Columbia University in New York to find out more about journalism as it relates to coverage of violence, trauma and war. I remain indebted to Dart Centre Asia-Pacific and the support they offer journalists in covering such stories responsibly—protecting themselves as well as their interviewees. On another occasion, I said too much. It was my last day inside the jail and one man in particular, 'Tom', wanted to say goodbye. I had interviewed him five times and developed a level of trust. We had talked to each other at length; he had expressed remorse on record. As an armed robber his crimes had been 'vicious'; now he was determined to turn his life around. I said he could contact me. In June, he did precisely that.

I recognised his voice immediately, when I answered his call on my private line at home. He was out in the desert, at a prison work camp near the opal fields of Andamooka. He had found a public telephone, called Telstra, and, after some guesswork regarding my address, they had given him my number.

'I just wanted to know when the program's going to be on.'

'Next month,' I replied, 'do you think they'll let you listen at the jail?'

'Don't know—you know that two of the guys busted out?'

'No I didn't ...'

'My money's running out. I bet you didn't think you'd hear from me again. I bet I've scared you.'

'No, not at all ...' the line went dead. My husband hit the roof. The next day I rang Telstra and requested our number be 'silent'.

Over the years, I have taken calls from Mark 'Chopper' Read, Australia's infamous gangland personality; interviewed drug dealers and addicts; and spent many hours recording inside various prisons. But there was something about 'Tom' and my encounter with him that worries me. My dilemma is ethical, personal and professional: for some reason, I suspect that he will come knocking at my door when he gets out, and I am unsure what I will do. I want to trust him, but I know I cannot. Immersion in the prison was one thing: ironically, I was safe within that environment. At home, I am not.

Silence now seems a safer option.

PART 3

APPLIED INVESTIGATIONS

Chapter 15: Politics   193
Case Study: In Search of a Truth Serum   204

Chapter 16: Crime Writing   208
Case Study: Intelligence-led Reporting   217

Chapter 17: On Flak, Balance and Activism: The Ups and
            Downs of Environmental Journalism   221

Chapter 18: Health Reporting: Opportunities and Challenges?   232
Case Study: Harnessing the Digital Era for Health Investigations   243

Chapter 19: Science Journalism   246

Chapter 20: Reporting Indigenous Affairs   254
Case Study: Taking Journalists on the Journey   267

Chapter 21: Investigative Essentials for Journalists in
            Multicultural and Diverse Communities   269

Chapter 22: Not Just About the Money   282
Case Study: BHP and Ok Tedi   291

Chapter 23: Industrial Relations   297
Case Study: IR reporting   305

Chapter 24: Investigative Journalism and Sports Reporting   308
Case Study: Harness Racing Exposé   318

Chapter 25: Publishing Your Work   320
Case Study: Tipping Point   330

15

Politics

NICK RICHARDSON

'In the face of canny politicians, tight-lipped bureaucrats and armies of spin merchants, rat cunning and the ability to bluff are sometimes all we've got'—veteran political journalist Laurie Oakes (2011)

'The line between spin doctors and panic merchants can be a thin one. Too often the government has spun itself dizzy, and failed to achieve any sustained focus on its good news'—political scientist Rodney Tiffen (2010)

'The two key rules that now govern the practice of Australian politics are: (1) Look like you're doing something and (2) Don't offend anyone that matters'—former federal Labor minister Lindsay Tanner (2011, p. 7)

One of the inescapable observations about the current political environment is the deep cynicism that exists in the relationship between politicians and the media. A corrosive corollary of this is the impact that cynicism has on the electorate, the institution of government, and inevitably, the Fourth Estate. While we could spend a great deal of time reflecting on the reasons for that cynical—even dysfunctional—relationship and its impact, this chapter will instead spend most of its time identifying some of the practical problems and then looking at ways to rehabilitate the situation by using the basic tools of journalism: curiosity, inquiry, commitment to the task, and lateral thinking. And an important part of this approach is utilising some of the tools, such as data journalism, that we have already identified to help renew the importance of investigative journalism in politics.

Politics, by its very nature, covers a range of activities and areas: many of the specialised chapters in this book—such as health, industrial relations, environment, finance and business, and even sport—join education, science and infrastructure as domains that become political because of the decisions and consequences that surround them. Governments make education policy, build schools and employ teachers. Trains, roads, bike lanes and buses—how you get to work, university or home—are inevitably about what governments do to support and invest in their communities.

This chapter's approach will involve circumventing what have become the standard rules of engagement between politicians and journalists. We will spend some time exploring those rules of engagement before we outline some possible new ways of finding and revealing political information.

This is not, however, about behaving unethically or with rogue intent. This is actually about remembering that there are many political stories that occur every day that are never reported. There is rich material for the journalist, especially if they work outside the mainstream media that is increasingly shackled to the routines and rhythms of the 24-hour news cycle. A determination to work outside this cycle and explore other legitimate stories will have its own rewards, most particularly in helping to rehabilitate the democratic compact that is at the heart of the journalist–politician connection. The more toxic that connection becomes, the harder it is for the average Joe to make sense of what is occurring in society.

Whatever we might think about politics and politicians, the job of the political journalist remains central to the understanding and functioning of a democracy. Electors in a compulsory voting system such as Australia have not only the right, but also a need, to be informed about the decisions that are made by all levels of government. How else can someone turn up at the ballot box and make an informed decision about who to vote for? As US journalism academic Jay Rosen said about political reporting in the USA and Australia: 'Things are out of alignment. Journalists are identifying with the wrong people. Therefore the kind of work they are doing is not as useful as we need it to be' (2011).

We, the public, need journalism to be committed to finding out what governments do and don't do. It is helpful to remember that one of the most memorable pieces of investigative journalism of the past six decades—the Pentagon Papers—was about revealing the truth behind a government's support for a foreign war. Investigative journalism at its finest can have profound consequences for the public good, and has, therefore, become more important this decade than ever.

HOW MOST POLITICAL STORIES OCCUR

There are few genuine political scoops generated through the federal or state press galleries. A check of the premier Australian journalism award, the Walkleys, reveal that in the investigative journalism category from 1991 to 2011 only two of the winners could be considered as Federal Press Gallery journalists. Yet the majority of the awarded stories had either a political dimension or a political consequence.

It is a simple fact that journalistic activity in the political environment is often about covering the story of the day, rather than the story behind the story. Political activity occurs at a public level that most journalists see and report on, whether it is a press release, a doorstop interview, parliamentary Question Time or a radio interview with a party leader. This conventional exchange is supplemented by conversations, either on or off the record, with MPs, ministers, councillors, party officials and bureaucrats who have a perspective—or in many instances, an agenda—to help shape the story. Over time, a political journalist will cultivate and develop those sources who will talk to them about particular political issues. Some political sources are happy to cooperate because they see the value in having their perspective in the public domain to advance their agenda or ambition with the audience of that particular media organisation.

There is, however, another subterranean level to these exchanges: it is a level that is actually more interesting because it is often about the deliberations, discussions and decisions about how power is used. Usually it takes a political player with a motive to reveal parts of this level, and because their motivation is political (and often about personal ambition) it can be difficult to feel certain that their information is reliable. Nonetheless, once this information finds its way into the public domain, other sources weigh in to the discussion, trying to shape the story, illuminate or exaggerate their own role, excoriate old rivalries or reach out to allies.

One of the best examples of this was the challenge Australian Foreign Affairs Minister Kevin Rudd mounted against Prime Minister Julia Gillard in February 2012. So much of the media coverage of the lobbying and jockeying was based on what Labor MPs were saying 'on background' to political reporters (meaning information that cannot be publicly attributed to a named source). Agendas of influence were peddled backwards and forwards from the Labor Caucus to the media in the battle to help identify who was supporting whom in the leadership ballot; to denigrate the contenders; or to elevate their claims on the job. Every political decision Gillard made during this time was viewed through the prism of the leadership rivalry, intensified by the events of June 2010 when Gillard rolled Rudd for the prime ministership. And in the end, such was the strength of the Gillard forces in 2012, the result of Rudd's failed attempt to return to his old job was known to the Gallery several days in advance of the Caucus vote.

The leadership challenge demonstrates one of the fundamental truths of political reporting: that many political stories develop, rather than break. They change incrementally through the media cycle as more sources—and more reaction—start to overlay the origins of the story. And with each incremental development, there will be a commentary to support it, so that the reader is left in no doubt about what it means. All of this is appropriate, in its way. It reflects the dynamic of the exchange between politicians and the media. But it has little to do with investigative journalism. It is, rather, the basic craft of following a developing story. And such a story will rarely tell us something we don't know because we, as news consumers, will know the cast of actors (the ministers and the MPs) and we will know their language and the way they express their position, views, reactions and motivations. So the challenge is how to get outside the conventions of this exchange. What are the obstacles journalists must identify before they can make progress and start to find new ways to reveal the story? And, more importantly, generate more informed political debate?

THE SEVEN DEADLY SINS OF POLITICAL JOURNALISM

Let's call them the Seven Deadly Sins of political journalism. Each of these 'sins' complicates investigative journalism in the political environment.

1 'FEED ME'

There is a mutual dependence between political journalists and politicians: journalists need stories and politicians need a platform. There is, in many ways, a tacit agreement of mutual exploitation, but at least each party knows what is going on. While there is some debate about whether the relationship is a 'snake pit' or a 'dance' (Savage & Tiffen 2007), there is no doubt that the dialogue takes place within an environment of often hostile (media) competition and mutual suspicion. The central problem in such a relationship is that the reader/viewer/listener, who are all voters, are often marginalised. And as veteran Canberra journalist George Megalogenis pointed out, it can reach a ridiculous level, most recently when Rudd was prime minister: 'Rudd feared that if a leader didn't feed the media it would eat the leader … The danger of saying "no" to the media even once was that they would not be asked back' (2010, p. 11). This sense of the media's importance really plays to the political media's self-perception—that it is the most important journalistic activity in the nation because it reports on national affairs. This is a somewhat skewed view, but many politicians feel they have to be part of that conversation. Silence, or non-engagement, may not help their career advancement or indeed help shape policy debate. In an era when it feels like we are in the middle of a perpetual election campaign, this kind of message-sending is considered vital.

Leaks that are usually managed for best effect are part of the deal, but behind each leak is a complex balancing act between source and reporter. Political leaders use the media to reach voters; other political players usually have a less altruistic motive for talking to political journalists. Either way, the relationship between the politician and the political journalist is complicated because it is rarely about a straight communication of information. It can be compromised by other agendas, including the journalist's or indeed the journalist's media organisation.

2 WADDYA KNOW?

This is perhaps one of the most important—and least asked—questions among press gallery reporters. Many inexperienced political reporters mistakenly believe they have all of a story when they have spoken to both sides of politics and worked their sources. The reality is that 'all' of the story is an elusive concept. There might be 20 people involved in any political or policy discussion. Can you ask them all? Consider the last time you attended a meeting or presentation and discussed it afterwards with a friend who was there. Did both of you remember the same thing in the same way? Even putting that aside, while there are layers of information that MPs, bureaucrats and councillors are happy to release, there is plenty that they are not prepared to publicise. Longstanding *Sydney Morning Herald* political columnist Alan Ramsey worked for five years as a press adviser to former Labor Leader Bill Hayden before Ramsey returned to the press gallery. He said: 'You can't know how little you know about everyday professional politics until you're on the inside ... Five years with Hayden established contacts, friends and a broad understanding of the essential self-serving nature of political behaviour that sustained me in political journalism for the ensuing 25 years' (Ramsey 2009, p. xix). Ramsey's path was a rare one: very few political journalists these days leave the fold, cross over in to political staff jobs, and then return to reporting. Those who do have an enormous benefit in understanding how much they don't know about what is really happening.

The flipside to this is how much journalists know that they cannot or will not publish because of legal or personal reasons. This was most clearly spelled out again during the Gillard–Rudd leadership challenge, when previously private details of Rudd's behaviour when he was prime minister were leaked. Canberra writer Christine Wallace wrote: 'To the outside world Kevin Rudd is a charming, intelligent Cheerful Charlie. People can't understand why he was dumped as leader in the first place and why there's such a terrific battle being waged to stop him becoming prime minister again. Insiders know he is not what he seems' (2012). The reality is only some of what the 'insiders' know is remotely interesting or relevant to the 'outsiders'.

3 SPIN CLASS

Spin is one of the most talked-about elements of political reporting. But it is also a problem for everyone, including the public and the politicians. Former federal Labor minister Lindsay Tanner is very clear on the problem: 'Spin is intensifying. Its significance is growing. Whereas once it reflected occasional embellishments and evasions, it now lies at the heart of the political process. People are complaining about something that they once ignored or took for granted, because it now dominates our public culture' (2011, p. 14). When MPs characterise news manipulation in such terms, we clearly have a problem. The issue is that spin has jumped the political fence, and is now part of a number of public debates—whether it is the big banks trying to explain not passing on the full interest rate fall; football coaches downplaying the extent of an injury to a star player; or a local councillor trying to portray an extensive local land development as a boost for the nearby shopping centre. Put simply, spin is pervasive and insidious. It also helps erode public trust in our key institutions. Spin has also become easier with the 24-hour news cycle (see below).

4 DO YOU FEEL LUCKY?

This is a simple and understated element in the mix. What are the stakes for the elected official, the MP or the bureaucrat in talking about a particular issue? And is it worth the risk? At state and local government level, this is a particular problem because bureaucrats in particular are rarely allowed to speak publicly about policy deliberations, either on or off the record. Federal public servants, especially departmental heads, have more leeway in this regard; but with the increasing politicisation of the bureaucracy, there is also less chance that the senior public servants will deliver information at odds with the government's thinking or priorities.

The risk problem is particularly prevalent at local government level, where the tension between the senior salaried council official (the chief executive officer) and a council made up of elected officials (many of whom have higher political ambitions) can lead to tensions within the council bureaucracy.

Who speaks for whom? And what they can say without putting pressure on themselves or their boss can make the local government reporter's job incredibly frustrating. Many local council stories are stymied by the attempts of council communications staff to delay, control or negate the political reporter's questions. The risk of saying something wrong, inappropriate or just stupid is so overwhelming as to reduce statements to banalities or eliminate access to sources. And almost all of these exchanges are conducted through the sterile channels of email Q&As. This means that the stakes internally (within council) outweigh the benefits of communicating the council's message externally. Just ask yourself this question—does that sound fair?

A key subtext to this discussion is the degree of trust on both sides of the exchange. Trust mitigates risk. If a source trusts the reporter to represent their position accurately, then there is less risk in speaking to the reporter. If, however, the source—whether they are council communications staff or a federal minister—feels the reporter has previously misreported their comments, has a particular agenda or is simply the new kid on the block, then the source will be aware of a heightened risk that the outcome may not go well. It is no surprise that the most experienced political reporters have the best sources because they have built up trusted relationships over time.

5 STOP THE CLOCK!

No you can't stop the 24-hour news cycle. If there is one element of political journalism that has become more demanding, it is the almost insatiable demand for content across all platforms. Journalists used to be mono-media: they were print journalists or radio reporters or television reporters. Now, journalists have to be adept at all three forms of media and file for online entities as well. Stories are short and constantly updated. Context and history drop away because there is no room for it. Whatever happens is reported only in the light of the story that came before it. As Gillard noted in 2010:

> We are in a media environment now where you could make a blockbuster announcement. Someone is tweeting about it while you are doing the press conference. Journalists can be doing a stand-up using you as a backdrop. By the time you get back to your office journalists are interviewing journalists about what the announcement may or may not mean. And two hours later someone will ring my press secretary and say: 'Have you got a story for us?' (quoted in Moore 2010).

Press gallery doyen Laurie Oakes describes it thus:

> Journalists have less time to think or draw on outside expertise. Their job description involves getting stuff on air or into print asap. The requirement for instant analysis can mean shallow analysis … politicians get less time to sell a message or explain a policy before being expected to move on to something new (2010, p. vii).

Political scientist Rod Tiffen agrees:

> The proliferation of news outlets, the constancy of deadlines, and the managerial pressures for ever greater productivity, all put increasing pressures on journalists for volume rather than depth. So there is more political reporting than ever, but neither its quality nor the quality of political debate show tangible improvement (2012, p. 21).

So in this instance, the constancy of coverage does not amount to quality of coverage. It also means that getting your message out first means that it is less likely to be published without a contrary voice. And it also increases the likelihood of you controlling the message during the news cycle. As social commentator Tim Dunlop explains: '[The politicians] also know that the very act of reporting something non-critically will give what they say authority and credence. They know that if their "version" is reported first, it will frame all future coverage no matter its truth value' (2012). The end result is that debate on public policy is often compromised and so too is the policy itself. This can lead to the next impediment.

6 LOOK AT ME, LOOK AT ME!

The constant demand for content—and the ceaseless transition from one soundbite to the next—can mean that the person who looks and sounds the best will have greater impact on steering the public debate. This is about appearance rather than message; entertainment rather than policy; notoriety rather than non-entity. It is a development that Tanner finds particularly galling. One of the more recent examples was the appearance of former Labor Leader Mark Latham on the election campaign for *60 Minutes*. Latham's behaviour when he imposed himself on the Gillard campaign became a story in its own right. Tanner wrote: 'As politics has been subsumed by entertainment, it has drifted inexorably in to the celebrity world … The power of celebrity has become a magnet for politicians and media' (2011, p. 77). While some of Tanner's perspective might be put down to disillusionment, it is fair to say that entertainment and celebrity are notable undercurrents in modern political journalism.

7 GIVE 'EM WHAT THEY WANT! (NOT)

Research from other Western democracies shows that public disenchantment with political media is widespread. A survey of the six US presidential campaigns to 2008 revealed that voters gave the media poorer grades than candidates, pollsters and campaign consultants (Farnsworth & Lichter 2011). The researchers' conclusion was damning: 'Reporters clearly have a different perspective about what citizens need to know than citizens themselves' (Farnsworth & Lichter 2011, p. 7). Voters apparently feel that the political media is not serving their interests in a way that serves them or their community.

As a voter, you might want to think about the last election campaign you observed. How much of what you heard or read addressed your priorities? How much of that content went to the bread-and-butter issues that helped make up your mind on who to vote for? Content is increasingly shaped by political scandals, the horse-race approach (especially evident in the reliance on the frequent public polling data) and journalists' opinion. Only some of that range of reporting will have what voters consider a direct impact on them. The rest is part of the loop of information and rumour that connects the political and the media class.

SEVEN SUPPORTIVE STRATEGIES

So what do we do about the Seven Deadly Sins of political reporting? If only it was as easy as avoiding the impediments and pitfalls we have just discussed. You need to be more assertive than that because the seven problems are oppressive and pervasive.

1 BE AN OUTSIDER

For all the talk of the benefits of being a 'political insider', it is rarely true these days that insider knowledge will trigger a groundbreaking piece of political investigative journalism. While it is true that what the Americans call the 'inside the Beltway' perspective can provide context and background, it is often reporters working outside the political round who actually reveal some of the bigger political stories.

A significant recent example is the 2011 Walkley Award for Scoop of the Year that went to Channel Ten reporter Matt Moran, who uncovered what became known as the 'Skype Scandal'. The story of how an 18-year-old female air force cadet's sexual liaison was Skyped to six other cadets became the focus of an investigation into the culture at the Australian Defence Force Academy, and turned into a significant political story that enabled Ten's Canberra correspondent Hugh Riminton to become part of the coverage. But it all started with Moran and the cadet.

Political journalists potentially risk their contacts—and rarely have the time—to investigate such issues to a depth. Most importantly, working outside the established political system of press secretaries and advisers means journalists risk not getting the same information or interviews that other political reporters receive. And not being in regular contact with those government mouthpieces minimises the risk of your story leaking out to your competitors.

2 BE SCEPTICAL

This seems like stating the bleeding obvious, but it is central to the journalistic activity and vitally important in politics, simply because there is so much information that is delivered in an official form. Just because it's official, however, doesn't mean that it cannot be tested and interrogated (see the case study at the end of this chapter). There are plenty of official inquiries, reports and documents that will carry the credibility of the department or agency that compiled them. That is as it should be, but it pays to remember that perhaps not every source has been consulted in the compilation of that report and that there may be additional information that subtly (or significantly) shifts the document's perspective. Once you deploy that scepticism wisely, the challenge then is to have the time to follow through on any doubts, omissions, mistakes or evidence that you think are worth exploring.

3 MINE THE PUBLIC DATA

As we have seen, there is a huge amount of material that is readily available to political reporters. But often the sheer volume of it becomes a tool for governments to create a blizzard of information that no political reporter has the time (or probably the inclination) to work through. One of the more telling examples of this was the Victorian Labor Government's decision in 2010 to release more than 200 agency and departmental reports to Parliament on one day. This became a story in its own right, and triggered a special investigation by Swinburne University journalism students in Melbourne who worked their way through the reports for *Crikey*, and revealed several significant stories that, without their work, would not have seen the light of day (*Crikey* 2010). This 'dumping' of reports is not uncommon, and as frustrating as it is for political reporters trying to find a story for their website, evening news or next day's paper, there will be plenty of gems among the dross if you're prepared to dig for them.

4 MINE THE NOT-SO PUBLIC DATA

So much information is now kept in online databases. As we have seen earlier in this book, it is very easy with the help of Excel spreadsheets to collate, filter and interrogate data sets. But the trick is actually finding the data and then making sense of it in a journalistic way.

Australia lags behind the UK in several useful government tools, such as the COINS database that details how the UK Treasury distributes money to departments and agencies. And all UK local government bodies have to reveal all their spending, contracts and tender documents valued over £500 (Brooke 2011). An Australian political journalist's life would be significantly better with such tools. But in the meantime—and putting aside campaigning for such innovations—the journalist needs to work Freedom of Information (FOI) hard and refuse to take 'no' for an answer.

Heather Brooke, the investigative journalist whose work in the UK on MPs' expenses triggered significant reform on the issue (and ended several MPs careers), started her investigation with an FOI request about MPs' expenses (Brooke 2011). The obstacle she faced was the official parliamentary view that such expense details compromised MPs' privacy. Her determination to find out the real picture led to a significant set of reforms in the UK. In this area, thankfully, Australian parliaments are far more robust: MPs' expenses have to be public and they are often a source of stories (see, for example the 2012 controversy over former Parliamentary Speaker Peter Slipper: Coorey 2012). The overall point is that journalists need to try to pinpoint where there are 'holes' in the public information system in the same way Brooke did. Ask yourself these questions: what don't you know and what should you know? Most importantly, what should the public know but what are they not being told? For instance: there is often a lack of specific detail and transparency around local government tendering contracts. This is a legitimate line of inquiry about councils' use of ratepayers' money. It is a subject that requires dedication and perseverance, but once you have the information, you have the basis of some unique and valuable content.

Whether journalists are working for community (suburban) titles, radio stations, metropolitan dailies, television stations or online sites, they all need to be aware how government decisions can impact on their audiences. A compelling example was the Federal Government's strategy when introducing the Carbon Tax from July 2012. Part of that strategy was that a federal agency, the Clean Energy Regulator, wrote to 104 local councils across the nation to notify them they were facing a special levy to deal with the greenhouse gases emitted from their large landfill sites (Priest 2012). These notifications did not detail which councils were facing the extra levy, and the Clean Energy Regulator initially refused to identify the councils. However, local community newspaper reporters could work it out by checking with their own council or submitting an FOI request to receive the full list. Initial reports suggested that some of the costs were up to $600 000—a significant and unbudgeted problem for some councils. It is worthwhile remembering that what the Federal Government does can have consequences for state and local governments. The information loop at the top might be narrow, but there are opportunities to find out more as the information trickles down through the different layers of government.

5 STATE OF MIND

This is not about what tools you have at your disposal; it's about really getting in to the frame of mind that prepares you to work outside the daily race of news and views. It can be a lonely existence, where the journalist is isolated from day-to-day contact with colleagues and rivals. It takes courage to sit outside the circus: the courage to accept that you don't need to be reporting on the daily events to be doing your job, and the courage to see the larger landscape and think creatively to identify the stories that are not being told. It means being proactive—a terrible word, but a useful approach for an investigative journalist. It means not being a passive receiver of information, shackled to a menu of political trivia and stunts. Search for the substance in political announcements and avoid the atmospherics. Stunts are increasingly frequent in politics. Whether it is former Family First Senator Steve Fielding pushing a mini supermarket trolley through Parliament House to highlight the cost of living, or Tony Abbott jogging through the surf in a pair of budgie smugglers, it's got little to do with what is really going on for most people.

Investigative journalism of all types demands time to think and time to reflect. 'If reporters lack the time to gather, analyze and reflect on information, then they will have less leverage to confront the institutions on their beat,' US journalism academic Dean Starkman noted in his revealing essay, 'The Hamster Wheel' (2010). It is also true that newsroom managers need to allow some of their journalists the time to develop story ideas, to research them and then write them in a compelling way for web or paper. It is almost impossible to be an investigative journalist if you are covering daily politics.

6 SOURCES

Journalists on a news round are only ever as good as their sources. Everyone can write a story from a press release, but the politics of the announcement, the Cabinet deliberations about the decisions, the Opposition party room debate—all of these things depend on having good sources.

It takes time to cultivate good sources. And the best way to behave in that relationship is as an ethical, honourable and accurate reporter. Some political sources will test a young journalist out with a story that has no great import and assess the likelihood of being able to trust the journalist in the long term. Others will make a decision on the political allegiances of the journalist or the media outlet they work for. For example, some Labor personnel feel uncomfortable dealing with *The Australian* because they believe the paper is not friendly to their side of politics, and they will turn to the Fairfax papers to give them what they believe is a fairer run.

Whatever the reason a source talks to a journalist, it is important to have people who can tell you what *else* is happening, outside the daily noise of the political battle. It is also important to remember that in the digital age there are many lobby groups that have their own websites. Many of them have sophisticated and detailed research around their particular topic that can be a useful starting point for a story. Equally important, the groups—whether they represent cyclists or the mining lobby—will have access to experts who can help the journalist understand and access data that is the cornerstone of many stories. Email, Twitter and Facebook also gives voters the chance to contact reporters with their own tips and feedback. Some of it will be useful and, most importantly, it gives the political journalist an insight in to what voters think is important. More than ever, the public is now a news source.

7 TAKE ADVANTAGE OF THE 24-HOURS NEWS CYCLE

The incessant nature of the news cycle means information is consumed like fast food. There is often little nourishment that goes with it, but in the ceaseless grind of the news machine, there will be plenty of information that is left behind or untouched. The value of this information is that it is still connected to the big issues of the day, but is rarely explored or investigated. This is particularly true about policy and budget innovations, which, by and large, are usually reported from a political perspective—who supports them, what they mean for the leader, what they mean for the bottom line—but rarely from the big picture perspective: whether the policies will work, where the money will come from, if they has been used elsewhere and with what effect, and how they fit in to a government's overall philosophy. So other reporters' discards can become fodder for fresh inquiries. And keep a diary of policy and budget announcements. When are they supposed to be delivered? If they don't turn up when they are supposed to, find out why. In a news cycle that destroys long-term memory, someone with diary-assisted recall can be priceless.

CONCLUSION

Knowing how the Labor factions work and who are their cheerleaders is helpful in understanding who supports whom (and what) in some of the internal party debates about public issues, such as the Carbon Tax or gay marriage. Having good contacts across the philosophical divide on the conservative side of politics will help a political journalist understand who has something to lose—and something to gain—internally from a particular decision the Liberal and National Party rooms make about, for example, welfare support for families or dental rebates for the elderly. But what use is that information to voters? How will it help voters understand their predicament? Voters are readers, listeners and viewers, and *they* are the journalist's first priority, not the politicians. Political journalists have a tendency to write for themselves. But investigating political issues through journalism helps re-establish the central role of the citizen because that form of journalism elevates the public good above the basic recording of events and personalities.

George Megalogenis believes the digital environment has created an anxiety among journalists who cling to their role as government watchdogs: 'Journalists fear their loss of authority will undermine their ability to hold governments to account' (2010, p. 79). The fear might exist but, if it does, it exists for the wrong reason. The digital age actually provides the courageous journalist with a great opportunity to find out more information that governments don't want revealed and agitate for more transparency. That is the role of the investigative journalist working in politics. The perceived erosion of this role and the debilitating decline in credibility that has accompanied it needs urgent attention. But the first few steps towards rehabilitating the reputation of political reporting are actually about ensuring that voters feel their concerns are central to the journalist's work. Oakes identified this as a cause for optimism: 'But [the voters are] not disengaged. They feel strongly. They're talking about politics. They want to know what's going on. The feedback I get in my job leaves no doubt about this' (Oakes 2011). This engagement is a vital first step for journalists to rebuild their coverage of politics in to a meaningful activity and explore the deeper issues that are at the heart of the public debate.

QUESTIONS TO CONSIDER

1   How are most political stories broken?

2   Identify the most recent political scoop in your state. How did the story come about? What effect did it have?

3   Why is it dangerous to completely trust your own knowledge of a political situation?

4   What is the best source of political stories?

5   What motivates political sources to talk to a political journalist?

TASK

1   Identify your local councillor. Do some research on them, including which party they represent (or if they're independent) and how long they've been in politics. Then go to the council website and look through the minutes of previous council meetings. Try to find a story within the minutes about what your councillor said or did. Then write a series of questions you would ask to find out why the councillor said or behaved the way they did.

REFERENCES

Brooke, H. 2011. *The Silent State*, London: Windmill Books.

Coorey, P. 2012. 'Day of Shame: Slipper Resigns', *The Sydney Morning Herald*, 10 October: www.smh.com.au/opinion/political-news/day-of-shame-slipper-resigns-20121009-27bda.html (accessed 6 December 2012).

Crikey. 2010. 'The Brumby Dump': www.crikey.com.au/the-brumby-dump (accessed 19 May 2012).

Dunlop, T. 2012. 'Have the Dark Arts of Spin Outflanked the Fourth Estate?', *The Drum*, 2 February: www.abc.net.au/unleashed/3805332.html (accessed 30 April 2012).

Farnsworth, S.J. & Lichter, S.R. 2011. *The Nightly News Nightmare: Media Coverage of US Presidential Elections, 1988–2008*, Maryland: Rowman & Littlefield.

Holmes, C.E. 2012. *Queensland Floods Commission of Inquiry – Final Report*, March, Brisbane: Queensland Government.

Megalogenis, G. 2010. *Trivial Pursuit: Leadership and the End of the Reform Era*, Melbourne: Black Inc.

Moore, T. 2010. 'Everything can be Reduced to a Tweet', *Brisbane Times*, 12 October: www.brisbanetimes.com.au/national/not-everything-can-be-reduced-to-a-tweet-20101012-16hh8.html (accessed 26 May 2012).

Oakes, L. 2010. *On The Record*, Sydney: Hachette.

Oakes, L. 2011. 2011 Andrew Olle Media Lecture, 21 October: www.abc.net.au/local/stories/2011/10/21/3345509.htm (accessed 30 April 2012).

Priest, M. 2012. 'Councils Grill Carbon Tax Chief on Costs', *Australian Financial Review*, 22 May, p. 5.

Ramsey, A. 2009. *A Matter of Opinion*, Crows Nest: Allen & Unwin.

Rosen, J. 2011. 'Why Political Coverage is Broken', *Pressthink*: http://pressthink.org/2011/08/why-political-coverage-is-broken (accessed 15 May 2012).

Savage, S. & Tiffen, R. 2007. 'Politicians, Journalists and "Spin": Tangled Relationships and Shifting Alliances', in S. Young, ed., *Government Communication in Australia*, Port Melbourne: Cambridge University Press, pp. 79–92.

Starkman, D. 2010. 'The Hamster Wheel', *Columbia Journalism Review*, October/November.: www.cjr.org/cover_story/the_hamster_wheel.php?page=all (accessed 10 April 2012).

Tanner, L. 2011. *Sideshow*, Melbourne: Black Inc.

Thomas, H. 2012, 'The Flood Uncovered', *The Weekend Australian*, 17 March, p. 1.

Tiffen, R. 2010, 'Time to Take A Deep Breath', *Inside Story*, 17 June: http://inside.org.au/time-to-take-a-deep-breath (accessed 14 April 2012).

Tiffen, R. 2012. 'Spin Doctors, News Values and Public Interest—The Bermuda Triangle of Policy Debate', in M. Ricketson, ed., *Australian Journalism Today*, South Yarra: PalgraveMacmillan, pp. 16–27.

Wallace, C. 2012. 'We Need to Talk about Kevin's Restoration Again', *The Australian*, 21 February, p. 10.

FURTHER READING

Jones, N. 1999. *Sultans of Spin*, London: Orion.

IN SEARCH OF A TRUTH SERUM

Hedley Thomas

The positive role of inquisitive reporters in causing the establishment of far-reaching Royal Commission-style inquiries is widely understood in modern journalism.

Journalists and members of the public have rightly viewed the media interest that leads to expert forensic legal and investigative scrutiny from a public inquiry as positive and necessary.

The public inquiry is usually a truth serum.

The stories that arise from the modern public inquiry are almost always newsworthy.

These stories can splash newspaper front pages, lead radio and television bulletins and provide an enviable public profile to those perceived to have run a good, robust inquiry.

Less well understood, however, is the educational benefit that can be derived by journalists from a well-run public inquiry.

For students of journalism, young journalists and even veterans, a stint at a public inquiry should be mandatory. I will discuss why.

One of the most celebrated Australian probes, the Fitzgerald Inquiry into Police Corruption in the 1980s, began as a result of the work of two journalists from competing media outlets—Phil Dickie of Brisbane's *The Courier-Mail* newspaper and Chris Masters of the ABC's *Four Corners* program.

In identifying rampant corruption at the highest levels, the outstanding work of Dickie, Masters, and the inquiry's head, Tony Fitzgerald QC, had a profound influence on many journalists.

It conditioned us to be more sceptical, more forensic, and stronger than some of our colleagues, whose timidity had permitted the corruption to flourish. We owe a debt of gratitude to this public inquiry, and those who made it happen.

The public inquiry is an outstanding classroom for journalists in other ways. A few days at a public inquiry may be more instructive than a month of routine tuition at a university journalism course.

What? When? Where? How? Why? These questions should guide journalists in everything they research and produce, and the public inquiry—freed as it is from the rules of evidence and law that limit free-flowing scrutiny in criminal trials—answers the questions best.

The unearthing and rigorous testing of facts by skilled lawyers, the range of cross-examination techniques used to question reluctant or lying witnesses, the balancing act by the inquiry's commissioner to maintain fairness—these are commonplace at a good public inquiry, and these are the most fundamental pillars of good, powerful journalism.

As journalists, we too must test the facts, play devil's advocate to ensure we are not being led astray by our sources, adopt clever strategies to question people who may be lying to us, and remain balanced even when the circumstances look black and white.

The public inquiry has helped me at formative stages of my career.

The first was the extraordinary Fitzgerald Inquiry, which I had watched unfold with wide-eyed awe as a junior reporter at the *Gold Coast Bulletin* and then *The Courier-Mail*.

The next was the lesser-known Trident Inquiry.

The Trident Inquiry examined allegations that police had broken the law and run amok in an undercover operation, Trident, which was supposed to identify a professional car-stealing racket.

In truth, the racket was one the police had themselves invented. They had helped steal about 70 luxury cars, corruptly enriched themselves by reselling the vehicles, and pretended at the end of the operation that they had done an outstanding job at public expense.

Having investigated and highlighted the wrongdoing in Operation Trident as a callow reporter, and been smeared by the then police commissioner for my trouble, I covered the subsequent inquiry over several months of public hearings.

The inquiry resulted in severe findings for the police and other wrongdoers involved. Some of the police were charged and convicted of criminal offences. The lucky ones avoided prison, but lost their careers.

In the supposedly cleaned-up post-Fitzgerald era, the Queensland Police Service shamefacedly admitted—along with the state's anti-corruption body, the Criminal Justice Commission—that its joint operation was a sham that orchestrated crime.

Some of the most powerful lessons for me were in observing the methods of the inquiry's examiners.

John Jerrard QC—the senior counsel who assisted the inquiry and went on to become a senior judge—used logical reasoning, wit, charm and doggedness to extract vital information from witnesses.

William Carter QC, a retired Supreme Court judge, had razor-sharp follow-up questions. He ensured civility in the court, and respect for those in the witness box.

Public inquiries such as this should be powerful teaching tools in journalism courses.

How many remarkable stories have never been written because the reporters failed to ask obvious follow-up questions, or lost the confidence of their source due to clumsy and poorly researched questions? The skilfulness and perceptiveness of reporters during interviews are vital to the outcomes.

How many false stories have been written because the reporters did not realise they were being spun, or lied to?

I strongly suspect that the statistics would be much more attractive if journalists became students of the public inquiry.

But if the public inquiry is an extraordinary refresher course for experienced journalists and a brilliant classroom for the inexperienced, it can also be a trap.

This is because royal commissions do get it wrong. They can make grave errors. They can be influenced by public prejudices and political currents.

And as a result of the symbiotic relationship between journalists and these inquiries, flaws can be deliberately overlooked by the same journalists and their outlets that took an unrelenting line in exposing the wrongdoing that led to the inquiry being set up.

In this way, journalists may self-censor or pull their punches about the worrying conduct of a public inquiry. They may accept, as holy writ, the evidence and findings of the inquiry. They may skew the public interest.

In effect, the journalists may become unknowing captives of the public inquiry, and beholden to the extent that every finding or utterance of the inquiry is regarded as the gospel truth.

Journalists have much to learn from the public inquiry, but they must remember that it is not a sacred cow. The judges and QCs who run these inquiries are not above the law. Their inquiries must be subjected by journalists to the same standards of rigour and healthy scepticism as other bodies.

Journalists owe it to the public to ensure that when the public inquiry goes off the rails, it is properly corrected by media showing neither fear nor favour.

I was reminded of this in striking fashion in the wake of one of Australia's most costly disasters, the January 2011 floods in Queensland where I live.

For much of 2011, the public Queensland Floods Inquiry (Holmes 2012) headed by a highly regarded Supreme Court judge, Cate Holmes SC, heard a great deal of evidence directly relevant to the inquiry's terms of reference—the operation of the Wivenhoe Dam.

Throughout 2011, there had been public disquiet about the operation of the dam, an enormous piece of public infrastructure.

The dam had released vast volumes of water into the Brisbane River at crucial times in the flood event. My reporting over much of 2011 sought to highlight significant anomalies and deficiencies.

By early 2012, however, the inquiry's public hearings had ended. The inquiry was set to release its final report, which was being prepared for the printers.

It was a report which found that the operators of the Queensland Government-owned dam had done everything right.

Before reaching this view, the inquiry had questioned each of the flood engineers in the witness box. Tens of thousands of pages in witness statements and other material had been extracted in evidence. Dozens of lawyers had pored over the evidence. The clearance verdict seemed a fait accompli.

Then something remarkable happened. In January 2012, a source contacted me to point out some fundamental evidence that the inquiry had overlooked.

We found much more that had been overlooked. After assembling the material in a lengthy dossier, I knew that the consequences would be significant. The evidence we had discovered was powerful because it was contemporaneous—in the form of emails and other documents created during the actual flood event.

The evidence that we discovered also directly contradicted the evidence that had been provided to the inquiry by the dam's operators when they claimed, falsely, that they ran the dam with clockwork precision.

Within 48 hours of *The Australian* publishing these revelations, the inquiry was suddenly reconvened. Public hearings restarted. More damning evidence was unearthed.

In late March 2012, the inquiry released its final report.

Justice Holmes concluded that her inquiry had been misled, and that the Wivenhoe Dam was operated in breach of the manual for a day and a half. Her conclusions were unavoidable.

In *The Weekend Australian* the day after the final report was released by Justice Holmes, I wrote:

> It is likely to usher in the largest class action in Australia's history. [Holmes'] finding of a cover-up, of 'recent invention' by the flood engineers in their attempts to justify their actions, have already triggered a referral of three of the four flood engineers to Queensland's anti-corruption body, the Crime and Misconduct Commission, for further investigation of alleged perjury-related offences relating to their preparation of documents, and statements to the inquiry.
>
> Holmes found that 'several things may have motivated the three engineers to present the false flood report, including a wish to protect their professional reputations from the damage that would be caused by a disregard of the manual'. There was also the fact that if the engineers were found to have breached the manual, SEQ Water's immunity from liability for massive damages would have ended.
>
> The inquiry's final report should bolster the hopes of thousands of Queenslanders that they may be compensated for some of their enormous property losses and hardships, arising from a negligent operation of the dam.
>
> It should also be a reminder that the experts get it wrong, self-interested parties lie, and the media's role in challenging the spin, and highlighting wrongdoing, is as vital as ever (Thomas 2012, p. 1).

These matters remain controversial. In August 2012, five months after the final report of the Queensland Floods Inquiry, the referral of three of the four flood engineers to the Crime and Misconduct Commission for consideration of possible criminal proceedings led to another legal opinion.

In this opinion, John Jerrard QC, now a retired judge, determined that any prosecution of the engineers would be oppressive. In his opinion, they were trying to follow a deeply flawed manual.

The legal opinion of Mr Jerrard was welcomed by the flood engineers, who have always strenuously denied any wrongdoing; however, it does not overturn or alter the findings of the Queensland Floods Inquiry. The evidence of Mr Jerrard is set to be tested in court as flood victims seek damages.

The outcome of the Queensland Floods Inquiry was enormously embarrassing and damaging for the inquiry's staff, the Queensland Government and the operator of the dam. It was also a reminder of what can go wrong when there is reluctance in the media to rigorously test the facts, even when they emerge from a public inquiry.

The issues were complex, revolving around hydrology, hydrodynamic modelling, and detailed release strategies, but they should have been subjected to better analysis in the media. Most journalists had concentrated their efforts instead on human-interest angles arising from those who were flooded, instead of how it happened.

The lack of rigour by journalists dovetailed with a quietly effective campaign of spin and misinformation.

If journalists had spent more time being sceptical, the truth could have emerged much sooner.

For a year, however, despite nuggets of evidence that pointed to the dam operator gilding the lily with many assertions about the scale and circumstances surrounding the event, the unvarnished truth remained elusive. Fortunately, the truth came out.

In summary, in my experience the public inquiry is a remarkable training ground for journalists. But the public inquiry should never be above reproach.

16

Crime Writing

ANDREW RULE AND NICK RICHARDSON

PART ❶ > NICK RICHARDSON

INTRODUCTION

There are some hardy preconceptions about investigative reporting: one of them is that crime—and corruption—are fertile areas for investigation and exposure. This preconception is based on sound evidence that dates back to several important examples in Australian journalism during the 1980s and 90s, such as waterfront crime, the Mr Asia drugs syndicate, and then the exposure of crooked police that helped trigger Queensland's Fitzgerald Inquiry. This reporting exemplifies the role of the Fourth Estate as the public watchdog. The journalists who were central to these revelations—including Bob Bottom, John Silvester, Phil Dickie and Chris Masters—and helped to glamorise what was, in reality, often dangerous and challenging work.

At the heart of this work was an implicit understanding that what was occurring had significant social and political impact. Across every state during the past 25 years, law and order has been a central plank of state political parties' attempts to win or hold on to power. Such is in the intersection between policing and politics. But this nexus is simply explained—personal security and issues of safety concern everyone. (Grabosky & Wilson 1989, p. 2). Arguably, these concerns about safety have increased in the aftermath of the terrorist attacks on the USA in 2001. These have made many communities more nervous and have inevitably triggered heightened vigilance among police services around the world, including Australia.

This has had consequences for crime reporting in the digital age. The foundation of all good investigative reporting—contacts and sources—are more wary of cooperating with journalists in an environment of suspicion and wariness. One reason is that telephone calls can be monitored and contacts between journalists and police can be scrutinised in a way that was neither possible (legally or technologically) nor considered desirable 20 years ago (*Herald Sun* 2011). Another consideration is that police reporters have less time to cultivate the police sources who may be able to help them with the kind of intelligence that forms the basis of good crime reporting. Journalists hooked into the 24-hour news cycle are constantly peddling to get the latest developments in ongoing stories, traffic accidents and emergencies, rather than being able to spend time cultivating sources and stories.

A third key element is the establishment of independent investigative bodies that provide scrutiny of police forces and the bureaucrats who work alongside them. In the past 25 years, most Australian states have established—or committed to establishing—an independent commission against corruption that seeks to monitor and penalise corruption in public life. In Victoria, for example, this scrutiny is built into the roles of the State Ombudsman and the Office of Police Integrity, which provide additional oversight of police activity. Police believe they have rarely been more accountable.

This doesn't mean that there are fewer stories among the criminal and law enforcement fraternity. Indeed, there are now more potential sources of information about criminal and police activity than ever, especially if they can be combined with information about the court system's operation. But access to information within these agencies is usually strictly controlled and it takes longer to be disseminated. All of which means that journalists have to work harder to find out exactly what is going on. Once again, this relies on the identification and sustained nurturing of trustworthy contacts.

This chapter is a unique part of the book—it combines an introduction to investigative crime reporting, followed by an analysis of how to write crime stories by one of Australia's most successful crime writers and investigative journalists, Andrew Rule. The rationale for Rule's contribution is the importance of telling the story well: the potential audience for investigative journalism about criminal activity is vast. It behoves the journalist to tell the story in a compelling fashion, regardless of the platform. Just how well that approach works is revealed in the case study at the end of this section, which is about an investigation into criminal activity among Queensland bikies, carried out by *The Courier Mail*. Both contributions are essential to understanding crime reporting.

TOOLS AND TECHNIQUES FOR THE CRIME REPORTER

First, let's spend some time looking at the tools you need in order to write and investigate crime. Like all good journalism, crime reporting starts with the simple act of understanding human motivation. And in crime, motivations of greed, revenge, loyalty and betrayal are common. Police, like journalists, see these motivations up close. It is also true that it is the exposure to human frailty—combined with the act of sleuthing—that is the basis of the common ground between reporters and police.

The daily routine of the police rounds reporter, which is built around regular interaction with the police's media unit, is rarely the fodder for the reporter interested in investigative journalism. A police media unit—by the nature of its monitoring and disseminating of information about routine incidents such as traffic accidents, burglaries and demonstrations—is neither equipped nor interested in deeper issues of probity or corruption (White 1996, p. 130). Yet it is likely that information the media unit distributes about some events—for example, the murder of a police informant—may pique the interest of the investigative journalist interested in the story behind the murder.

An area of growing exposure is white collar crime. This not only reflects a broader community interest in business, the share market and investments, but also the ever-present interest in the rich and powerful. Stories about fall from influence and loss of fortune—through simple mistake, ambition or greed—are worthwhile subjects for a journalist's investigation, especially when they lead to criminal charges and court appearances. Often journalists also need data journalism and well-developed research skills to mine the financial and company statements that hold some of the secrets behind such stories.

Yet as appealing as this kind of 'dollar drop' journalism is, it cannot rival the more lurid stories that are generated by the activities of criminal gangs. The notorious 'gangland' conflict that was part of Melbourne's almost daily news diet from 2004 to 2011 featured criminals being shot and feuds played out, while revenge, loyalty, greed and fear coalesced around an ever-dwindling number of crooks, most of whom were either killed or imprisoned as a result of their activities. But the coverage across all media was so extensive that it led a Supreme Court judge and former director of the National Crime Authority, Justice Betty King, to lament that some of these criminals had become celebrities (Buttler 2010). The situation was that the news coverage—and subsequent successful television drama *Underbelly*—helped foster the notion that criminals were often rich, exotic and dangerous. However, this was only a small part of what was actually going on within the criminal fraternity, and for the journalists reporting on this, there were also significant issues of public safety that needed to be considered, especially when criminal killings were taking place in suburban streets.

The problem for journalists dealing with lifelong criminals is the difficulty in knowing whether they are being told the truth. Criminals are usually practised liars. They will lie easily to journalists and to police, which is why journalists covering organised crime—or underworld activities—need to cultivate sources they know are dependable. The price for 'snitching' within the criminal fraternity can be high, but the reality is that criminals (like many people) also enjoy being notorious and talking (or gossiping) to journalists. A profile helps confer a certain status, including, in some instances, a cheap veneer of respectability. As Mick Gatto, one of Melbourne's legendary hard men, commented after the release of his autobiography: 'I'm recognised wherever I go: I can't go down to Lygon Street for a coffee without being asked for autographs or photos. I don't mind doing it—it's water off a duck's back—but it can get embarrassing' (Noble 2010). The antithesis of the high-profile crook is the sly, covert criminal who has no profile and no desire to speak on or off the record to journalists. They may be significant criminal figures, but they have no interest in cooperating with the media.

Allowing for the charm and propensity for deceit and exaggeration among criminals is one thing: the journalist also needs to be sure that no source, including police, has a particular agenda that skews a story. It is not uncommon in this highly charged law and order debate for various messages and intentions to be communicated, simply by knowing which source talks to which journalist and what information they dispense. It is, in some circumstances, vital that journalists proceed warily, for everyone's safety. Veteran Fairfax crime reporter John Silvester explains: 'There are times when crime reporters must withhold information because they don't want to destroy an ongoing investigation. The wrong story at the wrong time can allow someone to get away with murder' (Mann (Undated)). And an injudicious use of that inside knowledge can also jeopardise ongoing cooperation between the journalist and the source.

The final complicating factor for media disclosure of many criminal activities is the law, most particularly suppression orders (see Chapter 13). These orders, imposed by the courts, will prevent the reporting of names and details of some events on the grounds of ensuring a fair trial. Crime and court reporters can often be frustrated by suppression orders and they will try to write 'around' such impediments, so that they can at least tell some of the story. The end result is that crime reporters usually know far more than the law will ever allow them to publish or broadcast.

All of these factors ensure that it is usually only the most senior journalists who are suited to crime investigations. It is an activity that demands good sources, usually cultivated over years; a maturity to see the broader criminal landscape that is often the context for apparently isolated crimes; the knowledge to know the legal pitfalls associated with reporting about some criminals; and the instinct, built up over many years of journalism, to know the difference between the truth and a plausible deceit. A journalist who recognises those key elements will be able to write incisive, compelling and accurate investigations.

PART ❷ > ANDREW RULE

THE PITCH

'Here's the pitch. There's this guy in Little Italy, anywhere from Lygon Street to New York. He's got a long name that ends in a vowel but the guys call him Baz for short. Drives a V-8 muscle car, got biceps to match.

'Baz has the hots for this beautiful rich chick but he's punching above his weight. Her old man's a legit property developer. She lives in North Balwyn (or maybe New Jersey) and went to private school. Baz is so desperate to impress her he decides he has to get a Porsche but he has no dough. Then some Lebanese wise guy offers Baz a piece of the action in an import deal. The guy tells Baz if he puts in 30 grand up front, he'll turn it into 300 grand in three months. Problem: Baz is about 29 short of the 30. But he's desperate to get the Porsche to wow the hot chick and her parents.

'Baz tells his buddy Tony about the sure-fire import proposition, the Porsche and the hot chick. Tony says he'd like to help but he's got his own cash problems. So he gives Baz the number of a loan shark. The shark is not Italian and not a tough guy personally but he doesn't have to be: everyone knows what happens if you don't pay him on time. Big Mick visits you. Mick once hammered a three-inch nail into a guy's arm to make a point. That was over 300 bucks, so guess what happens when 300 grand is owing. The shark tells Baz he can have the money free for three months but then the clock starts ticking, big time. Two grand a day extra interest. And because he doesn't know Baz, he'll need Tony's IOU, thanks.

'The shark reminds the boys what happens to Tony if they don't pay. Micky and the boys come around with the blowtorch and bolt cutters and start on his toes. Baz isn't worried. He still can't think about anything but the Porsche. Besides, the Leb guys promised him the import rort is a walk in the park. Also, he's been snorting some excellent gear he gets from a guy in the drug squad, so he's feeling bulletproof.

'You can guess what happens. It all goes pear-shaped. Turns out the shark is playing both sides and tips off the Feds, who need a big pinch to hit the headlines to justify their travel budgets. The Feds follow a tonne of canned tomatoes from Naples across the world and open it up down at the docks one quiet day. Surprise, surprise, the cans are full of powders.

'Needless to say, Baz doesn't get his 300 grand. He gets a shotgun stuck in his ribs by a cop just before dawn and is looking at a couple of years for conspiracy. But, of course, that's not as bad as what happens to his buddy Tony, who loses all his toes. It turns out the loan shark always hated Tony's guts and was waiting for a chance to get his pound of flesh …'

End of pitch.

ONLY THE NAMES OF THE PLAYERS CHANGE

Tweak that story line any way you like and it works. Cast Matt Damon and Sean, say, in a gritty Boston or New York drama based on real gangsters' lives, directed by Scorsese. Or, for a fraction of the budget, shoot it around Carlton or King's Cross, with acres of bare breasts and violence choreographed with a rock soundtrack, and put another notch in the *Underbelly* belt. Give or take the clothes and cars and a few hundred years, the story is as strong as it was when a popular dramatist wrote it with a feather dipped in ink. His name was William Shakespeare and he called his yarn *The Merchant of Venice*. What could be truer crime than hacking off a pound of flesh? It's pure *Reservoir Dogs*. And it has as much sex, blood, money and racism as *The Wire*. It seems modern and edgy because crime never goes out of fashion.

This tells us that when it comes to crime writing, only the names of the players change. The themes remain the same, no matter how often they're reinvented and interpreted. All the world *is* a stage, all right, and crime writers worth reading know that. Shakespeare (and Scorsese and Mario Puzo, for that matter) didn't write 'true crime', but they did tell powerful stories, and powerful stories ring true.

There are too many bad true-crime writers. No other genre attracts so many hacks, amateurs and idiots, and these must be ignored. But at the quality end of the spectrum, the main difference between good true-crime writers and good fiction-crime writers is that the true-crime lot are probably sued more often. It seems clear that the best true-crime writers use the techniques of the crime novelist, while the crime novelists trawl newspapers and bulletins for real-life human tragedies to make their stories believable. Some hint that they conjure up every scenario and character in some sealed creative vacuum, but that's probably because they're nervous of being sued.

Observation is at least as important as imagination. This was revealed by Truman Capote's lament after his wealthy socialite patrons shunned him for writing thinly disguised versions of their lives. He said words to the effect of: 'I'm a writer. I have to write what I know.' To believe that Capote's non-fiction is faithful to every fact seems as naïve as believing his fiction was wholly imagined. It seems more likely he brought the same talents, skills and motives to all his work, regardless of the labels attached to it. Most of us do. There might not be a novelist inside every reporter, but there is most likely a reporter in every novelist. And every novelist worth their salt should be fascinated by crime, even if it is crime of the heart.

Crime is inherently interesting because it is at the core of being human. It's about life and death, sex and betrayal—subjects that have preoccupied us since our forebears grunted stories to each other sitting around fires in caves. Herd the words into the right order and you get stories people want to hear.

'TRUE-CRIME' JOURNALISM AND LITERATURE

It's a point worth making to condescending poseurs who roll their eyes, curl their lips and close their minds when they hear the words 'crime writing'. If these knee-jerk critics thought about it more than a few seconds, they might realise that crime of one sort or another—and the dilemmas it poses for people—is at the heart of all worthwhile drama and most literature. There might be more grotesque and terrible crime stories than *Oedipus Rex* or *Macbeth*, but not many. Sex, every sort of homicide, and superstition all get a run in the classics. *The Godfather* echoes Greek tragedy. *The Sopranos* is Shakespearean. Capote's *In Cold Blood* is as haunting and powerful as any of the Russian classics. What we think of as modern long-form journalism is more closely related to the literary novel than some suspect. There is as much powerful drama to be drawn from the world around us as was conceived by long-dead playwrights and novelists.

Some work resonates and leaves an impression that lingers in the minds of generations. For me and millions of others, Orwell's *1984*, Huxley's *Brave New World*, Salinger's *The Catcher in the Rye* and Golding's *Lord of the Flies* stood out. But, as a young reporter, I felt that the writing I could best learn from, that I could attempt to emulate in some way, was *In Cold Blood* and the wave of quality non-fiction it inspired. One of the earliest and best of these was *Beyond Belief*, a brilliant and chilling reconstruction of England's Moors murders by a Welsh playwright, Emlyn Williams. Capote and Williams found in terrible subjects a power that perhaps transcends their other work. Their sure touch for detail and dialogue, applied to meticulous research and reporting of the concrete, wove stories that resonate in the memory—as powerful now as when they were written in the 1960s. These writers, and the best of the many that followed them, provided a sort of blueprint for the long-form quality journalism we now expect to see every week.

In Cold Blood has inspired many imitators in the last 45 years, but still stands out. Its influence continues to carry, not just because of its quality, but because it was the first to do what it did so well: employ the novelist's eye and ear and rhythms to tell a true story of the sort that, until then, were nearly always told through conventional reportage.

To call Capote a 'true-crime writer' is, of course, like calling The Rolling Stones a popular musical ensemble. In reconstructing a mid-Western murder that barely made three paragraphs in the New York newspapers of the day, he found his most enduring subject and told a story that towered over everything else he did—and that still influences and informs those who followed him.

'True crime' is a broad church, one that includes John Berendt's *Midnight in the Garden of Good and Evil* and the non-fiction of our own Helen Garner. Like Berendt, Garner has probably never published a lame sentence, but in my view her most powerful work is when she turns her considerable talent to describing the effects of crimes. Here's the introduction to her essay on the death of the toddler Daniel Valerio more than 20 years ago, and the trial of the man who battered the little boy: 'What sort of man beats a two-year-old boy to death?' (1996, p. 185). There, in a dozen short words, is the perfect way to start that piece on that subject. Once read, it seems like the only way. Its sheer simplicity takes the reader straight to the heart of a story impossible to forget.

The perennial best-seller *Shantaram* is, strictly speaking, a novel. Unlike Garner, the former armed robber and heroin addict who writes under the name Gregory David Roberts packs his book with hundreds of sentences that would benefit from pruning or culling. Despite those faults, the story gains its force from the description of real events Roberts experienced in jail and on the run, and it is this force that makes it a cult book the world over, like the cocaine classic *Snowblind*, by Sabbag. *Shantaram's* opening paragraph, as long and ornate as Garner's is crisp and understated, is one of the most striking beginnings I've seen.

It took me a long time and most of the world to learn what I know about love and fate and the choices we make, but the heart of it came to me in an instant, while I was chained to a wall and being tortured.

It's a sentence worth quoting in a master class on how to write the arresting introduction, because it switches in a heartbeat from the philosophical and lyrical in a rhythmic phrase ('love and fate and the choices we make') to the shocking description of being chained and tortured. The effect is all the more shocking because Roberts has yoked them together in one brilliant sentence which begins a page that is, I think, as riveting as any I've read. A lot of other readers think so, it seems, and they apparently forgive the robber-turned-writer the 900 or so not-so-perfect pages that follow those first masterful words. There's a lesson there about how to start a story close to its most arresting point, and writers who aim to please an audience almost always know it.

MAKING IT REAL

People who have experienced crime in some form or another often write about it with verve and credibility. Few writers in any field write such addictively compelling copy as Thomas Harris, the man who brought us Hannibal Lecter. Harris is a former crime reporter. So is David Simon, who wrote the brilliant television series *The Wire*, which was born from a book based on a year spent with the Baltimore Homicide Squad when he worked for the *Baltimore Sun*. His collaborator on *The Wire* and other work is Ed Burns, one of the Baltimore homicide detectives he befriended on the street. These men know their subject and it shows. *The Wire* is one of the best pieces of drama ever made, let alone made for television. But why would anyone be surprised? It might be packaged as fiction for legal and dramatic reasons, but anyone who has read Simon's first-hand account of life with the 'murder police' knows it is all too real.

Carl Hiaasen is another former reporter. He might wink at the audience and play it for laughs in his Florida-based best-selling novels, but there's an edge to the humour that comes from knowing his beat and the street. Hiaasen served his time with the *Miami Herald* when it chronicled one of the most dangerous cities on Earth, and reading him is like watching a slick showman crack gags while juggling chainsaws: amusing, but never far from bloodshed. He worked alongside the legendary crime reporter Edna Buchanan, who carried a gun in her handbag and wrote true stories (including *The Corpse had a Familiar Face*) of the sort that no one could make up. P.J. O'Rourke wrote a cover line for Hiaasen— 'Better than literature'—that applies to them all. Another reformed journalist, Thomas Cook, wrote novels that drew on his real-life knowledge. His novel *Breakheart Hill* begins this way: 'This is the darkest story that I have ever heard. And all my life I have labored not to tell it.'

James Lee Burke, the evergreen Deep Southern crime writer, was a reporter and an oil-line pipe layer in a previous life. Both experiences inform his work. Burke scoffs at suggestions his stories are too violent. He once told a reporter: 'We hear it all the time, "Look at the violence in this." What kind of nonsense is that? It's just doo-dah. It's like saying, "My God, look at this Hamlet leaving all these bodies in the fifth act. Jeez, this is terrible"' (Burke, in Fuller 2011, p. 75).

Life is violent. It is human to be fascinated by it. This helps explain why the first feature-length film in the world, made in 1906, told the story of Ned Kelly. It was the first of (so far) 10 films and six plays about the bushranger, whose life has also inspired two successful novels and endless factual accounts and pieces of journalism. Sidney Nolan's 'Kelly' series of 27 paintings is probably Australia's most iconic art. And Western gunmen and East Coast gangsters have probably inspired Hollywood more than any other genre. The most powerful and successful films have mostly been based on true stories or identifiable prototypes, from *Bonnie & Clyde* to *Butch Cassidy and the Sundance Kid*; from *The Godfather* to *Goodfellas* and *Scarface*.

None of that would surprise the late Frank Galbally, revered defence lawyer to hundreds of people accused of serious offences from armed robbery to murder. The silver-tongued Galbally knew as much about telling crime stories as most writers and dramatists do. He knew about the power of words and using the techniques of the stage to capture his audience's imagination. His instructions to the accused who sought his services were to tell him a story 'that fits the facts'. This is the essence of the non-fiction writer's job. The story has to fit the facts—but telling it well is the key. Like jazz players who riff and improvise around a basic melody, the best writers use the facts as a foundation to build their story.

An example. Half a dozen books were written about the Falconio case—the abduction and presumed murder of a British tourist, Peter Falconio, and the remarkable escape of his terrified girlfriend, Joanne Lees, in the Northern Territory in 2001. The number of books was a predictable over-response to a story that captured headlines and fired imaginations all over Australia—and the UK. All but one of the books were 'quickies' of varying quality: from an emotive and nonsensical critique of the overwhelming case against the man convicted of Falconio's murder, Bradley John Murdoch, to competent hackery from competent hacks. These were published within days or weeks of Murdoch's trial in 2005, and so managed to spoil each other's sales. But the best Falconio book was not published until 2007. This was Paul Toohey's *The Killer Within*, a bleak and brilliant take on the crime and the accused and how they fitted into Top End culture. Toohey's reconstruction of the life of the convicted killer was as disturbingly good as the best long-form journalism can be. It was proof that the quality of the work is in direct proportion to the effort put into it. As the legendary US sports columnist Red Smith quipped: writing is easy—you just sit at the keyboard 'and open a vein'.

Old-time crooks used to say, if you can't do the time then don't do the crime, and the same applies to writing about it. If you can't spend time writing, don't do long-form crime writing. This applies to all serious, writing, of course. Of all the writers' rules this is the first: it takes time to herd words as finicky and flighty as cats and push them into the elusive order that transforms typing into writing. It's the literary equivalent of the alchemist turning lead into gold, and though not nearly so lucrative, it's rewarding in other ways. As someone once said, it's not the writing that's enjoyable, it's 'having written'—the after-glow of achievement. And the main achievement is to get it right. True crime is often about the mad, the bad and the sad—but as a general proposition it would be better if those people stuck to crime and left the crime-writing to others. The fact there is so much bad crime-writing about does not diminish the force and legitimacy of the best of it.

CONCLUSION

The best crime writing centres on the universal and timeless preoccupations of humanity: life and death, good and evil, right and wrong, loyalty and betrayal. And, often enough to keep it interesting, it's about sex—a short word that can cover a lot of ground, from the basest of brute behaviour to the most romantic courtly love. Crime writing can take the form of a morality tale, where good triumphs over evil, and in which people's sins find them out. And, increasingly, it is about moral dilemmas. The Scandinavian writer Jo Nesbo said recently that the sort of work he and other modern crime writers write is essentially about morality. In an increasingly godless and atheistic world, writers like Nesbo set up a moral framework for their characters—and their readers. True, Nesbo is a novelist; but the themes of right and wrong, of sex, death and betrayal, are universal.

One of the finest Australian novels of the last 20 years is Peter Temple's *Broken Shore*, a rare blend of literary merit and popular appeal that happens to be a crime thriller. And among the best Australian non-fiction of the 20th century is John Bryson's *Evil Angels*, which is technically true crime.

They endure because they are stories people want to read.

QUESTIONS TO CONSIDER

1   List three difficulties confronting crime reporters in the current climate.
2   What are some of the motivations for criminal behaviour that reporters need to be aware of to help identify stories about crime and criminals?
3   What do reporters need when they are interviewing criminals?
4   Why is crime so interesting to readers?
5   What does morality have to do with reporting on crime?

TASK

1   Find a crime that occurred in your local area (look in your local paper or on a news website). It could be a burglary or a hit-and-run. Try to find out more information than has been published (talk to local police, for example.) Write two versions of the story—a straight news story that could be published online; and another that contains all the facts but is told from the perspective of the perpetrator of the crime.

REFERENCES

Buttler, M. 2010. 'Supreme Court Judge Betty King Attacks Roberta Williams and Mick Gatto', *Herald Sun*, 3 May: www.heraldsun.com.au/news/special-reports/supreme-court-judge-betty-king-attacks-roberta-williams-and-mick-gatto/story-fn5ev9xr-1225861767099 (accessed 7 September 2012).

Cook, T. 1995. *Breakheart Hill*, New York: Bantam.

Fuller, R.R. 2011. *Angola to Zydeco: Louisiana Lives*, Mississippi: University Press of Mississippi.

Garner, H. 1996. *True Stories*, Melbourne: Text Publishing, pp. 185–92.

Grabowsky, P. & Wilson, P. 1989. *Journalism and Justice: How Crime is Reported*, Leichardt: Pluto Press.

Herald Sun. 2011. 'Overland Investigated *Herald Sun* Journalist after Whistleblower Leak', 3 June 3, p. 1.

Mann, E. Undated. 'Unmasking "Sly": Life and Crimes, as told by a Gun Reporter': http://deakin.edu.au/arts-ed/creative/writing/evolutions/showcase/nonfic/110323-Effie-Mann.pdf (accessed 7 September 2012).

Noble, T. 2010. 'Why We Love True Crime', *The Weekly Review*, 27 May, p. 5.

Roberts, G.D. 2003. *Shantaram*, Melbourne: Scribe.

Sabbagh, R. 1976. *Snowblind*, New York: Bobbs Merrill.

Simon, D. 1991. *Homicide*, Boston: Houghton Mifflin.

White, S.A. 1996. *Reporting in Australia*, South Melbourne: Macmillan.

FURTHER READING

Conley, D. 2002. *The Daily Miracle: An Introduction to Journalism*, Melbourne: Oxford University Press.

Tidey, J. 2012. *Class Act: A Life of Creighton Burns*, North Melbourne: Australian Scholarly Publishing.

INTELLIGENCE-LED REPORTING

Mark Solomons

Journalists have never been short of stories to write about outlaw motorcycle gangs. This is especially so in Australia, which is reputed to have more 'bikies' per head of population than anywhere else in the world and where historic outlaw figures such as Ned Kelly are a fixture in the public imagination.

Mostly these stories 'write themselves' as reporters would say—the outrageous exploits of easily identifiable rogues are easily translated into print. Those responsible for bringing them to heel are often more than willing to help. But in August 2011 *The Courier-Mail's* investigation team, which I had taken over the previous year, took a very different approach.

Within two months the team had detailed knowledge of hundreds of violent, habitual criminals and their associates, their business dealings, property assets and family ties. We had amassed a huge store of information and penetrated the 'code of silence' of bikie clubs. We had unearthed details of money-laundering schemes and had new leads in unsolved murders. We were mining a rich seam of story leads that provided real insight rather than just reinforcing stereotypes.

By the end of the project, in a reversal of roles, senior police investigators were *calling us* to find out what we knew. It was a refreshing change from the then-frosty relationship between the paper and Queensland Police spin doctors.

The bikies we profiled were convinced the whole shebang had been fed to us by the police. If only.

The big irony was that our success was partly due to us stealing techniques from law enforcement agencies. I call it intelligence-led reporting.

The project eventually generated a series of *Courier-Mail* articles and online packages described on ABC Radio as the best investigative journalism in the paper since the Fitzgerald era of the late 1980s.

Editors were delighted; some of the bikies were not.

Our work was interrupted briefly by threats made by a member of the Hells Angels to one of our journalists, prompting a review of our personal security.

There were also other costs—the paper spent tens of thousands of dollars buying company information and getting legal advice on what we could publish. But it was worth it. Which was a relief, because it could have gone the other way.

The brief in August from the editor, Michael Crutcher, had been open-ended.

'I want to talk about what you're going to be doing for the rest of the year. I want you and your team to find out what's happening in organised crime on the Gold Coast.'

He wants me to get killed, I thought at first, but I didn't dwell on it.

The Coast was then blighted by high youth unemployment, a decline in tourism, its economic mainstay, and a perceived rise in crime.

The Courier-Mail's pages were full of stories of the Coast's drug-dealing bikies, drunken hooning, tacky nightclubs and shonky tradespeople. The death in June 2011 of a police officer, Senior Constable Damian Leeding, after he was shot during a botched hold-up at the Pacific Pines Tavern, had brought an outpouring of public support and masses of coverage. *The Courier-Mail* had devoted its front page to the story for a week.

But there hadn't been much by way of explanation or insight into the reported crime wave. Michael told me there were suspicions of a bikie link to a brazen daytime shooting in a Gold Coast street a few weeks earlier. According to his police sources the alleged perpetrator had not spoken since his arrest. Also, the Coast chapter of the Finks outlaw motorcycle club had recently adopted new colours, adding a new 'Surfers Paradise' rocker to their patches, which some people on the Coast were interpreting as some sort of tribal signal.

But that was about it.

'Great,' I told him. 'We'd love to get involved in that.' A senior colleague later confessed that the same brief would have left him cold. Where to start and what exactly were we looking for? Drugs, crime, bikies, guns? How to find a way into this?

Sometimes a vague brief is a godsend. At least you can't be held to specifics. And we had a bit of time. Michael had said go away and think about it for a couple of weeks and come back with a plan. Our recently arrived news director, Steele Tallon, was supportive and told me to make it at least another six weeks before we ran anything. Longer if you need it, he said.

First I assigned Josh Robertson—a new recruit to the investigations team—the job of collecting up all the data he could find about Gold Coast bikies. 'Let's start with the bikies,' I said. 'They're easily identifiable. We'll get to the Russians, triads and whoever, later.' We agreed on basic sources of information he should use, including court records and databases of real estate and company information, and he set about the task with gusto. 'For now we talk to no one about what we're doing, including cops,' I told him. 'Especially cops.'

Now I needed a strategy, a structure, some direction. Some months earlier, an academic contact had recommended I get to know a criminologist in the Justice Department of Queensland University of Technology called Mark Lauchs, who I later found out 'taught' organised crime—intriguing in itself.

I met Lauchs for coffee at an Italian cafe in Milton and explained our problem.

I told him we had access to plenty of information about crime and criminals on the Coast, but not about how they were organised, nor the composition or activities of different criminal networks. 'You want to use Analyst's Notebook,' he said. 'We've got it. We'll help you. You'll see connections you never knew existed.'

Lauchs explained that Analyst's Notebook was the software program that produced the spidery maps showing the connections between criminals, their victims and others, featured on the credits to *The Wire*, the US television series about drug crime in Baltimore. The program is used by thousands of law enforcement bodies around the world. I'd never heard of it. 'I don't think it features in the actual show,' Lauchs said. I didn't care. I was a fan of the show, and this sounded cool. Plus he would do the grunt work of generating the maps after we provided him with our data. He'd even accept our very low-tech Microsoft Word files, he said.

The company that makes the software later told us it was the first time they had ever heard of Analyst's Notebook being used by a media organisation. 'And we can publish these maps?' I asked Lauchs. 'Sure,' he said. 'I can get an academic paper out of this some way down the track.' We had the back end sorted.

Then we went back to basics, interviewing police officers in Queensland and interstate, organised crime investigators, criminologists, lawyers, politicians, drug addicts, bikies and victims of crime. Some of the subjects probably occupied more than one of these categories. We made regular trips to the Coast. We compared notes with veteran *Courier-Mail* Gold Coast bureau chief Greg Stolz.

We even mulled over hiring a yacht to live on in Southport Marina—for about two hilarious minutes.

Josh buried himself in press clippings, court records and databases. He worked his network of contacts. Tuck Thompson, my deputy, sought out criminologists and other experts and made friends with some hard-case crims in rehab. I persuaded *The Courier-Mail's* motoring editor to fix me up with a series of large British and US motorcycles to review, taking them to drag-racing meets and hanging out in bike dealerships to pick up gossip and leads. He never ran any of the reviews, which didn't help my cover much.

There were raised eyebrows from colleagues in the newsroom, as I swaggered around in bike leathers, and we punctuated our strange work with conversations like: 'So he was running drugs for who? How much meth? And so why did the other guys kill him? Oh well, no wonder. What a dickhead. Can I have the Bandidos file when you're done please.'

A contact at the Crime and Misconduct Commission (CMC) told me that what we were doing was 'in law enforcement terminology, what's called a "collection plan"'.

At a later formal interview, the CMC's heads of organised crime and intelligence were concerned about a different kind of plan. 'Do you have a risk management plan?' one asked after I boasted of my team's previous success using surveillance, stake-outs and other covert methods on other assignments.

'What if you stumble into one of our operations?' another senior officer asked. A turf war with cops in some bikies' den would have been interesting. 'Also, our people are armed, trained and can call on back-up. With respect, none of that applies to you.'

The team had already taken a range of security precautions, but now we had official confirmation that we actually needed them. I thanked the officers for their concern and said I would pass it on to senior management. The bosses must have thought I was joking when they got my email—until we were threatened.

Our 'collection plan' and subsequent work ultimately produced a detailed analysis of seven Gold Coast outlaw motorcycle clubs. We had details of the criminal histories of members, their assets and business dealings going back 15 years. It was a massive amount of information.

But the real insight came from knowing how these people were connected to each other. We knew who had committed crimes with whom and who the victims were. We knew who was in business with whom and whose girlfriend did what. Best of all, we could see it at a glance on a map.

There were, as Mark Lauchs had predicted, some surprises. The big clubs made the most noise, but a couple of the smaller and lower-profile clubs appeared to have some of the wealthiest members. The Hells Angels were a tiny club, but the most disciplined and had the best business smarts, and everyone else was afraid of them, even though their clubhouse wasn't even on the Coast.

Some individuals with a big influence on particular clubs weren't even officially members or were serving long jail sentences. There were also links between clubs that had never previously been identified and some significant interstate and overseas connections.

We were stunned by the level of criminality among these groups. We knew that they traded on their bad-ass reputations, but it was hard to figure out how these people managed to function as a group at all when they appeared to spend so much of their lives in jail.

Another folk myth—that bikies were no-good layabouts with nothing to rub together except their bikes—also went out the window. Insiders said club members included 'psychos' as well as 'charming psychos', and it was unheard of to become a full member of a Gold Coast club without doing something criminal first.

But these people had jobs, businesses and some of them had quite a lot of money. They weren't the kingpins of the underworld, but they had a deeply entrenched and a lucrative—for some—role as its enforcers and its distribution network for illegal products. Motorcycles were just a common interest that gave them an excuse to hang out together and reinforced their outlaw perception of themselves. Bikes, like drugs, we discovered, were also a form of currency.

One of the most surprising things was that despite constant predictions of bikie 'war' on the Coast, the set-up was highly stable, with the main clubs each dominating tightly controlled territories with very little spill-over. Most of the disruption to this comfortable hierarchy was coming from interstate, and not local, rivalries.

We also saw some odd patterns. One example: there were hundreds of companies associated with the people on our maps, some controlled or owned by bikies, and some where the bikies' involvement was only peripheral. But the professional advisers who had set up the companies seemed to be drawn from a very small pool, with the same names cropping up again and again.

An insider explained: 'When you're moving in this kind of world, you're not going to involve just anybody in your business, you're going to use the bloke that you're introduced to by someone you trust.' *The Courier-Mail* published about a dozen major stories based on the team's work. Most appeared in a series of packages that ran in October and November 2011, culminating in the Queensland Police announcing that it planned to use controversial anti-gang laws against one of the Coast's clubs (The Finks). A double-page graphic ran, detailing the strength, criminal background and assets of each of the seven Gold Coast clubs, with an interactive version published on *The Courier-Mail's* website.

The graphic became a stick with which other News Ltd titles' news editors were to beat their reporters. 'This is the kind of thing you should be doing!' was what we heard was being shouted at our colleagues down south. We also published online heavily edited versions of the relational maps created using Analyst's Notebook. Getting the maps past News Ltd's lawyers was one of the most expensive parts of the whole exercise. To avoid the risk of contempt, we had to know whether any of the hundreds of people we were profiling were facing criminal charges.

We also had to exclude anyone whom we had no grounds to say was part of an organised criminal network. We knew that a senior bikie's wife was the front for his club's dodgy business deals, for example, but we couldn't name her because she'd never been convicted of a crime—which was exactly why she had this role.

Further stories were published in subsequent months as trials ended or new leads emerged.

We had made the investigation team's email address prominent in the coverage and some high-quality sources, as well as some cranks, soon availed themselves of the facility. A few days after the paper splashed with a story about a failed attempt by bikies to launder millions of dollars through a Gold Coast nightclub, Josh and I went to see Detective Superintendant John Sheppard, head of the organised crime unit at Queensland Police, at his invitation. There was a small issue of our use of confidential police sources. Couldn't possibly have been anyone under his command, he said. Of course not, we agreed. Sheppard also wanted to know more about the threat we had received.

At the end of the meeting I asked him what he thought of our use of Analyst's Notebook. 'You did a reasonable job of the maps,' he said. 'But some of those solid lines should have been dotted. I'm always telling our analysts that.'

WEBSITE REFERENCE

The Courier-Mail: Bikie Inc: www.couriermail.com.au/ bikieinc/.

17

On Flak, Balance and Activism: The Ups and Downs of Environmental Journalism

LIBBY LESTER

INTRODUCTION

In 1969, *The Age* established Australia's first environmental news round. Reporter John Messer was given the role. The late 1960s and early 70s was a crucial period in the formation of how we now think about 'the environment'. Public anxieties about pollution, water, population growth, wildlife protection and land use had begun to coalesce under an umbrella of 'environmental concern'. The contemporary environment movement in Australia, with its creative media tactics and strategic political lobbying, emerged from various campaigns across the country to protect landscapes—historic and natural—from development. Candidates began standing in elections on environmental platforms. As images of a fragile Earth were beamed from space for the first time, it became evident that there was now an environment to be saved.

Messer's brief was to 'save' the Little Desert, an arid bushland area in Victoria's north-west, from government plans to build a 25km road and subdivide the desert into farmland. Editor Graham Perkin was deeply concerned about these plans, and Messer was given full rein to investigate. Messer's breakthrough came in October 1969 when he discovered that the road ended at the 5000-plus-hectare farm of the brother-in-law of the Minister for Lands and Conservation, Sir William McDonald. The story ran on the front page. According to Perkin's biographer, Perkin was 'like a pig in shit', while to Premier Henry Bolte, Messer's story was the 'lowest filthiest piece of journalism' he'd ever seen (Hills 2010, pp. 298–9).

So began contemporary environmental reporting in Australia; a muddy mix of campaigning, bitter politics, complex legal, economic and scientific information, and old-fashioned dogged research.

This chapter examines the challenges facing contemporary journalists who routinely research and investigate environmental stories. It does so within the context of such history. History is important here because it provides insight into the relationship between journalistic practices and the social, political and technological contexts that influence the production and circulation of environmental issues in the news media. It is difficult to identify another area of journalism so prone to the vagaries of changing attitudes, to the peaks and troughs of public concern. And there is evidence that this dynamic, traceable over almost half a century, influences how journalists now go about their jobs. The chapter, therefore, discusses key challenges as identified by journalists researching environmental issues today,[1] but with an eye on the area's volatile past. The identified challenges are all interrelated, and, while not unique to environmental journalism, they are certainly sharpened when the focus of journalism is the environment.

FATIGUE

'Green fatigue' was first named as such in the late 1980s, when the wave of environmental interest that had included the release of the UN's *Brundtland Report* (1987) and its promotion of 'sustainable development' petered out in the face of the collapse of the Soviet Union, the first Gulf War and various other crises and diversions (Lester 2010, p. 2). Savvy reporters riding the wave of environmental interest in newsrooms around the Western world knew it wouldn't last; after all, the 1980s was also the decade when unprecedented displays of care and support for African famine victims had left publics, and news editors, inured to images of starving children. As had been the case with 'compassion fatigue', it was only a matter of time before editors' concern for ozone holes, logging protests, acid rain and toxic dumps also dissipated into a weary disinterest and the newspaper back pages.

It was also a phenomenon journalists and media scholars had previously identified specifically in relation to the environment. As early as 1972, Anthony Downs described what he called the Issue-Attention Cycle, or going 'Up and Down with Ecology'. For Downs, environmental issues are routinely engaged with by the public and media in such a way that 'alarmed discovery and euphoric enthusiasm' inevitably give way to concern over the costs—financial and to lifestyles—of fixing them (1972, pp. 39–41). Such issues enter a period of limbo, and eventually get overtaken by another concern that is entering the alarmed discovery phase. Later studies may have complicated the neatness of Downs' model—in particular, its notion that the level of public concern reflects the severity of the environmental risk itself, rather than how it is promoted or suppressed by various claims makers, such as NGOs or scientists (see especially Hilgartner & Bosk 1988)—but have confirmed again and again that environmental issues inevitably suffer a gradual decline in public attention, if not a complete disappearance (Hannigan 2006, p. 83). Notable declines have followed peaks of the late 1960s to early 70s, the late 80s, and the mid-to-late 2000s.

This is relevant to contemporary journalists' capacity to research and investigate environmental stories for several reasons. First, the number of journalists dedicated to the environmental round increases during periods of peak interest, and shrinks during troughs. Even *The Age*, the Australian newspaper with the deepest commitment to the round, has questioned whether the round should continue during some periods. It is difficult to identify another round so vulnerable to shifts in public opinion. While non-specialist journalists will often investigate environmental stories, it is hard to replace the in-depth knowledge and experience that the area demands. Less tangible is the role the round plays in extending the life of environmental issues on the public agenda; of signalling continued news media interest in matters environmental to the public and its political decision makers.

Second, environmental stories are given more time and space during periods of heightened public concern, and less during the troughs. This manifests itself in terms of the resources a newsroom will commit to covering an environmental issue, including journalists', photographers' or camera crews' time, and the expenses involved in investigations in regional or remote areas, such as hiring accommodation or helicopters. It is also evident in the space the story will be given, either in terms of word length in a newspaper, or minutes and seconds in a news bulletin, or placement within the news, webpage or broadcast. Much more rests on a journalist's capacity to pitch novel and interesting angles. The conundrum, however, is this: how to develop a succinct, newsworthy pitch without first having the knowledge or time to 'sniff around', and without becoming overly reliant on the claims of various vested interests and lobby groups.

This can leave the area's credibility and legitimacy prone to the vagaries of changing environmental attitudes. The round may be 'juniorised' at times of decreased interest by editors and the public, or—in extreme cases—the commitment to the round ends. As one longstanding environmental reporter notes:

> When you covered a major story, like the Franklin Blockade, the attitude was: Well done you. Now let's move you onto something more important that you can really get your teeth into … But not: Well done. Let's sit down and talk about where you can take this. It was more: Right, let's get you onto something really interesting (Personal interview 1 March 2012).

For this journalist's editors, 'something really interesting' meant investigating arts funding.

In short, journalists confirm it is much harder to get an environmental story up when the public is perceived by editors to have lost interest in environmental issues. Given the 'up and down' cycle in levels of environmental concern, this has ramifications on the capacity of journalists to carry out sustained and properly resourced investigation and research in the area.

BREADTH

A vast range of issues can be labelled 'environmental'. On any single day, mainstream media coverage might include the release of health-related science research; a protest regarding forests; river floods; a development application affecting marine reserves; claims for Indigenous hunting rights; a meeting over international whaling laws; water flows in irrigation zones; community concerns over toxic mining residue; and political and economic debate over the implications of the Carbon Tax. The skills required to comprehend this array of risks and concerns—let alone carry out a timely informative investigation— can be daunting. Moreover, with such a breadth of issues comes an equally wide range of potential sources, all competing to publicise their work or causes. Some are well-resourced institutions or groups, highly skilled promoters and media strategists; others are small informal groups formed to tackle a single issue. Journalists covering the environment need to be able to identify issues across a range of potential fields, to source diverse and accurate forms of information, and to be aware of the potential impacts of their selected angles and content.

The concept of media frames is useful here to help understand how such a wide range of information on the environment is sorted and presented by journalists to readers and viewers, and how readers and viewers in turn make meaning of media coverage. While a concept now commonly, if loosely, applied in academic studies of news media (Entman 1993; Vliegenthart & van Zoonen 2011), media framing can also in general terms be of use to journalists seeking to locate and promote their own stories and practice within broader contexts of changing media platforms, places and power. Climate change coverage, for example, can be framed as a scientific, political, economic or lifestyle issue, and these frames will change over time depending on events—such as droughts, cyclones, international negotiations or elections—or strategic interventions, such as Al Gore's film *An Inconvenient Truth* or Leonardo DiCaprio's *Vanity Fair* cover with Knut, the Berlin Zoo's polar bear cub (Brockington 2009). Nuclear energy frames may vary from highlighting the capacity of this form of power to help reduce greenhouse gas emissions, to locating it as one the world's most dangerous inventions—the choice of frame may depend on the recent occurrence of accidents, or NGO and industry lobbying. The journalist's decision—whether conscious or not—to highlight one frame over another, and therefore make some information more salient over other information, impacts on how editors and readers will respond to a pitch and resulting media coverage (Beck 2009).

We also know that framing varies across different media platforms and across different cultures and national boundaries. Research has found that the whaling dispute between Japan and Australia is framed more nationalistically in Australian media compared to Japanese media (Kudo 2008), while natural disasters are commonly framed by UK journalists as an 'act of God' compared to Swedish journalists, who are far more likely to attribute responsibility and blame to their political leaders (Robertson 2010, pp. 91–2). The application of frames is often based on broader social, political and physical factors (for example, territorial rights over the Southern Ocean; or whether a region is experiencing a period of drought), and as such supports the management and sorting of a vast array of information. However, journalists can also use particular frames to promote a story otherwise seen as uninteresting or unimportant; for example, an 'economic growth' frame can be applied to stories on renewable energies, ensuring climate change coverage that might otherwise have been dropped. It is also important that journalists are always aware of media framing to ensure that they are not unwitting slaves to dominant frames shutting out alternative interpretations of a situation or event (Smith 2005).

The breadth of the environmental issues also means that journalists routinely covering the environment necessarily rely on an extended network and a diverse range of sources. Any attempt to firmly categorise these sources is doomed to failure, given the blurred boundaries, overlaps and changing dynamics that exist in the area. Nevertheless, we can identify three broad groups. The first is institutional sources, such as universities, scientific organisations, local councils, courts, government departments and ministerial offices. These offer expert voices, such as scientists and other researchers; authoritative decision makers, such as politicians; and a range of official documentary sources, such as reports and statements. The second category includes organisations with varying levels of formality in their structure, such as environmental NGOs, community interest groups and industry lobby groups— all of which strategise to influence environmental decision making, if not always successfully. Beyond the public faces of their spokespeople or managed media events and protests, they increasingly provide access via signposting to a range of information relevant to their particular issues, such as weblinks to parliamentary reports or scientific papers. Journalists applaud this shift. One reporter notes:

> They're moving away from the older-style conservation groups who try to get in and lobby the media … You can go directly to reliable information—for example, somebody sends you to a government report that you may not have been aware of that shows the government did promise to act on something. You then develop a set of questions from that … It's exciting because it blows away a lot of the PR guff that we were getting and a lot of the campaign stunts that were clogging up environmental campaigns (Personal interview 1 March 2012).

A third important category of sources for environmental journalists is the non-expert voice. Here, lay knowledge is presented as a legitimate form of recognising or denying environmental consequences and risks (Beck 1992). A woman can describe the anguish of losing her child to preventable disease (Cottle 2000, p. 30); or a villager, seated in his kitchen in front of family memorabilia, speaks of the threat to his home caused by rising sea levels (Lester & Cottle 2009). Alternatively, once the floods arrive a farmer can deny that the drought has caused long-term environmental harm to a river system; or a long-time surf lifesaver can refute the claim that Bondi Beach has been altered by climate change (Lester 2010, p. 107).

Dealing with each of these types of sources requires a variation in approach. They have different expectations of what will result from their participation in journalism; different ambitions for their messages; and they work in different 'languages' and 'time zones', as will be discussed further in the next section. As with framing, an understanding of sources' roles, power and strategies helps journalists negotiate an unusually broad range of subject matter, and to provide in-depth, concrete knowledge to their viewers and readers.

COMPLEXITY

If the research and investigation of environmental stories requires looking across a vast and diverse range of issues and sources, it also requires a deep level of understanding of unusually complex subject matter. There is the science, of course: what exactly is the relationship between CO_2 and climate change? But there is also carbon accounting, coastal planning legislation, road or dam engineering, forest industry certification, biodiversity conservation and international laws, to name just a few potential topics. These are complicated fields that usually require years of education and expertise on the part of those working in the area, who—after years of education and expertise—often find it difficult to communicate their work or issues in simple and straightforward terms. Nevertheless, journalists are required to process and present aspects of these fields in comprehensible small packages—first, to their editors, and second to their readers and viewers.

Although universities and other research institutions have focused greater resources in recent years on communicating their research to a broader audience, journalists covering environmental issues continue to identify this as one of their main challenges:

> The obvious challenge is just telling a complicated story to a mainstream audience without dumbing it down. The key for TV is to keep it simple; turning a 1000-page report on some scientific analysis of climate change into a one-minute-forty story with three grabs and a piece to camera into palatable chunks for people to understand is the first complication (Personal interview 8 March 2012).

Journalists list a variety of tools to overcome the complexity of the area, such as selecting a contained, local angle on a transnational or global issue, and also say they often rely on their own background knowledge and expertise. Several journalists note the usefulness of having grown up in rural Australia. According to one reporter, it helps to 'talk fluent farm', but to also recognise one's limits:

> I can walk into a farming meeting, and I can not only understand what it is they are talking about, but I can understand the level of concern … But other times I'll be sitting there thinking, I know he's speaking English but that's all I know. It is really dense, head-turning stuff and if you want to understand it you've got to just climb onto the raft and hang on. It pulls your brain into 10 different directions. And if you hear somebody talking about that in the context of water reform, the temptation in newsrooms—where they're saying, Yeah, yeah, give me the skinny and give it to me now—is to blank that out, and say, I just don't want to know, I don't want to know (Personal interview 1 March 2012).

Understanding the processes behind scientific research is vital. Learning how peer review works is particularly important; that is, being able to judge the veracity and thoroughness of a peer review system and the standing of academic journals and other forums for research. Acknowledging 'science time' also helps (Allan 2002). Science and journalism work to very different deadlines—scientific research can take years to unfold and for its results to become certain, if ever (Pollack 2005). Misunderstandings can arise for both journalists and scientists over the concept of 'certainty'. To overcome such misunderstandings, journalists researching environmental topics with a heavy science bent say they often check back with the scientist to ensure they have accurately captured the elements of the research. They might also explain to the researcher that they need the 'pub' or 'beer coaster' version. While experienced media sources are aware that their research findings will be severely truncated in media coverage, it can be a shock for media novices.

Another noted challenge of the round is its heavy use of acronyms, generally avoided by news media as they are confusing to audiences if not in common use (such as CSIRO) and ugly in copy or spoken word. A broadsheet journalist describes limiting himself to one acronym per story (Personal interview 2 March 2012). All other organisational names and processes are then abbreviated—'the university', 'the institute', 'the society'—rather than used as an acronym. For news journalists with only 400 words or one-minute-thirty seconds, long organisational names (for example, the Institute for Marine and Antarctic Studies), academic research positions (Associate Professor of Agricultural Sciences at Charles Sturt University) and scientific, legislative or political processes (the Tasmanian Forests Intergovernmental Agreement Update and Progress Report) can take valuable space. Yet to ensure accuracy and fairness, and to avoid conflict from aggrieved interest groups or individuals, they must often be included in full.

The pitch to editors is particularly tricky for journalists researching in the area, both in terms of competing for publication or broadcast space, or for time and resources to carry out further investigation. An environment reporter at the ABC describes her weekly pitch:

> I run up briefs for the network editor … I might look at my week ahead and say, These are the five stories I want to follow this week. This is a trip I want to do this week. And I will do a three-paragraph brief on each story and give the reasons why we should be doing that story. And the next scenario for getting it over the line is to get the network editor to understand what the hell you're talking about because of the scientific sides of things. I've got to understand the science before I can pitch the story. That's the key (Personal interview 8 March 2012).

When journalists are unable to understand and relay the science, politics or economics behind an environmental issue, their stories become vulnerable to an over-reliance on the statements and interpretations provided by various sources. If the future of mainstream environmental journalism is its capacity to package informed, verified and fair research into a well-crafted story that helps readers understand and make decisions on the basis of media coverage, then the onus is on its practitioners to ensure the 'he said she said' style of reporting does not become its trademark. As such, the next section looks more deeply at the question of balance, and the pressures and ramifications that accompany a perceived lack of balance.

BALANCE AND FLAK

'Fair and balanced' is a phrase commonly applied to journalism as 'it should be'. We can take 'fair' to mean journalism that is ethical, takes all relevant information and viewpoints into account, and presents them in such a way that readers and viewers are provided with an informed and reasonable understanding of the issues or events. But what of 'balance'? Does balance mean that relevant information and viewpoints are considered equally while an issue is being researched; or that contending viewpoints will be given equal time or space in the final story?

The coverage of climate change through the later decades of the last century and the first decade of the twenty-first century—continuing into the second decade in some outlets—has highlighted the problem of balance and its openness to interpretation. In seminal research that drew on a sample of more than 5000 US newspaper and broadcast stories between 1988 and 2004, Maxwell and Jules Boykoff analysed how balance had become a form of bias (2004; 2007). They wrote:

> While international conferences, new scientific reports, and political promises might fuse into an amorphous swirl of cautious language that is unable to meet journalistic demands for freshness and novelty, the ever present dueling scientist could be relied upon for a dramatic dose of disagreement (2007, p. 1200).

This served to distort unfolding science and policy discourses, and to breed confusion within the general public about the difference between widely accepted knowledge and 'highly speculative claims' (Boykoff & Boykoff 2007, p. 1200).

Journalists routinely covering the environment continue to face the contentious issue of balance, and can clearly articulate how they incorporate it into their daily practice. According to a journalist who has covered environmental issues on and off since the early 1980s:

> I've always dug my heels in about that right from the start because I had gone from seeing my editors saying, This climate change thing, is it real? Is it really happening? to, If you can get climate change into that, it would be great ... So you do have to dig in when they say, We have to get balance in this, and you have to say, What is it you mean by balance? What is it you want? Yes, it's done if you've got an academic saying, We'll have to overhaul the building codes because of climate change. My idea of balance is to then go to someone from Master Builders and ask, Do you think this is something that should be done? How will it affect urban design? ... It's not going to someone who's vehemently opposed to climate change. That's just getting a comment from someone in the business of climate abuse, not climate research (Personal interview 1 March 2012).

The heightened awareness of the role of balance in environmental coverage is not isolated to climate change coverage. Nor is it coincidental that it is such an issue for environmental reporters. Since the inception of the round in the late 1960s, journalists reporting and researching the environment have faced a noticeably high level of scrutiny and negative feedback on their stories (Neuzil 2008). In interviews, environmental journalists suggest they are exposed to more scrutiny and negative feedback than many others in a newsroom. They describe receiving dozens of emails and letters to the editor; or aggrieved sources directly contacting their editors to complain of bias; or spending lengthy periods in formal complaints procedures arguing over details such as the size of an Olympic swimming pool (following an attempt to quantify for viewers how much waste water would be released daily into the ocean from a proposed industrial development).

Why environmental journalism? Environmental stories often highlight the risks and losses associated with growth and development—the cornerstones of industry and government and their measurements of success. Much is at stake: lifestyles, wealth, jobs, physical health, shared futures. Major conflict continues to play out over the use of landscapes and resources across the world. In developing nations, this is increasingly revealed through violence and other disciplinary measures against journalists who investigate environmental stories. The international organisation Reporters Without Borders found in a 2009 report that 15 per cent of the cases that the group monitors worldwide are now linked to the environment. The report claims:

> In many countries—especially, but not only, those that are not democracies—journalists who specialise in the environment are on the front line of a new war. The violence to which they are subjected concerns us all. It reflects the new issues that have assumed an enormous political and geostrategic importance (Reporters Without Borders 2009, p. 1)

While violence against journalists is uncommon in Western democracies, environmental journalists report facing high levels of negative feedback or 'flak', a term used by Herman and Chomsky in their 'manufacturing consent' model (1988). Some journalists say this 'flak' has had an insidious impact on their capacity to research and investigate environmental issues, for example:

> I can laugh about it now but the story I got the vilest abuse and indeed a death threat on was kangaroo culling in the ACT … And one of the editors said, Look there's too much contention about you covering these stories. I missed good stories, important stories (Personal interview 1 March 2012).

Others claim that, particularly with support from editors, their reporting is not affected. It is, nevertheless, a continuing challenge, for example:

> I get regularly accused of bias towards—I'm not sure exactly—but green causes … One of my great frustrations is we're talking about very complex issues with all sorts of shades of grey but it has been very successfully reduced by some people to either you being a made greenie or you're a realist (Personal interview 29 February 2012).
>
> It can be disheartening but at the same time I think the key is not to be afraid of those minority groups that certainly have targeted journalists in the environment speciality … When I would write a story and publish it online, there'd be 145 comments on it within an hour. I'd read the first page and my eyes would fall out. It was just too extraordinary to see your story being pulled apart and discredited so often (Personal interview 8 March 2012).

Journalists also note that constant negative scrutiny of their research and stories means they work to ensure accuracy and clarity. Lengthy attribution must remain:

> You credit the source in the intro. You say, The temperature's going to increase according to so and so, and you name them. You've got to pin it down to the organisation, to the person … And you've got to choose images carefully … You've got to set up shots that just don't focus on the cooling emissions of coal-fired power stations, for example (Personal interview 8 March 2012).

In short, environmental journalists always need to be prepared to defend their stories. It is inevitable that they will be asked to do so.

PERCEPTIONS

The final challenge identified by journalists researching environmental stories is one journalists rarely discuss openly. It concerns the often-hidden inner workings of a newsroom; the perceptions that circulate but rarely coalesce into a concrete form. As with flak, some environmental journalists believe they are more commonly exposed to this than other journalists working in newsrooms.

The condition relates to the murkiness surrounding ideas of campaigning and/or activist journalism in many contemporary mainstream media organisations. Many forms of investigative journalism, not just environmental journalism, have their roots in campaign-style reporting (Neuzil 2008; Neuzil & Kovarik 1996; Olesen 2008), and many reporters have left news rounds to work with political parties and lobby groups within their area of specialisation. But environmental journalists express concern about being perceived by colleagues and editors to be an 'environmentalist', or campaigning for action on the environment in general.

The external pressures already discussed are clearly a factor in creating a heightened awareness within newsrooms of possible accusations of bias, but only go so far in explaining internal newsroom dynamics, which may manifest in jokes about an environmental journalist carrying shopping in a plastic bag, to needing to 'manage expectations' about the motivation behind stories. The longstanding environment reporter quoted earlier continues recounting events surrounding her stymied coverage of kangaroo culling:

> There was also opposition from someone in the newsroom, who said, You shouldn't be covering these stories, you're behaving like a campaigner. I was outraged because it was a comment from a bloke who had no knowledge of the issue at all (Personal interview 1 March 2012).

The key, according to the journalists interviewed, is to investigate each issue on its own merits:

> There has been an expectation that this was a campaigning round. We often ask ourselves: Are we simply reporting on all aspects of environmental issues and taking a neutral position or are we pushing for better outcomes for the environment. I'm not sure that's been resolved … But our job, like all journalism, is to report and expose the truth in areas of public interest and I guess we still take the point of view that we report strongly on areas where there are environmental problems that need to be addressed; where expert opinion and scientific evidence tells us there are problems that need addressing (Personal interview 29 February 2012).

For those seeking to carry out meaningful investigations of environmental risks and harm, it is essential to be aware of the broader political and social contexts in which their journalism sits. Environmental concern among the public and in newsrooms can, like history, be fickle. Journalists who recognise this fickleness, and the role of their journalism within it, are better equipped to produce well-researched, quality journalism that stands a chance of impacting on the future.

1   Use only one acronym per story. Choose the most useful and least confusing for your story, then abbreviate other institutions, organisations or processes to, for example, 'the report', 'the university' or 'the group'.

2   Learn to talk 'farm' and understand 'science time' so that you are able to comprehend not only the severity of environmental risks and consequences, but also the level of concern sources and interest groups are expressing.

3   Be sensitive to changes in levels of environmental concern. You will need to alter your pitch, angle or overall frame depending on your editor's perceptions of social and political concern for environmental issues.

4   Select images with care. Illustrating environmental risks, consequences and concerns can be difficult. Commonly used images can be overused, inuring readers and viewers to their impact. Likewise, they can be misleading or needlessly expose your story to flak.

5   Be prepared to defend your stories. Double-check all facts, and ensure you have quoted and/or paraphrased your sources correctly. Attribute claims where there is still uncertainty.

6   Fix your story's angle before finding balance. Apply the principle of balance to your angle, not to the overall issue.

7 Find local angles on international issues to help break through complexity. Locate local scientists and local people dealing with the problem, while also ensuring they are credible sources with relevant experience and expertise.

8 Don't join environmental NGOs. Many great journalists initially joined the profession to 'save the world', but within newsrooms, environmental and social change is best achieved through strong journalism, not political activism.

QUESTIONS TO CONSIDER

1 To what extent has so-called 'green fatigue' impacted on environmental reporting since the 1960s?

2 What are the primary frames adopted by journalists when reporting on the environment?

3 Why is the 'non-expert voice' an important source for journalists covering the environment round?

4 What are the critical ethical issues that tend to arise in relation to environmental reporting?

5 To what extent is environmental journalism embraced by Australian media organisations? Will 'green fatigue' spell the end of environmental reporting, or is our interest in, and concern for, the environment strong enough to sustain it into the future?

TASK

1 Identify an environmental issue in your area. Prepare a story plan, listing the critical questions that need to be addressed, what sources/resources you need, where the possible answers could be found, and how the story can be tackled.

REFERENCES

Allan, S. 2002. *Media, Risk and Science*, Buckingham: Open University Press.

Beck, U. 1992. *Risk Society: Towards a New Modernity*, London: Sage.

Beck, U. 2009. *World at Risk*, Cambridge: Polity Press.

Boykoff, M.T. & Boykoff, J.M. 2004. 'Balance as Bias: Global Warming and the US Prestige Press', *Global Environmental Change*, 14, pp.125–36.

Boykoff, M.T. & Boykoff, J.M. 2007. 'Climate Change and Journalistic Norms: A Case-study of US Mass-media Coverage', *Geoforum*, 38, pp. 1190–204.

Brockington, D. 2009. *Celebrity and the Environment: Fame, Wealth and Power in Conservation*, London: ZED Books.

Cottle, S. 2000. 'TV News, Lay Voices and the Visualisation of Environmental Risks', in S. Allan, B. Adam & C. Carter, eds., *Environmental Risks and the Media*, London: Routledge, pp. 29–44.

Downs, A. 1972. 'Up and Down with Ecology: The "Issue-attention" Cycle', *The Public Interest*, 28, pp. 38–50.

Entman, R.M. 1993. 'Framing: Toward Clarification of a Fractured Paradigm', *Journal of Communication*, 43, pp. 51–8.

Hannigan, J.A. 2006. *Environmental Sociology*, London: Routledge.

Herman, E. & Chomsky, N. 1988. *Manufacturing Consent: The Political Economy of the Mass Media*, New York: Pantheon.

Hilgartner, S. & Bosk, C.L. 1988. 'The Rise and Fall of Social Problems: A Public Arenas Model', *American Journal of Sociology*, 94, pp. 53–78.

Hills, B. 2010. *The Golden Age of Graham Perkin*, Melbourne: Scribe Publications.

Kudo, M. 2008. 'A Comparative Analysis of the Press Coverage of the Whaling Conflict in Australia and Japan in 2005–2006', unpublished MA thesis in Journalism, Media and Communications, Hobart: University of Tasmania.

Lester, L. 2010. *Media and Environment: Conflict, Politics and the News*, Cambridge: Polity.

Lester, L. & Cottle, S. 2009. 'Visualizing Climate Change: Television News and Ecological Citizenship', *International Journal of Communication*, 3, pp. 17–26.

Neuzil, M. 2008. *The Environment and the Press: From Adventure Writing to Advocacy*, Evanston, Illinois: Northwestern University Press.

Neuzil, M. & Kovarik, W. 1996. *Mass Media & Environmental Conflict*. Thousand Oaks: Sage.

Olesen, T. 2008. 'Activist Journalism', *Journalism Practice*, 2, pp. 245–63.

Pollack, H.N. 2005. *Uncertain Science … Uncertain World*, Cambridge: Cambridge University Press.

Reporters Without Borders. 2009. *The Dangers for Journalists who Expose Environmental Issues*, Paris: Reporters Without Borders.

Robertson, A. 2010. *Mediated Cosmopolitanism*, Cambridge: Polity Press.

Smith, J. 2005. 'Dangerous News: Media Decision Making about Climate Change Risk', *Risk Analysis*, 25, pp. 1471–82.

UN. 1987. *Report of the World Commission on Environment and Development: Our Common Future* (the *Brundtland Report*), Oxford: Oxford University Press.

Vliegenthart, R. & van Zoonen, L. 2011. 'Power to the Frame: Bringing Sociology Back to Frame Analysis', *European Journal of Communication*, 26(2), pp. 101–15.

NOTE

1   Six senior journalists were interviewed for this chapter and for a larger investigation into environmental media and politics funded by the Australian Research Council (Discovery Grant DP1095173). The journalists are either dedicated environmental reporters or routinely cover environmental issues. Their employers include the national News Ltd-owned *The Australian* newspaper; the Melbourne-based Fairfax broadsheet *The Age*; the Fairfax-owned *Canberra Times*; the ABC; and a commercial national television network.

18

Health Reporting: Opportunities and Challenges?

TREVOR CULLEN

Health reporting is on the rise. This is evident from the steady increase in health publications, health programs on radio and television, and the soaring demand for online health information—showing that health is a popular topic and the media is where people turn to find it. Some researchers estimate that more than 80 per cent of people get their information on health from the media, and 55 per cent make decisions based on what they read (Pew Internet and American Life Project 2010). The demand for health information suggests that health journalism has a bright future. Yet, it places on journalists a responsibility to provide accurate and reliable content, especially since so many people make serious decisions based on what they read, hear or see on the media. This chapter focuses on this challenge and on ways to improve the content and context of health stories.

INTRODUCTION

Health is an important topic that affects everyone, either through their own personal experiences or those of their family, friends or work colleagues. Indeed, people are more interested in what hits closest to home, and they want information that is accurate and they can trust. Yet for a long time, reporting health consisted largely of statistics on the number of deaths and cases of disease, or reporting on epidemiological data that affects people we do not know. While this is important for health officials, it is of little interest to audiences who are increasingly demanding information that is useful to their daily lives. And conserving one's health is perhaps the most useful of all topics.

A survey in 2010 by the Pew Internet and American Life Project, revealed that 61 per cent of Americans searched for health information on the internet, and that six out of 10 respondents said the information they found online affected their decision about how to treat an illness or a medical condition. More than 55 per cent said it changed how they maintained their own health or the health of another.

The downside of reporting health is that there is saturation coverage of health topics, and nearly every possible news or feature angle seems to have been covered. This makes it hard to maintain interest and also credibility, especially when many health stories promote contradictory advice. It seems that nearly every week there is a new medical theory on whether the daily use of aspirin is effective or detrimental to one's health, or whether broccoli is a way to slow the spread of certain cancers.

So how reliable and well tested is the health information we read, hear or view? Surveys conducted in the USA and Australia show there is plenty of room for improvement.

THE UNHEALTHY STATE OF HEALTH JOURNALISM

Associate Professor Gary Schwitzer runs the *Health News Review* website, which has evaluated more than 1000 health stories in the US media. His May 2010 findings included a damning critique of the media's approach to covering health and medicine. Schwitzer argued that journalists tend to be cheerleaders rather than provide a critical analysis of health stories. He said there were too many fluffy, feel-good pieces, and unquestioning, awe-struck stories about breakthroughs; and not enough questioning of claims, investigating of evidence, and looking at conflicts of interests, especially with particular sources.

Another survey by the Australian Centre for Independent Journalism in Sydney analysed more than 200 health stories in the Australian press during a one-week period in September 2009, and found that more than half the stories were driven by PR events or media releases (Duxfield 2010). Also, a 2009 survey of health stories in *The Australian*, *The Sunday Times* and *The West Australian* by health journalism students at Edith Cowan University discovered a similar pattern—an unhealthy reliance on media releases (Callaghan 2010).

Several researchers argue that when it comes to health news, sober, reliable and expert reporting can be hard to find. As newsrooms cut numbers and reduce the time available for writing about health, there is often a rush to produce prepackaged stories, using wire services or relying on press releases as the primary and often only sources of research news (Mooney & Kirshenbaum 2009; Raward & Johnston 2009; Salleh 2009; Young 2009).

Increasing reliance by reporters on embargoes, press releases and wire copy encourages lazy journalism and bland reporting. Davies highlights the dangers of media groups relying on wire services, which may have a small pool of reporters producing high-speed but limited 'in-depth' reports, which then receive wide coverage (2008a). As journals adopt the use of publicity machines to promote their research, media outlets and wire services have every reason to rely too heavily on the easy media release to save time and effort in preparing science and health stories (Davies 2008a; 2008b; Mooney and Kirshenbaum 2009; Murcott 2009; Orange 2008).

Also, the engagement of PR firms in health organisations, the selective press releases sent out by medical organisations to the media, and the cost cutting approach of media organisations all foster what former *Guardian* reporter Nick Davies calls 'churnalism'—the churning out of stories with limited, if any, actual reporting by the journalist:

> more than ever in the past, we are likely to engage in the mass production of ignorance because the corporations and the accountants who have taken us over, have stripped out our staffing, increased our output and ended up chaining us to our desks so that generally we are simply no longer able to go out and make contacts or find stories or even check facts (2008b).

Another area of concern is how narrowly health stories are framed, with little or no reference to the social and economic determinants of health. For example, a study of media coverage of obesity in television news in Australia focused attention on personal responsibility for weight loss without reference to structural issues such as: economic pressures to work long hours in sedentary jobs; urban planning that fails to facilitate physical activity; poor public transport and inadequate provision of cycle paths; and inadequate provision of parks and other recreational facilities (Bonfiglioli et al. 2007). Yet the neglect of environmental and structural solutions suggests advocacy efforts may be needed to draw attention to how these factors, cumulatively, constrain individual choices and contribute to the obesity epidemic (Bonfiglioli et al. 2007, pp. 442–5).

Admittedly, this last point could be viewed as moving towards health promotion rather than the traditional journalist's role of reporting the facts. But with serious health epidemics such as adult diabetes, is it enough to report only 'what' is happening and omit the 'why' it is occurring, which provides a better understanding of the disease and ways to deal with it?

WAYS TO IMPROVE HEALTH REPORTING

Attempts have been made in Australia to try to improve the standard of health reporting. The website *Media Doctor* was created in 2004 to evaluate health stories that report on medications and treatments in the Australian media. It grades them according to a set list of criteria: the mention of potential adverse effects, the inclusion of alternative therapies, and the type of diagnostic tests. The panel includes a group of academics and also clinicians from the Newcastle Institute of Public Health, who have an interest in promoting better and more accurate reporting in the area of medical treatments. The aim is to improve the accuracy of health reporting by offering an evaluation of the quality of health stories, and providing feedback for journalists and media organisations on the quality of their stories.

In the USA, the *Health News Review* website provides health writers with a checklist to evaluate health claims and sources in news and feature stories:

- How strong is the evidence?
- Is this condition exaggerated?
- Who's promoting this?
- Do they have a conflict of interest?
- What's the total cost?
- How often do the benefits occur?
- Describe possible side effects.
- How often do the harms occur?
- Are there alternative options?
- Is this really a new approach?

Both websites encourage a more critical and proactive approach to health reporting with a strong emphasis on investigating claims and statements, rather than adopting a reactive response where the journalists wait for the story to come to them and seldom check the evidence (for more on the strategies PR companies use, see Chapter 12) .

Schwitzer refers to other pitfalls that health journalists need to avoid, including the use of words such as 'miracle', 'breakthrough' and 'cure' These words are misleading and unhelpful since the realities they refer to seldom occur. Also, Schwitzer points out that it is important to refer to more than one study, and to identify the sources of the studies as a way to weed out (or expose) bias and self-interest: for example, reveal which pharmaceutical company funded a particular project and challenge company media releases that look too good to be true.

There are other considerations. Ask yourself these questions before you write.

- What good is likely to result from your investigation?
- What harm could result?
- Is it fair, or does it favour someone over another?
- Are there alternatives to consider?

These questions point towards an important area—the ethics of health reporting. For example, when writing about depression, cancers or drug use and abuse, how far should a journalist go to acquire the story, especially when it involves intruding upon the privacy of reluctant participants?

In Australia, health writers are guided by the Media, Entertainment and Arts Alliance's Australian Journalists' Association Code of Ethics (MEAA 2001). This requires from journalists a commitment to honesty, fairness, independence and the respect for the rights of others. The code has 12 clauses, and, while it is not legally binding, it does provide guidelines about how to proceed or act. The code is covered in detail in Chapter 14, however, here is a summary of its implication for health journalists.

- **Clause 1** emphasises the need for fair and accurate reporting, getting facts straight and seeking comment.

- **Clause 2** is designed to prevent discrimination on the grounds of personal characteristics. Use terminology that you feel the community as whole would find acceptable and reasonable.

- **Clause 3** stresses the need to attribute information to its source. This can be tricky in health reporting. When investigating issues, a journalist may find that people making allegations about health system problems are unwilling to be named.

- **Clauses 4 and 5** overlap to an extent, and relate to not allowing personal interests or beliefs to affect balance and fairness. At its core, the ethics of health reporting is about being responsible for what we write and broadcast. Journalists should present information that is technically correct and morally sound.

- **Clause 6** relates to not allowing commercial interests to affect journalistic practice; for example, if a health writer was asked to produce a story focusing on a service, company or group advertised in a healthy lifestyle section.

- **Clause 7** focuses on chequebook journalism, in which news organisations pay for exclusive rights to a story; for example, about the separation of conjoined twins.

- **Clause 8** encourages the use of fair and honest means to secure a story. At times, a journalist can get more information from a health clinic or website by phoning or logging in as a potential patient or customer rather than as a journalist—hence the trap.

- **Clause 9** refers to digital editing techniques that allow cut-and-paste images and audio. Digital technologies have increased the potential for pictures and sound to be manipulated in ways that can mislead.

- **Clause 10** relates to plagiarism. A journalist should not lift the work of another from print, broadcast media or the internet. This issue is often overlooked or ignored. Plagiarism is stealing and any borrowed material should be sourced conscientiously. It is fair to say the huge amount of information on the internet has made this clause harder to police, but not impossible.

- **Clause 11** covers the areas of respect, grief and privacy and it is one of the most subjective clauses. For example: what is considered an intrusion? Stories of tragedy and suffering are an integral part of health writing and reflect society to itself. Health journalists should exercise their discretion, taking into account the particular circumstances of each case.

- **Clause 12** refers to correcting errors. To ensure trust, the media must repair errors. A prompt and fair correction (in time and prominence) retains the integrity of the journalist and publication.

THE DETERMINANTS OF HEALTH PROVIDE CONTEXT AND UNDERSTANDING

Often health stories are framed too narrowly, with little or no reference to the broader determinants of health—social, economic, cultural, religious and political factors—which provide both context and a better understanding of communicable and non-communicable diseases. As early as 1986, with the adoption of the *Ottawa Charter* (WHO 1986), the social and cultural dimensions of health became increasingly more mainstream. In more recent years social scientists have come to realise that socio-cultural factors influence complex health behaviours. Take, for example, the relationship between sexual behaviour and HIV infections. Beyond an individual's own social network, there are larger structural and environmental determinants that affect sexual behaviour, such as living conditions related to one's employment. Also, in some countries, there is a lack of sexually transmissible disease services, and condoms can be costly or unavailable. This puts pressure on many sex workers to act in unsafe ways to keep customers satisfied. All of these work against people adopting safer behaviours.

Kippax argues that individual behaviour and 'choice' is always mediated and structured by social relationships, which are in turn influenced by important differences of community, social status, class and other structural differences, such as gender and age. In other words, individual behaviour is always contextual, always socially embedded (2007, p. 5).

This is not a new insight. A special session of the United Nations General Assembly on HIV/AIDS in June 2001 adopted a Declaration of Commitment on HIV/AIDS and emphasised the important role of cultural, family, ethical and religious factors in the prevention of the epidemic and in treatment, care and support, taking into account the particularities of each country (United Nations 2001). This shift in thinking forms a key part of the social change communication (SCC) theory, where the focus is on seeing people and communities as agents of their own change. This theory is based on a belief that behavioural change is dependent on social change and is a long-term process (Deane 2002, p. 1). The social communication approach to understanding HIV, and the need to highlight the context in which the epidemic is embedded, has wide support (McKee et al. 2004, p. 41).

The implications of SCC theory, if adopted by editors and journalists, would widen the predominant narrow framing of HIV stories from a focus primarily on health to one that covers related issues, such as gender equality, domestic violence, inadequate access to treatment, poor health facilities, complex sexual networking, and challenging governments on their policies towards treatment, human rights and overall strategies. Indeed, this perspective on the disease provides a new and extensive list of news and feature stories for print, online and broadcast journalists.

Not everyone agrees, however, and questions remain about the role of journalism in health promotion and development contexts. For example, how does the media address extremely complex questions such as gender power and the connections between rising health costs and ecological sustainable development? While this remains an ongoing debate, the next section of this chapter focuses on the determinants of health. The author argues that this approach broadens the scope and context of health stories, and leads to a better understanding and discussion of effective measures to deal with communicable diseases such as HIV, sexually transmitted infections and tuberculosis. Press coverage of HIV in PNG is used as an example to highlight these points.

PRESS COVERAGE OF HIV IN PNG—WIDENING THE FRAME

The story of HIV is one of critical importance in many countries throughout the world. PNG, Australia's nearest neighbour, has a serious HIV epidemic, with up to 96 per cent of all HIV infections in the Pacific region. Up to 1.8 per cent of the adult population in PNG is infected with HIV and prevalence in urban areas maybe as high as 3.5 per cent (UNAIDS 2011). New infection rates have increased about 30 per cent each year since 1997. A report by the PNG National AIDS Council Secretariat (NACS) in May 2008 suggested an infection rate of over 100 000 people in PNG (which has a population of 5.5 million), and predicts that the country will eventually match the massive infection rates seen in several southern African countries). The author has chosen PNG as an example because he conducted an extensive longitudinal content analysis of press coverage of HIV in the country's two daily newspapers from 2000 to 2010 (Cullen 2010). One aim was to discover whether the journalists had tried to include the determinants of health in their HIV stories, rather than just report official facts and figures.

The focus on press coverage of HIV rather than a wider study on media coverage of the disease is due, in large part, to more effective access to archival print data. Print copy is easier to locate and avoids the long arduous task of trawling through broadcast tapes of the 1990s, when transcripts were not readily available. Also, newspapers are influential because news stories that appear in print or online are frequently used by radio and television news editors to provide background—and often actual content—for their daily broadcast news services. In addition, the press can keep issues and debates in the public forum, and move items onto and up the political agenda.

It is evident from the data on press coverage of the disease in PNG from 2000 to 2010 that a disproportionate emphasis was placed upon reporting infection rates, international funding and regional workshops, with little in-depth analysis of the disease or educational content (Cullen 2010, p. 171). Anna Solomon, a former newspaper editor in PNG, acknowledged that framing the disease in this way has narrowed debate of the topic and led to a lack of interest among readers. Solomon urged her fellow PNG journalists and editors to use imagination, initiative and sensitivity as a way to widen and inevitably improve the reporting of HIV in her country (2002).

In time, slight changes began to emerge. A content analysis by the author (Cullen 2007) analysed all online news items on HIV from the websites of the country's two national daily newspapers—*The Post-Courier* and *The National*—during a three-month period from September to November 2007. Surprisingly, while stories on HIV were similar in content to the author's earlier studies on press coverage of HIV in PNG (Cullen 2000; 2005), there was a new focus on domestic violence, with both newspapers including 10 items each on the topic in October and November 2007. This represented, for the first time, a small shift in the reporting of HIV in PNG and suggested that journalists had begun to link HIV with the wider social and cultural context of the disease.

The author also analysed all online news items on HIV from the websites of the country's two national newspapers during a three-month period from January to March 2010 (Cullen 2010). This revealed an interesting trend in the coverage—the recognition of the social stigma surrounding people with HIV in PNG. Several articles coded 'Person Living With AIDS' (PLWA) made it clear that the person described with the disease was not at fault. One notable article in *The Post-Courier* described the road to infection of a 29-year-old woman from Balimo who became the second wife of a 'well-built man who was a land-owner' from the region. It was only after her husband began losing weight rapidly that she discovered he had been diagnosed with HIV some time earlier, but had not disclosed it. The article directly addressed the societal pressure on her—both to remain with her husband and to hide the disease:

> She went back to her family and they are supportive in the situation and want to help raise [her HIV-infected daughter] who is four years old. She said she disclosed her status to the community and to date had not suffered stigma. The community is supportive and I believe that is due to ongoing awareness of the virus, she said (*The Post-Courier* 2010, p. 6).

Stories such this help to demystify the disease and gradually lessen the paralysing fear associated with it.

THE MISSING LINKS

While the press in PNG is slowly beginning to link the disease with the larger social and cultural context, there are other connected stories that are unreported—including in the area of gender equality—which reflect the complexity of the HIV situation in a developing country such as PNG, and expose how difficult it is to prevent and slow the spread of disease there. For example, sexual relations lie at the heart of the HIV epidemic in PNG. Women's lack of social or economic authority is underwritten by the sexual economy and enforced largely by violence. Current attitudes to sex pose serious barriers to the effectiveness of HIV interventions. Women in general, and those involved in sex work in particular, are blamed for HIV infection in PNG. It is true that this attitude is not limited to PNG, but also exists even in more developed countries. But the constant public scapegoating of sex workers has further entrenched the view that HIV can be attributed to 'filthy' and 'immoral' women. And yet, it is estimated that almost half of PNG men pay for sex at some time each year (Smith & Cohen 2000, p. 6).

For the same reasons, married women are the largest group of women at risk of HIV infection. Further, since most infected women are of childbearing age, they also carry the risk of infecting their children. These issues are directly linked to HIV and yet, until recently, there was rarely a news story or feature article on the topic in PNG's two main newspapers. It is difficult to give a clear explanation for this omission other than to state that gender equality was not considered newsworthy by the editors. Yet in-depth articles could expose the serious gender inequality in PNG and argue that if married women are to protect themselves and their children in such circumstances, they need precisely the same things as women need in general—access to education and training, removal of restrictions on employment, access to banking services, and credit on their own surety. In addition, they require drastic shifts in property rights, rights of divorced and widowed women, child custody rights, and protection against physical violence. The HIV epidemic is not simply about public health—it also is about basic human rights. There is a need, therefore, to ensure that when reporting on the HIV epidemic, wider links such as poverty reduction and gender equality are part of the coverage.

Other issues include the fact that, with increasing healthcare costs in countries hard hit by HIV, there is immense pressure to generate more income through mining, forestry and other environmentally degrading sources. Increased exploitation of natural resources will mean further degradation of water and ecosystems on which people depend for survival; so poverty increases, and the whole cycle of poverty fuels HIV transmission. Also, when family members in urban areas fall sick they often return to their villages, putting additional pressure on scarce resources and fragile environments. How many journalists would think of reporting these issues, or are able to link these issues? This is not due to an unwillingness to report, but rather a lack of awareness about the wider links to HIV. Unfortunately, the narrow conception and understanding of HIV to date has led to missed opportunities for wider coverage and debate.

Shining the spotlight on how local governments are coping—or not coping—with HIV is vital. Political leadership has proved a vital component in the struggle to stem the rise of HIV infections in other parts of the world. This is clear from the decline of infections in Uganda, Thailand and Gambia, where the political leaders have spoken openly and constantly about the epidemic. This has helped lessen the stigma surrounding HIV/AIDS in the local communities, and has galvanised these leaders into action as they defined the struggle against HIV as a national cause and campaign.

CONCLUSION

The growing interest in health information means that health writers are in demand. The findings of the Pew Internet and American Life Project (2010) put a responsibility on health journalists to provide accurate and reliable content, especially since so many people make serious decisions based in what they read, hear or see on the media. Yet, surveys in the USA and Australia that examined the state of mainstream and online health reporting exposed the extent of spin, the lack of medical evidence, and the narrow frame and context of many health stories, with little or no reference to the social determinants of health.

In an attempt to respond to such criticisms and challenges, this chapter looked at several ways to improve health reporting. These included a greater emphasis on critical analysis of evidence and claims; adherence to ethical and professional codes; and the need to widen the narrow frame and focus of many health stories through the inclusion of the determinants of health and human behaviour, which SCC theory advocates.

While this chapter did not examine the application of SCC theory to other communicable diseases, it did use the reporting of HIV in PNG as an example to show that HIV—like other communicable diseases, such as sexually transmitted infections—is not merely a medical problem, but operates like a magnifying glass on the exploitation of women, domestic violence, gender inequality, illiteracy, the lack of health facilities, and the kind of rampant poverty that forces people to migrate. These connections have important implications for political and financial reporters, editorial page writers, television producers and radio journalists, especially if they want to engage in meaningful coverage of the HIV epidemic and its broader ramifications. For now, the most challenging aspect for health journalists is to realise the complexity and interconnectedness of the web of issues linked to reporting HIV, together with other communicable and non-communicable diseases.

GETTING STARTED

There are various types of health news and feature stories, but four common ones are: research-based, healthcare system-based, preventative, and informative stories.

The research-based approach focuses on the extensive amount of new research on health practices, policies and treatments. The findings of such research can be found on numerous health databases and websites, some of which are listed at the end of this chapter. Stories could focus on new studies, new developments or new claims; or they could put the research into context or present more information about how the studies were conducted.

Healthcare system-based stories normally deal with health services and government policy, and stories under this heading usually focus on hospital management issues in terms of budgets, available beds, or waiting times for operations. Debate over federal or state funding is always an ongoing contentious issue, as is the area of patient safety and certain clinical practices.

The other two areas—preventative and informative health stories—are popular and tend to highlight risk factors such as smoking, excessive drinking, unhealthy diets and lack of exercise, and also the benefits of a healthier lifestyle.

The next question is how you develop the idea for a health feature. One way is to start with a question, because the more precise your topic is, the sharper the feature will be as you do not have to try to cover every angle. So for example, questions concerning cancer could include:

- Can science cure cancer?
- What is the latest research that could fight cancer?
- How do survivors of cancer learn to live with the disease?
- Why has life expectancy of children with leukaemia improved, when adults with the disease have such a poor chance of survival?

Or with drug abuse:

- How has illegal drug use changed in the past 10 years?
- What are the dangers of ecstasy?
- Why are so many marijuana users ending up with drug-induced psychosis?
- How do you tell that you have a drinking problem? What are the signs?

Or with obesity:

- What can we do to encourage overweight adults to exercise more?
- How has child obesity changed in the past 10 years?
- Should parents be banned from driving children to school?
- Do diets really make a long-term difference?

QUESTIONS TO CONSIDER

1   Why does the author believe that health reporting is 'on the rise'?
2   Why is Schwitzer critical of US health reporting? Do you believe the same criticisms can be directed at Australian health reporting? Why or why not?
3   Why does Schwitzer warn against the use of loaded language?
4   What does the HIV–PNG case study suggest about the significance of health reporting and the ethical issues involved?

TASK

1   Identify a recent health story covered by a number of different media organisations. How does the media reporting differ across the various media outlets? To what extent do these stories lend weight to the author's concerns about the need for more ethical health reporting?

REFERENCES

Bonfiglioli, C., Smith, B., King, L., Chapman, S. & Holding, S. 2007. 'Choice and Voice: Obesity Debate in Television News', *The Medical Journal of Australia*, 187(8), pp. 442–5.

Callaghan, R. 2010. *Health Journalism: Students Unravel the Hype and Laziness in Health Research Reporting*, peer-reviewed conference paper delivered at the Journalism Education Association of Australia Conference, Perth, Australia, 1 December.

Cullen, T. 2000. *Repeating Mistakes: Press Coverage of HIV/AIDS in Papua New Guinea and the South Pacific*, unpublished PhD thesis, St Lucia: University of Queensland.

Cullen, T. 2005. 'Press Coverage of HIV in PNG: Is It Sufficient to Report Only the News?', *Australian Studies in Journalism*, 15, pp. 133–50.

Cullen, T. 2007. '25 Years of Reporting HIV: What Can Pacific Journalists Learn?', peer-reviewed paper presented at the JEANZ Conference in Wellington, New Zealand, 11December.

Cullen, T. 2010. 'Reporting HIV in Papua New Guinea: Trends and Omissions from 2000–2010', *Pacific Journalism Review*, 16(2), pp. 163–78.

Davies, N. 2008a. 'Churnalism has Taken the Place of What We Should Be Doing: Telling the Truth', *PressGazette*: www.pressgazette.co.uk/story. asp?storycode=40117 (accessed 20 October 2011).

Davies, N. 2008b. 'Our Media Have Become Mass Producers of Distortion', *The Guardian*: www. guardian.co.uk/commentisfree/2008/feb/04/ comment.pressandpublishing (accessed 10 October 2012).

Deane, J. 2002. 'Approaches to HIV and AIDS Communication Strategies': www.healthcomms. org/comms/hiv-aids/hiv02.html (accessed 7 January 2008).

Duxfield, F. 2010. 'Spinning the Media: Spin Doctors Have Plenty to Say in Health Reporting', *Crikey*: www.crikey.com.au/2010/03/17/spinning-the-media-spin-doctors-have-plenty-to-say-in-health-reporting (accessed 28 November 2012).

Kippax, S. 2007. *Reflections of a Social Scientist on Doing HIV Social Research*, Sydney: The National Centre in HIV Social Research.

Las Vegas Sun. 2010. 'Do No Harm': www.lasvegassun. com/hospital-care/part-one/.

McKee, N., Bertrand, J. & Benton-Becker, J. 2004. *Strategic Communication in the HIV/AIDS Epidemic*, London: Sage Publications.

Media Entertainment and Arts Alliance (MEAA). 2001. *Australian Journalists' Association Code of Ethics*: www.alliance.org.au/code-of-ethics.html (accessed 21 November 2011).

Mooney, C. & Kirshenbaum, S. 2009. 'Unpopular Science', *The Nation*: http://groups.yahoo.com/ group/Net- Gold/message/29734?var=1 (accessed 8 October 2011).

Murcott, T. 2009. 'Science Journalism: Toppling the Priesthood', *Nature*, 459(10), pp. 1054–5.

National AIDS Council Secretariat (NACS). 2008. *Annual STI, HIV & AIDS Surveillance Report*, Port Moresby, Papua New Guinea: NACS.

Orange, R. 2008. 'Beware the Spin Doctors', *PressGazette*: www.pressgazette.co.uk/story.asp?sec tioncode=1&storycode=40441 (accessed 20 August 2009).

Pew Internet and American Life Project. 2010: http:// pewinternet.org/Data-Tools/Get-The-Latest-Statistics.aspx (accessed 3 September 2011).

The Post-Courier (PNG). 2010. 'Sad Tale but True in PNG', 25 March.

Raward, D. & Johnston, J. 2009. 'FM Radio News: Spreading the News or Spread Too Thin?', *Australian Journalism Review*, 31(1), pp. 63–76.

Salleh, A. 2009. 'Scientists Risk becoming "PR Hacks"', *ABC Science*: www.abc.net.au/science/ articles/2009/07/03/2613817.htm (accessed 22 July 2009).

Schwitzer, G. 2010. 'The Future of Health Journalism', *Public Health Forum*: www.resoundinghealth.com/ static/Schwitzer%20health%20journalism.pdf/.

Seale, C. 2002. *Media and Health*, London: Sage.

Smith, S. & Cohen, D. 2000. *Gender, Development and the HIV Epidemic*, Geneva: UNDP.

Solomon, A. 2002. Former editor of *The Independent* newspaper, interviewed in Port Moresby, PNG, 18 September.

UNAIDS. 2011. *Report on the Global AIDS Epidemic*, Geneva: UNAIDS/WHO.

United Nations. 2001. *Declaration of Commitment on HIV/AIDS*, United Nations Special Session on HIV/AIDS, New York, 25–27 June.

USC Annenberg: Reporting on Health. 2012. 'Matter: How a Sci/Tech Investigative Reporting Startup Raised $140 000 on Kickstarter': www.reportingonhealth.org/blogs/2012/04/05/matter-how-scitech-investigative-reporting-startup-raised-140000-kickstarter/.

WHO. 1986. *The Ottawa Charter for Health Promotion*, Geneva: World Health Organization.

Young, E. 2009. 'On Cheerleaders and Watchdogs—The Role of Science Journalism', *ScienceBlogs*: http://scienceblogs.com/notrocketscience/2009/07/on_cheerleaders_and_watchdogs_-_the_role_of_science_journali.php (accessed 10 August 2009).

WEBSITE REFERENCES

ABC Health & Wellbeing: www.abc.net.au/health/.

ABS: www.abs.gov.au/.

Australian Government Department of Health and Ageing: www.health.gov.au/.

BBC: Health: www.bbc.co.uk/health/.

British Medical Journal: http://www.bmj.com/.

The Community Guide: www.thecommunityguide.org/index.html/.

Government 2.0 Taskforce: http://gov2.net.au/.

Health Is Everything: Using Data to Report Great Stories on Your Community's Health: www.reportingonhealth.org/reporting-community-health/.

Health News Review: www.healthnewsreview.org/.

The Lancet: www.thelancet.com/.

Matter: http://readmatter.com/.

Media Doctor: www.mediadoctor.org/.

Medical Journal of Australia: www.mja.com.au/.

ProPublica: Dollars for Docs: http://projects.propublica.org/docdollars/.

Research on AIDS Reporting: www.aidsreporting.com/.

Therapeutic Guidelines: www.tg.com.au/.

The University of Sydney: Medical Sciences Databases: www.library.usyd.edu.au/databases/health.html/.

US Global Health Policy: www.globalhealthreporting.org/.

World Health Organization: www.who.int/.

FURTHER READING

Brodie, M., Hamel, E.B., Kates, L.A., Altman, J. & Drew, E. 2004. 'AIDS at 21: Media Coverage of the HIV Epidemic', *Columbia Journalism Review*, 42(6), p. A1.

UNESCO. 2011. *Strategy for HIV/AIDS Prevention Education*, Paris: UNESCO.

HARNESSING THE DIGITAL ERA FOR HEALTH INVESTIGATIONS

Melissa Sweet

The health round is huge and complex. Its most-explored territory spans research, clinical practice, service delivery, health policy and politics, and public health. Although the mainstream media often conflates health with health services, many of the determinants of any population's health lie outside the health sector. These include the so-called social determinants of health—the social, cultural and economic factors that have a large influence on the health of populations and individuals.

When considered in this light, there are very few issues that can't be considered potential fodder for a health investigation: the construction of a new prison, the building of suburbs without public transport, the quality of public education in poorer areas—these all have significant health implications that merit investigation. The public health methodology of health impact assessment—which, as its name suggests, investigates the health consequences of wider policies and developments—can also be useful for journalists.

The constant deluge of health and medical news—from journals, researchers, conferences, and a multitude of professional and other vested interests—means that reporters on the daily beat are often overwhelmed, and have little opportunity to conduct longer investigations. There are rich pickings for those with the time and capacity to dig deeper. The major challenge is not that there is any shortage of subjects, but in sifting through the many options to find those with maximum public interest value.

Another challenge lies in providing audiences with sufficient context to help them make sense of what are often complex issues. An investigation into failings in care at a particular health or aged care service, for example, is lacking if it does not include some wider understanding of the research and policy that has developed around healthcare safety and quality over the past 20 years. An investigation into a test or treatment is likewise lacking if it is not informed by a basic understanding of epidemiology, and does not include enough context to enable its audience to assess the quality of evidence given about the intervention.

Fortunately, the digital age makes it easier than ever to do such research. Web tools and sites worth checking include Google Scholar; the Cochrane Collaboration (for the evidence basis of health interventions); the Campbell Collaboration (for the effects of interventions in education, crime and justice, social welfare and international development); PubMed Health, a US-based collection of systematic reviews from various sources; and The Community Guide, another US-based repository of evidence for public health interventions.

Increasingly, there are online resources enabling reporters to put Australian health and the healthcare system in context—for example, how we compare with other countries. The Global Health Data Exchange at the Institute for Health Metrics and Evaluation in Seattle, Washington state, and the World Health Organization's Global Health Observatory are worth a look. The so-called 'grey literature', which includes research and reports that have not been formally published, can also be worth digging into. When investigating research or clinical stories, it is also worth checking the US health journalism watchdog site, Health News Review, which includes a list of questions and issues to consider when reporting on tests, treatments and other interventions.

Another advantage of the digital age is that journalists now have easier access to more information than in the past, when powerful lobby groups such as the Australian Medical Association tended to be the major source of health and medical news. The ease and affordability of social media channels mean that a wider range of groups and interests are able to engage in public debate around health; while the rise of social media is slowly breaking down some of the barriers of access to public sector employees.

The Government 2.0 agenda and some of the drivers of healthcare reform internationally—including moves for greater transparency and accountability for financing and health service performance—mean that an increasing amount of data is becoming available to help inform investigations. In Australia, the MyHospitals website, for example, enables comparison of hospitals' performance, while the new primary healthcare organisations known as Medicare Locals will also be required to publish data about services and health in their areas. There are plans for a My Aged Care website. Similarly, the international push for a greater focus on population health—understanding the forces that shape the health of specific communities, as well as their access to health-promoting environments and services—is also opening up new sources of data and other material for investigations. There is increasing potential to look across multiple sources of data to investigate the factors contributing to poor health in specific communities—for example, around health, education, transport, food supply and urban planning. Again, the challenge for journalists is to put meaning and context around the data while engaging audiences in complex issues.

The digital age is also enabling new ways of conducting investigations. It enables crowdsourcing of story ideas and can also be used to enlist the help of the community in actually doing some of the work—whether crunching data, creating data visualisations, or helping to check and disseminate investigations. The nature of online publishing also means that investigations can become an ongoing process rather than a one-off publishing event, and allow for multiple presentations in multiple formats. For example, ProPublica's investigations of pharmaceutical company payments to doctors in the USA, entitled appropriately 'Dollars for Docs', has a news app that lets readers look up their own doctors and see the payments they've received. Collaboration and co-production—two of the buzz words of the digital age—were also enlisted by the 'Dollars for Docs' team, which made their data widely available to other news organisations and journalists. More than 125 local news organisations did their own local investigations using the 'Dollars for Docs' data. ProPublica also broke new ground in transparent, collaborative, open journalism with its launch of a Facebook site for patients harmed by healthcare. The site—which is also open to other journalists, health professionals and more widely—is billed as an example of 'service journalism', meaning it provides a service to a particular community, rather than simply being a mechanism for providing story fodder to ProPublica.

Another example of online innovation comes from the *Las Vegas Sun's* 2010 'Do No Harm' series on hospital care , which is profiled in the introduction to the 2012 *Data Journalism Handbook*. The reporters investigated more than 2.9 million hospital billing records, which revealed more than 3600 preventable injuries, infections and surgical mistakes. They obtained data through a public records request and identified more than 300 cases in which patients died because of mistakes that could have been prevented. They went through painstaking checking to 'clean' the data and ensure its integrity. Their findings were published along with an interactive graphic that allows users to sort data by preventable injuries or by hospital.

Two USA-based organisations, the Association of Health Care Journalists and the Reporting on Health group at the University of Southern California Annenberg, have a wealth of excellent resources for those looking for ideas for health investigations, or for advice on how to do them. Reporting on Health has published a free-ebook to help journalists, bloggers, health communicators, and researchers find data to illuminate stories on their local communities. Although the ebook—*Health Is Everything: Using Data to Report Great Stories on Your Community's Health (Bass*—has a US-focus, the general ideas could be adapted elsewhere. It covers, for example, how data can be used to answer questions about how air pollution levels in one part of town compare with another; and how many infants die before their first birthday and how this varies from place to place. It emphasises the importance of transparency, and recommends including a 'nerd box', or methodology section on investigations. The ebook's author, Pulitzer Prize-winning journalist Frank Bass, says:

> Typically, a nerd box contains between 500 and 1000 words of text explaining the procedures used to obtain and analyse the data, although it can and often should run longer. Remember, very few journalists get into trouble for being transparent; all journalists suffer when one is secretive.

One of the advantages of the digital era is that audiences can double-check your work. While the digital age has brought many challenges—not least the threat to the business model that has traditionally sustained journalism—it is also bringing many new opportunities, as might be expected in an era of rapid change and innovation. For example, according to the Reporting on Health blog (USC Annenberg: Reporting on Health 2012), journalists in the USA used the fundraising platform for creative ventures, Kickstarter, to raise $50 000 in just over two days to start *Matter*, a website for investigative reporting on science and technology.)

There are many new opportunities for investigating stories or beats that may not have appealed to mass media editors, but are able to find niche audiences online. Journalists need to work hard to stay abreast of the digital revolution. Engaging in Twitter and other social media is critical for staying up to date with the changes that are occurring—and not only in our own industry. We also have much to learn from how other sectors are applying digital innovation in their fields, and 'old-fashioned technologies'—aka books—can also be helpful for this.

Melissa Sweet acknowledges and thanks Barbara Feder Ostrov, a veteran health journalist in the US and deputy editor of Reportingonhealth.org, for reviewing this article and providing useful suggestions.

REFERENCES

Association of Health Care Journalists: www.healthjournalism.org/.

Campbell Collaboration: www.campbellcollaboration.org/.

The Cochrane Collaboration: www.cochrane.org/.

Data Journalism Handbook. 2012: http://datajournalismhandbook.org/.

Institute for Health Metrics and Evaluation: Global Health Data Exchange: www.healthmetricsandevaluation.org/ghdx/.

MyHospitals: www.myhospitals.gov.au/.

ProPublica: Introducing the ProPublica Patient Harm Community on Facebook: www.propublica.org/article/introducing-the-propublica-patient-harm-community-on-facebook/.

PubMed Health: www.ncbi.nlm.nih.gov/pubmedhealth/.

University of Southern California Annenberg: Reporting on Health: www.reportingonhealth.org/.

World Health Organization: Global Health Observatory: http://apps.who.int/ghodata/?theme=country/.

19

Science Journalism

KARINA KELLY

INTRODUCTION

My path to being a science reporter started with five years in television news. At first I was wildly enthusiastic about being part of such an all-consuming business. But as the years rolled by, I began to wonder about the personal tragedies we sometimes packaged up as news. I came to realise that in the yearly news cycle, there are stories that roll around like clockwork. They are virtually the same each year. Only the names and faces change. Whether it's the St Patrick's Day parade or the opening of the David Jones Christmas Sale, you know how the story will play out. Perhaps I am too easily bored. Whatever the reason, I found myself exasperated by the repetitiousness of daily news and the limitations set by those deciding what was a story and what wasn't.

When I went to report for ABC Television's science program, *Quantum*, a whole universe opened up for me. It's strange to think that by specialising, the breadth of one's reporting would widen, but that's how it seemed to me. I could report on genetic modification of pigs one week, and the structure of the universe the next. I was bringing back news from the frontiers of science and it was fascinating, inspiring and important. I got to talk to some of the brightest people in the world who were, more often than not, good company and pleasant to deal with. Many, being teachers, were very patient about me quizzing them intensely so that I could get up to speed on their particular subject. I felt the need to understand them well in order to be able to condense years of their work into a few minutes on television. And as the years went on, I became better at being able to distinguish which were the really important stories to tell.

THE TWO CULTURES

In 1959, C.P. Snow delivered a lecture at Cambridge University called *The Two Cultures*. Snow was a British physicist who worked in the Cavendish Laboratory at Cambridge, and also a well-known novelist. He argued that there was a divide between the 'literary intellectuals', whom he regarded as 'natural Luddites', and the scientists. He was speaking about his own country in his own time, but Pulitzer Prize-winning US science writer Jon Franklin also felt this 'social seismology' in the 1960s: 'there is one thing that any science writer can tell you for certain: the laboratory was on one side of the fault line, and the newsroom the other' (1997, p. 145).

But that was all very long ago and far away. In the second decade of the new millennium, the dynamism of our society is built on scientific innovation. The foundations of our medicine; our understanding of the workings of our bodies, of climate change, of power generation; and the way we communicate with each other—all continue to be improved by the brightest of our scientific minds. And yet if the attitudes of editors and heads of media organisations are anything to go by, the two cultures are alive and well and still not talking to each other.

Most people who become journalists and make their way up the editorial ladder are arts-oriented rather than science-oriented. Simply put, they prefer words to numbers. They value their own experience, which they see as allowing them to judge others' motives and morality. They are men and women of the world. They do not have their heads in the clouds and their bodies in ivory towers. They tend to feel uncomfortable with scientists, whose motives they cannot easily judge and whom they suspect know too much about Very Important Things. As Jon Franklin eloquently puts it:

> Scientists saw the world as theory and fact, observation and prediction, statistical significance and probability. The rest of the world titrated experience in terms of motive and morality, right and justice, miracles and fate (2007, p. 146).

In *Thinking, Fast and Slow* (2011), Economics Nobel Laureate Daniel Kahneman (who is a psychologist) suggests we humans have two different systems for thinking. With echoes of Dr Seuss, Kahneman has dubbed them System 1 and System 2. System 1 is fast, intuitive and emotional. System 2 is slow, more deliberative and more logical. Fast works for us most of the time. If a large carnivore is chasing you, slow thinking will turn you into lunch. But slow thinking has its place in our world. And, as Kahneman points out, it can give you startlingly different answers to your questions. Slow thinking is what is required if you are going to get to the bottom of a great problem. This kind of thinking requires the thinker to consider each and every possibility, no matter how superficially stupid, in order not to miss something that may be counter-intuitive, but may also just happen to be right. It was slow, deliberative thinking that made people realise the Earth moved around the sun, that stars are like the sun only much further away, and that fossils were once living animals that have been preserved by geological processes.

Now imagine that you are one of those men and women running a media organisation. They know how the world works: people are corruptible, politicians lie, and money is influence. How does this deliberative kind of thinking look from their perspective? The most positive interpretation is that these people are naïve. The harsher take on it is that they are certifiable, as though they are prepared to entertain even the most ludicrous scenario. It evokes Lemuel Gulliver's visit to the Grand Academy of Lagado:

> The first man I saw was of a meagre aspect, with sooty hands and face, his hair and beard long, ragged and singed in several places. His clothes, shirt, and skin were all of the same colour. He had been eight years upon a project for extracting sunbeams out of cucumbers, which were to be put into vials hermetically sealed, and let out to warm the air in raw inclement summers. He told me, he did not doubt that in eight years more he should be able to supply the Governor's gardens with sunshine at a reasonable rate; but he complained that his stock was low, and entreated me to give him something as an encouragement to ingenuity, especially as this had been a very dear season for cucumbers (Swift 1726 (2005), p. 206).

SEEKERS OF THE TRUTH

The public perception of science is that it seeks the truth. But whatever science uncovers can be upset by the next piece of research. So it is probably more accurate to say that science provides us with 'today's truth'—the best available explanation we have right now. We used to think that women were born carrying their lifetime's supply of eggs already formed inside them. We now think that's not the case, and stem cells may produce new ones as women age. Lycopene, the wonder ingredient in tomato sauce was thought to ward off prostate cancer, if you happen to have a prostate. Now the US Food and Drug Administration says there is very little scientific evidence for this claim.

For people who don't understand how science works, this looks like the scientists don't know what they are doing. Mostly the process is iterative; repeated studies get closer and closer to the best answer we have. But sometimes, science ploughs through human knowledge, turning up new things and burying others that we might have believed were the truth for hundreds of years. Science is disruptive. It causes change, and this has been unsettling to society since society was first invented.

I'm sure there were those who weren't at all happy about the advent of agriculture 12 000 years ago and who hankered after the romance of the hunt. The massive changes to society during the industrial revolution shifted populations, built big cities, and transformed trade and manufacture. They also took away a lot of people's livelihoods and rebalanced the social structure, giving greater power to the industrialists and taking it away from the landed gentry. Sail had to give way to steam ships, and steam ships to air travel. Telegrams, telexes and fax machines have given way to texts and emails. Smartphones and laptops now give us unprecedented and, to me, astonishing access to information. We are living through the third great transformation of human society: agriculture, manufacture and now information. It's as if the Earth is growing its own brain with trillions of interconnections and a perfect memory. The thought of it is simultaneously thrilling and unnerving.

We employ the by-products of science with predilection. We prize the access to information that a machine the size of a pack of cards can give us as it nestles warmly in our pockets. But most of us are still wary of where science will lead us next.

So where does all of this leave the science journalist? Are they journalists or are they scientists? On which side of the 'seismic divide' do they stand? The broader community of journalists aren't quite sure what to make of science journalists. Some colleagues at the ABC referred to those of us working on *Quantum* as 'you scientists'. We communicated with scientists, we mingled with them and tried to translate their argot to the vernacular; and so, to these other journalists, we *were* scientists. They could not see that we were story-tellers, journalists and program makers just like them.

Benevolently disposed media heads regard the journalists who work on the science program or the science page as a strange breed who should be nurtured like an unusual orchid at the back of the greenhouse. But upholders of the bastions of old media think science journalists are not quite part of the team and not entirely to be trusted. In these organisations, the two cultures are well and truly separate. To them, the science journalist has been smeared with the pheromones of the other tribe. Either way, kindly or hostile, as the UK Science and the Media Expert Group found in 2010, 'science is clearly not seen as a priority' (p. 14). Many people in the media don't think science journalists are journalists at all. They think science journalists are not combative or judgmental enough to qualify as 'real' journalists. Mainstream journalists don't think they need to watch the science media for breaking news. I remember preparing a story on work being done by the Bureau of Meteorology on possible mechanisms causing the lack of winter rains in southern Australia for ABC's *Catalyst*. A lot of negotiation went on with the meteorologists about what was going to be said, and the story took our team weeks to prepare. After it went to air, it was picked up about 10 days later in the features section of *The Australian* newspaper. That night, ABC Television news ran it, interviewing the same meteorologist who had appeared on *Catalyst* a week-and-a-half before. Through the vector of a daily newspaper, a science story had miraculously been transformed into 'news'.

Science journalists need to be 'ambidextrous': both able to relate to the rigours and processes of scientific endeavour, and also to turn the process into an engaging yarn—with a beginning, a middle and an end. But in the final analysis they must be journalists first, no matter how advanced their scientific training. Science journalists tell stories and the source of their stories is science.

Science stories fall into four broad categories: science politics stories, scientist-as-hero stories, stories of scientific controversies, and stories about new ideas in science.

SCIENCE POLITICS STORIES

Science politics stories might relate to science fraud, or public science research influenced by commercial interests, or breaches in safety protocol, to give a few examples. These stories should be dealt with using the same research and interviewing skills that would be used by a mainstream journalist. The UK Science and the Media Expert Group felt that this was an area of weakness.

> As well as bringing scientific controversy and wonder to mass audiences, the media can also hold science to account in a very public way. The media's classic role of 'speaking truth to power' should be as true for the science establishment as it is of the political elites; a constant theme in evidence from journalists was the unique role for media in questioning and scrutinizing science. Far from threatening to undermine science, the media's role in holding it to account can make science better, more honest and more accountable, though the group found that, with a few honourable exceptions, this form of investigative journalism was by far the weakest area of science reporting today (2010, p. 3).

Science politics stories involve conflict and human frailty—themes with which the public is familiar.

SCIENTIST-AS-HERO STORIES

This is also true of the scientist-as-hero story. For example, in 1984 West Australian medical researcher Barry Marshall drank a Petri dish of *Helicobacter pylori* and made himself quite ill. Fourteen days later, following his unorthodox theory, he cured himself with antibiotics the medical world said would never work. In this rather adventurous way, Marshall managed to upturn long-held views about the cause of stomach ulcers. It led to his being awarded the Nobel Prize in Physiology.

This is a wonderful David and Goliath story. It is the kind of tale we have been taught to appreciate since we first sat proudly on a parent's lap and were entertained by a story. A character triumphs against the odds, and his life and that of those around him are changed forever.

STORIES OF SCIENTIFIC CONTROVERSIES

One step removed from the political science and scientist-as-hero stories are stories of scientific controversy—climate change, for example.

Within the science community there is much conflict and disagreement about how to interpret the information on climate change. But this is a scientific argument, not a political or emotional one. The battle is raging, but it's taking place in the scientific journals—and it is there that scientists are being convinced about the evidence. When mainstream journalists report on climate change, the lazy ones interview one person representing the vast majority of scientists and then they find a 'climate sceptic' in order to introduce 'balance' to the story. But this does exactly the opposite. It unbalances the story away from the majority scientific viewpoint and so misrepresents the state of understanding on the subject, hindering the public's knowledge of the debate. So these stories need to be researched and approached differently. Science journalists understand that peer-reviewed journals hold the key to understanding the scientific arguments. If the paper gets through the peer-review process, then it means that other experts in the area have accepted the article.

It is true that some older scientists who have invested decades of their lives in supporting a particular theory will do their best to hinder the progress of the new ideas put forward by their younger colleagues. The machinations of human politics don't bypass university science departments. But niggling and frustratingly slow as it is, peer review is the mechanism set up to make sure that 'today's truth' will eventually make it out into the open. Gradually, those in the field reading these reports become convinced that the new theory has some merit and they are, sometimes one by one, swayed from the old to the new. The articles are written in deliberately non-rhetorical language. For those of us who want to be persuaded by a piece of writing, they can seem impenetrably dull. That's why even if you could figure out the jargon, most scientific papers are very difficult for the uninitiated to read.

There is a limit to what a science journalist can do in this environment. It is not up to the journalist to judge the scientific merit of a published paper. But in reporting the findings in a reputable journal, the science journalist can at least be assured that other scientists in the field have taken a good close look at it and let it through.

STORIES ABOUT NEW IDEAS IN SCIENCE

Fourth on the list are stories about new ideas. These were always my favourite, even though they stretched my story-telling skills to their limits. What makes a good story? From Homer's *Odyssey* to Jane Austen's *Pride and Prejudice*; from J.K. Rowling's *Harry Potter* to Stieg Larsson's *The Girl with the Dragon Tattoo*, good stories all hinge on transformation. The main character starts the story in one state and finishes the story in a different state. Along the way, the character is put to the test. Their beliefs or their physical endurance or their emotional strength are robustly challenged. It is cathartic, and they come out of the story a changed person. Stronger, weaker, for worse or for better, they have been transformed. And so have we by reading or hearing or watching their transformation. That's what happens to the characters in fiction, and most of us find the process emotionally satisfying.

Imagine for a moment that you could apply this same process to the world of ideas; in other words, ideas themselves become the characters in a story. What would that look like? Ideas have a beginning. There is a status quo—the old belief. Then someone has a new idea that challenges the old idea. The questioning and doubting of the old idea is a traumatic process. It is uncomfortable for people who have been taught something to contemplate wiping the slate clean and starting again. It is both terrifying and exhilarating at the same time. The story ends with a new equilibrium—just as a fictional story does. In fiction, the transformation and our engagement with it is emotional. In the story of the new idea, the shift is intellectual.

Is there room for this kind of story on television or in generalist newspapers and magazines? Absolutely. People who are likely to read or watch stories about science are inquisitive. They are interested in new ideas and apply them to their understanding of the greater world.

THE FUTURE FOR SCIENCE JOURNALISM

Very few science journalists get promoted to editor of a mainstream newspaper. But I can't help wondering if things might have turned out differently for some of our great media organisations if they had been. Or even if the editors had bothered to consult their own science and technology writers about what was happening online. Media proprietors around the world have been caught out by the massive and disruptive technological changes taking place in their own businesses. They have lost their 'rivers of gold' in classified advertising to online operations with much lower overheads and no commitment to journalism. But while the web was threatening their livelihood, it also offered these publishers more readers than they might ever have dreamed of—with whom they could communicate at no cost. Most of these publishers did not think of buying the online advertisers as a form of insurance. Instead they stuck to printing newspapers and throwing them on our front steps. As purveyors of information, presumably in touch with social trends, their failure to grasp the threat posed by online media to their own businesses is breathtaking. For many organisations, this neglect will mean their demise. And a lot of journalists of all stripes will need to find new employment.

While the media proprietors might not listen to their own science journalists, what's happening on the other side of that fault line? The finance reporter, the arts reporter and other specialists can expect to be invited to a soirée or two, to ingest the occasional glass of grassy sauvignon blanc or a morsel of cheese. According to the UK Science and the Media Expert Group, 'there are more journalism courses for those wanting to go into sports journalism than science journalism' (2010, p. 14). And you get tickets to the big games. If you are looking to be lionised, flattered or chatted up, don't go into science journalism. Scientists regard science journalists as fairly dangerous creatures who are likely to trip them up, quote them out of context or make them look silly. So despite having learned to be bilingual, the science journalist can find themselves on the outside of both cultures. Why then do so many people want to spend the rest of their lives doing it? Did I mention that it is the most interesting job in the world? As Tim Radford, a former science editor of *The Guardian*, writes: 'Science writers—alone of the tribe of scribes—usually have a new story to tell' (2007, p. 95).

In every story I have ever reported, I have learned something new. I have stood at the top of Mount Mauna Kea on the Big Island of Hawaii discussing astronomy and gazing down at the tropical cloud banks a kilometre below. I have trundled inside the rail cart of a medieval silver mine in the Japanese Alps to report on an experiment searching for neutrinos. I have sat in a little boat off the coast of New Zealand watching a giant sperm whale anchored in the sea like an aquatic Uluru, until it spouted and dived into the bay, its tail waving goodbye. I have seen the great red spot of Jupiter with my own eyes through the 10-inch lens of a telescope at Siding Spring. I have taken a camera crew deep inside the red caves of the Coonawarra to see the skeletons of extinct animals lying intact after tens of thousands of years, the enamel of their teeth still shining.

Science journalists inhabit the frontier of new ideas. And they help to convey what it's like there to the wider world. It is simply the greatest fun. There is a goose-bump-producing frisson that comes from understanding something for the first time which inspires one to want to pass the favour on. And it's addictive. The more you do it, the more you want to.

There has been a fashion in the last decade to cast science reporters as if they were contestants in reality television programs. Let's make the reporter do a lie detector test, or see if shaving makes hairs on the leg grow back faster than waxing. These attempts to engage the audience by putting the reporter through some embarrassing experience so that the audience will empathise with them has, it seems to me, two results. The first is that once the viewers have seen the reporter hanging upside down from a bungy cord, or being sick into a bucket, they begin to feel they have seen more of this person than they ever really wanted to. So the short-term gain of attracting viewers through curiosity can turn into long-term fatigue. From the reporter's point of view, it is not a path leading to a long and distinguished career in science journalism. Second, these unseemly grabs for the audience's emotional engagement sit uncomfortably with the main thrust of the information a science program ought to be conveying. It's the ideas that are most important. And asking an audience to think emotionally about scientific ideas moves their brains to Kahneman's fast thinking when we should be encouraging the more deliberative kind (2011).

The business of journalism is undergoing a rapid and radical change as communication switches from ink and paper and broadcast to the electrons of web-based communication. But as this transformation occurs, the need for good science journalists will become greater, not less. As the bulk of the world's population becomes better educated and gains access to the web, the demand for news from the frontiers of science will only increase. According to a 2012 report of the US National Science Foundation, more Americans now get science and technology information online than from television. The world will always need good research and thoughtful interpretation of science. No matter what editors think, most people want to know what is going to happen next in the greatest story of them all: the fate of the universe and all the creatures in it.

TIPS

1   In science, peer-reviewed journals are the gold standard. If someone has published their work in a well-respected peer-reviewed journal, you know that people who understand the work have taken a good long look at it and let it through. So, barring science fraud (see Tip 6), the likelihood is that the work stacks up. But …

2   Science journal articles make fairly poor copy from the journalist's perspective. These articles are concerned with conveying the methods used by the researchers so that fellow scientists can compare this work with other work in the field. Talk to the scientist (and others) about the *implications* of the work. Science is concerned with process, but journalists need an end to their stories.

3 Never be afraid to spend time on the phone or in person asking questions. Scientists have been trained to write in non-speculative, unemotional language. What you are looking for in an interview is everything they *didn't* put into their journal article: How did you feel? What was it like? What are the implications?

4 Never pretend you understand something when you don't. Most scientists are also teachers and are happy to keep explaining until you get it. You cannot explain something to your readers, listeners or viewers if you don't understand it yourself.

5 If you want to know who disagrees with a scientist's work, ask them. They will know better than anyone and more often than not will happily tell you. It is likely that this doubter will have challenged them publicly at a conference, so it won't be a deep and troubling secret to them.

6 Investigative science journalism (for example reporting on allegations of science fraud) requires an inside source, a great deal of care and a lawyer by your side.

QUESTIONS TO CONSIDER

1 To what extent does the 'social seismology' that divides science and the newsroom continue to exist today? Why do you believe that is the case?

2 What are the various categories of science story identified in this chapter?

3 To what extent do you consider the stereotypes of science reporters are justified? Is what they do that different from other forms of journalism?

4 To what extent do you believe the latest scientific breakthroughs have launched science journalists into the mainstream?

TASK

1 Go online to the Bureau of Meteorology website and select some long-term weather data. Write this up as a story plan, indicating who you need to talk to add further dimensions to the story (including an agricultural dimension).

REFERENCES

Franklin, J. 2007. 'The End of Science Writing', in M.W. Bauer & M. Bucchi, eds, *Journalism, Science and Society: Science Communication between News and Public Relations*, New York: Routledge.

Kahneman, D. 2011. *Thinking, Fast and Slow*, New York: Farrar, Straus and Giroux.

National Science Foundation. 2012. *Science and Engineering Indicators 2012*, Ch. 7: www.nsf.gov/statistics/seind12/c7/c7s1.htm/.

Radford, T. 2007. 'Scheherazade: Telling Stories, Not Educating People', in M.W. Bauer & M. Bucchi, eds, *Journalism, Science and Society: Science Communication between News and Public Relations*, New York: Routledge.

Snow, C.P. 1959 (2102). *The Two Cultures*, Cambridge: Cambridge University Press.

Science and the Media Expert Group, UK. 2010. *Science and the Media: Securing the Future*, January: www.scribd.com/doc/25528355/Science-and-the-Media-Securing-the-Future/.

Swift, J. 1726 (2005). *Gulliver's Travels*, New York: Bantam edition.

WEBSITE REFERENCE

Bureau of Meteorology: www.bom.gov.au/.

20

Reporting Indigenous Affairs

MICHAEL MEADOWS

INTRODUCTION

> There is a diversity of peoples and opinions in Indigenous Australia; however not all voices are heard at the same volume (McCallum et al. 2012, p. 109).

One of the biggest continuing challenges for Australian journalists is to find more effective ways of representing Australia's cultural diversity. And nowhere is this more apparent than in the misrepresentation of Indigenous people in mainstream news and current affairs. Aboriginal and Torres Strait Islander people still struggle both to be heard and to have their issues accurately represented in the Australian media (Meadows 2001; Stewart et al. 2010; Waller 2010; McCallum et al. 2012). Fortunately, there are exceptions—where well-researched, engaging articles about Indigenous affairs provide audiences with information relevant to these communities beyond prevailing ideas and assumptions. But they are in the minority and stereotypes are never far below the surface, emerging quickly when journalists select easy pathways for story outcomes. Journalism is 'the primary method of framing experience and forming public consciousness of the here and now' (Adam 1993, p. 45). And perhaps most importantly for the focus of this chapter, treating marginalised people *equally* often means treating them *differently* (Husband 2000, p. 212).

Journalism that is based on predictability and 'commonsense' explanations for frequently complex issues is often not all that far away from an alternative approach that seeks to uncover the 'good sense' embedded in most arguments (Meadows et al. 2009). However, this is not a simple process of weighing up positive and negative stories—far from it. What it requires is a fundamental shift in thinking about journalism practice that has the potential to flow through to a journalist's overall approach to the craft. Put simply, this means doing journalism well. In this chapter, I will consider some strategies that might help you to negotiate your way through what can be a difficult, yet rewarding aspect of journalism practice—reporting responsibly and effectively on Indigenous affairs.

To do this, I will suggest a problem-based approach which, I believe, fits admirably with notions and objectives of both good journalism practice and research (Meadows 1997a; Lindgren & Phillips 2011).

A problem-based approach to reporting essentially applies a framework for assessment, judgment and analysis of a particular topic to produce a desired outcome—in this case, a news or feature-length story across a range of multimedia platforms. Drawn from problem-based learning (PBL) approaches now used in a wide range of professional disciplines—including medicine, nursing, law, engineering and journalism education—it offers a useful framework for everyday journalism practice, particularly in a vexed area such as reporting Indigenous affairs.

But what evidence exists for a need to revise current journalism practices in Australia and beyond when covering Indigenous affairs?

FRAMING INDIGENOUS AFFAIRS

Although the contemporary news media do allow space for reliable and accurate images of Indigenous affairs and people, the overall tenor of coverage tends to frame Indigenous people as problems; the coverage is almost always negative and usually associated with antisocial activities. Media are arguably the major source—and in many cases the only source—of information about issues that are beyond our normal, everyday experiences. And yet all of us will have developed particular attitudes and opinions, despite limited interactions with particular sections of society. Nowhere is this more powerfully evident than in the representations of race relations (Hall 1981; Husband 2000; Meadows 2001; Waller 2010). This places a particularly heavy responsibility on journalists to provide accurate, well-informed and carefully constructed stories that deal with these issues.

Ideas and assumptions about particular cultural groups in society tend to build on prior frameworks. For example, media coverage of protests in the north Queensland Palm Island community in 2004 have routinely been reported as a 'riot' ever since the event. And while the term 'riot' has variable meanings— from 'any disturbance of the peace by an assembly of persons' to 'wild, or violent disorder and confusion' (*Macquarie Dictionary* 2008, p. 1050)—it was quickly attached to the event on Palm Island, probably because a police station was burned down. Significantly, despite the angry protests involved, no one was injured in the melee. Interestingly, the 'riot' has always been called the 'resistance' by the Palm Island community—a response to the tragic death in police custody of a young local man, Cameron Doomadgee (Meadows et al. 2007, p. 64; Hooper 2008).

Despite two very different frameworks of understanding of the event, it was the stereotypical 'riot' that seduced—and continues to influence—mainstream media coverage of this event and its aftermath. The role played by the media and journalism in this process is clear, as Gandy suggests:

> [It] takes place through a multidimensional structure of routinized relationships that are governed by well-structured systems of beliefs and opinions. Those beliefs and opinions are generated, integrated into cognitive structures and reinforced by direct and indirect experiences. The mass media are the primary source of those indirect or mediated experiences (1998, p. 155).

Such frameworks or 'faces of truth' (Alia 1996) are able to take hold because they represent a 'commonsense' interpretation of events. It was a much easier story to write from the 'riot' framework because all major sources used for journalists—the government, police, emergency services, and other media, etc.—dutifully accepted this as an explanation. If the story had been based on the idea of the 'resistance', then it becomes a more complex undertaking, requiring journalists to access sources beyond their usual contacts: representatives of north Queensland's Indigenous communities. The few journalists who attempted to establish some communication with Palm Island residents—primarily and perhaps, predictably, from the national broadcasters, ABC and SBS—were at least able to reflect some alternative viewpoints in their stories. One senior Palm Island resident explained why the community felt compelled to turn to Indigenous media—a local community radio station in Townsville—to get their message across:

> It was a case of getting the facts right and that was important for our mob. Last year [2004], we had every man and his dog against Palm Island at that particular time—we had the police union against Palm, we had the Premier talking against Palm, we had the Minister for Aboriginal Affairs talking against Palm, so the mainstream media were getting *their* story rather than the community's story (Palm Island Interview 2005).

While overt racism might be more of a rarity these days, it is institutionalised racism that is of most concern, mainly because it is invisible. It is embedded in practices, organisational structures and processes that enable the framing of such events in a particular way, most often supporting the status quo. The day-to-day, routine representation of Indigenous affairs and people in this way creates and reinforces stereotypes which, in the absence of alternative ideas and assumptions about how to interpret the world, are easily digested by media audiences (Said 1993, p. 26; Meadows 2001). As such, they become 'commonsense' explanations—if Indigenous people are involved and there is some disruptive activity, then framing it as a riot makes it much easier for audiences to accept. Besides, who, apart from those in positions of relative power in the community—a trade union leader or prominent representative of a community organisation, for example—can challenge that interpretation?

Australian journalism continues to represent Indigenous people within a narrow range of possibilities stemming from a long 'history of indifference' from the time of the European invasion (Stanner 1977). Since the first Aboriginal prisoner was taken on New Year's Eve in 1788, the framing of Indigenous people being associated with crime, social problems and public disorder has been difficult to shift. Early descriptions of Indigenous people in explorers' journals depicted them as having less-than-human characteristics, so perhaps it is not surprising that the stereotype of 'the drunken Aborigine' was firmly established by 1830. Representations of Indigenous people in the colonial press have been described variously as 'perhaps one of the most malignant collection of writings ever' (Gibson 1984, p. 157) and examples of 'virulent racism and white supremacy' (Cryle 1992, p. 67). Indigenous women were effectively invisible. *The Bulletin* magazine projected racist stereotypes from its inception in 1881, and from 1908 proclaimed 'Australia for the white man' on its masthead. This remained unchanged until Donald Horne took over as editor in 1960 (*The Bulletin* 1980, p. 279)! Success in sport and the arts are exceptions, arguably because successful Indigenous people are seen to have become 'just like us'. More often than not, their Indigenous heritage is unspoken and invisible unless participants themselves draw attention to it for a particular reason—for example, an Indigenous 'all stars' sporting competition providing role models for young people—or for a particular achievement, such as Cathy Freeman's Olympic gold medal in 2000.

This is the historical context from which Indigenous affairs reporting in Australia emerged—and largely remains locked. While the most overt racist depictions have mercifully disappeared from Australian media coverage, institutionalised racism remains just below the surface. For example, land rights—and some have perhaps more accurately termed these 'human rights'—have been a long-running area of dispute between Indigenous and non-Indigenous Australia from 1788. This was clearly evident in the 1990s, following the High Court cases around Native Title, *Mabo* and *Wik*—journalists at the time were seriously reporting that people's backyards would be subject to Aboriginal land claims. This created a climate of hate and division in Australian society, regardless of the truth or otherwise of the assertions. In another example, Pauline Hanson's fortunately short-lived One Nation Party tapped into institutionalised racism—some of it overt—in an attempt to gain political leverage within the Australian community (Meadows 1997b).

This bears a striking similarity to the stereotyping, patronising, romanticising, and ignorance identified by Weston in her study of press images of Native Americans (1996, p. 163). Both here and there, First Nation people are framed within constrained stereotypes, largely defined by non-Indigenous people (including journalists) who have had little to do with Indigenous people of their societies. African Americans, too, experience the same kind of framing in stories about their affairs, reinforcing the view by scholars globally that media 'fail to perform responsibly as an agent of its minority consumers' (Gandy 1998, pp. viii, 5). Gandy usefully describes stereotypes as 'distillations of complexity'—a term that partly explains why journalists struggle with alternatives. Journalism can and does deal with complex issues, but increasingly a preference for shorter and simpler stories has pushed longer, more thoughtful investigative and feature stories off the agenda. The economic bottom line that drives celebrity-driven news values globally, coupled with an increasingly voracious appetite for copy by online publications, leave little room for more considered articles that are able to tackle complex and locally-relevant issues, creating a notable 'democratic deficit' (Hackett & Carroll 2006; McChesney & Pickard

2011). On a related tack, a national study of urban, regional and remote Indigenous community media audiences in 2007 revealed that the community radio and Indigenous television sectors are making a significant contribution to managing community mental health by empowering audiences to better understand and control issues that impact on their emotional and social wellbeing. The study reinforces a claim that mainstream media need to be more aware of a growing dissatisfaction with their inability to 'connect' with their diverse audiences on such issues (Meadows et al. 2007; Meadows & Foxwell 2011).

And so the challenge remains. Indigenous issues continue to be framed in routine and predictable ways, and are often played out in classic 'moral panics' that can have a significant impact on public perceptions (McCallum 2010; Waller 2010, p. 22). Ideas and assumptions suggested by media frames are more likely to be adapted and applied by audiences for news according to their own local understandings and experiences (McCallum 2007; 2010). Some have looked to so-called 'citizen' journalism as the saviour, but analysis of the bulk of this activity reveals a primary focus on self, celebrity and recycling existing mainstream news (Lowrey 2006; Reese et al. 2007; Meadows 2012). Perhaps one of the best hopes for change lies at the level of the local, with independent community-based journalism providing opportunities for giving alternative viewpoints to growing audiences around Australia (Forde et al. 2009; Forde 2011; Meadows 2012). With a continuing dominance and concentration of ownership of mainstream media in Australia, the onus on journalists in 'framing experience and forming public consciousness' has never been more important (Adam 1993, p. 45).

At the end of this chapter, I list a number of resources for journalists reporting on Indigenous affairs in Australia which underpin the suggestions that follow.

A PROBLEM-BASED APPROACH

- What is the central problem or question you are dealing with?
- How can you begin to address the problem or question?
- What do you already know that might help you to deal with the problem or question?
- What information/knowledge do you need to help you solve the problem or answer the question?
- Where can you find this information?
- How can you best achieve this?

This framework identifies a series of questions or problems which are essential, not only to learn more about a topic of investigation itself, but also to assist in producing a better story. I will deal with each question separately, offering some concrete examples of how each might be applied to Indigenous affairs journalism.

WHAT IS THE CENTRAL PROBLEM OR QUESTION YOU ARE DEALING WITH?

'A discourse of risk and crisis' continues to dominate public discussion of Indigenous affairs in Australia, with the news media playing a central role in this (Meadows 2001; McCallum 2010; Waller 2010). As suggested earlier, the media response to reporting such issues remains trapped within the framework of conflict. Stepping away from this framework and trying to reformulate the issue by exploring the 'why?' and the 'how?' might reveal a deeper and more meaningful response. For example, the 'riot' on Palm Island was an expression of spontaneous outrage by people in the region who quite simply felt they had few other options open to them. Why was this the case? What prompted this particular community to respond in the way it did?

For the Palm Island community, it was not *only* the loss of one young man that prompted the response—tragic though it was—but that it was *another* death in custody. Why is this still happening in Australia despite a 1991 Royal Commission into Aboriginal Deaths in Custody? The pioneering investigative work by West Australian journalist Jan Mayman influenced the establishment of the 1991 Royal Commission because she stepped beyond the framework to identify a pattern of other largely unexplained Indigenous deaths in custody. This broadened the story to one of international significance. Australia is still being criticised internationally for its continuing treatment of Indigenous people (Minority Rights Group International 2010). Despite our continuing efforts to 'close the gap' between Indigenous and non-Indigenous people, our actual achievements in terms of Indigenous health and wellbeing remain appalling (Productivity Commission 2009).

Based on this context, other options for news stories apart from the 'riot' become evident.

HOW CAN YOU BEGIN TO ADDRESS THE PROBLEM OR QUESTION?

Existing guidelines in the Media Entertainment and Arts Alliance Australian Journalists' Association Code of Ethics (2001, Clause 2) offers a very broad 'template of virtue' in which to operate:

> Do not place unnecessary emphasis on personal characteristics, including race, ethnicity, nationality, gender, age, sexual orientation, family relationships, religious belief, or physical or intellectual disability.

However, the code offers little else in relation to reporting on Indigenous affairs. Fortunately, Indigenous journalists working for the national broadcasters, ABC and SBS, have produced sets of detailed reporting protocols. Although these are aimed particularly at remote community interactions, the principles espoused apply across a broad range of Indigenous–media relations (ABC 2012; SBS 2012; Oxfam Australia (undated)).

For most journalists, finding appropriate Indigenous sources is the greatest challenge. The absence or omission of Indigenous sources in articles dealing with Indigenous affairs has become commonplace, with Indigenous voices regularly making up just one-fifth of all sources quoted in such stories (Meadows 1994; 2000; 2001; Hippocrates et al. 1996). But keep in mind that even where Indigenous sources are used, the 'loudest voices' may not necessarily be the most appropriate for a story (Weston 1996; Meadows 2001). Unfortunately, journalists covering Indigenous affairs settle too often and too easily for the most accessible sources rather than the right ones. There are many 'resourceful, creative and persistent' Indigenous sources available and willing to help you with your story if you approach them in the right way (McCallum et al. 2012, p. 109).

Why do Indigenous sources seem so hard to find?

One reason why Indigenous sources seem so hard to find is that there is a widespread view across Indigenous communities that journalists and mainstream media simply cannot be trusted. As I have suggested, there is ample evidence to support this view. But some journalists manage to make contact with Indigenous sources on a regular basis, which suggests that this issue can be overcome by a willingness to engage more deeply with community affairs (Waller 2010). So how can this happen?

Most often, it is a matter of making contact with communities or sources through someone who already knows you, and/or being persistent but polite. Knowing something about the story background—and not just relying on your news organisation's archives—will help to convince potential sources that you are genuinely trying to produce something worthwhile, rather than producing yet another predictably framed response. Knowing who is the right source for a story comes from knowledge of this specialised area of journalism practice. It is no different from any other specialised area, such as politics, the environment, sport, etc. Unless you have developed and maintained sources, you will find it difficult to find them, particularly in Indigenous communities because of the distrust and even dislike for media and journalists. This is an obstacle which can be overcome by building up a regular source list, and then using this network where you are trusted to locate other Indigenous experts when required.

The Indigenous media network that covers the continent is arguably one of the best—and largely untapped—resources for mainstream journalists. Indigenous media provide a first level of service to Indigenous communities while acting as a cultural bridge between Indigenous and non-Indigenous

Australia (Roth & Valaskakis 1989; Meadows 1994; 2001; Rankine & McCreanor 2004; Wilson & Stewart 2008; Forde et al. 2009). Find out when and where local talkback programs are being broadcast and tune in to identify the issues of concern for Indigenous people in your area of interest. Try, for example, *TalkBlack* (4K1G) from Townsville which is streamed online; *Let's Talk with Tiga Bayles* (98.9FM), available through the National Indigenous Radio Service (NIRS) in some areas; and National Indigenous Television (NITV) News.

But it will take time to become accepted as someone who can be trusted if you are new to the area. Remember too that fundamental to traditional and modern Indigenous society is the idea of reciprocity. Put simply, this means an exchange. If you expect to always be taking—asking for information while offering nothing in return—then you will quickly outstay your welcome. This is where you need to be aware of possible ways in which you might be able to balance the relationship: for example, offering media training to an organisation; assisting with editing an Indigenous publication; suggesting ways in which such tasks might be undertaken; or putting your source in touch with another of your sources who may be able to help with an unrelated problem—education, health, housing, etc.—using your own 'knowledge networks' to 'give something back'.

Locating the right source for the right story is as important when covering Indigenous affairs as any other specialised area—you would seldom ask a state treasurer to comment on an environmental story, for example. The principle is the same.

WHAT DO YOU ALREADY KNOW THAT MIGHT HELP YOU TO DEAL WITH THE PROBLEM OR QUESTION?

This is where your specialist knowledge is crucial. If you have an interest in this specialisation—and you should if you are covering it—then you will be able to draw from your existing knowledge to think about some possible angles for your story. What has been published about this previously? Who has been interviewed? Are they the right people with appropriate expertise, or one of the 'usual suspects'? A broad knowledge of current affairs, but particularly of issues of concern to the Indigenous community is central here. What are the issues of current concern in the Indigenous community? How might these relate to your story?

If you are well-informed in your specialist area, you will know how to correctly identify local Indigenous sources. If you are not sure, ask. How do they prefer to be identified? Are the terms 'Murri' (Queensland) or 'Koori' (New South Wales, Victoria and South Australia), 'Nungar' or 'Nyungar' (Western Australia) preferred over local language names such as 'Jagera' (parts of Brisbane), 'Kombumerri' (Gold Coast region) or 'Murray Islander' (Torres Strait)? Each Indigenous community has a sense of its own identity, with 'Indigenous', 'Aboriginal' or 'Torres Strait Islander' being viewed as imposed European terms. But some of your interviewees may opt for this latter form of identification.

Aboriginal people are referred to in more than 700 pieces of legislation, most of them created after the 1967 referendum which originally gave First Nation people here the right to vote (McCorquodale 1986, p. 9). The 'official' definition of an Indigenous person is one who is a descendant of Indigenous people, who identifies as Indigenous, and who is identified by the Indigenous community as such.

So ask your sources how they prefer to be identified. In this way, identity becomes more of a shared concept rather than an imposed and often stereotypical tag. Note also that some Indigenous people find the term 'leader' offensive.

WHAT INFORMATION/KNOWLEDGE DO YOU NEED TO HELP YOU SOLVE THE PROBLEM OR ANSWER THE QUESTION?

This is where you try to identify what is missing from your existing knowledge of the topic or issue to enable you to write the story. Make a list of the key information you will need. Do you need to locate prior reports, inquiries or studies that might provide some background to your topic? Do you need to identify experts in a particular area? What about relevant and available audio or visual material?

Using your list of information gaps as a guide, write down possible sources. Researching the background to a story should not be confined to your own organisation's archives because you then run the risk of assuming the same framework in interpreting any new information. Try to go beyond the usual sources. Universities and other research-based institutions have numerous Indigenous and non-Indigenous experts who have spent years—some, their entire academic careers—delving into aspects of Indigenous affairs. It is your job to find them, and all universities have media relations officers whose job it is to help with this task. Many Indigenous experts are not working within such institutions, but may be employed in a community organisation—a legal, housing or health service, or a local media organisation, for example.

Use your knowledge of online sources and local libraries to further enhance your knowledge and understanding of the region, the people and the issues involved. Librarians are invaluable resources who are vastly under-utilised by journalists. Like other experts in a particular area, librarians can help you to locate online and on-the-shelf sources in a fraction of the time it would otherwise take you to do so. Again, unless you have developed contacts in these areas, you will struggle when the time comes to get information quickly. Do not rely on Google alone. Many crucial documents relating to Indigenous affairs are not available online. This is where your sources' knowledge and your network of experts come into play.

You may need to organise a meeting with the local Indigenous Council of Elders. Most large centres have such an organisation which meets regularly to discuss issues of concern to the local community. Again, contacts with such an organisation will be crucial if you are to do your job properly and thoroughly. But remember, you will most often need to work to their timetables, which may not accord with your own story deadlines. Ensure you establish the timeline early in conversations you have with your source.

You need to prioritise your information needs against your sources' ability to provide the necessary material. For example, some information may have to be 'authorised' by a council of elders before it can be used. This can take time—a day or even a week—so plan for it if you can. Otherwise, perhaps factor in a follow-up story with information that may take longer to obtain. It may well be that the information you wait for produces a better, more complete account of the issue.

Underpinning this approach is the crucial dimension of informed consent. Journalist Lisa Waller argues that this 'goes to the heart of what establishing a meaningful and equal relationship actually means' (2010, p. 25). For many journalists, this is a grey area where they are reluctant, for example, to delete or change factual information gathered during an interview after the interview has been completed. There is no ethical basis for such a stance. If your interviewees, for any reason, decide at a later time that something they have told you is either inaccurate or puts them at risk, then you have an ethical duty to correct it. Some journalists might interpret this as 'editorial interference'.

But what is more important here: a good accurate story that might not lead a broadcast news bulletin or make page one in a newspaper, or an inaccurate story that might cause significant problems for your source who has given you an exclusive? 'Who benefits from this?' is a question you must constantly ask yourself when you are working as a journalist, even more so when dealing with sensitive issues. The old adage 'When in doubt, find out, or leave it out' is good journalistic practice.

Reading back a draft of your story to a source is frowned upon by many journalists—the potential for 'editorial interference' rears its head yet again. But if you make it clear to a source that this is solely to check accuracy, then it is difficult to see where the problem lies. And publishing something which, even unintentionally, damages your relationship with your source may result in you losing access to an entire information network. Word travels quickly on the 'bush telegraph' in Indigenous Australia!

ALTERNATIVE APPROACHES

Indigenous and non-Indigenous Australia represent parallel universes which seem to intersect only at times of conflict and crisis. The very nature of non-Indigenous journalistic inquiry is in direct conflict with traditional knowledge-management processes in Indigenous societies (Ginsburg 1993, p. 574;

Avison & Meadows 2000; Meadows 2005), which suggests that journalists may need to adopt more appropriate methods to effectively access the 'parallel universe' of Indigenous Australia. What many journalists do not understand is that when they enter Indigenous communities, it is akin to going to another country with different frameworks of understanding and cultural protocols. If we physically travel out of Australia, we find it much easier to accept this—the difficulty lies in that Indigenous 'countries' are in our own backyard.

Although ethnography itself has many dimensions, engaging in observation and participation align reasonably well with journalistic practice. In fact, it may be necessary to embrace such approaches more effectively to reclaim the kind of 'public conversation' that journalism seems to have lost in terms of Indigenous affairs reporting. Journalism and media play a central role in the meaning-making processes of the broader public sphere, which itself is comprised of a multitude of smaller, overlapping spheres (Fraser 1999). An Indigenous public sphere (or spheres) is part of this network. Indigenous public spheres can be seen as providing opportunities for people who are regularly subordinated and ignored by mainstream public sphere processes. They enable Indigenous people to deliberate together, to develop their own counter-discourses, and to interpret their own identities and experiences. This is one explanation for the emergence, growth and continuing strength of Indigenous media that serve their audiences because of a failure by the mainstream media to do so (Meadows 2005).

If we accept the existence of an Indigenous public sphere, then we need to rethink ways of accessing it that go beyond the 'usual' journalistic approaches. As Husband suggested earlier in this chapter, treating people *equally* often means treating them *differently* (2000, p. 212). Bird argues that one way of achieving this is to set aside 'the protective cloak' of objectivity and news values by adopting alternative newsgathering methods akin to ethnography (2005, p. 305). The elusive ideal of objectivity for journalists means being fair to everyone; for anthropologists, it means being fair to the truth (Bird 2005, p. 304–5). Which is more important? Ethnography thus requires greater empathy and involvement with sources than is usual for journalists and, for some, this may seem threatening or unsettling. One danger is becoming too identified with sources and their interests. The flipside is that an empathetic approach may be more effective in enabling communication and a deeper understanding of the issues involved (Bird 2005, p. 303). It is a fine balance. Bird concludes that when journalists become aware of their sources 'as people', perhaps then they also become more critical of the kinds of easy answers that claim the story must come first (2005, p. 304). At the very least, it encourages journalists to become more self-reflective of their role.

An ethnographic approach, which some have usefully defined as 'active listening' (Downing 2007; Dreher 2010), places importance on connections and context, demanding a constant reframing of questions, revision of ideas, and the cultivation of new sources (Bird 2005, p. 304). By contrast—as with the Palm Island 'riot'—journalists often start and finish with a particular framework for their stories, shaped by previous coverage. The ethnographic process is thus dialectical (a two-way process) rather than linear.

CONCLUSION

Journalists' claims of fairness and accuracy alone are not enough when covering this sensitive area of journalistic activity because such claims inevitably involve value judgments about the selection of information from the vast array available (Waller 2010). The ease with which stereotypes can prevail is perhaps the most compelling reason to critique journalistic practices that produce particular ideas and assumptions about Indigenous people and their affairs. It is also a compelling reason to explore ways of establishing a dialogue between Indigenous and non-Indigenous people—practitioners and audiences alike—based on an expectation of improved cross-cultural understanding. While mainstream media continues to struggle with such ideas, journalism at a local level may be in a better position to engage with Indigenous communities and sources, perhaps because of its stronger local links and, thus, greater level of accountability.

1   Question prevailing frameworks: Husband's (2000) conclusion that treating marginalised people equally often means treating them differently underpins journalistic coverage of this specialised area. Applying a problem-based framework might enable you to look beyond the obvious angles for stories. Focussing on the 'how?' and 'why?' will enable you to satisfactorily address the questions: 'Who benefits from this?' and 'Why is this a news story?'

2   Seek, build and maintain sources and networks: spend time building relationships with sources and networks if you are to win their trust. In some cases, this will involve more time than with other source networks. You must be prepared to counter a widespread negative perception of mainstream media and journalism, and its stereotypical, superficial treatment of Indigenous affairs.

3   Make use of Indigenous media outlets: these represent an excellent resource for accessing Indigenous networks and information about local issues of concern, but you must be prepared to engage in an exchange—reciprocity—rather than expecting to take information for nothing.

4   Be aware of how Indigenous people prefer to be identified: Simply ask. Beware of using generic terms such as 'Indigenous', 'Aboriginal' or 'leaders' without first checking on how your sources would like to be acknowledged.

5   Always include the context for events you describe in your story where possible: don't assume it is part of your audience's 'commonsense' understanding of the issue.

6   Be prepared to go beyond your usual parameters to obtain informed consent: this may involve checking story details with your sources—essential, particularly with sensitive issues.

7   Consider alternative approaches: ethnographic methods such as observation and participation take more time but will result in a deeper understanding of the issues and stronger source relationships—and better, more informed stories.

QUESTIONS TO CONSIDER

1   What is the 'fundamental shift in thinking' identified in this chapter?
2   How have stories about Indigenous people traditionally been framed?
3   What are the author's concerns about 'institutionalised racism'?
4   How does the author's problem-based model work?
5   Describe how 'active listening' works and how it can be applied to coverage of Indigenous issues.

TASK

1   Locate some historical examples of media coverage of Indigenous issues (dating from the 1950s to the 1970s. Identify the key themes covered in these stories and the language employed. Next, obtain some examples of recent Indigenous stories and see how/if the frames and language have changed. Summarise your findings.

REFERENCES

ABC. 2012. *Cultural Protocol*: www.abc.net.au/indigenous/education/cultural_protocol.htm (accessed 30 March 2012).

Adam, S. 1993. *Notes Towards a Definition of Journalism: Understanding an Old Craft as an Art Form*, The Poynter Papers No. 2, St Petersburg: The Poynter Institute.

Alia, V. 1996. 'The Rashomon Principle: The Journalist as Ethnographer', in V. Alia, B. Brennan & B. Hoffmaster, eds, *Deadlines and Diversity: Journalism Ethics in a Changing World*, Halifax: Fernwood, pp. 98–109.

Avison, S. & Meadows, M. 2000. 'Speaking and Hearing: Aboriginal Newspapers and the Public Sphere in Canada and Australia', *Canadian Journal of Communication*, 25, pp. 347–66.

Bird, S.E. 2005. 'The Journalist as Ethnographer', in E.W. Rothenbuhler & M. Coman, eds, *Media Ethnography*, Thousand Oaks: Sage, pp. 301–8.

The Bulletin. 1980. 'Centenary Issue', Vol. 101, No. 5186, 23 January.

Cryle, D. 1992. 'Snakes in the Grass: The Press and Race Relations at Moreton Bay 1846–47', in R. Fisher, ed., *Brisbane: The Aboriginal Presence 1824–1860*, Brisbane: Brisbane History Group Papers, No. 11, pp. 69–79.

Downing, J. 2007. 'Grassroots Media: Establishing Priorities for the Years Ahead', *Global Media Journal: Australian Edition*, 1(1), pp. 1–16: www.commarts.uws.edu.au/gmjau/2007_1_toc.html (accessed 3 April 2012).

Dreher, T. 2010. 'Speaking Up or Being Heard? Community Media Interventions and the Politics of Listening', *Media, Culture and Society*, 32(1), pp. 85–103.

Forde, S. 2011. *Challenging the News: The Journalism of Alternative and Independent Media*, London: Palgrave Macmillan.

Forde, S., Foxwell, K. & Meadows, M. 2009. *Developing Dialogues: Indigenous and Ethnic Community Broadcasting in Australia*, London: Intellect; Chicago: University of Chicago Press.

Fraser, N. 1999. 'Rethinking the Public Sphere: A Contribution to the Critique of Actually Existing Democracy', in C. Calhoun, ed., *Habermas and the Public Sphere*, Cambridge MA: MIT Press.

Gandy, O.H. Jr. 1998. *Communication and Race: A Structural Perspective*, London: Arnold.

Gibson, R. 1984. *The Diminishing Paradise: Changing Literary Perceptions of Australia*, Sydney: Sirius.

Ginsburg, F. 1993. 'Aboriginal Media and the Australian Imaginary', *Public Culture*, 5, pp. 557–78.

Hackett, R.A. & Carroll, W.K. 2006. *Remaking Media: The Struggle to Democratize Public Communication*, New York and London: Routledge.

Hall, S. 1981. 'The Whites of their Eyes: Racist Ideologies and the Media', in G. Bridges & R. Brunt, eds, *Silver Linings: Some Strategies for the Eighties*, London: Lawrence and Wishart, pp. 28–52.

Hippocrates, C., Meadows, M. & van Vuuren, K. 1996. *Race Reporter*, Brisbane: Queensland Anti-Discrimination Commission.

Hooper, C. 2008. *The Tall Man: Death and Life on Palm Island*, Camberwell: Penguin.

Husband, C. 2000. 'Media and the Public Sphere in Multi-ethnic Societies', in S. Cottle, ed., *Ethnic Minorities and the Media*, Buckingham: Open University Press, pp. 199–214.

Lindgren, M. & Phillips, G. 2011. 'Conceptualising Journalism as Research: Two Paradigms', *Australian Journalism Review*, 33(2), pp. 73–83.

Lowrey, W. 2006. 'Mapping the Journalism–Blogging Relationship', *Journalism*, 7(4), pp. 477–500.

McCallum, K. 2007. *Public Opinion about Indigenous Issues in Australia: Local Talk and Journalistic Practice*, Gold Coast: Griffith University Press.

McCallum, K. 2010. 'News and Local Talk: Conversations about the Crisis of "Indigenous Violence" in Australia', in S.E. Bird, ed., *The Anthropology of News and Journalism: Global Perspectives*, Bloomington: Indiana University Press.

McCallum, K., Waller, L. & Meadows, M. 2012. 'Raising the Volume: Indigenous Voices in News Media and Policy', *Media International Australia*, 142, pp. 101–11.

McChesney, R.W. & Pickard, V. 2011. *Will the Last Report Please Turn Out the Lights: The Collapse of Journalism and What Can Be Done to Fix It*, New York: The New Press.

McCorquodale, J. 1986. 'The Legal Classification of Race in Australia', *Aboriginal History*, 10(1), pp. 7–24.

Meadows, M. 1994. 'The Way People Want to Talk: Indigenous Media Production in Australia and Canada', *Media Information Australia*, 73, pp. 64–73.

Meadows, M. 1997a. 'Taking a Problem-based Approach to Journalism Education', *Asia Pacific Media Educator*, 3, pp. 89–107.

Meadows, M. 1997b. 'Perfect Match: The Media and Pauline Hanson', *Metro*, 109, pp. 86–90.

Meadows, M. 2000. 'Deals and Victories: Newspaper Coverage of Native Title in Australia and Canada', *Australian Journalism Review*, 22(1), pp. 81–105.

Meadows, M. 2001. *Voices in the Wilderness: Images of Aboriginal People in the Australian Media*, Westport: Greenwood Press.

Meadows, M. 2005. 'Journalism and Indigenous Public Spheres', *Pacific Journalism Review*, 11(1), pp. 36–41.

Meadows, M. 2012. 'Putting the Citizen Back into Journalism', *Journalism (Online)*:1–18: http://jou.sagepub.com.libraryproxy.griffith.edu.au/content/early/2012/04/17/1464884912442293.full.pdf+html (login required).

Meadows, M. & Foxwell, K. 2011. 'Community Broadcasting and Mental Health: The Role of Local Radio and Television in Enhancing Emotional and Social Wellbeing', *The Radio Journal*, 9(2), pp. 89–106.

Meadows, M., Forde, S., Ewart, J. & Foxwell, K. 2007. *Community Media Matters: An Audience Study of the Australian Community Broadcasting Sector*, Brisbane: Griffith University.

Meadows, M., Forde S., Ewart, J. & Foxwell, K. 2009. 'Making Good Sense: Transformative Processes in Community Journalism', *Journalism*, 10(2), pp. 154–69.

Media Entertainment and Arts Alliance (MEAA). 2001. *Australian Journalists' Association Code of Ethics*: www.alliance.org.au/code-of-ethics.html (accessed 23 November 2001).

Minority Rights Group International. 2010. *State of the World's Minorities and Indigenous Peoples 2010—Australia*: www.unhcr.org/refworld/docid/4c33312034.html (accessed 30 March 2012).

Oxfam Australia. Undated. *Aboriginal and Torres Strait Islander Protocols*: https://docs.google.com/viewer?url=http://www.terrijanke.com.au/img/publications/pdf/14.OxfamAus-AboriginalTorresStraitCulturalProtocols-1207.pdf (accessed 28 November 2012).

Palm Island Interview. 2005. With senior island representative, conducted by M. Meadows, 19 August.

Productivity Commission. 2009. *Overcoming Indigenous Disadvantage: Key Indicators 2009*: www.pc.gov.au/gsp/reports/indigenous/keyindicators2009 (accessed 30 March 2012).

Rankine, J. & McCreanor, T. 2004. 'Colonial Coverage: Media Reporting of a Bicultural Health Research Partnership', *Journalism*, 5(1), pp. 5–29.

Reese, S.D., Rutigliano, L., Hyun, K. & Jeong, J. 2007. 'Mapping the Blogoshphere: Professional and Citizen-based Media in the Global News Arena', *Journalism*, 8(3), pp. 235–61.

Roth, L. & Valaskakis, G. 1989. 'Aboriginal Broadcasting in Canada: A Case Study in Democratisation', in M. Raboy & P.A. Bruck, eds, *Communication For and Against Democracy*, Montreal: Black Rose Books.

Said, E. 1993. *Culture and Imperialism*, New York: Vintage.

SBS. 2012. *Corporate Protocols*: www.sbs.com.au/aboutus/corporate/view/id/106/h/The-Greater-Perspective (accessed 30 March 2012).

Stanner, W.E.H. 1977. 'The History of Indifference Thus Begins', *Aboriginal History*, 1(1–2), pp. 3–26.

Stewart, H., Meadows, M., Bowman, L., van Vuuren, K. & Mulligan, P. 2010. 'Indigenous Voice: A Work-integrated Learning Case Study in Journalism Education', *Australian Journalism Review*, 32(2), pp. 59–72.

Waller, L. 2010. 'Indigenous Research Ethics: New Modes of Information Gathering and Storytelling in Journalism', *Australian Journalism Review*, 32(2), pp. 19–31.

Weston, M.A. 1996. *Native Americans in the News: Images of Indians in the Twentieth Century Press*, Westport: Greenwood Press.

Wilson, P. & Stewart, M. 2008. *Global Indigenous Media: Culture, Poetics and Politics*, Durham: Duke University Press.

WEBSITE REFERENCES

Australian Indigenous Communications Association: http://aicainc.org.au/.

Australian Legal Information Institute: Online Index: www.austlii.edu.au/.

Indigenous Remote Communications Association: www.irca.net.au/.

Mindframe: Reporting Suicide and Mental Illness—A Resource for Media Professionals: Indigenous Australians: www.mindframe-media .info/site/index.cfm?display=84360.

WARU: Remote Indigenous Media Resources and Background: www.waru.org/organisations/ media.php/.

CASE STUDY

TAKING JOURNALISTS ON THE JOURNEY

Heather Stewart

My first story about an Aboriginal and Torres Strait Islander issue involved a racial slur at a Dubbo rugby football match in New South Wales in the early 1990s. Even back then I had the sense of how journalism could be used to make a difference. That passion has remained with me throughout the decades as I have striven to uncover new stories that can raise awareness about humanity, social equity and humility.

In 1993 I moved to the Northern Territory and was based in Darwin, where more than 30 per cent of the population was of Aboriginal and Torres Strait Islander descent. I spent 13 years there.

Culture was rich and the people in communities generous and open-hearted and it was not hard to find a good story, but these were overshadowed by news about the highest rate of incarceration, STDs, child abuse, suicide, renal disease, traucoma, poor education outcomes, and alcohol, kava, gunja and other substance abuse. Then there were the housing stories, gang stories and land rights stories. There were the native title stories, tribal punishment stories, Stolen Generations stories and finally the intervention stories.

Almost every story had the potential to involve an Indigenous element. Yet dictated to by the ABC editorial policies and Sydney-centric decision makers, surrounded by Aboriginal and non-Aboriginal colleagues, I faced a daily paradox regarding what was fair and accurate coverage of *any* issue. How much should I include the element that was screaming to be told—the real story behind the story? One Sydney colleague warned: 'Watch out for too many "poor bugger me Black" stories'. At the time, I was sitting in a room for a conference call with a colleague who was Aboriginal. It enraged me. My colleague remained silent. I argued the case that things were different in the Northern Territory because of our demographic. This appeared to fall on closed ears. I never felt we made a difference at that level, as opinions were set. We continued covering the stories we felt needed to be covered. But actually I didn't think things were different because of the demographic—I felt we were just covering stories that deserved to be told.

The divide between common Australian perceptions and what I began to understand and appreciate in terms of culture and knowledge grew larger the longer I spent covering the issues. Finding a simple sentence to provide an objective representation became a paradox. It was a relief to move to long-form documentaries to let people tell their own stories. But the reality is that many reporters covering Indigenous stories may not have any knowledge about Australian history, the Stolen Generations, Native Title—the context. They cover the 'what', barely embedding or even realising the 'why'. But I learned to listen not with my ears but my heart; and to see not with my eyes but with my mind.

I continue to seek knowledge and I have learned to always be open to new information and ways of looking at life. The more I embraced this approach, the fuller the stories became.

I made mistakes—I did all the things an over-zealous White reporter does. I entered communities thinking I had permission when I didn't, and I spoke too much instead of listening. I tried to get short sentences and interrupted in all the pauses. I wore the wrong clothes, and arrived in choppers and big cars. I am surprised anyone spoke to me when I think back.

But then I also sat in the dirt and went down to the water holes and watched the kids swim and laugh until the right people came along and shared their stories. They wanted a voice. I went looking for long bums (a local shellfish) and had mud crab on the open fire; I ate mangrove worms, went turtle hunting and camping; I went to corroborees and met some beautiful artists, now long gone.

I attended land council meetings and Federal Court hearings and the Gurinji walk-off celebration and the opening of the Mutujulu Cultural Centre.

It was not until I entered the academic world that I found validation for my instincts about journalism being used as a way to even the playing field. But sadly, I found many studies in the literature proving that misrepresentation of Aboriginal and Torres Strait Islander issues are still leading to reinforcement of stereotypes and ignorance in mainstream Australia.

The answer has to be more Aboriginal and Torres Strait Islander people in the media telling stories (not just Indigenous stories), and every Australian journalist being armed with the tools to make informed choices about covering Indigenous stories in an informed way. Not everyone will be as fortunate as I and spend 13 years learning on the job, but there are many of us who have done so who are united in passing on our skills to the next generation. Less than 1 per cent of Australian journalists are Indigenous ... that's despite the ABC and SBS developing stringent reconciliation action plans and embarking on cross-cultural training. Modern technology is empowering Indigenous Remote Community broadcasters to have a voice. The National Indigenous Radio Service and National Indigenous Television have Aboriginal and Torres Strait Islander people telling their own stories. But the majority of reporters remain non-Indigenous. They need to be taken on the journey.

21

Investigative Essentials for Journalists in Multicultural and Diverse Communities

ANGELA ROMANO

INTRODUCTION

Discussions about investigative journalism often focus on the role of journalists as watchdogs. Watchdog journalists add to the 'record of the day' about the known activities of political and business leaders and institutions by shining a light on hidden behaviours in the circles of power. These include corrupt, inefficient, incompetent or otherwise inappropriate conduct.

There is however a second type of investigative journalism that is often overlooked. Investigative journalism also involves identification, deep observation and analysis of trends across society that would otherwise remain hidden or obscured. In this type of journalism, it is as if reporters sit in helicopters that hover over communities. From this big-picture view, investigative journalists scrutinise more than society's major political and business institutions. They map human activities, landmarks, patterns and changes in the landscape, and connections across the whole of society. These journalists can also land their helicopters in many and varied communities, including minority and marginalised communities. From this close-up view, journalists add depth, richness, colour and character to the 'record of the day' by reporting on the personalities, problems, achievements, values, ways of life, and pressing issues in sub-communities. They also trace how sub-communities link and relate to the broader society.

This chapter will explore some of the tools that these types of investigative journalists use to uncover news in ethnic and religious communities. The chapter draws from best practice as outlined by journalists and research reports from Australia and abroad, as well as data from a major Australian research project: the Vulnerability and the News Media project (see Romano 2011).[1]

One comment by a participant in focus groups that were conducted for the Vulnerability and the News Media project offers an example of the potential for this type of journalism to generate cutting-edge revelations into significant public issues. The person commented on how regularly Australia's news media run follow-up stories about major issues that had been broken by the BBC or other large international news organisations in relation to conflict and conditions in Afghanistan. The participant pointed out that Australian journalists could easily have broken the same stories themselves. 'We have all the people who fought in the war and who have been victims of war—they are here in Australia and they still have their families down at the battlefield,' he said. 'Those incredible stories are here.' He expressed concern that journalists rarely know how to tap into the potential of local communities to provide the types of information and connections that they need to identify, research and fact-check stories. 'I think the way that the media conducts its business here is separate from real-life experiences,' he said.

EMBEDDING CULTURAL KNOWLEDGE INTO NEWS ROUNDS

There are two different approaches to investigating issues in ethnic and religious communities. One is to have specialised reporters who have a specific round focusing on ethnic- and faith-based communities. The other is to embed such reporting into all rounds so that all reporters take responsibility for it.

Relatively few Australian media organisations have journalists who are specifically assigned to cover ethnic or religious minorities. When such reporters do exist, they tend to work for organisations that specifically target diverse communities or offer special-interest programming, such as ABC Radio National's 'Religion and Ethics Report'. Apart from this, reporters rarely focus specifically on religious and ethnic sub-communities unless they are working on special projects that address multiculturalism or minority-group issues.

One notable example of this type of special project was 'The Cultural Divide', a 50-story series that *The Australian* newspaper published over a period of 11 weeks in 2002. The series provided a colourful but in-depth exploration of ethnic identity and immigration during the turbulent period that followed the September 11 attacks, when such issues had heavily polarised Australian society. Some participating reporters were removed from regular duties to spend days or even weeks with communities with high levels of ethnic diversity or concentrations of minority groups in order to identify significant issues from those communities' viewpoints (Romano 2006, pp. 180–1).

It is often assumed that embedding reporters in a minority group to gather stories is a time-consuming and thus expensive way to create stories (Colbert 2003, p. 26). Few media organisations can sustain the expenses involved with this option. By contrast, it can be highly practical and cost effective for reporters on different rounds to embed cross-cultural content into their rounds by diversifying their approach to journalism.

This happens when reporters who are assigned to the politics, crime and courts, health, education, business, and other rounds make an active effort to establish simple but significant routines that build connections with minority communities. This approach is sometimes called 'mainstreaming', because sources from minority communities are not used just for overtly 'ethnic' or 'religious' issues, but also for 'mainstream issues' such as employment, economics, business and politics (Itule & Anderson 1997, pp. 285–9). The following sections explain how such mainstreaming can become part of newsroom routines.

BASIC MAINSTREAMING

At the most basic level, it is easy to mainstream sources from minority communities into the recurring stories that form the bread and butter of a rounds reporter's work. For example, almost every rounds reporter is required to cover stories that result from the regular release of official figures, statistics or data. Depending on the round, there will be a regular drip-feed of figures, statistics and other data about unemployment, inflation, balance of payments, consumer confidence, building approvals, crimes and offenders, car accidents, suicide rates, drug and alcohol use, health conditions, health services, educational institutions, gender equity, or many other issues. Rounds reporters quickly learn the routines about who releases such data and when it is circulated. They prepare themselves by developing contact lists of reliable sources with the expertise to analyse the data's significance. It becomes a very simple matter for rounds reporters to develop a list of groups or individuals among minority constituencies who can similarly interpret the facts and figures and explain how trends affect different community sectors.

For example, when economic figures are released, journalists habitually call on strategists and economists from the major banks and similar institutions to provide analysis and evaluation. However, a savvy journalist could just as easily interview sources from the Muslim Business Network, Indigenous Business Australia, Chinese Entrepreneurs and Small Business Association, or many other similar organisations for variety. Even bilateral trade centres and chambers of commerce, such as the Australia Arab Chamber of Commerce and Industry, can provide contacts with business people whose ethnic background or cross-national business experience gives them different cultural perspectives when discussing exchange rates, inflation and other 'mainstream' issues.

Such basic mainstreaming opens the potential for new perspectives on what the figures mean for an interviewee's specific ethnic or religious community. Each source's cultural background and life experiences also provide an opportunity for fresh, illuminating ways of understanding the issues and evaluating their causes and impact in society in general. Journalists are more likely to gain more colour, depth and originality from such interviews than from the predictable comments commonly provided by the strategists, economists and other 'usual suspects' from banking organisations.

Ethnic and religious organisations with expertise in business, health, social services and other fields can be found via basic internet searches. Additionally, each state government's department of multicultural affairs compiles comprehensive lists of groups that represent, serve, or are made up of people from ethnic and religious minorities. Ethnic communities' councils—and other peak bodies that represent diverse communities at national, state and local level—also collect similar lists of contacts. Some government and peak organisations will even provide searchable directories that categorise different groups according to their fields of activity or expertise. One example is the Queensland Government's *Multicultural Resource Directory*. Journalists can effectively use these directories as user-friendly, pre-packaged contact lists.

Additionally, reporters can sometimes uncover interesting elements to a story by analysing 'mainstream' statistics and asking what they show about different types of communities. One example of how using a cultural lens can unearth new perspectives was evident when a US newspaper, the *Hartford Courant*, analysed figures on 'traffic stops'—a term that describes police officers pulling over a motorist. Analysis of 100 000 traffic stops in 2011 found that Black and Hispanic drivers who were stopped by police in the state of Connecticut were significantly more likely to be ticketed or charged than White motorists (Kauffman 2012a). The story's author noted that the article covered a highly sensitive issue that 'struck a nerve' with readers, immediately stimulating a 'visceral' reaction in local communities (Kauffman 2012b).

MAPPING THE COMMUNITIES

For coverage of minority communities that permeates through a wider range of media stories, journalists need to map the many layers that exist within these communities. Editor Karen Lin Clark notes that journalists tend to spend time only in the top and bottom layer of communities (2001). Journalists interact with the top layer when they report on official meetings and similar activities; and they connect with the bottom layer when they meet with individuals in their living rooms, particularly when tragedies occur. Clark suggests that journalists who learn to report on the layers in between will find important stories before those issues hit the official public agenda (2001, p. 42). Those in-between layers are commonly found in places such as cafés, coffee shops, pubs, hairdressers, shopping malls, bookstores and post offices. Ray Oldenburg calls these the 'third places' where people congregate in between work and home. He argues that 'third places' form anchors for community life by providing spaces for creative social interaction and grassroots democratic discussions and activities (1991; 2000). When considering ethnic and religious minorities, journalists need to learn not only how to report about in-between layers and 'third places', but also how to find them in the first place.

For a reporter who is attempting to identify these in-between layers, a common starting point is to look at physical maps and telephone directories that provide an indication of key landmarks, places and organisations. Journalists can learn a lot from physical settings—the age, architectural style and types of buildings—about both the history and current state of communities. Journalists also need to have conversations with community members about where they go to talk, resolve problems, or satisfy their social, health, educational, economic and other needs. The type and number of facilities in an area can be sufficient to provide an indication of trends and issues affecting the various communities there. For example, when new types of groups move into communities, support centres will materialise to assist newcomers in locating suitable housing, building English-language skills, searching for jobs, overcoming isolation, and developing social connections. For those communities with a high concentration of older citizens, certain stores and cafés deliver not just commercial services such as food or groceries, they also supply seniors with life-enhancing attributes such as social connections, friendship networks, and advice or assistance in relation to problems (Rosenbaum 2006). Therefore, in each community there will be very different patterns in terms of where community members live, how concentrated their populations are, the lifestyles they lead, and the types of services and 'third places' they use and value.

Cheryl Gibbs and Tom Warhover suggest that when meeting with people in 'third places' or other community settings, reporters should ask the same kinds of questions that people ask when they first move to an area: 'what the area is like, what people do for fun, what they most like about the area, what they like least, what kinds of community issues concern them—questions designed to give you an overview of what is important to people there' (2002, p. 74). Distilling useful information from such conversations and observations can be challenging for journalists who are accustomed to asking questions or gathering facts that relate to a specific story, rather than thinking about the broader context. Clark suggests that 'journalists do not listen well' because they ask questions and listen for the best quote or soundbite, without hearing or considering what other insights the interviewee has to offer (Clark 2001, p. 43). By contrast, Gibbs and Warhover's questions are not asked with the expectation of identifying an immediate story. Instead, these questions help reporters to 'learn about what makes the community like others and what makes it unique' (2002, p. 82). Journalists can build an even stronger sense of the community members' economic activities, shared identity, social life and physical wellbeing if they couple information from these conversations with details gleaned from documents created by government departments, academic researchers, businesses, interest groups and community members themselves.

An example of the value of exploring in-between layers and 'third places' can be seen in the results of the 'Big Night Out of Research'. The Big Night Out was organised by researchers from the GENERATE! project in Western Sydney (Butcher & Thomas 2001), who light-heartedly named the activity after the Australian–New Zealand Big Day Out annual outdoor music festival. The Big Night Out researchers aimed to showcase 'the popular culture of young people from migrant backgrounds by taking journalists to the places where young people meet and mingle, such as karaoke bars and nightclubs and an esplanade where young people cruise in modified cars' (Dreher 2003, p. 128). The 'Big Night Out' team succeeded in attracting much media attention. This included magazine and newspaper features, with the most notable being a front-page story in *The Sydney Morning Herald*. There were also radio interviews, segments on talkback programs, and international media requests (Dreher 2003, p. 128).

Such a project illustrates how in-depth coverage of lifestyles and issues in ethnic and minority communities is not confined to dull sermons on the benefits of multiculturalism, or 'happy stories' to make up for 'bad stories' that stereotype or misrepresent minority groups. Although the Big Night Out was initiated by university-based researchers rather than reporters themselves, it demonstrates how the in-between layers of diverse communities can provide dynamic stories that are interesting, useful and relevant to both minority and non-minority group members.

TAKE ME TO YOUR LEADER?

Reporters in any round rely heavily on community leaders to provide story ideas, information, depictions of events and issues, and quotable quotes. The Harwood Institute for Public Innovation has identified five types of leaders that journalists can use: official leaders, civic leaders, experts, connectors and catalysts (see Table 22.1) (Harwood & McCrehan 2000; Kuhr & Harwood 2006). The first three are relatively easy to find. They include leaders from government departments and business organisations, spokespeople from religious and non-profit groups, and academic experts. Finding the final two types of leaders requires a more sustained engagement with communities and deeper probing of the ways in which they are organised. These include unofficial leaders who build networks within their communities, provide guidance or information, or help others to solve their problems

TABLE 21.1: TYPES OF COMMUNITY LEADERS

TYPE OF LEADER	CHARACTERISTICS AND ROLES
Official leaders are the elected leaders and appointed heads of government agencies or large institutions, politicians, public servants, CEOs, business bosses, board members, union chiefs, etc.	**Official leaders** make policy decisions, manage the operations of major institutions, and monitor activities that affect communities. Their decisions and actions may have considerable impact on community wellbeing, but they may be disconnected from ordinary people.
Civic leaders are people who hold important leadership positions in the community. These include religious leaders such as priests, rabbis and imams; heads of community centres, NGOs, non-profit groups and special-interest groups; etc.	**Civic leaders** represent the interests of groups of people within communities. They can provide journalists with the point of view of their interest group on official issues and are generally knowledgeable about trends in their community. The Harwood Institute found that journalists generally go to these types of leaders when trying to expand their source networks.
Experts are people with specialised or high-level professional knowledge, such as researchers, university professors, planners, lawyers, doctors, etc.	**Experts** are usually easy to find and interview, and can provide essential context, background and history about issues. However, they rarely help journalists to explore how people in the community feel or think about an issue.
Connectors are people who interact with a wide number or variety of people, organisations or groups. They spread ideas and build relationships between different people, organisations and groups.	**Connectors** can help journalists to identify and meet leaders and community members who may be less visible than official and civic leaders, but are still influential or significant. Connectors are knowledgeable about what is happening within communities, including the activities, trends and relationships in different sectors.
Catalysts may have no official leadership title, but they are a community's unofficial experts or managers. Other people often go to catalysts for information, guidance or help.	**Catalysts** can usually provide a realistic and nuanced picture of what is happening in a community. They can express the community's voice about what issues people care about, what dilemmas they wrestle with, what issues people talk about, and what they do and don't know.

Source: Adapted from Harwood & McCrehan 2000; Kuhr & Harwood 2006.

When covering ethnic and religious communities, journalists should recognise that the most significant leaders in minority communities may not be elected or appointed figures with official titles. A valued community leader may be a teacher, religious leader or hairdresser who helps people with an array of problems, such as negotiating with council for approval for neighbourhood developments, fundraising for facilities for a local school, or mediating disputes between families. These informal leaders are often better sources than official leaders for describing their group's circumstances and voicing the community's opinions and moods.

GETTING THE CONTEXT AND FACTS CORRECT

When conversations with community leaders or ordinary people in 'third places' lead journalists to a story, extra attention must be paid to the source's and the story's context. Journalists need to establish sufficiently deep and broad connections with ethnic or religious community to be aware of the diversity of people within such groups. Focus group research from the Vulnerability and the News Media project found that participants felt the journalism corps as a whole had little understanding of the general nature of their communities, let alone the nuances and changes occurring within them, or how contextual factors affect identity. One common symptom is that journalists interview an individual from a minority group, but they are unable to tell whether that person's comments or experiences represent a predominant trend within that community or whether they are highly personalised or atypical. This regularly leads to journalistic reports that are shallow or misleading.

One participant in focus groups conducted for the Vulnerability and the News Media project provided an example of this. Some of the news reports about the appointment of the new Grand Mufti of Australia in 2007 suggested that there were 'battles' between Muslims in New South Wales and Victoria over who should hold the position. In reality, there was little state-based rivalry about the issue. The focus group participant, who was acquainted with many of the individuals involved in the stories, concluded that a small number of people's perspectives were presented as typical of overall community views, and 'that actually hurts the whole community'.

Just as government and business leaders may engage in spin, so too can community leaders provide slanted views of their communities. Much research has shown that leaders of minority communities will sometimes build their position and power by presenting their own preferred images of their cultures to the outside world, and concealing differences and developments within their communities (Burlet & Reid 1998, p. 273). This again highlights the need to cross-check information from all sources for factual accuracy and context.

Many organisations exist that can help journalists to understand community structures. An example is the African Communities Council (ACC), which helps to coordinate and strengthen relationships between different African communities and organisations in various Australian states. While the ACC and similar bodies have their own agendas and biases, they form a starting point for journalists trying to understand the interests and structures within communities.

Kent Collins' recommendations about how to report on the elderly is also useful for journalists who report on ethnic and religious communities (2003). Collins, a former reporter and newsroom manager, notes that special handling is required when journalists use individuals' stories and specific examples to provide vital, humanising elements to stories. No individual or example can represent the whole of the community, but if journalists add qualifiers and background about the subset, this helps audiences to better understand the overall community (2003, p. 125). Collins also cautions reporters to beware of individuals and groups that claim to represent—or are eager to profit from—senior citizens, retirees and the elderly. He warns reporters that unless they carefully source information from everyone who claims to be a community representative, those individuals' or groups' motives will remain hidden (2003, p. 127). While Collins was talking about the reporting of seniors, retirees and the elderly, his advice is applicable to journalists who want to get their facts and context right when reporting on ethnic or religious issues.

Documents from government departments, research institutions, representative organisations and informal groups also help journalists to corroborate, contextualise or background the details that they have gathered from communities. Because people's recollections can be distorted due to faulty recall or deliberate manipulation of the details, journalists should try to check claims from interviews and conversations against the 'paper trail' that individuals and organisations collect. Depending on the story, this may include parliamentary and other government records, government and business financial reports, budget audits, official figures and statistics, research reports, historical records, planning documents, minutes of meetings, opinion poll findings, outcomes of official investigations and inquiries, and similar kinds of data.

DEALING WITH SOURCES

Journalists need to be aware that people in religious and ethnic communities may not deal with the media very frequently, if at all. This is very different from the well-groomed, articulate spokespeople from government, business and similar associations, who often undergo media training so that they are confident when talking with journalists, and can communicate in a coherent, concise, convincing style. Journalists who 'cold call' ethnic and religious organisations for comments on the day that newsworthy data is released or a critical incident occurs will often find that nobody is available to answer the telephone. If someone does answer, they often cannot provide a person who is willing or able to comment at short notice.

Further issues arise among communities where members may have particularly poor connections with the news media due to their isolation, cultural factors, or suspicions of journalists due to substandard coverage of their community in the past. For example, these problems often surface when journalists report on asylum seekers and refugees. Access to asylum seekers in immigration detention centres has been extremely limited since 2002, when the Federal Government began routinely rejecting almost all journalists' requests to enter the centres to see conditions or speak with asylum seekers (Herman 2002; Miller 2011). In 2012, new policies allowed access only to those media organisations that signed a highly restrictive deed of agreement with the Immigration Department (Dorling 2012, p. 5). Even asylum seekers and refugees outside immigration centres often hesitate to talk with journalists. They may fear that if their names or images appear in news media stories, this may jeopardise their residency within Australia or threaten the safety of relatives and friends who may still be at risk in their countries of origin. Some asylum seekers and refugees may be suspicious that journalists are affiliated with the government, because this is often the case in their home countries. Some may feel distress in revisiting past traumas, and exposing indignities that they have suffered to public scrutiny. Newly arrived asylum seekers and refugees may simply lack the fluency or confidence to speak in English in a public forum (Romano 2007, pp. 186–7).

Organisations that support asylum seekers and refugees may also be diffident about providing assistance to journalists on days when big issues, controversies or crises attract media attention. Many support organisations are small, with limited opening hours due to their restricted funds and reliance on volunteer labour. These organisations' staff may lack the time or skills to deal with journalists. On days when contentious issues erupt, staff may also be reluctant to submit asylum seekers or refugees in their networks to a torrent of requests from journalists who all request same-day access for interviews and photographs in order to meet deadlines (Romano 2007, p. 187). They are most likely to help journalists who have developed a reputation for quality reporting on the subject, or who have previously interacted with the organisation or its circle of contacts.

When reporters engage with grassroots levels of communities of any kind, they can rarely think of their connections as a 'one and done' activity (Remalay 2009, p. 30). This is particularly true when dealing with minority communities. For journalists trying to conduct 'basic mainstreaming' for routine stories on statistics and similar data, it is wise to sound out relevant people from community organisations and cultivate them as contacts prior to the release of data. This gives the organisations' staff time to nominate suitable speakers with the capacity and confidence to comment on the specific topics on the day that they will be needed. Similarly, when dealing with communities that may be difficult to access or reticent to speak publicly—such as asylum seekers or refugees—journalists need to establish connections on 'quiet' news days if they expect that sources will be forthcoming when crises, conflict or other major issues make headlines. Developing a connection through repeated conversations and contacts over time also allows journalists to develop a better understanding of the community's structures and contextual factors.

Past projects with minority communities also indicate the value of explaining the news process to minority sources, so that they understand how the comments that they make in interviews and images they provide will be handled by media organisations. Sources who rarely deal with the media will have little understanding of how their story will compete with a large pool of other stories for space within a publication or bulletin; how sub-editors may rewrite stories for impact or slash selected stories for length; or why stories may be dropped at the last minute for breaking news or late advertisements. For example, academic researchers who brokered a cooperative collaboration between Queensland's *Courier-Mail* and ethnic and Indigenous organisations found that the community partners expressed confusion and disappointment when the newspaper failed to run several stories that had involved much effort from the community members. The community members were unaware that their articles were spiked because they were not as newsworthy as other stories that were available on the day (Romano & Hippocrates 2001, p. 177). This example indicates why it is worthwhile explaining to sources from ethnic and religious minorities why an interview that took an hour may only lead to a few sentences being quoted in the final story, or may not lead to any story at all. If sources understand newsroom processes, they are more likely to continue to offer information to the reporter in the future, rather than abandon the relationship if their initial connections failed to yield fruit.

UNLEASHING CREATIVITY

When the facts from minority communities are woven into stories, reporters often need to be more creative and inventive than they would with 'run-of-the-mill' stories. Reporter Sara Persinger notes that Australian editors are less interested in specialised knowledge about Islam than in a contentious or shocking comment by a Muslim leader (2010, pp. 52–3). In an environment in which reporters generate more stories than can possibly be published, editors seek attractive images, sensational stories or significant developments that will make easy headlines, breaking news, scoops, exclusives, and big splashes (Collins 2003, p. 127; Jacubowicz & Seniveratne 1996, pp. 9–10; Persinger 2010, pp. 52–3).

Stories about minority communities will also often require additional contextual information if audiences are to appreciate the nuances and background of issues. This will cause editors and producers who are accustomed to 400-word or 45-second stories to cringe. As former reporter and editor Jan Colbert notes: 'it takes time and precious space to go beyond the conventional. To many editors and producers, context means the story becomes more expensive' (2003, p. 26).

Reporters thus need to create stories that editors and audiences cannot easily dismiss as being 'worthy but dull'. This requires creativity and innovation to find the compelling features of stories, condense the necessary contextual information into a few words or sentences, and develop new story-telling strategies without resorting to sensationalised, stereotyped or shallow storylines. The important and interesting nature of everyday stories from ethnic and religious communities will not emerge as easily as they will in conventional stories about controversies, crimes, conflict and crises, which have obvious dramatic elements and fit neatly into clichéd story-telling formulas.

CONCLUSION

This chapter has explored a form of investigative journalism that helps reporters to probe issues in ethnic and religious communities by identifying the significant places in communities where people meet and talk, and engaging in extended conversations with community members. Research shows that when reporters spend time on connection-building conversations and interactions with communities, they can enjoy long-term benefits in terms of improved contacts and story ideas (Romano 2001, pp. 57–9).

US journalist Leon Dash's reporting of teenage pregnancy among African Americans is a powerful example of how extensive grassroots community conversations combined with meticulous fact-checking led to a substantial shift in how a major socio-economic issue was framed in his country (2003). Dash spent 17 months studying the causes and effects of teenage pregnancy, including one year living in one of the poorest ghettos in Washington DC. In the preceding decade, the US media had consistently portrayed the issue of teenage pregnancy as one of ignorance about birth control and inadequate access to contraceptives (Colbert 2003, p. 25). After listening to Black teenagers describe their cultural values, motivations and struggle with poverty and parenthood, Dash found that teens generally knew how to prevent pregnancy. Instead, conceiving a child was connected to their need for self-esteem and someone to love (2003). His journalism helped to reshape public understandings of the causes for the ever-lowering age of teen parents—not just among poor Black youths, but among poor and disadvantaged US communities in general.

The example illustrates the possibilities of this form of investigative journalism, when it is conducted in a rigorous and sophisticated way. Such journalism does not simply record pertinent issues, grassroots political movements, demographic changes and social trends if or when they become clearly visible due to their size, impact or controversial nature. Instead, this form of journalism exposes such issues as they evolve, and potentially offers more frequent, more accurate and more comprehensive portrayals of ethnic and religious communities.

TIPS

1   Move away from stereotyped topics and images. Expand coverage of ethnic and religious communities from stories about multicultural festivals or 'problem people'. Embed people and issues from these communities into stories about politics, business, economics, health and all other topics. Provide ongoing coverage of community issues based on ideas gained from the group's leaders and significant meeting places.

2   Avoid stereotyping individuals and communities. Be aware of difference within communities. Don't portray one person's opinions or behaviour as if it is typical of everyone from the same faith or ethnic group.

3   Interviews are not a 'one and done' event. Continue your interactions and exchanges with interviewees, community leaders, and people in 'third places' over time, so that you are attuned to cultures and issues.

4   Cover 'both sides of the story' when it is relevant, but be aware that many issues may have multiple sides. By being open to perspectives from a wide variety of sides, you may encounter a different story to the one you initially imagined.

5   Only identify a person's religious or ethnic background if it is relevant to the story. A source's culture and upbringing should affect a story indirectly, as it affects their priorities, understandings, perspectives, values, word choices and similar factors.

6   Be careful to check and attribute information carefully. People from minority communities are often burdened by labels that are associated with their being 'different'. The damage can be easily compounded by false or misleading allegations, facts and figures.

QUESTIONS TO CONSIDER

1   What are the pros and cons of the various approaches to ethnic and religious reporting discussed in this chapter?

2   What are the ethical issues surrounding the mainstreaming of sources in ethnic communities?

3   How can the internet be used to background stories about ethnic and religious communities?

4   What does the 'mapping the community' strategy involve? What are the risks associated with not properly understanding the various layers in communities?

5   Why should journalists seek to instil a degree of creativity into the stories about ethnic and religious communities? What are the risks?

TASK

1   Locate some recent stories involving multicultural groups in Australia. What are the main frames used by journalists in covering these stories? How many sources do they employ, and do these sources adequately reflect the complexity of the issue being reported on?

REFERENCES

Burlet, S. & Reid, H. 1998. 'A Gendered Uprising: Political Representation and Minority Ethnic Communities', *Ethnic and Racial Studies*, 21(2), pp. 270–88.

Butcher, M. & Thomas, M. 2001. *GENERATE*, Institute for Cultural Research, University of Western Sydney: www.uws.edu.au/_data/assets/pdf_file/0009/196335/generate.pdf/.

Clark, K.L. 2001. 'Civic Mapping can Ignite a Reporter's Curiosity', *Nieman Reports*, 55(1), pp. 42–4.

Colbert, J. 2003. 'Women, Gender and the Media', in F. Cropp, C.M. Frisby & D. Mills, eds, *Journalism Across Cultures*, Iowa: Iowa State Press, pp. 23–38.

Collins, K.S. 2003. 'Just Don't Call 'em "Old Folks"', *Journalism Across Cultures*, in F. Cropp, C.M. Frisby & D. Mills, eds, *Journalism Across Cultures*, Iowa: Iowa State Press, pp. 113–30.

Dash, L. 2003. *When Children Want Children: The Urban Crisis of Teenage Childbearing*, Urbana: University of Illinois Press.

Dorling, P. 2012. 'US Prison Inspired Media Rule', *The Age*, 14 March, p. 5.

Dreher, T. 2003. 'Speaking Up and Talking Back: News Media Interventions in Sydney's "Othered" Communities', *Media International Australia*, (109), pp. 121–37.

Gibbs, C.K. & Warhover, T. 2002. *Getting the Whole Story*, New York: Guildford Press.

Harwood, R.C. & McCrehan, J. 2000. *Tapping Civic Life*, 2nd edn, Washington DC: Harwood Institute for Public Innovation and Pew Center for Civic Journalism.

Herman, J.R. 2002. 'Access to Refugees', *Press Council News*, 14(1), pp. 1–2.

Itule, B.D. & Anderson, A.A. 1997. *News Writing and Reporting for Today's Media*, Boston: McGraw-Hill.

Jacubowicz, A. & Seniveratne, K. 1996. *Ethnic Conflict and the Australian News Media*: www.multiculturalaustralia.edu.au/doc/jakubowicz_3.pdf/.

Kauffman, M. 2012a. 'Unequal Enforcement', *Hartford Courant*, 25 February: http://articles.courant.com/2012-02-25/news/hc-traffic-stops-0226-20120223_1_black-drivers-white-drivers-black-motorists/.

Kauffman, M. 2012b. 'Race + Data Journalism = Angry Readers', *Hartford Courant*, 29 February: http://courantblogs.com/investigative-reporting/race-data-journalism-angry-readers/.

Kuhr, P. & Harwood, R. 2006. 'Find Community Leaders', in *Covering Communities*, William Allen White School of Journalism and Mass Communication, Harwood Institute of Public Innovation, and the Knight Foundation: www.coveringcommunities.org/PDFs/find_community_leaders.pdf/.

Miller, B. 2011. 'Media Detention Centre Access Now a Critical Threat', *PM*, ABC, 11 May: www.abc.net.au/pm/content/2011/s3220536.htm/.

Oldenburg, R. 1991. *The Great Good Place*, New York: Marlowe & Company.

Oldenburg, R. 2000. *Celebrating the Third Place*, New York: Marlowe & Company.

Persinger, S.S. 2010. 'Reporting on Islam for the Australian Media', in H. Rane, J. Ewart & M. Abdalla, eds, *Islam and the Australian News Media*, Melbourne: Melbourne University Press, pp. 50–65.

Remaley, M.H. 2009. 'Fifteen Things Every Journalist Should Know about Public Engagement', *Kettering Review*, 27(1), pp. 26–35.

Romano, A. 2001. 'Inculcating Public Journalism Philosophies into Newsroom Culture', *Australian Journalism Review*, 23(2), pp. 43–62.

Romano, A. 2006. 'Public Journalism and the "Frugal Correspondent" in Multicultural Societies', *Australian Studies in Journalism*, (6), pp. 169–88.

Romano, A. 2007. 'The News Media's Representation of Asylum seekers', in D. Lusher & N. Haslam, eds., *Yearning to Breathe Free: Seeking Asylum in Australia*, Annandale, Sydney: Federation Press.

Romano, A. 2011. 'Seeking Inclusion: Views from "Vulnerable" Communities about Reporting by the Australian News Media', presented to the International Unity in Diversity Conference, 18–19 August, Townsville, North Queensland: http://eprints.qut.edu.au/55213/.

Romano, A. & Hippocrates, C. 2001. 'Putting the Public Back into Journalism', in S. Tapsall & C. Varley, eds, *Journalism Theory in Practice*, Melbourne: Oxford University Press, pp. 166–84, 255–81.

Rosenbaum, M.S. 2006. 'Exploring the Social Supportive Role of Third Places in Consumers' Lives', *Journal of Service Research*, 9(1), pp. 59–72.

NOTE

1   The Australian Research Council Linkage grant project, 'Vulnerability and the News Media', was conducted by the University of South Australia, University of Wollongong, Bond University, Griffith University, Queensland University of Technology, the Dart Centre Asia Pacific, Hunter Institute of Mental Health, Response Ability for Journalism Education, Journalism Education Association of Australia, Australian Press Council, Media Entertainment and Arts Alliance, Special Olympics Australia, and Australian Multicultural Foundation.

Not Just About the Money

NIGEL MCCARTHY

INTRODUCTION

Many, if not most, business people are honest. Others, however, will seek to gain advantage or extra profits through selfish—and sometimes illegal or unethical—behaviour. In this, they might often seek justification in the writings of the eighteenth-century Scottish philosopher Adam Smith, who was a pioneer in the study of political economy, later to become economics. Smith, his modern disciples tell us, advocated self-interest. Further, Smith believed that individuals pursuing self-interest would benefit society overall. In recent years, though, the pursuit of self-interest in business, further refined in the doctrine of neoliberalism, has been thrown into question by the activities of financiers and others who brought about the global financial crisis (GFC). The GFC was a dramatic display of the economic and social costs of self-interest.

One way of dealing with excessive self-interest that damages vital institutions, such as the financial system, is through public revelation that leads to debate, opprobrium and sanction. Revelation can come about through enforcement institutions and agencies, whistle-blowers (who may or may not be encouraged through leniency provisions in legislation), and the media, through highlighting public concerns or through exposing unethical and illegal behaviour through investigative journalism.

A friend who has had a lifelong involvement with business tells me that media business sections and programs should report only 'technical issues', such as price movements, legislation, regulation, taxation, and profit and loss. Other issues—such as moral behaviour, human rights, the environment, and the equitable distribution of wealth—do not have to be covered in the financial pages, he argues, as they are usually reported in other parts of the newspaper (or television program or internet site).

I disagree. A major challenge in financial and economic journalism today is recognising that finance and economics are strongly linked to issues such as those mentioned above. Finance and economic news does not exist in a vacuum, but is shaped, and helps shape, what surrounds it. Practices and attitudes—such as PR, the changing media, secrecy, corruption and lack of ethics, exclusion of different groups or attitudes, the unwillingness to look beyond the superficial and the need for investigative journalism—are the topics of this chapter. So too are approaches to reveal and overcome these practices and attitudes.

The GFC and the Euro crisis have focused massive attention on business and economics, and highlighted public disillusionment—displayed by movements such as Occupy Wall Street—with much corporate behaviour and values. This makes investigative business journalism more relevant than ever.

THE MECHANICS OF INVESTIGATIVE BUSINESS JOURNALISM

In this chapter we will consider the mechanics of investigative reporting for business, some recent examples of investigative reporting, the tools and approaches of investigative business reporters, and the issues surrounding investigative reporting for business. One of these issues is that many media organisations around the world are businesses themselves and are driven by the same needs as non-media businesses to respond to consumer demands, satisfy legislative requirements, reduce costs and maximise profits. This can create conflict between independent journalism and profits, and acceptance or challenge of government policy.

Investigative business reporting includes examination of the behaviour and character of business leaders; corporate ethical, legal and financial performance; scrutiny of products and markets; business relations with workers, regulators and governments; global operations; and social and environmental behaviour. Journalists investigating business examine and compare corporate and institutional performance through data analysis and by examining records. Their sources include business people, regulators, independent analysts such as accountants and academics, politicians and other government figures, and NGOs such as environmentalists, human rights campaigners and ethicists. Journalists' tools can include software programs such as spreadsheets; finance and economic glossaries to find their way through technical terms and jargon; guides to formulas for analysing business numbers; copies of business regulation and laws; and contact lists of business and accounting experts. Investigative business journalists need to be tuned in to market dialogue. They are required to have perseverance, attention to detail, and a nose for unethical or illegal behaviour, as well as the ability to spot trends and patterns, and to recognise that shiny facades can be built on shallow foundations.

Day-to-day stories in finance news come from market movements, such as the stock exchange or commodity prices, and company announcements, such as financial results, exploration or production figures and personnel changes. The investigative financial reporter, however, has to go far beyond these to uncover stories such as the loss-making performance that a company would rather cover up, unscrupulous behaviour by company managers or directors, and unethical or illegal activities such as dumping of polluted materials or the bribe paying that the company wishes to hide. Some examples of these, to be considered in later pages, include fraudulent accounting practices that led to the collapse of the giant US energy company Enron, or bribery allegations against the Australian currency-printing company Securency, which was uncovered by investigative reporters and resulted in charges and court appearances for Securency executives.

Investigative business journalists uncover stories in a number of ways. One is to respond to tips from whistle-blowers or to listen to complaints from customers, clients and business partners. Spectacular corporate success or disappointing failure are indicators that should be examined by investigative business reporters. Rapid business expansion or acquisition programs, radical changes of direction, or the introduction of new products or approaches also warrant scrutiny by journalists.

Business journalists should also follow the 'money trail'; a forensic examination of a company's accounts or activities aimed at discovering whether the company is, for example, actually spending money on plant and equipment for production, or on high living for the directors. Investigative journalists can also, for example, turn to engineering specialists to check that the 'space-age fuel additive that will give motorists 100 kilometres to the litre' that corporate promoters are spruiking to raise funds from investors actually works. Careful examination of company behaviour tested against corporate regulations can reveal corporate behaviour that has crossed the line of legality. Corporate performance can be researched by data kept by regulators such as the Australian Stock Exchange (ASX), the Australian Securities and Investments Commission (ASIC), and the Australian Competition & Consumer Commission (ACCC) (see Chapters 5 and 11).

PROTEST AND COVERAGE

The Occupy Wall Street protest, which saw demonstrators occupy Zuccotti Park near Wall Street in New York, highlights some of the issues surrounding finance and economics, and how these issues are also social and political. The coverage of the protest also illustrates some different directions and slants of media reporting and commentary.

The protest started in September 2011, with hundreds of people camping in Zuccotti Park and thousands of others joining in for demonstrations and marches. The protest was unstructured, postmodern perhaps, and without a clear leader or single message. The overall message, however—to me at least when I visited the site in October 2011—was clear. The protestors were angry at the excesses of Wall Street. They felt they had been let down by politicians. They felt that they had been denied the opportunity and success promised by the American dream. The protestors identified with the 99 per cent of Americans who feel they have missed out on the affluence and power that the super-wealthy 1 per cent of Americans enjoy. The Occupy Wall Street movement was echoed by demonstrations in 80 countries around the world, although there was no formal coordination and many of those other demonstrations reflected ongoing social unrest.

The demonstrations focused attention on the media in terms of how it was reporting the protest and the surrounding issues. Reporter Brian Stelter wrote in *The New York Times*:

> Newspapers and television networks have been rebuked by media critics for treating the movement as if it were a political campaign or a sideshow—by many liberals for treating the protesters dismissively, and by conservatives, conversely, for taking the protesters too seriously. The protesters themselves have also criticized the media—first for ostensibly ignoring the movement and then for marginalizing it (2011, p. 1).

Examples of conservative coverage include hosts and guests on the Fox network describing the protesters as a 'group of nuts and lunatics and fascists' (Karl Rove), 'demonic loons' (Ann Coulter) and 'a bunch of wusses' (Greg Gutfeld). On the liberal MSNBC, came comments such as 'it is what working people are talking about' (Ed Schultz) and 'it has the support of tens of millions of Americans' (Michael Moore) (in Stelter 2011, p. 1).

The Occupy Wall Street protestors relied heavily on social media. By the end of November, just after the protestors were removed from Zuccotti Park, there were 1.7 million videos on YouTube that had been downloaded 73 million times. There were 400 pages related to the protests on Facebook that had attracted 2.7 million viewers. The main Twitter account of the protest, @occupywallstnyc, had 94 000 followers. Posts were running at 400 000 to 500 000 a day. Social media contributors also challenged media traditions in another way: were they journalists or not? Perhaps half the people who said they were journalists covering the protest and who were arrested by police were without any press credentials. An Occupy Wall Street organiser, Patrick Bruner, said: 'We're fighting a system, and this media is a part of the system. And when this media doesn't cover us in a fair light, the desire isn't to shame them, it's to create an alternative' (in Stelter 2011, p. 1).

TRUST AND ETHICS

The GFC and the European debt crisis should pose serious doubts and questions on the values of Western capitalism for even the most casual observer of finance, economics, politics or the media. Occupy Wall Street was an attempt to articulate deep-felt concerns about financiers abusing their customers, and politicians who are far removed from the concerns of ordinary voters, and unable or unwilling to cut through the complexities of self-interest, factions, and lobbyists and interest groups (both often represented by PR companies) to bring about change. The media, as seen by Occupy Wall Street protesters such as Patrick Bruner, is one part of the system and one part of the problem; and there is a need for an alternative.

People other than the protestors have also identified problems with the financial and political system. This is why the protest resonated so widely. At the time Zuccotti Park was occupied, for example, a *New York Times* article highlighted the problem. Journalist Jessie Eisinger reported that investment bank Morgan Stanley had more capital and lower leverage than it did at the height of the financial crisis. Eisinger wrote, however: 'Yes, Morgan Stanley by any measure is a safe and solid investment bank. Except for one: The amount of trust people have in the whole financial and political system. It's just about zero' (2011).

Eisinger added that Morgan Stanley's shares had fallen by 42 per cent over 2011 and that shares in all the big banks had also fallen by double digits. The essential problem, Eisinger said, was:

> a slow burn beneath the global financial system that flares up at the worst moments. Banks don't have faith in other banks, investors are deeply scarred and wary, and nobody believes that the governments around the world could grapple with the magnitude of the problems, even if they wanted to (2011).

The issue of trust in US banks is felt even in the White House. In a landmark speech in Kansas in December 2011, President Barack Obama said he would pursue stronger penalties for business that break the law. He added:

> The fact is this [banking crisis] has left a huge deficit of trust between Main Street and Wall Street. And major banks that were rescued by the taxpayers have an obligation to go the extra mile in helping to close that deficit of trust.

(By way of background, a major cause of the GFC was sub-prime lending. The finance industry made loans to people they knew would be unlikely to meet the repayments, without making the repayment terms clear. These debts were then bundled with other debts, given top-grade ratings and sold on to other financial institutions.)

Public trust in business in the USA has also been damaged over the past decade by criminal acts by high-profile businesspeople, who have been found guilty of fraud and related charges and sentenced to jail. Examples included Raj Rajaratnam, Galleon hedge fund (11 years); Bernie Madoff, Madoff Investment Services (150 years); Bernard Ebbers, WorldCom (25 years); Jeffrey Skilling, Enron (24 years); and Dennis Kozlowski, Tyco International (eight to 25 years).

Most recently, trust in the media has been seriously damaged by the phone-hacking scandal at *The News of the World* in the UK. *The Guardian's* investigative journalist Nick Davies played a key role in exposing the scandal. Journalists and a private investigator working for the Sunday tabloid hacked into the mobile phones of as many as 4000 people, including celebrities, politicians, and relatives of dead British soldiers and of murdered schoolgirl Milly Dowler. Davies was alerted to the scale of phone-hacking at the paper by two tip-offs: one by a former *News of the World* journalist; and the second from a senior policeman who casually referred to 'thousands of names' being involved. Davies scanned back copies of the paper for 'interesting' stories that may have come from hacking, then contacted the journalists. Many willingly spoke to Davies because of bullying at the paper, but did not want to be identified because of the power of News Corporation boss Rupert Murdoch. Police were also criticised for being too close to journalists, receiving payments for information, and for failing to pursue their initial investigations into hacking. Several journalists have already been jailed and a number of other journalists and serving and former high-level executives have been arrested. The paper was closed in 2011 as a result of the scandal.

Crisis, illegal and unethical behaviour, posturing, collapse and bailouts—all often followed by inquiries—have become a feature of business in recent years. One cause is an excess of neoliberalism that promotes the relaxation of business regulation, the maximisation of profits over other values, and the enrichment of the elite. As mentioned at the start of this chapter, neoliberals argue that their position is supported by the writings of Adam Smith. One of Smith's most famous quotes is: 'It is not from the benevolence of the butcher, the brewer, or the baker, that we expect our dinner, but from their regard to their own self-interest' (1776 (1937), Book 1, p. 14). Neoliberals have also sought justification in Smith's comments that individual pursuit of self-interest brings unintended benefits to the wider society: 'By pursuing his own interest [an individual] frequently promotes that of the society more effectively than when he really intends to promote it' (1776 (1937), Book 5, p. 488).

Smith can hardly be held responsible for the excesses of the salespeople, financiers, traders, ratings agencies and investors who contributed to the GFC. Or can he? Should journalists have paid more attention to those other interpretations of Smith, and pointed out that were they are at odds with the self-interest that motivated many of the financial players?

INVESTIGATIVE REPORTING AND ENRON

In December 2001, the giant US energy company Enron declared bankruptcy—the largest corporate collapse in US history. Enron investors lost US$74 billion, US$40–45 billion of which was blamed on fraud. Enron's share price collapsed from US$90 to 12 cents between August 2000 and January 2002. Investigative journalists were key players in revealing the accounting loopholes and poor financial practices by Enron.

In July 2000, Texas-based *Wall Street Journal* reporter Jonathan Weil received a call from a contact suggesting he should examine Enron's earnings. His response is detailed in a *New Yorker* magazine article by Malcolm Gladwell (2007), which is a step-by-step account of investigative reporting.

Enron had been named the USA's most innovative company by *Fortune* magazine for six years in a row. Weil spent a month examining Enron's annual reports and quarterly filings to cut through what he called 'a lot of noise in the financial statements'. He learned that Enron used mark-to-market accounting. This values future earnings at today's prices; if prices drop in the future, earnings will be lower than estimated. Weil sought outside help, including a university professor in accounting, an analyst at Moody's investment-rating agency, and representatives from the Financial Accounting Standards Board. Weil also met Enron officials to discuss his findings. He said later: 'There was no dispute about the numbers. There was only a difference in how you should interpret them.' Weil found, in brief, that Enron was listing income it expected to make as money that it was actually making. In one three-month period of 2000 alone, $747 million in its accounts was money that Enron executives expected to make at some future time.

Weil's approach highlights several key tasks of investigative reporting. He displayed willingness to act on his contact's insights. He spent a month looking into Enron's statements—time and effort are a necessary and crucial part of investigative reporting. He also sought out experts. A journalist's key skills include writing, researching, asking questions, having broad general knowledge, knowing what is happening in their community or area of reporting, and having good news sense. Only a few specialist journalists are likely to be as knowledgeable as professionals working in a particular field on a daily basis. Experts can guide a journalist through material, inform them of industry practice, provide details of legal aspects and so on. They can also be quoted as 'expert witnesses' in the report. Weil also asked Enron officials themselves about their practices. This can be a problematical approach in investigative journalism. On one hand, it is a valuable way to confirm facts and conclusions. On the other hand, contacting the subject of the investigation can reveal the journalist's interest, allow the subject to prepare defensive action, take action to prevent publication of the material, or change practices, or remove or destroy evidence. In this example, Weil was able to add to his report by approaching Enron.

Weil's investigation, the follow-up and Enron's collapse are also a lesson in how the media and the business world forget the past. The conversations between Weil and the accounting professor included discussion on how some finance companies in the 1990s had used mark-to-market accounting on sub-prime loans. The risks imposed by mark-to-market accounting, sub-prime loans and the Enron collapse were forgotten by most journalists, business and the public ahead of the sub-prime crisis of 2008. An example of this is provided by Lewis in his account of the sub-prime crisis, *The Big Short* (2010). He explains how money managers Charlie Ledley and Jamie Mai recognised in advance that the sub-prime crisis was likely. They explained their concerns to reporters they knew at *The New York Times* and *The Wall Street Journal*, but found no interest. They explained their concerns to the market regulator, the Securities Exchange Commission, and likewise found no interest.

AUSTRALIAN FIRMS AND ILLEGALITY

The willingness of Australian businesspeople—whom we may presume are relatively well-educated, affluent, travelled, and otherwise responsible members of society—to engage in illegal and unethical behaviour gets regular coverage in the Australian media. This behaviour is at different times exposed by the authorities, by whistle-blowers, by lucky breaks and by investigative journalists.

QANTAS

The Australian airline Qantas was one of 21 global airlines involved in a massive price-fixing scandal investigated by regulators in the USA, the UK, the European Union and Australia. The airlines, threatened by a downturn, plotted together between 2000 and 2006 to fix passenger and freight-fuel surcharges between the USA and Europe, Asia, South America and Australia. The price fixing inflated the surcharge on a return ticket from the UK to Europe, for example, from US$7 to $94, or by more than 12 times. The scam cost US passengers and freight customers alone hundreds of millions of dollars.

The revelation of the price fixing in 2005 started a series of investigations, hearings and court cases in a variety of countries. The 21 airlines were fined more than US$1.7 billion in the USA. The European Union fined airlines US$1.1 billion. In the UK, the Office of Fair Trading fined British Airways a record US$246 million. The Australian airline Qantas's share of the US fines was US$61 million. Qantas also paid US$26 million in the USA to settle a class action brought against it in relation to the price fixing. In Australia, the ACCC fined Qantas A$20 million. US regulators charged 19 airline executives in relation to the scam and four, including a Qantas executive, were sentenced to jail.

The airlines' price-fixing scheme involved large group meetings in different parts of the world, smaller meetings, and emails and phone calls. One investigator said some of the airline executives tried to hide or destroy incriminating material.

The price fixing was first brought to the attention of regulators when Lufthansa made a confession to the US Justice Department. Virgin then disclosed its price-fixing agreements with British Airways. Both Lufthansa and Virgin sought to reduce penalties against themselves by confessing and turning in their co-conspirators. The former US Associate Attorney-General Kevin O'Connor told Associated Press that companies which confessed might be trying to limit liabilities from illegal conduct. 'Generally speaking, if they have an inkling they might get caught, they come in. The theory might be that eventually these things will be exposed and why risk continuing?' O'Connor said (in Caldwell 2011).

VISY

The A$20 million fine against Qantas is the second-largest penalty for price fixing handed down in Australia. The largest is the A$36 million fine against the packaging company Visy, owned by the late Melbourne businessman Richard Pratt. Visy and competitor Amcor dominate the Australia cardboard packaging market. Over a lunch in 2001, Pratt and the managing director of Amcor agreed to implement a price-fixing deal. As detailed by Pratt biographers Kirby and Myer (2009), the companies would not poach each other's major customers and would act together on price rises. Agreements of this nature are illegal in Australia. According to some estimates, the cost of the agreement to Visy and Amcor customers—among them popular consumer names such as Nestlé, Foster's, Gillette, Parmalat and Cadbury Schweppes—was A$700 million. When the deal was exposed, Amcor's stock price fell.

The price-fixing deal came unstuck when Amcor's lawyers accidentally found details of the agreement in documents. As in the USA and the UK, Australian law offers leniency—indeed, immunity from prosecution—to price fixers who confess. The lawyers took the material to Amcor's board, which confessed to the ACCC in late 2004. The ACCC investigations into the agreement discovered secret meetings between representatives of the two companies had taken place in locations such as parks and motels. Pratt at first denied knowing about the agreement. In late 2007, however, he changed his story and admitted to knowing about the deal. In his decision to fine Visy A$36 million, Justice Peter Heerey said of Pratt and the Visy executives: 'None of the most senior people hesitated for a moment before embarking on obviously unlawful conduct' (in Kirby & Myer 2009, p. 177). The ACCC later moved to take criminal proceedings against Pratt—who, incidentally, was then ill with cancer—for providing them with false and misleading information. The case, however, was withdrawn one day before Pratt's death in April 2009.

SECURENCY

One recent example of investigative journalism in Australia that exposed illegal corporate behaviour won the 2011 Walkley Award in Investigative Journalism for *The Age* journalists Richard Baker and Nick McKenzie. They uncovered a range of dubious practices in attempts to win foreign sales by the Australian note-printing companies Securency and Note Printing Australia, amounting to Australia's biggest bribery scandal. A number of Australian officials face bribery charges: that between 1999 and 2010 they helped gain overseas contracts to sell Australian-produced banknotes. In Vietnam, Australian officials were alleged to have paid up to A$20 million in bribes. These allegations extended to similar arrangements in Malaysia, Indonesia and Nepal. Activities in India and Africa are also being investigated.

It is illegal for Australians to pay bribes to do business in foreign countries. The Reserve Bank of Australia owns 50 per cent of Securency and 100 per cent of Note Printing Australia, and the directors of both companies at the time of the bribes included serving and former Reserve Bank officials. The judges of the Walkley Award noted that Baker and McKenzie had undertaken meticulous research to unravel the complex money trail in the case and had exposed an international network of corruption.

The story started with a tip-off from a source, who became known as Mr X, who had concerns about corruption involving Securency. Baker and McKenzie had to prove to Mr X they could be trusted, and at the same time confirm that Mr X was telling them the truth. McKenzie told Peter Clarke of *Inside Story*:

> How do you know anything is true in journalism? You start with a nugget of information and you begin to try to corroborate that. You do it through the most simple of means; by making phone calls, by Googling names, by checking things out.
>
> If our source, Mr X, had told us that a contract had happened on this date, and there was corruption surrounding that contract, then the first thing we'd do [is find out] … did that contract happen on that date? If it did, we've got one tiny piece of corroboration telling us that what he was telling us was true. Then we would try to corroborate the rest of it. And that was effectively the process (Clarke 2010).

CONCLUSION

The GFC shocked people in most Western countries. Riddled with self-interest, the finance industry, ratings agencies, regulators, politicians, journalists and members of the public had all been happy not to examine the financial system too closely while the system was—apparently—going well. Global major media organisations were tightly connected to the financial system. Investigative journalism at the time was suffering as newspapers experienced a downturn and as media organisations focused on increasing reach and profits that looked possible from new technology, rather than investing in journalism.

The shock of the GFC should cause a rethink on both counts. The self-interest that drove the markets close to collapse is showing signs of re-emerging, with bonuses paid on Wall Street in 2010 averaging US$125 000—more than in any year between 1985 and 2004. Illegal and unethical behaviour in business continues, and needs to be exposed. Past wrongdoings need uncovering, and current practices need ongoing scrutiny. Regulators and politicians need to recover the public's trust. Investigative journalists can help uncover the greedy, illegal and unethical activities of businesspeople and shine a light on the areas where change is needed.

TIPS

1. Follow the money trail.
2. Listen to tips and research them carefully.
3. Research key people in companies and uncover their history.
4. In business and finance, if it 'looks too good to be true', it probably is and could be a good topic for an investigative report.
5. Learn to read financial statements (the basics are fairly simple) and analyse data and numbers.
6. Turn to independent experts—such as academics and accountants—for help.
7. Consider how changing circumstances such as interest rates, exchange rates or commodity prices could impact on a company.
8. Follow local and global trends and consider how they might impact on companies (look what happened to video rental stores).
9. Note companies undergoing big changes such as ownership or expansion and revisit them to examine the outcome.

QUESTIONS TO CONSIDER

1. What approaches to investigative journalism are highlighted in the Enron and Securency examples?
2. How is the media industry tied into the financial system? How does this impact on journalism?
3. What are the costs of illegal and unethical behaviour in business?
4. Compare and contrast the philosophies that underpin business values and journalism values.

TASK

1. Summarise the *News of the World* phone-hacking scandal and the impact this has had on media and politics in the UK and elsewhere.

REFERENCES

Caldwell, A. 2011. '21 Airlines Fined in Price-fixing Scheme', Associated Press, 3 May: www.msnbc.msn.com/id/41926712/ns//travel-news/t/airlines-fined-price-fixing-scheme/#/.

Clarke, P. 2010. 'Digging Up a Scandal', *Inside Story*, 18 June: http://inside.org.au/wp-content/uploads/2010/06/investigate.mp3ark/.

The Economist. 1999. 'Business: Mea Copper, Mea Culpa', 352(8133), p. 58.

Eisinger, J. 2011. 'Between the Lines: Wall St Banks Face a Deficit of Trust', *The New York Times*, 12 October: http://dealbook.nytimes.com/2011/10/12/between-the-lines-morgan-stanley-faces-deficit-of-trust/.

Gladwell, M. 2007. 'Enron, Intelligence, and the Perils of Too Much Information', *The New Yorker*, 8 January, 82(44).

Kirby, J. & Myer, R. 2009. *Richard Pratt: One Out of the Box—The Secrets of an Australian Billionaire*, Milton: John Wiley & Sons Australia Ltd.

Lewis, M. 2010. *The Big Short: Inside the Doomsday Machine*, New York: W.W. Norton & Co.

Mathews, M.R. 1997. 'Twenty-five Years of Social and Environmental Accounting Research: Is There a Silver Jubilee to Celebrate?', *Accounting, Auditing and Accountability Journal*, Vol. 10. No. 4, pp. 481–531.

Smith, A. 1776 (1937). *The Wealth of Nations*, New York: Modern Library.

Stelter, B. 2011. 'Protest Puts Coverage in the Spotlight', *The New York Times*, 21 November.

FURTHER READING

Evensky, J. 2005. *Adam Smith's Moral Philosophy: A Historical and Contemporary Perspective on Markets, Law, Ethics, and Culture*, New York: Cambridge University Press.

Lux, K. 1990. *Adam Smith's Mistake: How a Moral Philosopher Invented Economics and Ended Morality*, Boston: Shambhala.

Preston, J. 2011. 'Protestors Look at Ways to Feed the Web', *The New York Times*, 25 November.

Shakespeare, W. *Hamlet*, Act 3, scene 1.

Smith, A. 1759 (1976). *The Theory of Moral Sentiments*, Indianapolis: Liberty Classics.

Watson, T. & Hickman, M. 2012. *Dial M for Murdoch: News Corporation and the Corruption of Britain*, London: Allen Lane.

BHP AND OK TEDI

Mary Kaidonis

Introduction

This case study will focus on the limitations of financial reports and the role that journalism can play in addressing the question of corporate accountability. The context for this discussion is Generally Accepted Accounting Principles (GAAP), which seek to ensure that company reports provide regulators, shareholders and other interested parties with a degree of transparency when looking at a company's activities over the previous 12 months.

One question in particular arises: if a corporation is the subject of media scrutiny, should the issues raised by journalists be covered in the annual report or reports that cover the period in question? This case study will look at the accounting treatment of the then BHP-owned Ok Tedi Mine in PNG in an attempt to answer questions surrounding the role of journalists and media organisations in holding major corporations to account for policy decisions that may have had a significant social and economic cost. When media coverage of an issue disagrees with the so-called 'reality' conveyed by the financial reports, important questions need to be raised about the capacity of large corporations to down play the impact of such disasters on their balance sheets and in their role as responsible corporate citizens.

The case: the Ok Tedi mine and environmental damage

The environmental damage and pollution from the Ok Tedi mine in PNG, managed by BHP,[1] was described as 'one of the world's worst mine disasters' (Mining Policy Center et al. 1999, p. 1). Journalists' articles such as 'Big Ugly Australian: Ok Tedi, BHP and the PNG Elite' (Lafitte 1995) reflected the sentiment towards those responsible. The ABC's *Four Corners* program 'After the Gold Rush' (Fowler, 2000) presented several perspectives on this case. Twelve years later, the case is still newsworthy (see Walker 2012).

The environmental damage was largely revealed by journalists and resulted in BHP being publicly castigated (Andrew 2000), forcing the company to engage in a PR counter-offensive via its annual reports, media releases, discussion papers and websites (see, for example, BHP 1999; BHP Billiton 2002; 2003). All focused on the benefits to flow from the mine, including the substantial health, educational and other benefits to infrastructure which was specific to the Western Province of PNG. Financial benefits in the form of royalties and taxes paid to PNG were also highlighted (BHP 1999).

It is not unusual for a corporation to make disclosures in its annual reports about its social responsibility. Whether it is an attempt to mitigate unfavourable media attention (Deegan et al. 2002; Patten & Crampton 2004) or not, such disclosures communicate a particular reality that can augment or deflect from issues not addressed in the financial reports.

In essence BHP did not account for liabilities related to the environmental damage caused by OTML in its 1995 financial reports, yet it did recognise its investment in OTML as an asset (see Chapter 11 for a discussion of what constitutes an 'asset', and other financial terms). Does the lack of accounting of a liability mean that responsibility does not exist? The environmental damage is still occurring. It is still in a public interest and the mine is still 'an environmental sink, spilling millions of tonnes a year of tailings downstream' (Walker 2012, p. 23). If the environmental damage is still occurring, then who bears the responsibility?

To account for the asset but not the liability

OTML was partly owned by both BHP and the Independent State of PNG. Investment in OTML was growing, and by 1994 BHP accounted for this asset, stating that its '[b]eneficial interest in ordinary shares increased to 60% from 30% and in preference shares increased to 69.4% from 34.7%' (BHP 1994, p. 24). This represented a majority shareholding, and OTML was acknowledged as an entity BHP controlled as it had been acquired at fair value (BHP 1994; BHP 1999).[2] The asset had been taken into account—but acknowledging any liability was another matter.

In a discussion paper, BHP acknowledged that the environmental damage resulted in forest dieback of over 1000 square kilometres (BHP 1999). Despite this damage, there was no requirement to record a liability for two reasons. The first is that the environmental consequences were so-called 'externalities',[3] which GAAP would consider to be outside of the organisational boundaries (Hines 1988) and, as such, were not part of the reporting requirements. The second reason is that the OTML mining operations were in accordance with the *Mining (Ok Tedi Agreement) Act 1976* (Cth) and legislative exemptions (see Kaidonis & Stoianoff 2011). Since the environmental pollution was 'neither an issue of compliance, nor a consequence of failure to enforce legislation' (Kaidonis & Stoianoff 2011, p. 595), no liability was recorded.

Neither was any liability recorded when local villagers sought $4 billion in compensation from BHP and OTML for the environmental damages resulting from the Ok Tedi Mine (Engineers Australia 1994, p. 9). However, there was a note in the BHP 1994 financial reports under the heading 'contingent liabilities' which stated:

> Whilst liability (if any) of the defendants in relation to these proceedings cannot be quantified it is not expected that the outcome of these proceedings will have a material adverse effect on the BHP group (p. 24).

The notes to the financial reports form part of the financial reports, therefore any reference to an item or issue in the notes is considered to be taking that item or issue into account. However, in this case the note says that BHP does not have to take into account any liability, since the liability itself is not clear and neither is the amount.

In BHP's 1996 annual reports, there was no specific mention of liabilities, although there were references to 'resolutions, progress and compensation to villagers affected by the Ok Tedi Mine (pp. 7–8). BHP's 1999 annual reports had a section under the heading 'Environmental Regulation' and referred to costs of compliance: 'although they may be substantial, [they] will be unlikely to have a material adverse effect on BHP's financial position or results of operations (p. 29).

In order for a transaction or event to be taken into account, GAAP requires that an event or transaction be significant enough to warrant being included in the financial reports. Usually this means the item impacts on the profit. Materiality or significance is not considered from stakeholders' perspectives. Therefore, BHP did not transgress GAAP requirements. However the social and environmental consequences of BHP's actions—as highlighted by journalists—suggest that the company was able to use the accounting standards to play down its obligations. In fact, it seems that rather than account for a liability, BHP chose to divest their shares in OTML.

Not to account for an asset

In 1999 BHP announced that there was no longer sufficient future financial benefit in OTML for it to retain its interest on its books. The financial returns for OTML had 'not provided an acceptable direct financial return to its private shareholders' (BHP 1999, p. 10). The OTML project in total cost US$1.9 billion (BHP Billiton 2002). According to a BHP news release: 'BHP Billiton wrote-off its entire investment in the Ok Tedi project', including 'its share of the net assets in the project' (BHP Billiton 2002, p. 6). The investment in OTML was no longer an asset, and since this asset was written off, it no longer needed to be taken into account.

BHP divested its 52 per cent shareholding in OTML in February 2002 (BHP Billiton 2002; Walker 2012). The Chairman of BHP stressed that the company was keen to exit PNG 'in a way that minimises the costs to shareholders while meeting the social and environmental obligations you would expect of us' (Porter 2001, p. 1).

From a journalistic perspective, there are a number of issues that need to be underscored. Not accounting for the asset is reasonable, since OTML no longer represents future economic benefits for BHP. Writing off an asset is reasonable. Further, the asset should be taken off BHP's books, since BHP no longer has any shares in OTML. However, it does not follow that relinquishing shares also means relinquishing responsibilities associated with OTML. Further, it is interesting that withdrawal of BHP from PNG included provision for:

> permanent dredging of sediments from the Lower Ok Tedi (at a current cost of US $35 million per year), or implementation of an approved superior alternative mitigation measure, for the life of the mine (BHP Billiton 2002, p. 2).

It is not clear how this release from future liabilities can be sustained when mitigation efforts are also expected. The following discussion provides some explanation, although justification may be another thing.

Still no liabilities were accounted

Arguments about future liabilities were all linked to the relinquishing of shares. The then Chairman of BHP explained this strategy: 'as we will have no future financial benefits coming from the mine's operations, the agreement will also provide protection for us against future liabilities' (Porter 2001, p. 1).

This approach was supported (it seems) by PNG's Minister of Mining, who argued that BHP's exit from PNG needed to be 'acceptable to all the shareholders of the Ok Tedi Mining Limited' (Haivetta 2001, p. 2). This was achieved by a 'series of releases, indemnities and warranties [which] protect BHP Billiton from legal liability for the period after its exit' (Porter 2001, p. 3).

Therefore, the agreement, related releases and indemnities are important and worth investigating further. These instruments ensured that BHP was released from any legal action relating to the regulatory compliance by the PNG Government (Porter 2001, p. 4). The PNG government knew this, BHP knew this, the banks knew this, but the actual term 'liability' for the environmental damage was avoided in the financial reports.

The first principle of any GAAP is the separation of ownership and liability, which is the point of limited liability corporate structures.[4] BHP transferred its equity in OTML to PNG Sustainable Development Program Ltd (PNGSDP) (Walker 2012). The PNGSDP has the role of funding 'sustainable development projects in PNG' (Porter 2001, p. 2) and a range of financial and social benefits accrued to the Western Province of PNG (Walker 2012).

According to Walker (2012) the present owners of the Ok Tedi Mine are PNGSDP (which is the majority shareholder) and the Independent State of PNG. It is therefore appropriate that the annual report of PNGSDP be submitted to its owners. However, the PNGSDP's annual report was also submitted to BHP Billiton Ltd (PNG Sustainable Development Ltd 2010). This is curious, since PNGSDP was supposed to be 'an independent entity with no connection to BHP Billiton or the State' (Haivetta 2001, p. 3). Another reference is made to independence in the BHP Billiton background briefing on Ok Tedi, which specified that PNGSDP would have 'seven independent directors with three appointed by each of BHP Billiton [sic]' (Porter 2001, p. 3). Further, '[a]pproval of projects will require a majority of directors appointed by BHP Billiton and the PNG agencies' (Porter 2001, p. 3). The emphasis on the independence of PSGSDP from BHP is not convincing and is certainly worthy of journalistic investigation.

Was independence ever intended? The appendix to BHP's 2002 news release stated that legal arrangements provided for the:

> Program Company to indemnify BHP Billiton and the PNG Government against any claims for damages relating to loss from pollution or damage to the environment arising from the operation of the Ok Tedi mine (in the case of BHP Billiton) following the exit date and (in the case of the Government) prior to the exit date (BHP Billiton 2002, pp. 5–6).

This indemnity is also confirmed in PNGSDP's 2010 annual report (before the table of contents) under the heading 'Assurance and indemnification'. The question arises: why is the report submitted to BHP Billiton, which supposedly no longer holds a beneficial interest in the company, having disposed of its shares in 2002—eight years earlier. Perhaps the question is not whether to account or not, but rather who is accountable to whom?

Conclusion

The case of Ok Tedi demonstrates that financial reports alone are not adequate to ensure that corporate responsibilities are highlighted in company reports. The long-term environmental damage arising from the Ok Tedi Mine was given prominence by journalists. However, any corresponding liability was not evident in BHP's financial reports, despite it being the major shareholder in OTML and having managed the Ok Tedi Mine when the environmental damage began.

A journalist wishing to investigate questions of liability would need more than the notes to the accounts, although that is a good place to start. In the case of the Ok Tedi Mine, BHP relinquished shares in OTML, rather than account for any liability for environmental damage. However, the assurance against any future liability had to be achieved by legislative instruments. One could trace ownership of OTML to find that PNGSDP and the Independent State of PNG were the shareholders. Although BHP was no longer a shareholder, it is not clear why PNGSDP submitted their annual reports to BHP (as well as the shareholders of OTML).

Ownership and control are usually linked to responsibility and an expectation of accountability. It is lamentable that corporate accountability can only be partially fulfilled by financial reports. Some would say that financial reports are 'woefully inadequate' in discharging accountability, even if they are prepared in accordance with GAAP (Neimark 1995, p. 4). The financial reports and GAAP are social constructions as much as the annual reports. Journalists play a crucial role in highlighting competing perspectives, since the financial reports can only show a reality as constructed by an interpretation of a given set of GAAP. In the case of BHP and its interest in the Ok Tedi Mine, perhaps there is scope for more journalistic scrutiny.

Notes

1   BHP Ltd, with headquarters in Melbourne, merged in 2001 with Billiton PLC, with headquarters in London, to become the BHP Billiton Group or BHP Billiton, with its headquarters in Melbourne. In this case study, BHP Ltd and BHP Billiton will be referred to as BHP.

2   It is not within the ambit of this case study to discuss valuation of assets.

3   These externalities have been brought within the realm of annual reports, but only on a voluntary basis and only since social and environmental accountability has gained prominence (see Mathews 1997).

4   It is clear that accounting and legal systems play a significant role in sustaining each other, but the discussion of this is not within the ambit of this case study.

REFERENCES

Andrew, J. 2000. 'Denying Accountability? Australia's International Mining Shame', *News Journal of APCEA*, Vol. 6, No. 1, March, pp. 7–10.

BHP. 1994. *BHP Report to Shareholders 1994: Financial Statements*, The Broken Hill Proprietary Company Limited.

BHP. 1996. *BHP Report to Shareholders 1996: Financial Statements*, The Broken Hill Proprietary Company Limited.

BHP. 1999. *BHP and Ok Tedi: Discussion Paper*, August, pp. 1–20: www.bhp.com.au/copper/oktedi/oktedi.htm (accessed 10 September 1999).

BHP Billiton. 2002. 'BHP Billiton Withdraws from Ok Tedi Copper Mine and Establishes Development Fund for Benefit of Papua New Guinea People', *News Release*, 8 February, No. 06/02, pp. 1–6.

BHP Billiton. 2003. 'Ok Tedi Sustainable Development Program': www.bhpbilliton.com/bb/sustainableDevelopment/environment/okTedi.jsp (accessed 24 May 2003).

BHP Billiton. 2012. 'BHP Billiton Results for the Half Year Ended 31 December 2011', *News Release*, No. 05/12, pp. 1–17.

Deegan, C. 2007. *Australian Financial Accounting*, 5th edn, North Ryde: McGraw-Hill Australia Pty Ltd.

Deegan, C., Rankin, M. & Tobin, J. 2002. 'An Examination of the Corporate Social and Environmental Disclosures of BHP from 1983–1997: A Test of Legitimacy Theory', *Accounting, Auditing & Accountability*, Vol. 15, No. 3, pp. 312–44.

Drillbits & Tailings. 2001. 'BHP Billiton Runs from Responsibilities in Papua New Guinea', Vol. 6, No. 10, 30 December: www.moles.org/ProjectUnderground/drillbits/6_10/2.html/.

Engineers Australia. 1994. '$4 Billion Claim against BHP over Ok Tedi', June, p. 9.

Fowler, A. 2000. 'After the Goldrush', ABC, *Four Corners*, 10 April, transcript: www.abc.net.au/4corners/stories/s117535.htm/.

Haivetta, C. 2001. 'Mining (Ok Tedi Continuation (Ninth Supplemental) Agreement) Bill', *Second Reading Speech to Parliament, Papua New Guinea*, 11 December, pp. 1–5.

Hines, R.D. 1988. 'Financial Accounting: In Communicating Reality, We Construct Reality', *Accounting, Organisations and Society*, 13(3), pp. 251–61.

IASB. 2003. *International Financial Reporting Standards (IFRSs) 2003*, London: International Accounting Standards Committee Foundation.

Independent State of Papua New Guinea. 2001. 'Mining (Ok Tedi Continuation (Ninth Supplemental) Agreement) Bill 2001', *Draft of 15/11/01 as Supplied by the PNG Bills Office 17/12/01, after the Passing of the Act, No. 7 of 2001*, pp. 1–14.

Kaidonis, M.A. 2008. 'The Accounting Profession: Serving the Public Interest or Capital Interest?', *Australasian Accounting Business and Finance Journal*, 2(4), pp. 1–5.

Kaidonis, M.A. & Stoianoff, N.P. 2011. 'Legislation, Citizens' Rights and the Self-determination of a Developing Country: A Papua New Guinean Case Study', in L. Paddock, D. Qun, L. Kotze, D.L. Markell, K.J. Markowitz & D. Zaelke, eds, *Compliance and Enforcement in Environmental Law, Toward More Effective Implementation*, The IUCN Academy of Environmental Law Series, ISBN 978 1 84844 831 5.

Lafitte, G. 1995. 'Big Ugly Australian: Ok Tedi, BHP and the PNG Elite', *Arena Magazine*, October–November, No. 19, pp. 18–19.

Mining Policy Center, MiningWatch Canada, MineWatch UK. 1999. 'One of the World's Worst Mine Disasters Gets Worse', *Joint Press Release*, 11 August, pp. 1–3.

Murray, G. & Williams, I. 1997. 'Implications for the Australian Minerals Industry: A Corporate Perspective', in G. Banks & C. Ballard, eds., *The Ok Tedi Settlement: Issues, Outcomes and Implications*, Canberra: National Centre for Development Studies and Resources Management in Asia-Pacific, pp. 196–204.

Neimark, M.K. 1995. *The Hidden Dimensions of Annual Reports*, Princeton: Markus Wiener Publishers.

Patten, D.M. & Crampton, W. 2004. 'Legitimacy and the Internet: An Examination of Corporate Web Page Environmental Disclosures', in M. Freedman & B. Jaggi, eds, *Advances in Environmental Accounting & Management*, 2, pp. 31–57.

PNG Sustainable Development Ltd. 2010. *Annual Report 2010*.

Porter, R. 2001. 'BHP Billiton Background Briefing on Ok Tedi', *BHP Billiton*, pp. 1–5.

Richardson, A.J. 1989. 'Corporatism and Intraprofessional Hegemony: A Study of Regulation and Internal Social Order', *Accounting, Organizations and Society*, 14(5/6), pp. 415–31.

Rudkin, K. 2007. 'Accounting as Myth Maker', *Australasian Accounting Business and Finance Journal*, 1(2), 2007: http://ro.uow.edu.au/aabfj/vol1/iss2/2/.

Salmon, R. & AAP. 1995. 'BHP Pins Hopes on Revised Ok Tedi Agreement', *The Australian Financial Review*, 30 November, p. 9.

Unerman, J., Bebbington, J. & O'Dwyer, B., eds, 2007. *Sustainability Accounting and Accountability*, Oxford & New York: Routledge.

Upper Middle Fly Villages, Families and Clans of Membok, Karemgo, Erecta, Yulawas, Moian Villages. 2004. 'Affidavit between Opt Out Persons, Individuals, Families and Groups and Clans of the Upper Middle Fly Villages and The Broken Hill Proprietary Company Limited—First Defendant and Ok Tedi Mining Limited—Second Defendant January 12 2004', *Fax to The Supreme Court of Victoria at Melbourne (Common Law Division) Australia*, 13 January, pp. 1–3.

Walker, T. 2012. 'PNG on the Fly', *The Australian Financial Review Magazine*, March, pp. 22–7.

Williams, S.J. 2003. 'Assets in Accounting: Reality Lost', *The Accounting Historians Journal*, 30(2), pp. 133–74.

23

Industrial Relations

KAYT DAVIES

INTRODUCTION

Industrial relations (IR) reporting makes front pages because it's about conflict and, in many cases, it impacts on the daily lives of readers—or of people in their communities. The world of IR is also populated by colourful characters, usually keen to use the megaphone of media coverage; and so it's relatively easy for journalists to get good talent willing to make strong statements. Increasingly, IR is moving beyond coverage of awards—the wages and conditions under which people work—to include broader issues such as bullying and sexual harassment. These are legitimate issues that sadly confront many workers across the nation every day. Reporting on these problems is an important contribution to shaping a better working experience for many Australians.

The failure of much contemporary IR reporting is that it simply churns press releases (and, more recently, video statements) from the conflicted parties. Done well though, IR reporting can stimulate public debate about disputes by analysing the claims made by the parties and checking them against real facts and figures found in reports, parliamentary *Hansard* and awards. This kind of reporting holds the colourful characters to account for what are sometimes wildly inaccurate claims about the demands of the other party, and supports the progress of reasoned arguments about why better pay and conditions should or shouldn't be granted.

As well as remembering that IR matters are fundamentally newsworthy—because they deal with gruesome workplace deaths and agreements that force some families into crippling poverty, while others are left struggling with decisions about how to spend their 'play money'—it helps in this field to remember the journalistic commitment to fair and balanced reporting. Disputes have more than one side, and so should articles about them.

ABOUT IR

So who are the players in an IR dispute? In the simplest terms, the players are employees/workers, usually banded together into a union, negotiating with employers, who are either private sector (companies) or public sector (governments). The bargaining tends to be about workers wanting more pay and/or better working conditions, and employers not wanting to increase what they spend on wages, training, safety equipment or legal liability.

In Australia, many union victories are embedded in industrial awards—a term that in this context means legally binding documents that set out the minimum entitlements for workers in most industries. Awards are often published online.

The first award was granted in 1908 after action by the Australian Workers Union (AWU), and it protected shearers who had suffered terrible deterioration of wages and conditions in the 1897 Depression. Sick leave started to appear in awards in the 1920s. In 1936 a campaign by printing workers resulted in the first paid annual leave. Penalty rates were established in 1947, when unions convinced the Arbitration Commission that people deserved to be paid more for working outside their normal hours. In 1971 the AWU campaigned on behalf of an unfairly sacked worker, and since then unfair dismissal protection has been embedded in state and federal legislation. Long service leave, shift and uniform allowances, redundancy pay, health and safety workers compensation, superannuation, parental leave and equal pay for women are other issues unions have successfully campaigned for (Unions Australia website).

The name of the body that makes rulings about awards and industrial matters has changed over the years. From 1904 to 1956 it was the Commonwealth Court of Conciliation and Arbitration. From 1956 to 1973 it was the Commonwealth Conciliation and Arbitration Commission. From 1988 to 2009 it was the Australian Industrial Relations Commission; and since 1 January 2010, it has been Fair Work Australia. As the federal ruling body has evolved, responsibility for some aspects of IR law has been handed back to the states, and so it is now worth checking whether a specific dispute has relevant state and/or federal legislation.

Another of the most important changes to Australian IR law was the introduction of enterprise bargaining (a specific form of collective bargaining) in the 1990s. This was introduced as part of the Price and Incomes Accord (Mark VII) negotiated between the unions' peak body, the Australian Council of Trade Unions (ACTU), and the Federal Labor Government, with the support of the Australian Democrats in the Senate. The Accord was part of a move away from centralised wage fixing into a more 'flexible' IR system, and it is credited with effectively 'deunionising' the mining industry in the Pilbara in Western Australia by making it possible to offer higher wages for work in remote locations. The Accord is still controversial in some union circles, as it allows workers and their unions to negotiate directly with their employers over pay and conditions.

In seeking good descriptors about unions and disputes, distinctions can be drawn between blue collar and white collar unions, with blue tending to be for manual or trade workers, and white for professional or office workers. The blue collar unions are often adversarial and militant in their strategies, and therefore attract media attention; but a much higher proportion of members are represented by white collar unions that are less adversarial, rendering the stereotype of a sweaty industrial unionist fairly inaccurate. It's also worth noting that you can't always tell which union a worker is in by just looking at where they work. One employer might have workers in a range of unions, so it's worth checking which unions are involved in a dispute—because the one that sent you a press release might be a relatively minor player seeking to steal a bit of glory (and possibly some members) from a rival union.

Australia has about 45 trade unions federally registered with Fair Work Australia and 50 registered with the umbrella organisation, the ACTU, as well as other unions registered with state Fair Work and other peak bodies Overall, they represent 1.87 million members. The proportion of employees in Australia who were union members in their main jobs in August 2010 was around 18 per cent. This breaks down into 20 per cent of full-time employees and 14 per cent of part timers; and 41 per cent of government employees and 14 per cent of company employees (ABS 2010). In some industries however, such as waterfront, police and fire fighting, union membership is 90–99 per cent.

The ACTU is the peak body for unions in Australia. This means that unions pay for membership of the ACTU and, in return, it offers its members services, such as hosting a website that explains the role and function of unions; tempting workers to find and join unions; and lobbying when governments seek to change laws that relate to how unions and employers can negotiate. The ACTU (in conjunction with its member unions) runs an online service for unions called Unions Australia. The site is primarily for workers who can use it to sign up for union membership. Unions Australia then connects them with the most appropriate union for their workplace and role. This site, and its state-based counterparts, can also help journalists find the unions involved in disputes and their phone numbers, as most unions are listed under 'members and affiliates'; but bear in mind that not all unions are members of the ACTU and some prominent unions, such as the Australian Nursing Federation, are not on its list. The Fair Work Australia websites have fuller lists, but these don't include contact details.

Another reason to check out these sites is that the IR sector is replete with jargon and terminology that sounds generic but has specific meaning in the IR context, so get familiar enough with it to follow what your interviewees are saying—but not so familiar that you forget to decode it into plain English for your readers. The Unions Australia website has a handy glossary under the 'about unions' tab that should be a reference point for journalists new to the round. There is also a good glossary of IR terms on the Fair Work Australia website.

There are a few other ways of classifying unions that are worth noting if you are trying to gauge the newsworthiness of their executives' comments or the extent to which the union organisers can speak for their workers. These include the size of the union and its density. 'Density' refers to how many of the workers in the industry or company are in the union, as this dictates how likely it is that a significant number of members would follow instructions by union organisers about industrial action such as strikes.

BANTER AND DOG WHISTLES

To understand how IR plays out in the Australian media, it is worth looking back at the touchstones of economic theory that underlie the positions taken. Adam Smith, the Scottish philosopher discussed in Chapter 22, wrote in 1776 that he thought that society worked best when supply and demand were allowed to operate freely, and that when this happened the market would dictate how much of what products it wanted and the fair price for those products. In the 1930s, British economist John Maynard Keynes argued that the main problem with following Smith's neoclassical economic theory to the letter was that the old, sick and unemployed were left income-less and hungry; great gaps between rich and poor were emerging; and this led to political instability. His idea was to balance free market capitalism with taxes and government services (such as universal healthcare). This is the philosophy that the Labor Party holds dear.

The historical importance of IR policies to the development of our current political situation is evident in the names of our major political parties. If you look in a dictionary you'll see that the term 'liberal' in all contexts—not just political—means 'freedom loving'. In contrast the Liberal Party in Australia is socially conservative. The 'liberal' in its name refers to its belief that free market trading, unfettered by big taxes and rules about how much workers must be paid, is best for Australia.

The Labor Party was formed in the late 1800s to represent the interests of the labour movement in Parliament. This was a time when the movement was growing in strength and the failure of a few key strikes had made it evident that parliamentary intervention was required to protect workers' rights (MacIntyre 2001, p. 24). State Labor parties formed first and ran candidates for the first federal election in 1901. In all, 24 Labor members were elected and they formed the first Labor Caucus. With the Labor Party attracting about half of the vote in the early 1900s, it didn't take long for the conservative paries to realise that Labor would be easier to defeat if they worked together (Janensch 1994).

With our current politicians coming from these core philosophical and historic positions, the political tug of war in Australia continues to play out as the Liberals and Nationals push for companies to have the power to negotiate individual workplace agreements with workers, while the Labor Party insists on maintaining unions' place at the negotiating table. There have been some notable exceptions to this, with Hartcher (2011) noting that Labor was responsible for a major deregulation of the labour market in 1992 that saw the introduction of enterprise bargaining. This meant that workers could negotiate with employers at the level of individual organisations, rather than a whole-of-industry level, as collective bargaining had previously operated.

In the past two decades, IR reform has played a key role in Australian federal election outcomes, and threatens to be a major issue at a state level in the future, with scandals involving the Health Services Union (HSU) in New South Wales, and the dispute between construction giant Grollo and the Construction, Forestry, Mining and Energy Union (CFMEU) in Victoria. The latter case is providing a real test of Australia's IR laws, in particular the capacity of the parties to reach a decision in a dispute under arbitration.

Arbitration is the process of hearing both sides of a dispute and helping the parties come to an agreement, usually by imposing a legally-binding settlement. Under the current legislation Fair Work Australia has powers of compulsory arbitration in limited circumstances outlined in the *Fair Work Act 2009* (Cth), such as in cases where a dispute is disrupting national interests. Fair Work Australia also offers voluntary arbitration when both parties want a dispute settled.

One of the big IR stories of 2011 was Qantas CEO Alan Joyce's decision to ground the airline's entire fleet and to lock out all of its workers until disputes with three unions were resolved. In grounding the fleet, Joyce effectively forced the government to refer the dispute to Fair Work Australia for arbitration, putting an end to the process of enterprise bargaining that was already under way. The referral meant that all industrial action had to stop while the issue was being looking into. This cut short the strategies the unions were using to attempt to win over the Qantas board.

The grounding of all flights presented news editors with dilemmas about which angle of the story to focus on. Angry travellers were an easy and colourful source of news, and coverage of their reactions showed the widespread impact of Joyce's decision. It was easy for viewers to relate to the ordinary people suddenly inconvenienced. Many television stations took this approach, with the time constraints of the television news format precluding deeper coverage. Able to run more extensive coverage, newspapers and online outlets took their reportage a step deeper and explained what the workers in the three unions were asking for, what action they had previously taken to try to convince Qantas to yield to their demands, and the reasons Qantas had given for saying 'no'.

Only a few news outlets took the final step and explored the long-term legal implications of Joyce's decision to do something so dramatic that the Federal Government was forced to step in and intervene in the dispute. They also speculated on what Joyce's actions revealed about the new Fair Work legislation. While this kind of reporting is undoubtedly harder work for journalists—as it requires time spent speaking to legal experts to get a thorough understanding of the situation—it is ultimately the kind of reporting that holds powerbrokers, governments and policy makers to account.

The brevity requirements of much news programming makes it possible, and in some cases necessary, for journalists to create packages that simply take a grab from each side of politics; but this does have a downside. It enables skilled media manipulators within the political parties to use IR disputes as 'dog whistles' to shout out quick messages to sections of the community who they know have their ears tuned to the topic. This reduces complex issues to banter and point scoring, and does little to promote better understanding of the validity of the claims being made by the parties to the dispute.

Media coverage of IR stories often falls into easy political slogans—the Liberals are 'good for business' and Labor is 'good for workers'—and obscure many issues in the IR arena. In addition, this kind of simplistic reporting can overlook reality, which often sees parties act in ways at odds with the slogans.

HOW TO TACKLE IR STORIES

Journalists keen to explore deeper issues can find out more about the implications of decisions and disputes by contacting the union peak bodies; interviewing legal experts from university business schools; subscribing to specialist IR media outlets such as Workplace Express and CCH; and by cultivating contacts—which means making time to have conversations with experts in the field and taking them up on offers to help contextualise events. Critical contact-building strategies include doing research before calling for help, and being absolutely trustworthy about on-the-record/off-the-record material. Trying to understand what are often complex matters demonstrates good faith with your contacts. They will appreciate the effort. And if you take this approach, you are likely to find ample help from the network of IR people. Developing good working relationships like this enables you to call experts in unions and law firms who will become resources for the story you are working on, and who will deliver story tips and introductions to the right people.

The office of the Fair Work Ombudsman is another valuable source of help and advice for journalists. This should not be confused with the Fair Work Australia office. The Ombudsman and the office staff are there to provide advice about workplace rights and responsibilities. The office was established by the *Fair Work Act*, but operates independent of government. It can get involved with individual cases in ways that Fair Work Australia can't, because Fair Work Australia has to remain impartial and detached in order to function properly as a tribunal that arbitrates.

In addition to federal laws, some IR issues are legislated by state governments. For example in Western Australia, Greens MLC Alison Xamon introduced a bill seeking to have employers made legally responsible for deaths on their worksites. The Bill's official title is the Occupational Safety and Health Amendment Bill, but its unofficial name is the Industrial Manslaughter Bill, and it seeks to have employers with substandard safety procedures chargeable with manslaughter if one of their employees is killed at work. This bill is an example of a growing trend of support for workers' rights from The Greens, and raises questions among some political commentators about the strength of Labor's traditional links with unions and workers.

In seeking to win IR arguments employers (and conservative politicians) often make dramatic claims about the risk of business closures and the potential need to cut staff if union demands for better pay and conditions are granted. For example after Fair Work Australia's February 2012 decision to grant 150 000 social and community workers wage increases of up to 45 per cent over eight years (in order to correct their longstanding underpayment), Liberal state premiers—who provide about 45 per cent of the sector's funding—responded with lines such as this from Victoria's Ted Baillieu: 'This has the potential to have significant impact on state finances. The bottom line is the choice for state governments, and private sector bodies, to fund this or cut services' (Skulley 2012, p. 8). It is important for journalists to investigate such claims and not simply take them on face value. One way of looking into these claims is to look at state budgets—or, when a company involved is publicly listed on a stock exchange, to find its latest financial report—and to look at how much profit it is making and how much it is spending on staff and salaries. It is then easier to calculate how much the percentage increase the union is asking for would have on the state's/company's financial position. Once you've found that out, you have a good question to take to your next interview.

That's not to say that companies and governments don't sometimes face hard times for a number of reasons—including increasing material costs, increasing competition, movements in the exchange rate for companies that rely on export earnings, and supply/demand considerations—with their consequent impact on the prices companies can ask for their products. This was highlighted in mid-2012 when the spot price for iron ore fell to below $90 a tonne, causing major mining companies to defer expansion plans and lay off employees. Such factors can see once-prosperous workplaces teetering on the brink of unprofitability, as we saw in 2011 and 2012 with Bluescope Steel. If the hard time is temporary, it can be in the workers' best interests to tighten their belts for a while to get through the rough patch, rather than insisting on pay rises that could jeopardise the company's future and their jobs.

BLUFF AND BLUSTER

The IR rhetoric from both sides of a dispute is characterised by companies threatening collapse and job cuts, while unions threaten industrial action. Industrial action can include a number of activities. Strikes are just one option. An example of a non-strike industrial action was the refusal of Qantas pilots to wear Qantas neckties during the 2011 dispute and to wear red ties instead, as a mark of protest. Pilots also explained the dispute to passengers during flights. When unions are deciding on what action to take, they have a number of issues to take into consideration. The Qantas pilots could have gone on strike, as the baggage handlers did, grounding planes and inconveniencing passengers; but instead they chose non-disruptive measures in a bid to appear reasonable and civic-minded.

The persuasive power of unions depends on their size and density. These factors influence how likely the union members are to strike if the union asks them to, and how much a strike will inconvenience the employers. For example the Maritime Union of Australia represents around 90 per cent of eligible maritime workers, so 20 striking workers can close a port with a significant commercial impact on employers. Workers who handle perishable goods (such as dairy products), or who work in industries with chemical processes also have potential to cost their employers a lot of lost revenue, even if only a few of them stop work. This means that a strike is a powerful bargaining tool in these cases.

Nurses and school teachers can also go on strike, but their situation is very different. They are employed by state governments who are keenly aware of the impact on the public if hospitals and schools are affected. Governments don't necessarily lose money for every day of strike action, but inconveniencing the general public can be risky. It is a risk that teachers and nurses are usually loathe to take, and their reluctance to push their case becomes a powerful weapon in helping convince the public that strike action is only the last resort for the so-called 'caring' professions. This can provide a moral high ground for teachers and nurses during the political debate, but only if used sparingly.

In trying to win the media war in these disputes, some unions are turning to digital and social media—crafting statements and making videos for viral release that explain their cases for better hours, smaller classes and more workplace support. In response, health, education and IR ministers, and PR people working for companies, are using similar tools to present their arguments, furnishing journalists with pre-prepared packages. The upside of this is that it can save newsrooms time; but the downside is that it gives journalists little or no opportunity to decide what questions they want answered—to develop competing statements that illuminate the issues and details at the centre of the dispute. Journalists who want to do more than simple cut-and-paste 'churnalism' seek insight through conversations with informed sources; read the awards and relevant reports; and conduct their own interviews. The potential reward for journalists who do this is the in-depth exclusive that goes beyond what their cut-and-paste rivals have done.

The publication of videos by sources presents technological challenges that require journalists to be able to manipulate and reconcile footage of differing quality from different sources and to bring it together in a single piece. This means that journalists now need a working understanding of audio and video editing, as well as writing and photography skills. In addition, social media can be used to gauge public opinion, source story ideas, and to find people whose lives are affected by the dispute. Social media tools can also be used to allow affected audiences to opt to follow the story in more depth than the general audience may want to.

CONCLUSION

The art of IR reporting is in remembering that it's all about people going about their lives, working for a living, and either feeling ripped off and short-changed or not. Think about this next time you're at work.

In addition to following political events, journalism has a public service role to play by simply letting people know what the legislation means to them, what their entitlements are, and the channels they can use to have them recognised and protected. This can be done through magazine-style 'how to' pieces, infographics, and human interest stories about everyday issues such as 'what to do about a sleazy boss' and 'how to handle a workplace bully'.

The trick to not being manipulated by parties in any dispute is to always seek another perspective. Don't take information at face value. Use your contacts and engage with the complexity of the legislation.

1   Remember the basics of journalism. IR issues are newsworthy because they're about conflict and they impact on the lives of readers—as workers, as community members and as tax-paying citizens.

2   Always get both sides of the story, and present them equally. Don't simply let the most charismatic speaker's voice prevail. Remember there are independent experts, such as academics, lawyers and think-tank executives, who can offer depth and an alternative perspective.

3   Build contacts and find people you can call on when you need advice. Nurture your relationships by not revealing to anyone what they tell you off the record.

QUESTIONS TO CONSIDER

1   Give some examples of the IR 'banter' identified in this chapter.

2   To what extent can it be argued that Australia's IR battlegrounds are defined by the political philosophies of the Labor and Liberal Parties?

3   Do you believe that ideology rather than commonsense influences the direction in which Australia's IR policies move?

4   To what extent was this the case with the Qantas dispute discussed in this chapter?

5   How do the roles of the Fair Work Ombudsman and Fair Work Australia differ?

TASK

1   Identify a recent industrial dispute and summarise how it is reported in the media. What are the main frames employed? How many voices are reported? To what extent do you believe the coverage is fair and balanced? How could the story be improved?

REFERENCES

ABS Cat 6310.0. 2010. *Employee Earnings, Benefits and Trade Union Membership, Australia*, August 2010: www.abs.gov.au/ausstats/abs@.nsf/mf/6310.0

Hartcher, P. 2011. *The Sweet Spot*, Melbourne: Black Inc.

Janensch, D. 1994. *Power Politics: Australia's Party System*, 3rd edn, Sydney: Allen & Unwin.

MacIntyre, S. 2001. 'The First Caucus', in J. Faulkner & S. MacIntyre, eds, *True Believers*, Sydney: Allen & Unwin, pp. 17–29.

Skulley, M. 2012. 'Industry Rounds on Wage Ruling', *The Australian Financial Review*, 2 February, p. 8.

Smith, A. 1776 (1904). *An Inquiry into the Nature and Causes of the Wealth of Nations*, E. Cannan, ed., Library of Economics and Liberty: www.econlib .org/library/Smith/smWN13.html (accessed 6 February 2012).

WEBSITE REFERENCES

ACTU: www.actu.org.au/.

CCH: www.cch.com.au/.

Fair Work Australia: www.fwa.gov.au/.

Fair Work Ombudsman: www.fairwork.gov.au/.

Unions Australia: www.unionsaustralia.com.au/.

Unions Australia: About Unions: Achievements by Australian Unions: www.unionsaustralia.com.au/ about.aspx/.

Workplace Express: www.workplaceexpress.com.au/.

FURTHER READING

Childs, F. 2006. *Research Note No. 2, 2006–07: Federal Government Advertising 2004–05*: www.aph.gov .au/library/pubs/rn/2006-07/07rn02.htm (accessed 6 February 2012).

Kitney, G. 2012. 'Libs' Internal Battle Heats Up', *The Australian Financial Review*, 2 February, p. 7.

O'Brien, S. 2011. 'WA Teachers Losing Pay', *Media Release*, 1 September: www.mediastatements.

wa.gov.au/Pages/WACabinetMinistersSearch .aspx?ItemId=143812&minister=O'Brien&admin= Barnett (accessed 7 February 2012).

Wynhausen, E. 2011. *The Short Goodbye*, Melbourne: Melbourne University Publishing.

IR REPORTING

Mark Skulley

In 2011, I was asked to participate in a panel discussion that was entitled The Death of the IR Round.

The theme was mostly right because, nowadays, only a handful of journalists cover IR full time. But the timing of the discussion was spectacularly wrong because it came just before Qantas management snuffed out disputes with three aviation unions by grounding its entire fleet. That was a global story covered by the BBC and *The New York Times*, as well as being Australia's biggest IR story since the 1998 waterfront dispute.

The IR round used to be one of the most coveted beats in any big news organisation. Back in the 1970s and early 80s, there were vastly more strikes, a bigger section of the workforce were union members, and national wage rises were set by a central workplace tribunal. But structural changes in the economy— more casual jobs, the shrinkage of traditional blue collar work, more working women, more independent contractors, and a shift to bargaining in individual workplaces—changed that. The IR round morphed into 'workplace' coverage as part of the osmotic shift by the major newspapers into lifestyle and social reportage from the mid-1980s onwards.

That's the archaeology of the recent past. It's worth recapping because many common notions—such as 'a fair day's pay for a fair day's work'—have deep roots in Australian public and private life. Debates about arbitration of industrial disputes, and striking a balance between labour and capital, pre-date Federation and have played a more prominent role than in otherwise comparable nations, such as the UK and the USA. Interest in workplace issues runs deep and wide in Australia, where there are about 10 million workers, plus many more retirees, the unemployed, and kids in school who will soon be heading out to work.

So, fewer journalists are covering work and working life, despite having wonderful new tools made possible through digital technology. But this case study argues that journalists still have to do the old stuff—such as reading a court list and court judgments—as well as following Twitter and social media to do the job. All reporting still begins with Rudyard Kipling's Six Honest Men (what and why and when and how and where and who). And it's worth remembering that 'IR' reporting is an amalgam of traditional rounds that include national and state politics, workplace politics, the law and courts, business and, at times, police.

An industrial dispute in 2012 involving the big Melbourne-based building company Grocon shows how new and old are intertwined. Grocon is run by a young businessman named Daniel Grollo. The company has had periodic disputes during the past decade with Australia's most militant union, the Construction Forestry Mining and Energy Union (CFMEU). Grocon said it could not allow the union to nominate safety representatives and shop stewards from outside its immediate workforce. The CFMEU alleged the company was nominating 'yes men' for delegate roles while employing a former nightclub bouncer as a safety manager.

The CFMEU blockaded four Grocon projects in Melbourne that were worth hundreds of millions of dollars. Legal strikes can only be taken during formal bargaining over new workplace agreements, meaning the blockades were illegal. The barricades were manned by CFMEU members, not Grocon workers, and remained in place in defiance of two injunctions from the Victorian Supreme Court. The company enlisted police support to get some workers back on site, but this failed after police horses were punched and police used capsicum spray to prevent four officers from being injured.

Grollo and CFMEU leadership agreed to private talks before the workplace tribunal, Fair Work Australia. The talks were due to start at 4.30pm on Thursday, 30 August. I wrote a draft page-one story, which left a space for the result of the talks. The parties gave brief comments on the way in to the meeting, and then a waiting game began against the deadline for the next day's newspapers. SMS messages to the parties in the talks went unanswered.

Finally, at about 9.40pm, Grollo emerged to say the talks had broken down because the CFMEU refused to first stop the blockade. The union responded by criticising Grollo for rejecting a truce recommended by Fair Work Australia president Iain Ross. I scrambled to come up with a new slant, using an iPhone to file for the final edition. A new version of the story was filed for the paper's website, along with a copy of the recommended truce that Grocon rejected. (Internet users love hyperlinks to core documents, and in IR the details always matter.)

But it was a mixture of new and old. The benefits of simply hanging about are often overlooked in the race to file web updates and to call contacts on their mobiles. In this case, the gossip outside Fair Work Australia was that the Victorian police had cancelled all leave and would have a massive presence at Grocon's Emporium site the following day in anticipation of trouble.

After getting home at 1am, it was down to the Emporium site at 6.30am in drizzling rain and cold. Thousands of unionists gathered and I took up position near a ute equipped with loudspeakers to follow what the union leaders said. I was packed shoulder-to-shoulder with protestors under an awning, and my first take on the iPhone was shaky as a persistent drip-drip fell on my head. Here's how it unfolded through my iPhone reports. The spelling mistakes and literals are real.

6.43am

A massive police contingent has assembled in the melb CBd this morning as Preparations are made to bust the blockade by construction workers at a grocon project.

Police have fenced off the myer empprium project, withhubdredofoffpicer inside the perimeter fence.

Outside are scores of mounted police and a observe helicopter overhead.

6.47am

Hundred of cfmeu members have been told that grocon will soon bring bus loads of employees to break the blockade which has been running for 10 days.

Cfmeu Victorian president ralph Edwards told hundred of building workers that it would be along campaign and they were not there to 'punch on' with the police.

'we're not here for custer's last stand,' mr Edwards told the crowd.

'we're here to give to give Daniel grollo's 'heroic employees' a bit of a hard time.

But mr Edwards appealed for the protesters to show disciple Saying that anyone looking to fight should 'piss off now'.

This basic copy was sent from an iPhone to a sub-editor in Sydney, where it was blended with other copy. I could have sent my own photos, but we had a proper photographer who filed using his laptop. Regular updates followed, which were posted straight away. A colleague worked the crowd, talking to unionists and police. I emailed a statement from Grocon to the news desk and another colleague attended a police press conference.

The upshot was that Grocon managed to get 30 employees on site but the blockade continued for another week. The company is now seeking more than $10 million in damages from the CFMEU, which has an elephantine memory for grudges.

This coverage was infinitely faster and easier due to digital technology. But that only relates to the reportage, the means of writing the story and publishing it. The full impact of digital technology has yet to hit IR reporting. This reporter must admit to having been a Luddite, but he has seen the light.

Working with a colleague who specialises in data mining led to a feature showing that one-fifth of the membership of the Australian Workers Union were still on the books, even thought they were not financial. This data was publicly available through Fair Work Australia, and was mashed with information on union membership from leaked ACTU records.

Digital technology is also great for fact-checking. A prominent player on a Brisbane picket line claimed to be a concerned citizen who was not aligned with construction unions. That might wash in the courts, but a quick internet search showed that the man had been praised in union journals as 'The Agitator' in an earlier dispute. Indeed, the union website included a photograph of him in a union T-shirt, wielding the tongs at a union sausage sizzle. But how to check his identity? We went to Facebook, where he had posted his own snap.

And this checking cuts both ways. The same building company protested when it was initially reported that a blockade on a big Brisbane project was costing $100 000 a day. However, Fair Work Australia records later showed the builder had given evidence that the real cost was $300 000 a day.

Another little-explored field, union finances, came to prominence through allegations of credit card abuse and misconduct at the Health Services Union (HSU). The biggest breaks in the HSU story came from old-style internal whistle-blowers giving primary information, such as credit card statements, to *The Sydney Morning Herald*. But social media kept the HSU story running hot, with crucial new information coming out first on Twitter and guerrilla websites.

So, the old IR round is brimming with stories, contrary to rumours of its demise. So far, the Australian union movement has outstripped the news media in the use of digital technology, let alone employers and the Coalition. The ACTU's Your Rights at Work campaign that helped Labor win the 2007 federal election was built on detailed voter research, and pushed through paid television commercials and social media. The grassroots campaign included identifying the marginal seats where union members lived and then door-knocking them individually.

The point being: use digital technology, but do not neglect direct personal contact. Like police rounds, IR reporting is often conducted at times of stress. And in such circumstances, it helps if you have previously had 'face time' with a source.

24

Investigative Journalism and Sports Reporting

ROGER PATCHING

INTRODUCTION

Sport plays a significant role in Australian society and culture. It has been suggested that sport defines the country's 'global image' (Stewart et al. 2004); while Harte and Whimpress contended that Australia's national heroes have, in the main, been connected with sport:

> The country can relate to a Don Bradman more than any politician: to a Dawn Fraser rather than to an artist; to athletes, swimmers, boxers, footballers of varying codes and even to a racehorse such as Phar Lap (2008, p. 1).

The colonial poet Henry Lawson referred to Australia as 'a land where sport is sacred' (cited in Lynch & Veal 2006, p. 261). Historian Donald Horne, in his seminal work *The Lucky Country*, observed that 'sport to many Australians is life and the rest is shadow' (1964, p. 40). Modern-day journalists and opinion writers have always been quick to remind their audiences, usually in discussing the latest sports star to fall from grace, of the important role sport plays in the national identity. Middendorp suggested that 'most Australians would agree that sport is not just good for us, it is our driving national passion, our true religion' (2010).

DISCUSSION

For a country with a relatively small population, to use a sporting cliché, Australia 'punches well above its weight' on the international sporting stage. But there is more to sports reporting than the chronicling of results, medal tallies and the like. There are also many scandals and controversies off the playing field—resulting from in-depth investigative reporting of both individuals and teams involved in the myriad of sports that draw the crowds to the major venues and to the couches in front of their televisions.

Sport fills countless space in the mainstream media. Special preview and review lift-out sections almost every day give wide coverage to horse racing. Specialist sports magazines line shelves in every newsagency. Sports stories can be heard or seen on almost every mainstream radio and television news bulletin. There are 16 sports channels on Australian subscription television (Leys 2012). Free-to-air channels pay vast sums for the rights to the popular sports, and well as the Olympic and Commonwealth Games and various sports' World Cups. The major national sporting events—such as the Melbourne Cup, and the AFL Grand Final, National Rugby League (NRL) Grand Final and their respective State of Origin series—make the list of the most-watched television programs every year. Three made the Top 10 in 2011: the Melbourne Cup was the sixth most-watched program, the AFL Grand Final was seventh, and the third State of Origin clash was eighth (*The Australian* 2011, p. 26).

Nothing fills the front pages of the nation's papers faster than sporting success, unexpected failure, scandal or controversy. While previous chapters of this book have contained lengthy and sound advice on how to access information from various sources for in-depth stories, the purpose of this chapter is to put some of that into a sporting context and discuss some aspects of information gathering and journalism ethics that pertain particularly to sports reporting. It also gives readers some tips on the major issues that sports journalists need to know about.

In the hierarchy of professional journalism, the sports department may be seen as what academic Raymond Boyle once characterised as the 'toy department' (2006), but there is no doubt sports coverage consistently fills more space in the daily media than any other specialist reporting round.

Some sports stories fall into your lap; others take a lot of digging, research and patience. The Melbourne Storm salary cap-rorting scandal of 2010 was not the result of exhaustive investigative journalism; but another salary cap scandal eight years earlier, involving the Sydney-based Canterbury Bankstown Bulldogs NRL team, did result from investigative journalism by *The Sydney Morning Herald*. The *Herald* revealed that the Bulldogs had breached the salary cap by about $1.5 million over two seasons (McClymont et al. 2002). The competition front-runners at the time (late in the season), were stripped of 37 premiership points, guaranteeing them the dreaded 'wooden spoon' for finishing last, and fined $500 000 (Davies et al. 2002). The story originated from the reporters being leaked club documents that detailed the extra payments to key players (McClymont & Davies 2002).

DEVELOPING AND MAINTAINING CONTACTS

Central to all major (and minor) investigative pieces are contacts—they are the lifeblood of all good journalism. The all-important contacts in sport include the players, their managers, the club or association management, the umpires or referees, and the team doctors, trainers, coaches and physiotherapists. Even the fans—commenting on a story online, or talking to a reporter at a game or over a drink afterwards—can point journalists in the direction of a major story. From day one on the job, reporters need to start collecting people's contact details for future reference.

Nurturing contacts is an ongoing challenge. It might be a former school friend you later discover has an important position in a team or part of a sporting management group who tips you off to what becomes a big story. It was a former member of the Pakistani cricket team's management that led *News of the World* investigative journalist Mazher Mahmood to the match-fixing scandal of 2010 that ultimately led to the jailing of three Pakistani cricketers. The renowned journalist, who uses various forms of entrapment to snare his victims, said rumours had abounded for years that some Pakistani players and officials were in league with bookmakers in India, but it was a simple tip-off that led him to the players' manager/'fixer' (Mahmood 2011).

The chief sports columnist for *The Sydney Morning Herald*, Richard Hinds, believes the importance of contacts in helping break major stories is fundamental to modern-day journalism, 'particularly in an age where cyberspace allows armchair pundits to blog/tweet opinions that are, most often, based merely on opinion' (2012). Hinds says this can be a challenge: 'The increased difficulty in gaining first hand access to administrators, coaches and athletes makes the cultivation of inside contacts harder, yet at the same time even more valuable' (2012). He adds that contact with those possessing 'insider knowledge', or those in authority, is what separates journalism from the many opinion-based blogs.

The extra challenge in this environment relates to the propensity of some sports journalists to regard themselves as part of the sports community they cover, rather than independent operators paid to write, analyse and report. Being the journalistic equivalent of a cheerleader for football, swimming, rugby, netball or cricket will compromise a journalist's capacity to see issues around the team—and the sport—objectively. Sports journalists who are uncritical fans, or who get too close to the sports stars they cover, are sometimes prone to ignoring negative stories. This is why some of the more incisive pieces of investigative sports reporting have come from outside the ranks of sports reporters.

A compelling example is the ABC's *Four Corners* exposé on sexual scandals within the NRL that aired in 2009. Although the program's starting point was a series of stories that appeared in Sydney's daily papers, *Four Corners* managed to reveal new dimensions to the allegations. The reporter was Walkley Award-winning investigative journalist Sarah Ferguson, who not only took the time to unearth the new allegations but also had no fear of 'burning' any NRL contacts.

Similarly, *The Age* investigative journalists Nick McKenzie and Richard Baker scrutinised the Victorian racing industry in 2012 with a series of allegations about corruption and race fixing. Once they started the revelations—again on ABC's *Four Corners*—the racing writers who had not written about these allegations were obliged to follow them up.

RESEARCH AND STATISTICS

Successful journalists are able to research relevant information quickly, either from their own files, or by knowing where to get it—be that from a contact, their organisation's online information database, or any one of the thousands of sports-related websites. When Michael Clarke was heading towards that memorable triple century in Sydney in early January 2012, the cricket broadcaster, the Nine Network, kept ticking off the milestones the young Aussie captain was achieving as they rolled by. Access to accurate statistics was vital for their ongoing coverage.

Much sporting coverage is about statistics—the method used to gauge one performance against another. The sporting journalist needs to know where to get their hands on the important (and sometimes little-known) statistics that will set their story apart from another's coverage. In the electronic era, the journalist's task is made much easier by the existence of online sites that are dedicated to the collection and interpretation of sport-specific data. For example, the official AFL website provides readily accessible data that covers not only the competition, but also a wealth of information covering both teams and individual players.

Richard Hinds believes that statistics should be used to emphasise or underline a point, and not be the source of the story itself. He prefers to use statistics 'to further justify a judgment made with your own eyes' (2012).

But there is another important role for statistics—as a genuine tool for measuring sporting talent. One of the most revealing pieces of investigative journalism in the past decade was Michael Lewis' *Moneyball*, which took a fresh look at US baseball by focusing on the success of one baseball team. As Lewis wrote: 'It began, really, with an innocent question: how did one of the poorest teams in baseball, the Oakland Athletics, win so many games?' (2003, p. 1). Finding the answer to this innocent question illustrated the vital role of applying different statistical measurements to reveal players who had the most efficient skills in the league. Lewis subtitled the book 'the art of winning an unfair game', and he documented how this creative approach to evaluating performances led Oakland to recruit players with particular skills at lower prices, while increasing their success. Baseball, like cricket, is rich in statistics so the basic material was all there. But it took a journalist posing a simple question to reveal how important those statistics can be (for more on the use of statistics, see Chapter 8).

UNDERSTANDING YOUR STORY

The importance of Australian sport means that stories centring on sporting figures will often migrate from their usual spot at the end of the news bulletins or the back pages to the front. The author's doctoral research is analysing newspaper coverage of the private lives of five leading Australian cricketers, from Don Bradman to Michael Clarke. When Clarke, at the time the national vice captain, broke up with his bikini-model fiancée, Lara Bingle, the story ran for about a fortnight. In eight capital city newspapers from Brisbane to Adelaide, the private life of Australia's cricket captain-in-waiting rated more than 230 mentions in 13 days—including almost 130 news stories and about 75 opinion pieces or features. That's more than five pieces (aside from the ongoing news-related coverage) a day, to say nothing of the broadcast and online coverage (Patching 2012). This extra-curricular coverage only increases a sportsperson's profile, and arguably adds to the audience interest in their on-field exploits.

An integral part of all journalism is interviewing. In sport, interviewing poses unique problems for journalists. Audiences have long been used to seeing sporting superstars giving monosyllabic responses. Nowadays, however, when sports, teams and athletes have sponsors, more often than not the sporting celebrity will be coached on how to handle interviews and how to avoid controversial answers. But feature or investigative stories require interviewing to much greater depth. Getting beneath the superficial veneer of the athlete's comfort zone takes patience. Often, sporting celebrities will only 'open up' to journalists they respect, and who they know are not just after a quick headline but are genuinely interested in their views. Gaining their respect takes time.

It is easy to interview sports stars when they have just won a championship or an Olympic gold medal. More tact is needed when their sporting dream has been shattered by a poor performance or an injury, or they have been cut from the team. The athlete may have been given a 'rough time' by the media and they may not be in the mood to talk to reporters. You need to convince them, perhaps through a third party such as their manager or coach, that you really are interested in their side of the story and want to give them an opportunity to explain what's brought about the downturn in their form, or how long the injury might keep them away from competition.

Major journalism pieces require a mix of facts, opinions and anecdotes. It is the individual reporter's choice how they weave the various components into their stories. Anecdotes—such as recalling a particular incident in a game or backgrounding a particular memorable result—are commonly used to begin major sporting features. But facts are still the primary focus, supplemented by the opinions of all those involved in the story.

Investigative journalism applied to sport requires all these elements, but it also requires an understanding of the audience for a story: sport, in its simplest form of winning and losing, is always interesting to fans of the winners and losers. But sports journalism draws a bigger audience when it peels back the layers to reveal how our sports really operate and the role our sports stars play in the billion-dollar business. As we have seen, there are plenty of news consumers who are interested in jockey Danny Nikolic, footballer Ben Cousins and swimmer Nick D'Arcy—not just because they are talented sportsmen, but rather because they have lives outside sport that reveal human desires and failings. It is around such frailties that some meaningful sports investigation can begin. For example, Cousins' drug predicament could become the basis for investigating recreational drug use in Australian sport. Or the brawl with a fellow swimmer that saw D'Arcy omitted from the 2008 Olympic team could become the starting point for a story on how sporting administrators deal with the impact of such incidents on team dynamics.

Whatever the issue, journalists undertaking an investigation into sport still need to observe the basics. It is valuable to consider sport through the prism of some of the key issues.

KEY ISSUES

There are a number of ongoing issues that sports reporters must keep accurate, up-to-date files on—be they actual newspaper clippings or official reports, or digital versions kept on USBs or portable hard drives, or simply a list of the URLs where the information can be readily accessed. Sporting injuries, sports personalities as role models, drugs in sport, unsporting behaviour, discrimination in any form, sport and politics, the business aspects of sport and gambling are all areas that provide major stories for whatever platform you're filing for.

SPORTING INJURIES

Elite sports competitors drive their bodies to the limit, and will be injured from time to time. A basic knowledge of the most common forms of injury in a particular sport (or where to get the information quickly) is essential for a journalist to be able to gauge the likely length of an athlete's recovery, and whether it is season-ending, or worse, career-ending. Some club officials and coaches will try to downplay or disguise the extent of their athlete's injury for some competitive advantage. Being sceptical about recovery and rehabilitation can be a useful approach in such circumstances.

Another area that impacts elite sport is depression, often referred to as the 'black dog'. One in five Australians will experience a mental illness at some time in their lives (Mindframe website), and for many athletes this is after they retire. NRL greats Andrew Johns (Linnell 2008), Mat Rogers (*The Gold Coast Bulletin* 2006) and Wally Lewis (*ABC News* 2008) are among those who have publicly admitted to battles with depression. Four-time Olympic gold medallist Libby Trickett told a Sunday paper that her entire family had had a decade-long struggle with depression (Marcus 2010). The problems can be a legitimate reason for an athlete's change in behaviour and performance at critical times.

ROLE MODELS

Sports stars, like it or not, are role models. Youngsters look up to their idols and expect them to behave off the field the way they usually perform on the field—to set an example of the right way to play, and live. Sports columnist with *The Australian* Patrick Smith noted that sporting icons have no option but to be role models—'Their choice is whether they are good ones or bad ones' (Smith 2005). The Nine Network's Ken Sutcliffe, one of the doyens of sports reporting in Australia, had a similar view: 'if you are an elite sports star, reaping the financial benefits and other opportunities that your ability has provided, it is a given—you are a role model: it comes with the territory' (Sutcliffe & Heads 2009, p. 237).

The private lives of sporting stars are seen as being 'in the public interest' for the tabloid media. There has been a serious debate UK as to what constitutes 'the public interest' as opposed to what the public 'might be interested in'. It is an ongoing ethical debate that often involves sporting personalities: how much privacy do they deserve? A useful guide when investigating the behaviour of sporting identities is to ask who is most affected by that behaviour: only the individual? Their family? Their club? If there is a wider impact, then there is probably a legitimate reason to investigate further.

ILLEGAL DRUGS IN SPORT

The use of illegal drugs in sport is one of the biggest ongoing scandals worldwide. Olympians lose gold medals, and a winner can be stripped of their Tour de France title after failing a drug test. Footballers of all codes are not exempt. In Australia in recent years, footballers at the top of their respective codes— Ben Cousins (AFL), Andrew Johns (NRL) and Wendell Sailor (NRL and rugby union)—have all been exposed as drug takers. When Australia's most successful bowler, Shane Warne, admitted on the eve of the cricket World Cup in South Africa in 2003 that he had tested positive to taking a diuretic, there would have been a scramble among the reporters in the touring party to find out what 'taking a diuretic' meant. Warne claimed his mother had given him the pill for 'cosmetic reasons' (*ABC News* 2003), but he was still banned from playing for a year. Diuretics are banned by international sporting bodies because of their potential to conceal performance-enhancing substances (*The Gold Coast Bulletin* 2003). Six months before the 2012 London Olympics, British authorities announced they would be analysing more than 6250 samples during the Games, more than any other Games (Hanna 2012).

The taking of drugs in sport in its many forms—from performance-enhancing substances to the taking of so-called 'recreational' drugs—is a continuing story as some athletes strive for that extra, illegal edge against their competitors. Keep the Australian Sports Anti-doping Authority (ASADA) website on your 'favourites' list for the latest news in the fight against illegal drugs, plus reports and general background. The World Anti-doping Authority website is also worth a regular visit.

The danger for the sports journalist trying to extract a story from this particular area is often the issue of confidentiality: most of the major Australian sporting codes will never identify those who are in any way associated with the taint of drugs. The other complicating factor is the burden of proof. Sophisticated testing can reveal many things and sometimes, despite numerous negative tests, do little to eradicate the suggestion of being a drug cheat. Cycling legend Lance Armstrong fits neatly in to this category. Despite a record consecutive seven Tour de France victories, and numerous clean drug tests, the US Anti-Doping Agency banned Armstrong for life in August 2012. Armstrong denied the allegations until confessing to US talk show host Oprah Winfrey in 2013.

UNSPORTING BEHAVIOUR

Unsporting behaviour on or off the field will always be a big story and give rise to potential investigative pieces. Sometimes it is the fans who provide the story, such as the behaviour of visiting fans on the Gold Coast at the 2011 Boxing Day A-League soccer clash, when the local team, Gold Coast United (at that stage bottom of the table) defeated the defending premiers and rivals from 'up the motorway', the Brisbane Roar, 1-0 (Pangallo 2011). Roar fans let off orange (the team's dominant jersey colour) flares and brawled with local fans after the game, as outnumbered police struggled to contain the violence (Pangallo et al. 2011).

DISCRIMINATION

Discrimination is covered in most sports' codes of conduct, which ban vilification in any form, be it racist, sexual, religious or ethnic. Racist sledging became the sports scandal of the 2007–08 Australian summer when Indian spinner Harbhajan Singh was reported for sledging Andrew Symonds, allegedly calling him a 'monkey'. He was later cleared after days of front-page tour-threatening coverage (Gould, 2008). A racial storm engulfed the NRL showpiece event, the State of Origin series, in 2010 when former star Andrew Johns was forced to quit as assistant coach of the New South Wales team after he made a racist remark about Queensland Aboriginal star Greg Inglis (Badel 2010). There have also been racist issues with the AFL, and with players in the English Premier Football League.

Women are discriminated against in a number of sporting contexts. Their games are given scant coverage on free-to-air or subscription television and—unless they are a big name, such as grand slam tennis winner Sam Stosur, golfer Karrie Webb, former athlete Cathy Freeman, or Beijing Olympics triple gold medallist Stephanie Rice—they will struggle to attract sponsorship dollars. The latest statistics available suggest coverage of women's sport accounts for 2 per cent of total sports broadcasting on television, 1.4 per cent on radio and 10.7 per cent in newspapers (Broderick 2010).

Sexual harassment is another serious issue with a sporting application. Coaches are particularly vulnerable because of the close physical and emotional relationships they develop with their charges. Fans and parents can also be guilty of discrimination—a Sydney junior soccer player's dad was banned from the game after yelling 'you should have been wiped out during the war' at parents from a rival Jewish club (Dale 2008).

SPORT AND POLITICS

It is a cliché that sport and politics don't mix, but they do. Politics in sport and surrounding sporting activities has a long history. In Australia, the infamous bodyline cricket series in 1932–33 strained diplomatic relations with England, the 'Mother Country'. Most modern Olympic Games have had their share of political dramas, from as early as the 1936 Games in Berlin that saw embarrassment to Hitler's 'Aryan superiority' when African American athlete Jesse Owens won four gold medals (*The Weekend Australian* 2004). There have been boycotts of various Games, including Australia's first Olympics in Melbourne in 1956; the boycotting by some Western countries of the 1980 Games in Moscow; and the reciprocation by the Soviet Bloc in boycotting the 1984 Los Angeles Games. Politics has impacted on cricket in 2003 and 2007 when pressure was placed on the Australian team not to play in Zimbabwe in protest at that country's dictator, Robert Mugabe (Milne 2007).

Terrorism has also been a danger, ranging from the massacre of 11 Israeli athletes at the 1972 Munich Olympics *The Weekend Australian* 2004) to the 2009 attack on the Sri Lankan cricket team in Pakistan, which saw six policemen and two civilians killed and seven members of the Sri Lankan team injured (*The Courier Mail* 2009). A major part of the budget of any Olympic or Commonwealth Games is spent on security. Various aspects of how sport and politics intersect—even government funding of major sporting facilities—are potential topics for investigation.

SPORT IS BIG BUSINESS

Huge amounts are paid for the television rights to major sports, and the high Australian (male) achievers in each sport are paid handsomely for their endeavours. *Business Review Weekly* annually publishes a list of the top 50 Australian sports earners. Topping the list in 2010 was basketballer Andrew Bogut, who earned $13 million, followed by former World Moto-GP champion Casey Stoner with $9.5 million. Formula One driver Mark Webber finished third on $9 million (2011–12). To put their earnings into perspective, the average Australian in 2011 was earning a little more than $53 000 a year (Jenkin 2011). Gold Coast golfer Adam Scott won a four-day tournament in the USA that August and pocketed A$1.35 million (*The Sydney Morning Herald* 2011)—earning more in four days than the 'average Australian' would earn in 25 years.

Access to events for the media is also a news story because television networks guard their exclusive rights—especially at high-profile international events. There are any number of surveys that provide news stories about sport. The ABS regularly surveys participation rates in sport and other aspects of the business of sport, such as how many people volunteer to help run sporting clubs.

GAMBLING

Illegal gambling on cricket has already been mentioned. But legal gambling is big business too, hence the large lift-out sections in the daily newspapers devoted to results and previews of various race meetings around the country. According to *The Economist*, Australians are the world's worst gamblers, with each person over the age of 17 losing an average of $1300 a year (2011). There's also the issue of individual sportspeople gambling on games, which has seen both the AFL and NRL take action against players; and the issue of gambling agencies sponsoring sporting teams (and having their name or logo appearing on the club jersey) and venues.

On the eve of the 2012 Olympic year, the UK's Olympics Minister Hugh Robertson warned that the activities of illegal betting syndicates trying to fix events by bribing athletes was the biggest threat to the reputation of the London Games (Caroe 2012). A few months earlier the father of Wayne Rooney, one of soccer's best-known players, and eight others, including the soccer star's uncle, were arrested for their part in a betting scam (Davenport 2011). Wayne Rooney senior was later found to have no case to answer. Cricket match fixing, horserace fixing and numerous other examples of so-called 'exotic' betting have become significant stories during the past 15 years.

CONCLUSION

This chapter looked at the importance of sport to Australians and to the Australian media, and highlighted some of the areas that regularly provide stories for the back pages of the nation's newspapers (and air-time on radio and television). It has also looked at the major areas and issues that will often appear on the front pages or as in-depth features inside the papers, or in their weekend glossy magazines, as well as providing stories for the major daily and weekly current affairs radio and television programs. There will always be room for a good sports story.

A sport story that highlights the erosion of a game—or player's high standards—because of gambling, drugs or sex will always make a splash in the media. And that is because most of us have an idealised view of sport and competition—that it is pure and its participants are equally untarnished by human frailties. The truth is somewhat more prosaic than that and such moments represent the basis of an investigative journalist's approach to sport.

QUESTIONS TO CONSIDER

1 Identify several key areas in sport where an investigative journalist may find a useful lead.

2 You are a general reporter but you think there are some stories in sport that the sports reporters aren't getting. How and where would you develop contacts to help you research those stories?

3 What represents the best test of public interest in a sportsperson's private life?

4 How would you go about identifying and researching a positive story or series of stories on women's sport in your local area? What are the issues you need to think about and how would you deal with them?

TASK

1 Think about a sports story you have read, heard or watched recently. What is the larger issue behind it? (Money, draft picks, drugs, etc.) How would you construct an investigative feature around that larger issue?

REFERENCES

ABC. 2009. 'Code of Silence', *Four Corners*, 11 May, transcript: www.abc.net.au/4corners/content/2009/s2567972.htm/.

ABC. 2012. 'Inside Mail', *Four Corners*, 7 August: www.abc.net.au/4corners/stories/2012/08/05/3561019.htm (accessed 25 February 2013).

ABC News. 2003. 'Warne Admits to Second Offence', 25 February: www.abc.net.au/news/2003-02-25/warne-admits-to-second-offence/1221254 (accessed 14 January 2012).

ABC News. 2008. 'I Thought About Ending It: Lewis', 19 February: www.abc.net.au/news/stories/2008/02/19/2166233.htm (accessed 19 February 2008).

The Australian. 2011. 'The Year in Television', 28 November.

Badel, P. 2010. 'Racial Storm Engulfs Origin', *The (Qld) Sunday Mail*, 13 June, p. 3.

Boyle, R. 2006. *Sports Journalism: Context and Issues*, London: Sage.

Broderick, E. 2010. 'Women in Sport Hit the Grass Ceiling', *The Sydney Morning Herald*, 21 May, p. 13.

Business Review Weekly. 2011–12. 'Top 50 Sports Earners', 15 December 2011–26 January 2012.

Caroe, L. 2012. 'Olympics Organisers Fear Betting Scandal', *The (London) Sun*, 1 January: www.thesun.co.uk/sol/homepage/news/4031635/Olympics-organisers-br-fear-betting-scandal.html (accessed 12 January 2012).

The Courier Mail. 2009. 'Ambushed: Terror Declares War on Sport', 4 March, p. 1.

Dale, A. 2008. 'Soccer Dad Banned for Anti-Jew Slur', *The Daily Telegraph*, 28 February: www.news.com.au/dailytelegraph/story/0,22049,23286968-5001021,00.html (accessed 28 February 2008).

Davenport, J. 2011. 'Rooney's Father and Uncle Held in Betting Scam', *London Evening Standard*, 6 October, p. 1.

Davies, A., McClymont, K. & Walter, B. 2002, August 24–25. 'The Day League's Heart Broke', *Sydney Morning Herald (weekend edition)*, p. 1.

The Economist. 2011. 'The Biggest Losers', 16 May: www.economist.com/blogs/dailychart/2011/05/gambling (accessed 2 February 2012).

The Gold Coast Bulletin. 2003. 'Doctor: Diuretic Can Mask', 12 February, p. 4.

The Gold Coast Bulletin. 2006. 'Mat Fears the Black Dog's Bite', 16 February, p. 1.

Gould, R. 2008. 'India Fans the Flames', *MX (Brisbane)*, 12 February, p. 13.

Hanna, L. 2012. 'London 2012 Anti-doping Lab Opens as It Prepares to Fight Olympic Drug Cheats', *The (London) Mirror*, 19 January: www.mirror.co.uk/news/london-2012-olympic-games/2012/01/19/london-2012-anti-doping-lab-opens-as-it-prepares-to-fight-drug-cheats-115875-23707843 (accessed 21 January 2012).

Harte, C. & Whimpress, B. 2008. *The Penguin History of Australian Cricket*, Melbourne: Penguin.

Hinds, R. 2012. Email to author, 8 May.

Horne, D. 1964. *The Lucky Country*, Harmondsworth: Penguin.

Jenkin, C. 2011. 'Average Weekly Pay Packet Hits $1000', *Herald Sun*, 14 May: www.heraldsun.com.au/news/national/average-weekly-pay-packet-hits-1000/story-e6frf716-1226055693989 (accessed 21 September 2011).

Lewis, M. 2003. *Moneyball: The Art of Winning an Unfair Game*, New York: W.W. Norton.

Leys, N. 2012. 'Summer of Sport', *The Australian*, 11 January: www.theaustralian.com.au/media/summer-of-sport/story-fnab9kgi-1226241633892 (accessed 11 January 2012).

Linnell, G. 2008. 'Andrew Johns Talks of his "Dark Places" of Depression', *The Daily Telegraph*, 6 September: www.news.com.au/dailytelegraph/story/0,22049,24301659-5001021,00.html (accessed 6 September 2008).

Lynch, R. & Veal, A. 2006. *Australian Leisure*, fourth edn, Frenchs Forest: Pearson.

Mahmood, M. 2011. 'How I Broke the Spot-fix Scandal', *The Sunday Times*, republished in *The Australian*, 7 November, p. 41.

Marcus, C. 2010. 'Libby Trickett Tells of Family's Battle with Depression', *The Sunday Telegraph*, 5 September: www.dailytelegraph.com.au/national/im-fighting-the-blues-libby-trickett-tells-of-familys-battl-with-depression/story-e6freuzr-1225914300066 (accessed 17 May 2011).

McClymont, K. & Davies, A. 2002. 'Bulldogs Bust the Bank to Stay On Top', *The (Weekend) Sydney Morning Herald*, 17–18 August, p. 1.

McClymont, K., Davies, A. & Masters, R. 2002. 'NRL Salary Cap Crisis: The Dogs are Barking', *The Sydney Morning Herald*, 19 August, p. 19.

Middendorp, C. 2010. 'Forget Drug Cheats, Sport Stars Fail the Other Sort of Dope Test', *The Sydney Morning Herald*: www.smh.com.au/opinion/society-and-culture/forget-drug-cheats-sport-stars-fail-the-other-sort-of-dope-test-20100909-1533g.html (accessed 10 September 2010).

Milne, G. 2007. 'You're Out: Downer Bans Aussie Cricket Team from Zimbabwe Tour', *The (Qld) Sunday Mail*, 13 May, p. 1.

Pangallo, M. 2011. 'Trouble Flares as Local Soccer Derby Becomes Euro Football Nasty', *The Gold Coast Bulletin*, 27 December, p. 3.

Pangallo, M., Tuttiett, H. & Elder, J. 2011. 'Flare Idiots Hooli-gones', *The Gold Coast Bulletin*, 28 December, p. 4.

Patching, R. 2012. Incomplete PhD thesis, Bond University.

Smith, P. 2005. 'Good or Bad, Footballers Must Accept They are Role Models', *The Australian*, 29 July, p. 33.

Stewart, B., Nicholson, M., Smith, A. & Westerbeek, H. 2004. *Australian Sport: Better by Design?*, Abington: Routledge.

Sutcliffe, K. & Heads, I. 2009. *The Wide World of Ken Sutcliffe*, Crows Nest, Sydney: Allen and Unwin.

The Sydney Morning Herald. 2011. 'Adam Scott Wins by Four Shots', 8 August: www.smh.com.au/sport/golf/adam-scott-wins-by-four-shots-20110808-1ii1v.html (accessed 8 August 2011).

The Weekend Australian. 2004. 'State & Politics', 7–8 August.

WEBSITE REFERENCES

ABS: www.abs.gov.au/.

Australian Football League: www.afl.com.au/.

Australian Sports Anti-doping Authority (ASADA): www.asada.gov.au/[REMOVED HYPERLINK FIELD].

Mindframe: www.mindframe-media.info/.

World Anti-doping Authority: www.wada-ama.org/.

FURTHER READING

Craddock, R. 2010. 'Big Risk to Pick Yuppie Michael Clarke', *Herald Sun*, 30 December: www.heraldsun.com.au/sport/the-ashes/big-risk-to-pick-yuppie-michael-clarke/story-fn67wltq-1225979024765 (accessed 30 December 2010).

HARNESS RACING EXPOSÉ

Caro Meldrum-Hanna

Harness racing in Australia has been tarnished by allegations of corruption, doping and race fixing since its inception. Known colloquially as the 'red hots', the trotting community is particularly passionate about their sport, and in recent times many have worked to clean up its image.

In New South Wales, prize money for race wins was earmarked to leap in 2011. In response, Harness Racing New South Wales, the regulator of the sport in the state, sharpened its focus on integrity.

Come August 2011, the regulator released an unexpected and brief media release announcing that two of its stewards, the police of the sport, had tendered their resignations and that an internal investigation was under way. There was a brief and vague reference to possible misconduct. No more details were given.

My task, as an investigative reporter, was to find out why the stewards had resigned, what the possible misconduct could be, and what the regulator was investigating. At this point, Harness Racing New South Wales was a closed shop. Management were not talking, and no more details were being given to the media.

Faced with an information vacuum, I needed to find people who would talk. I spent time at paceways talking to locals, speaking off the record at first. Suspicions were high; the industry was awash with rumours. Allegations of horse doping and race fixing began to mount. Names were mentioned but nothing was concrete. Races and paceways were mentioned. Some tip-offs proved wildly off the mark; others more useful.

Some individuals were more cautious, refusing to meet me at the track. I was an outsider and I was investigating something many didn't want exposed. They didn't want to be seen talking to a journalist. Some conversations had to occur in private and out of eyeshot and earshot. Gaining the trust of people inside harness racing circles was no easy task, but their cooperation was vital. Research was key. These people were my main source of information, and I needed to know what I was talking about if they were going to talk to me.

Only a few sports journalists were following the story and no one had pieced together what was going on. Once I had found reliable sources and allegations were corroborated, the conversations continued for several weeks. Each time, crumbs of new information came to light. I was told to look at particular tracks and particular races where some believed doped horses had won. I then matched the dates of race meets to which stewards were on duty. How had they missed doped horses? Why didn't they swab them? Were swabs ever taken? Or could the stewards be complicit in a doping and gambling ring? It seemed like a wild allegation at first.

When I began to collect data on races meets, times and places, the names of two stewards consistently popped up as being on duty at the allegedly suspicious race meets—and they were the two stewards who had recently resigned. The picture suddenly grew much clearer.

This was the breakthrough point—the moment you realise your journalistic hunch is right. The moment you realised you could be on to a big story.

The next step was to approach the regulator with my account and what I believed the scam was, how it was operating, and who was involved. I needed to corroborate and confirm. Most importantly, I needed to separate fact from fiction and get it on the record. Once the interview with Harness Racing New South Wales was filmed, the final pieces of the puzzle fell in to place. The two stewards who recently resigned were the alleged runners of an underground doping and race-fixing ring.

The task of telling how the alleged scam worked was complex. There were legal restrictions on what we could report and how we could report it. Television is a challenging medium when it comes to telling a story with no visual evidence or archive footage of people and places. Pieces to camera were incorporated to reveal and punctuate information, and the cameraman shot a race meet for an entire day, riding on the track and entering the stables. The editor added effects to certain visuals, injecting mood and tone.

The best way to tell the story was to follow the process of discovery. Piece by piece, information was revealed on camera. Following the story, New South Wales police continued investigating. Several months later, charges have been laid against several people allegedly involved in the scam. These cases are now before the courts.

25

Publishing Your Work

LAWRIE ZION

INTRODUCTION

Why develop multimedia skills? Addressing this question in the *Walkley Magazine*, journalist Kimberley Porteous offered four main reasons: it empowers journalists to produce better journalism; mastering new story-telling forms is both inspiring and exciting; smart news websites stand out and are likely to draw bigger audiences; and, at a time when newsrooms are shrinking, a broad skill base will make you more employable (Porteous 2009).

Following Porteous' lead, this chapter takes as a given that these days journalists need to be able to work in a multimedia environment, irrespective of their specific roles or skills. We'll also assume that the more skills you have, the better. What needs fleshing out, however, is how all journalists can develop a mindset that will foster thinking about how the stories they tell can take full advantage of the changing media-scape.

WHAT IS MULTIMEDIA JOURNALISM?

The focus here will be on the questions that underpin all of this. What exactly do we mean by 'multimedia journalism'? Which kinds of stories best fit which different media formats? How can text, audio, photos, video and graphics be combined to enhance the stories you want to tell, or even to develop new kinds of story-telling? And how should we think about audiences, especially given the opportunities for interactivity and user-generated content?

One of the challenges of writing about multimedia journalism is that technology has advanced so quickly, journalists have been forced to come up with a new language to describe new ways of telling stories (Wenger & Potter 2008, p. 2). Consequently, a number of terms have evolved to describe emerging journalistic forms and practices in the digital age. In this chapter, the term 'multimedia journalism' is used as a catch-all to describe what otherwise might be referred to as 'convergence', 'cross-platform', and 'multi-platform journalism'.

A simple definition of multimedia is 'the integration of text, images, sound, video, and graphics to tell a journalistic story' (Berkey-Gerard 2009). It follows that a straightforward way of understanding multimedia journalism is: 'the practice of gathering news and reporting it across multimedia' (Wilkinson et al. 2009, p. 2). In a literal sense, multimedia journalism pre-dates online journalism. As Mark Deuze reminds us: 'journalists in for example public broadcasting organizations such as the BBC in the UK have always worked in a multiple media capacity, and there are plenty of examples of "combo-journalism" in the mid-20th century when newspaper journalists were also expected to wield a photo camera' (2004, p. 143).

But the internet is the main force behind multimedia journalism. It enables the 'expansion of the amount of news coverage available well beyond the limits of the newspaper and broadcast news holes'; provides opportunities to distribute almost any type of content; and allows interactivity so that users can experience content differently, as well as changing and contributing to it, and faster and more frequent updating than in any other medium (Wilkinson et al. 2009, p. 3). Perhaps the most important of these in practical terms 'is the opportunity to provide any combination of text, pictures, graphics, audio and video' (Wilkinson et al. 2009, p. 3).

For some time, much of what was understood as multimedia consisted of additions to a print story that were included in the online version of the same masthead. And different publications might have different definitions of what constitutes multimedia. *The New York Times* website, for example, classifies any non-textual stand-alone presentation as 'multimedia'; therefore a video story is classified as multimedia, but a single photograph that accompanies a written story is not. As Jacobson says: 'The characteristic shared by all of these packages is that they could not appear as-is in the printed newspaper' (2012, p. 4).

Multimedia journalism isn't just the repurposing of content for different platforms. It has also led to the emergence of entirely new ways of telling stories, such as the nonlinear format, in which the information presented in each medium is complementary. 'Nonlinear' means that instead of a rigidly structured single narrative, stories are designed to give users the choice of how to navigate through the elements of a story according to their own interests (Stevens 2011b; Grabowicz 2012).

Multimedia stories can be driven by anything from a single reporter—think the 'backpack' or 'multiskilled' journalist—to journalists working as part of a large team. In the case of the former, a journalist will gather all the main ingredients—such as video clips, still photos, audio and other information—and then edit and produce the story. In the latter, a story editor or producer assigns a team that may include a reporter, a photographer, a videographer and a graphic artist to deliver elements of a story that are assembled and edited to their direction (Stevens 2011a; Wilkinson et al. 2009, pp. 3–4).

The most important role of the journalist in a multimedia environment, however, is 'to be able to look at a situation and determine what elements are needed for the various ways that might be used to disseminate the story' (Wilkinson et al. 2009). p. 7.

THE 'MULTIMEDIA MINDSET'

But it's not just about how many pieces of equipment or what software you can master. Whether working alone or as part of a team, a more important attribute is what's come to be known as a 'multimedia mindset' (Wenger & Potter 2008; Wilkinson et al. 2009; Currie 2010; Quinn 2005). This means both a capacity to understand how different media can complement each other to create new kinds of story-telling, and an 'audience first' appreciation of who the story is for and how it might be consumed.

This is more challenging than it used to be. The changing habits of what Jay Rosen famously described as 'the people formerly known as the audience' (Rosen 2006) have been the subject of much debate. With research constantly illuminating how media consumption is being transformed, the very concept of 'audience' is becoming harder to pin down, and more complicated to audit.

In one sense, demonstrating the uptake of online media is relatively straightforward. For example, a recent survey found that more than three-quarters of adult internet users in Australia said that the internet was an important or very important source of news to them, while fewer than half the respondents said the same thing about newspapers (Ewing & Thomas 2011). A 2011 Nielsen report found that:

> Australians continue to increase their consumption of rich media content online, with 71% accessing audio or video content online in 2010 and 35% doing so on a weekly basis. The proportion of those consuming video content online increased from 41% in 2009 to 60% in 2010.

Of greater significance, however, is the question of *how* users actually connect with multimedia journalism. One of the most profound recent shifts in the media is the extent to which journalism has turned into a conversation where engagement with audiences shapes the quality of the journalism. According to Currie:

> News organisations that have built highly engaged communities have a natural support network for their journalism. They are positioned to get better stories, find more informed sources, achieve greater accuracy in their reporting, and have a more loyal audience base (2010, p. 122).

The public used to be the audience that received the completed story. 'For the new media model, journalism should be a more co-operative project of citizens and journalists' (Ward 2011, p. 214).

Even when users aren't involved in the creation of content, their changing consumption habits still need to be grappled with. The challenge now is not just to find audiences and hold on to them, but also to figure out which format or formats they're going to use to digest the content you're producing.

This is no simple matter. Each technological advance has added a new layer of complexity—and a new set of players—in connecting that content to consumers and advertisers. By 2011, nearly half of all Americans (47 per cent) were getting some form of local news on a mobile device (Pew Research Center's Project for Excellence in Journalism 2011). One consequence of this is that content creators have to factor in not just which applications will work in which browsers, but how complex forms of story-telling will render on a smartphone screen.

Then there is the issue of attention span (are you still with me?). What are the best ways to engage with audiences that snack and scan for information? One concern has been that narrative story-telling will be replaced by constant bursts of information lacking in any context, and a flood of raw video and data.

But Paul Grabowicz, who heads the New Media Program at the UC Berkeley Graduate School of Journalism, cites several studies that suggest that the reverse might actually be the case.

> Rather than undermining the traditional narrative, the Internet is an opportunity to experiment with multi-dimensional storytelling that provides context and depth and also is more compelling. Instead of a single linear narrative, a story can be broken down into a series of narratives organized as topical subsections that people can explore according to their own interests (2012).

What skills and attributes are required to develop these kinds of stories? Certainly, a competency in more than one media platform is essential (Currie 2010, p. 119). British journalist and author Andy Bull reflects the general consensus when he suggests that multimedia journalists should be able to write basic news reports, take pictures and create still picture stories, film and edit a video story, and record and edit a podcast (Bull 2010, p. 2; see also Wilkinson et al. 2009, pp. 6–7).

MULTIMEDIA IN ACTION: 'BLIZZARD HITS MELBOURNE'

But most importantly, journalists need to understand which media formats are best suited to which kinds of stories. Consider this scenario (hypothetical at the time of writing). After a warmer-than-average July, an unexpected blizzard hits Melbourne, blanketing the entire metropolitan area in snow, and bringing the city to a standstill. For anyone familiar with Melbourne, it's obvious that this would be big news—despite the city's reputation for having a 'four seasons in one day' climate, it's only snowed three times in the city during the last 80 years, and in each instance the falls were light.

Traditional media have well-established ways of handling this kind of story. We know television news would feature footage of snow falling around city landmarks, kids making snowmen, astonished and irritated commuters battling the floundering transport system, any accidents or deaths linked to the event, and interview grabs with someone from the weather bureau. Radio would be 'snowed in' with listener accounts of the blizzard, details of any disruptions or emergencies, on-the-spot reporting, and traffic and weather updates. The next day's papers would frame the event in context. This means not only providing an account of what happened, but also the how and the why—photos and snow maps would be used in conjunction with a news feature and, in all likelihood, a discussion about the possible climate change implications.

But how might these media formats be deployed in a multimedia context? Understanding their traditional strengths and weaknesses is an essential requirement of the multimedia mindset. So too is appreciating how these attributes shift in an interactive online environment.

TEXT

Text is usually the glue of a multimedia piece—it's the best way to provide an anchor for a story that contains other elements, or is developing swiftly. For breaking news, newspapers have long been overshadowed by broadcast, but text is essential for such stories online. The moment the blizzard hits Melbourne, initial reports would break on a social media platform such as Twitter, so your own report needs to verify these tweets as well as deliver constant text updates as other details come to hand (see Chapter 7 and the accompanying case study for more on this). Text is also the medium best suited to generating audience involvement; linking to other materials or sources (Bull 2010, pp. 31–4); and providing headlines and tags that make your piece searchable. Sharp writing skills are essential—not only for the body of your story, but also for everything from captions for audiovisual material to summaries and social media updates.

But text isn't usually the best way to convey character or emotion. And nor can you assume that much of it will be read: a 2008 study by Nielsen found that for much of the time, users only read about 20 per cent of text on any given screen (also cited by Benedetti 2010, p. 187). If text is your main format, think of how it can be 'chunked' with subheadings and bullet points (Porteous 2009). For news-driven pieces, consider how the most important information should be written. That stalwart of newspaper news, the inverted pyramid—which was designed to deliver the most important information at the top of the story—is still a generally sound model for online news stories (Benedetti 2010, p. 188), although different views have emerged about how best to adapt it to stories designed to be read on screens (Wilkinson et al. 2009, p. 38).

PHOTOGRAPHS

If your background is primarily text or broadcast, think of the impact that still photographs can have at all stages of a story's lifespan. 'Use photography when you need to show the story to readers to capture them,' says Kimberley Porteous. 'Take advantage of the infinite space on the online platform and run a photo essay or slideshow with a narrative arc; don't just dump a pile of images in random order (Porteous 2009).

Multimedia journalists need to be able to curate user-generated content. It's now standard practice for the online sites of major mastheads and television networks to actively encourage photos from their readership, and to include them alongside the work of staff photographers in photo galleries (see, for instance, the gallery published in *The Age* online after Melbourne's 2011 Christmas Day storm: *The Age* 2011).

MOVING IMAGES

Moving images are ideal for showing events as they unfold, and for capturing the immediacy of dramatic situations (Bull 2010, p. 34). Tornadoes, tsunamis and sporting highlights are obvious examples. Yet video can be just as important in interviews where emotion or body language might be more revealing than what is said (Porteous 2009). If resources are tight, the costs and benefits need to be weighed up, but video in a multimedia package doesn't have to be as polished as television (Currie 2010, p. 119). Remember, user-generated content, CCTV footage and video captured on a smartphone can all be used to better effect online than on television.

AUDIO

Audio provides the immediacy of video without the disadvantage of requiring the audience's full attention (Bull 2010, pp. 31–4). For packaged pieces, it's a great medium when your audience needs to hear the voices involved, or when a particular noise is the story's subject (Porteous 2009). In live-to-air situations, audio remains a powerful way to connect with the audience—consider the longevity of talkback, the first form of interactive media, which has been on the airwaves for more than half a century. Meanwhile, podcasting has opened opportunities to reach niche audiences across the globe.

The internet has also spawned a new story-telling format: the audio slideshow. This 'true child of multimedia journalism and the web' (Bull 2010, p. 36) can be more effective than a video (Currie 2010). As Porteous enthuses: 'Sound adds authenticity and emotion and is extremely powerful when combined with still photography in an audio slideshow: a storytelling tool much greater than the sum of its parts. They're a natural for newspapers with photojournalists on staff and easy access to images (2009). One example is photojournalist Andrew Meares' Polaroid-style commentary of the Gillard campaign for the 2010 election, which he shot using his iPhone camera. Meares' commentary also provides a fascinating account of how a seasoned practitioner has adapted to the multimedia environment.

GRAPHICS

Whether they include maps, statistics, timelines, or other ways of putting complex information into context, graphics have long been essential to print media as well as television. In a multimedia environment, the same rules apply, but with interactivity built in wherever possible.

Some of the richest possibilities are being realised through interactive mapping. The static map that appears in print can now be layered with an interactive GPS so that users can see what's happening in their own neighbourhood, thus strengthening the possibilities of providing information to a range of communities through a single story (Stevens 2011a). For example, when snow blanketed the UK in December 2010, *The Guardian's* website took the best photos sent in from the public and geotagged them on an interactive map with two key features: a clickable slideshow chronicling the evolution of the weather pattern that led to the cold snap); and a summary of the country's worst-hit areas, using a combination of embedded travel advisories and crowdsourced photos.

Be careful, however, to ensure that the graphics help to clarify the issue at hand. Problems quickly arise if users become confused—an issue discussed in some detail in the excellent online documentary *Journalism in the Age of Data* (McGhee 2010).

NONLINEAR STORY-TELLING

A multimedia mindset requires an understanding of the dynamics of nonlinear forms of story-telling. Even if you control all the elements that are published, you need to accept that you're not going to be able to determine how they are consumed. That's because users can now choose how to navigate through the elements of a story (Stevens 2011b).

In large-scale pieces especially, users may enter and leave the story from a variety of pages. The challenge is to maximise their experience (Benedetti 2010, p. 193). 'Your user may watch all the video first; may read all the stories, but not in order; may check out the audio clips and then the photo gallery; or do any combination of the above' (Benedetti 2010, p. 194).

Journalists who are used to traditional story formats may find that this takes some getting used to, but it's worth embracing the challenge. For rather than undermining the traditional narrative, the internet has opened up opportunities to provide more compelling in-depth stories (Grabowicz 2012).

An excellent example of this is the ABC's *Black Saturday* website, which was launched a few months after the devastating fires of 2009 ripped through Victoria. Go to the home page and you'll see a 'mosaic' screen filled with pictures of people affected by the fires. Scroll below the mosaic and you will find the 'About' section, which describes the intentions of the project:

> Hundreds of people have shared their stories and experiences of the fires and the aftermath online. Residents of fire-affected communities, volunteer fire fighters, journalists, community leaders, politicians, volunteers, academics, experts and tourists have posted their photos, videos, and opinions online through blogs, websites and social media spaces.
>
> Through these first person accounts we can gain insight into what these communities were like before and after the fires. The Black Saturday website offers a collection of the most compelling and significant of these stories and places them alongside official accounts and records about key events. It provides a central space to explore the event from all angles. It gives us a way to make sense of what happened and to understand what it was like to experience a firestorm the size of Black Saturday.
>
> By interweaving user-generated media with professional media sources and official documents, this website provides a 360° view of the Black Saturday bushfires and the aftermath. Organising the media content on a map, a timeline or by a particular topic allows us to piece together the over-arching story of Black Saturday as told from the perspectives of countless individuals.
>
> The site also features a series of moving video portraits in which survivors relate their experience of the day. Each of these portraits gives us an insight into life before and after the fires and shows some of the many different ways fire can affect an individual and a community. Some of these stories are about a struggle to come to terms with loss, trauma and life after the fires. Others share inspiring stories of survival and compassion.

This site shows how a relatively new form of story-telling can make strategic use of archival material—in this sense an in-depth multimedia package can also be an online repository designed not just for the present, but also for the future.

Yet, while the site incorporates ABC radio and television segments that went to air during the bushfire period, this isn't simply an aggregation of previously broadcast material. In concept and design it is something that could only have been made for an online environment. The 14-person project team built the site from scratch with a mission to provide a rich, exploratory and nonlinear experience.

But how does the nonlinear form of this project work for the user? Here's something to try in a small group. Allow 15 minutes for everyone to explore the site separately, beginning at the homepage. Then each person should describe how they used the site. The chances are that no two responses will be the same. You might have ended up watching home videos taken of the billowing smoke as filmed at Kangaroo Ground in Melbourne's north-east (ABC: *Black Saturday*: 'Ring of Fires'),while someone else viewed the 14-minute documentary profile of Lex, a goat farmer from the West Gippsland town of Callignee, talking about why she's only returned to her former home three times since the fires devastated her property (ABC: *Black Saturday*: 'Lex').

There may be something random about the possible range of experiences, but nonlinear stories still need to be especially well thought-through. You have to road-test for potholes, even if you're no longer in the driver's seat. Provide a clear map of the story, including links to all story parts on every page to ensure that users get a sense of the scale of the piece. And avoid 'dead-ending', whereby users find themselves on a screen with no links to the rest of the piece or related stories (Benedetti 2010, p. 194).

Even if you're not an expert in design, it's important to understand how the architecture of a multimedia story will work. Think again about the organising principles behind the *Black Saturday* site. Did the 'mosaic' homepage provide you with enough visual cues to understand the breadth of content in the package? What made it possible to traverse from one section of the site to another? What made you decide to choose the elements of the package that you visited?

REALISING YOUR STORY

How can all these principles be best realised? One strategy to organise your structure is to storyboard the piece in the planning stage. Jane Stevens recommends dividing the story into its logical, nonlinear parts, such as: a lead/nut graph/blurb paragraph that sums up why this story is important; profiles of the main people in the story; the event or situation; a description of a process or how something works; pros and cons; the history of the event or situation; and any other related issues raised by the story (Stevens 2011a). Prepare by doing background interviews, anticipate what to expect in the field, look up anything the sources have published, and collect as many available visuals as you can to get an idea of what the story's components may be (Stevens 2011b).

At both the planning and editing stage, be conscious too of what you *don't* need. A lot of material can be harvested in a short time, but packaging it will be much more difficult if you don't make strategic decisions at each stage of the production. Editing skills and editorial judgment are both just as critical in the multimedia realm as in traditional story-telling forms; perhaps more so if you're collecting material in multiple formats.

Where possible, use hyperlinks to provide context and depth, especially in nonlinear stories. As journalist and computer scientist Jonathan Stray explains:

> In print, readers can't click elsewhere for background. They can't look up an unfamiliar term or check another source. That means print stories must be self-contained, which leads to conventions such as context paragraphs and mini-definitions ('Goldman Sachs, the embattled American investment bank.') The entire world of the story has to be packed into one linear narrative (2010).

Whatever your story, consider the ethical or best-practice considerations of how material is to be gathered and published. How will you generate and manage user-generated content? What comments need to be moderated to weed out abusive or defamatory responses? How do you verify material that's been sent in from anonymous users? Be mindful too of the principles of fair usage and the requirements of copyright—what can and can't be used without clearance will vary across different platforms, and in different countries too (Aufderheide 2012).

Always credit photos or other material, including user-generated content. When mistakes happen, acknowledge and correct them: 'The posted story is not the end of the process. It is the start of an online dialogue whereby everyone is free to critique the story and enrich its sources, facts, and perspectives' (Ward 2011, p. 213). So be clear about how changes to a story will be signalled to the user, and acknowledge where information needs further verification.

And keep in mind that not every story needs the multimedia treatment. As *The Washington Post's* national innovations editor Mark S. Luckie puts it, some stories are just 'un-webbable'. It's not that you can't enhance them with a multimedia package; it's that the results aren't worth the effort: 'When you can't do everything for every story, the key is to "filter and prioritize"' (Kirchner 2010).

TECHNICAL PROFICIENCY

So you're not a tech junkie or a computer programmer. Join the club. But with technology constantly shaping how stories can be told, some basic skills are essential. This goes beyond being able to gather news using multiple devices. As a multimedia journalist, you also need to regularly evaluate new story-telling tools and applications. One of the most popular to emerge in 2011 was the social curation tool Storify (Newman 2011; Fincham 2011) that quickly became popular with both bloggers and news sites (Tenore 2011). By the time this book goes to print, there will be many others.

Get into the habit of using apps that can be downloaded to your smartphone—you can edit photos and shoot video on the same device that you use to record them and watch the news on (as well as making the occasional phone call).

Become familiar with HTML, CSS and JavaScript. While not every journalist is going to be a web developer, knowing the basics of all of these will help you to see the possibilities of what can be done—and, perhaps more importantly, the restrictions and complications (Scanlon 2012).

1 Blogging is a practical way to develop multimedia skills. If you haven't done so already, set up a blog that features video, audio, photos, graphics and user engagement in your posts. Tell the world about your new posts on social media platforms such as Facebook and Twitter. And keep track of your audience through site stats.

2 Collaborate with people who have different skill sets. Use the rock band model—if you're a drummer, you're going to need to find a guitarist.

3 But if you're a guitarist, get a drum kit. In other words, if your strength is writing, start taking photos and video and build stories around them. By playing with the technology, you'll be learning the basic principles of editing and story-telling, working out how to do more with less and, most importantly, developing a multimedia mindset.

4 Follow sites with multimedia-rich content. As well as the mastheads of Australia's daily newspapers, the ABC, and *ninemsn*, keep track of how *Slate*, NPR, the BBC, *The Guardian* and *The New York Times* are using multimedia content. Keep up with sites that specialise in discussing web and multimedia journalism, including *Mashable*, *10 000 Words* and *MediaShift*.

5 Keep track of the journalists whose work you admire on Twitter and/or other social media platforms.

6 Follow the ethics and best-practice discussions and be transparent about which codes of practices you subscribe to.

7 Experiment. One challenging dimension of multimedia story-telling is that there are relatively few ground rules. That's also the best thing about multimedia story-telling.

QUESTIONS TO CONSIDER

1 How has the internet informed the development of multimedia journalism?

2 What are the strengths of the internet over traditional broadcast media when it comes to managing content?

3 What is the difference between linear and nonlinear story-telling?

4 List a number of the features identified in this chapter regarding the capabilities of multimedia as a story-telling medium.

5 What are the options to Storify that have emerged since this chapter was written? How do they work?

TASK

1 Tackle the Black Saturday challenge identified in this chapter—either in a group or individually.

REFERENCES

ABC. 2008. 'Tipping Point', *Four Corners*: www.abc
.net.au/4corners/special_eds/20080804/arctic/
default.htm/.

The Age. 2011. *Storm Rolls Over Melbourne*: www
.theage.com.au/photogallery/environment/weather/
storm-rolls-over-melbourne-20120216-1tba2.
html?selectedImage=0 (accessed 23 February 2012).

Aufderheide, P. 2012. *Journalists Should Learn Best
Practices for Fair Use in Digital Age*: www.pbs
.org/mediashift/2012/02/journalists-should-learn-
best-practices-for-fair-use-in-digital-age046.html
(accessed 16 February 2012).

Benedetti, P. 2010. 'Structure and Story Online', in
P. Benedetti, T. Currie & K. Kierans, eds, *The
New Journalist: Roles, Skills and Critical Thinking*,
Toronto: Emond Montgomery Publications.

Berkey-Gerard, M. 2009. *Assignment—What is
Multimedia Journalism?*: http://mbgjournalism
.wordpress.com/2009/10/08/assignment-what-is-
multimedia-journalism (accessed 5 February 2012).

Bull, A. 2010. *Multimedia Journalism: A Practical
Guide*, Oxford: Routledge.

Currie, T. 2010. 'Roles and Skills for Cross-platform
Reporting', in P. Benedetti, T. Currie & K. Kierans,
eds, *The New Journalist: Roles, Skills and Critical
Thinking*, Toronto: Emond Montgomery
Publications.

Deuze, M. 2004. 'What is Multimedia Journalism?'
Journalism Studies, 5, pp. 139–52.

Ewing, S. & Thomas, J. 2011. *Online Media Use in
Australia 2007–2011: Submission to the Independent
Media Inquiry*: http://cci.edu.au/sites/default/
files/sewing/CCI_ISR%20submission%20to%20
independent%20media%20inquiry.pdf (accessed
25 January 2012).

Fincham, K. 2011. *Using Storify for Journalism
Education*: http://storify.com/kellyfincham/
using-storify-for-journalism-education (accessed
6 January 2012).

Grabowicz, P. 2012. *Multimedia Journalism—The
Transition to Digital Journalism*: http://multimedia
.journalism.berkeley.edu/tutorials/digital-
transform/multimedia-storytelling (accessed
31 January 2012).

The Guardian. 2010. 'UK Snow: An Interactive Map':
www.guardian.co.uk/uk/interactive/2010/dec/01/
uk-snow-map-weather/.

Jacobson, S. 2012. 'Transcoding the News: An
Investigation into Multimedia Journalism published
on nytimes.com 2000–2008', *New Media & Society*,
14, August, pp. 867–85.

Kirchner, L. 2010. 'Some Stories are "Un-Webbable"',
Columbia Journalism Review: www.cjr.org/the_
news_frontier/some_stories_are_un-webbable.php
(accessed 23 January 2012).

McGhee, G. 2010. *Journalism in the Age of Data*,
Stanford University: http://datajournalism.stanford
.edu (accessed 10 February 2012).

Meares, A. 2010. *On Tour with Julia Gillard*: www
.theage.com.au/multimedia/federal-election/
on-tour-with-julia-gillard-20100810-11xho.html
(accessed 10 February 2012).

Newman, C. 2011. *Tips for using Storify in your
Reporting in Digital Storytelling*: http://storify
.com/craignewman/tips-for-using-storify-in-you-
reporting (accessed 5 January 2012).

Nielsen. 2011. *Nielsen's State of the Online Market:
Evolution or Revolution?*: www.nielsen-online
.com/pr/OCR_mr-mar11_FINAL.pdf (accessed
25 January 2012).

Nielsen, J. 2008. *Alertbox: How Little do Users Read?*:
www.useit.com/alertbox/percent-text-read.html
(accessed 17 January 2012).

Pew Research Center's Project for Excellence in
Journalism. 2011. *The State of the News Media
2011: Overview*: http://stateofthemedia.org/2011/
overview-2/ (accessed 1 February 2012).

Porteous, K. 2009. *What is News Multimedia*,
The Walkley Foundation: www.walkleys.com/
features/491 (accessed 20 January 2012).

Quinn, S. 2005. *Convergent Journalism: The
Fundamentals of Multimedia Reporting*, New York:
Peter Lang.

Rosen, J. 2006. *The People Formerly Known as the
Audience*, Jay Rosen: http://archive.pressthink.
org/2006/06/27/ppl_frmr.html (accessed
25 January 2012).

Scanlon, C. 2012. Personal communication with the author, 12 February.

Stevens, J. 2011a. *Storyboarding*, Knight Digital Media Centre: http://multimedia.journalism.berkeley.edu/tutorials/starttofinish/storyboarding/.

Stevens, J. 2011b. *What is a Multimedia Story?* Knight Digital Media Centre: http://multimedia.journalism.berkeley.edu/tutorials/starttofinish/choose (accessed 16 December 2011).

Stray, J. 2010. *Why Link Out? Four Journalistic Purposes of the Noble Hyperlink*, Harvard University: www.niemanlab.org/2010/06/why-link-out-four-journalistic-purposes-of-the-noble-hyperlink (accessed 28 February 2012).

Tenore, M.J. 2011. *The 5 Types of Stories that make Good Storifies*, Poynter: www.poynter.org/how-tos/newsgathering-storytelling/153697/the-5-types-of-stories-that-make-good-storifys (accessed 31 January 2012).

Ward, S.J.A. 2011. *Ethics and the Media: An Introduction*, Cambridge: Cambridge University Press.

Wenger, D.H. & Potter, D. 2008. *Advancing the Story: Broadcast Journalism in a Multimedia World*, CQ Press: Washington DC.

Wilkinson, J.S., Grant, A.E. & Fisher, D.J. 2009. *Principles of Convergent Journalism*, New York; Oxford: Oxford University Press.

WEBSITE REFERENCES

ABC: *Black Saturday*: www.abc.net.au/innovation/blacksaturday/.

ABC: *Black Saturday*: 'Lex': www.abc.net.au/innovation/blacksaturday/people/lex/default.htm/.

ABC: *Black Saturday*: 'Ring of Fires': www.abc.net.au/innovation/blacksaturday/default.htm#/timeline/sequence/chapter/1/showid/0000064/.

ABC: *Four Corners*: www.abc.net.au/4corners/.

ABC: *Four Corners*: 'A Bloody Business': www.abc.net.au/4corners/content/2011/s3228880.htm/.

The New York Times: www.nytimes.com/.

Storify: www.storify.com/.

TIPPING POINT

Ruth Fogarty

Original idea

When *Four Corners* broadened its reach beyond 45 minutes of television to the digital platform, the decision was made to create a series of special online editions designed to offer the audience a more interactive story-telling experience. Programs were chosen on the currency and scope of their subject matter, and their source material was mined, presenting an assortment of unseen footage and interviews, documentary evidence, and other research in an easy-to-use Flash template. The aim was to encourage a more in-depth examination of a topic, give the program a longer shelf life, and also take advantage of the developing medium.

The program used this approach for the first time in 2004 with a special edition on 'Islamist Terrorism— From September 2001 to 2004'; it a took a two-person team three months to design, edit and produce— re-cutting six *Four Corners* programs on terrorism, editing dozens of interviews, and developing various interactive features in Flash. This was an immense assignment, but it was well received and it paved the way for a recurrent and more efficiently produced series, which would focus on one program at a time. A good example of this format was the online edition of 'Tipping Point' (ABC 2008).

'Tipping Point'

The decision to produce a special edition to accompany Marian Wilkinson's 2008 report 'Tipping Point'— about the effects of global warming on the Arctic icecap—was a simple one. 2008 was the year of the *Garnaut Climate Change Review* and governments and communities around the world were increasingly aware of the growing climate crisis.

At the time, Marian was a senior environment reporter at *The Sydney Morning Herald*, and had spent months trying to get to the Arctic Circle so she could witness firsthand the vanishing of the vast sea ice. She pressed various scientific groups in Germany, Norway, the USA and Canada, before finally securing a ride on board a Canadian icebreaker, the *Louis S. St-Laurent*. The *Louis* was taking a team of scientists on an expedition through the legendary shipping route known as the Northwest Passage, where many early explorers lost their lives. In 2007, the Arctic waters were virtually ice-free for the first time on record— and this would be only the second time the passageway had been opened up to sea vessels.

Marian was joined by a two-man *Four Corners* team (cameraman Neale Maude and sound recordist Daniel O'Connor), and they boarded the *Louis* in Dartmouth Harbour, Nova Scotia. The journey took 10 days, and during that time Marian spoke to several experts on the political, economical and environmental implications of the Arctic melt. She also kept a diary narrating their voyage, observing small details—such as the day-to-day life on board an icebreaker—and some of the more drastic weather changes. It was this diary—along with the interviews, and the scientific data donated by the National Snow and Ice Data Center (NSIDC) and NASA—that furnished us with the content needed to produce the website. And it was the cameraman's dramatic stills and footage of the polar melt, and of the natural world dependent on those waters, which proved the perfect backdrop.

Extended interviews

In a topic as divisive as climate change, it was important to present the viewpoints of those on the frontline of their scientific field. 2008 was International Polar Year and on board the *Louis* were scientists from 60 different nations, who were sailing through the Arctic with the aim of mapping and communicating some of the changes happening across the region.

As the Arctic waters warm, a complex set of scenarios arise. One of the biggest questions being asked in 2008 was how the loss of the summer sea ice might impact on global weather patterns. On land, Marian spoke to sea ice specialists at the US Army's Cold Regions Research & Engineering Laboratory (CRREL) in New Hampshire, the NSIDC in Colorado, and the International Arctic Research Centre (IARC) in Fairbanks, Alaska. All stressed the same point: the sea ice is melting at an accelerated rate and a change in climate is an explicit cause.

Many alarming questions were raised in Marian's interviews: such as the impact on the atmosphere of a thawing permafrost; the environmental cost if there is a territorial 'cold rush' on the Arctic's energy reserves; and the threat to the survival of the polar bear—and other wildlife and birds—as their habitat shrinks. I wanted to zoom in on these concerns, and this informed the selection process when editing the interviews. The interview on these issues formed the basis of the online narrative and collectively presented a powerful record of the potential impacts of the melt.

Mapping the journey

The aim of mapping the route was to create a dramatic sense of the journey—to convey the remoteness of the region, and the enormity of the distances travelled up the Northwest Passage. Their route took the *Four Corners* team from Dartmouth, past Newfoundland, through the Gulf of St Lawrence and up the Strait of Belle Isle; onto the entrance to the Labrador Sea, north to the Davis Strait and past the Arctic Circle. After 10 days in rough and sometimes hazardous waters, they entered the eastern entrance to the Northwest Passage and finally disembarked in Resolute Bay, Nunavut.

To create the map, I worked with an experienced ABC web developer, Tim Madden, who produced the template. Back in 2008, Google Maps hadn't yet evolved to its present level of functionality, and so much of the technical aspects were made possible by inserting a Google Map inside a Flash-based template.

One concern was achieving geographical accuracy, which meant I needed to source the precise longitude and latitude coordinates. To do this, I sought access to the *Louis'* log, and this allowed me to accurately transcribe the voyage.

On the map, we marked the passage from Nova Scotia to Resolute Bay, placing individual icons at key locations along the route. We also placed icons at locations where the team made noteworthy sightings or observations along the route, and these were illustrated with some of the unique footage, stills and other media that personalised their trip.

The icons were then 'tweened', a Flash animation process that forges a connection between anchor points and creates a dynamic motion between them. A pop-up window was placed at each key location and this was where any type of media could be hosted.

Once the technical elements had been established, I curated all of the pertinent content that would best re-animate the voyage, such as a photo of the first glimpse of ice, a diary entry noting the weather extremes, or an interview with the ship's captain.

The most forceful piece of footage turned out to be a short and simple animation produced by the NSIDC, showing the drastic reduction in sea ice over the Arctic from 1979 to 2007. This 30-second clip became the symbol of an environmental 'tipping point'.

Afterthoughts

The world of reporting has been changed irrevocably. Because of its narrative flexibility, online journalism opens up interesting ways of story-telling. Assembling the unique elements of a story and putting them on display lets the viewer behind the scenes of the program-making process, and makes it possible to tell a story in a multi-dimensional way using different points of view.

The *Four Corners* website extends and enriches program content and its life span, and gives audiences a chance to delve deeper into a program's themes. It also provides a platform on which to chronicle any important developments.

If there's a component of a story that can't be explored within the 'broadcast' piece, the matter can be dealt with online—and often a topic will gather its own momentum. Sarah Ferguson's controversial report 'A Bloody Business', on the alarming conditions in Indonesia's slaughterhouses, had one of the lowest viewer ratings in 2011; but in the following weeks and months the report's website became a central reference point for those engaged in the debate. With over 320 000 page views, the story was the most popular visited on the website that year.

Interactive story-telling can also be a powerful tool in educative terms, as it provides a way of breaking down complex issues into their component parts. And the freedom to use a variety of media to tell a story means there are more ways to engage your audience and to encourage their own inquiries.

An online audience is much more participatory than a television or print audience, and increasingly they demand a right to more information and a right of reply. An evolving social media culture—plus the rise of the 'citizen journalist'—have broken down the boundaries between old media formats and new.

The digital platform is no longer a font of derivative and secondary news and information, and it will continue to shape the form and practice of journalism in the future—but the credibility and veracity of the source and content must always remain important.

INDEX

Aaron, Mark   16
Abbott, Tony   158, 200
ABC
   The Age and   19
   agenda setter   157
   Black Saturday website   325
   online story Walkley   19
   radio   16
   Radio Current Affairs   91, 178
   television   16
   see also specific programs
ABC Innovation   91
Aboriginals and Torres Strait Islanders
   Indigenous journalists   258–9, 261
   Indigenous radio and television   257–9, 261
   land rights   256
   marginalisation   254
   Palm Island community   255, 257
   see also Indigenous affairs journalism
abortion   13
acronyms, use of   225, 228
Adelaide Advertiser   17, 178
Aeropagitica (Milton)   5
'Afghan War Diary'   40
African Communities Council (ACC)   274
'After the Gold Rush'   291
Age, The   10, 12, 14, 16, 19, 25–6, 33, 79, 169, 221, 288, 310
   'The Age tapes'   15–16
Al Jazeera   40
al-Asaad, Riad   94
All Ordinaries Index (All Ords)   140
Allen, Allen and Hemsley   169
al-Sharif, Manal   91
AM   16, 91, 155, 178
Amcor   287
American Airlines   159
Analyst's Notebook   218, 220
Andersen, Arthur   149
annual reports   142
Apublica   42
Arab Spring   91, 101–2
arbitration   298
ArcGIS   132
archives   81–4
ArcMap   119
Armstrong, Lance   313
Asahi Shimbun   42
Associated Whistle-blowing Press (AWP)   43
Association of Health Care Journalists   244

'astroturfing'   94, 158–9
asylum seekers   275
Attorney-General for the State of New South Wales v John Fairfax Publications Pty Limited   172
AusAID   68
AustLII   74
Australian, The   13, 16, 19, 112, 206, 233, 248, 270
Australian, The [not current publication]   11
Australian Associated Press (AAP)   145, 157
Australian Bureau of Statistics   72, 105, 132
Australian Cemeteries Index   83
Australian Centre for Independent Journalism   4, 34, 68, 71, 152, 233
Australian Competition and Consumer Commission (ACCC)   141, 283, 287–8
Australian Conservation Foundation   80
Australian Council of Trade Unions (ACTU)   298–9, 306–7
Australian Defence Force Academy   198
Australian Dictionary of Biography   79
Australian Financial Review   12, 17–18
Australian Journalists' Association   82, 171, 235, 258
Australian Law Reform Commission   167
Australian Legal Information Institute   74
Australian Medical Association   243
Australian Prudential Regulation Authority (APRA)   141
Australian Science Archives Project   82
Australian Securities and Investments Commission (ASIC)   69–71, 140–1, 149, 283
Australian Securities Exchange (ASX)   71, 149
Australian Sports Anti-doping Authority (ASADA)   313
Australian Stock Exchange (ASX)   139–42, 283
Australian Taxation Office (ATO)   141
Australian War Memorial   82
Australian Women's Weekly   78
Australian Workers Union (AWU)   298

Background Briefing   16
Bacon, Wendy   14, 34
Baillieu, Ted   26, 301
Baker, Mark   19
Baker, Richard   19, 25–7, 33, 288, 310
balance and bias   226
balance sheets   143
Baltimore Sun   213
Bankstown Bulldogs   309
Barnett, Colin   158
Barrass, Tony   170

Barry, Paul   17
Bass, Frank   244
BBC Social Media Summit   88, 92–3, 96
BBC User-Generated Content Hub   96
#BBCSMS   92–3, 95–6
Bedder, Sharon   159
Bedford, Anthony   137
Bentley, David   17
Berendt, John   212
Bernstein, Carl   7, 14
Beveridge, John   149–50
Beyond Belief (Emlyn Williams)   212
BHP Billiton   141, 291–4
'Big House, The'   188–9
'Big Night Out of Research'   272
Big Short, The (M. Lewis)   286
'Big Ugly Australian: Ok Tedi, BHP and the PNG
         Elite'   291
Bingle, Lara   311
Bird, S.E.   261
Birnbauer, Bill   20, 72
Bjelke-Petersen, Sir Joh   16
Black (Justice)   45
Black Saturday website   325
Blackboard   66
Blainey, Geoffrey   80
blogging   152, 159, 166, 326–7
         blogs as data sources   125
Blogging and Tweeting Without Getting Sued
         (Pearson)   166
'Bloody Business, A' *Four Corners*   332
Bluescope Steel   301
Bob Hawke Prime Ministerial Library   82
'Body of Evidence'   30
Bogut, Andrew   314
Bolte, Henry   221
Bond, Alan   17
Bonnie & Clyde   213
Bottom, Bob   208
Boykoff, J.M.   226
Boykoff, M.T.   226
Boyle, Raymond   309
Bracken, John   32
Bradshaw, Paul   94
Brave New World (Huxley)   212
Bray, Sir Theodore   12
Breakheart Hill (Cook)   213
Broken Shore, The (Temple)   215
Brooke, Heather   199
Brumfield Bird and Sandford's (BBS)   152
Brundtland Report (United Nations)   222
Bruner, Patrick   284
Brunswick Research   125

Bryson, John   215
Buchanan, Edna   213
Budd, Joe   170
budgets   145–7
Bull, Andy   322
Bulletin, The   11, 15–16, 256
Bureau of Investigative Journalism   40
Burke, James Lee   213
Burson-Marsteller   159
Burton, B.   158
Business Review Weekly   314
business sector   139–47, 149–50
         see also financial journalism
Butch Cassidy and the Sundance Kid   213
'Butcher of Bega'   17
Button, John   181
Butts, B.   33
Byrne, Andrew   170

cabinet minutes   80–2
California Watch   29
Calley, William   50
Campbell Collaboration   243
Capitol News Connection   32
Capote, Truman   211–12
Carbon Tax   200
Carlton, Mike   16–17
Carlton, Richard   16
Carnegie, Andrew   30
Carnegie Corporation   33
Carroll, Vic   11, 13
Carter, William (QC)   205
Carvin, Andy   93
cash flow statements   144
Catalyst   248
Catcher in the Rye, The (Salinger)   212
Catt, Roseanne   67–8, 181
CCH   300
census   111
Center for Investigative Reporting (CIR)   29–30
Center for Public Integrity (CIP)   29, 31
Centre for Independent Journalism (CIJ)   152
Chamberlain, Lindy   80
Chandler, Sol   13
Channel Nine   17, 168
Channel Seven   17, 170
Channel Ten   17
Chartered Institute of Public Relations (CIPR)   159
Chifley Government   79
Chmagh, Saeed   39
Chomsky, N.   227
Christians, C   182
Chubb, Philip   14

'churnalism'   4, 233, 302

Clark, Karen Lin   271

Clark, Manning   80

Clarke, Michael   310–11

Clarke, Peter   288

Clean Energy Regulator   200

climate change review   330

CNN   171

'Coalition for Clean and Renewable Energy'   159

Cochrane Collaboration   243

Cocklin, Wolf   91

Coco v A.N. Clark (Engineers) Ltd   169

codes of ethics   171, 183, 185, 235, 258

COINS database   199

Cold War   11–12

collaborative journalism   6–7, 91
  see also Twitter; *WikiLeaks*

'Collateral Murder' video   39

Collins, Kent   274

Colonial Times   11

Color of Money, The (Dedman)   117

Colvin, Mark   91

Commsec   141–2

Community Guide, The   243

community mapping   271–2

companies and business records   69–71, 80, 139–47,
  149–50, 283, 291–4
  see also financial journalism

Competition and Consumer Act 2010 (Cth)   168

computer-assisted reporting (CAR)   116–17

confidentiality   54, 75, 168–9, 175, 179, 313

Connor, Rex   15

Construction, Forestry, Mining and Energy Union
  (CFMEU)   300, 305–6

Consumer Price Index   104–5

contempt   172

Conversation, The   35

Cook, Thomas   213

Cornwall, Deborah   171

corporate (private) sector   139–40
  see also financial journalism

Corpse had a Familiar Face, The (Buchanan)   213

Costigan Royal Commission   15

Coulter, Ann   284

Coulthart, Ross   17–18

Courier Mail, The   12, 16–17, 170, 204, 209, 217–19

Cousins, Ben   311–12

Crabb, Annabel   91

Crikey news website   34–5, 68, 73, 152, 199

Crime and Misconduct Commission (Qld)   206,
  218–19

crime writing   208–15

Crouch, Wallace J.   13

crowdsourcing   43–5, 90–2, 244

Crutcher, Michael   217–18

CSR   14

cultural diversity and journalism
  269–77

'Cultural Divide, The'   270

Current Affair, A   168, 170

Currie, T.   322

Dangerous Ground website   34, 72

Danziger Bridge shootings   30–1

D'Arcy, Nick   311

Darling, Ralph   11

Dart Center for Journalism and Trauma   189

Darville, Helen   17

Darwin creative industries   132–3

Dash, Leon   277

data journalism   116–21, 123–35
  content analysis   130
  data analysis   117–19
  definition   125
  discussion list sources   125
  social media sources   125
  spreadsheets   118–19
  text analysis tools   130
  text databases   125–6
  Twitter   125

Data Journalism Handbook   244

Dateline   17

Davies, Nick   233, 285

Davis, Kevin   34

Davis, L.   157

Daylight, Ruth   12

De relationibus novellis (Peucer)   5

Dedman, Bill   117

defamation   173–4

Demidenko, Helen   17

Dempster, Quentin   16

Der Spiegel   40

detention centres   69

Deuze, Mark   181, 321

diaries   173, 201

Dickie, Phil   16, 204, 208

Didion, Joan   55

'Dispatches' (Channel 4)   40

'Do No Harm'   244

'Dollars for Docs'   244

Doomadgee, Cameron   255

Dowler, Milly   285

Downs, Anthony   222

Doyle, John (Chief Justice)   179

'Dr Death'   49

Dunlop, Tim   197

Ebbers, Bernard   285
EBIT   142, 149–50
EBITDA   142, 149–50
Economist, The   314
'Eco-Skies'   159
Edmonds, R.   32
Eisinger, Jessie   285
Electronic Frontier Foundation   57
Ellsberg, Daniel   171
Engelberg, Stephen   31
Enron   149, 283, 285–6
enterprise bargaining   300
environmental journalism   221–9
    see also Ok Tedi, PNG
ethics
    codes   171, 183, 185, 235, 258
    investigative journalism   182–6, 188–9
ETrade   141–2
Euro Crisis   283–4
Evans, Harold   12
Evidence Act (Cth)   56
Evil Angels (Bryson)   215
Excel   118–19

Facebakers   97
Facebook
    Occupy Wall St   284
    usage   89
    use by PR people   4
Factiva   68
Fair Work Australia   298–301, 306–7
Fair Work Ombudsman   301
Fairfax, Warwick Jr   13
Fairfax Media
    closure of presses   19
    investigative journalism   16, 18
    National Times, The   13
    outsourcing editorial roles   33
    shareholders   3
    staff cuts   19
    use of *WikiLeaks*   18
Falconio, Peter   214
Farrow, Nick   17
federal budgets   145
Federal Communications Commission   32, 34–5
Federated Ships, Painters and Dockers' Union   15
Felt, W. Mark   6–7
Ferguson, Sarah   310, 332
Fielding, Steve   200
financial journalism   282–9, 291–4
    interpreting documents   139–47, 283, 291–4
Fitzgerald, Tom   12
Fitzgerald, Tony   204
Fitzgerald Inquiry into Police Corruption   16, 204–5

Flash software   330–1
Fleishman-Hillard   154
Flink Labs   137
Flynn, K.   49
Fogarty, Ruth   330–2
Foot, Paul   181
Ford, Edsel   30
Ford, Henry   30
Fordham, Ben   170
Foreign Correspondent   17
Fortune   286
forums as data sources   125
Four Corners   12, 16, 68, 204, 291, 310
    digital platform   330–2
Fourth Estate   5, 12, 18, 134, 153, 193, 208
Fox network   284
Franklin, B.   18, 151–3, 157–8
Franklin, Jon   246–7
Fraser, Malcolm   15
Fraser Government   15
Freedom of Information Act 1982 (Cth)   81
Freedom of Information (FOI) requests   66, 74, 168, 199–200
Freeman, Cathy   256, 313
Frontline (PBS)   29, 31
Funabiki, J.   32

Galbally, Frank   213–14
Game, Peter   15
Gandy, O.H. Jr   152, 255–6
Garnaut, Ross   330
Garner, Helen   212
Gatto, Mick   210
Generally Accepted Accounting Principles (GAAP)   291–4
GENERATE! project   272
Gerard, Robert   18
GetUp   35
Gibbs, Cheryl   272
Gillard, Julia   158, 194–5, 197–8
Gillard Government   69
Gilligan, Andrew   173–4
Gillmor, D.   89
GIS (geographic information systems) software   132
Gladwell, Malcolm   286
global financial crisis (GFC)   143, 282–5, 289
Global Health Data Exchange   243
Global Health Observatory   243
Global Industry Classification Standard (GICS)   140–1
Global Mail, The   33, 35, 89
Glover, Henry   30–1
Godfather, The   213
Gold Coast Bulletin   204

Gollin group   14
Goodfellas   213
Google   68
Google Docs   66
Google Fusion Tables   119
Google Maps   331
Google News archive   69
Google Scholar   243
Gore, Al   223
Government 2.0   244
government information   72–3, 80, 163–5
Grabowicz, Paul   322
'green fatigue'   222–3
Greenpeace   159, 181
Greenpeace Australia   80
Greens, The   33, 301
Greenslade, Roy   184
greenwashing   158–9
GRM International   68, 71
Grocon   305–6
Grollo, Daniel   300, 305–6
group researching   66
Guardian, The
        data journalism   123–4
        MPs expenses exposé   44
        partnership with *Wikileaks*   40, 42–3
        Twitter apology   92
        website   324
Gutfeld, Greg   284
Guthrie, Bruce   14

Haigh, Gideon   3
Hale, Clive   17
Hall, Edward Smith   11
Hamer/Thompson Government (Vic.)   14
'Hamster Wheel, The'   200
Hansard   73, 78, 80
Hanson, Pauline   256
Harris, Thomas   213
Hartcher, P.   299
Harte, C.   308
Hartford Courant   271
Harwood Institute for Public Innovation   272
Haxton, Nance   178–80
Hayden, Bill   196
Health Is Everything: Using Data to Report Great Stories on Your Community's Health (Bass)   244
health journalism   232–40
        online information   232, 234, 243–5
        PR generated   233–4
Health News Review   233–4, 243
Health Report, The   16
Health Services Union (HSU)   300, 307
Henninger, Maureen   73

Herald, The   12, 14–15
Herman, E.   227
Herrington, Donnell   30
Hersch, Seymour   50
Hewitt, Gavin   174
Hiaasen, Carl   213
Hickey, Simon   78
Hickey, Sir Justin   78
Hidden Web (Henninger)   73
Hill, Jess   89–91, 93–5, 101–2
Hills, Ben   14
Hinch, Derryn   172
Hinch v Attorney-General [Victoria]   172
Hinds, Richard   309–10
Hindu Times, The   42
HIV   236–9
HMAS *Sydney*   78
Hockey, Joe   90
Hoffman, Toni   49
Hogan, Allan   16
Hogg, Lionel   12
Holmes, Cate (SC)   205–6
Holmes, Johnathan   17
Horin, Adele   14
Horne, Donald   308
Hosken, Ben   138
Houston, Brant   32
Howard, John   18
Howe, Jeff   91
Hudson, Fiona   137–8
Huffington Post, The   29
Hughes, Gary   25, 79
human sources   48–58
HUMINT (human intelligence)   48, 58
Hurricane Katrina   28–9
Husband, C.   261–2
Hutton Inquiry   174
Hydro Quebec   159

Ides of March, The   160
I.F. Stone Medal for Journalistic Independence   34
In Cold Blood (Capote)   212
Inconvenient Truth, An (Gore)   223
Independent Commission Against Corruption (ICAC)   80, 171
Indigenous affairs journalism   254–62, 267–8
        ethnographic approach   261
        framing   255–7
        Indigenous public sphere   261
        mistrust   258
        terminology   259
industrial relations journalism   297–303, 305–7
informed consent   260
Inglis, Greg   313

Initial Public Offering (IPO)   140
Inside Story   35, 288
intellectual disability and justice   178–80
intelligence-led reporting   217–20
International Covenant on Civil and Political
  Rights   167
interview techniques   154–5
inverted pyramid   323
investigative journalism
  Australian history   10–21
  deception   183–4
  definitions   6–8
  ethics   182–6, 188–9
  paying for information   184
  roles   181–2
  see also research
Investigative News Network   34
Investigative Reporters and Editors (IRE)   6–7, 32,
  117, 124
Investigative Reporting Workshop   29
Iraq Body Count   40
'Iraq War Logs'   40
'Islamist Terrorism—From September 2001 to 2004'
  Four Corners   330

Jacobson, S.   321
Jaspin, Elliot   117
'Jerilderie Letter'   78
Jerrard, John (QC)   205–6
John Curtin Prime Ministerial Library   82
John S. and James L. Knight Foundation   30–4
Johns, Andrew   312–13
Jones, Caroline   16
Josephi, B.   33
journalism
  balance and bias   226
  context   274
  flak   226–7
  history   5–21
  informed consent   260
  talking to leaders   272–3
  working with communities   271–2, 275–6
  see also collaborative journalism; crime writing;
  data journalism; environmental journalism;
  financial journalism; health journalism;
  Indigenous affairs journalism; industrial
  relations journalism; investigative journalism;
  multicultural journalism; multimedia
  journalism; sports journalism
Journalism in the Age of Data (McGhee)   324
Journalist's Guide to Media Law, The (Pearson &
  Polden)   166, 169
Joyce, Alan   300

Kahneman, Daniel   247, 251
Kaidonis, Mary   291–4
'Katrina's Hidden Race War'   30
Kaye, Bill   13
Kelly, David   174
Kelly, Ned   78, 213
Kerr, Sir John   15
Keynes, John Maynard   299
Khemlani, Tirath   15
Kieran, Matthew   185
Killer Within, The (Paul Toohey)   214
King, Betty (Justice)   209
Kippax, S.   236
Kirby, J.   287
Knight Foundation *see* John S. and James L. Knight
  Foundation
Knightley, Phillip   12–13
Koch, Tom   124
Kozlowski, Dennis   285

La Repubblica   42
Lamb, Sir Larry   16
Land Titles Searches   72
Lane, Sabra   155
Larkin, John   14
Las Vegas Sun   244
Lateline   17
Latham, Mark   198
@lauandomar   94–5
Lauchs, Mark   218–19
Lawson, Henry   78, 308
Le Monde   40
Ledley, Charlie   286
Leeding, Damian   217
Lees, Joanne   214
legal information   74, 80
legal issues   166–75
Lenah Game Meats case   167
Lenz, Widukind   13
Let's Talk with Tiga Bayles (98.9FM)   259
Leveson Inquiry   182
Lewis, C.   29, 32–3
Lewis, J.   152
Lewis, M.   286, 310
Lewis, Sir Terence   16
Lewis, Wally   312
Leximancer   130–1
L'Expresso   42
Liberty of the Press (Mill)   5
library usage data   126–9
Libya   101
LinkedIn   68
Listening Devices Act 1984 (NSW)   16, 170

Littlemore, Stuart   17
Lloyd, C   5
'loans affair'   15
local government budgets   146
Lockwood, Douglas   12
Lombardi, K.   184–5
Longley, Billy 'The Texan'   15
Lord of the Flies (Golding)   212
Luck, Peter   16
Luckie, Mark S.   326
Lucky Country, The (Horne)   308

Mabo   256
Mabo, Eddie   80
McBride, William   13, 16
McDonald, Sir William   221
McKenzie, Nick   19, 26, 33, 288, 310
McKew, Maxine   17
McKnight, D.   11
McLean, Bethany   149
Madden, Tim   331
Madoff, Bernie   285
Mahmood, Mazher   309
Mai, Jamie   286
mainstreaming   270–1
Majeed, Mazhar   184
Manning, Bradley   171
Manning, Peter   17
Marais, Simon   3
Maritime Union of Australia   302
Marr, David   13
Marshall, Barry   249
Martin, Catherine   14
Mascall-Dare, Sharon   188–9
Masters, Chris   16–19, 166, 179, 204, 208
Matter website   245
Maude, Neale   330
Mayman, Jan   16, 257
Meadlo, Paul   50
Meares, Andrew   324
Media Doctor   234
Media, Entertainment and Arts Alliance   171, 183,
     185, 235, 258
media framing   223–4, 236–7, 254, 256
media training   154–5
Medianet   156
medical reporting   232–40
Medicare Locals   244
Megalogenis, George   195
Megarry, (Justice)   169
Melbourne 'ganglands'   209–10
Meldrum-Hanna, Caro   318–19
Mellish, Morgan   18

Melville, Henry   11
Menzies Government   79
Messer, John   221
Meyer, Philip   116–17
Miami Herald   116–17, 213
Microsoft Access   119, 127
Microsoft Excel   118–19, 199
Middendorp, C.   308
Midnight in the Garden of Good and Evil
     (Berendt)   212
Mill, John Stuart   5
Miller, Lisa   154
Milton, John   5
Mitchell, Harold   145
mobile devices   322
Monash University Records and Archives Service   82
'Money Makers'   19
Monitor, The   11
Moodle   66
Moon, N.   111
'Moonlight State, The'   16
Moore, Jo   157
Moore, Michael   284
Moran, Matt   198
Morgan Stanley   140, 285
Morton, Tom   34
motorcycle gangs   217–20
MSNBC   284
muckraking journalism   5–6, 10–11, 13, 21
Mugabe, Robert   314
multicultural journalism   269–77
Multicultural Resource Directory (Qld)   271
multimedia journalism   320–7
     audio   324
     creative process   326–7
     graphics   324
     moving images   323–4
     nonlinear story-telling   324–5
     photographs   323
     text   323
     tools   326
     user-generated content   320, 323–6
Municipal Association of Victoria (MAV) finance
     workshop   146
Murdoch, Bradley John   214
Murdoch, Rupert   285
     Australian, The   13
Murphy, Lionel   15–16
Musselwhite, K.   33
'My Lai Massacre'   50
Myer, R.   287
MyHospitals website   244
MySQL database manager   119

Nation   12
Nation, The magazine   30
Nation Institute, The   30
National Archives of Australia   80, 82
National Crime Authority   15
National Disability Awards   179
national film and sound archive   82
National Indigenous Radio Service (NIRS)   259, 268
National Indigenous Television (NITV)   259, 268
National Institute for Computer-Assisted Reporting
        (NICAR)   117, 124
National Library of Australia   78–80, 82
National Party Government (Qld.)   16
National Science Foundation (US)   251
'National Smokers Alliance'   159
National, The   237
National Times, The   13–15, 18
Negus, George   16
neoliberalism   282, 285
'Net Bet affair'   17
New America Media   30
New Journalism   6, 13
New Matilda   35
New York Times, The
        Occupy Wall Street protest   284–5
        partnership with *ProPublica*   20
        partnership with *Wikileaks*   40
        partnerships   28
        Pentagon Papers   44–5, 171
New Yorker   286
Newcastle Institute of Public Health   234
News Limited   19, 220
News of the World   167, 184, 285, 309
Newsbank   68
newspaper circulation decline   28
Newton, Eric   34
Newton, Max   12
Nicholls, Chris   170
Nielsen research   322–3
1984 (Orwell)   212
Nixon, Richard   6–7, 10
Noel Butlin Archives Centre   82
Nolan, Sidney   213
non-profit US news centres   28–33
        charitable status   32–4
Noor-Eldeen, Namir   39
Norton, John   11
Note Printing Australia   19, 26, 288
Noyes, D.   32
NPAT   149–50
Nvivo   130

Oakes, Laurie   49, 193, 197, 202
Obama, Barack   285

O'Brien, Denis   13
O'Brien, Kerry   17
O'Brien, Michael   167
Occupy Wall Street   283–5
O'Connor, Daniel   330
O'Connor, Kevin   287
Ok Tedi, PNG   291–4
Oldenburg, Ray   271
Olle, Andrew   17
One Nation Party   256
open verification   89
OpenAustralia website   73–4
'Operation Wallah'   17
Opes Prime   18
opinion polls   111–13
oral history   83
O'Rourke, P.J.   213
OurSay   35
Owens, Jesse   314

Packer, James   71
Packer, Kerry   15
Page One   17
Pakistani cricket scandal   184
Palm Island community   255, 257
Papua New Guinea   236–9, 291–4
Paranyuk, Nina   12
parliamentarians' salaries   104–7
parliamentary information   73
Pat, John   16
Patel, Jayant M.   49
Peach, Bill   16–17
Pearson, Mark   166
pecuniary interest registers   73
peer review   225, 251
Penberthy, Jefferson   13
'Pentagon Papers'   171
Perkin, Graham   12–14, 221
Perl   120
Persinger, Sara   276
Peucer, Tobias   5, 7
Pew Internet and American Life Project   232
Philadelphia Inquirer   29
Philby, Kim   12
Phillip Morris   159
phone-hacking scandal   285
Pickering, Larry   170
Pilger, John   14, 181
Pillemer, Tracy   67
Pleasance, P.   183
PM   91, 93, 95, 178–9
PNG National AIDS Council Secretariat   236
Pol Pot regime   14
Polden, M.   166

policy communications   163–5
Political Fictions (Didion)   55
political journalism   193–202
    see also industrial relations journalism
Porteous, Kimberley   320, 323–4
Post-Courier, The   237
Poynter Report   32
Pratt, Richard   287–8
Precision Journalism (Meyer)   116
Price and Incomes Accord   298
privacy   134, 167, 184, 235
problem-based approach to reporting   254–5, 257–60
property records   72
ProPublica
    A.C. Thompson   30–1
    collaborations   31
    'Dollars for Docs'   244
    funding   31–2
    non-profit investigative news outlet   29
    partnership with *New York Times*   20
Protess, D.   6
provenance   81–2
Provis, C.   185
public companies   71
Public Eye   17
Public Interest Disclosure Act 2010 (Qld)   56
Public Interest Lawyers   40
public relations (PR)
    'astroturfing'   158–9
    greenwashing   158–9
    leaks and tip-offs   158
    media alerts   156
    media conferences   156
    media releases   152, 155–6, 233–4
    PR generated journalism   4, 233–4
    press kits   156
    scoops   157
    tools   155–6
    working with PR industry   151–60
Public Relations Institute of Australia
    (PRIA)   159
PubMed Health   243
Pulitzer Prize   20, 29, 117
Pyramid Building Society   17
Python   120

Qantas   287, 300–2
Quantum   246, 248
Queensland Floods Inquiry   205–7
Quinn, Karl   170

racism   256, 313
Radford, Tim   250
Radio National   270

Rainbow Warrior   181
Rajaratnam, Raj   285
Ramsey, Alan   78, 196
Real Life   17
Reeves, Graeme Stephen   17
refugees   275
'Religion and Ethics Report,' Radio National   270
Reporters Without Borders   227
Reporting on Health group   244–5
research
    information sources and tools   69–74
    peer-reviewed journals   225, 251
    primary and secondary sources   79
    process   65–75
    strategies   77–84
Reserve Bank of Australia   19, 26, 33, 141, 288
Reservoir Dogs   211
Reuters   39
Reverse Google Image Search   97
Rice, Stephanie   313
Richards, David   15
Rivkin, Rene   18
Roberts, Gregory David   212–13
Robertson, Hugh   314
Robertson, Josh   218, 220
Robinson, Paul   14, 17
Rockefeller, John D.   30
Rogers, Mat   312
Rooney, Wayne   314
Roosevelt, Theodore   11
Rosen, J.   89, 194, 321
Rosenthal, Robert   29
Ross, Iain   306
Rove, Karl   284
Royal Commission files   82
Royal Commission into Aboriginal Deaths in
    Custody   257–8
Rudd, Kevin   194–5
Rule, Andrew   209
Rush, Geoffrey   154–5
Ryan, Morgan   16
Ryle, Gerald   79

Sailor, Wendell   312
Salaries and Allowances Tribunals   104
salary cap scandal   309
Saltman Engineering Co Ltd v Campbell Engineering
    Co Ltd   169
Sandler, Herbert   31
Sandler, Marion   31–2
SAS data analysis software   119, 134
SBS   17, 157
Scarface   213
Schembri, Adrian   137

Schultz, Ed   284
Schwitzer, G.   233–4
science, understanding   223–8, 248
Science and the Media Expert Group   248–50
science journalism   246–51
    controversies   249
    new discoveries   250
    science politics stories   248–9
    scientist-as-hero story   249
    see also environmental journalism
Scott, Adam   314
ScreenSound Australia   82
Securency   19, 26, 283, 288
7.30   17
sexual crimes   172
Shantaram (Roberts)   212
share market   139–41
Sheppard, John   220
Shin, J-H.   151, 153
Silvester, John   208, 210
Simon, David   213
Sin index   137–8
Singh, Harbhajan   313
60 Minutes   17, 68, 198
Skilling, Jeffrey   285
Skulley, Mark   305–7
'Skype Scandal'   198
Slessor, Kenneth   80
Slipper, Peter   199
Sloan, W.D.   79
smartphones   322, 326
Smith, Adam   282, 285, 299
Smith, Patrick   312
Smith, Red   214
Smith's Weekly   11
Snow, C.P.   246
Snow, Deborah   14
Snowblind (Sabbag)   212
Sobhraj, Charles   170
social change communication (SCC) theory   236, 239
social media   4
    see also Facebook; Twitter
Solomon, Anna   237
Solomons, Mark   217–20
sources, protecting   56–7, 170–1
Spatial Information Exchange (NSW)   72
#Spill   88, 91
spin   196
sports journalism   308–15
    contacts   309–10
    coverage   309
    drug use   312–13
    financial aspects   314

    gambling   314
    harness racing   318–19
    players' health   312
    politics and   313–14
    racism   313
    research and statistics   310
    terrorism   314
SPSS data analysis software   134
Standard and Poors   140
Starkman, Dean   200
Startt, J.D.   79
state budgets   145
statistics   103–14
    basis points   109
    degree of tolerance   112
    mean   103–4
    median   106–7
    mode   108–9
    percentage change   110
    percentage difference   109–10
    percentage points   109
    percentile   110
    sample size   112
    standard deviation   108
Steiger, Paul   31
Stelter, Brian   284
Stevens, Glen   19
Stevens, Jane   326
Stewart, Heather   267–8
Stewart Royal Commission   16
stock exchange   139–42, 149
    indices   140
    sectors   140–1
Stockwell, S.   152
Stolz, Greg   218
Stone, Gerald   16–17
Stoner, Casey   314
Storify   326
Storm Financial   18
Stosur, Sam   313
strategic communications   163–5
Stray, Johnathan   326
sub judice   172
Sudd/Thompson case   11
Suffer the Children ('Insight' team)   13
Suich, Max   13
Summers, Anne   14
Sunday   17
Sunday Age   17
Sunday Night   17
Sunday Sun   14
Sunday Telegraph   13
Sunday Times (London)   12

Sunday Times (Perth)   170, 233
Sunderland, Alan   167
Sunshine System, The   16
surveillance   169–70
Surveillance Devices Act (NSW)   170
Sutcliffe, Ken   312
SVT (Sweden)   40
Swan, Norman   16
Sweet, Melissa   243–5
Sydney Gazette and New South Wales Advertiser,
    The   10
Sydney Morning Herald, The (SMH)   10, 12, 19, 74,
    78–9, 169–72, 272, 307, 309
Symonds, Andrew   313
Syria   102

TalkBlack (4K1G)   259
Tallon, Steele   218
Tanner, Lindsay   18, 193, 198
Tanner, William   30
Tasmanian Police Offences Act 1935   168
Telegraph, The   42–3
Temby, Ian   80
Temple, Peter   215
Tesoriero, Nino   163–5
thalidomide   6, 13, 16
The World Today   91
Thinking, Fast and Slow (Kahneman)   247
This Day Tonight   16
Thomas, Hedley   17, 19, 204–7
Thomas, Peter   67–8
Thompson, A.C.   29–32, 34
Thomson Reuters   29
Tidey, John   14
Tiffen, R.   158, 193, 197
Tiffen, Rod   151
'Timber Mafia'   19
Times Picayune, The   31
'Tipping Point' *Four Corners*   330–1
Today   154
Today Tonight   170
Tomal, Saleh Matasher   39
Toohey, Brian   13
Toohey, Paul   214
Topsy   97
Trade Practices Act 1974 (Cth)   168
trade unions   297–303
Trendsmap   97
trespass   167–8
Trickett, Libby   312
Trident Inquiry   204–5
Tronado microwave machine   14
Trove, National Library of Australia   78–9, 84

Truin, D.   156
Truth   11, 13
Tuchman, Barbara   79
Turner, Graeme   16
Twitter
    Advanced Twittersearch   97
    changes to journalistic practice   89–91
    crowdsourcing   44
    data journalism   125
    direct message (DM)   89, 95
    false reports   95
    Guardian, The   92
    'hashtagged' conversations   89
    media releases   156
    Occupy Wall St   284
    open verification   89
    re-tweeting (RT)   92–3
    Twitstorms   94
    usage   89
    use by journalists   90–7
    use by PR people   4
    verification   92–6
Twtpoll   97

UN Educational, Scientific and Cultural
    Organization   236
Underbelly   209, 211
'UniMuckraker'   34
Unions Australia website   299
Universal Declaration of Human Rights (United
    Nations)   167
university-based journalism   28–30, 32–4
University of Melbourne Archives   82
University of New South Wales Archives   82
University of Tasmania Archives   82

Valerio, Daniel   212
Vanity Fair   223
Vietnam War   11, 14, 50, 55
Virgin   287
Visy   287–8
'Vulnerability and the News Media'   130–2, 269,
    274, 281

Wage Price Index   104–5
Wainer, Bertram   13
Waldman, Steve   32
Walker, T.   293
Walkley Awards   12–14, 17, 19–20, 25, 167, 198, 288
    Business Journalism Award   18
    Gold Walkley   14, 16–18
Walkley Magazine   320
Wall Street Journal   286

Wallace, Christine   196
Waller, Lisa   260
Wardell, Robert   11
Warhover, Tom   272
Warne, Shane   312
Washington Post   7, 14, 28
        'Pentagon Papers'   171
Watergate affair   6–7, 10, 14
Watts, Susan   173–4
Webb, Karrie   313
Webber, Mark   314
Weekend Australian, The   206
Weil, Johnathan   286
Weitenberg, Calliste   71
Wentworth, William Charles   11
West Australian, The   14, 233
Weston, M.A.   256
Westpac v John Fairfax   169
Whimpress, B.   308
whistle-blowers   48–58
Whitlam, Gough   15
Whitlam Government   14–15
Whittaker, Paul   17
Whitton, Evan   11–13, 20
Wik   256
WikiLeaks
        'Afghan War Diary'   40
        anonymous online dropbox   56
        collaboration with traditional media   20
        'Collateral Murder' video   39
        connective publishing   42, 46
        crowdsourced declassification   43–6
        'Iraq War Logs'   40

leaked diplomatic cables   39–44, 171
partnerships   40–3
use by Fairfax   18
Wilkinson, Marian   14, 330–1
Willesee, Mike   16
Williams, A.   152
Williams, Emlyn   212
Williams, Pamela   17
Wilmot, Chester   80
Winfrey, Oprah   313
Wire, The   211, 213
Witness   17
Wittenoom Trust   14
Wolfe, Tom   13
Wong, Penny   155
Wood, Gordon   170
Wood, Graeme   33
Woodward, Bob   7, 14
Worker, The   11
Working Group on the Information Needs of
        Communities   32
Workplace Express   300
World Anti-doping Authority   313
World Health Organization   243
World Today, The   178

Xamon, Alison   301

yellow journalism   11
Yooralla Media Award for Excellence   179
Yoshihara, N.   32
YouTube   4, 92, 156, 284